The
Hard Disk
Technical
Guide

The Hard Disk Technical Guide

Contributors:	Douglas T. Anderson
	Pat Dawson
	Sandra Honomichl
	Michael Tribble
Research Assistance:	Ofra Albalak
	Sandra Honomichl
	David Vehrs
Cover:	Danny Brand
Illustrations:	Michael Tribble
	Anni Wildung

 MICRO HOUSE **Micro House International, Inc.**

P.O. Box 17515
Boulder, CO 80301-9679

Twelfth Revision S-D., October 1996

ISBN 1-880252-30-9

Printed in the United States

Table of Contents

Trademarks

Adaptec, ASPI	Adaptec Corporation
BTC	Behavior Tech Computer Corporation
CDC	Control Data Corporation
DTC	Data Technology Corporation
DTK	Datatech Enterprises Co.,Ltd.
Everex	Everex Computer Systems, Inc.
IBM, IBM PC, PC/XT, PC/AT, PS/2, OS/2	International Business Machines Corporation
HP	Hewlett-Packard Company
Maxtor	Maxtor Corporation
Microsoft, MS-DOS, Windows, Windows 95, Windows NT	Microsoft Corporation
Phoenix	Phoenix Software Assoc., Ltd.
Quantum	Quantum Corporation
Seagate	Seagate Technology, Inc.
Western Digital	Western Digital Corporation

All other trademarks respective to their owners.
Most hard drive and controller card model names are trademarks of their respective manufacturers.

Limits of Liability and Disclaimer of Warranty

The authors have used their best efforts in preparing this book. These efforts include the compilation and research of information contained within. None of the source information in this guide has been electronically or mechanically reproduced in any way. All specifications and information have been compiled through years of research and testing. The authors and publisher are not responsible for errors or omissions contained in this guide.

Introduction

Thank you for selecting the *Hard Disk Technical Guide*, from the industry's leading authority on the installation, set up, and trouble-shooting of hard drives.

The purpose of this text is to be a practical how-to guide and an easy to use reference for today's most popular hard disk drive formats used by desktop computers. Whether you are a novice performing a do-it-yourself PC upgrade or a technician in need of a handy reference, we hope you will find this text a valuable tool.

The *Hard Disk Technical Guide* contains complete set-up information and procedures for the industry's most common hard drives and controllers. It focuses on the four most prevalent hard drive interface formats in use today: IDE, SCSI, ESDI, and ST-506/412. In addition to installation procedures, the guide offers related information ranging from IDE logical translation tables to a comprehensive glossary of terms.

What this text is *not* intended to be is a nuts and bolts hardware dictionary. Due to the large number of hard drive manufacturers and the various models they make, it would be prohibitive to detail the technology involved, especially considering the rate at which the industry is moving forward. However, we do provide some basic information on the common workings of the generic hard drive. For more information on hardware technology, please consult the recommended reading list provided in the appendices.

As a bonus, we have included a CD-ROM which contains some of our most popular utilities and demonstrations of our award-winning products. A fully-functional copy of *EZ-Drive*™ is included for hassle-free installation of your IDE drives. We know you will find the utilities extremely useful and hope the demonstrations spark your interest in our other indispensable software products.

The research staff at Micro House sincerely hopes that you find the *Hard Disk Technical Guide* a valuable tool for your hard drive needs!

About This Book

This book is arranged into seven chapters. Each chapter has been designed to help you with every aspect of hard drive and hard drive controller installation and trouble shooting.

- **Chapter 1** covers basic hard drive components and concepts common to many hard drives.

- **Chapter 2** will aid you in choosing the right hard drive for your needs, as well as help you understand the various specifications that describe a hard drive's capabilities.

- **Chapter 3** contains comprehensive information on the four major interface types.

- **Chapter 4** offers step-by-step installation procedures for the four major interface types, including partitioning and high-level formatting.

- **Chapter 5** contains specifications and jumper settings for the most commonly used hard drive controller cards.

- **Chapter 6** contains jumper settings for the most commonly used hard drives.

- **Chapter 7** contains solutions to problems that are encountered most often, as well as methods you can use to get the most out of your hard drive.

In addition, the appendices included with this text cover everything from logical specifications for hundreds of drives to a directory of manufacturers. There is also a comprehensive glossary for fast reference of terms you may not be familiar with.

How to Use This Text

Our goal for this text is for it to be a useful reference, no matter what level of technical expertise you may possess. We realize no one is interested in reading a reference book cover-to-cover, especially if they are looking for a specific piece of information. With this in mind, we have organized the *Hard Disk Technical Guide* according to the level of detail the information requires. If you require very basic information on how a disk drive works, the information is available. If you are already familiar with the basics, or don't care, you will not have to sift through technical details just to get how-to instructions.

Because it is sometimes annoying to sift through explanations of every acronym or technical term, and just as annoying when the author assumes the reader is fluent in computerese, we have used bold type-face to reflect words which are covered in the glossary.

Another handy reference feature is the symbols located next to section heads and important information. If you are looking only for essential information, simply skip the sections that have the Nice-To-Know symbol. Pay close attention to the passages that are marked by the card with a lightning bolt through it and the broken floppy disk – they could save you from a tragic episode.

Conventions

- There are several variations of the term "**hard disk drive**" in common use. This text will use either "**hard disk drive**," "**hard drive**," or simply "**drive**."

- Unless otherwise noted, the terms "**controller**," "**host adapter**," and "**adapter**" all refer to the printed circuit board which provides the interface to the host system.

- The term **computer** refers to the main-board and all of the components native to it (Central Processing Unit, memory, Basic Input/Output System).

- The term **peripheral** refers to any input or output device attached to the computer.

- The term **embedded** means that the facility referred to is built-in and not removable.

- 1**MB**, unless otherwise noted, denotes 10^6 bytes in this text.

Information Level Symbols

Warning

Denotes failure to take proper precautions could result in damage to hardware.

Data Loss

Denotes improper use of procedure could result in permanent loss of data.

Important

Denotes key technical information the reader should become familiar with.

Technical Information

Denotes non-essential technical information.

Nice-To-Know

Denotes anecdotal/historical, non-essential information.

Back-Up

This symbol is a prompt to back-up the information on your hard drive in preparation for a procedure that could or will destroy data on the drive.

CD-ROM

The information contained in this passage refers to one or more of the supplemental programs found on the CD-ROM included with this text.

Micro House Product

The text under this logo refers to one of our excellent products. Please contact our sales staff for details. Address and telephone information can be obtained in Appendix D.

Understanding the Basic Hard Drive

Chapter One Contents:

A hard drive is a mass-storage device on which data is magnetically written to and read from a platter (disk) spinning at a high rate of speed

Hard drives are the predominant media used for data storage and retrieval in desktop computers today. A hard drive is a mass-storage device on which data is magnetically written to and read from a platter (disk) spinning at a high rate of speed. The platter is written to/read from by means of a head which the platter spins underneath. The platter itself is coated with a magnetic medium, much like the film that coats audio tapes.

Over the years, there have been several variations on the hard disk drive theme. By far the most popular hard drive format is the so-called **Winchester** drive. The term Winchester drive is a commonly accepted industry term that originated from IBM drives that were manufactured in the 1960s. These drives could store 30 **megabytes** of data on removable media and another 30 megabytes on fixed media − thus the designation "30-30," which was the caliber of a famous rifle made by the Winchester firearms factory. This book specifically covers Winchester-type drives.

Hard drives have experienced explosive growth in popularity and capability recently due to a combination of factors. Each new jump in **CPU** technology is met with more powerful software, which in turn requires more data storage space. The relatively static price of system memory has prompted increased use of hard drive **virtual memory** in multitasking operating systems. In turn, this increased demand for storage has spurred more competition and development in hard drive technology, bringing hard drive capability up and prices down. In 1994, a high-end IDE drive was typically in the 400-500MB range and went for about $300. The same amount in 1996 bought a drive in the 2GB range.

Basic Drive Components

Physically, the different types of hard drives in this book are the same. They all write to and retrieve data from magnetic media bonded to hard (usually metal or glass) platters which spin at high **rpms** (**rotations per minute**). The major differences lie in the electronics and instructions that they use to communicate with the host computer, comprehensively known as the **interface**. In fact, many hard drives on the market today are sold in both **SCSI** and **IDE** versions (see Chapter 2 for general interface descriptions) that are mechanically identical.

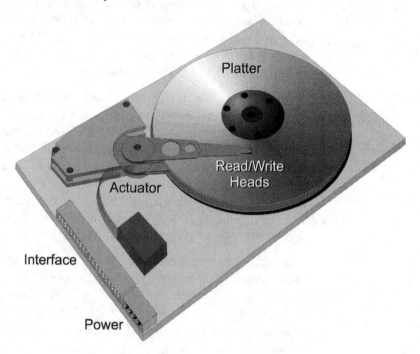

Figure 1-1: Disk Drive Basic Physical Layout

Platters

The **platter**, or **disk,** in a hard drive is usually non-removable (as opposed to a removable floppy diskette). There are several disks stacked vertically and fixed to the spindle of a high-speed electric motor, called the **spindle motor**. The **substrate** is the material each platter composed of. The substrate must be highly resistant to the stress imposed by high rotation speeds and temperature. It is usually metal, although glass and ceramic have been used.

Because the hard drive's metallic platter is much more resistant to change than the plastic disk of a floppy drive, it can be subjected to higher stress with more reliable results. This means that the disk on a hard drive can be spun at speeds of 5,000 rpm and greater, while traditional 1.2MB and 1.44MB floppy drives are limited to around 300 rpm. Faster rotation speeds allow faster data **access times** and **throughput**.

The substrate is thinly coated or plated on both sides with a magnetic substance (iron oxide or thin-film metal media) for non-volatile data storage. Surfaces of disks are usually lubricated to minimize wear during drive start-up or power-down. Plated media are also extremely hard and much less susceptible to damage due to head crashes (the head coming into contact with the surface of the platter). A plating will hold more than double the magnetic particles of a coating in the same amount of space, allowing greater storage capacity and throughput. This brings up another important parameter used to describe hard drive capability: **areal density**.

Areal density describes the physical amount of data that can be held on an area of the disk, measured in **bits per inch^2**. Areal density is obtained by multiplying the **bit density** (**bits per inch**) by **track density** (**tracks per inch**), yielding the bits per square inch on the disk surface. Bit density is measured radially around a track, and track density is measured linearly across the face of the disk (see **Figure 1-2**). Please see the section titled "Basic Drive Concepts" on page 15 for detailed explanations of some of the terms used in this paragraph.

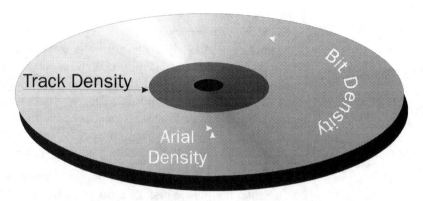

Figure 1-2: Bit Density vs. Track Density

Heads

Data is written to or extracted from the drive by means of **data heads** that sense the magnetic fluctuations on the **platter** spinning beneath it. These fluctuations are interpreted as the 1s and 0s of the **binary** data format that a computer understands. When the disk spins, a cushion of air only microns thick forms underneath the head. This is the reason that hard drives are factory sealed and basically have to be replaced in the event of a physical media failure. The tolerances are so tight that even microscopic damage to the disk surface will permanently degrade or even destroy the drive. Foreign particles, such as dust, invading the drive assembly can be disastrous.

When looking at the capabilities of different types of data heads, the most important specification is the **areal density** (see page 5) of the magnetic media that the heads are capable of reading from or writing to. Two types of heads are in common use today: **inductive**, and **magnetoresistive** (**MR**).

Inductive heads have been the mainstay of the industry since hard drives were invented. A **monolithic** inductive head is basically an electromagnet, that is, a ferrous core wound with current carrying wire. The core is shaped in order to bring the poles together, separated by a small gap (see **Figure 1-3**).

When the head is used for writing data, an electrical current is sent through the wire, producing a magnetic field in the gap. The magnetic flux extends from the gap and is imparted to an area of the recording medium along the track the head is over.

The same head is used to read data by inducing a current in the coils when the gap passes over a change in the magnetic flux over the recording medium. The drive control circuitry controls the switch between read and write operations.

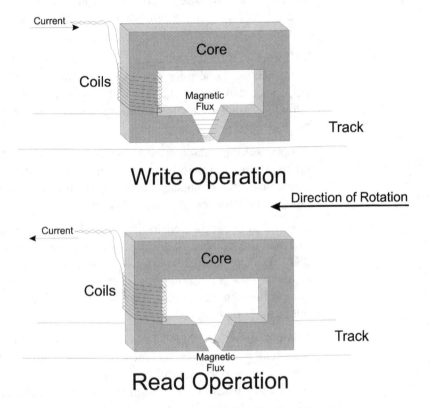

Figure 1-3: Monolithic Inductive Head

Increasing areal densities of the recording media have required improvements in head technology. Higher areal density means that that the individual magnetic fluxes are smaller and therefore weaker. This means that read heads must be more sensitive, and write heads must be capable of producing smaller, more accurate fields. Inductive heads have progressed since the days when they were simply U-shaped electromagnets. Technological improvements have allowed them to become smaller and more sensitive. **Composite** heads use the heavier ferrous material only where needed, with the bulk of the structure made up of a lighter, non-magnetic substance.

Thin-film is the last in the line of inductive-type heads. Thin-film heads use the same micro-circuitry technology used to manufacture chips such as CPUs. The advantage is small size and light weight, allowing greater accuracy in read/write operations and head placement.

Simply making inductive heads smaller and lighter is effective only up to a point. Inductive single-head technology puts faster data access and greater capacity at odds because of conflicting physical requirements for read and write operations.

In order to boost the sensitivity of read operations, it is possible to increase the number of turns in the coil, or rotation speed of the disk. Both methods increase the inductance of the current passing through the coil, hindering high-speed write operations. A compromise between coil turns and disk rotation speed is necessary, but limits performance.

Magnetoresistive (**MR**) heads use a material that changes its electrical resistance in the presence of a magnetic field. A small direct current is constantly passed through the MR element. When the element passes over a magnetic field, a voltage change occurs in proportion to the change in the MR element's resistance. The change in resistance depends on the direction of the magnetic field the MR element encounters. The resulting change in voltage is interpreted as a bit 1 or bit 0. This is a simplistic explanation for MR head operation, but illustrates the basic concept.

MR heads are extremely sensitive, but can only be used for read operations. Thin-film inductive heads are still used for write operations. Since read and write operations use separate elements, no compromises have to be made regarding these components.

Table 1-1 outlines the increasing performance of the different types of heads:

Table 1-1: Typical Read Head Type Capacities	
Head Type	**Areal Density (BPI x TPI)**
Monolithic Inductive	$3,600,000$bits/in^2
Composite Inductive	$12,000,000$bits/in^2
Thin-Film Inductive	$500,000,000$bits/in^2
Magneto-resistive	$1,000,000,000,000$/in^2 +

There are usually several read/write heads in a hard drive. On larger drives, a single head and platter surface is reserved for the **servo**. The servo contains information for feedback head positioning systems. When looking at drive specifications, the term "heads" usually only pertains to actual data heads, those that read or write the data usable by the computer. Such is the case with the drive listings in this guide. There may be eight platter surfaces but only seven data heads. Only one of the several read/write heads is in use at any one time. The controller can only handle data from one head at a time, which in itself does not result in any data transfer delays, as the other elements involved in the transfer of data can only take in so much data at one time.

Actuator

The **actuator** is a device that provides head positioning over the platter surfaces (see **Figure 1-1**). The actuator anchors the **carriage assembly**, which in turn holds the read/write heads.

Two kinds of actuators have been commonly used, **stepper motor actuators** and **voice-coil actuators**.

A **stepper motor actuator** uses a motor that moves the actuator arm in discrete steps. The heads are positioned by rotating the motor a precise number of steps and then converting these steps into linear motion. This means that misalignments can eventually occur due to overheating or mechanical wear. Most older hard drives, especially inexpensive ones, use this kind of actuator. Floppy drives also use this kind of actuator.

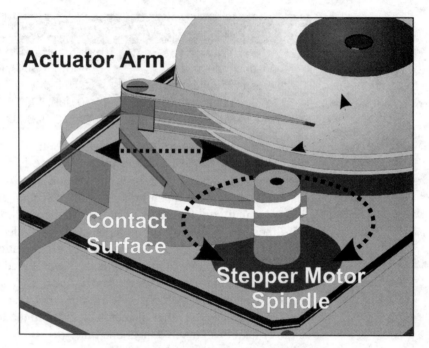

Figure 1-4: Stepper Motor Actuator

All modern hard drives use the **voice-coil actuator** because it is the faster and more reliable of the two types. A voice-coil actuator uses a solenoid (a magnet that pulls on a metal rod) to pull the heads toward the center of the platter. The heads are placed on a hinge mechanism with a spring that pulls in the other direction. The amount that the actuator moves the carriage assembly is regulated by the amount of current sent through the voice coil motor. When the solenoid is released, the heads get pulled back to the outer edge of the platters. Powering off the drive results in the actuator automatically "parking" the data heads. The term "voice-coil" is used because speakers operate in much the same way – using an inductive voice coil and permanent magnet to displace the sound-producing cone. Voice-coil actuators are much faster than stepper actuators because they don't have to use incremental steps – they go directly to their destination. They are also more accurate because actuator arm positions are not mechanically preset and therefore less subject to misalignment. Positioning information (**servo**, see below) is located on the platters themselves and is used for constant realignment of the heads.

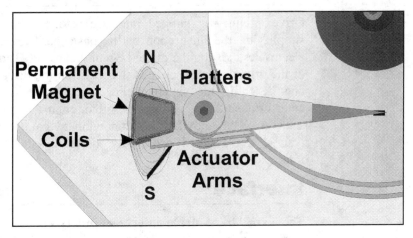

Figure 1-5: Voice-Coil Actuator

To give you an idea of the speed difference between a voice-coil and stepper motor, consider that a drive using the stepper motor takes from 65 to 100ms (65 to 100 thousandths of a second) to move from one track to another, as compared to the voice-coil actuator that usually only requires 10 to 40ms – more than twice the speed of the stepper motor.

Head positioning in a voice-coil actuator drive is provided by a feedback system known as the **servo**. Servo information is pre-recorded position reference data that is located on a disk. The drive uses this information and compares it against the actual head position, then makes corrections as necessary to place the head at the correct track. There are two general types of servo systems: **dedicated servo head/disk** and **embedded servo data.**

Some of the larger capacity drives use an entire platter surface (dedicated servo) to store this information. This is why you will see a drive that has only seven data heads but four platters (there are usually two heads for every platter). The eighth disk surface is reserved for the servo platter. Hard drives with an odd head count will have a dedicated servo. **Embedded servo** data does not require an additional disk and head, instead using added servo data on every cylinder. The voice-coil actuator knows what track it's on by reading positioning information (**servo**) that has been permanently placed between the tracks.

Drive Control Circuitry

Drive circuitry is lumped into one category for the purpose of simplifying the illustration of the basic hard drive. Most of the electronics exist on the printed circuit board (PCB) on the underside of the drive. Typical circuits that exist on the drive involve coding and decoding the signals being sent to/received by the heads, actuator positioning, and spindle motor control. "Intelligent" drives, such as SCSI and IDE, contain onboard control circuitry, while "dumb" (ST-506/412) drives rely on control circuitry located on an intermediary adapter.

Interface

The term "**hard drive interface**" refers collectively to both the hardware used to make the physical connection between the drive and the computer, and the electronic instructions that manage the transfer of data. The four hard drive interface types most commonly used in the microcomputer environment are: **ST-506/412** (sometimes called **MFM**), **Enhanced Small Device Interface (ESDI)**, **Small Computer System Interface** (**SCSI**), and **Integrated Drive Electronics** (**IDE**).

Of the four common interface types, both the ST-506/412 and ESDI are no longer widely available. The ST-506/412 was the first to be developed and was made obsolete by the performance limitations of its design. Even when upgraded with improved RLL recording technology (see page 18), its maximum data transfer rate was only 7.5 **Mb/s** (**Megabits per second**), far short of that now achieved by current IDE and SCSI models. ESDI, a high-performance version of ST-506/412, is much faster, reaching speeds of up to 24 Mb/s. ESDI drives were also considered quite reliable and available with as much as a **gigabyte** of storage capacity. These factors made it the prime choice for a network drive prior to the advanced development of SCSI. Unfortunately, for those with an interest in ESDI, the full benefits of the ESDI interface were never realized and it was eventually surpassed by SCSI in flexibility and performance.

The remaining types, SCSI and IDE, account for the vast majority of drives sold today. In their present forms, SCSI drives are usually seen in high-end applications such as network servers, while IDE drives are the Original Equipment Manufacturer's (**OEM**) choice for systems intended for the popular market, such as home computers and work stations. Please refer to Chapter Two for details on the differences between SCSI and IDE and how to choose the interface that best fits your needs.

There are other hard drive interfaces that are not covered in this manual. Those interfaces are usually found in minicomputers and mainframe systems. Most are designed for non-PC bus types such as VMEbus, S-Bus, STD Bus, and Multibus. **SMD** (Storage Modular Device) and **IPI** (Intelligent Peripheral Interface) are two examples of common interfaces that are used in the mini and mainframe environments. **PC-Card** drives are usually small **form-factor** IDE drives that use the **PCMCIA** (**Personal Computer Memory Card International Association**) bus. These are **Plug and Play** (**PnP**) devices that are designed to be used in the laptop computer environment.

Buffer

All modern hard drives have some amount of on-board memory, which is termed the **buffer**. The buffer is a way-station for requested data after it is read from a location on disk. On older drives, a **Track Buffer** was used to allow the drive to operate at an optimum level without having to a wait for a relatively slow (8088/8086 CPU) system to process each read/write sequence to or from memory. Rather than having to wait for the first track to be processed by the host system before moving on to the next, the drive puts the contents of the first track into the track buffer and moves on. See the description of **interleaving** on page 21 for more information on how system speed can affect drive performance.

Newer systems are fast enough that even high-performance drives can sometimes seem inadequate. In this case, the advantage of a disk buffer is that it decreases system delays due to the physical limits of the drive speed. Read sequences can be sped up by having the buffer hold information that it anticipates the system will request. There are varying levels of sophistication in the methods buffers use to predict what data will be requested. A **Lookahead Buffer** simply loads requested data and some of the following information located sequentially on disk. A **Segmented Lookahead Buffer** is the same thing, except that it can hold several read sequences simultaneously to avoid repetitious read operations.

Basic Drive Concepts

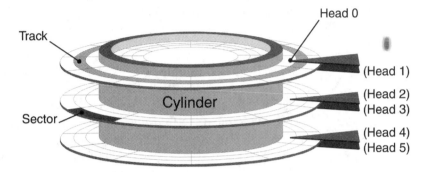

Figure 1-6: Disk Physical Organization

Cylinders

The physical organization of a hard disk is fairly straight-forward. In order to multiply capacity, there are usually several platters stacked vertically in the unit. The largest unit of organization is the **cylinder**. A cylinder is a surface formed by the same track number on vertically stacked disks. At any location of the head positioning arm, all the tracks at that position compose that particular cylinder. See **Figure 1-6** for an illustration.

Tracks

The concentric circles that hold data on a disk platter are called **tracks**. A track is composed of a circle of adjacent magnetic flux domains. Each track is divided into **sectors**, which are normally 512 bytes in length.

Sectors

A section of one track is called a sector. Each sector is defined with magnetic markings and an identification number (this identification number is contained in the sector header). All sectors contain a **sector header**, (usually) 512 bytes of data, and an **Error Correction Code** (**ECC**) (See **Figure 1-7**).

The **sector header** is the address portion of a sector. The sector header (ID field) is written during the format operation. It includes the cylinder, head, and sector number of the current sector. This address information is compared by the disk controller with the desired head, cylinder, and sector number before a read or write operation is allowed.

The **Cyclical Redundancy Check (CRC)** value is placed at the end of the sector header and is used by the drive to verify sector address integrity. In a typical scheme, 2 CRC bytes are written to each sector. After the drive finds the address it is instructed to look for, it calculates a CRC value that it checks against the CRC value in the sector. The two CRC values should match, meaning the drive is looking in the correct place for the requested data. If the values do not match, an error code is reported back, causing drive access to halt.

The **Error Correction Code (ECC)** is placed after the data portion of the sector, and is used to verify that the data being read is valid. The ECC hardware in the controller used to interface the drive to the system can typically correct a single burst error of 11 bits or less. This maximum error burst correction length is a function of the controller. With some controllers (not SCSI or IDE) the user is allowed to the select this length. The most common selection is 11 bits.

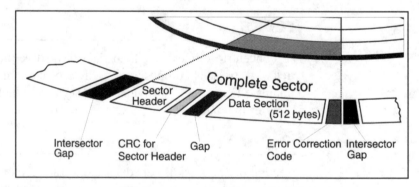

Figure 1-7: Sector Detail

On most drives, all the tracks have the same amount of sectors even though the tracks are much larger near the outside of the platter than the inside. This arrangement simplifies the organization of the sectors on the drive, but has the draw-back of giving up potential disk space. More advanced recording methods have been introduced such as **ZBR™** (**Zone Bit Recording**), a trademark of Seagate Technology, in which tracks on the outside cylinders have more sectors per track than the inside cylinders, although each sector still contains 512 bytes of data.

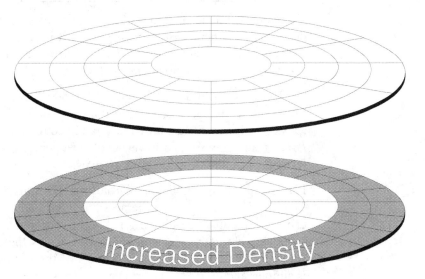

Figure 1-8: Zone Bit Recording

Advanced Drive Concepts

This section is an introduction to some drive concepts that you may want to familiarize yourself with. Some of the terms describe obsolete technology, but still show up from time to time on some manufacturer's drive specification sheets.

Addressing

There are two major methods of data **addressing**. Addressing is the organization scheme used to assign data to locations on the drive. The addressing methods are: **CHS (Cylinders, Heads, Sectors)** and **Logical Block Addressing (LBA).**

CHS is used on most IDE, and all ST-506/412 and ESDI drives. Information is accessed according to the three-dimensional (physical) location (head, cylinder, and sector) it falls under. The **BIOS** (see page 33) and lower levels of operating systems use this format to communicate with hard drives.

LBA is used by SCSI and **Enhanced IDE** drives (see Chapter Three). This addressing scheme simply assigns each sector in the drive a sequential one-dimensional number or logical address. LBA is a desirable addressing scheme because it is the format used by software applications and higher levels of the **operating system**; it is simpler and easier to perform calculations with LBA than with the three-dimensional CHS format. LBA addressing requires a host system BIOS which supports it or a **controller** that bypasses the host system BIOS with a replacement block device driver or its own on-board BIOS ROM.

See the Technical Information sections about IDE and SCSI in Chapter Three for examples which may aid you in understanding CHS and LBA.

Encoding

Encoding is the method used to convert the **binary** information (0s and 1s) used by the computer into the flux reversals (or transitions) that can be stored and read from magnetic media. As drive technology improves, newer encoding schemes are being employed to allow data to be packed more densely on the disk.

Frequency Modulation (FM) encoding is an outdated encoding scheme that is no longer in use. It used up to half of the disk space with timing signals for the encoding process.

FM encoding was replaced by **Modified Frequency Modulation (MFM)** encoding. As the name implies, MFM is a refinement of FM. MFM does away with the need for timing signals, allowing it to pack twice as much data as FM encoding on the same drive. MFM does this by using a fixed length encoding scheme. Flux reversals on the disk will always be evenly spaced in time so that the beginning of one bit can be separated from another. This type of scheme also allows even single bit errors to be detected easily and corrected by the controller electronics, where the encoding/decoding process is performed. MFM encoding was replaced by RLL encoding for use in hard drives, although MFM is still widely in use for floppy drives.

FM and MFM use a 1:1 relationship between flux reversals and the bits they represent. This simplifies encoding/decoding logic, but makes the drive more susceptible to the physical limits of the media and electronics. The drive circuitry needs time to react to each flux reversal – the more flux reversals, the slower the performance of the drive. This also means that each flux reversal needs more space to be detected properly. A better way is to maximize the space between flux reversals.

Run Length Limited (RLL) is a type of encoding scheme that requires fewer flux reversals for a given amount of data as well as reducing the amount of data-checking information taking up disk space. The logic used is far more complicated than that used in MFM, but allows much more data to be placed on the disk. RLL encoding represents data in bytes instead of individual bits. Bytes are in turn represented by 256 selected 16-bit combinations. These 16-bit combinations are chosen for having the maximum amount of space between 0s and 1s. The "run-length" in RLL refers to the number of consecutive 0s in a 16-bit combination prior to the appearance of a 1. The extra spacing between flux reversals gives the read/write circuitry more time perform an operation. RLL uses twice as many bits to represent a byte of data as MFM, but the efficient spacing of flux reversals more than makes up for the extra bits by allowing the use of smaller magnetic domains.

There are several types of RLL encoding. In RLL 2,7 the run-length of 0s in each 16-bit code is at least two and limited to a maximum of seven. This allows for a fifty percent increase in disk space over MFM encoding. RLL 3,9 (commonly called Advanced RLL, or ARLL) is also available, which further increases disk space (up to 100% from MFM).

Partial Response Maximum Likelihood (PRML) is not really an encoding scheme, but an advanced type of analog read channel used to reliably pick out the weaker signals that result from higher areal densities (see "Analog Read Channels" below). The use of a PRML read circuit enables the use of a more efficient RLL encoding scheme that allows consecutive 1s to exist in the bit sequence. For example, PRML/RLL 0,4,4 encoding means that 1 bits can occur consecutively, up to four 0 bits can exist between 1 bits. The last 4 is used to limit the number of 0s between 1s for some specific sequences.

Where the encoding takes place also has an effect on drive performance. On ST-506/412 drives, the encoding/decoding process was performed on the controller card, instead of at the drive itself. ESDI drives reversed this state because of the drawbacks of having a raw signal becoming degraded over the length of the cable from the drive to the controller (see the ESDI section of Chapter 3 for more information). All modern hard drives (IDE and SCSI) perform the encoding/decoding process on the drive instead of the controller. In addition to the benefits stated above, host adapters are less expensive and can have more features packed in the space not taken up by drive-controller circuits.

Analog Read Channel

Most drives still use a simple analog peak detection scheme to pick out digital information from the analog signal received from the heads. The peak detection scheme runs into problems when combined with newer media and head technologies that enable high areal densities. In such cases, the individual magnetic fluxes are so close together that some overlap occurs. A less sophisticated read circuit that simply looks for individual analog peaks may experience errors due to this overlap.

A **Partial Response Maximum Likelihood** (**PRML**) circuit can overcome signal overlap and background noise by sampling the signal at several locations along the curve, then projecting the shape to more accurately determine the location of the peaks.

Interleave

In the past, most hard drives could transfer data faster than the computer could process it. **Interleaving** alleviated this problem by forcing the drive to read the data a little slower. Interleaving slows down the rate at which sectors come under the data heads by skipping one or more sectors between sector read/write operations.

For example, Figure 1-9 shows sectors that are non-interleaved on top, while the diagram on the bottom has sectors interleaved at 1:3. If the interleave is 1:3 then the sectors are renumbered: **1**-7-13-**2**-8-14-**3**-9-15-**4**-10-16-**5**-11-17-**6**-12. This allows the CPU to store the data for sector #1 while #7 and #13 are under the head, and then continue with sector #2 when it's ready. In one revolution, approximately six sectors of 512 bytes will have been read and stored by the CPU. In three revolutions, all of the sectors will have been read and stored. Most 8088/8086-based systems use an interleave of three or four. Most 80x86-based systems use an interleave of 1 or 2. The interleave required depends on several factors, including the speed of the interface, CPU, and the controller electronics.

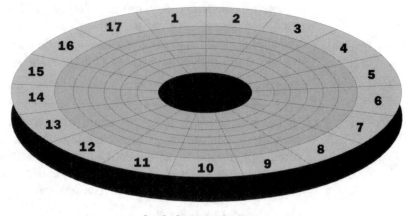

1:1 Interleave

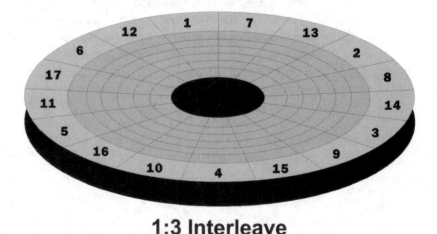

1:3 Interleave

Figure 1-9: Interleaving

The computer systems on the market today can easily accommodate the throughput, or data transfer rate, of even the fastest drives. In addition, all drives of recent manufacture use interfaces that can handle data throughput at rates greater than the mechanical part of the drive is capable of. For these reasons, no interleaving is used for current drives. Another way of saying this is that the interleave of modern hard drives is 1:1.

Landing Zone

This is the section of the disk that is designed as the safe zone for head parking after power is removed from the drive, usually the highest cylinder on the drive. Depending on the actuator, the head parking procedure can be an active or passive process.

If the actuator is a stepper motor type, when the power is turned off the drive's heads will remain over the track where the last read/write action was performed. If the drive is jolted, data under the heads can be lost. The stepper motor drive heads must be parked through software that places the head at a safe (for data) landing zone. Some later model stepper actuator drives used the residual energy of the rotating disks to move the heads to the landing zone after power-down.

Voice-coil drives automatically park themselves due to the design of the solenoid-spring mechanism. Head parking software is not needed on these drives and should not be used.

Low-Level Formatting

Low-level formatting physically divides the hard drive's disks into tracks and sectors in preparation for the reception of data and records the sector header data that organizes the tracks into sequential sectors on the disk surfaces.

Low-level formatting is the first step in preparing a drive to store information. The process sets up the "handshake" which allows communications between the drive and the controller. Low-level formatting physically divides the hard drive's disks into tracks and sectors in preparation for the reception of data and records the sector header data that organizes the tracks into sequential sectors on the disk surfaces. Sector header information identifies the sector number and contains the head and cylinder address. This information is never altered during normal read/write operations.

In an 8088/8086 system, the low-level format is usually done using DOS's debug utility. In an 80x86 system, 80x86 advanced diagnostics are typically used (most of the "clone" 80x86 BIOSes have a built in low level program). Third party software may also be used to perform low-level format on both 8088/8086 and 80x86-type machines.

Most IDE and SCSI drives are low-level formatted at the factory using special equipment, therefore the end-user should not attempt low-leveling these drives. See Chapter 4 for specific interface low-level information.

Partitioning

Partitioning is a mandatory operation which organizes the physical drive into logical volumes.

Partitioning and **high-level formatting** prepare a hard drive for use with a specific **operating system**. Partitioning is a mandatory operation which organizes the physical drive into logical volumes. All drives must have a primary partition, and may optionally have one or more extended partitions.

Partitioning a drive is necessary today for several historical reasons. The current level of industry standardization didn't exist in the early days of the personal computer, so it was more common to see several different operating systems being used to run the various applications available. Because of the expense of mass data storage in the past, a single hard drive often had to be shared by several operating systems. Each of these operating systems required a separate partition. In addition, on some older systems it was necessary to partition a drive into several logical volumes because the operating system could not handle the capacity of larger drives in a single volume.

Some DOS (see "Operating Systems") partitioning terms you might want to become familiar with are:

- **Primary Partition**: This is the volume designated as the boot drive (C:) and contains the **Master Boot Record** (**MBR**). The MBR contains information on the locations and parameters of all of the partitions on the drive as well as pointers to the location of boot information for the operating system (boot code). Although there can be several partitions designated as primary, only one of them at a time can be the active primary partition.

- **Extended Partition**: All other partitions on the drive are considered extended partitions.

See the next section for information on DOS partition limits.

High-Level Formatting

High-level formatting, also known as DOS formatting, organizes the drive partitions for a filing system by constructing a **root directory** from which sub-directories can be created. The other function of high-level formatting is to write a master record that keeps track of the location of the files, empty space, and defective areas on a partition. The dominant PC operating systems, DOS and Windows, call this master record the **File Allocation Table** (**FAT**). One way to look at it is to say the FAT is to the hard drive what a table of contents is to a text.

Partition Limits

Due to the number of bits allocated (16), the FAT currently limits the size of a single partition to 2.1GB. Windows for Workgroups (WFW) uses an optional system called 32-bit disk access, and Windows 95 uses the VFAT (Virtual File Allocation Table). These file systems are also bound by the 2.1GB limit. If a drive is under the 2.1GB limit, then multiple partitions are not necessary (although the partitioning process is still required).

Some operating systems do not have this limitation because they use more advanced file access systems for keeping track of file locations. Windows 95 uses FAT-32, Windows NT uses a system called NTFS (NT File System), and OS/2 uses the HPFS (High Performance File System). These are 32-bit file systems that are not limited to 2.1GB partitions. These advanced file systems are not compatible with the DOS 16-bit FAT.

The following information details the partition limits of the various DOS versions:

- DOS versions 2.0 to before 3.00 support a single partition of up to 16MB.
- DOS 3.00 to before 3.30 support a single partition of 32MB.
- DOS versions from 3.30 to before 4.00 may have multiple partitions no greater than 32MB. Therefore, when using these versions, a 100MB drive will have to be partitioned into four parts: 32MB, 32MB, 32MB and 4MB.
- DOS versions from 4.00 to before 5.00 may have partition sizes up to 2.1GB.
- Versions 5.00 and 6.x allow partitions of 2.1GB and support for up to eight physical drives.

Table 1-2: DOS Version Partition Limits		
Version	**Number of Partitions**	**Max Partition Size**
2.x	1	16MB
3.00-3.29	1	32MB
3.30-3.99	4	32MB
4.x	4	2.1GB
5x-6.2	8	2.1GB

Note that while later versions of DOS theoretically allow partitions of up to 2.1GB, none of the DOS versions can handle a hard drive with over 1,024 cylinders unaided (see page 34). This results in the capacity of an individual IDE drive being limited by combined DOS/BIOS/IDE constraints to 528MB (see page 60).

Even DOS 6.x is still affected by this limit. To access more than 1,024 cylinders on an IDE drive, you will need specific hardware support, such as may be found in some newer translating or LBA BIOSes. The alternative is using a software package such as **EZ-Drive™** or **DrivePro™** from Micro House.

ON THE CD

Clusters

Although data is physically divided into sectors of 512 bytes on a hard disk, the operating system keeps track of available disk space by organizing the drive into **clusters** or **allocation units**. A single cluster, composed of several sectors, is the smallest unit of drive space that an operating system can work with. A cluster can be used, unused, or defective (contain bad sectors).

The reason that the operating system does not work with individual sectors is that it would significantly degrade system performance. Organizing groups of physical sectors into logical clusters streamlines **FAT** processing chores and keeps the FAT down to a more manageable level, allowing DOS to run faster. The drawback to using clusters is that more physical disk space is wasted. Since a file *must* take up at least one cluster and usually several, there will almost always be some unused sectors in the last cluster allocated for that file, called **slack space**. The result is that much more physical space will remain unused than if the drive could be allocated by the sector.

The number of sectors composing a cluster depends on the DOS version and size of the partition. Note that a significant disadvantage of using larger partitions is that DOS assigns an increasing number of sectors per cluster according to partition size in order to keep the FAT size from degrading system performance. This means that as partition size goes up, slack space increases proportionally.

For example, say one partition uses eight sectors/cluster and wastes an average of half the last cluster in slack space. Another partition uses 64 sectors/cluster and has the same portion of the last cluster wasted. The smaller partition would waste 4 sectors, or 2,048 bytes per file, while the larger partition would waste 32 sectors, or 16,384 bytes per file. Multiply this times thousands of files and you can see that a significant amount of storage space can be lost in this manner.

The following table illustrates the progressive increase in cluster size relative to partition size for DOS:

Table 1-3: DOS Cluster Sizes	
Partition Size	**Cluster Size (512 bytes/sector)**
16 - 127 megabytes	2KB
128 - 255 megabytes	4KB
256 - 511 megabytes	8KB
512 - 1,023 megabytes	16KB
1,024 - 2,047 megabytes	32KB

Sector Sparing

Sector sparing is a method used on most newer drives to mask the presence of defective sectors on a disk. Sector sparing effectively reduces the number of usable sectors on each track by one and re-allocates the spare sector for substitution in place of a defective sector. The system will see fewer defects because only the drive is aware of the spare sectors. Sector sparing reduces the total capacity of a drive but is useful if the drive has a relatively large amount of defects and you run applications that require a defect-free drive.

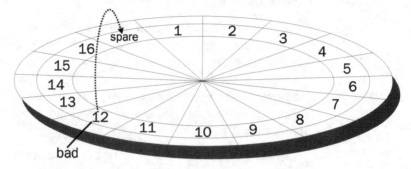

Sector Sparing For A 36-Sector Drive

Operating system sees 35 good sectors and no bad sectors

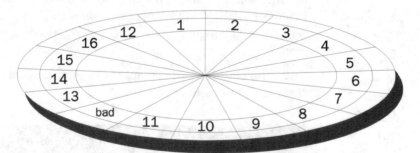

Same Drive Without Sector Sparing

Operating system sees 35 good sectors and 1 bad sector

Figure 1-10: Sector Sparing

Head and Track Sector Skewing

Consider that hard drive disks spin at thousands of rpms. After completing the read/write of a track, the head must reposition itself to start operating on an adjacent track. The head must then make sure it is on the correct track by identifying the first logical sector of that next track. If the first logical sector of every track on the platter is lined up radially along a disk, then the head probably will not be able to re-position itself quickly enough to catch the first sector of the new track after finishing the last sector of the previous track. The head must then allow the disk to spin under it almost a complete revolution before starting with the first sector of the new track. If this is occurring, the drive is not operating optimally.

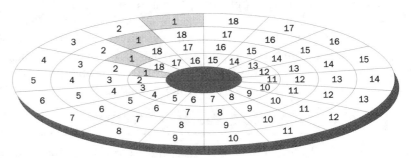

Figure 1-11: Head and Sector Skewing

Sector skewing is the repositioning of the first logical sector on each track to allow the data heads time to switch tracks before coming upon the first sector of the new track. The head does not have to wait an entire revolution after jumping to an adjacent track because there is an adequate amount of space between the last sector of the previous track and the first sector of the new track. A skew factor is added when formatting a disk to improve performance by reducing wasted disk revolutions. Because most newer drives are low-leveled at the factory, this is not usually necessary. For those wishing to change the skew factor on older drives, sector skew values must be obtained from the drive manufacturer.

No matter how fast the actuator assembly may be, it takes more time to move the heads physically as opposed to switching operation from one head to another. **Head skew** is the term applied to the organization of tracks among all of the disks in a drive that allows the drive to switch read/write heads in order to minimize actuator movement. For example, a drive locates requested information on the first track of the upper surface of the top disk. After finishing the first track, it switches to the head located on the bottom surface of the same disk and begins reading the next track. The drive goes through all of the heads until it has to switch back to the first head, finally being forced to move the actuator assembly. If the tracks are arranged optimally, the drive will read all of the requested information with no wasted revolutions. If the tracks are not arranged optimally, during one of the head switches, the head will not catch the first sector of the track under it on the first pass and another revolution will be required. The tracks on adjacent surfaces can be offset to ensure that after a switch, the next head assembly catches the first sector of the track it is over. Head skew can be set to 0 if the drive does not support it.

Reduce Write Current

On some older drives, the **Reduced Write Current** (**RWC**) is a signal input that decreases the amplitude of the write current at the actual drive head. Normally, this signal is specified to be used during inner track write operations to lessen the effect of adjacent bit "crowding." When installing a drive in a system, the RWC number requested by the CMOS setup utility is the first track number to begin the area of RWC. That track and all subsequent tracks will be written with RWC. This parameter is ignored for setting up modern drive types.

Write Precompensation

Write precompensation (**WPC**) is a method used on older drives to compensate for the increased density of data on tracks closer to the spindle. Because tracks on the inside of the disk have to hold the same amount of data as the outer tracks, the data must be packed more densely on the inner tracks. Depending on factors like encoding method and areal density of the magnetic media, increasing data density results in some drawbacks.

Packing more signals in less space means that weaker flux reversals must be used, which can result in read/write heads not being able to perform properly. In some cases, WPC means that the inner tracks are written with stronger magnetic fields to provide clear signals.

Bit-shifting is another side-effect of packing magnetic fields more densely on the inner tracks. Magnetic fields that are placed in close proximity can affect each other. Bit-shifting can cause data heads to misinterpret the exact position of individual fluxes.

WPC is also the term applied to varying the timing of the head current from outer tracks to the inner tracks of a disk. This process makes up for the bit-shifting that occurs on the inner cylinders that pack more data into a smaller area.

Although you will sometimes still see a place to enter a WPC value in the CMOS set-up, modern drives do not need it. For this reason, this value should usually be set to 0. WPC is only required on large form-factor drives using oxide magnetic media.

The Data Transfer Chain

There are several steps involved in extracting data from its physical location on the disk to placing it in the host memory (and vice-versa). All of the data handling elements in this chain represent potential bottlenecks to overall performance. Simply installing a bigger, faster drive may not give you the results you expected. This section presents a simplification of the process for those wishing to become more familiar with the way a hard drive works.

There are basically five players in the data transfer chain:

1. Mass storage device (disk drive)

2. Device **controller**

3. **Basic Input/Output System** (**BIOS**)

4. **Operating System** (**OS**)

5. Host memory (**RAM**).

Each of these is detailed in the sections below.

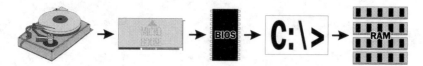

Figure 1-12: Data Transfer Chain

Controller/Host Adapter

A controller is the printed circuit board required to interpret data access commands from the host computer (via the bus), and send track seeking, read/write, and other control signals to and from a hard drive. SCSI and IDE host adapters do not perform drive control and encoding/decoding functions, as these are accomplished by circuits on the drive itself. These types of adapters are sometimes termed "dumb" controllers. ST-506/412 controllers are "intelligent" in that they must tell the drive where to find a read/write location, as well as perform the encoding and decoding of raw signals into data.

BIOS

The **Basic Input/Output System** (**BIOS**) is the interpreter that sets up a specific computer to allow the operating system (such as DOS) to communicate with peripherals.

The **Basic Input/Output System** (**BIOS**) is the interpreter that sets up a specific computer to allow the operating system (such as DOS) to communicate with peripherals. The BIOS can be thought of as the "glue" that holds together hardware made by a variety of manufacturers. The BIOS is firmware, that is, the instructions are permanently written on a Read Only Memory (ROM) chip. Newer BIOSes often use a Flash ROM, a non-volatile memory chip that can be written-to in order incorporate upgrades and bug-fixes.

Because system parameters are changed often, a method of updating the parameter information used by the BIOS is needed. The **CMOS** (**Complementary Metal Oxide Semiconductor**) RAM stores this information, which can be changed through a BIOS utility often called the CMOS Setup. A small battery is used to power the CMOS when the computer is turned off. During the boot sequence, the BIOS refers to the information contained in CMOS to initialize (boot) the computer and performs a **Power On Self Test** (**POST**).

Most 80286 and 80386-type computers use two BIOS chips. Each chip only has a data path 8-bits wide, but the CPU can handle a 16-bit data path. If the designers were to put the whole BIOS on one chip, access to it would be through a slow 8-bit path. By dividing the BIOS between two 8-bit chips, data can be transferred from each chip at the same time, creating a 16-bit BIOS data path. The access order is altered for each byte of data. One chip contains all the odd numbered bytes and the other contains all the even numbered bytes. If you were to look at the BIOS area with DOS debug (use the command DF000:0), you would probably see a copyright message such as:

```
CCOOPPYYRRIIGGHHTT
```

This is because each of the two chips has a copyright message in it and when meshed together form this composite message.

More current system designs (80486 and above) use only one BIOS chip. They get by the 8-bit BIOS data-path problem by utilizing BIOS Shadow RAM. Shadow RAM is fast RAM memory that is set aside for the placement of a copy of the BIOS contents. The Shadow RAM can then be accessed through 16, 32, or even 64-bit data paths. In these types of systems, ensure that the shadow feature is turned on.

Most systems that use two chips use 27256-type chips. The "256" is the number of **kilobits** that the chip can hold. If you divide this number by 8 you can get the number of bytes that the chip holds, which is 32KB. So two of them together equal 64KB, the normal size for current BIOSes. Some older systems use two 27128-type chips, which is a total of 32KB (16KB x 2), and a few newer systems use two 27512 chips which is a total of 128KB (64KB x 2). The systems that use a single BIOS chip usually have one 27512 (64KB).

BIOS Imposed Limits

Please read this section of information on BIOS/DOS-imposed drive limits.

The original IBM (80x86 CPU) BIOS originally allocated just enough bits for 1,024 cylinders, 255 heads, and 63 sectors/track in its drive parameter look-up table. The 1,024 cylinder limit was commonly exceeded in hard drives long ago. Drives that are accessed through the system BIOS can get around this limit by performing a translation (see page 59).

Older BIOSes (regardless of the operating system) limited the acceptable number of cylinders in a drive to 1,024. Some BIOSes provided for 4,096 cylinders, but this feature was useful only with newer operating systems other than DOS. This is because of the interface originally provided between the BIOS and the OS, called INT 13h.

The method that is provided for applications (such as an OS) to access hard drives through the BIOS is the software **Interrupt 13h** (**INT 13h**). Issuing an INT 13h call allows an application to let the BIOS know when it needs to use the hard drive. Note that this is not the same as a hardware interrupt request (IRQ). Due to the number of bits allocated for drive parameters, INT 13h also only provides for 1,024 cylinders. Because DOS uses INT 13h for disk access, it and related OSes are subject to the 1,024 cylinder limit.

Newer BIOSes (Enhanced BIOS) use a translation scheme at the INT 13h interface to enable DOS-based OSes to work with large capacity drives (see page 64). These translation schemes allow the use of new large-capacity drives while maintaining INT 13h compatibility for older DOS-based software.

Another way of getting around BIOS-imposed limits is to bypass the system BIOS altogether. SCSI controllers with an onboard BIOS do not normally use the system BIOS for drive access.

Operating System (OS)

The **Operating System** (OS) consists of a series of programs that allow interaction between the user, software, and hardware. As there are many excellent resources available for more information on the various operating systems, this text only deals with OS matters specifically relating to hard drives.

The **Operating System** (OS) consists of a series of programs that allow interaction between the user, software, and hardware.

The OS provides a standardized way for programs to access the computer's resources (usually through the BIOS), even though peripherals are made by a multitude of manufacturers. Just as the BIOS is the hardware "glue," the OS can broadly be thought of as the software glue. The advantage is that consumers have a reasonable assurance of buying hardware/software products that are compatible with their systems. The disadvantage to this compatibility is that the peripherals must have parameters within OS limits.

The **Disk Operating System** (DOS) is the traditional OS for the personal computer market, and is still in widespread use. DOS-imposed limits have traditionally not been a problem for the average user because the cost of high-capacity (>2GB) drives kept them mostly in the commercial applications arena. Recent developments, however, have made >2GB drives available to even entry-level home computer users.

Some DOS terms you will see used frequently in this text are covered in the section in this chapter titled "Advanced Drive Concepts." Please refer to that section for information on **Low-Level Formatting**, **Partitioning**, and **High-Level Formatting**.

Chapter Review:

- All modern hard disk drives are considered Winchester-type drives.

- Hard drives are mechanically simple , using platters, actuators, and read/write heads to perform physical access tasks. Technological advancements that have improved drive performance have largely been in the recording media and electronics.

- Hard drives are physically organized by cylinders, tracks, and sectors.

- Some important concepts to be familiar with are: addressing, encoding, low-level formatting, partitions, high-level formatting, and clusters.

- Data must be handled through several elements between system memory and disk media. Overall performance is determined by the limiting component of the data transfer chain.

Selecting a Drive

Chapter Two Contents:

Which Interface Should I Choose?

When choosing between IDE and SCSI, your basic consideration is cost vs. performance. How much hard drive do you really need and how much are you willing to spend for it?

The first place to begin when selecting a drive, whether as original equipment, replacement or upgrade, is with the type of interface that best fills your needs. Because ST-506/412 and ESDI have been superseded by IDE and SCSI, the choice is between the latter two interfaces in today's market.

Your basic consideration is cost vs. performance. How much hard drive do you really need and how much are you willing to spend for it? If money is no object and you only want the biggest and fastest, SCSI is your choice. If cost is the limiting factor, then go with IDE. The greater likelihood is that you are probably somewhere in-between these extremes and need to consider other factors, which are covered below.

Capacity

The first specification that will jump out at you is drive capacity. This is actually not much of a factor when considering which interface is best for your needs. In the past, it was true that SCSI drives were capable of much greater storage volume than IDE. Newer IDE drives, however, are theoretically capable of capacities up to 8.4GB, which closes the gap with SCSI. In either case, the currently most popular operating systems (DOS, Windows) are limited to 2.1GB partitions, although an update that overcomes this limitation will soon be available for Windows 95 (FAT-32).

You may want to consider the risks of depending on a single massive drive for your storage needs. If your storage requirements are in the multiple gigabyte range, you may want to consider several drives of smaller capacity rather than a single large drive. Besides cutting your potential losses in case of mechanical failure, back-up and restoration tasks take less time when data is divided among smaller drives. Remember, IDE controllers are limited to 4 attachments on newer models (2 on older ones), while SCSI can attach up to 7 devices in a daisy-chain. An option for high-end installations is to employ a storage array scheme. See the explanation of **RAID** under the SCSI Interface section of Chapter 3 for more information.

Speed

As mentioned earlier, SCSI and IDE drives are often mechanically identical. This means that in many cases the performance is correspondingly similar. Although **caching** utilities and hardware exist to increase the performance of IDE drives, a SCSI drive with similar options will usually out-perform an IDE due to the efficiency of the SCSI interface. This makes SCSI the more desirable option for use in environments that require high-performance, such as network file servers and CAD workstations.

Number of Attachments

SCSI can support up to seven of these devices on a single controller, or even 15 in the case of some dual-channel models, as opposed to the two or four drives supported by the *typical* IDE controller. Some BIOSes already support four IDE channels in anticipation of a new ATA specification. Again the consideration is how much do you really need? Larger capacity drives alleviate the need to attach additional units, and some people will never need to attach more than two IDE devices. On the other hand, if internal space is becoming a consideration because available expansion slots are scarce, SCSI is a viable solution.

Variety of Peripherals

SCSI provides greater flexibility than IDE. Although IDE tape drives and CD-ROMs have recently become available under the **ATA Packet Interface** (**ATAPI**) specification, the SCSI interface has supported about every peripheral imaginable for quite some time. CD-ROM's, Digital Audio Tape (DAT) decks, and Optical/Floptical drives are all presently available with SCSI interfaces. Note that data transfer performance can degrade as more peripherals are added on the chain.

Reliability

If you want to know which drive type will last longer, SCSI or IDE, the answer is that the interface has no effect on reliability. Reliability is a factor when considering which model to purchase, but not interface type. See the section below on **Mean Time Between Failure** (**MTBF**) for information on drive reliability.

Cost

Despite all of SCSI's advantages, IDE still accounts for the majority of drives sold in the PC market. This is because its performance has always been adequate when compared to cost and ease of use.

Recent developments, however, are heating up the IDE vs. SCSI debate. The proliferation of multi-media systems and higher performance CPUs has increased the demand for drives that push and even exceed the limits of the old IDE format. At first glance, the SCSI interface, with its multi-device capacity and higher performance, seems like the logical choice in the multimedia environment.

In order to narrow the performance gap, several major drive manufacturers have coordinated an updated version of the IDE format. The official name for the new specification is ATA-2, which is defined by the X3T13 subgroup of the X3 Accredited Standards Committee. The ATA-2 standard concentrates on standardizing methods used to make the IDE interface faster. These changes allow for drive capacities of over 8GB and data transfer rates exceeding 10MB/s. Seagate calls the drives that support this standard "Fast ATA" products.

The **Enhanced IDE** (**EIDE**) camp, led by the Western Digital Corporation, is a comprehensive update. EIDE drives incorporate the ATA-2 standard, but go further by requiring changes in a system's hardware, BIOS, and operating system. EIDE requires this because, in addition to increased data transfer rates, it also provides a standardized method to break the old IDE capacity barriers. In addition to increases in performance and capacity, EIDE specifies an additional channel, allowing a total of four IDE devices to be installed in a system. Another major issue addressed by EIDE is the ability to attach devices other than hard drives. The IDE CD-ROM interface that utilizes the ATA Packet Interface (ATAPI) basically adapts parts of the SCSI command set for use in the ATA interface. This is desirable because it eliminates the need for an additional adapter and has the potential of providing a standard CD-ROM interface for the industry. See the IDE section of Chapter 3 for details on ATA-2 and EIDE features.

Although the outcome remains to be seen, the net effect of Enhanced IDE will probably be to maintain the status quo, with SCSI being relegated to more demanding, yet less popular applications. Enhanced IDE merely narrows the performance gap with SCSI in order to address the increased needs of the average end-user.

 # How to Shop for a Drive

Advances in CPU technology have had a ripple effect on the rest of the computer industry. More capable CPUs have spurred the development of more complex and storage-hungry software, especially in the multimedia segment. The demand for more space has spurred disk drive manufacturers to roll out bigger, faster drives at a seemingly breakneck pace. In 1994, a 528MB drive was considered adequate storage space for most applications. In 1996, 1GB+ drives were found even in entry-level systems, and the high-bar is always being raised.

While all this is good for the consumer, it does mean that shopping for a new drive involves becoming informed. First, you should know about the system that the drive is destined for. Will it natively support large drives? Does it support the latest data transfer modes? Also educate yourself on the current drive market.

For each category of drive, there are models from several different manufacturers with varying quality and price. Perhaps the best way to become familiar with the quality of different drives is through product reviews. Every few months one of the major computer periodicals, such as *PC Magazine*® or *Byte*®, will review hundreds of drives and list their findings. Because many performance specifications may be misinterpreted or misleading, having this kind of objective performance data is very valuable. See the section below for information on drive specifications.

Recent Technological Advances

Hard drive capabilities have advanced to keep up with the demands of faster systems running larger and more complex applications. Consider looking for some of the technology mentioned in this section when looking to upgrade your data storage.

More capacity is at the forefront of development efforts of the major drive manufacturers. Achieving a higher capacity may require improvements in everything from the recording media all the way to the operating system. Some of the current technology being employed to increase drive capacity includes MR heads and PRML read channels (see Chapter One).

Multitasking operating systems and multimedia applications place increased demands on hard drives. Higher throughput is just as important a consideration as increased capacity. Improvements in manufacturing methods have allowed disk rotation speeds to go over 7,000rpm. Updates in both the IDE and SCSI interfaces have specified improved data transfer modes (see Chapter Three). Drives and controllers are also using larger caches with more sophisticated algorithms.

Today's drives are extremely reliable and rugged. Improved manufacturing methods have led to tighter mechanical tolerances and much better quality control. However, don't base a comparison of drive reliability on MTBF (see next section) numbers provided by the manufacturers. MTBF is a specification that is open to interpretation, so you may not be making a fair comparison (see page 46).

Keeping a recent backup is the only real insurance against data loss. Other protective measures are only effective for reducing down-time.

ON THE CD

A copy of *EZ-SMART™* is included on the CD-ROM that came with this text.

Although current hard drives are dependable, they are not infallible. Being mechanical devices, they are subject to wear and will all eventually fail. Keeping a recent backup is the only real insurance against data loss. With that in mind, other protective measures are effective for reducing down-time. Some RAID levels (see the SCSI section in Chapter Three) provide real-time data mirroring and the ability to hot-swap failed drive modules. An industry effort at device failure management is a combined hardware/software system called **Self-Monitoring, Analysis and Reporting Technology** (**SMART**). SMART aware-devices monitor themselves and report any operating degradation or fault conditions that could lead to data loss with continued operation.

What Do Drive Specifications Mean?

Read this section to familiarize yourself with the general definitions of drive specifications. For specific information on specifications that relate to the various interfaces, refer to the appropriate section of Chapter 3.

Capacity

Capacity is the total storage space available on the hard disk, usually presented in megabytes, gigabytes, and sometimes even terabytes. The following table defines some common measures of data capacity:

Table 2-1: Data Unit Definitions	
Bit:	A binary digit. The smallest unit of data, either a 1 or a 0.
Byte	8 bits.
Kilobyte	1,024 bytes.
Megabyte	1,048,576 bytes.
MB (million bytes)	1,000,000 bytes.
Gigabyte	1,073,741,824 bytes.
GB (billion bytes)	1,000,000,000 bytes
Terabyte	1,099,511,627,776 bytes.

There is some minor confusion associated with binary measurements due to a lack of standardization in the computer industry. Computers use the binary (base 2) numeric system, while the terms kilo, mega, and giga are borrowed from the decimal (base 10) numeric system. Because describing capacities in bytes can become cumbersome, hardware and software makers have taken to using larger units. Most drive manufacturers don't use megabytes and gigabytes in their specification sheets, as described in the table above, for a couple of reasons. Dividing everything by 1, 048,576 is not as easy as simply moving the decimal point six places, and the binary figures have a tendency of making the drive look smaller to the uneducated consumer.

For example, some manufacturers will present a drive with a capacity of 428,067,840 bytes as having approximately 428 million bytes (total bytes divided by 1,000,000), while you will see others describe the same product as having 408 megabytes (total bytes divided by 1,048,576 bytes per megabyte). Which is correct? Once again, there is no real standard, but be sure to keep this in mind when comparing drives in order to be sure you are not looking at two different types of numbers.

> Since many of the figures you may want to use in this text come from drive manufacturers, we will use MB to represent 1 million bytes (decimal) and spell out megabyte when referring to binary figures. Likewise, GB represents 1 billion bytes, while gigabyte is spelled out to refer to the binary-based value.

Be sure to consider the **formatted capacity** when shopping for a drive. The unformatted capacity is the total capacity of the drive before being prepared for use. The formatted capacity is the usable space after the drive is organized for use. You could lose over 50MBs on a large drive after formatting due to the space taken up by defining the sector boundaries. For example, the Maxtor XT-4380E has 384MB of unformatted space but only 319MB of formatted space available to the user. This is a 65MB difference!

MTBF

One specification that many people have come to misunderstand is **Mean Time Between Failure** (**MTBF**). Many assume this spec is given to help them estimate the life expectancy of a drive and therefore place a great deal of importance on it when shopping for a drive. MTBF doesn't really estimate a drive's life-span, therefore it shouldn't be used for this purpose. It would be truly useful to have a specification based on actual performance *in the field* to help establish an average life expectancy for a drive. MTBF, however, is established in a very clean and climate controlled test lab with brand new drives.

The figure is arrived at like this: a given number of new hard drives are run for a given length of time. The number of drives is multiplied by the number of hours they're run, yielding **Total Power-on Hours** (**TPOH**). Next, the TPOH is divided by the total number of drive failures during that period. For instance, if they run 1000 new drives for 30 days (720 hours) and one fails, the MTBF would be 720K POH (1000 drives x 720 hours / 1 failure = 720,000). Now, 720,000 hours is equal to 82 years and 10 weeks of non-stop operation. Does this test indicate that one of these drives can be expected to last for 82 years? No, it means that there is a one in a thousand chance that the drive *won't last a month*. Of course, one who understands this process may find this spec useful in establishing the reliability of a particular drive family.

Be careful when comparing this spec between different drive manufacturers. There is no set standard on how many drives to use or how long to keep them running in order to come up with the figures. Just because one manufacturer's numbers may be more impressive than another's does not necessarily mean the drive with the lower MTBF is less reliable. Because of the lack of standardization on calculating MTBF values, this figure has been open to interpretation by some manufacturers out to enhance the appeal of their product.

Regularly perform a backup of all data on your system!

Keep in mind that proper precautions prevent a drive failure from being a catastrophe (see Chapter Seven). Foremost among these precautions should be to regularly perform a backup of all data on your system.

Aside from taking precautions against drive failure, the best sense of security may come from buying the drive with the best warranty.

Throughput

The true measure of hard drive performance is known as the **Data Transfer Rate** (**DTR**). The DTR, sometimes called **throughput**, is the speed at which data is transferred from the drive to host memory, and is typically measured in megabytes per second. The data transfer rate is affected by a variety of factors from the rotational speed of the disks to the type of CPU installed in the system.

Be aware that there are two different types of DTR, internal and external. **Internal Transfer Rate** is the speed from the disk media to the drive's on-board **cache memory** or **buffer**, and **External Transfer Rate** is from the drive's cache to the computer.

Latency is the measurement of how long a drive must wait before a specified sector rotates under the heads. The **average latency** is the time it takes to complete one-half of a platter rotation, and is measured in milliseconds. If a drive turns at 60 revolutions per second (or 3,600 revolutions per minute) the average latency for that drive is 8.33 thousands of a second (milliseconds).

Average latency is significant when considering factors that affect the data transfer rate. The data transfer rate can be slowed if data is being read or written sporadically, such as happens with inefficient software, so that the average latency period has to pass again and again. This can noticeably affect the performance of even "fast" drives.

Another specification that people sometimes put too much importance on is **Average Seek** or **Access Time,** usually measured in milliseconds (ms). This is the average time it takes for the drive to position the read/write heads above the requested data. If there is a gross disparity in this figure on comparable drives then it probably will affect performance, but the spec that most accurately illustrates performance is **DTR.**

Physical Dimensions

The physical size of the drive may be a consideration if it is an internal model, due to the size of the drive bays that are available in the computer casing. **Form Factor** is the width of the drive, usually expressed in inches. 3.5 in. and 5.25 in. are the two most common form factors.. 2.5 in. and smaller form factor drives are largely used in laptop computers. Although 2.5 in. drives may seem small, their capacities are not much less than that of larger form factor drives.

Height is expressed as a fraction, such as full, half or third-height. Full-height is approximately 3 inches.

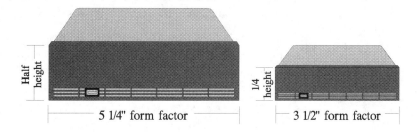

Figure 2-1: Form Factor

Chapter Review:

- Two major interfaces dominate the disk drive market – SCSI and IDE. Choosing between them involves assessing relative benefits versus cost. IDE drives are the most popular and are usually packaged by OEMs for personal computer and workstations.

- The disk drive market advances at a rapid pace. Shopping for a drive involves becoming an educated consumer. Find out if your system can support the features of the current crop of drives. Look over the drive market by consulting a recent issue of a computer magazine that involves drive comparisons.

- Know what the drive specifications mean. General marketing terms such as "fast" and "reliable" are meaningless without a standard basis for comparison.

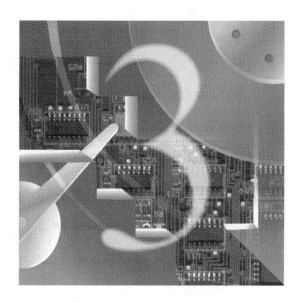

Interface Technical Information

Chapter Three Contents:

Hard Drive Interfaces

The purpose of this section is to provide technical details and historical information on the four major interface types.

The IDE Interface

IDE General Description

IDE stands for "**Integrated Drive Electronics**." The term simply means that all the electronics required to control data transfer exist on the drive's circuit board. The alternative would be to have the necessary hardware reside on the controller card. IDE is not the actual interface name, but the term has become commonly accepted in the industry to encompass the various facets of the format. The interface itself is actually called the **ATA**, or **AT Attachment** (as in IBM AT), and is defined by a set of standards laid down by boards of industry engineers currently called the X3T13 committee and the ATA Working Group.

Because the drive electronics are self-contained, IDE drives (like SCSI drives) are said to be intelligent. This is a distinct advantage to the manufacturer, because they don't have to sacrifice performance to ensure wide compatibility. It is also a benefit to the end-user, where, in contrast to ST-506/412 and ESDI drives, controller compatibility is not an issue of concern.

The electronic instructions of IDE drives are installed on the drive. Because of this, the card (controller) that plugs into the I/O expansion bus is just a "dumb" adapter. This adapter card serves little purpose other than connecting the drive to the computer. Incidentally, the absence of drive electronics on the adapter leaves room for other applications. This is how manufacturers are able to put a floppy drive, two serial ports, a game port, and parallel port on a single half-length IDE card. Most new motherboards even have an embedded IDE drive connector, eliminating the need for an adapter and freeing up an additional bus slot.

IDE drives perform a translation, converting the logical information which the drive and the BIOS tables can agree on into the actual information concerning where information is physically stored on a disk. This translation became necessary because most IDE drives started using 36 or more sectors per track, which at the time was not supported in BIOS drive-type tables. Other physical parameters have also exceeded the DOS-defined limits due to advances in drive technology. See the section below concerning IDE drive capacity for details on physical and logical specifications.

If you have recently been shopping for an IDE drive, you may have experienced some confusion regarding the terms **Enhanced IDE** (**EIDE**), **ATA-2**, and **Fast ATA**. These are all terms that relate to drives incorporating updates of the ATA interface. As explained previously, the term ATA refers to the actual interface, while IDE refers to the storage format that implements the ATA interface. Correspondingly, the updated interface, which is standardized and approved by an ANSI-sponsored sub-committee, is known as ATA-2. ATA-2 is sometimes being marketed as Fast ATA. Enhanced IDE refers to the standard being pushed by the Western Digital Corporation which, in addition to incorporating ATA-2, has features that allow increased drive capacity.

The goal of ATA-2/Enhanced IDE is to provide performance upgrades at minimal cost, both to the manufacturer and end-user. ATA-2 ensures backward-compatibility with IDE (AT) products through the use of the standard 40-pin connector and the same signal definitions. Enhanced IDE is more comprehensive, requiring BIOS and controller upgrades to take full advantage of the new drive's capabilities.

Although there are IDE controllers on the market that allow up to 4 drive attachments, most IDE controllers still only provide for a maximum of two drives. The reason for this is that even though IDE has always provided for an alternate address, the BIOS only supports two IDE drives off of the primary address.

Enhanced IDE controllers allow up to four IDE devices. In addition to an EIDE controller, taking advantage of this capability requires BIOS support, which will add to the cost when upgrading.

In the past, the only devices that used the ATA interface were IDE hard drives. The ATA-2 standard has addressed this shortcoming. The reason for wanting a greater variety of IDE devices is to eliminate the need for a separate expansion board for some commonly attached peripherals. In addition to simplifying device installation, this has an additional advantage of freeing up more expansion slots.

The ATA-2 convention already supports the attachment of CD-ROM and tape drives to standard IDE connectors via the **ATA Packet Interface** (**ATAPI**). Proponents of ATA-2/Enhanced IDE are hoping that both manufacturers and end-users will flock to their format as an economical solution to the compatibility jungle of the multi-media environment.

History of the IDE Interface

This interface originated in 1988 when a number of peripheral suppliers formed the **Common Access Method** (**CAM**) **Committee** to push an industry-wide effort of adopting a standard software interface for SCSI peripherals. Part of their goal was to specify what is now known as the ATA (AT Attachment interface), which would allow an interface to be designed into the new low cost AT-compatible motherboards. The ATA interface is usually not mentioned because it is encompassed in the term IDE. ATA refers to the interface itself and IDE to the hard drive. A standard was established and approved by the **X3T9** committee and sent to **ANSI** for approval.

The original IDE convention was designed to meet the mass-storage needs of the mid-1980s. As the convenience and low cost of IDE started to be overcome by its limitations, end-users desiring more speed and capacity from their hard drives have increasingly turned to the SCSI interface. In a move to protect their market share, several major manufacturer's of IDE drives have, in recent years, coordinated to set a new IDE standard under the banner of the **Small Form Factor Committee (SFF)**. The revised IDE interface, properly known as ATA-2 was approved by ANSI under the **X3T10** specification in 1994. The ATA standards have since moved to its own X3 subgroup **X3T13**. ATA-2 is the latest approved standard, but **ATA-3** and **ATA-4** are currently in the works. The goal of participating **SFF** members was to address the advantages that have made SCSI increasingly the interface of choice, while keeping IDE's strong points intact – low cost and ease of use.

The complete ATA standards documents can be obtained from **Global Engineering Documents**.

IDE Physical Characteristics

See the section in Chapter One titled "Basic Drive Components" for information regarding the basic workings of a hard drive. IDE drives vary widely in physical dimensions, but are commonly seen in 3.5 in., third or half-height formats in order to fit in the drive bays of most PC cases manufactured today.

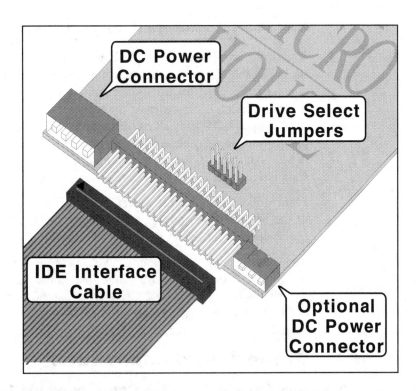

This diagram depicts the under-side of a typical IDE drive. This layout will vary from drive to drive, but the basic connections will always be present.

Figure 3-1: IDE Connection Diagram

Cabling

IDE drives normally attach to the computer via a 40-pin connector (44-pin and 72-pin connectors have also been used) and a controller card. The controller is often embedded in the motherboard, meaning the drive cable connects directly to the motherboard. See the end of this section for cable and pin-out descriptions.

Drive Select Jumpers (Master/Slave)

The drives connected to the IDE interface are called **Master** and **Slave**. The relationship between the two drives (which is master and which is slave) is usually determined by jumper settings on the drives. The physical order of the drives on the cable connector is irrelevant. ATA and ATA-2/Enhanced IDE hard drives may be paired on a single cable. With the old IDE (XT) interface, up to two drives may be installed in a system, but the controller must have a separate connector and port address for each drive.

Some drives offer a **Cable Select** option, which overrides the setting of the Master/Slave jumpers and designates Master/Slave based on the position of the drives relative to the cable.

The jumpers for master and slave selection are located on the underside of the drive, close to the data cable. These jumpers are almost always set to "Single Drive Only" at the factory, and usually need to be altered according to the Master/Slave designation for each drive installed on the cable.

IDE Technical Information

How to Calculate Disk Capacity on IDE Drives

Cylinders, Heads, and Sectors Per Track (**CHS**) are the parameters used to determine the capacity of a hard drive. See the section titled "Basic Drive Concepts" in Chapter One for definitions on cylinders, heads, and sectors per track.

The following formula can be used if your BIOS does not supply the capacity for the drive types, or if you have two of the drive's parameters and need the third.

Capacity in megabytes =

(cylinders) (heads) (sectors per track) (sector size) / (1,048,576 bytes/megabyte)

Table 3-1: IDE Drive Parameters (Specifications)	
Cylinders	Total usable drive cylinders
Heads	Drive's data heads
Sectors/Track	Usually variable in recently manufactured drives. Maximum value is 63 sectors/track
Sector Size	Usually 512 bytes. This figure is supplied by DOS, rather than the BIOS

Physical vs. Logical Specifications

The **physical parameters** are the actual values. The **logical** (translated) specifications are the heads, cylinders, and sectors that both the BIOS and DOS can work with.

Calculating capacity is perhaps the most confusing and least understood aspect of IDE drives. The reason for this confusion is that two contradictory sets of parameters appear to exist that are used to calculate drive capacity. This dual set of parameters became necessary when IDE drives began to use more than 1,024 cylinders, which was the old BIOS/DOS-imposed maximum. A translation scheme therefore became necessary to get the BIOS to think that the drive's parameters were within its limits.

The **physical parameters** (or specifications) are the actual values. If you opened up the hard drive and looked inside and saw 4 heads, that would be the physical (actual) number of heads. The logical (translated) specifications are the heads, cylinders, and sectors that both the BIOS and the IDE interface can work with. Ideally, both the physical and logical specifications can be plugged into the capacity formula (see below) and reach the same figure.

When setting up an IDE drive, the BIOS must be informed of the drive's specifications. The logical specifications are entered into the BIOS as the Drive Type. The hard drive then performs all translations from logical to physical values. The manufacturer will usually have a recommended logical translation for its drives that can be provided by its technical support department. A list of the IDE manufacturers' recommended logical translations for popular drives is in **Appendix A**.

In the example below, the physical cylinders exceed 1,024 cylinders, so the drive performs a translation, reducing the cylinders and increasing the heads and SPT count in order to arrive at the same capacity.

Table 3-2: Physical vs. Logical Specifications Example					
Spec. Type	Heads	Cylinders	Sectors Per Track	Sector Size	Capacity
Physical	4	1,985	62	512	252.04MB
Logical	10	895	55	512	252.03MB

Notice that .01MB of capacity has been lost due to the translation. Because specifications must be whole numbers, logical translations rarely match the potential physical capacity, and some of that capacity must be sacrificed. Manufacturers' recommended logical translations are designed to minimize lost capacity.

We have included a list of the manufacturers' recommended parameters for some popular drives, and a chart of universal translations for those BIOSes that have a user-definable drive type in **Appendix A**. Simply look up the drive's size in megabytes and choose or enter a drive type in your BIOS that matches the heads, cylinders and sectors. To be safe, you *may* want to select a type from the table that is one megabyte less than your drive's capacity. The values in this table may not always be those the manufacturer supplies, but in most cases they will work.

IDE Capacity Barriers

The capacity of IDE drives is limited by the highest common values of the parameters acceptable to the host system BIOS, OS and the IDE drive itself.

Drives that meet the ATA-1 specifications are limited to a capacity of 528MB. The 528MB barrier exists because of the number of bits allocated for specifying the cylinder, head, and sector address information at both the BIOS and the IDE interface levels. At the BIOS level, 10 bits are allocated for the cylinder number, 8 bits are allocated for the head number, and 6 bits are allocated for the sector number. At the ATA-1 interface level, 16 bits are allocated for the cylinder number, 4 bits are allocated for the head number, and 8 bits are allocated for the sector number. The IDE and BIOS limits cannot be taken individually, however. The lesser of the IDE/BIOS bit values allocated to a parameter is what determines the actual capacity limit of the ATA-1 interface. **Figure 3-2** may help you understand this process.

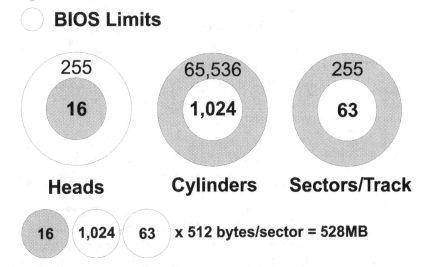

IDE Limits
BIOS Limits

Figure 3-2: ATA-1/BIOS Parameter Limits

The actual ATA-1 capacity limit is calculated by taking the lesser of the parameter limits between the BIOS and the IDE interface. The capacity of drives in the IDE format is determined by the highest common values of the parameters acceptable to both the host system BIOS and the IDE drive itself.

	Heads	Cylinders	Sectors Per Track	Sector Size (DOS)	Capacity
Table 3-3: ATA-1/BIOS Imposed Limits					
IDE	16	65,536	255	512	136.9GB
BIOS	255	1,024	63	512	8.4GB
ATA-1 (Lesser Value)	16	1,024	63	512	528MB

EZ-Drive is a software solution that will allow large IDE hard drives to be compatible with systems that do not natively offer large drive support or LBA

IDE drives can be instructed to use parameter translations, these utilize the entire disk with no loss of disk space if they do not exceed 528MB. The IDE 528MB limit is not necessarily written in stone. With *EZ-Drive*, it is possible to use drive parameters outside the values a particular BIOS allows. *EZ-Drive* will perform a translation that halves the number of cylinders and doubles the heads so that the BIOS thinks the drive is within allowable limits. See the IDE section of Chapter Three for more information on "large" IDE drives.

Almost all IDE drives manufactured today have parameters that are greater than 16 heads, 1,024 cylinders, and 63 sectors/track. This means the capacity of these drives exceeds the ATA-1 528MB limit. Enhanced IDE hardware offers support for large drives, but requires native support for more than 1,024 cylinders by the BIOS (Enhanced BIOS). Most older BIOSes do not allow a user to enter parameters larger than those above, therefore third-party software support such as a replacement DOS block device driver or *DrivePro*'s Large Drive Master Boot Record (MBR) is required. *EZ-Drive* also provides large drive support.

EZ-Drive is a software solution that will allow large IDE hard drives (>528MB) to be compatible with systems that do not natively offer large drive support. *EZ-Drive* features support for large drives with capacities between 512MB and 8GB.

If you have a BIOS that has large drive support, you will not need to use *EZ-Drive*'s large drive support feature to access the full capacity of your hard drive. If this is the case, you can still use it for hassle-free installation. If you are not sure of your system's ability to support hard drives, it is completely safe to use *EZ-Drive*. In-doubt? Use *EZ-Drive*.

WARNING: If an IDE drive is told to use parameters that exceed the DOS restrictions (number of cylinders greater in number than 1,024), DOS (and DOS-based OSes) will accept and *use these parameters* with no error message. Some BIOS tables, in fact, even have entries that are invalid.

For example, some BIOS tables have 15 x 1,224 x 17 as parameters for type 46. These parameters may even be the physical parameters for some drives, but if you select these parameters for a drive and the drive is told to write to a logical sector beyond the 1,024 cylinder limit, DOS will write to the drive's cylinder 0 in a "wrap-around" effect **without giving any error to the user**. This is due to a little known anomaly in DOS. Writing to this location can be disastrous, since it will write over, in approximate order, the Master Boot Code and Partition Table, the DOS Boot Record, the FATs, the Root Directory, and then user data! Note that the drive will perform correctly until the disk is filled to the point that it begins to wrap around. So, even though the drive boots and can be written-to and read-from, the DOS restrictions still apply. The results could become disastrous in time. Note also that this is a DOS software limitation and does not necessarily apply to newer systems that specifically support more than 1,024 cylinders, and with operating systems other than DOS. Using *EZ-Drive* will completely overcome this problem.

The capacity barrier that currently causes the most concern for drive manufacturers and system vendors is the DOS 2.1GB partition limit.

The capacity barrier that currently causes the most concern for drive manufacturers and system vendors is the DOS 2.1GB partition limit (see "High-Level Formatting" on page 25). The most obvious solution is to divide the drive into multiple partitions smaller than 2.1GB. In addition to overcoming the partition size limit, this solution has the advantage of using more efficient cluster sizes (see page 26). Operating systems that use a more advanced file allocation scheme (such as OS/2 Warp or Windows NT) do not have this limit.

One final note about IDE capacity limits: at the rapid rate of IDE capacity increase, the 8.4GB limit (see Table 3-3) imposed by the BIOS will quickly go from the realm of theory to reality. Overcoming this barrier will require a comprehensive change in the IDE/BIOS interface.

IDE Addressing Schemes

The IDE interface has traditionally used CHS addressing (see page 18). CHS originally used the physical specifications to perform disk addressing, but physical limits prompted the use of logical translation schemes. Some BIOSes simply translate CHS to under 1,024 cylinders to get around the INT 13h limit, but the natural progression is to simply translate CHS addresses into linear block numbers that are easier to work with.

IDE **Logical Block Addressing** (**LBA**) is also a translation scheme, but only uses one dimensional sequential sector addresses rather than the three-dimensional CHS system. LBA is the disk access method used by Enhanced IDE for large-capacity (>528MB) disk drives. LBA is a comprehensive change over the old IDE format, and requires specific support from the host-system's BIOS (**Enhanced BIOS** or **EBIOS**) and the drive's firmware.

IDE LBA works like this: On power-up, the host system's BIOS performs a Power-On Self Test (POST) during which it interrogates the drive with the Identify Drive command. The BIOS checks the drive response to see if it supports the LBA mode. IDE LBA consists of a 28-bit address for up to 268,435,456 sectors of 512 bytes, making the interface theoretically capable of capacities of up to 137,438,953,472 bytes or 128 gigabytes. Please note that DOS-based file systems still limit individual partitions to 2.1GB.

After confirming that the drive supports LBA addressing, the BIOS constructs an **Enhanced Drive Parameter Table** (**EDPT**). The EDPT is actually two tables – one that accepts CHS information from the drive's response to the Identify Drive command, and another that is filled with translated (LBA) information for the operating system. From this point, the BIOS and the drive communicate using the LBA format.

IDE Data Transfer

There are two methods whereby data transfer is accomplished in IDE drives. The first is **Processor Input/Output (PIO).** There are several PIO modes defined that allow increased transfer rates, the most recent being **PIO Mode 4**. The other method is called **Direct Memory Access (DMA).** There are two variations on DMA: **Single-word DMA** and **Multi-word DMA**. These two DMA categories are further divided into modes that allow for increased performance. Further details on PIO and DMA are provided in the following sections.

Another way to speed up data transfer is through **caching**. **Caching** is the process where the system loads data from the hard disk to the **RAM** set aside as **cache memory**. The system may then refer to **cache memory** for information instead of going back to the hard disk, thereby increasing the processing speed. Please read on for more information on caching.

PIO Modes

PIO is the transfer method used on most IDE drives. PIO relies on the CPU to handle data transfer tasks. **PIO Modes 0, 1, and 2** are considered "blind" transfer modes, because the amount of data sent to the CPU is not modulated. In the case of PIO Modes 0-2, the CPU and drive do not have a means to monitor the availability of data transfer resources, and accordingly lack a means to "throttle" the amount of data transferred. Because of this, the amount of data sent by the drive in response to the CPU during a given transfer cycle must be fixed. In addition, the amount of the transferred data must be limited to the worst case of the amount of the drive's memory buffer which is guaranteed to be available for host transferring duties. PIO Modes 0, 1, and 2 are defined to provide increased performance levels within the limits of the blind transfer format.

Block PIO (BPIO), sometimes called **multi-sector data transfer**, is supported by local-bus controllers (and needs BIOS support as well) and counts the 512-byte transfer unit of normal PIO as a portion of a block that consists of n times 512-bytes. This feature greatly reduces interrupt overhead because more than one sector is processed per interrupt call. This has the effect of improving system performance. A compatible drive and controller that support the **Read Multiple** and **Write Multiple** commands, as well as a software package (such as *EZ-Drive*) that enables multi-sector data transfers, is required in order to take advantage of this feature.

PIO Mode 3 is defined in the ATA-2 update and is available on newer IDE drives. There are presently **PIO Mode 4** drives on the shelves, and **PIO Mode 5** is right around the corner. PIO Modes 3 and higher are also called **Programmed I/O**, **Throttled PIO, or Flow Control**, because they allow modulation of the amount of data being transferred in a cycle. This is accomplished through the use of a signal issued by the drive known as the **I/O Channel Ready** (**IORDY**), which is used to control data throttling.

PIO Modes 3 and greater require support by the drive, local-bus controller, and BIOS. If any one of these elements is not PIO Mode 3 capable, then only a blind transfer (PIO Modes 0, 1, or 2) can be enabled. This means that simply plugging in an Enhanced IDE drive into an older system will not result in higher drive performance.

	Table 3-4: PIO Modes		
PIO Mode	**Average Transfer Rate**	**Cycle Time**	**Flow Controlled?**
0	3.3MB/s	600ns	No
1	5.2MB/s	383ns	No
2	8.3MB/s	240ns	No
3	11.1MB/s	180ns	Yes
4	16.6MB/s	120ns	Yes

DMA Modes

DMA is usually offered as an option on IDE drives that can be enabled by jumpers. DMA allows the drive to bypass the CPU and control data transfer with the host memory directly. There are two types of DMA: **Single Word DMA** and **Multi-Word DMA**. DMA uses two handshaking signals, **DMA Request** (**DMARQ** or **DRQ**) and **DMA Acknowledge** (**DMACK** or **DACK**) to control the flow of data between the drive and host memory. DMARQ is asserted by the drive when it is ready to transfer data to or from the host. DMACK is returned by the host when the data transfer cycle is completed. The drive must wait until the host asserts the DMACK signal before negating the first DMARQ signal and asserting another DMARQ, if there is more data to transfer.

Single-word DMA means that a data string of specified length is transferred per DMARQ/DMACK handshake cycle. **DMA Modes 0, 1**, and **2** define progressive performance increases.

	Table 3-5: Single-Word DMA Modes		
DMA MODE	**AVERAGE TRANSFER RATE**	**CYCLE TIME**	**REQUIREMENTS**
0	2.08MB/s	960ns	DMA support
1	4.16MB/s	480ns	DMA support
2	8.33MB/s	240ns	DMA support

Multi-word DMA is more sophisticated. Multi-word DMA means that the host withholds the DMACK signal while there is data remaining to be transferred between the host and drive. Multi-Word DMA requires a local bus controller that supports the defined **Multi-Word DMA Modes 0** and **1**.

	Table 3-6: Multi-Word DMA Modes		
MULTI-WORD DMA MODE	**AVERAGE TRANSFER RATE**	**CYCLE TIME**	**REQUIREMENTS**
0	4.16MB/s	480ns	DMA support/Local-bus controller
1	13.33MB/s	150ns	DMA support/Local-bus controller

Why are there two data transfer methods supported on modern IDE drives? The main reason is to maintain backwards-compatibility for the vastly diverse IDE hardware on the market today. In the past, advances in processor and data-bus technologies have alternately made PIO or DMA the most practical way to increase data transfer speeds.

Which mode should you choose? You should enable the highest performing mode that your system supports. As of the time this text was written, hardware that complies with the ATA-2 standard is readily available. If your equipment is not of very recent manufacture, it may not support PIO Mode 3 or greater, or either of the Multi-Word DMA modes. Remember, the best data transfer rate your system is capable of depends on the highest PIO or DMA mode that is supported by the drive, controller, and BIOS.

IDE Encoding

IDE drives use RLL encoding. See page 18 for more information on encoding.

IDE Identify Drive Command

The **Identify Drive** command is supported by almost all newer IDE drives. It allows the host system to interrogate the IDE drive concerning its parameters and available data transfer modes. Automatic detection of drive type requires that the drive support this command. The Micro House utility **MHIDE**, which is included on the CD-ROM that comes with this text, gives concise information derived from the Identify Drive command.

Low-Level Formatting IDE Drives

All IDE drives are low-level formatted by the factory. Reformatting these drives is not recommended as it may erase the factory defect map and may even destroy the drive.

You may come across programs that claim to low-level IDE drives. These programs simply erase the areas of the disk that contain data. They do not re-initialize the sector boundaries. These programs can be quite helpful when nothing else will get the drive running.

IDE Drive Interleave

Modern IDE drives do not require interleaving, or, in a technical sense, IDE drives use an interleave of 1:1. Please see page 21 for an explanation of interleaving.

ATAPI

ATA-2 addresses a major shortcoming of the original ATA specification in that it allows for the attachment of peripherals other than hard drives. The ATA Packet Interface (ATAPI), is incorporated into the ATA-2 specification for this purpose. ATAPI, which was derived from parts of the SCSI-2 command set, offers a more standardized way of connecting some of the most popular peripherals – making the use of proprietary adapter cards unnecessary. No other system hardware support is required – simply attach the ATAPI device to an available IDE channel and use the appropriate driver for the OS. IDE tape drives and CD players are now commonly available.

IDE Connector and Pin-Outs

This interface uses one 40-pin cable that must not exceed 24" in length. This interface is bus-specific. Two types of IDE interfaces are covered in this section: ATA and (obsolete) IDE(XT) types. The ATA type is per X3T9 committee specifications. The ATA-2 pin-outs are identical to that of the ATA.

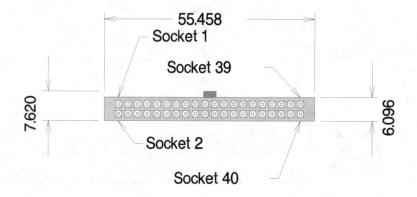

Figure 3-3: IDE Connector (dimensions specified in mm)

ATA/ATA-2 Signal Descriptions

Table 3-7: ATA/ATA-2 Pin Assignments

Pin	Signal	Description	Pin	Signal	Description
1	RESET	»Drive Reset	2	Ground	Ground
3	DD7	«»Data Line Bit 7	4	DD8	«»Data Line Bit 8
5	DD6	«»Data Line Bit 6	6	DD9	«»Data Line Bit 9
7	DD5	«»Data Line Bit 5	8	DD10	«»Data Line Bit 10
9	DD4	«»Data Line Bit 4	10	DD11	«»Data Line Bit 11
11	DD3	«»Data Line Bit 3	12	DD12	«»Data Line Bit 12
13	DD2	«»Data Line Bit 2	14	DD13	«»Data Line Bit 13
15	DD1	«»Data Line Bit 1	16	DD14	«»Data Line Bit 14
17	DD0	«»Data Line Bit 0	18	DD15	«»Data Line Bit 15
19	Ground	Ground	20	key pin	Unused (used for keying)
21	DMARQ	« DMA Request	22	Ground	Ground
23	-DIOW	»I/O Write Data	24	Ground	Ground
25	-DIOR	»I/O Read Data	26	Ground	Ground
27	-IORDY	»I/O Channel Ready	✪28	SPSYNC/CSEL	»Spindle Sync/Cable Select
29	-DMACK	»DMA Acknowledge	30	Ground	Ground
31	INTRQ	«Interrupt Request	32	-IOCS16	«Host 16 Bit I/O
33	DA1	»Host Address Bus Bit 1	✪34	-PDIAG	«»Passed diagnostics
35	DA0	»Host Address Bus Bit 0	36	DA2	»Host Address Bus Bit 2
37	CS1FX-	»Host Chip Select 0	38	-CS3FX	»Host Chip Select 1
✪39	-DASP	«Drive active/Drive 1 Present	40	Ground	Ground

The "-" preceding the signal description indicates an active low signal.
"«" = output from drive,
"»" = input to drive,
"«»" = bi-directional.
"✪" denotes drive intercommunication signals.

See below for drive intercommunication signal flow:

Table 3-8: IDE Intercommunication Signal Flow

Host		Drive 0		Drive 1
28	—→	28	<-SPSYNC->	28
34	═	34	<-PDIAG-->	34
39	<—	39	<-DASP-->	39

ATA/ATA-2 Signals

Drive Reset (RESET): This signal from the host system is asserted for at least 25ms after voltage levels have stabilized during power on and is negated thereafter, unless some event requires that the drive(s) be reset following power on.

Drive Data Bus (DD0-DD15): This is an 8- or 16-bit bi-directional data bus between the host and the drive. The lower 8 bits are used for 8-bit transfers, e.g. registers and ECC bytes. All 16 bits may be used for data transfers.

Drive I/O Write (-DIOW): This is the Write strobe signal. The rising edge of -DIOW clocks data from the host data bus, DD0-DD7 or DD0-DD15, into a register or the data port of the drive.

Drive I/O Read (-DIOR): This is the Read strobe signal. The falling edge of -DIOR enables data from a register or the data port of the drive onto the host data bus, DD0-DD7 or DD0-DD15. The rising edge of -DIOR latches data at the host.

DMA Acknowledge (-DMACK - Optional): This signal is used by the host in response to DMARQ to either acknowledge that data has been accepted, or that data is available.

DMA Request (-DMARQ - Optional): This signal, used for DMA data transfers between host and drive, will be asserted by the drive when it is ready to transfer data to or from the host. The direction of data transfer is controlled by -DIOR and -DIOW. This signal is used in a handshake manner with -DMACK, i.e., the drive will wait until the host asserts -DMACK before negating DMARQ and before re-asserting DMARQ, if there is more data to transfer.

When a DMA operation is enabled, -IOCS16, -CS1FX and -CS3FX will not be asserted and transfers will be 16 bits wide.

NOTE: ATA products with DMA capability require a pull-down resistor on this signal to prevent spurious data transfers. This resistor may affect driver requirements for drives sharing this signal in systems with unbuffered ATA signals.

I/O Channel Ready (IORDY - Optional): This signal is negated to extend the host transfer cycle of any host register access (Read or Write) when the drive is not ready to respond to a data transfer request. When IORDY is not negated, IORDY will be in a high impedance state.

Spindle Synchronization (SPSYNC - Optional): This signal may be either input or output to the drive depending on a vendor-defined switch. If a drive is set to MASTER, the signal is output and if a drive is set to SLAVE, the signal is input.

There is no requirement that each drive implementation be plug-compatible to the extent that a multiple vendor drive subsystem be operable. Mix and match of different manufacturers' drives is unlikely because RPM, sync fields, sync bytes, etc., need to be virtually identical. However, if drives are designed to match the following recommendation, controllers can operate drives with a single implementation.

There can only be one MASTER drive at a time in a configuration. The host or the drive designated as master can generate SPSYNC at least once per rotation, but may be at a higher frequency.

SPSYNC received by a drive is used as the synchronization signal to lock the spindles in step. The time to achieve synchronization varies and is indicated by the drive setting DRDY. If the drive does not achieve synchronization following power on or a reset, it will not set DRDY.

- A master drive or the host generates SPSYNC and transmits it.
- A slave drive does not generate SPSYNC and must be responsible to synchronize its index to SPSYNC.
- If a drive does not support synchronization, it will ignore SPSYNC.
- In the event that a drive previously synchronized loses synchronization, but is otherwise operational, it does not clear DRDY.

Prior to the introduction of this standard, SPSYNC was defined as DALE (Drive Address Latch Enable) and used for an address-valid indication from the host system. The host address and chip selects, DAO through DA2, -CS1FX, and -CS3FX were valid at the negation of DALE. Because of this, the drive did not need to latch these signals with DALE.

Cable Select (CSEL): The drive is configured as either Drive 0 or Drive 1, depending on the value of CSEL:

- If CSEL is grounded then the drive address is 0
- If CSEL is open then the drive address is 1

Special cabling can be used by the system manufacturer to selectively ground CSEL. For example, CSEL of Drive 0 is connected to the CSEL conductor in the cable, and is grounded, thus allowing the drive to recognize itself as Drive 0. CSEL of Drive 1 is not connected to CSEL because the conductor is removed, thus the drive can recognize itself as Drive 1.

Drive Interrupt (INTRQ): This signal is used to interrupt the host system. INTRQ is asserted only when the drive has a pending interrupt, the drive is selected, and the host has cleared nIEN in the Device Control Register. If nIEN=1, or the drive, is not selected, this output is in a high impedance state, regardless of the presence or absence of a pending interrupt.

INTRQ is negated by:

- Assertion of -RESET, or
- The setting of SRST of the Device Control Register, or
- The host writing the Command Register, or
- The host reading the Status Register.

NOTE: Some drives may negate INTRQ on PIO data transfer completion, except on a single sector read or on the last sector of a multi-sector read.

On PIO transfers, INTRQ is asserted at the beginning of each data block to be transferred. A data block is typically a single sector, except when declared otherwise by use of the Set Multiple Command. An exception occurs on Format Track, Write Sector(s), Write Buffer and Write Long commands, and -INTRQ will not be asserted at the beginning of the first data block to be transferred.

Drive 16-bit I/O (-IOCS16): Except for DMA transfers, -IOCS16 indicates to the host system that the 16-bit data port has been addressed and that the drive is prepared to send or receive a 16-bit data word. This signal is an open collector output.

- When transferring in PIO mode, if -IOCS16 is not asserted, transfers are 8-bit using DD0-7.
- When transferring in PIO mode, if -IOCS16 is asserted, transfers are 16-bit using DD0-15 for 16-bit data transfers.
- When transferring in DMA mode, the host uses a 16-bit DMA channel and -IOCS16 will not be asserted.

Passed Diagnostics (-PDIAG): This signal will be asserted by Drive 1 to indicate to Drive 0 that it has completed diagnostics. A 10K pull-up resistor will be used on this signal by each drive.

Following a power-on reset, software reset or -RESET, Drive 1 will negate -PDIAG within 1 msec (to indicate to Drive 0 that it is busy). Drive 1 will then assert -PDIAG within 30 seconds to indicate that it is no longer busy and is able to provide status. After the assertion of -PDIAG, Drive 1 may be unable to accept commands until it has finished its reset procedure and is ready (DRDY=1).

Following the receipt of a valid Execute Drive Diagnostics command, Drive 1 will negate -PDIAG within 1 msec to indicate to Drive 0 that it is busy and has not yet passed its drive diagnostics. If Drive 1 is present, then Drive 0 will wait for up to 5 seconds after the receipt of a valid Execute Drive Diagnostics command for Drive 1 to assert -PDIAG. Drive 1 should clear BSY before asserting -PDIAG, as -PDIAG is used to indicate that Drive 1 has passed its diagnostics and is ready to post status.

If -DASP (see below) was not asserted by Drive 1 during reset initialization, Drive 0 will post its own status immediately after it completes diagnostics and clears the Drive 1 Status Register to 00h. Drive 0 may be unable to accept commands until it has finished its reset procedure and is ready (DRDY=1).

Drive Address Bus (DA0-DA2): This is a three-bit, binary-coded address asserted by the host to access a register or data port in the drive.

Drive chip select 0 (-CS1FX): This is the chip select signal decoded from the host address bus used to select the Command Block Registers.

Drive chip select 1 (-CS3FX): This is the chip select signal decoded from the host address bus used to select the Control Block Registers.

Drive Active/Drive 1 Present: (-DASP): This is a time-multiplexed signal that indicates that a drive is active, or that Drive 1 is present. This signal is an open collector output and each drive must have a 10K pull-up resistor.

- During power on initialization or after -RESET is negated, -DASP will be asserted by Drive 1 within 400 msec to indicate that Drive 1 is present.
- Drive 0 will allow up to 450 msec for Drive 1 to assert -DASP. If Drive 1 is not present, Drive 0 may assert -DASP to drive an activity LED.
- -DASP will be negated following acceptance of the first valid command by Drive 1 or after 31 seconds, whichever comes first.
- Any time after negation of -DASP, either drive may assert -DASP to indicate that a drive is active.

NOTE: Prior to the development of this standard, products were introduced which did not time-multiplex the -DASP signal. Some used two jumpers to indicate to Drive 0 whether Drive 1 was present. If such a drive is jumpered to indicate Drive 1 is present, it should work successfully with a Drive 1 that complies with this standard. If installed as Drive 1, such a drive may not work successfully because it may not assert -DASP to indicate that the drive is active.

IDE(XT) Signal Descriptions

	Table 3-9: IDE(XT) Pin Assignments				
Pin	**Signal**	**Description**	**Pin**	**Signal**	**Description**
1	RESET	»Drive Reset	2		Ground
3	DD7	«»Data Line Bit 7	4		Ground
5	DD6	«»Data Line Bit 6	6		Ground
7	DD5	«»Data Line Bit 5	8		Ground
9	DD4	«»Data Line Bit 4	10		Ground
11	DD3	«»Data Line Bit 3	12		Ground
13	DD2	«»Data Line Bit 2	14		Ground
15	DD1	«»Data Line Bit 1	16		Ground
17	DD0	«»Data Line Bit 0	18		Ground
19	Ground	Ground	20	key pin	Unused
21	AEN	»Address Enable	22		Ground
23	-DIOW	»I/O Write Data	24		Ground
25	-DIOR	»I/O Read Data	26		Ground
27	-DACK	»DMA Acknowledge	28		Ground
29	DRQ	»DMA Request	30		Ground
31	INTRQ	«Interrupt Request	32		Ground
33	DA1	»Address Bus Bit 1	34		Ground
35	DA0	»Address Bus Bit 0	36		Ground
37	-CS1FX	»Drive Chip Select 0	38		Ground
39		Unused	40		Ground

The "-" preceding the signal description indicates an active low signal.
"«" = output from drive
"»" = input to drive
"«»" = bi-directional

IDE(XT) Signals

Drive Reset (-RESET):   This signal from the host system is asserted for at least 25 msec after voltage levels have been stabilized during power on, and is negated thereafter unless some event requires that the drive(s) be reset.

Drive Data Bus (DD0-DD07):   This is an 8-bit, bi-directional data bus between the host and the drive.

I/O Write (-DIOW):   This is the Write strobe signal. The rising edge of -DIOW clocks data from the host data bus, DD0-DD7, into a register or the data port of the drive.

I/O Read (-DIOR):   This is the Read strobe signal. The falling edge of -DIOR enables data from a register or the data port of the drive onto the host data bus, DD0-DD7 or DD0-DD15. The rising edge of -DIOR latches data at the host.

DMA Acknowledge (DACK): This is a System I/O channel signal which is asserted to indicate that a DRQ signal has been honored. -DACK will clear the DRQ signal, and in conjunction with either -IORD or -IOWR, will cause DMA data to be read from or written to the device.

Address Enable (AEN): This is a System I/O channel signal that is asserted during a DMA cycle. It is used to disable the decoding of I/O port addresses during DMA cycles.

Interrupt Request (INTRQ): This signal is used to interrupt the host system. INTRQ is asserted only when the drive has a pending interrupt, the drive is selected, and the host has cleared nIEN in the Device Control Register. If nIEN=1, or the drive is not selected, this output is in a high impedance state, regardless of the presence or absence of a pending interrupt.

INTRQ is negated by:

- Assertion or -RESET, or
- The setting of SRST in the Device Control Register, or
- The host writing the Command Register, or
- The host reading the Status Register.

On PIO transfers, INTRQ is asserted at the beginning of each data block to be transferred. A data block is typically a single sector, except when declared otherwise by use of the Set Multiple Command. An exception occurs on Format Track, Write Sector(s), Write Buffer and Write Long commands. -INTRQ will not be asserted at the beginning of the first data block to be transferred.

Drive Address Bus (DA0-DA2): This is a three-bit binary-coded address asserted by the host to access a register or data port in the drive.

Drive chip select 0 (-CS1FX): This line is the Card Select to the drive. It is generated from a Decoder external to the drive and is used to enable the programmed I/O operations.

The SCSI Interface

SCSI General Description

SCSI stands for "**Small Computer Systems Interface**." The SCSI interface can more accurately be described as a bus. This is because the so-called device interface, or host adapter, leaves most of the interfacing functions to the devices attached to it. Up to seven (fifteen on some recent variations) SCSI peripherals, such as hard drives, tape drive units, CD-ROM drives, and even printers, can be daisy-chained together through one interface. Each device must have its own **Logical Unit Number** (**LUN**) so that the interface can identify it. Note that the host or host adapter is considered a device.

SCSI drives are usually found in high-end systems that require the maximum available performance. SCSI drives are generally more expensive than their IDE counterparts, and are more difficult to install.

SCSI drives, like IDE, are considered "intelligent" devices, meaning all the electronics used to control drive functions are self-contained on the drive unit itself. The SCSI interface goes a step further by incorporating the instructions needed to communicate with the host system. This is an advantage over IDE, which depends on instructions contained in the BIOS in order to communicate with the host (see page 34). It is also the reason that a mechanically identical SCSI drive is more expensive than its IDE counterpart. Because the BIOS is not used in communicating between the drive and the host system, the Drive Type in CMOS is set to "0" or "Not Installed" for SCSI installation. The drive firmware or installed device driver handles communication tasks.

Each of the seven SCSI devices can theoretically have up to eight subdevices (providing your SCSI devices and software support this configuration – fifty-six devices!). Commands are associated with an LUN and sent down the SCSI bus. The device (drive) with that LUN will accept the commands and it perform the requested task.

Some SCSI devices require you to use a device driver in the CONFIG.SYS file. If you are experiencing difficulties, check with the controller or peripheral manufacturer to see if a driver is required.

SCSI Variations

One of the reasons that SCSI has not enjoyed the popularity of the IDE interface is the wide scope of the standard itself. In the past, SCSI device vendors have liberally interpreted the specification, resulting in compatibility problems and adding to the difficulty of set-up operations. The bewildering array of required device drivers can intimidate even experienced technicians.

There can be many variations of the SCSI theme. The **SCSI-1** interface can basically be configured as single-ended or differential. **SCSI-2**, on the other hand, has provisions for straight SCSI-2, on up to **Differential Wide Fast SCSI**. Each variation is hardware-specific and is not compatible with the others. This section covers the specifics of the various SCSI versions.

SCSI-1 vs. SCSI-2 and SCSI-3

SCSI-1 is the original industry standard published by ANSI in 1986. **SCSI-2** encompasses the previous SCSI-1 standard, meaning it is backwards-compatible. SCSI-2 not only adds technical improvements, it also addresses compatibility issues by incorporating the **Common Command Set**. **SCSI-3** is not a recognized standard at the time this text is being written, but it is anticipated to be approved soon. Improvements include provisions for up to fifteen devices from a single SCSI adapter, and maximum data transfer rates better than 100MB/s.

Single-Ended SCSI vs. Differential SCSI

Single-Ended and **Differential** refer to the type of cable employed for the SCSI bus. Single-ended accounts for the vast majority of SCSI devices. Differential SCSI is designed for specialized environments that require cable lengths of up to 25 meters (single-ended is good for no more than 6 meters). Differential cabling is used to overcome the signal degradation that can occur over relatively long cables.

Differential cables use twice as many signal lines as single-ended cables. All signals sent by the host adapter along the SCSI bus are accompanied by mirror-image (inverted) signals along corresponding wires. The SCSI device attached to the other end takes the difference (differential) between the two signals to determine the intended input. Any noise introduced into the line between the host adapter and SCSI device should affect both lines equally and be canceled out by the differential process.

Note that differential and single-ended SCSI devices are not compatible and require different host adapters. Attempting to connect a differential drive to a single-ended host adapter (or vice-versa) will result in damage to the system.

Standard vs. Fast SCSI

Fast SCSI is a feature of SCSI-2 that effectively doubles the average throughput over the same 50-pin cable by using synchronous (vs. asynchronous) data transfer. Fast SCSI allows transfers up to 10MB/s. Other Fast SCSI flavors include Fast 20 (20MB/s) and Fast 40 (40MB/s).

Standard vs. Wide SCSI

Wide SCSI uses a 68-pin **P-cable** to allow a 16-bit data path (vs. 8-bits on the 50-pin **A-cable**). Average data transfer rates of up to 20MB/s can be attained with Wide SCSI. Combining Wide data paths with Fast transfer techniques results in Fast Wide SCSI, enabling possibilities in the 80MB/s transfer range.

Serial SCSI

The SCSI variations in the preceding sections transport signals along parallel lines. Drive manufacturers have been eyeing high-bandwidth serial techniques as the next step in advancing drive throughput. Serial data transfer involves transporting data in packets, similar to techniques used in local area networks (LANs). New interfaces such as **SSA** (**Serial Storage Architecture**) and **FC** (**Fiber Channel**) provide up to 100MB/s on a single channel and are designed to eventually provide a single high-speed peripheral interface. SSA and FC in their present incarnations basically replace the parallel physical transport layer with the serial format. The command structure (internal drive logic) is still SCSI-2.

Table 3-10: SCSI Variations

SCSI Type	SCSI Spec.	Connector	Max. LUNs	Bits	Max. Throughput
Standard	SCSI-1/SCSI-2	A-cable	8	8	5 MB/s
SCSI Fast	SCSI-2	A-cable	8	8	10 MB/s
SCSI Wide	SCSI-2	P-cable	16	16	10 MB/s
SCSI Fast-20 (Ultra SCSI)	SCSI-3	A-cable	8	8	20 MB/s
SCSI Fast-40	SCSI-3	P-cable	16	8	40 MB/s
SCSI Fast-Wide	SCSI-3	P-cable	16	16	80 MB/s
SSA	N/A	SSA	127	serial	80 MB/s
Fiber Channel	N/A	Fiber Channel	127	serial	100 MB/s

RAID

RAID is a general scheme to increase I/O performance by making a modular array of hard drives appear as a single storage unit. The term **RAID** stands for "**Redundant Array of Inexpensive** (or **Independent**) **Disks**." RAID is most useful in high-end applications such as network file servers, where numerous I/O requests compete for drive access, or graphics intensive environments, where sequential file retrievals monopolize I/O resources.

The primary advantage to RAID is that it improves I/O performance by enabling faster data transfer. The scheme basically consists of an array of standard hard drives installed to create one large logical drive. Data files are broken into segments and distributed throughout the array so drive heads can access data segments in parallel (simultaneously).

The other advantage is that RAID provides options to guard data against media failure by simultaneously duplicating complete data sets or through the use of parity schemes from which data may be reconstructed. Some RAID versions even allow "hot-swapping" – meaning the ability to pull out a bad drive and install a new one while the array is still in use.

Coordinating multiple hard disks to operate as one logical unit is typically achieved through a RAID controller. Most controllers house processors that manage data access and distribution functions, as well as parity checking functions used in data recovery. Some even have their own CPU and RAID BIOS, allowing drive arrays to be initialized and managed independently of the host computer. On the lower-end, RAID controllers can reside on a bus within the host computer. Hard drives attached to this controller comprise the RAID array. On high-end RAID systems, both the controller and hard drives are housed in an external cabinet. In both systems, the RAID unit operates with all internal functions transparent to the host computer.

Although RAID is not intended to be interface-specific, SCSI drives are generally used by default due their availability and high performance. Typically, RAID controllers support multiple SCSI interfaces that include both 8-bit and 16-bit data paths (see "Standard vs. Wide SCSI" above). On most external RAID cabinets, the power and interface connection between the host computer and cabinet is accomplished via a single 80-pin **Single Connector Attachment** (**SCA**) connector. Some manufacturers use proprietary 100 and 120-pin connectors.

RAID accomplishes the formation of a single logical drive from multiple units through a process called "**striping**." Striping involves arranging information so that individual files are divided into segments that are then interleaved (distributed) among drives in the array. An individual file, for example, may have one segment on Drive 1, a second segment on Drive 2, and so on. The portion of the file that exists on a single drive is a stripe segment. A stripe segment can be as small as a single byte, or as large as multiple sectors.

The size of stripe segments has considerable effect on the performance of a RAID system. In I/O environments that process large files, such as graphics, it is desirable to select smaller stripe segments (such as a byte) so that data from a single file is distributed across all disks. All drive heads can then operate simultaneously to retrieve or write segments of the same file, increasing throughput substantially. In network environments, where there are many I/O requests for smaller files, a larger stripe segment is preferable. Smaller stripe segments would tie up all drive heads on a single operation. If a stripe segment is large enough to allow a single small file to fit on a single drive, then multiple files may be accessed across the array simultaneously.

Data recovery is available on most RAID systems. When a drive within an array fails, one of two options exist depending on the RAID level:

1. If data has been duplicated on pairs, RAID switches data access to the duplicate drive.
2. If parity information has been saved, the lost data is rebuilt on a spare drive that is brought into the array.

Some systems require manual intervention to add this drive and initiate the rebuild process. Newer high-end versions support back-up drives that automatically come online whenever a drive fails.

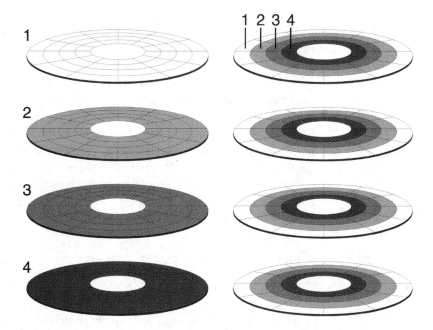

The platters on the left represent non-striped disks. The platters on the right are striped. Both would contain the same information, but the striped disks have the data arrayed across all five platters, rather than sequentially arranged (Disk 1, then Disk 2, etc.).

Figure 3-4: RAID Striping

There are six levels of RAID offered, each with unique functions:

RAID 0 is the simplest and has the fastest data transfer rates. RAID 0 distributes (stripes) data across the array without any duplication. Data throughput is faster because stripe segments are transferred in parallel between array elements and the controller. RAID 0 is in effect a misnomer because it does not offer the protection of redundancy against mechanical failure. If one drive module goes down, the entire array is down.

RAID 1, in contrast to RAID 0, consists of a pair of drives to which duplicate information is written simultaneously, a process known as **data mirroring**. The smallest unit of RAID 1 is two drives, called a mirrored pair. The simplest form of RAID 1 consists of a single mirrored pair containing duplicate data. When more than one mirrored pair exists in the array, data is striped across one side of the array, with the stripes being mirrored on the other half. Each mirrored pair contains identical stripes. If one half of a mirrored pair experiences a fault condition, the other is there for error recovery. Like RAID 0, read/write operations occur in parallel, significantly increasing throughput. The advantages of RAID 1 are that it offers automatic, real-time backup of data and faster access. The disadvantage is that it doubles the number of drives required in order to operate.

RAID 2 has been superseded by RAID 3, over which it offers no advantages.

RAID 3 combines data striping with a dedicated parity drive for error recovery. It requires at least three drives per array: two for striped data and one for parity information. The data is striped in smaller segments, down to one byte, and drives are accessed in parallel. Because of this, the drive spindles must be synchronized to avoid delays. The advantages to RAID 3 are that long records can be accessed quickly and it provides some protection against media failure. The disadvantage is that the format is a poor choice for networks, as each I/O operation occupies the entire array.

RAID 4 is similar to RAID 3, except that the striping process uses longer segments and the drive's spindles are not synchronized to facilitate simultaneous file access.

RAID 5 does not require a separate parity drive because data and parity information are striped together across the array. Although the size of stripe segments is optional at this level, a large stripe segment that confines individual files to one or two drives is preferable for the same reason as RAID 4.

History of the SCSI Interface

This interface originated as the SASI (Shugart Associates System Interface) in 1979. It was one of several disk interfaces that worked at a logical level instead of the widely accepted device level. Working at a logical level allowed for a stable interface while the disk devices could change rapidly.

In 1980, Shugart Associates attempted to replace IPI (Intelligent Peripheral Interface) through the X3T9 Standards Committee, but was not able to do so because of limited industry acceptance. NCR added features to Shugart's original interface and in 1982 the X3T9 decided to start a project for SCSI based on SASI. During the project, optical WORM (Write Once, Read Many) commands were added, no longer limiting SCSI to hard drives.

In 1984 NCR released the NCR 5380. This chip includes on-chip, single-ended drivers/receivers that allowed the industry to produce inexpensive SCSI interfaces. This is the chip that Apple Computer originally implemented in their Macintosh computers, which gained SCSI widespread acceptance.

In 1986, ANSI approved SCSI as ANSI X3.131-1986. Also in 1986, X3T9 began the SCSI-2 project to incorporate the CCS (Common Command Set) into SCSI, plus numerous other improvements and additions.

After years of delay, ANSI approved the SCSI-2 standard (X3.131-1994) in 1994. In addition to technical improvements and the ability to connect a wider variety of devices, SCSI-2 addresses the need for better compatibility among the various manufacturers' products. New SCSI standards are currently being worked on the the X3T10 subgroup of the X3 Accredited Standards Committee. Further advances are being addressed by SCSI-3, which is presently under development. The complete SCSI standards documents can be obtained from ANSI.

 # SCSI Physical Characteristics

See the section in Chapter One entitled "Basic Drive Components" for information regarding the basic workings of a hard drive. SCSI drives vary widely in physical dimensions, but are commonly seen in 3.5 in., third or half-height formats in order to fit in the drive bays of most PC casings being manufactured today.

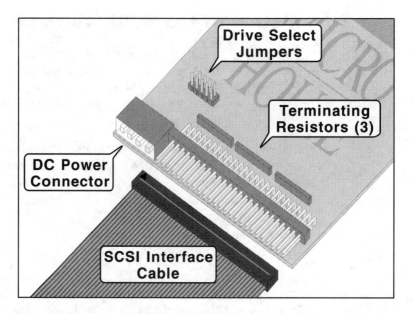

This diagram depicts the under-side of a typical SCSI drive. This layout will vary from drive to drive, but the basic connections will always be present.

Figure 3-5: SCSI Connection Diagram

SCSI Cabling

There are basically two types of SCSI cables in use today, along with their corresponding differential versions. The most common is the 50-pin **A-cable**. SCSI-2 specifications accommodate the 68-pin **P-cable** for **Wide SCSI**, which will be standardized under SCSI-3. Among the differences from ST-506/412 and ESDI cabling are that no separate data cable exists, there are no twisted wires, and multiple connectors may be present on the cable for the installation of multiple devices. There are actually many variations of SCSI cables, depending on the application. Please see the section in this chapter titled "SCSI Variations" and the SCSI Cables and Pin-outs section in this chapter for more information.

Terminating Resistor Packs

These are socketed resistor packs, sometimes called terminators, that are usually yellow and sometimes black or blue. On SCSI drives there are several of these on each hard drive. They can be found on the underside of the drive near the drive header cable. Terminating resistors for the first and last drives in the chain should be installed. All resistors for drives connected in the middle of the daisy-chain should be removed. SCSI controllers are considered one of the eight devices allowed and so have terminators on them to terminate the start of the chain. On some drives the resistors are not socketed or intended for removal – if this is the case, the resistors can usually be enabled internally by jumper or switch settings.

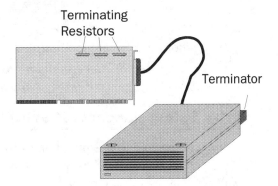

Terminator configuration: Single Drive Only (Internal or External).

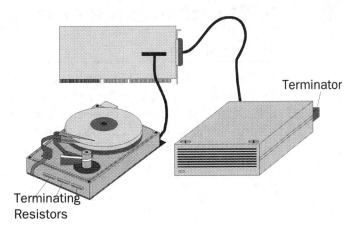

Terminator configuration: Internal and External Drives.

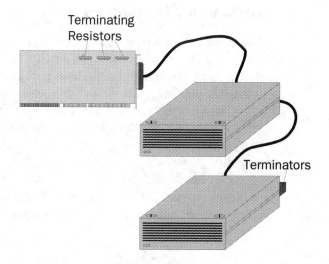

Terminator configuration: Multiple Internal or External Drives.

Figure 3-6: SCSI Terminating Resistor/Drive Select Configurations

Drive Select Jumpers (SCSI ID)

There will three or four 2-pin jumpers for the Drive Select function. These jumpers are used to set a drive select number (SCSI ID) between 0 and 7 (15 for Wide SCSI), with each jumper representing a binary unit, or bit. In most cases a SCSI boot drive should be set to SCSI ID 0, which would leave all jumpers open.

SCSI Technical Information

SCSI Adapters

Recall that SCSI drives, like IDE models, are intelligent and do not depend on the host adapter for drive controlling functions. Unlike IDE, SCSI host adapters do not depend on the interfacing programs resident in the computer's BIOS. This means that SCSI adapters must have their own method of communicating with the host system. This is part of the reason for the greater cost of SCSI over IDE.

Due to a lack of standardization in the past, manufacturers of SCSI adapters have had more freedom in choosing how their products accomplish an interface. Because of this, the software used to set up SCSI adapters, such as device drivers, was usually specific to a particular model. SCSI-2 has attempted to address this problem with the **Advanced SCSI Programming Interface (ASPI)**. The intent of ASPI is to standardize SCSI devices so that a device driver for any ASPI-compatible peripheral will work for any ASPI-compatible adapter, regardless of the manufacturer.

BIOS Drive Type Selection

Almost all SCSI controllers do not use the host system BIOS, therefore the drive type selection in the CMOS setup should be set to "0" or "Not Installed."

SCSI Drive Addressing

SCSI drives access data through **Logical Block Addressing (LBA)**. This means that the LBAs, or sectors, are ordered sequentially, instead of the three-dimensional **CHS** addressing format used in drives using other interfaces. See page 18 for more information on CHS and LBA addressing.

To find the capacity of SCSI drives, simply multiply the number of sectors by the sector size (usually 512 bytes). For example:

1,032,192 sectors x 512 bytes/sector = 528,482,304 bytes

Although SCSI drives "think" in terms of LBA, the host system BIOS does not usually support this type of addressing. Generally, SCSI adapters bypass the host system BIOS either through a BIOS-ROM installed on the adapter itself, or through a replacement block device driver that is specific to the adapter model.

SCSI controllers with a replacement BIOS ROM perform a translation from CHS into LBA in order to remain compatible with standard BIOS **INT 13h** software interrupts. This means that in this case the drive is still subject to the limitations imposed on CHS parameters by the bits allocated to INT 13h (see below). Therefore SCSI drives using this type of controller are limited to approximately 8GB, the same as Enhanced IDE drives. See page 60 for information on BIOS-imposed CHS limits.

Low-Level Formatting

All newer SCSI drives are low-level formatted by the factory. Reformatting these drives is not usually necessary.

Low-level software for SCSI drives is specific to the host adapter model because of wide variations at the register level. The low-level program is usually resident in the adapter's firmware. Consult the user's manual that came with your SCSI adapter for information on accessing the low-level program.

SCSI INT 13h Handling

When implemented in a DOS-based system, SCSI drives access the host system through software **Interrupt 13h (INT 13h)** to remain compatible with the manner in which hard drives were intended to be interfaced through the AT BIOS. Usually, the programs necessary to access the hard drive reside in the computer's BIOS and are invoked through this software interrupt. In the case of SCSI drives, the host BIOS is bypassed by the firmware on the SCSI controller or the loaded SCSI device driver which redirect INT 13h calls to themselves. This is the reason that the "Drive Type 0" or "Not Installed" is selected for most SCSI drives in the CMOS setup.

Caching

Due to the high-performance applications that SCSI drives are being used for, cost is generally less of a consideration than for IDE systems. Because of this, SCSI controllers with on-board cache are fairly common.

Interleave

Modern SCSI drives do not require interleaving, or, in a technical sense, SCSI drives use an interleave of 1:1. Please see page 21 for an explanation of interleaving.

SCSI Connectors And Pin-Outs

SCSI A-Cable Connector and Pin Assignments

This interface uses one 50-pin cable. For a single-ended cable, a 50-conductor flat cable or a 25-signal twisted-pair cable is used. The maximum cable length is 6 meters. For a differential cable, a 50-conductor cable or 25-signal twisted-pair cable is used. The maximum cable length is 25 meters.

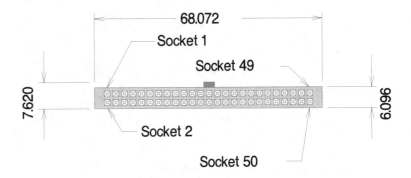

Figure 3-7: SCSI A-Cable Connector

(dimensions specified in mm)

Table 3-11: SCSI Single-Ended A-Cable Pin Assignments

Pin	Assignment	Pin	Signal	Assignment
1	Ground	2	-DB(0)	Data line 0
3	Ground	4	-DB(1)	Data line 1
5	Ground	6	-DB(2)	Data line 2
7	Ground	8	-DB(3)	Data line 3
9	Ground	10	-DB(4)	Data line 4
11	Ground	12	-DB(5)	Data line 5
13	Ground	14	-DB(6)	Data line 6
15	Ground	16	-DB(7)	Data line 7
17	Ground	18	-DB(P)	Parity line (data)
19	Ground	20	Ground	Ground
21	Ground	22	Ground	Ground
23	Ground	24	Ground	Ground
25	No connection	26	TERMPWR	Terminator power
27	Ground	28	Ground	Ground
29	Ground	30	Ground	Ground
31	Ground	32	-ATN	Attention
33	Ground	34	Ground	Ground
35	Ground	36	-BSY	Busy
37	Ground	38	-ACK	Acknowledge
39	Ground	40	-RST	Reset
41	Ground	42	-MSG	Message
43	Ground	44	-SEL	Select
45	Ground	46	-C/D	C/D
47	Ground	48	-REQ	Request
49	Ground	50	-I/O	I/O

Shield ground is optional on some cables.

Some shielded flat ribbon cables use pin 1 as a connection to the shield.

The "-" preceding the signal description indicates an active low signal.

Table 3-12: SCSI Differential A-Cable Pin Assignments

Pin	Signal	Assignment	Pin	Signal	Assignment
1	SG	Shield Ground	2	Ground	Ground
3	+DB(0)	Data Line 0	4	-DB(0)	Data Line 0
5	+DB(1)	Data Line 1	6	-DB(1)	Data Line 1
7	+DB(2)	Data Line 2	8	-DB(2)	Data Line 2
9	+DB(3)	Data Line 3	10	-DB(3)	Data Line 3
11	+DB(4)	Data Line 4	12	-DB(4)	Data Line 4
13	+DB(5)	Data Line 5	14	-DB(5)	Data Line 5
15	+DB(6)	Data Line 6	16	-DB(6)	Data Line 6
17	+DB(7)	Data Line 7	18	-DB(7)	Data Line 7
19	+DB(P)	Parity Line	20	-DB(P)	Parity Line
21	DIFFSENS	Differential Sense	22	Ground	Ground
23	Ground	Ground	24	Ground	Ground
25	TERMPWR	Terminator Power	26	TERMPWR	Terminator Power
27		Ground	28		Ground
29	+ATN	Attention	30	-ATN	Attention
31		Ground	32		Ground
33	+BSY	Busy	34	-BSY	Busy
35	+ACK	Acknowledge	36	-ACK	Acknowledge
37	+RST	Reset	38	-RST	Reset
39	+MSG	Message	40	-MSG	Message
41	+SEL	Select	42	-SEL	Select
43	+C/D	C/D	44	-C/D	C/D
45	+REQ	Request	46	-REQ	Request
47	+I/O	I/O	48	-I/O	I/O
49		Ground	50		Ground

Shield ground is optional on some cables.
Some shielded flat ribbon cables use pin 1 as a connection to the shield.
The "-" preceding the signal description indicates an active low signal.

SCSI P-Cable Connector and Pin Assignments

This interface uses one 68-pin cable. The maximum single-ended cable length is 6 meters. The maximum differential cable length is 25 meters.

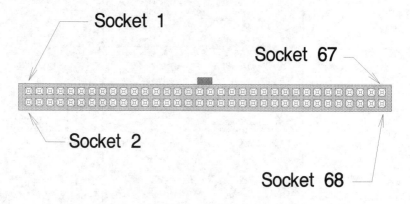

Figure 3-8: SCSI P-Cable Connector

(dimensions specified in mm)

Table 3-13: SCSI Single-Ended P-Cable Pin Assignments

Pin	Assignment	Pin	Signal	Assignment
1	Ground	35	-DB(12)	Data line 12
2	Ground	36	-DB(13)	Data line 13
3	Ground	37	-DB(14)	Data line 14
4	Ground	38	-DB(15)	Data line 15
5	Ground	39	-DB(P1)	Parity line 1
6	Ground	40	-DB(0)	Data line 0
7	Ground	41	-DB(1)	Data line 1
8	Ground	42	-DB(2)	Data line 2
9	Ground	43	-DB(3)	Data line 3
10	Ground	44	-DB(4)	Data line 4
11	Ground	45	-DB(5)	Data line 5
12	Ground	46	-DB(6)	Data line 6
13	Ground	47	-DB(7)	Data line 7
14	Ground	48	-DB(P 0)	Parity line 0
15	Ground	49	Ground	Ground
16	Ground	50	Ground	Ground
17	TERMPWR	51	TERMPWR	Terminator Power
18	TERMPWR	52	TERMPWR	Terminator Power
19	Reserved	53	Reserved	Reserved
20	Ground	54	Ground	Ground
21	Ground	55	-ATN	Attention
22	Ground	56	Ground	Ground
23	Ground	57	-BSY	Busy
24	Ground	58	-ACK	Acknowledge
25	Ground	59	-RST	Reset
26	Ground	60	-MSG	Message
27	Ground	61	-SEL	Select
28	Ground	62	-C/D	C/D
29	Ground	63	-REQ	Request
30	Ground	64	-I/O	I/O
31	Ground	65	-DB(8)	Data line 8
32	Ground	66	-DB(9)	Data line 9
33	Ground	67	-DB(10)	Data line 10
34	Ground	68	-DB(11)	Data line 11

The "-" preceding the signal description indicates an active low signal.

Table 3-14: SCSI Differential P-Cable Pin Assignments

Pin	Signal	Assignment	Pin	Signal	Assignment
1	+DB(12)	Data line 12	35	-DB(12)	Data line 12
2	+DB(13)	Data line 13	36	-DB(13)	Data line 13
3	+DB(14)	Data line 14	37	-DB(14)	Data line 14
4	+DB(15)	Data line 15	38	-DB(15)	Data line 15
5	+DB(P1)	Parity line 1	39	-DB(P1)	Parity line 1
6	Ground	Ground	40	Ground	Ground
7	+DB(0)	Data line 0	41	-DB(0)	Data line 0
8	+DB(1)	Data line 1	42	-DB(1)	Data line 1
9	+DB(2)	Data line 2	43	-DB(2)	Data line 2
10	+DB(3)	Data line 3	44	-DB(3)	Data line 3
11	+DB(4)	Data line 4	45	-DB(4)	Data line 4
12	+DB(5)	Data line 5	46	-DB(5)	Data line 5
13	+DB(6)	Data line 6	47	-DB(6)	Data line 6
14	+DB(7)	Data line 7	48	-DB(7)	Data line 7
15	+DB(P0)	Parity line 0	49	-DB(P0)	Parity line 0
16	DIFFSENS	Differential Sense	50	Ground	Ground
17	TERMPWR	Terminator Power	51	TERMPWR	Terminator Power
18	TERMPWR	Terminator Power	52	TERMPWR	Terminator Power
19	Reserved	Reserved	53	Reserved	Reserved
20	+ATN	Attention	54	-ATN	Attention
21	Ground	Ground	55	Ground	Ground
22	+BSY	Busy	56	-BSY	Busy
23	+ACK	Acknowledge	57	-ACK	Acknowledge
24	+RST	Reset	58	-RST	Reset
25	+MSG	Message	59	-MSG	Message
26	+SEL	Select	60	-SEL	Select
27	+C/D	C/D	61	-C/D	C/D
28	+REQ	Request	62	-REQ	Request
29	+I/O	I/O	63	-I/O	I/O
30	Ground	Ground	64	Ground	Ground
31	+DB(8)	Data line 8	65	-DB(8)	Data line 8
32	+DB(9)	Data line 9	66	-DB(9)	Data line 9
33	+DB(10)	Data line 10	67	-DB(10)	Data line 10
34	+DB(11)	Data line 11	68	-DB(11)	Data line 11

The "-" preceding the signal description indicates an active low signal.

SCSI Bus Signals

There are eighteen signals on the SCSI-1 Bus; nine are control and nine are data. (The optional parity signal is a data signal.) For SCSI-2, there are a total of twenty-six signals, the same nine control signals as SCSI-1 and seventeen data.

Busy (BSY): An "OR-tied" signal that indicates the bus is being used.

Select (SEL): A signal used by an initiator to select a target or by a target to re-select an initiator.

Control/Data (C/D): A signal driven by a target that indicates whether CONTROL or DATA information is on the DATA BUS. True indicates CONTROL.

Input/Output (I/O): A signal driven by a target that controls the direction of data movement on the DATA BUS with respect to an initiator. True indicates input to the initiator. This signal is also used to distinguish between SELECTION and RESELECTION phases. A signal driven by a target during the MESSAGE phase.

Request (REQ): A signal driven by a target to indicate a request for a REQ/ACK data transfer handshake.

Acknowledge (ACK): A signal driven by an initiator to indicate an acknowledgment for a REQ/ACK data transfer handshake.

Attention (ATN): A signal driven by an initiator to indicate the ATTENTION condition.

Reset (RST): An "OR-tied" signal that indicates the RESET condition.

Differential Sense (DIFFSENS - optional): Differential Alternative only. All signals consist of two lines denoted +SIGNAL and -SIGNAL. A signal is true when +SIGNAL is more positive than -SIGNAL, and a signal is false when -SIGNAL is more positive than +SIGNAL. All assigned signals must be terminated at each end of the cable.

NOTE: As an option, the DIFFSENS signal of the connector is reserved for an active high enable for the differential drivers. If a single-ended device or terminator is inadvertently connected, this signal is grounded, disabling the drivers.

Terminator Power (TERMPWR – optional):

Single-ended SCSI devices providing terminator power (TERMPWR) will have the following characteristics:

4.0 volts DC to 5.25 volts DC (VTerm): 800 milliamps minimum source drive capability 1.0 milliamp maximum sink capability (except for the purposes of providing power to an internal terminator) with 1.0 amp recommended current limiting (e.g., a fuse).

Differential SCSI devices providing terminator power (TERMPWR) will have the following characteristics:

600 milliamps minimum source drive capability, 1.0 milliamp maximum sink capability (except for the purposes of providing power to an internal terminator), with 1.0 amp recommended current limiting (e.g., a fuse).

The use of keyed connectors is recommended in SCSI devices that provide terminator power to prevent accidental grounding or mis-connection of terminator power.

SCSI devices that supply terminator power do so through a diode or similar semiconductor that prevents reverse-flow of power into the SCSI device.

Data Bus (DB(15-0,P)): Eight data bit signals (sixteen for SCSI-2), plus a parity-bit signal that form a DATA BUS. DB(7) is the most significant bit (DB(15) for SCSI-2) and has the highest priority during the ARBITRATION phase. Bit number, significance, and priority decrease downward to DB(0). A data bit is defined as 1 when the signal value is true and is defined as 0 when the signal value is false.

Data parity DB(P) is odd. The use of parity is a system option (i.e., a system is configured so that all SCSI devices on a bus generate parity and have parity detection enabled, or all SCSI devices have parity detection disabled or not implemented). Parity is not valid during the ARBITRATION phase.

The ESDI Interface

ESDI General Description

The **Enhanced Small Device Interface** (**ESDI**) was designed to address the limitations of ST-506/412 drives. At the time the ST-506/412 drives were developed, internal data transfer rates exceeded the ability of the computer to process data. Processor speeds and other electronic advances have since reversed this state. ESDI is similar to the ST-506/412 interface in that it uses the same cables and many of the same pin signals, but this is where the similarity ends.

The ESDI interface is a comprehensive improvement over ST-506/412. ESDI drives can transfer data up to 24 Mb/s, although most transfer at 10 Mb/s. ESDI controllers are more flexible than ST-506/412 in that they can *potentially* handle not only hard drives, but also floppy drives and tape backup units, and they can perform direct file transfers between these devices. This interface also features dramatically improved error checking over the ST-506/412, standard and is used mostly on larger capacity hard drives.

The circuitry that separates the data from the signal being read from the drive's read/write heads is called the **clock-data separator**. On ESDI drives, it is contained on the hard drive itself and not on the controller card. Signal/noise margins are improved because the data is separated from the signal before the degradation (which results from traveling longer distances down the cable to the interface) sets in. In addition, ESDI drive manufacturers are able to incorporate a clock-data separator that is specifically matched to the capabilities of the hard drive. The benefit is much greater throughput than could be achieved on the ST-506/412 format.

Data on these drives is stored in much higher densities than on ST-506/412 drives. The **sectors per track** (**SPT**) are usually 33, 34, 35, 48, or higher and may even have variable sectors. That is, the outer tracks may have more SPT than the inner tracks.

As with IDE and SCSI drives, the ESDI drive is somewhat "intelligent." It will accept commands (**opcodes**) to perform various functions on its own and will report back when done.

History of the ESDI Interface

An ad hoc group of controller and device manufacturers (led by Maxtor Corporation) met to develop a standard that would increase the data capacity and speed of the existing ST-506/412 interface.

The first standard's document was released in 1983. This initial release defined the **Enhanced Small Disk Interface**, but after the **Enhanced Small Tape Interface** was defined, it was decided in October, 1983, to merge the two standards into one. This new interface became the **Enhanced Small Device Interface (ESDI)**.

In 1985, a version suitable for optical disks was released.

In 1987, it was agreed that the ESDI definition for tape did not have enough acceptance and would not be incorporated in the standard.

The ESDI standard has been approved by the **ISO (International Organization for Standardization)** as ISO 10222:198x, and X3T9 standard X3.170. The complete ESDI standards document can be obtained from the X3T9 committee or **Global Engineering Documents** (see **Appendix C: Directory of Manufacturers** for address information).

Although ESDI drives still compare favorably with many IDE and SCSI products, for various reasons ESDI never gained the momentum of the other two formats. ESDI is no longer supported by the major drive manufacturers.

ESDI Physical Characteristics

See the section in Chapter One entitled "Basic Drive Components" for information regarding the basic workings of a hard drive.

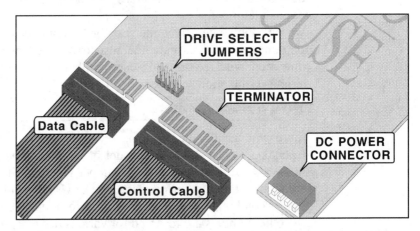

Figure 3-9: ESDI Connection Diagram

This layout will vary from drive to drive, but the basic connections will always be present.

ESDI Cabling

ESDI requires two interface cables: the control cable and the data cable. The data cable is the smaller 20-pin ribbon cable. One data cable is required for each hard drive attached to the controller.

The control cable is the large 34-pin ribbon cable. One control cable is required for every two hard drives. There are several types of drive control cables. The type of cable used dictates the settings of drive select jumpers and termination resistors. The different cables and their associated jumper and termination resistor settings are described in Chapter Four.

Terminating Resistor Pack

This is a socketed resistor pack that is usually yellow and sometimes black or blue. It can be found on the underside of the drive or near the drive control and data cables. Remove these only according to the instructions for the type of control cable used (twisted or non-twisted). On some drives the resistors are not socketed or intended for removal. In this case the resistors are enabled internally by jumper or switch settings. Please see Chapter Four for details on the various termination settings.

Drive Select Jumpers

There will usually be three or seven 2-pin drive select jumpers, depending on the make and model of the hard drive. The position on the far left or far right of the jumper block will be drive select 0 (sometimes the numbering starts at 1). Usually only four of these jumper combinations are actually used for the drive select function. The other jumpers are reserved for various drive parameters.

ESDI Technical Information

BIOS Drive Type Selection

The BIOS set-up is also called the CMOS set-up. When installing an ESDI drive into a system the CMOS drive type should usually be set to "1" and firmware on the ESDI interface will handle any compatibility problems.

ESDI Controllers

When implemented in a DOS system, ESDI drives access the host system through **Interrupt 13h** (**INT 13h**) in order to remain compatible with conventional hard drive interfaces. The programs necessary to access the hard drive are invoked through this interrupt.

ESDI controllers are typed according to the manner in which they implement INT 13h, and fall into two basic categories:

1. **Auto-typing** controllers actually replace the computer's own BIOS INT 13h programs. INT 13h is redirected to the controller's own set of programs contained in its firmware. This firmware knows exactly how to handle an ESDI drive. You must set the computers drive type (in the CMOS set-up) to "1" so that this firmware can locate it. Type 1 is normally a 10MB drive, but not in this case. Most controllers issue an ESDI General Configuration command to the drive to get its actual parameters.

2. **WD1005** and compatible controllers are accessed in the same manner as ST-506/412 controllers. There is no INT 13h replacement and the drive type (in CMOS) must be set to the drives actual heads, cylinders and sectors. This type of ESDI controller is not as common due to the fact that it may only be used with drives that fall within the limits of the computer's BIOS and DOS limitations (no more than 1,024 cylinders, 16 heads, and 63 sectors, giving 528MB).

There are ESDI controllers in use that do not have an on-board BIOS. These controllers neither translate nor low-level format drives. For installation purposes, these drives should be treated as ST-506/412 drives, in that they need to be low-leveled with software (not firmware). Also, this type of ESDI drive is limited to 1,024 cylinders unless using some type of third-party software support, such as *DrivePro*.

Some ESDI controllers have installed firmware that is only compatible with a specific ESDI hard drive. Also, some controllers are rated at a certain MHz speed (10MHz, 15MHz, 20MHz, or 24Mhz). In all cases, always ensure that the controller is compatible with the drive being installed.

Interleave

ESDI hard drives usually use an interleave of one. See page 21 for a description of interleaving. An interleave of three should be fine for most 8086/8088 installations, and two for most 80286 installations. 80386s and above use an interleave of one, provided the controller is designed for a 1:1 interleave.

There are several software packages that allow you to adjust the interleave after the low-level is done. They will even find an optimum interleave for the system and drive you are using.

Bad Sectors

Because of the early technology used in ESDI drives, no sector-sparing (relocation of defects on the disk surface) nor automatic bad-sector mapping is used. Due to the lack of these features, it is very important that defects are entered into a bad-track table before the drive is low-level formatted. Defect locations are usually printed on the drive casing by the manufacturer.

ESDI Connectors and Pin-Outs

This interface uses two cables: a 34 pin flat ribbon *control cable* (3 meters maximum) and a smaller 20 pin flat ribbon *data cable* (3 meters maximum). Although the same two cables are used with the ST-506/412 interface, the pin assignments are completely different.

(This material is reproduced with permission from American National Standard ISO 10222:198x, copyright 1986 by the American National Standards Institute. Copies of this standard may be purchased from the American National Standards Institute at 1430 Broadway New York, N.Y. 10018.)

ESDI Control Cable Connector and Pin Assignments

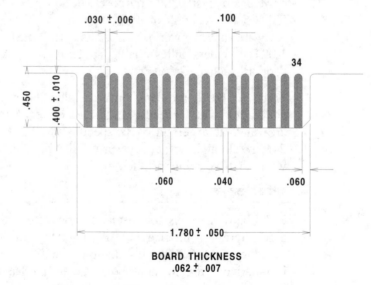

Figure 3-10: ESDI Control Cable Card Edge

(dimensions specified in inches)

Table 3-15: ESDI Control Cable Pin Assignments

Pin	Assignment	Pin	Assignment
1	Ground	2	» -HEAD SELECT 3 (2^3)
3	Ground	4	» -HEAD SELECT 2 (2^2)
5	Ground	6	» -WRITE GATE
7	Ground	8	« -CONFIG/STATUS DATA
9	Ground	10	« -TRANSFER ACKNOWLEDGE
11	Ground	12	« -ATTENTION
13	Ground	14	» -HEAD SELECT 0 (2^0)
15	Ground	16	« -SECTOR/ADDRESS MARK FOUND
17	Ground	18	» -HEAD SELECT 1 (2^1)
19	Ground	20	« -INDEX
21	Ground	22	« -READY
23	Ground	24	» -TRANSFER REQUEST
25	Ground	26	» -DRIVE SELECT 0 (2^0)
27	Ground	28	» -DRIVE SELECT 1 (2^1)
29	Ground	30	» -DRIVE SELECT 2 (2^2)
31	Ground	32	» -READ GATE
33	Ground	34	» -COMMAND DATA

"-" = an active low signal
"«" = output from drive
"»" = input to drive

ESDI Data Cable Connector and Pin Assignments

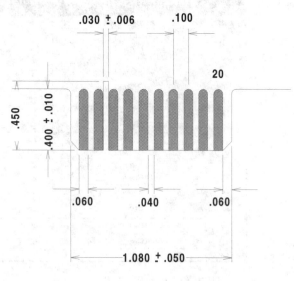

BOARD THICKNESS
.062 ± .007

Figure 3-11: ESDI Data Cable Card Edge

(dimensions specified in inches)

Table 3-16: ESDI Data Cable Pin Assignments			
Pin	**Assignment**	**Pin**	**Assignment**
1	-DRIVE SELECTED	2	-SECTOR/ADDRESS MARK FOUND
3	-COMMAND COMPLETE	4	-ADDRESS MARK ENABLE
5	RESERVED FOR STEP MODE	6	Ground
7	WRITE CLOCK +	8	WRITE CLOCK -
9	CARTRIDGE CHANGED	10	READ / REFERENCE CLOCK +
11	READ / REFERENCE CLOCK -	12	Ground
13	NRZ WRITE DATA +	14	NRZ WRITE DATA -
15	Ground	16	Ground
17	NRZ READ DATA +	18	NRZ READ DATA -
19	Ground	20	-INDEX

"-" = an active low signal
"«" = output from drive
"»" = input to drive

ESDI Control Output Signals

The control out signals are of two types: those to be multiplexed in a multiple drive system and those intended to do the multiplexing. The control signals to be multiplexed are WRITE GATE, READ GATE, HEAD SELECT 2(2^0), HEAD SELECT 2(2^1), HEAD SELECT 2(2^2), HEAD SELECT 2(2^3), TRANSFER REQ and COMMAND DATA. The signals to do the multiplexing are DRIVE SELECT 2(2^0), DRIVE SELECT 2(2^1), and DRIVE SELECT 2(2^2).

ADDRESS MARK ENABLE (D-x) is a control output in the radial cable. It is not multiplexed.

Any lines not used should be terminated.

DRIVE SELECT 0, 1 , 2: The three drive select lines are to be decoded for drive select. Decode 000 is "no" select. Drive should be deselected prior to power down as insurance against destructive writing.

Table 3-17: ESDI Drive Select Matrix							
Drive Selected	None	1	2	3	4	5	6	7
Drive Select 2 (2^2)	0	0	0	0	1	1	1	1
Drive Select 1 (2^1)	0	0	1	1	0	0	1	1
Drive Select 0 (2^0)	0	1	0	1	0	1	0	1

HEAD SELECT 0, 1, 2, 3: These four lines allow selection of each individual read/write head in a binary coded sequence. Head Select 2 (2^0) is the least significant line. Heads are numbered 0 through 15. When all Head Select lines are negated (high), head 0 will be selected. Addressing more than 16 heads is allowed by use of the Select Head Group command.

Head addressing is continuous from 0 through both removable and fixed drives. If a removable drive is present, head 0 will be on the removable media drive.

Addressing more heads than contained in the drive will result in a write fault when attempting to perform a write operation.

WRITE GATE: This signal allows data to be recorded on the disk. The assertion of this signal creates a "write splice" and initiates the writing of the header or the data Phase Lock Oscillator (PLO) Sync field by the drive. The write splice is defined as the point at which WRITE GATE turns on or off, relative to Index or Sector pulse.

When formatting, WRITE GATE should be negated for 2 bit times minimum between the address area and the data area to identify to the drive the beginning of the data PLO sync field.

READ GATE: This signal allows data to be read from the disk. READ GATE should only be asserted during a PLO Sync field, and at least the number of bytes defined by the drive prior to the ID or Data Sync Bytes. The PLO sync field length is determined by the response to the Request PLO Sync Field Length command. READ GATE will be negated when passing over a write splice area.

COMMAND DATA: When presenting a command, 16 information bits of serial data plus parity, will be presented on this line. This data is to be controlled by the handshake protocol with signals TRANSFER REQ and TRANSFER ACK. Upon receipt of this serial data, the drive performs the required function as specified by the bit configuration. Data is transmitted MSB (Most Significant Bit) first.

The parity utilized in all commands is odd. The parity bit will be a "1" when the number of "1's" in a 16 bit command is an even number.

No communications should be initiated, and the drive will ignore any attempt, unless the COMMAND COMPLETE line is asserted.

TRANSFER REQUEST: The Transfer Request line functions as a handshake signal in conjunction with TRANSFER ACK during command and configuration/status transfers.

ADDRESS MARK ENABLE: This line will be permanently terminated in the drive.

DISK SOFT SECTOR (Address Mark Enable, optional): For soft sectored drives, this signal, when WRITE GATE is asserted, causes an Address Mark to be written. ADDRESS MARK ENABLE is asserted for 24 +/-1 bit times. See Figure 24 for timing. The Address Mark written is left to the drive manufacturer's discretion.

ADDRESS MARK ENABLE, when asserted without WRITE GATE or READ GATE, causes a search for Address Marks. If WRITE GATE is asserted, the negation of this signal causes the drive to begin writing the ID PLO Sync field.

DISK FIXED SECTOR (Address Mark Enable, optional): In fixed sector drives, ADDRESS MARK ENABLE does not cause an Address Mark to be written on the media. The trailing edge of ADDRESS MARK ENABLE, with WRITE GATE asserted, initiates the writing of the header PLO sync field.

The beginning of a Header PLO Sync field is defined at format time by using ADDRESS MARK ENABLE, or by the leading edge of WRITE GATE assertion.

ESDI Control Input Signals

All control cable input signals are enabled by their respective DRIVE SELECT decodes. All data cable input lines are always enabled.

DRIVE SELECTED: This is a status line provided at the data cable connector to inform the controller of the selection status of the drive. The DRIVE SELECTED line is driven by a driver. This signal is asserted only when the drive is selected. The DRIVE SELECT output lines on the control cable are asserted by the controller.

READY: This signal indicates only that the spindle is up to operating speed. Specifically, when this interface signal is asserted, it indicates that the drive spindle is up to speed and when this signal is negated, it indicates that the drive spindle is not up to speed.

CONFIGURATION/STATUS DATA: The drive presents serial data on the Configuration/Status Data line upon request from the controller. This config/status serial data is presented to the interface and transferred using the handshake protocol with signals TRANSFER REQ and TRANSFER ACK. Once initiated, 16 bits plus parity are transmitted MSB first. The parity utilized is odd.

TRANSFER ACKNOWLEDGE: The TRANSFER ACKNOWLEDGE signal functions as a handshake signal along with TRANSFER REQ during COMMAND and CONFIGURATION-STATUS transfers.

ATTENTION: This signal is asserted when the drive wants the controller to request its standard status. Generally, this is a result of a fault condition or a change of status.

If a selected device encounters a condition which causes it to become busy and unable to respond to the controller, it will assert ATTENTION in conjunction with the negation of COMMAND COMPLETE.

Writing is inhibited when ATTENTION is asserted.

ATTENTION is negated by the Control Command with the Reset Interface Attention modifier, set only if the condition which caused it to occur no longer exists.

INDEX: This pulse is provided by the drive once per revolution to indicate the beginning of a track. This signal is asserted to indicate INDEX. Only the transition at the leading edge of the asserted pulse is accurately controlled. This signal is available on the control cable (gated) and on the radial data cable (ungated), and will be implemented on both cables by the drive manufacturer.

SECTOR / ADDRESS MARK FOUND: This signal is available on the control cable (gated) and on the radial data cable (ungated), and is implemented on both cables by the drive manufacturer.

DISK and OPTICAL HARD SECTOR (SECTOR): This interface signal, which is mutually exclusive with ADDRESS MARK FOUND, indicates the start of a sector. The leading edge of the asserted sector pulses is the only edge that is accurately controlled. The index pulse indicates sector zero. No short sector lengths are allowed.

DISK SOFT SECTOR (ADDRESS MARK FOUND): This interface signal, which is mutually exclusive with SECTOR, indicates the detection of the end of an address mark.

COMMAND COMPLETE: This is a status line provided at the radial data cable connector. This ungated input to the controller allows the drive's COMMAND COMPLETE status to be monitored during overlapped commands, without selecting the drive.

This signal will be negated in the following cases:

- During a power-up sequence, this line will stay negated until the power-up sequence is complete.
- Upon receipt of the first COMMAND DATA bit. COMMAND COMPLETE will stay negated during the entire command sequence.
- Whenever the drive is unable to respond to the interface (e.g. during recovery from internally detected error conditions). If this should occur during the time that the device is selected, then ATTENTION will be asserted to advise the controller that the device is busy and unable to respond to the interface.

If COMMAND COMPLETE was negated due to an error condition, when the drive is able to respond to the interface, it will continue to assert ATTENTION and COMMAND COMPLETE.

If COMMAND COMPLETE was negated due to a normal, non-error condition, when the drive is able to respond to the interface, it will negate ATTENTION and then assert COMMAND COMPLETE.

This signal is driven by an open collector driver.

ESDI Data Transfer Signals

All lines associated with the transfer of data between the drive and the controller are differential in nature and may not be multiplexed. These lines are provided at the radial data cables of each drive.

Four pairs of balanced signals are used with magnetic and optical disks for the transfer of data and clock: WRITE DATA, READ DATA, WRITE CLOCK, and READ/REFERENCE CLOCK.

Magnetic disks support only NRZ transfers. Optical disks optionally provide the capability for the READ DATA and WRITE DATA signals to transfer either NRZ or Synchronized Encoded Data.

NOTE: Providing the Encoding/Decoding to be used in the controller allows the bit patterns for Sync bytes and Resync fields to be passed across the interface. This simplifies the handling of these unique fields and may reduce the control electronics required in the optical disk.

NRZ WRITE DATA: This is a differential pair that defines the data to be written on the track. This data will be clocked by the WRITE CLOCK signal.

NRZ READ DATA: The data recovered by reading previously written information is transmitted to the controller via the differential pair of READ DATA lines. This data is clocked by the READ CLOCK signal. READ DATA will be held at a zero level until PLO sync has been obtained and data is valid.

NOTE: READ DATA carries erasure pointer data during an erasure read in an optical disk drive. Erasure pointer data is useful information to an optical disk in the event that extended error recovery procedures are necessary.

READ/REFERENCE CLOCK: The REFERENCE CLOCK signal from the drive determines the data transfer rate.

REFERENCE CLOCK is present and stable when READY is asserted (the drive is spinning).

READ CLOCK is valid when READ GATE is active and PLO Synchronization has been established.

REFERENCE CLOCK is valid when READ GATE is inactive.

All transitions between REFERENCE CLOCK and READ CLOCK must be performed without glitches. Two missing clock cycles are permissible.

NOTE: Extended Clocks may occur with the High Speed port and on optical disks in which the negated period of the clock varies, i.e., is not symmetrical in width with the asserted period. This occurs on a repetitive basis, but not necessarily on every clock cycle. The leading edge of the signal will be used to clock data.

WRITE CLOCK: WRITE CLOCK is provided by the controller and will be at the bit data rate. This clock frequency is dictated by the READ/REFERENCE CLOCK during the write operation.

WRITE CLOCK need not be continuously supplied to the drive. WRITE CLOCK should be supplied before beginning a write operation, and should last for the duration of the write operation.

Optical disks may not produce a symmetrical wave form due to device specific implementations. Both standard and extended period wave forms are permitted.

The ST-506/412 Interface

ST-506/412 General Description

ST-506/412 drives were popular in the desktop PC environment in the 1980s. The ST-506/412 interface is now obsolete and has since been superseded by the other interface types covered in this text. Drives using this interface are often termed MFM drives in reference to the simple encoding scheme. ST-506/412 is the more correct label for these devices, since RLL encoding has also been employed for them.

These drives are not very "intelligent." There are no opcodes or special features as with the other interface types. The host adapter (controller) contains virtually all of the logic used to access data. Unlike the other interface types, the controller must match the encoding scheme used by the drive. See page 18 for details on encoding.

When installed in XT-type systems, ST-506/412 drives utilize the firmware installed on the controller card that contains a table of hard drive parameters. The hard drive to be installed must match one of the drive parameters in the table, though some controllers allow user-definable parameters.

When implemented in 80x86 or Pentium compatible systems, the BIOS in the host computer has a table of hard drive parameters. The hard disk to be installed must match one of the drive parameters in the table. Most BIOSes made in the nineties have a user-definable drive type that allows you to set a type to match the drive.

History of the ST-506/412 Interface

This interface was developed by Seagate Technologies (originally Shugart) in 1980 solely for use with their ST-506 5MB hard drive. It was later revised in 1981 for their ST-412 , a 10MB drive, with a feature called "buffered seek." Although this interface had considerable size and speed limitations by today's standards, it was well suited for the original PCs. With a transfer rate of 5Mbits/sec (Mb/s) for MFM and 7.5Mb/s for RLL, one was seldom waiting for the drive while working on a 4.77MHz IBM PC. In fact, its throughput was fast enough that interleaving (see page 21) was necessary to maximize system/drive performance.

ST-506/412 Physical Characteristics

See the section in Chapter One entitled "Basic Drive Components" for information regarding the basic workings of a hard drive.

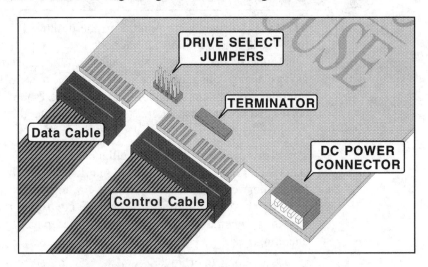

Figure 3-12: ST-506/412 Connection Diagram

This layout will vary from drive to drive but the basic connections will always be present.

ST-506/412 Cabling

ST-506/412 requires two interface cables: the control cable and the data cable. The data cable is the smaller 20-pin ribbon cable. One data cable is required for each hard drive attached to the controller.

The control cable is the large 34-pin ribbon cable. One control cable is required for every two hard drives. There are several types of drive control cables. The type of cable used dictates the settings of drive select jumpers and termination resistors. The different cables and their associated jumper and terminating resistor settings are described in Chapter Four.

Terminating Resistor Pack

This is a socketed resistor pack that is usually yellow and sometimes black or blue. It can be found on the underside of the drive or near the drive control and data cables. The correct setting is essential for proper drive operation. Install terminating resistors on the drive at the end of the cable, remove resistors on drives in the middle of the cable. On some drives, the resistors are not socketed or intended for removal. In this case, the resistors are enabled internally by jumper or switch settings.

Drive Select Jumpers

Of the various option jumpers or switches on the drive (there may be many), only four may be called drive select jumpers/switches. Of these four, however, only two can be used on ST-506/412 interface drives. The position to the far left or far right of the drive select jumper/switch block will be drive select 0 (sometimes the numbering starts at 1). The other jumpers are reserved for various drive parameters. The drive number to be selected depends on the desired DOS drive designation (C: or D:), and the type of cable used for connection to the controller.

ST-506/412 Technical Information

ST-506/412 Encoding

It is important that the correct encoding method is matched when pairing a hard drive and controller. MFM drives always have 17 sectors and RLL usually have 26 or more. Even though the firmware on an MFM interface card may allow sector values greater than 17, or the drive may be set for a type in CMOS with more than 17 sectors per track, the electronics will only use 17 SPT. So, a 30 megabyte RLL drive used on an MFM controller will only format out to 20 megabytes, since it's using only 17 sectors per track instead of its optimum 26. This costs disk space, but is better than throwing away an RLL drive if you only have an MFM controller.

Do not use an MFM drive with an RLL controller. MFM drives are designed to use only 17 sectors per track and forcing it to use 26 or more will cause excessive bad sectors, and possibly permanently damage the electronics. You may get 30 megabytes out of a 20 megabyte drive, but it will substantially reduce its life.

Interleave

See Chapter One for a complete description of **interleaving**. An interleave of three should be fine for most 8086/8088 installations, and two for most 80286 installations. 80386s and above use an interleave of one, provided the controller is designed for a 1:1 interleave.

There are several software packages that allow you to adjust the interleave after the low-level is done. They will even find an optimum interleave for the system and drive you are using.

INT 13h

When the computer accesses the ST-506/412 hard drive, it does so through software interrupt used for hard drives, INT 13h. The programs necessary to access the hard drive are located in the computer's BIOS and are accessed through this interrupt. ST-506/412 controllers never have an on-board BIOS, so ST-506/412 drives are accessed through the standard host system BIOS.

Bad Sectors

Because of the early technology used in ST-506/412 drives, no sector-sparing (relocation of defects on the disk surface) nor automatic bad-sector mapping is used. Due to the lack of these features, it is very important that defects are entered into a bad-track table before the drive is low-level formatted. Defect locations are usually printed on the drive casing by the manufacturer.

ST-506/412 Connectors and Pin-Outs

This interface uses a 34-pin *control cable* and a smaller 20-pin *data cable*.

ST-506/412 Control Cable Connector and Pin Assignments

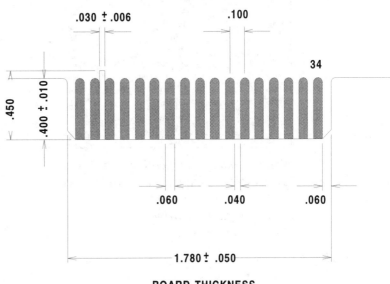

Figure 3-13: ST-506/412 Control Cable Card Edge Diagram

(dimensions specified in inches)

Table 3-18: ST-506/412 Control Cable Pin Assignments

PIN	ASSIGNMENT	PIN	ASSIGNMENT
1	Ground	2	» -HEAD SELECT 8 (2^3)
3	Ground	4	» -HEAD SELECT 4 (2^2)
5	Ground	6	» -WRITE GATE
7	Ground	8	« -SEEK COMPLETE
9	Ground	10	« -TRACK ZERO
11	Ground	12	« -WRITE FAULT
13	Ground	14	» -HEAD SELECT 1 (2^0)
15	Ground	16	TO DATA CABLE PIN 7
17	Ground	18	» -HEAD SELECT 2 (2^1)
19	Ground	20	« -INDEX
21	Ground	22	« -READY
23	Ground	24	» -STEP
25	Ground	26	» -DRIVE SELECT 1
27	Ground	28	» -DRIVE SELECT 2
29	Ground	30	» -DRIVE SELECT 3
31	Ground	32	» -DRIVE SELECT 4
33	Ground	34	» -DIRECTION IN

Note: on older specifications Pin 1 was the -REDUCED WRITE CURRENT signal and Pin 3 was Reserved.
"-" = an active low signal
"«" = output from drive
"»" = input to drive.

ST-506/412 Data Cable Connector and Pin Assignments

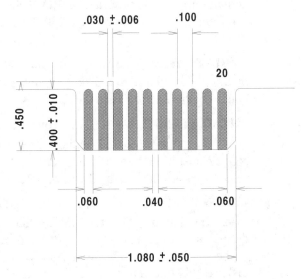

Figure 3-14: ST-506/412 Data Cable Card Edge Diagram

(dimensions specified in inches)

PIN	ASSIGNMENT	PIN	ASSIGNMENT
\multicolumn{4}{c}{*Table 3-19: ST-506/412 Data Cable Pin Assignments*}
1	DRIVE SELECTED	2	Ground
3	Reserved	4	Ground
5	Reserved	6	Ground
7	To Control Cable Pin 15	8	Ground
9	Reserved	10	Reserved
11	Ground	12	Ground
13	+ MFM WRITE DATA	14	- MFM WRITE DATA
15	Ground	16	Ground
17	+ MFM READ DATA	18	- MFM READ DATA
19	Ground	20	Ground

"-" = an active low signal.

ST-506/412 Control Input Signals

The Control Input Signals are latched into the drive by the activation of the appropriate -DRIVE SELECT line. Each Control Input Signal is terminated by a 220/330 ohm resistor network in the drive.

- **WRITE GATE:** The true (low) state of this signal enables write data to be written on the disk. The false state of this signal enables data to be transferred from the drive.

- **HEAD SELECT:** These lines provide a means to select read/write heads in a binary coded sequence. Head Select 2^0 is the least significant bit. Heads are numbered 0 through 15. When all head select lines are false, head 0 will be selected.

- **DIRECTION IN:** This signal defines the direction of motion of the read/write heads when the -STEP line is pulsed. A high-level defines the direction as "out." At this time, when a pulse is applied to the -STEP line, the heads will move away from the center of the disk. If this line is a low, the direction of motion is defined as "in," and the step pulses will cause the read/write heads to move toward the center of the disk.

- **STEP:** This control signal causes the read/write heads to move in the direction defined by the -DIRECTION IN line. The drive is able to accept step pulses in two modes: track-to-track and buffered. In the track-to-track mode, step pulses should be sent at a 3ms rate or greater to access the desired track. In the buffered mode, step pulses must be sent at a 2ms to 200ms rate. In this mode, step pulses are accumulated until no new pulses have been received for 210ms An optimized seek algorithm is then executed to minimize access time. Pulses that occur after the 210ms period and prior to completion of seek will be ignored. The drive automatically decides which mode to use based on the incoming step pulse rate. The direction line should be maintained at the desired level of 100ns before the first step pulse and until 100ns after the last step pulse has been issued.

- DRIVE SELECT 1, 2, 3, and 4: When low, this signal connects the drive to the control lines and allows step or read/write operations. When -DRIVE SELECT is active, the drive responds by turning on the activity LED. Placing a jumper across the appropriate pins on the drive's PC board selects the drive, when the corresponding -DRIVE SELECT line is low.

ST-506/412 Control Output Signals

The Control Output Signals are latched from the drive by the activation of the appropriate -DRIVE SELECT line. Each Control Output Signal should be terminated in the controller with a 220/330 ohm resistor network.

- SEEK COMPLETE: This signal will go true (low) when the read/write heads have settled on the desired track following a seek. A Read or Write operation should not be attempted when -SEEK COMPLETE is false. The following conditions will cause a -SEEK COMPLETE to go false:

- If the +5 or +12 volt line becomes unsafe or is momentarily lost.
- If the drive attempts a seek retry after settling on a track.
- If a step pulse greater than 1µs in width is sent.
- When a recalibration sequence is initiated (by drive logic) at power on because the read/write heads are not at Track Zero.

- WRITE FAULT: This signal is used to indicate that a condition exists in the drive that will result in improper writing on the disk. When this signal is true, further writing is inhibited at the drive until the condition is corrected. Once corrected, the controller can reset this line by deselecting the drive. Any of the following conditions may cause -WRITE FAULT to go true:

- An open or shorted head in the drive.
- No transitions on the WRITE DATA line when -WRITE GATE is true.
- DC voltages are out of tolerance with -WRITE GATE active.
- More than one seek retry between seek commands from the controller.
- Step pulses are received when -WRITE GATE is active.

- INDEX: This 300μs (typical) interface pulse is provided by the drive once per revolution (16.67ms nominal) to indicate the beginning of the track. Normally, this signal is a high-level and makes the transition to the low-level to indicate -INDEX. Only the transition from high to low is valid.

- READY: This interface signal, when true (low) together with -SEEK COMPLETE, indicates that the drive is ready to read, write, or seek, and that the I/O signals are valid. When this signal is false, all writing and seeking are inhibited.

- TRACK ZERO: This interface signal is true (low) only when the drive's read/write heads are positioned at Track Zero (the outermost data track).

- DRIVE SELECTED: This signal will go true (low) only when the drive is programmed as drive *n* (*n*=1,2,3, or 4) and the -DRIVE SELECT *n* line is asserted by the controller.

ST-506/412 Data Transfer Signals

All signals associated with the transfer of data between the drive and the controller are differential. Two pairs of balanced signals are used for the transfer of data: WRITE DATA and READ DATA.

WRITE DATA: This is a differential pair that defines the transitions to be written on the track. The transition of the + WRITE DATA line going more positive than the - WRITE DATA line will cause a flux reversal on the track, provided at the selected head. In recording, to optimize data integrity and meet the error rate specified, the write data presented by the controller to the drive must be precompensated from the write precompensation cylinder to the ending drive cylinder.

READ DATA: The data recovered by reading a pre-recorded track is transmitted to the controller via the differential pair of **READ DATA** lines. The transition of the + READ DATA line going more positive than the - READ DATA line represents a flux reversal on the track of the selected head.

Chapter Review:

- IDE is the dominant interface used for hard drives. PC type computers almost always have native support for this interface.

- The SCSI interface is the choice for servers and high-end work stations. SCSI is superior to IDE in many ways, but is more expensive and requires more knowledge to set up and maintain.

- The ESDI and ST-506/412 interfaces are obsolete and no longer supported by drive manufacturers.

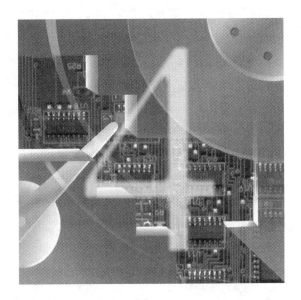

Drive Installation

Chapter Four Contents:

Overview

This section covers installation procedures for the four major interface types.

Installation of hard drives can be divided in two major steps: hardware and formatting/partitioning. This section gives step-by-step procedures and tips to make set-up as easy and trouble-free as possible.

Hardware jumper settings will vary depending on manufacturer and model. This means you will need documentation on your main-board, controller card, and hard drive prior to beginning installation procedures.

If this is an upgrade or addition of a secondary drive, before proceeding, make a back up of the entire original disk

Items You Will Need:

✓ Phillips screwdriver
✓ Flat-head screwdriver
✓ Additional/replacement hard drive
✓ Drive cable
✓ Controller card (if upgrading)
✓ Manufacturer's (or MHI) documentation on your:

> hard drive
> controller card
> main-board

✓ DOS Boot-disk with FDISK.EXE and FORMAT.COM files (DOS installation only)

Items That Will Make Your Life Much Easier:

✓ *Micro House Technical Library*™
✓ Micro House *DrivePro* or *EZ-Drive*

Safety Precautions

Take some time to perform some safety precautions prior to moving on to the following steps. These basic precautions could save you from potential financial loss or even personal injury.

• If possible, work over an anti-static mat. In any case, be sure to discharge any static-electricity on your body by touching a grounded object prior to touching any component on your computer. Discharging static into computer components can result in permanent data loss or even damage.

• Turn off the computer and make sure it is not plugged in.

• Use only proper tools and do not attempt to force anything into place.

• Handle the hard drive gently.

• Double check all connections *prior* to plugging in to a power source and turning on.

IDE Drive Installation

If this is an upgrade or addition of a secondary drive, back up the original drive in its entirety.

If you are installing more than one drive, it is recommended that you accomplish all of the steps outlined below sequentially for each drive, rather than installing all of the drives at once. This will make trouble-shooting much easier if you encounter any problems.

IDE Installation Summary

The following outline is a general instruction for installing IDE drives. Please read the entire section for a step-by-step installation guide.

1. Install the hard drive(s), setting the appropriate jumpers and connecting the drive(s) to the controller via the IDE cable.

ON THE CD

Note: *EZ-Drive* can perform the last three steps for you!

2. ***DrivePro*** and ***EZ-Drive*** from Micro House are highly recommended hard drive set-up utilities. The use of these excellent programs could save you some time and/or headaches. Refer to **Appendix D: *EZ-Drive*** User's Guide for information on *EZ-Drive* installation.

3. If you are proceeding manually, enter the CMOS set-up utility and define the drive-type.

4. Set up the desired partitions, then format the drive using the appropriate FDISK and FORMAT commands.

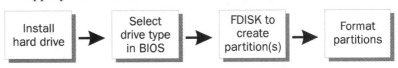

Figure 4-1: IDE Drive Installation

IDE Step-by-Step Installation

Hardware Installation

1. Take the general precautions listed in this chapter under the heading "Safety Precautions" prior to proceeding.

2. Remove the outer casing from the computer chassis. The retaining screws are usually located in the back or underneath.

3. Take some time to familiarize yourself with the organization of the chassis and some of the components prior to proceeding. Chassis organization can vary depending on manufacturer, size, and tower or desk-top orientation.

4. If you are upgrading or attaching a new IDE controller, first remove the old one and find an appropriate expansion slot to install the new one. Prior to installation, configure the controller according to the options you would like enabled. Jumper settings can be found in the manufacturer's documentation or, in some cases, Chapter Six of this text.

ON THE CD

If you cannot find the documentation and do not know the manufacturer of your controller, the *Micro House Technical Library* contains jumper settings for many of the most popular hard drives, controllers, and main boards manufactured. This handy reference contains the equivalent of thousands of pages of hardware documentation on a single CD-ROM. A demonstration of this highly acclaimed tool has been included on the CD-ROM that came with this text.

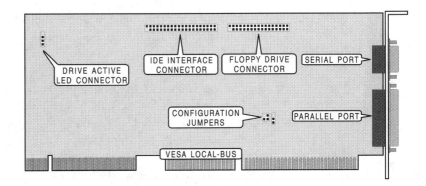

This diagram depicts some typical features of after-market IDE controllers, which may have other I/O options. This layout will vary among adapters, but the illustration should help you recognize basic features.

Figure 4-2: IDE Controller Connection Diagram

If you wish to install more than two drives (other than SCSI) on your system, you will need native support such as found in Enhanced IDE systems. The alternative is to enable a secondary controller through third-party software, such as the copy of *EZ-Drive*, which is included with this text.

The additional controller card <u>must</u> support secondary port addressing or it cannot be used. To determine if your card does, refer to your documentation to see if there is a jumper for this feature. If you are still unsure, ask the manufacturer. If the card does not support it, you must get one that does. Some points about secondary adapter support:

- One or two drives can be used on the secondary adapter. The drives on the secondary card are not usually set in CMOS.
- IDE drives on the secondary card can be set up by *EZ-Drive* while on the secondary port.
- Note that any duplicated ports, such as floppy, parallel, or serial will have to be disabled to avoid conflicts. Some floppy controllers have a jumper for disabling, but this is often not reliable. A more reliable method is setting the floppies to the secondary address where the computer will not find them.

- In most cases, the secondary card must have its IRQ disabled. An exception is that some multi-tasking operating systems require IRQ15 to be enabled for the secondary adapter.
- Some controllers have a jumper to disable IRQ, some set the port address and IRQ with the same jumper. If your card has a jumper that sets IRQ14 or IRQ15, you can often completely disable it by removing the jumper completely. If your secondary card does not have a jumper to disable IRQ14, you can disable it manually by taping over the connection. On a 16-bit controller, the IRQ14 line is found on the back side card edge, on the 16-bit (short) extension. It is the 7th contact from the left or 12th from the right (D7). Placing a piece of simple transparent tape over that contact will disable IRQ14. If you choose to perform this operation, be sure to take the proper safety precautions.

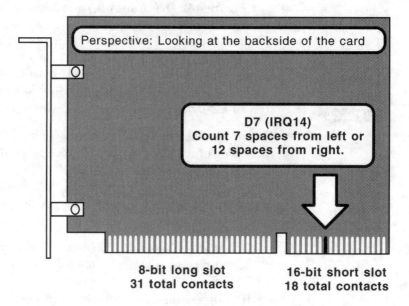

Perspective: Looking at the backside of the card

D7 (IRQ14)
Count 7 spaces from left or
12 spaces from right.

8-bit long slot
31 total contacts

16-bit short slot
18 total contacts

Note: Many manufacturers only plate the contacts that will be needed on the card. Be sure to count the spaces for contacts whether they are plated or not, not just the plated contacts.

Figure 4-3: Disabling IRQ14

Most current main-boards have an embedded IDE controller. If you are upgrading the controller, the embedded controller must be disabled. Consult the documentation for your mainboard to find the correct jumper settings to disable its embedded controller. If you do not have the manual, contact the manufacturer or reseller. Address and telephone information for major manufacturers can be found in **Appendix C**.

Some important IDE controller settings of which you should be aware:

- The IDE port enable/disable jumper should be enabled.
- If you intend to use PIO Mode 3 or higher on your IDE drive, the IORDY signal <u>must</u> be enabled. See the section on PIO modes under the heading "IDE Data Transfer" in Chapter 3 for information on PIO Modes and the IORDY signal.
- If you wish to use one of the DMA data transfer modes, make sure that both the DMARQ and DMACK jumpers are enabled for the DMA channel you will be using.

5. Prior to installation, configure the drive according to the options you would like enabled. Jumper settings can be found in the manufacturer's documentation or, in some cases, Chapter Seven of this text. Address and telephone information for major manufacturers can be found in **Appendix C**.

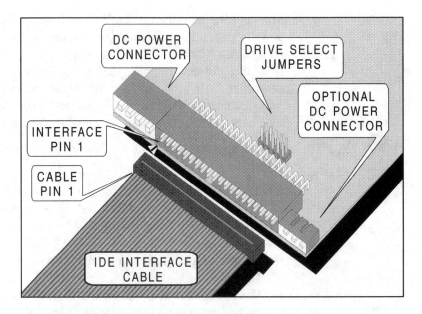

Although most IDE interface connectors will be oriented this way with respect to the drive, this is not always the case. Be sure to look for a Pin 1 indicator on the interface connector, such as a notch in the connector shroud at that location.

Figure 4-4: IDE Connection Diagram

Configure the Drive Select Jumpers according to the priority you wish to assign to the drive(s): **single drive only, master in a two drive system,** or **slave in a two drive system**. Note that the drive which is designated as the master will be the boot drive. See the sub-section titled "Drive Select Jumpers (Master/Slave)," located under the section "IDE Physical Characteristics" in Chapter 3 for an explanation of the drive priorities.

IDE drives vary widely in options and their corresponding jumpers. Some IDE drive settings of which you should be aware are as follows:

- If you intend to use PIO Mode 3 or higher on your IDE drive, the IORDY signal must be enabled. See the section on PIO modes under the heading "IDE Data Transfer" in Chapter 3 for information on PIO Mode 3 and the IORDY signal.

- If you wish to use one of the DMA data transfer modes, make sure that both the DMARQ and DMACK jumpers are enabled.
- A few IDE drives offer two choices on activating the spindle motor: activate on system power-up, or activate on command only.

Some IDE drives offer spindle synchronization in a two-drive system for special applications. Note that this feature is subject to compatibility problems if the drives are not identical. See the IDE: Connectors and Pin-outs section of Chapter Three for information concerning the SPSYNC signal on IDE drives.

6. There are three connectors on the typical IDE drive cable. Attach the appropriate end to the controller connector (the two drive connectors are fairly close together). Determine which connector you will be attaching to the drive(s) according to where the drive(s) will be housed in the computer casing. The cable connector has no bearing on which drive is master or slave in a two drive system.

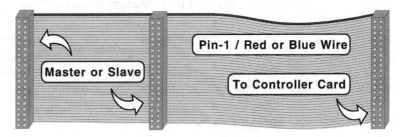

This is the data cable attached to an IDE hard drive. It has 40 pins (Some computers use a 44- or 72-pin connector) and should not exceed 24" in length. The location on the cable is irrelevant to selection of Master or Slave drive.

Figure 4-5: IDE 40-Pin Cable

Locate pin 1 on the IDE cable. It can be found by one of three possible markings: a triangle stamped on the connector close to pin 1, a colored stripe on wire #1 (usually red or blue), or a keying tab inside the connector that will not allow the cable to be inserted incorrectly. Orient the cable connector so that it corresponds to pin 1 on the drive interface connector and join the two connectors. Refer to **Figure 4-4** for an illustration.

7. Each drive requires its own power cable. The cable is attached to the computer's power supply. The connector is keyed so that it can only be inserted one way.

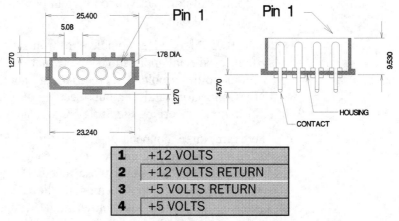

1	+12 VOLTS
2	+12 VOLTS RETURN
3	+5 VOLTS RETURN
4	+5 VOLTS

Figure 4-6: DC Power Connector

8. Fix the drive(s) into the appropriate drive bays. Most drives can be mounted in any orientation except upside-down, but be sure to check for restrictions if you are not mounting the drive upright and flat (platters parallel to the plane of the floor). Remember that hard drives operate under high tolerances. The selection of an internal location away from hot components and/or with access to good air circulation will help increase the life span of the drive.

9. Perform a quick check to make sure that all connectors are in place. Also make sure all tools and other loose objects are removed from inside the computer chassis.

10. Replace the casing over the computer chassis and complete re-assembly with the appropriate fasteners.

11. Plug the computer back in.

You are now ready to proceed to the BIOS set-up portion of the installation process.

Micro House *DrivePro* and EZ DRIVE

ON THE CD

- At this point, all you have to do is run the copy of *EZ-Drive* provided with this text, and choose the automatic installation option. That's it! *EZ-Drive* automatically detects your drive's parameters, enters a BIOS drive type, partitions and formats your drive. Refer to **Appendix D** for information on *EZ-Drive* installation.

- *DrivePro* contains all the features of *EZ-Drive* and much more. Please run the *DrivePro* demonstration included with the purchase of this text for a hands-on preview of this powerful program's easy-to-use features.

- If you are going to finish installing the drive manually, please go on to the following steps:

BIOS Set-Up Procedure

The BIOS set-up is also called the CMOS set-up. This procedure enables the BIOS to work with the drive by letting it know the drive's parameters.

1. Double-check all of the connectors prior to plugging in. Power-up the computer and perform the procedure required to enter the CMOS set-up. The CMOS set-up entry procedure can vary depending on the BIOS manufacturer, but is typically accomplished by one of these actions:

    A. Pressing and holding down the escape (Esc) key during the Power-On Self-Test (POST).
    B. Pressing and holding down the delete (Del) key during the POST.
    C. Pressing the (Ctrl), (Alt), and (Esc) keys at the same time while in DOS.
    D. Pressing the (Ctrl), (Alt), and (S) keys at the same time while in DOS.
    E. Pressing the (Ctrl), (Alt), and (Ent) keys at the same time while in DOS.
    F. Some BIOS types will automatically go into the CMOS set-up if a system configuration change is detected, which would include hard drive alterations.

2. Go into the hard drive set-up portion of the CMOS set-up.

3. Select the Drive Type. This can be done one of three ways: automatic type selection, pre-defined drive type, or user definable drive type.

    A. Newer BIOS types and IDE drives support automatic detection of the drive parameters. This option is easiest and least open to error. If you are not sure if your drive supports the Identify Drive command, try this option anyway. If automatic selection does not work, you will have to go to one of the other two types selection methods.

    B. A user-defined drive type should be used if the drive-type table in your BIOS does not include the parameters of your drive. If your BIOS allows manual parameters to be entered, then enter the manufacturer's recommended logical heads, cylinders, and sectors per track for the drive. Be sure to enter the *logical* parameters of your drive. These values are usually printed on the drive casing. If you cannot find the logical values on your drive, look for the specifications in **Appendix A** of this text. If you cannot find your drive listed under its manufacturer, match the values corresponding to the drive's capacity in the IDE Quick Reference Table. By doing this you, will be able to minimize wasted capacity.

    C. Look for the values that match your drive in the BIOS Drive-Type Table. If your BIOS has a defined type that matches your drive's capacity exactly, then use it.

In some instances, you may find that your BIOS does not support automatic type detection or a user-definable drive type, and you cannot find the exact matching type in the table. If this is the case, then try selecting the drive type in the table that most closely matches the parameters of your drive, but has a capacity that is <u>less than or equal</u> to your drive's capacity. This procedure also applies if you don't have the logical conversion information, but know the capacity, because most IDE drives do a translation so that they may be used in systems that do not support the drive type needed.

For example, if the IDE hard drive to be installed is 22 megabytes in size, type 2 would be selected in the BIOS setup for this drive as it is the closest match in megabytes to the IDE drive.

ON THE CD

Remember, the physical information is the actual heads, cylinders, and SPT of the hard drive. The logical information is the heads, cylinders, and SPT that the drive and BIOS table can agree on. Although this will result in a working IDE drive, it is not optimal because in some cases you could lose drive space by having to choose a type that is far less than the drive's potential size.

> **Note**:   Be safe – don't go over the correct capacity by even one byte!

Of course, you can simply use **EZ-Drive** and disregard the preceding passage.

4. Exit the drive set-up menu, save the settings, and exit the CMOS set-up. The drive(s) are now ready to be partitioned and formatted.

Low-Level Formatting

> IDE drives have been factory low-leveled and only need to be FDISKed and DOS formatted. Low-leveling the drive may wipe out the factory-marked defect list and might even render the drive unusable!

Most IDE drives have variable sectors per track and use sector sparing. They may also utilize wedge servos. These servos mark the track and sector boundaries. Wedge servos are written to the platters by a special machine. The drive itself is unable to re-create these. It is impossible to low-level this type of IDE drive because there is no way to rewrite these servos unless the special machine is used. The drive electronics are intelligent enough to refuse a low-level command. On these types of drives a low-level program will simply scrub the data areas clean.

DOS Partitioning

EZ-Drive will perform this step for you!

Please see Chapter One for details on partitioning. **FDISK** is the utility provided with DOS-based OSes to partition a drive. There are different partitioning limitations for each DOS version, the latest supporting partitions of up to 2GB.

Surprisingly, DOS does not yet support more than 1,024 cylinders, despite the fact that it has been discussed since before the release of version 5.0. To access over 1,024 cylinders (in effect > 528MB) you will need either hardware or software support such as *DrivePro* or *EZ-Drive*. Please see the section on IDE Technical Information in Chapter Three for more information on DOS-imposed capacity limits.

> You can lose a significant amount of drive capacity by using a large partition. There is usually a portion of the last cluster used for a file which ends up being wasted. Because DOS uses more sectors per cluster for large partitions, there is a proportional increase in the amount of unused sectors in larger clusters. Please refer to page 26 for a more detailed explanation of clusters and how they affect wasted drive capacity.

1. If you are installing a master drive only or a master/slave combination, boot from a DOS disk containing the files `FDISK.EXE` and `FORMAT.COM`. If you are only installing a slave drive, boot normally from the master drive.

2. Run the FDISK program by typing FDISK at the prompt.

3. Use the menu to set the desired partitioning options for your drive(s), depending on the DOS version you are using (see above). Note that the latest version of DOS allows partitions of up to 2GB, which is enough to allow a single (primary) partition on just about every IDE drive manufactured today. Please see Chapter One for an explanation of primary and extended partitions.

4. For the master or sole drive, set the boot partition to "active" if it's not done automatically.

5. Exit FDISK. The partition(s) are now ready for high-level formatting.

High-Level Formatting

EZ-Drive will perform this step for you!

Once the drive is partitioned, each partition must be high-level formatted with the operating system that you will be using. To format under DOS, use the **FORMAT** command, specifying the partition to be formatted. For example, type FORMAT C: to format the partition designated as "C:" drive.

If you want to make this the boot drive, save a step and use the command **FORMAT /S** to automatically transfer the system files after formatting. If the partition is already formatted, then use the **SYS** command to transfer the system files to the partition and make it bootable. Simply put:

- If the partition is unformatted, type FORMAT C: /S at the prompt.

- If the partition is already formatted type SYS C: at the prompt.

Problems?

- Make sure that pin 1 on the interface connector corresponds with pin 1 of the cable connector.

- Double check that the Drive Select jumpers are set properly. It is easy to inadvertently look at the jumper block from the wrong perspective.

- If you manually entered the drive-type in the BIOS table, it is possible that one or more of the cylinders, heads, or SPT values is not supported by the system.

- If you encounter other problems during the installation procedure, refer to Chapter Eight, which contains some of the more common set-up problems you may encounter and their solutions.

SCSI Drive Installation

If this is an upgrade or addition of a secondary drive, back up the original drive in its entirety.

If you are installing more than one drive, it is recommended that you accomplish all of the steps outlined below sequentially for each drive, rather than installing all of the drives at once. This will make trouble-shooting much easier if you encounter any problems.

SCSI Installation Summary

The following outline is a general instruction on installing SCSI drives in a DOS environment. Please read the entire section for a step-by-step installation guide.

1. Connect the drive to the controller via the cable (see the SCSI section of Chapter Three).

2. If you are proceeding manually, enter the CMOS set-up utility and define the drive-type as "0" or "Not Installed."

3. The SCSI controller you are using may require a replacement block device driver. Additionally, some SCSI drives may need to be low-level formatted. Refer to the user's manual, which came with it, to find out how to install it.

4. Set up the desired partitions, then format the drive using the appropriate FDISK and FORMAT commands.

Figure 4-7: SCSI Drive Installation

SCSI Step-by-Step Installation

Hardware Installation

1. Take the general precautions listed in this chapter under the heading "Safety Precautions" prior to proceeding.

2. Remove the outer casing from the computer chassis. The retaining screws are usually located in the back or underneath.

3. Take some time to familiarize yourself with the organization of the chassis and some of the components prior to proceeding. Chassis organization can vary depending on manufacturer, size, and tower or desk-top orientation.

4. If you are upgrading or attaching a new SCSI controller, first remove the old one and find an appropriate expansion slot to install the new one. Prior to installation, configure the controller according to the options you would like enabled. Jumper settings can be found in the manufacturer's documentation or Chapter Five.

ON THE CD

> If you cannot find the documentation and do not know the manufacturer of your controller, the ***Micro House Technical Library*** contains jumper settings for many of the most popular hard drives, controllers, and main boards manufactured. This handy reference contains the equivalent of thousands of pages of hardware documentation on a single CD-ROM. A demonstration of this highly acclaimed tool has been included on the CD-ROM which came with this text.

DRIVE ACTIVE
LED CONNECTOR

FLOPPY DRIVE
CONNECTOR

SCSI INTERFACE
CONNECTOR

CONFIGURATION
JUMPERS

TERMINATING
RESISTORS

SCSI INTERFACE
CONNECTOR

VESA LOCAL-BUS

Figure 4-8: SCSI Controller Connection Diagram

5. Terminating resistors are socketed resistor packs, sometimes
    called terminators, that are usually yellow and sometimes black
    or blue. On SCSI drives there are several of these on each hard
    drive. They can be found on the underside of the drive or near
    the drive header cable. Leave terminating resistors installed for
    the last drive on the chain. In the case of a single-drive system,
    the drive must be terminated. Remove all resistors for drives
    connected in the middle of the daisy-chain. SCSI controllers
    are considered one of the (usually) eight devices allowed on the
    chain and so have terminators on them to terminate the start of
    the chain. On some drives the resistors are not socketed or
    intended for removal – if this is the case, the resistors can
    usually be enabled internally by jumper or switch settings.
    Please see Figure 3-6 for an illustration of terminating resistor
    configuration.

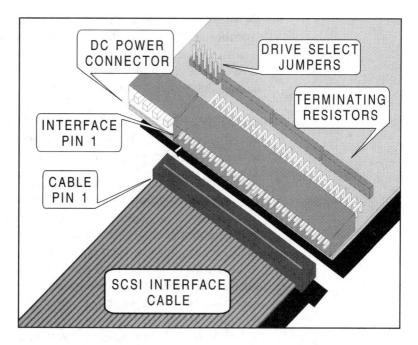

DC POWER CONNECTOR

DRIVE SELECT JUMPERS

TERMINATING RESISTORS

INTERFACE PIN 1

CABLE PIN 1

SCSI INTERFACE CABLE

Although most SCSI interface connectors will be oriented this way with respect to the drive, this is not always the case. Be sure to look for a Pin 1 indicator on the interface connector, such as a notch in the connector shroud at that location.

Figure 4-9: SCSI Connection Diagram

6. Prior to installation, configure the drive according to the drive number assigned and the options you would like enabled. Jumper settings can be found in the manufacturer's documentation. Address and telephone information for major manufacturers can be found in **Appendix C**.

   SCSI drives vary widely in options and their corresponding jumpers. Some SCSI drive settings of which you should be aware:

- **Drive Select** jumpers are used to select the **Logical Unit Number (LUN)** of the device in the SCSI chain. The LUN is also called the "SCSI ID" and consists of a number between 0 and 7, with 7 being assigned to the controller and having the highest priority. All devices in the chain must have a unique SCSI ID. In most cases a SCSI boot drive should be set to SCSI ID 0, which would leave all jumpers open. Drive Select jumpers usually consist of three 2-pin jumpers, with each jumper representing a binary unit, or bit.

- **TERMPWR** jumpers are used to specify the *source and destination* of terminator power on the SCSI drive. Three settings commonly found on many drives address how on-board terminators are to be powered: terminator power (TERMPWR) is to be supplied by (**1**) the drive itself, (**2**) by the SCSI bus, or by (**3**) both drive and SCSI bus. If the bus uses an A-cable, termination power is supplied by pin 26. The pin assignment varies on other cable types. Another common jumper setting allows the drive to supply power to the SCSI bus. If this option is available, keep in mind that at least one device on the SCSI cable must provide power to the bus. Usually it is the SCSI adapter.

- Some SCSI drives have **spindle motor power-up option** jumpers. There are two options: spindle motor starts on power-up, or spindle motor starts on command only. Enabling the spindle motor starts on command function allows a compatible controller to stagger the spindle motor power-up according to the SCSI ID number assigned to the drive. The reason for this is to avoid overloading the power supply by having all the motors start at once.

- On some SCSI drives, a **spindle-motor power-up delay** function is included. This is much the same as the spindle motor starts on command function, except that the drive does not need to be told by the controller when to start the spindle motor, instead delaying power-up according to the SCSI ID number. Lower number drives have shorter delays.

- **SCSI parity** should be enabled if your drive *and* controller support this feature. SCSI parity is simply an error checking function which increases the reliability of data transfers.

7. There are two or more connectors on the SCSI drive cable. The connectors on the SCSI cable are inter-changeable, meaning either end can be attached to any device. The order in which SCSI devices are attached to the daisy-chain has no bearing on device priority. The SCSI ID number is the sole method of assigning device priority.

There are basically two types of SCSI cables in use today, along with their corresponding differential versions. The oldest and most common is the 50-pin A-cable. SCSI-2 specifications accommodate the 68-pin P-cable for Wide SCSI.

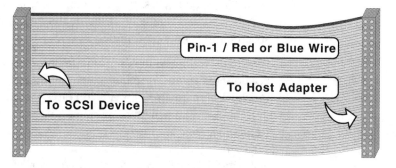

This is the 50-pin cable attached to a SCSI-1 or SCSI-2 hard drive or other SCSI device.

Figure 4-10: SCSI Internal A-Cable

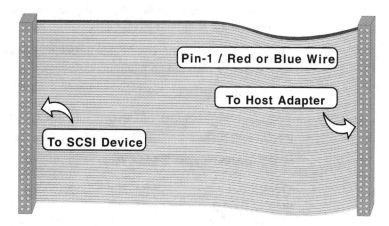

This is the 68-pin cable attached to a Wide SCSI-2 hard drive or other SCSI device.

Figure 4-11: SCSI Internal P-Cable

Locate pin 1 on the SCSI cable. It can be located by one of three possible markings: a triangle stamped on the connector close to pin 1, a colored stripe on wire #1 (usually red or blue), or a keying tab inside of the connector that will not allow the cable to be inserted incorrectly. Orient the cable connector so that it corresponds to pin 1 on the drive interface connector and join the two connectors. Refer to Figure 4-9 for an illustration.

8. Each drive requires its own power cable. The cable is usually attached to the computer's power supply, but in the case of multiple, external-SCSI device systems, a separate power supply may be necessary. The connector is keyed so that it can only be inserted one way. Electrical assignments and connector specifications may be found in Figure 4-6 on page 138.

9. Fix the drive(s) into the appropriate drive bays. Most drives can be mounted in any orientation except upside-down, but be sure to check for restrictions if you are not mounting the drive upright and flat (platters parallel to the plane of the floor). Remember that hard drives operate under high tolerances. The selection of an internal location away from hot components and/or with access to good air circulation will help increase the life span of the drive.

10. Perform a quick check to make sure that all connectors are correctly configured and secure. SCSI cables can be damaged if connected backwards. Also make sure all tools and other loose objects are removed from inside the computer chassis.

11. Replace the casing over the computer chassis and complete re-assembly with the appropriate fasteners.

12. Plug the computer back in.

You are now ready to proceed to the BIOS set-up portion of the installation process.

BIOS Drive Type Selection

The BIOS set-up is also called the CMOS set-up. When installing a SCSI drive into a system, the CMOS drive type should be set to "0" or "NOT INSTALLED" since most SCSI host adapters have a BIOS that supplies the drive type for the drive and handles the read/writes for the drive. If the version of DOS being used is earlier than 5.0, a special software driver will need to be used if more than two SCSI hard drives are installed.

1. Power-up the computer and perform the procedure required to enter the CMOS set-up. The CMOS set-up entry procedure can vary depending on the BIOS manufacturer, but is typically accomplished by one of these actions:

   A. Pressing and holding down the escape (Esc) keys during the Power-On Self-Test (POST).
   B. Pressing and holding down the delete (Del) keys during the POST.
   C. Pressing the (Ctrl), (Alt), and (Esc) keys at the same time while in DOS.
   D. Pressing the (Ctrl), (Alt), and (S) keys at the same time while in DOS.
   E. Pressing the (Ctrl), (Alt), and (Ent) key at the same time while in DOS.
   F. Some BIOS types will automatically go into the CMOS set-up if a system configuration change is detected, which would include hard drive alterations.

2. Go into the hard drive set-up portion of CMOS set-up.

3. Select Drive Type "0" or "Not Installed" from the BIOS Drive Type Table.

Low-Level Formatting

The controllers that do support low-level formatting may usually be accessed through the DOS debug command G=C800:5, or with special firmware that comes with the controller. Refer to the documentation that came with your controller for information on this matter.

SCSI Device Drivers

Some SCSI controllers use a replacement block device driver to set up communication between the operating system and the disk drive. If this is the case, the device driver is specific to the controller model and should come packaged with it. Consult the user's manual of your particular controller for information on how to install the device driver.

DOS Partitioning

Please see Chapter One for details on partitioning. **FDISK** is the utility provided with DOS to partition a drive.

1. If you are installing a new boot drive, boot from a DOS disk containing the files **FDISK.EXE** and **FORMAT.COM.** If you are installing additional (non-boot) drive(s), boot normally from the drive that is already installed.

2. Run the FDISK program by typing FDISK at the prompt.

3. Use the menu to set the desired partitioning options for your drive(s), depending on the DOS version you are using.

4. For the boot or sole drive, set the boot partition to "active" if it's not done automatically.

5. Exit FDISK. The partition(s) are now ready for high-level formatting.

High-Level Formatting

Once the drive is partitioned, each partition must be high-level formatted with the operating system that you will be using. To format under DOS, use the **FORMAT** command, specifying the partition to be formatted. For example, type FORMAT C: to format the partition designated as C: drive.

If you want to make this the boot drive, save a step and use the command **FORMAT /S** to automatically transfer the system files after formatting. If the partition is already formatted, then use the **SYS** command to transfer the system files to the partition and make it bootable. Simply put:

*   If the partition is unformatted, type FORMAT C: /S at the prompt.

*   If the partition is already formatted type SYS C: at the prompt.

Problems?

*   *Before applying power*, make sure that pin 1 on the interface connector corresponds with pin 1 of the cable connector.

*   Double-check that the SCSI ID jumpers are set properly. It is easy to inadvertently look at the jumper block from the wrong perspective.

*   If you encounter other problems during the installation procedure, refer to Chapter Eight, which contains some of the more common set-up problems you may encounter and their solutions.

ESDI Drive Installation

If this is an upgrade or addition of a secondary drive, back up the original drive in its entirety.

If you are installing more than one drive, it is recommended that you accomplish all of the steps outlined below sequentially for each drive, rather than installing all of the drives at once. This will make trouble-shooting much easier if you encounter any problems.

ESDI Installation Summary

The following outline is a general instruction for installing ESDI drives. Please read the entire section for a step-by-step installation guide.

1. Install the hard drive(s), setting the appropriate jumpers and connecting the drive(s) to the controller via the ESDI data and control cables.

2. *DrivePro* and from Micro House is a highly recommended hard drive set-up utility. The use of this excellent program could save you some time and/or headaches.

3. If you are proceeding manually, enter the CMOS set-up utility and define the drive-type. This is usually, though not always, Type 1. Refer to the ESDI portion of Chapter Three for information on the different controller types and which Drive Type should be selected accordingly.

4. Set up the desired partitions, then format the drive using the appropriate FDISK and FORMAT commands.

Figure 4-12: ESDI Drive Installation

ESDI Step-by-Step Installation

Hardware Installation

1. Take the general precautions listed in this chapter under the heading "Safety Precautions" prior to proceeding.

2. Remove the outer casing from the computer chassis. The retaining screws are usually located in the back or underneath.

3. Take some time to familiarize yourself with the organization of the chassis and some of the components prior to proceeding. Chassis organization can vary depending on manufacturer, size, and tower or desk-top orientation.

4. If you are upgrading or attaching a new ESDI controller, first remove the old one and find an appropriate expansion slot to install the new one. Be sure that you are using a compatible controller, typed according to the MHz rating (refer to the ESDI section of Chapter Three for more information). Prior to installation, configure the controller according to the options you would like enabled. Jumper settings can be found in the manufacturer's documentation.

ON THE CD

> If you cannot find the documentation and do not know the manufacturer of your controller, the *Micro House Technical Library* contains jumper settings for many of the most popular hard drives, controllers, and main boards manufactured. This handy reference contains the equivalent of thousands of pages of hardware documentation on a single CD-ROM. A demonstration of this highly acclaimed tool has been included on the CD-ROM that came with this text.

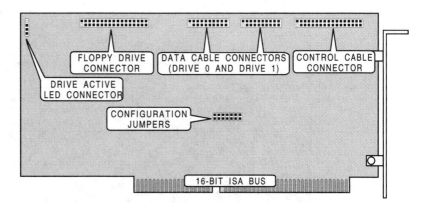

Figure 4-13: ESDI Controller Connection Diagram

5. Terminating resistors are socketed resistor packs, sometimes
    called terminators, that are usually yellow and sometimes black
    or blue. On ESDI drives, there are several of these on each hard
    drive. They can be found on the underside of the drive or near
    the drive control and data cables. The terminating resistors on
    ESDI drives are configured according to the type of cable used
    to attach the drive to the controller. Look through step 7 to find
    the proper setting for your system's configuration. On some
    drives the resistors are not socketed or intended for removal – if
    this is the case, the resistors can usually be enabled internally by
    jumper or switch settings.)

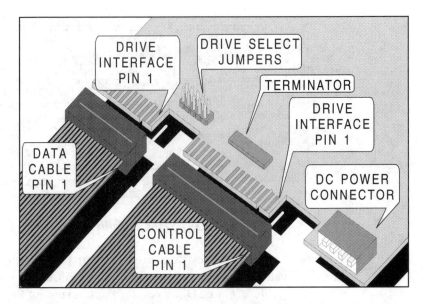

Although most ESDI interface connectors will be oriented this way with respect to the drive, this is not always the case. Be sure to look for a Pin 1 indicator on the interface connector, such as a notch in the connector shroud at that location.

Figure 4-14: ESDI Connection Diagram

6. Prior to installation, configure the drive according to the drive number assigned and the options you would like enabled. Jumper settings can be found in the manufacturer's documentation. Address and telephone information for major manufacturers can be found in **Appendix C**.

ESDI drives vary widely in options and their corresponding jumpers. Some ESDI drive settings of which you should be aware are as follows:

- Some ESDI drives offer two choices on activating the spindle motor: activate on system power-up, or activate on command only.

- Some ESDI drives offer spindle synchronization in a two-drive system for special applications. Note that this feature is subject to compatibility problems if the drives are not identical.

- There will be three or seven 2-pin **Drive Select** jumpers, depending on the make and model of the hard drive. The position to the far left or far right will be drive select 0 (sometimes the numbering starts at 1). Usually only four of these jumper settings are actually used for the drive select function. The other jumpers are reserved for various drive parameters.

Because the type of cable used depends on the system's hard drive configuration, please see step 7 for the proper jumper setting of your configuration.

7. ESDI drives require two interface cables: the control cable and the data cable. The data cable is the smaller 20-pin ribbon cable. One data cable is required for each hard drive attached to the controller.

The control cable is the large 34-pin ribbon cable with three connectors. One control cable is required for every two hard drives. There are several types of drive control cables. The type of cable used dictates the settings of drive select jumpers and termination resistors. The different cables and their associated jumper and termination resistor settings are described below:

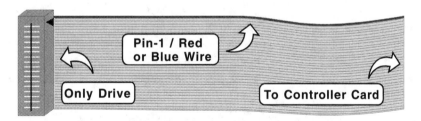

Figure 4-15: ESDI Single-Drive Control Cable

The ESDI Single Drive Control Cable is used in systems with only one hard drive. Jumper and termination resistor settings for single-drive ESDI configuration are as follows:

- Configure the drive select jumpers for drive select one.
- Leave the termination resistor installed on the drive.

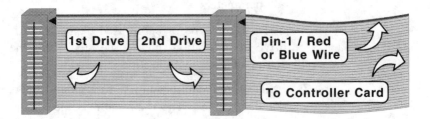

Figure 4-16: ESDI Dual-Drive Control Cable With No Twist

The ESDI Dual Drive Control Cable is used in systems with one or two hard drives. The connector on the end of the cable is for the first or only hard drive. The connector in the middle of the cable is for the second hard drive.

Jumper and termination resistor settings for dual-drive control cable with no twist are as follows:

- For the first or only hard drive, set the drive select jumpers for drive select one. Leave the termination resistor installed.
- For the second hard drive, set the drive select jumpers for drive select two and remove the termination resistor.

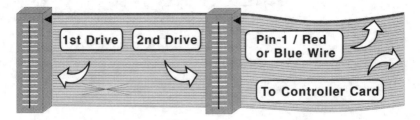

Figure 4-17: ESDI Dual-Drive Control Cable With Twist

The ESDI Dual Drive Control Cable With Twist is used in systems with one or two hard drives. With the connector on the end of the cable being for the first or only hard drive. The connector in the middle of the cable is for the second hard drive.

Jumper and termination resistor settings for dual-drive control cable with a twist are as follows:

- For the first or only hard drive, set the drive select jumpers for drive select two and leave the termination resistor installed.
- For the second hard disk, set the drive select jumpers for drive select two and remove the termination resistor.

The drive select jumpers are set to the second position on both the drives in this case because the cable twist reverses the drive select pins. This cable was developed in order to eliminate the need to change the drive select jumpers. Both drives are always set for drive select two, and can be interchangeably designated drive C: or drive D:, depending on cable position.

Locate pin 1 on both the data and control cables. Pin 1 can be located by one of three possible markings: a triangle stamped on the connector close to pin 1, a colored stripe on wire #1 (usually red or blue), or a keying tab inside of the connector that will not allow the cable to be inserted incorrectly. Orient cable connectors so that they correspond to pin 1 on the drive interface connectors and join data and control connectors. See **Figure 4-14** for an illustration.

8. Each drive requires its own power cable. The connector is keyed so that it can only be inserted one way. Electrical assignments and connector specifications may be found in Figure 4-6 on page 138.

9. Fix the drive(s) into the appropriate drive bays. Most drives can be mounted in any orientation except upside-down, but be sure to check for restrictions if you are not mounting the drive upright and flat (platters parallel to the plane of the floor). Remember that hard drives operate under high tolerances. The selection of an internal location away from hot components and/or with access to good air circulation will help increase the life span of the drive.

10. Perform a quick check to make sure that all connectors are in place. Also make sure all tools and other loose objects are removed from inside the computer chassis.

11. Replace the casing over the computer chassis and complete re-assembly with the appropriate fasteners.

12. Plug the computer back in.

You are now ready to proceed to the BIOS set-up portion of the installation process.

Micro House *DrivePro*™

ON THE CD

- The drive set-up utilities from Micro House offer no-headache drive installation of ESDI drives.

- Please run the *DrivePro* demonstration included with the purchase of this text for a hands-on preview of this powerful program's easy-to-use features.

- If you are going to finish installing the drive manually, please go on to the following steps:

BIOS Drive Type Selection

The BIOS set-up is also called the CMOS set-up. When installing an ESDI drive into a system, the CMOS drive type should usually be set to "1" and the firmware on the ESDI interface will handle any compatibility problems.

1. Power-up the computer and perform the procedure required to enter the CMOS set-up. The CMOS set-up entry procedure can vary depending on the BIOS manufacturer, but is typically accomplished by one of these actions:

   A. Pressing and holding down the escape (Esc) key during the Power-On Self-Test (POST).
   B. Pressing and holding down the delete (Del) key during the POST.
   C. Pressing the (Ctrl), (Alt), and (Esc) keys at the same time while in DOS.
   D. Pressing the (Ctrl), (Alt), and (S) keys at the same time while in DOS.
   E. Pressing the (Ctrl), (Alt), and (Ent) keys at the same time while in DOS.
   F. Some BIOS types will automatically go into the CMOS set-up if a system configuration change is detected, which would include hard drive alterations.

2. Go into the hard drive set-up portion of CMOS set-up.

3. Select Drive Type 1 from the BIOS Drive Type Table.

Low-Level Formatting

The low-level format is the first step in preparing the drive after the physical installation is complete. This process sets up the "handshake" between the drive and the controller. Most of these drives <u>must</u> be low-leveled via the controller's on-board firmware which usually can be accessed through the DOS debug command G=C800:5. The drive specifications are usually encoded on the drive by the factory. These specifications are read from the drive by the controller. The controller may also do a conversion to increase the sectors and decrease the cylinders, bringing them within the BIOS/DOS 1,024 cylinder limit.

Most ESDI drives are low-level formatted for variable sectors per track. They also use a technique called sector skew. This moves the sectors slightly from track to track to account for track-to-track seek time and head switch time. The skew factor is calculated by dividing the track-to-track seek time and/or head switch time of the drive by 16.6ms and then multiplying this number by the number of sectors per track. The final figure is rounded to the next whole number to obtain the optimum sector skew value. Before you start to worry, you can relax knowing that controllers that support this feature do so automatically. If you would like to implement skewing on your drive, then you will need to run the low-level code on the controller's BIOS or software included with the card (if available).

There is also another factor that comes into play: sector sparing. Drives/controllers that support this feature reduce the number of sectors on each track by one and place defect information on the drive. Applications will see fewer defects since only the drive is aware of the spare sectors. This reduces the total capacity of your drive but is useful if the drive has a large amount of defects and your application requires a defect-free drive.

DOS Partitioning

Please see Chapter One for details on partitioning. **FDISK** is the utility provided with DOS to partition a drive. There are different partitioning limitations for each DOS version, the latest of which supports partitions of up to 2GB – enough to use one large partition for just about every ESDI manufactured.

You can lose a significant amount of drive capacity by using a "large" partition. There is usually a portion of the last cluster used for a file which ends up being wasted. Because DOS uses more sectors per cluster for large partitions, there is a proportional increase in the amount of unused sectors in larger clusters. Please refer to the page 26 for a more detailed explanation of clusters and how they affect wasted drive capacity.

1. If you are installing a new boot drive, boot from a DOS disk containing the files **FDISK.EXE** and **FORMAT.COM.** If you are installing additional (non-boot) drive(s), boot normally from the drive that is already installed.

2. Run the FDISK program by typing FDISK at the prompt.

3. Use the menu to set the desired partitioning options for your drive(s), depending on the DOS version you are using.

4. For the boot or sole drive, set the boot partition to "active" if it's not done automatically.

5. Exit FDISK. The partition(s) are now ready for high-level formatting.

High-Level Formatting

Once the drive is partitioned, each partition must be high-level formatted with the operating system that you will be using. To format under DOS, use the **FORMAT** command, specifying the partition to be formatted. For example, type FORMAT C: to format the partition designated as C: drive.

If you want to make this the boot drive, save a step by using the command **FORMAT /S** to automatically transfer the system files after formatting. If the partition is already formatted, then use the **SYS** command to transfer the system files to the partition and make it bootable. Simply put:

- If the partition is unformatted, type FORMAT C: /S at the prompt.

- If the partition is already formatted type SYS C: at the prompt.

Problems?

- Make sure that pin 1 on the interface connector corresponds with pin 1 of the cable connector.

- Double check that the drive-select jumpers are set properly. It is easy to inadvertently look at the jumper block from the wrong perspective.

- Make sure that you are using the proper type of cable according to your system's drive configuration, and that your drive is properly terminated.

- Are you using the correct type of controller for your drive? See the ESDI section of Chapter Three for information on the different controller types.

- If you encounter other problems during the installation procedure, refer to Chapter Eight, which contains some of the more common set-up problems you may encounter and their solutions.

ST-506/412 Drive Installation

If this is an upgrade or addition of a secondary drive, back up the original drive in its entirety.

If you are installing more than one drive, it is recommended that you accomplish all of the steps outlined below sequentially for each drive, rather than installing all of the drives at once. This will make trouble-shooting much easier if you encounter any problems.

ST-506/412 Installation Summary

The following outline is a general instruction on installing ST-506/412 drives. Please read the entire section for a step-by-step installation guide.

1. Install the hard drive(s), setting the appropriate jumpers and connecting the drive(s) to the controller via the ST-506/412 data and control cables.

2. **DrivePro** from Micro House is a highly recommended hard drive set-up utility. The use of this excellent program could save you some time and/or headaches.

3. If you are proceeding manually, enter the CMOS set-up utility and define the drive-type.

4. Set up the desired partitions, then format the drive using the appropriate FDISK and FORMAT commands.

Figure 4-18: ST-506/412 Drive Installation

ST-506/412 Step-by-Step Installation

Hardware Installation

1. Take the general precautions listed in this chapter under the heading "Safety Precautions" prior to proceeding.

2. Remove the outer casing from the computer chassis. The retaining screws are usually located in the back or underneath.

3. Take some time to familiarize yourself with the organization of the chassis and some of the components prior to proceeding. Chassis organization can vary depending on manufacturer, size, and tower or desk-top orientation.

4. If you are upgrading or attaching a new ST-506/412 controller, first remove the old one and find an appropriate expansion slot to install the new one. Be sure that you are using a compatible controller, according to the appropriate encoding (MFM or RLL). Prior to installation, configure the controller according to the options you would like enabled. Jumper settings can be found in the manufacturer's documentation.

It is important that you correctly match the encoding when pairing a hard drive and controller. MFM drives always have 17 sectors and RLL usually have 26 or more. Even though the firmware on an MFM interface card may allow you to enter in a sector value greater than 17 or you may set the drive for a type in CMOS with more than 17 sectors per track, the electronics will only use 17. So a 30 megabyte RLL drive used on an MFM controller will only format out to 20 megabytes, since its using only 17 sectors per track instead of its optimum 26. This costs you disk space, but is better than throwing away an RLL drive if you only have an MFM controller.

Do not use an MFM drive with an RLL controller. MFM drives are designed to use only 17 sectors per track and forcing it to use 26 or more will cause excessive bad sectors, and possibly permanently damage the electronics. You may get 30 megabytes out of a 20 megabyte drive but it will substantially reduce the life of the drive.

If you cannot find the documentation and do not know the manufacturer of your controller, the **Micro House Technical Library** contains jumper settings for many of the most popular hard drives, controllers, and main boards manufactured. This handy reference contains the equivalent of thousands of pages of hardware documentation on a single CD-ROM. A demonstration of this highly acclaimed tool has been included on the CD-ROM that came with this text.

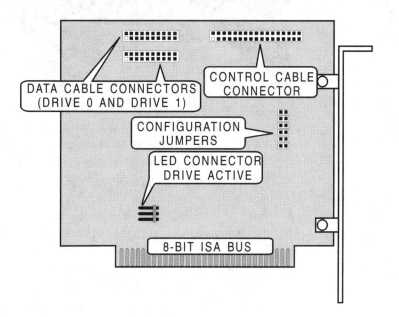

Figure 4-19: ST-506/412 Controller Connection Diagram

5. Terminating resistors are socketed resistor packs, sometimes called terminators, that are usually yellow and sometimes black or blue. On ST-506/412 drives, there are several of these on each hard drive. They can be found on the underside of the drive or near the drive control and data cables. The terminating resistors on ST-506/412 drives are configured according to the type of cable used to attach the drive to the controller. Look through step 7 to find the proper setting for your system's configuration. On some drives the resistors are not socketed or intended for removal – if this is the case, the resistors can usually be enabled internally by jumper or switch se ings.

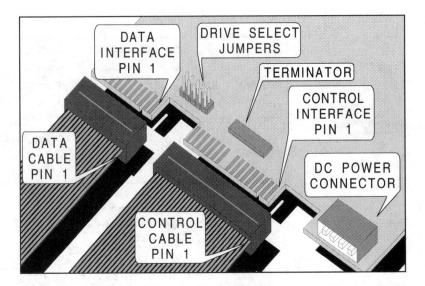

*Although most ST-506/412 interface connectors will be oriented this
way with respect to the drive, this is not always the case. Be sure to
look for a Pin 1 indicator on the interface connector, such as a
notch in the connector shroud at that location.*

Figure 4-20: ST-506/412 Connection Diagram

6. Prior to installation, configure the drive according to the drive
    number assigned and the options you would like enabled.
    Jumper settings can be found in the manufacturer's
    documentation. Address and telephone information for major
    manufacturers can be found in **Appendix C**.

    Of the various option jumpers or switches on the drive (there
    may be many) only four may be called drive select
    jumpers/switches. Of these four, however, only two can be
    used on ST-506/412 interface drives. The position to the far left
    or far right of the drive select jumper/switch block will be drive
    select 0 (sometimes the numbering starts at 1). The other
    jumpers are reserved for various drive parameters. The drive
    number to be selected depends on the desired DOS drive
    designation (C: or D:) and the type of cable used for connection
    to the controller.

Because the type of cable used depends on the system's hard drive configuration, please see step 7 for the proper jumper setting for your configuration.

7. ST-506/412 drives require two interface cables: the control cable and the data cable. The data cable is the smaller 20-pin ribbon cable. One data cable is required for each hard drive attached to the controller.

The control cable is the large 34-pin ribbon cable with two or three connectors. One control cable is required for every two hard drives. There are several types of drive control cables. The type of cable used dictates the settings of drive select jumpers and termination resistors. The different cables and their associated jumper and termination resistor settings are described below:

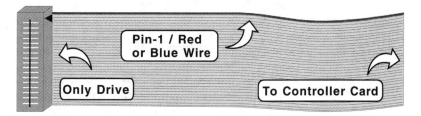

Figure 4-21: ST-506/412 Single-Drive Control Cable

The ST-506/412 Single Drive Control Cable is used in systems with only one hard drive. Jumper and termination resistor settings for single-drive ST-506/412 configuration are as follows:

- Configure the drive select jumpers for drive select one.
- Leave the termination resistor installed on the drive.

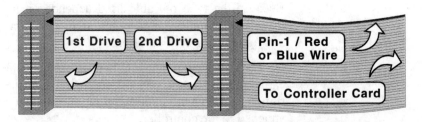

Figure 4-22: ST-506/412 Dual-Drive Control Cable With No Twist

The ST-506/412 Dual Drive Control Cable is used in systems with one or two hard drives. The connector on the end of the cable is for the first or only hard drive. The connector in the middle of the cable is for the second hard drive.

Jumper and termination resistor settings for dual-drive control cable with no twist are as follows:

- For the first or only hard drive, set the drive select jumpers for drive select one. Leave the termination resistor installed.
- For the second hard drive, set the drive select jumpers for drive select two and remove the termination resistor.

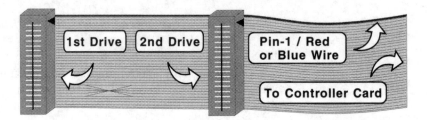

Figure 4-23: ST-506/412 Dual-Drive Control Cable With Twist

The ST-506/412 Dual Drive Control Cable With Twist is used in systems with one or two hard drives. With the connector on the end of the cable being for the first or only hard drive. The connector in the middle of the connector is for the second hard drive.

Jumper and termination resistor settings for dual-drive control cable with a twist are as follows:

- For the first or only hard drive, set the drive select jumpers for drive select two and leave the termination resistor installed.
- For the second hard disk, set the drive select jumpers for drive select two and remove the termination resistor.

The drive select jumpers are set to the second position on both the drives in this case because the cable twist reverses the drive select pins. This cable was developed in order to eliminate the need to change the drive select jumpers. Both drives are always set for drive select two, and can be interchangeably designated drive C: or drive D:, according to cable position.

Locate pin 1 on both the data and control cables. Pin 1 can be located by one of three possible markings: a triangle stamped on the connector close to pin 1, a colored stripe on wire #1 (usually red or blue), or a keying tab inside of the connector that will not allow the cable to be inserted incorrectly. Orient cable connectors so that they correspond to pin 1 on the drive interface connectors and join data and control connectors. See Figure 4-20 on page 168 for an illustration.

8. Each drive requires its own power cable. The connector is keyed so that it can only be inserted one way. Electrical assignments and connector specifications may be found in Figure 4-6 on page 138.

9. Fix the drive(s) into the appropriate drive bays. Be sure to check for restrictions if you are not mounting the drive upright and flat (platters parallel to the plane of the floor). Remember that hard drives operate under high tolerances. The selection of an internal location away from hot components and/or with access to good air circulation will help increase the life span of the drive.

10. Perform a quick check to make sure that all connectors are in place. Also make sure all tools and other loose objects are removed from inside the computer chassis.

11. Replace the casing over the computer chassis and complete re-assembly with the appropriate fasteners.

12. Plug the computer back in.

You are now ready to proceed to the BIOS setup portion of the installation process.

Micro House *DrivePro*

- The drive set-up utilities from Micro House offer no-headache drive installation of ST-506/412 drives.

- Please run the **DrivePro** demonstration included with the purchase of this text for a hands-on preview of this powerful program's easy-to-use features.

- If you are going to finish installing the drive manually, go on to the following steps:

Low-Level Formatting

The low-level format is the first step in preparing the drive after the physical installation is complete. This process sets up the "handshake" between the drive and the controller.

Some BIOSes include a low-level format utility in the CMOS set-up. Also, ST-506/412 controllers sometimes have the low-level program in their firmware (XT-type controllers will always have low-level software built-in). If you cannot locate the low-level software in either of these places, you will have to use a third-party software package that contains this feature, such as **DrivePro** from Micro House. Please note:

- The ST-506/412 hard drive controller cards used in XT systems have an on-board BIOS.
- Most XT controller low-level software can be accessed through the DOS DEBUG command: G=C800:5.

ST-506/412 drives have a manufacturer's defect list printed on the casing. This list contains information about which sectors have been found to be unreliable during factory tests. ST-506/412 low-level programs allow the user to enter this list into a table to mark these sectors and prevent data from being written to them. You may also want to run your own surface scan periodically to see if any additional defects have appeared, and enter this new information during the next low-level procedure you perform.

See page 21 for a complete description of **interleaving**. An interleave of three should be fine for most XT installations, and two for most 80286 installations. 80386s and above can use an interleave of one, provided the controller is designed for a 1:1 interleave.

There are several software packages that allow you to adjust the interleave after the low-level is done. They will even find an optimum interleave for the system and drive you are using.

BIOS Drive Type Selection

The BIOS set-up is also called the CMOS set-up. This procedure enables the BIOS to work with the drive by letting it know the drive's parameters. The AT system has the drive-type table contained in its motherboard BIOS. The drive to be installed must match one of these table entries. Most BIOS tables have a user-definable drive type so that you may define your own type. If your BIOS does not have a type that matches your drive, or a user-definable drive type then you must use a software package that will overcome this limitation. *DrivePro* from Micro House is one such product.

1. Power-up the computer and perform the procedure required to enter the CMOS set-up. The CMOS set-up entry procedure can vary depending on the BIOS manufacturer, but is typically accomplished by one of these actions:

   A. Pressing and holding down the escape (Esc) key during the Power-On Self-Test (POST).

   B. Pressing and holding down the delete (Del) key during the POST.

   C. Pressing the (Ctrl), (Alt), and (Esc) keys at the same time while in DOS.

   D. Some BIOS types will automatically go into the CMOS set-up if a system configuration change is detected, which would include hard drive alterations.

2. Go into the hard drive set-up portion of CMOS set-up.

3. Select Drive Type according to the parameters of your drive, or enter a user-defined drive type if your BIOS supports this feature. ST-506/412 drives do not perform a translation, so simply knowing the capacity of the drive is not enough. See **Appendix A** for drive parameter information.

Additionally, you will have to enter some other parameters here for ST-506/412 drives, such as Write Precompensation, Reduced Write Current, and Landing Zone. See **Appendix A** for explanations of these parameters.

DOS Partitioning

Please see Chapter One for details on partitioning. **FDISK** is the utility provided with DOS to partition a drive.

1. If you are installing a new boot drive, boot from a DOS disk containing the files **FDISK.EXE** and **FORMAT.COM**. If you are installing additional (non-boot) drive(s), boot normally from the drive that is already installed.

2. Run the FDISK program by typing FDISK at the prompt.

3. Use the menu to set the desired partitioning options for your drive(s), depending on the DOS version you are using.

4. For the boot or sole drive, set the boot partition to "active" if it's not done automatically.

5. Exit FDISK. The partition(s) are now ready for high-level formatting.

High-Level Formatting

Once the drive is partitioned, each partition must be high-level formatted with the operating system that you will be using. To format under DOS, use the **FORMAT** command, specifying the partition to be formatted. For example, type FORMAT C: to format the partition designated as C: drive.

If you want to make this the boot drive, save a step and use the command **FORMAT /S** to automatically transfer the system files after formatting. If the partition is already formatted, then use the **SYS** command to transfer the system files to the partition and make it bootable. Simply put:

- If the partition is unformatted, type FORMAT C: /S at the prompt.
- If the partition is already formatted type SYS C: at the prompt.

Problems?

- Make sure that pin 1 on the interface connector corresponds with pin 1 of the cable connector.

- Double check that the Drive-Select jumpers are set properly. It is easy to inadvertently look at the jumper block from the wrong perspective.

- The type of encoding used by the drive and controller should be the same. Please review the section on low-level formatting ST-506/412 drives for this information.

- Make sure that you are using the proper type of cable according to your system's drive configuration, and that your drive is properly terminated.

- If you encounter other problems during the installation procedure, refer to Chapter Eight, which contains some of the more common set-up problems you may encounter and their solutions.

Chapter Review:

- Review the safety precautions outlined on page 130 prior to servicing any hardware.

- Set-up utilities, such as **EZ-Drive** and **DrivePro**, can greatly simplify the installation process.

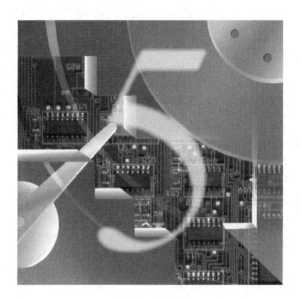

Controller Settings

Chapter Five Contents:

General Controller Information

Interface Connections

Please consult Chapter Three for specific details on connectors for IDE, SCSI, ESDI, and ST-506/412 interfaces.

Controller to Drive Power Connections

The following connections are common to all controllers with an on board power source.

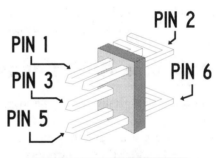

PIN	DESCRIPTION
1	+12 Volts DC
2	+12 Volts DC
3	+5 Volts DC
4	Not used
5	Ground
6	Ground

Figure 5-1: Controller Onboard Power Connector

Drive Activity Connector

The following connections are common to all controllers with a 4-pin drive activity connector. A LED may be connected to either ground pin (pin 1 or pin 4) and either signal pin (pin 2 or pin 3).

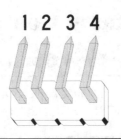

PIN	DESCRIPTION
1	Ground
2	+5 Volts DC
3	+5 Volts DC
4	Ground

(Lines 2 and 3 only go high during disk activity)
Figure 5-2: Controller Drive Activity LED Connector

Common BIOS Debug Format Codes

The following table is a general guide to the controller BIOS entry points (debug codes) on many of the listed manufacturers' products. They are not always the same and are usually only available on 8-bit RLL and MFM controllers. Note that if the BIOS address is changed on the controller, then the entry point listed below will also change (i.e.: BIOS address was C800, entry point was C800:5. Address changed to CC00, entry point changes to CC00:5).

Table 5-1: Common BIOS Debug Format Codes	
Adaptec	G=C800:ccc or G=C800:6
Scientific Micro Systems-OMTI	G=C800:6
Seagate	G=C800:5
Western Digital	G=C800:5

To use one of the above enter the DOS Debug utility and type the corresponding code at the dash (-) prompt.

Common Hardware Settings

Default Jumper Settings

The default or most common jumpers positions are denoted by the ⇨ symbol. Pin-1 and jumper 1 are indicated by an arrowhead symbol (▲).

Base I/O Address

This option allows the selection of the base I/O address from among the choices given. Available addresses are usually standardized to avoid conflict with other peripherals.

IRQ

IRQ is short for Interrupt Request, which is the standard method used by peripherals to access the CPU. Available IRQs are usually standardized to avoid conflict with other peripherals

BIOS Address

Controller cards with an onboard BIOS usually have an option to set the BIOS address. BIOS address is sometimes called "memory address."

Data Transfer Modes

Some controllers allow the selection of the data transfer mode between PIO and DMA. The native mode for most IDE controllers is non-throttled PIO (see page 65). Be sure that the transfer mode selected is supported by all hardware elements in the system.

Non-Hard Drive I/O Options

Many controllers bundle other I/O options, such as floppy, parallel, and serial ports. Be sure to de-conflict any IRQ or base I/O address settings between these ports and any ports that may already exist in the system. COM refers to serial ports, and LPT refers to parallel ports.

Undocumented Jumpers

Some jumper settings are specified as "unidentified," "factory configured – do not alter," or may have a dash. Information was not available on these jumpers or settings and their configuration should not be altered.

Selected Controller Settings

The remainder of this chapter contains information on specific hardware settings for selected controllers.

ACCULOGIC, INC.
SIDE-2/PCI

Data bus: 32-bit PCI
Size: Half-length, half-height card
Hard drive supported: Four IDE(AT) drives
Floppy drives supported: None

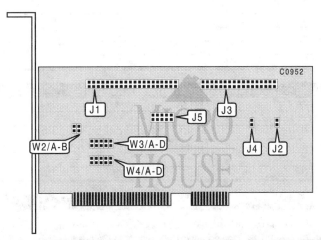

CONNECTIONS	
Function	**Location**
40-pin primary IDE (AT) connector	J1
2-pin connector - drive active LED	J2
40-pin secondary IDE (AT) connector	J3
10-pin ISA IRQ board connector	J5

USER CONFIGURABLE SETTINGS		
Function	**Location**	**Setting**
⇨ Factory configured - do not alter	J4	N/A

ADDRESS MODE SELECTION		
Mode	**W2/A**	**W2/B**
⇨ ISA IDE	Off	On
Native mode	On	Off

Continued on next page. . .

ACCULOGIC, INC.
SIDE-2/PCI

. . .continued from previous page

PCI PRIMARY INTERRUPT SELECTION				
INT	W3/A	W3/B	W3/C	W3/D
⇨ ISA IRQ 14	Off	Off	Off	Off
A	On	Off	Off	Off
B	Off	On	Off	Off
C	Off	Off	On	Off
D	Off	Off	Off	On

PCI SECONDARY INTERRUPT SELECTION				
INT	W4/A	W4/B	W4/C	W4/D
⇨ ISA IRQ 15	Off	Off	Off	Off
A	On	Off	Off	Off
B	Off	On	Off	Off
C	Off	Off	On	Off
D	Off	Off	Off	On

MISCELLANEOUS TECHNICAL NOTES
If IRQ 14 or 15 is selected, the ISA IRQ board is required. This board connects the primary IDE interrupt to the ISA bus IRQ 14 and secondary IDE interrupt to ISA bus IRQ 15.

ACCULOGIC, INC.
SIDE-2/VL

Data bus: 32-bit VL-bus
Size: Three-fourth length, half-height card
Hard drive supported: Four IDE(AT) drives
Floppy drives supported: None

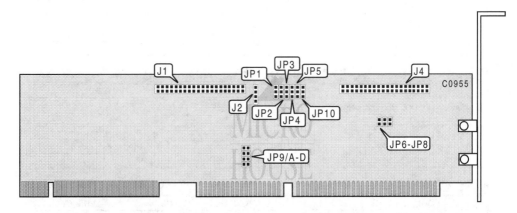

CONNECTIONS	
Function	**Location**
40-pin VESA primary IDE(AT) connector	J1
4-pin connector - drive active LED	J2
40-pin ISA secondary IDE(AT) connector	J4

USER CONFIGURABLE SETTINGS		
Function	**Location**	**Setting**
⇨ VESA IDE(AT) interface enabled	JP3	Pins 1 & 2 closed
VESA IDE(AT) interface disabled	JP3	Pins 2 & 3 closed
⇨ VESA IDE primary address is 1F0h	JP4	Pins 1 & 2 closed
VESA IDE secondary address is 170h	JP4	Pins 2 & 3 closed
⇨ VESA I/O address is 078h	JP5	Pins 1 & 2 closed
VESA I/O address is 178h	JP5	Pins 2 & 3 closed
⇨ ISA secondary IOCHRDY signal disabled	JP8	Open
ISA secondary IOCHRDY signal enabled	JP8	Closed
⇨ ISA secondary IDE(AT) interface disabled	JP10	Pins 1 & 2 closed
ISA secondary IDE(AT) interface enabled	JP10	Pins 2 & 3 closed

ACCULOGIC, INC.
SIDE-2/VL

. . .continued from previous page

BIOS ADDRESS SELECTION		
Address	JP6	JP7
⇨ C800h	Off	Closed
D000h	On	Open
D800h	Off	Open
Disabled	On	Closed

PRIMARY IDE INTERRUPT SELECTION		
IRQ	JP1	JP2
⇨ VESA is primary IDE (IRQ 14) and ISA is secondary IDE	Pins 1 & 2 closed	Pins 1 & 2 closed
VESA is primary IDE (IRQ14)	Pins 1 & 2 closed	Pins 2 & 3 closed
VESA is secondary IDE	Pins 2 & 3 closed	Pins 2 & 3 closed
Note: Jumper J9 selects the IRQ for secondary VESA/ISA IDE.		

SECONDARY IDE INTERRUPT SELECTION				
IRQ	JP9/A	JP9/B	JP9/C	JP9/D
⇨ IRQ15	Closed	Open	Open	Open
IRQ10	Open	Closed	Open	Open
IRQ11	Open	Open	Closed	Open
IRQ12	Open	Open	Open	Closed

MISCELLANEOUS TECHNICAL NOTE
The location of pin 1 on all jumpers is unidentified.

ACCULOGIC, INC.
SIDE-4/HP

Data bus:	16-bit ISA
Size:	Half-length, full-height card
Hard drive supported:	Two IDE(AT) interface drives
Floppy drives supported:	Two 360KB, 720KB, 1.2MB, 1.44MB or 2.88MB drives

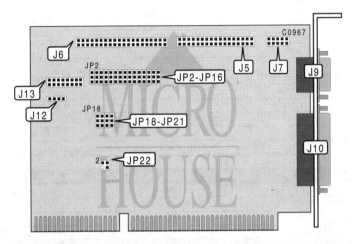

CONNECTIONS	
Function	**Location**
34-pin cable connector - floppy drive	J5
40-pin IDE(AT) connector	J6
10-pin serial port 2 - internal	J7
9-pin serial port 1 - external	J9
25-pin parallel port - external	J10
4-pin connector - drive active LED	J12
Internal power connector	J13

USER CONFIGURABLE SETTINGS		
Function	**Location**	**Setting**
⇨ IDE primary address enabled	JP2	Pins 2 & 3 closed
IDE secondary address is 170h	JP2	Pins 1 & 2 closed
⇨ IDE(AT) interface enabled	JP3	Pins 1 & 2 closed
IDE(AT) interface disabled	JP3	Pins 2 & 3 closed
⇨ Factory configured - do not alter	JP6	N/A
⇨ Factory configured - do not alter	JP7	N/A
⇨ Floppy primary address enabled	JP9	Pins 2 & 3 closed
Floppy secondary address enabled	JP9	Pins 1 & 2 closed
Floppy secondary address enabled	JP9	Pins 1 & 2 closed
⇨ Factory configured - do not alter	JP11	N/A
⇨ Factory configured - do not alter	JP12	N/A
⇨ Floppy drive interface enabled	JP15	Pins 1 & 2 closed
Floppy drive interface disabled	JP15	Pins 2 & 3 closed

Continued on next page. . .

ACCULOGIC, INC.
SIDE-4/HP

. . .continued from previous page

USER CONFIGURABLE SETTINGS (CONTINUED)		
Function	**Location**	**Setting**
⇨ Parallel port IRQ 7 select	JP16	Pins 1 & 2 closed
Parallel port IRQ 5 select	JP16	Pins 2 & 3 closed
⇨ IOCHRDY signal disabled	JP17	Open
IOCHRDY signal enabled	JP17	Closed
IDE(AT) IRQ 15 select - normal	JP18	Pins 1 & 2 closed
IDE(AT) IRQ15 select - delayed	JP18	Pins 2 & 3 closed
⇨ IDE(AT) IRQ 14 select - normal	JP19	Pins 1 & 2 closed
IDE(AT) IRQ14 select - delayed	JP19	Pins 2 & 3 closed
⇨ Serial port 1 IRQ4 select	JP22	Pins 1 & 2 closed
⇨ Serial port 2 IRQ3 select	JP22	Pins 3 & 4 closed
Note: The location of jumper JP17 is unidentified. It may be soldered on the board in some models.		

SERIAL PORT 1 ADDRESS SELECTION		
COM	**JP8**	**JP14**
⇨ COM1 (3F8h)	Pins 1 & 2 closed	Pins 1 & 2 closed
COM2 (2F8h)	Pins 1 & 2 closed	Pins 2 & 3 closed
COM3 (2F8h)	Pins 2 & 3 closed	Pins 1 & 2 closed
Disabled	Pins 2 & 3 closed	Pins 2 & 3 closed

SERIAL PORT 2 ADDRESS SELECTION		
COM	**JP10**	**JP13**
⇨ COM2 (2F8h)	Pins 1 & 2 closed	Pins 1 & 2 closed
COM1 (3F8h)	Pins 1 & 2 closed	Pins 2 & 3 closed
COM4 (238h)	Pins 2 & 3 closed	Pins 1 & 2 closed
Disabled	Pins 2 & 3 closed	Pins 2 & 3 closed

PARALLEL PORT ADDRESS SELECTION		
LPT	**JP4**	**JP5**
⇨ LPT1(378h)	Pins 1 & 2 closed	Pins 2 & 3 closed
LPT2(278h)	Pins 1 & 2 closed	Pins 1 & 2 closed
Disabled	Pins 2 & 3 closed	Pins 2 & 3 closed

PARALLEL PORT DMA SELECTION		
Channel	**JP20**	**JP21**
1	Pins 1 & 2 closed	Pins 1 & 2 closed
3	Pins 2 & 3 closed	Pins 2 & 3 closed

MISCELLANEOUS TECHNICAL NOTES
Location of pin 1 on all jumpers is not available.

ACCULOGIC, INC.
SIDE-4/*PLUS*

Data bus: 16-bit, ISA
Size: Half-length, full-height card
Hard drives supported: Two IDE(AT) drives
Floppy drives supported: Two 360KB, 720KB, 1.2MB or 1.44MB drives

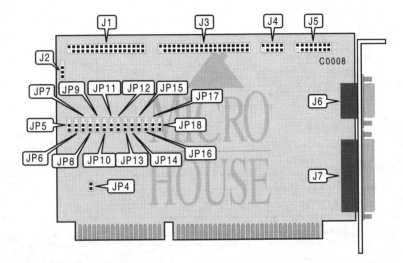

CONNECTIONS	
Function	**Location**
34-pin control cable connector-floppy drive	J1
4-pin connector-drive active LED	J2
40-pin AT Interface (IDE) connector	J3
9-pin serial port 2-internal	J4
15-pin game port-internal	J5
9-pin serial port 1-external	J6
25-pin parallel port-external	J7

Continued on next page . . .

ACCULOGIC, INC.
SIDE-4/*PLUS*

. . . continued from previous page

USER CONFIGURABLE SETTINGS		
Function	**Location**	**Setting**
⇨ I/O Channel Ready signal disabled	JP4	open
I/O Channel Ready signal enabled	JP4	closed
⇨ Floppy drive enabled	JP5	pins 1 & 2 closed
Floppy drive disabled	JP5	pins 2 & 3 closed
⇨ Floppy drive port address is 3F0-3F7h	JP6	pins 1 & 2 closed
Floppy drive port address is 370-377h	JP6	pins 2 & 3 closed
⇨ Single speed floppy drives supported	JP7	pins 1 & 2 closed
Dual speed floppy drives supported	JP7	pins 2 & 3 closed
⇨ Hard drive enabled	JP8	pins 1 & 2 closed
Hard drive disabled	JP8	pins 2 & 3 closed
⇨ IDE select mode enabled	JP9	pins 1 & 2 closed
Not used	JP9	open
⇨ Hard drive port address is 1F0-1F7h	JP10	pins 1 & 2 closed
Hard drive port address is 170-177h	JP10	pins 2 & 3 closed
⇨ Not used	JP11	open
⇨ IRQ14 normal	JP12	pins 1 & 2 closed
IRQ14 delayed until ACTIVE- signal is removed	JP12	pins 2 & 3 closed

SERIAL & PARALLEL PORT CONFIGURATIONS		
Function	**Location**	**Setting**
⇨ Serial port 1 (CN6) enabled	JP13	pins 1 & 2 closed
Serial port 1 (CN6) disabled	JP13	pins 2 & 3 closed
⇨ Serial port 1 (CN6) set to COM1	JP14	pins 1 & 2 closed
Serial port 1 (CN6) set to COM3	JP14	pins 2 & 3 closed
⇨ Serial port 2 (CN4) enabled	JP15	pins 1 & 2 closed
Serial port 2 (CN4) disabled	JP15	pins 2 & 3 closed
⇨ Serial port 2 (CN4) set to COM2	JP16	pins 1 & 2 closed
Serial port 2 (CN4) set to COM4	JP16	pins 2 & 3 closed
⇨ Parallel port (CN7) enabled	JP17	pins 1 & 2 closed
Parallel port (CN7) disabled	JP17	pins 2 & 3 closed
⇨ Parallel port (CN7) address is LPT1	JP18	pins 1 & 2 closed
Parallel port (CN7) address is LPT2	JP18	pins 2 & 3 closed

ADAPTEC, INC.
AHA-1740A, AHA-1742A

Data bus:	32-bit, EISA
Size:	Full-length, full-height card
Hard drive supported:	Up to seven SCSI devices
Floppy drives supported:	Two 360KB, 720KB, 1.2MB, or 1.44MB drives

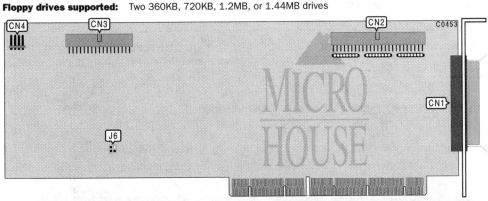

CONNECTIONS	
Function	**Location**
50-pinSCSI connector - external	CN1
50-pinSCSI connector - internal	CN2
34-pin control cable connector - floppy drive	CN3
4-pin connector - drive active LED	CN4

USER CONFIGURABLE SETTINGS		
Function	**Location**	**Setting**
⇨ Floppy drive enabled	J6/jumper 1	closed
Floppy drive disabled	J6/jumper 1	open
⇨ Floppy drive port address is 3F0-3F7h	J6/jumper 2	open
Floppy drive port address is 370-377h	J6/jumper 2	closed

ADAPTEC, INC.
AHA-1740/AHA-1742A (VER. 2)

Data bus:	32-bit EISA
Size:	Three-quarter length, Full-height card
Hard drive supported:	Up to fourteen SCSI devices
Floppy drives supported:	360KB, 720KB, 1.2MB, 1.44MB

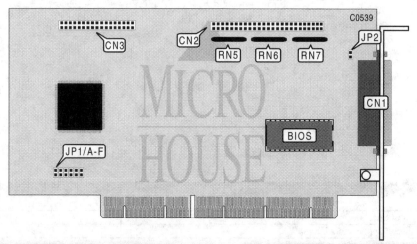

CONNECTIONS	
Function	**Location**
50-pin SCSI interface - external	CN1
50-pin SCSI interface - internal	CN2
34-pin control cable connector - floppy drive	CN3
Terminating resistor 1	RN5
Terminating resistor 2	RN6
Terminating resistor 3	RN7

USER CONFIGURABLE SETTINGS		
Function	**Location**	**Setting**
⇨ Factory configured - do not alter	JP1/A	N/A
⇨ Factory configured - do not alter	JP1/B	N/A
⇨ Factory configured - do not alter	JP1/C	N/A
⇨ Factory configured - do not alter	JP1/D	N/A
⇨ Floppy drive primary address select	JP1/E	open
Floppy drive alternate address select	JP1/E	closed
⇨ Floppy drive interface enabled	JP1/F	closed
Floppy drive interface disabled	JP1/F	open
⇨ TERMPWR supplied by host interface	JP2	closed
TERMPWR not supplied by host interface	JP2	open

ADAPTEC, INC.
AHA-2944W

Data bus: 32-bit PCI
Size: Half-length, full-height card
Hard drive supported: Up to fifteen SCSI-2 devices
Floppy drives supported: None

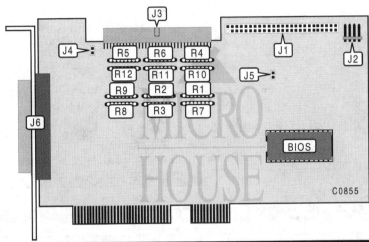

CONNECTIONS	
Function	**Location**
50-pin SCSI connector - internal	J1
4-pin connector - drive active LED	J2
68-pin SCSI connector - internal	J3
68-pin SCSI connector - external	J6

USER CONFIGURABLE SETTINGS		
Function	**Location**	**Setting**
Termination power for J3, when power off enabled	J4	closed
Termination power for J3, when power off disabled	J4	open
Termination power for J1, when power off enabled	J5	closed
Termination power for J1, when power off disabled	J5	open
Low byte & high byte set to off	R1-R12	removed
Low byte & high byte set to on	R1-R12	installed
Low byte set to off, high byte set to on	R9, R12, R3, R6	installed
	R1, R2, R4, R5, R7, R8, R10, R11	removed

MISCELLANEOUS TECHNICAL NOTES
R1, R2, R9, R10, R11, R12 are 330-ohm. R3, R4, R5, R6, R7, R8 are 150-ohm. When using only the 68-pin external connector low & high bytes must be set to on. When using the 68-pin internal & external connectors or when using the 50-pin & 68-pin internal connectors low byte must be set to off, high byte to on. When using the 50-pin internal & 68-pin external low & high bytes must be set to off.

ADAPTEC, INC.
AMM-1570

Q3/95

Data bus:	16-bit ISA
Size:	Full-length, full-height card
Hard drive supported:	Up to seven SCSI drives
Floppy drives supported:	Two 360KB, 720KB, 1.2MB, 1.44MB, or 2.88MB drives

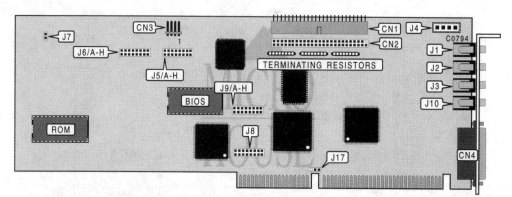

CONNECTIONS	
Function	**Location**
50-pin SCSI connector - internal	CN1
50-pin SCSI connector - external	CN2
4-pin connector - drive active LED	CN3
15-pin game port - external	CN4
Headphone/speaker jack	J1
Line out	J2
Line in	J3
CD audio in	J4
Mic in	J10

USER CONFIGURABLE SETTINGS		
Function	**Location**	**Setting**
⇨ Factory configured - do not alter	J5/A	open
⇨ INT 19h reroute enabled	J5/B	closed
INT 19h reroute disabled	J5/B	open
⇨ Factory configured - do not alter	J5/C	open
⇨ Fast SCSI disabled	J5/D	open
Fast SCSI enabled	J5/D	closed
⇨ Synchronous negotiation disabled	J5/E	open
Synchronous negotiation enabled	J5/E	closed
⇨ SCSI disconnection enabled	J5/F	closed
SCSI disconnection disabled	J5/F	open
⇨ Floptical support disabled	J5/G	open
Floptical support enabled	J5/G	closed
⇨ Extended translation disabled	J5/H	open
Extended translation enabled	J5/H	closed
⇨ Factory configured - do not alter	J6/F	open

Continued on next page. . .

ADAPTEC,INC.
AMM-1570

. . .continued from previous page

USER CONFIGURABLE SETTINGS		
Function	**Location**	**Setting**
↻ Factory configured - do not alter	J6/G	open
↻ SCSI parity checking enabled	J6/H	open
SCSI parity checking disabled	J6/H	closed
↻ Floppy drive enabled	J7	closed
Floppy drive disabled	J7	open
↻ Factory configured - do not alter	J8	open
↻ I/O port address is 340h - 35Eh	J9/E	open
I/O port address is 140h - 15Eh	J9/E	closed
↻ Host adapter BIOS enabled	J9/H	closed
Host adapter BIOS disabled	J9/H	open

SCSI ID CONFIGURATION			
ID	**J6/A**	**J6/B**	**J6/C**
↻ 7	closed	closed	closed
0	open	open	open
1	closed	open	open
2	open	closed	open
3	closed	closed	open
4	open	open	closed
5	closed	open	closed
6	open	closed	closed

INTERRUPT SELECTION						
IRQ	**J6/D**	**J6/E**	**J9/A**	**J9/B**	**J9/C**	**J9/D**
↻ 11	open	closed	open	closed	open	open
9	open	open	open	open	open	closed
10	closed	open	open	open	closed	open
12	closed	closed	closed	open	open	open

BIOS BASE ADDRESS SELECTION		
Address	**J9/F**	**J9/G**
↻ DC000h - DFFFFh	closed	closed
C8000h - CBFFFh	open	open
CC000h - CFFFFh	open	closed
D8000h - DBFFFh	closed	open

SOUND CHIP BASE ADDRESS	
Address	**J17**
↻ 220h	pins 1 & 2 closed
240h	pins 2 & 3 closed
Invalid	open

ALWAYS TECHNOLOGY CORPORATION
AL-7048

Data bus: 32-bit, VL-bus
Size: Full-length, full-height card
Hard drive supported: Up to seven SCSI devices, and two IDE (AT) interface drives
Floppy drives supported: Two 360KB, 720KB, 1.2MB or 1.44MB drives

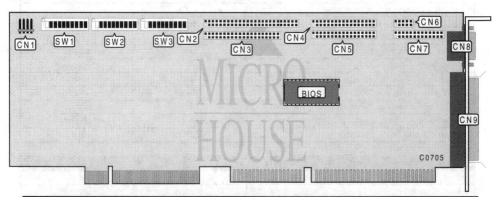

CONNECTIONS	
Function	**Location**
4-pin connector - drive active LED	CN1
50-pin SCSI-2 connector - internal	CN2
40-pin IDE (AT) interface connector - port 1	CN3
34-pin control cabled connector - floppy drive 1	CN4
34-pin control cabled connector - floppy drive 2	CN5
10-pin serial port 2 - internal	CN6
26-pin parallel port connector	CN7
9-pin serial port 1 - external	CN8
50-pin SCSI-2 connector - external	CN9

USER CONFIGURABLE SETTINGS		
Function	**Location**	**Setting**
Factory configured - do not alter	SW1/9	N/A
Multiple drive support enabled	SW1/10	on
Multiple drive support disabled	SW1/10	off
Factory configured - do not alter	SW3/1	N/A
Standard parallel port mode enabled	SW3/2	On
Enhanced parallel port mode enabled	SW3/2	off
Enhanced parallel port DMA1 enabled	SW3/3	on
Enhanced parallel port DMA3 enabled	SW3/3	off
SCSI synchronous negotiation enabled	SW3/4	on
SCSI synchronous negotiation disabled	SW3/4	off
Factory configured - do not alter	SW3/5	N/A
Factory configured - do not alter	SW3/6	N/A

Continued on next page . . .

ALWAYS TECHNOLOGY CORPORATION
AL-7048

. . . continued from previous page

USER CONFIGURABLE SETTINGS		
Function	**Location**	**Setting**
16 transfers/BUS Grant enabled	SW3/7	on
2 transfers/BUS Grant enabled	SW3/7	off
32-bit VESA mode enabled	SW3/8	on
16-bit VESA mode enabled	SW3/8	off
Boot ROM enabled	SW3/9	on
Boot ROM disabled	SW3/9	off
Active termination enabled	SW3/10	on
Active termination disabled	SW3/10	off

BIOS ADDRESS			
Address	**SW1/1**	**SW1/2**	**SW1/3**
C800h	on	on	on
CC00h	off	on	on
D000h	on	off	on
D400h	off	off	on
D800h	on	on	off
DC00h	off	on	off
Disabled	on	off	off
Disabled	off	off	off

I/O ADDRESS			
ISA Address	**VESA Address**	**SW1/4**	**SW1/5**
110h	E800h	on	on
200h	D800h	off	on
220h	C800h	on	off
100h	F800h	off	off

IRQ SELECT			
IRQ	**SW1/6**	**SW1/7**	**SW1/8**
IRQ9	off	on	off
IRQ10	on	on	off
IRQ11	off	off	on
IRQ12	on	off	on
IRQ14	off	on	on
IRQ15	on	on	on
Disabled	on	off	off
Disabled	off	off	off

Continued on next page . . .

ALWAYS TECHNOLOGY CORPORATION
AL-7048

. . . continued from previous page

SERIAL PORT 1 CONFIGURATION		
COM/Address	SW2/1	SW2/2
COM1/3F8h	off	off
COM2/2F8h	on	off
COM3/3E8h	off	on
Disabled	on	on

SERIAL PORT 2 CONFIGURATION		
COM/Address	SW2/3	SW2/4
COM2/2F8h	off	off
COM1/3F8h	on	off
COM4/2E8h	off	on
Disabled	on	on

PARALLEL PORT CONFIGURATION		
LPT/Address	SW2/5	SW2/6
LPT1/378h	on	off
LPT2/278h	off	off
Disabled	on	on

IDE PORT		
Setting	SW2/7	SW2/8
Primary controller enabled	off	on
Secondary controller enabled	off	off
Disabled	on	on

FLOPPY DRIVE		
Setting	SW2/9	SW2/10
Primary floppy drive enabled	off	on
Secondary floppy drive enabled	off	off
Disabled	on	on
Disabled	on	off

ALWAYS TECHNOLOGY CORPORATION
IN-2000

Data bus: 16-bit, ISA
Size: Half-length, full-height card
Hard drives supported: Up to seven SCSI devices
Floppy drives supported: Two 360KB, 720KB, 1.2MB, or 1.44MB

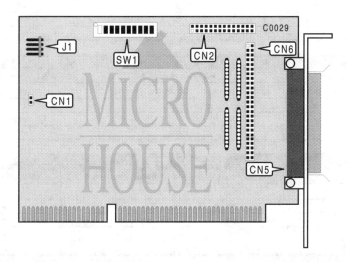

CONNECTIONS	
Function	**Location**
2-pin connector-drive active LED	CN1
34-pin data cable connector-floppy drive	CN2
25-pin SCSI connector-external	CN5
50-pin SCSI connector-internal	CN6
4-pin power connector-controller power	J1

USER CONFIGURABLE SETTINGS		
Function	**Location**	**Setting**
⇨ Asynchronous operation enabled	SW1/switch 8	off
Synchronous operation enabled	SW1/switch 8	on
⇨ Floppy drive enabled	SW1/switch 9	on
Floppy drive disabled	SW1/switch 9	off
⇨ Not used	SW1/switch 10	off

Continued on next page . . .

ALWAYS TECHNOLOGY CORPORATION
IN-2000

. . . continued from previous page

BIOS ADDRESS		
Address	SW1/switch 1	SW1/switch 2
⇨ C800-CBFFh	off	off
D800-DBFFh	on	off
D000-D3FFh	off	on
Disabled	on	on

I/O PORT ADDRESS		
Address	SW1/switch 3	SW1/switch 4
⇨ 220-22Fh	off	off
200-20Fh	on	off
110-11Fh	off	on
100-10Fh	on	on

INTERRUPT REQUEST			
IRQ	SW1/switch 5	SW1/switch 6	SW1/switch 7
⇨ 15	off	off	off
14	off	on	off
11	off	off	on
10	off	on	on
Disabled	on	off	off

ATC/UNITRON COMPUTERS & COMPUTER PARTS
SCSI-2/IDE/MULTI-IO (REV.1.3 & 1.4)

Data bus:	32-bit VL-Bus
Size:	Three/quarter-length, full-height card
Hard drive supported:	Two IDE(AT) interface drives plus up to 7 SCSI devices
Floppy drives supported:	Two 360KB, 720KB, 1.2MB, 1.44MB or 2.88MB drives

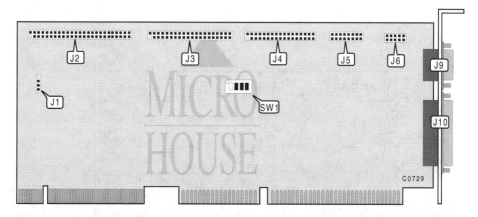

CONNECTIONS	
Function	**Location**
4-pin connector - drive active LED	J1
50-pin SCSI-2 interface	J2
40-pin IDE(AT) interface	J3
34-pin floppy drive controller	J4
16-pin game port	J5
10-pin serial port - internal	J6
9-pin serial port - external	J9
25-pin parallel port - external	J10

BIOS ADDRESS SELECTION				
Address	**SW1/1**	**SW1/2**	**SW1/3**	**SW1/4**
C8000h	off	on	off	off
D0000h	off	off	on	off
D8000h	off	off	off	off
Disabled	off	on	on	off

BOCA RESEARCH, INC.
IDE300

Data bus: 16-bit ISA
Size: Half-length, half-height card
Hard drive supported: Two EIDE drives
Floppy drives supported: Two 360KB, 720KB, 1.2MB, 1.44MB, or 2.88MB drives

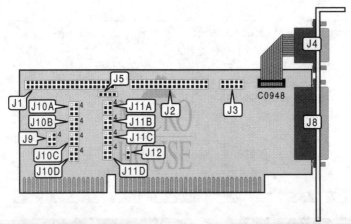

CONNECTIONS	
Function	**Location**
40-pin primary IDE(AT) connector	J1
34-pin cable connector - floppy drive	J2
10-pin serial port 2 - internal	J3
9-pin serial port 1 - external, 10-pin serial port 1 internal	J4
4-pin connector - drive active LED	J5
25-pin parallel port - external	J8

USER CONFIGURABLE SETTINGS		
Function	**Location**	**Setting**
⇨ Serial port 1 IRQ4 select	J9	Pins 1 & 2 closed
Serial port 1 IRQ3 select	J9	Pins 4 & 5 closed
Serial port 1 IRQ5 select	J9	Pins 5 & 6 closed
Serial port 1 IRQ7 select	J9	Pins 2 & 3 closed
⇨ Serial port 1 is COM1	J10A	Pins 1 & 2, 4 & 5 closed
Serial port 1 is COM2	J10A	Pins 1 & 2, 5 & 6 closed
Serial port 1 is COM3	J10A	Pins 2 & 3, 4 & 5 closed
Serial port 1 disabled	J10A	Pins 2 & 3, 5 & 6 closed

Continued on next page. . .

BOCA RESEARCH, INC.
IDE300

. . .continued from previous page

USER CONFIGURABLE SETTINGS (CONTINUED)		
Function	Location	Setting
➪ Serial port 2 is COM2	J10B	Pins 1 & 2, 4 & 5 closed
Serial port 2 is COM1	J10B	Pins 1 & 2, 5 & 6 closed
Serial port 2 is COM4	J10B	Pins 2 & 3, 4 & 5 closed
Serial port 2 is disabled	J10B	Pins 2 & 3, 5 & 6 closed
➪ Serial port 2 IRQ3 select	J10C	Pins 4 & 5 closed
Serial port 2 IRQ4 select	J10C	Pins 1 & 2 closed
Serial port 2 IRQ5 select	J10C	Pins 5 & 6 closed
Serial port 2 IRQ7 select	J10C	Pins 2 & 3 closed
➪ Floppy drive interface enabled	J10D	Pins 1 & 2 closed
Floppy drive interface disabled	J10D	Pins 2 & 3 closed
➪ IDE(AT) IRQ 14 select	J10D	Pins 4 & 5 closed
IDE(AT) IRQ 15 select	J10D	Pins 5 & 6 closed
➪ Parallel port address is 378h	J11A	Pins 1 & 2, 4 & 5 closed
Parallel port address is 278h	J11A	Pins 1 & 2, 5 & 6 closed
Parallel port address is disabled	J11A	Pins 2 & 3, 4 & 5 closed
➪ Parallel port is unidirectional	J11B	Pins 1 & 2, 4 & 5 closed
Parallel port EPP mode select	J11B	Pins 1 & 2, 5 & 6 closed
Parallel port ECP mode select	J11B	Pins 2 & 3, 4 & 5 closed
Parallel port IEE1284 select	J11B	Pins 2 & 3, 5 & 6 closed
➪ No DMA channel selected	J11C	Open
DMA channel 1 select	J11C	Pins 1 & 2, 4 & 5 closed
DMA channel 3 select	J11C	Pins 2 & 3, 5 & 6 closed
➪ IDE(AT) interface is primary	J11D	Pins 1 & 2, 4 & 5 closed
IDE(AT) interface is secondary	J11D	Pins 1 & 2, 5 & 6 closed
IDE(AT) disabled	J11D	Pins 2 & 3, 4 & 5 closed
➪ Parallel port IRQ7 select	J12	Pins 1 & 2 closed
Parallel port IRQ5 select	J12	Pins 2 & 3 closed

BOCA RESEARCH, INC.
IDE PLUS: IDEVL2

Data bus: 32-bit, VL-bus
Size: Three/quarter-length, half-height card
Hard drive supported: Four IDE (AT) Interface drives
Floppy drives supported: Two 360KB, 720KB, 1.2MB, 1.44MB, or 2.88MB drives

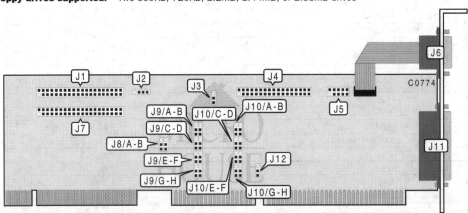

CONNECTIONS	
Function	**Location**
40-pin IDE(AT) interface connector A	J1
4-pin connector - drive active LED	J2
34-pin control cable connector - floppy drive	J4
10-pin serial port 2 - internal	J5
10-pin serial port 1 - external	J6
40-pin IDE(AT) interface connector B	J7
25-pin parallel port	J11

USER CONFIGURABLE SETTINGS		
Function	**Location**	**Setting**
⇨ Floppy drive enabled	J3	pins 1 & 2 closed
Floppy drive disabled	J3	pins 2 & 3 closed
⇨ Parallel port uses IRQ7	J12	pins 1 & 2 closed
Parallel port uses IRQ5	J12	pins 2 & 3 closed

IDE PORTS A & B CONFIGURATION - J8			
Port A (J1)	**Port B (J7)**	**Jumper A**	**Jumper B**
Primary address	Disabled	pins 1 & 2 closed	pins 1 & 2 closed
Secondary address	Disabled	pins 2 & 3 closed	pins 2 & 3 closed
Primary address	Secondary address	pins 1 & 2 closed	pins 2 & 3 closed
Disabled	Disabled	pins 2 & 3 closed	pins 1 & 2 closed

IDE PORTS A & B INTERRUPT SELECT - J10			
Port A (J1)	**Port B (J7)**	**Jumper G**	**Jumper H**
IRQ14	Disabled	pins 1 & 2 closed	all pins open
IRQ15	Disabled	pins 2 & 3 closed	all pins open
IRQ14	IRQ15	pins 1 & 2 closed	pins 2 & 3 closed
IRQ15	IRQ14	pins 2 & 3 closed	pins 1 & 2 closed

Continued on next page. . .

BOCA RESEARCH, INC.
IDE PLUS: IDEVL2

. . . continued from previous page

SERIAL PORT 1 CONFIGURATION - J9		
COM/Address	**Jumper A**	**Jumper B**
COM1/3F8h	pins 1 & 2 closed	pins 1 & 2 closed
COM2/2F8h	pins 1 & 2 closed	pins 2 & 3 closed
COM3/3E8h	pins 2 & 3 closed	pins 1 & 2 closed
Disabled	pins 2 & 3 closed	pins 2 & 3 closed

SERIAL PORT 1 INTERRUPT SELECT - J9		
IRQ	**Jumper E**	**Jumper F**
IRQ4	pins 1 & 2 closed	all pins open
IRQ3	all pins open	pins 1 & 2 closed
IRQ5	all pins open	pins 2 & 3 closed
IRQ7	pins 2 & 3 closed	all pins open
Disabled	all pins open	all pins open

SERIAL PORT 2 CONFIGURATION - J9		
COM/Address	**Jumper C**	**Jumper D**
COM2/2F8h	pins 1 & 2 closed	pins 1 & 2 closed
COM1/3F8h	pins 1 & 2 closed	pins 2 & 3 closed
COM4/2E8h	pins 2 & 3 closed	pins 1 & 2 closed
Disabled	pins 2 & 3 closed	pins 2 & 3 closed

SERIAL PORT 1 INTERRUPT SELECT - J9		
IRQ	**Jumper G**	**Jumper H**
IRQ3	all pins open	pins 1 & 2 closed
IRQ4	pins 1 & 2 closed	all pins open
IRQ5	all pins open	pins 2 & 3 closed
IRQ7	pins 2 & 3 closed	all pins open
Disabled	all pins open	all pins open

PARALLEL PORT CONFIGURATION - J10		
LPT/Address	**Jumper A**	**Jumper B**
LPT1/378h	pins 1 & 2 closed	pins 1 & 2 closed
LPT2/278h	pins 1 & 2 closed	pins 2 & 3 closed
Disabled	pins 2 & 3 closed	pins 1 & 2 closed

ENHANCED PARALLEL PORT MODES - J10		
Mode	**Jumper C**	**Jumper D**
Standard	pins 1 & 2 closed	pins 1 & 2 closed
Enhanced Parallel Port (EPP)	pins 1 & 2 closed	pins 2 & 3 closed
Extended Capabilities Port (ECP)	pins 2 & 3 closed	pins 1 & 2 closed
IEEE 1284 (all of the above)	pins 2 & 3 closed	pins 2 & 3 closed

ENHANCED PARALLEL PORT DMA CHANNEL SELECT - J10		
DMA Channel	**Jumper E**	**Jumper F**
Disabled	all pins open	all pins open
DMA1	pins 1 & 2 closed	pins 1 & 2 closed
DMA3	pins 2 & 3 closed	pins 2 & 3 closed

BUSLOGIC, INC.
BT-757C, BT-757CD

Data bus: 32-bit EISA
Size: Three-quarter length, full-height card
Hard drive supported: Up to fifteen SCSI devices
Floppy drives supported: Two 360KB, 720KB, 1.2MB, or 1.44MB drives

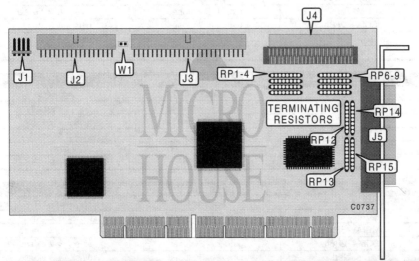

CONNECTIONS	
Function	**Location**
4-pin connector-drive active LED	J1
34-pin connector-floppy drive interface	J2
50-pin connector-SCSI interface (internal)	J3
68-pin connector-SCSI interface (internal)	J4
68-pin connector-SCSI interface (external)	J5

USER CONFIGURABLE SETTINGS		
Function	**Jumper**	**Setting**
⇨ Floppy drive interface enabled	W1	closed
Floppy drive interface disabled	W1	open
Note: The location of W1 is different in the C and CD models. For the C model, W1 is located between the floppy drive interface and the drive active LED connector.		

TERMINATION POWER CONFIGURATION	
Setting	**Terminators Installed**
Data bits 0-7 terminated	RP1, RP2, RP3, RP4, RP6, RP7, RP8, RP9
Data bits 8-15 terminated	RP12, RP13, RP14, RP15
All signals terminated	All installed
Note: These settings apply only to the BT-757CD.	

MISCELLANEOUS TECHNICAL NOTES
The BT-757C and BT-757CD differ in that the 'C' model incorporates a single-ended interface and software controlled active termination, while the 'CD' model utilizes a differential interface and standard (i.e. differential) termination.

BUSLOGIC, INC.
BT-757D, BT-757S

Data bus: 32-bit, EISA
Size: Full-length, full-height card
Hard drive supported: Up to seven SCSI devices
Floppy drives supported: Two 360KB, 720KB, 1.2MB, 1.44MB, or 2.88MB drives

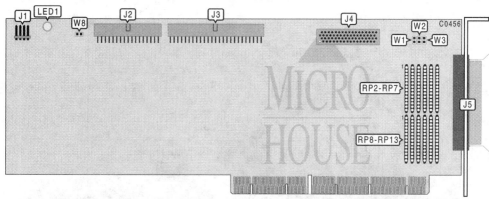

CONNECTIONS	
Function	**Location**
4-pin connector - drive active LED	J1
34-pin control cable connector - floppy drive	J2
50-pin SCSI connector - internal	J3
68-pin SCSI connector - internal	J4
68-pin SCSI connector - external	J5

USER CONFIGURABLE SETTINGS		
Function	**Location**	**Setting**
⇨ Termination power to 50-pin connector enabled	W1	closed
Termination power to 50-pin connector disabled	W1	open
⇨ Termination power to internal 68-pin conn. enabled	W2	closed
Termination power to internal 68-pin conn. disabled	W2	open
⇨ Termination power to external 68-pin conn. enabled	W3	closed
Termination power to external 68-pin conn. disabled	W3	open
⇨ Floppy drive enabled	W8	closed
Floppy drive disabled	W8	open

STATUS LED		
LED	**Status**	**Function**
LED1	on briefly after start-up	Self-test successful
LED1	blinking	SCSI active
LED1	3 blinks, pause, 3 blinks sequence	Searching for SCSI device

MISCELLANEOUS TECHNICAL NOTES
BT-757D is a differential SCSI controller. Terminators RP2, 4, 6, 8, 10, and 12 contain 150ohm resistors. Terminators RP3, 5, 7, 9, 11, and 13 contain 330ohm resistors. BT-757S is shipped with three resistor packs on-board, at the same locations as RP6, 7, and 13. Each pack contains 110ohm resistors.

BUSLOGIC, INC.
BT-956C

Data bus: 32-bit PCI
Size: Half-length, full-height card
Hard drive supported: Up to fifteen SCSI devices
Floppy drives supported: Two 360KB, 720KB, 1.2MB, or 1.44MB drives

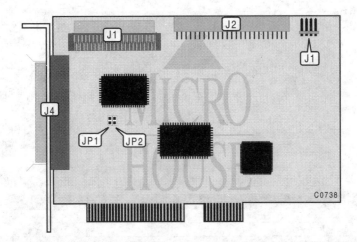

CONNECTIONS	
Function	**Location**
68-pin connector-SCSI interface (internal)	J1
50-pin connector-SCSI interface (internal)	J2
4-pin connector-drive active LED	J3
68-pin connector-SCSI interface (external)	J4

BASE MEMORY ADDRESS SELECTION		
Address	**JP1**	**JP2**
⇨ System BIOS	open	open
C800h	closed	open
D800h	open	closed
DC00h	closed	closed

BUSLOGIC, INC.
BT-956CD

Data bus: 32-bit PCI
Size: Half-length, full-height card
Hard drive supported: Up to fifteen SCSI devices
Floppy drives supported: Two 360KB, 720KB, 1.2MB, or 1.44MB drives

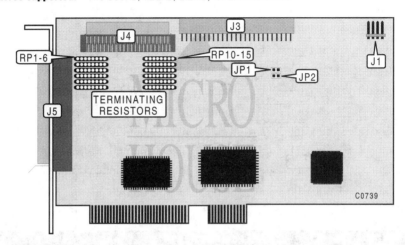

CONNECTIONS	
Function	**Location**
4-pin connector-drive active LED	J1
50-pin connector-SCSI interface (internal)	J3
68-pin connector-SCSI interface (internal)	J4
68-pin connector-SCSI interface (external)	J5

BASE MEMORY ADDRESS SELECTION		
Address	**JP1**	**JP2**
⇨ System BIOS	open	open
C800h	closed	open
D800h	open	closed
DC00h	closed	closed

TERMINATION POWER CONFIGURATION	
Setting	**Terminators Installed**
Data bits 0-7 terminated	RP1, RP2, RP3, RP4, RP10, RP11, RP12, RP13
Data bits 8-15 terminated	RP5, RP6, RP14, RP15
All signals terminated	All installed

DATA TECHNOLOGY CORPORATION
DTC2280 PLUS

Data bus: 16-bit ISA
Size: Half-length, half-height card
Hard drive supported: Two IDE(AT) interface drives
Floppy drives supported: Two 360KB, 720KB, 1.2MB, 1.44MB

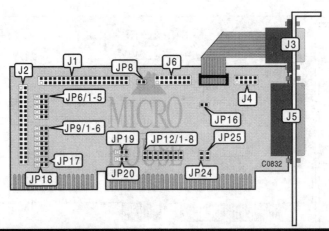

CONNECTIONS	
Function	**Location**
40-pin IDE(AT) interface connector	J1
34-pin cable connector - floppy drive	J2
9-pin serial port 1 - external	J3
10-pin serial port 2 - internal	J4
25-pin parallel port - external	J5
16-pin game port - internal	J6
2-pin connector - drive active LED	JP8

USER CONFIGURABLE SETTINGS		
Function	**Location**	**Setting**
⮩ Floppy drives A & B normal	JP6/1	pins 1 & 2 closed
Floppy drives A & B reversed	JP6/1	pins 2 & 3 closed
⮩ Floppy drive interface address is 3F0h	JP6/2	pins 2 & 3 closed
Floppy drive interface address is 370h	JP6/2	pins 1 & 2 closed
⮩ IDE(AT) interface enabled	JP6/3	pins 1 & 2 closed
IDE(AT) interface disabled	JP6/3	pins 2 & 3 closed

USER CONFIGURABLE SETTINGS(CONTINUED)		
Function	**Location**	**Setting**
⮩ IDE(AT) interface address is 1F0h	JP6/4	pins 2 & 3 closed
IDE(AT) interface address is 170h	JP6/4	pins 1 & 2 closed
⮩ Floppy drive interface enabled	JP6/5	pins 1 & 2 closed
Floppy drive interface disabled	JP6/5	pins 2 & 3 closed
⮩ Game port enabled	JP16	closed

Continued on next page. . .

DATA TECHNOLOGY CORPORATION
DTC2280 PLUS

. . . continued from previous page

USER CONFIGURABLE SETTINGS(CONTINUED)		
Function	**Location**	**Setting**
Game port disabled	JP16	open
⇨ Factory configured - do not alter	JP17	N/A
⇨ Factory configured - do not alter	JP18	N/A
⇨ Hard drive interrupt IRQ14 select	JP19	pins 1 & 2 closed
Hard drive interrupt IRQ15 select	JP19	pins 2 & 3 closed
⇨ Factory configured - do not alter	JP20	N/A
⇨ Factory configured - do not alter	JP24	N/A
⇨ Factory configured - do not alter	JP25	N/A

SERIAL PORT 1 CONFIGURATION		
Port 1	**JP9/1**	**JP9/2**
⇨ COM1	pins 1 & 2 closed	pins 2 & 3 closed
COM3	pins 2 & 3 closed	pins 1 & 2 closed
Disabled	pins 2 & 3 closed	pins 2 & 3 closed

SERIAL PORT 2 CONFIGURATION		
Port 2	**JP9/3**	**JP9/4**
⇨ COM2	pins 1 & 2 closed	pins 2 & 3 closed
COM4	pins 2 & 3 closed	pins 1 & 2 closed
Disabled	pins 2 & 3 closed	pins 2 & 3 closed

PARALLEL PORT CONFIGURATION		
LPT	**JP9/5**	**JP9/6**
⇨ 1 (378h)	pins 2 & 3 closed	pins 1 & 2 closed
2 (278h)	pins 1 & 2 closed	pins 2 & 3 closed
3 (BCh)	pins 1 & 2 closed	pins 1 & 2 closed

SERIAL PORT 1 INTERRUPT SELECTION			
IRQ	**JP12/1**	**JP12/2**	**JP12/3**
⇨ IRQ4	closed	open	open
IRQ3	open	closed	open
IRQ5	open	open	closed

SERIAL PORT 2 INTERRUPT SELECTION			
IRQ	**JP12/4**	**JP12/5**	**JP12/6**
⇨ IRQ3	closed	open	open
IRQ4	open	closed	open
IRQ5	open	open	closed

PARALLEL PORT INTERRUPT SELECTION		
IRQ	**JP12/7**	**JP12/8**
⇨ 7	closed	open
5	open	closed

DISTRIBUTED PROCESSING TECHNOLOGY
PM2041W, PM2041FW

Data bus: 16-bit ISA
Size: Half length, full-height card
Hard drive supported: Fifteen SCSI-Wide, or eight SCSI-Wide with seven SCSI-2 Narrow
SCSI-3 and Fast SCSI devices also supported
Floppy drives supported: Two 360KB, 720KB, 1.2MB, or 1.44MB drives (PM2041WF only)

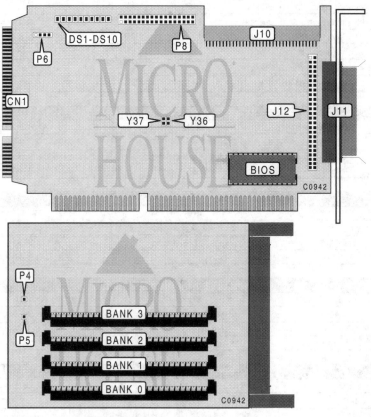

RC4040 - Optional RAID/Caching Module

CONNECTIONS	
Function	**Location**
68-pin SCSI connector - internal	J10
68-pin SCSI connector - external	J11
50-pin SCSI connector - internal	J12

Continued on next page. . .

DISTRIBUTED PROCESSING TECHNOLOGY
PM2041W, PM2041FW

. . .continued from previous page

CONNECTIONS CONTINUED	
Function	**Location**
RC4040 connector	CN1
LED - ECC enabled (green)	P4
LED - memory fault (red)	P5
4-pin connector - drive active LED	P6
34-pin cable connector - floppy drive (PM2041WF only)	P8
LED - adapter busy	DS1
LED - computer bus transfer to adapter	DS2
LED - computer bus transfer from adapter	DS3
LED - cache hit	DS4
LED - disk read/ahead active	DS5
LED - disk read	DS6
LED - disk write	DS7
LED - adapter reset	DS8
LED - interrupt to computer pending	DS9
LED - DRQ to computer asserted	DS10

BIOS ADDRESS SELECTION		
Address	**Y36**	**Y37**
⇨ C8000h	closed	closed
D8000h	closed	open
DC000h	open	closed
Disabled	open	open

DRAM CONFIGURATION				
Size	**Bank 0**	**Bank 1**	**Bank 2**	**Bank 3**
1MB	(1) 256K x 36	None	None	None
1MB	None	(1) 256K x 36	None	None
1MB	None	None	(1) 256K x 36	None
1MB	None	None	None	(1) 256K x 36
2MB	(1) 256K x 36	(1) 256K x 36	None	None
2MB	None	(1) 256K x 36	(1) 256K x 36	None
2MB	None	None	(1) 256K x 36	(1) 256K x 36
3MB	(1) 256K x 36	(1) 256K x 36	(1) 256K x 36	None
3MB	None	(1) 256K x 36	(1) 256K x 36	(1) 256K x 36
3MB	(1) 256K x 36	None	(1) 256K x 36	(1) 256K x 36
3MB	(1) 256K x 36	(1) 256K x 36	None	(1) 256K x 36
4MB	(1) 256K x 36	(1) 256K x 36	(1) 256K x 36	(1) 256K x 36

Continued on next page. . .

DISTRIBUTED PROCESSING TECHNOLOGY
PM2041W, PM2041FW

. . .continued from previous page

DRAM CONFIGURATION CONTINUED				
Size	Bank 0	Bank 1	Bank 2	Bank 3
4MB	(1) 1M x 36	None	None	None
4MB	None	(1) 1M x 36	None	None
4MB	None	None	(1) 1M x 36	None
4MB	None	None	None	(1) 1M x 36
8MB	(1) 1M x 36	(1) 1M x 36	None	None
8MB	None	(1) 1M x 36	(1) 1M x 36	None
8MB	None	None	(1) 1M x 36	(1) 1M x 36
12MB	(1) 1M x 36	(1) 1M x 36	(1) 1M x 36	None
12MB	None	(1) 1M x 36	(1) 1M x 36	(1) 1M x 36
12MB	(1) 1M x 36	None	(1) 1M x 36	(1) 1M x 36
12MB	(1) 1M x 36	(1) 1M x 36	None	(1) 1M x 36
16MB	(1) 1M x 36	(1) 1M x 36	(1) 1M x 36	(1) 1M x 36
16MB	(1) 4M x 36	None	None	None
16MB	None	(1) 4M x 36	None	None
16MB	None	None	(1) 4M x 36	None
16MB	None	None	None	(1) 4M x 36
32MB	(1) 4M x 36	(1) 4M x 36	None	None
32MB	None	(1) 4M x 36	(1) 4M x 36	None
32MB	None	None	(1) 4M x 36	(1) 4M x 36
48MB	(1) 4M x 36	(1) 4M x 36	(1) 4M x 36	None
48MB	None	(1) 4M x 36	(1) 4M x 36	(1) 4M x 36
48MB	(1) 4M x 36	None	(1) 4M x 36	(1) 4M x 36
48MB	(1) 4M x 36	(1) 4M x 36	None	(1) 4M x 36
64MB	(1) 4M x 36	(1) 4M x 36	(1) 4M x 36	(1) 4M x 36

Notes: Although not shown above, 1MB, 4MB and 16MB SIMMs can be combined and DPT ECC SIMMs

can replace parity SIMMs of 4MB or 16MB.

Single sided SIMMs are preferred, but low-profile double sided 2M and 8MB increments are supported.

DISTRIBUTED PROCESSING TECHNOLOGY
PM2122

Data bus: 32-bit EISA
Size: Three-quarter length, Full-height card
Hard drive supported: Up to seven SCSI devices
Floppy drives supported: 360KB, 720KB, 1.2MB, 1.44MB

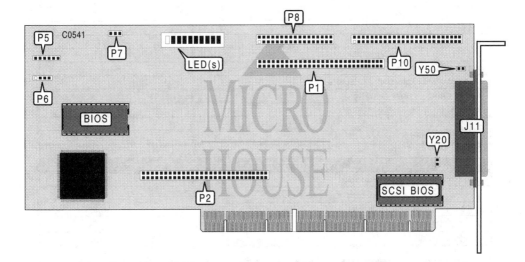

CM 4000 Module

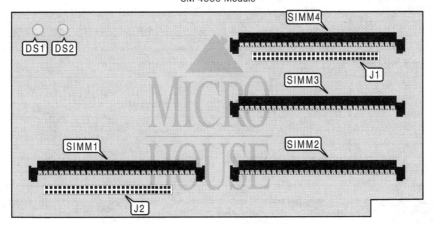

Continued on next page. . .

DISTRIBUTED PROCESSING TECHNOLOGY
PM2122

. . .continued from previous page

CONNECTIONS	
Function	**Location**
58-pin CM4000 expansion connector	J1
58-pin CM4000 expansion connector	J2
50-pin SCSI interface - external	J11
10-piece LED	LED(s)
58-pin CM4000 expansion connector	P1
58-pin CM4000 expansion connector	P2
6-pin DM4000 expansion connector	P5
4-pin connector - drive active LED	P6
3-pin DM4000 expansion connector	P7
34-pin control cable connector - floppy drive	P8
50-pin SCSI interface - internal	P10

USER CONFIGURABLE SETTINGS		
Function	**Location**	**Setting**
▷ Floppy drive interface enabled	Y20	closed
Floppy drive interface disabled	Y20	open
▷ TERMPWR enabled	Y50	closed
TERMPWR disabled	Y50	open

DIAGNOSTIC LED(S)		
LED	**Status**	**Condition**
1-10	Blinking in rotating pattern	SCSI activity has ceased
1-8	Blinking quickly in rotating pattern	EISA adapter has not been configured
9	on	IRQ is pending
1-4	Blink once per second at power-up	Trap error in processor
1, 2, & 8	Blink once per second at power-up	No SIMM in socket 1 of CM4000
2 & 8	Blink once per second at power-up	Largest SIMM is not in socket 1 of CM4000
3 & 8	Blink once per second at power-up	Parity SIMM is not in socket 1
Other combination	Blink once per second at power-up	Firmware trap has occurred
DS1	on	Fault has occurred with CM4000 module
DS1	off	No fault has occurred
DS2	on	ECC enabled
DS2	off	ECC disabled

MISCELLANEOUS TECHNICAL NOTES
Note: The manufacturer does not provide a diagram of the DM 4000 module.

DISTRIBUTED PROCESSING TECHNOLOGY
PM3021

Data bus: 16-bit ISA
Size: Three-fourth length, full-height card
Hard drive supported: Up to seven SCSI-2, SCSI-3 or Fast SCSI devices
Floppy drives supported: Two 360KB, 720KB, 1.2MB, or 1.44MB drives

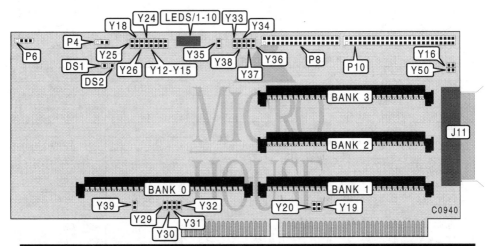

CONNECTIONS	
Function	**Location**
3-pin connector - remote alarm	P4
4-pin connector - drive active LED	P6
34-pin cable connector - floppy drive	P8
50-pin SCSI connector bus 0 - internal	P10
50-pin SCSI connector bus 0 - external	J11
ECC or Parity Error LED - red	DS1
ECC enabled LED - green	DS2
LED - adapter busy	LEDS/1
LED - computer bus transfer to adapter	LEDS/2
LED - computer bus transfer from adapter	LEDS/3
LED - cache hit	LEDS/4
LED - disk read/ahead active	LEDS/5
LED - disk read	LEDS/6
LED - disk write	LEDS/7
LED - adapter reset	LEDS/8
LED - interrupt to computer pending	LEDS/9
LED - DRQ to computer asserted	LEDS/10
Note: The configuration of the 10-segment LEDS is unidentified.	

Continued on next page. . .

DISTRIBUTED PROCESSING TECHNOLOGY
PM3021

. . .continued from previous page

USER CONFIGURABLE SETTINGS		
Function	**Location**	**Setting**
⇨ Bus-On time is 12.8µs and Bus-Open time is 1.6µs	Y15	Open
Bus-On time is 6.4µs and Bus-Open time is 1.6µs	Y15	Close
⇨ SCSI active termination enabled	Y16	Close
SCSI active termination disabled	Y16	Open
⇨ Drive address lines SA17-19 and LA17-19 enabled	Y19	Close
Drive address lines LA17-19 only enabled	Y19	Open
⇨ Floppy drive interface enabled	Y20	Close
Floppy drive interface disabled	Y20	Open
⇨ ISA bus mastering enabled	Y24	Close
ISA bus mastering disabled (PIO enabled)	Y24	Open
⇨ Floppy controller address is primary (3F0h)	Y34	Open
Floppy controller address is secondary (370h)	Y34	Close
⇨ SCSI BIOS ROM size is 8K	Y38	Open
SCSI BIOS ROM size is 16K (factory upgrade)	Y38	Close
⇨ External cable detection disabled	Y39	Open
External cable detection enabled	Y39	Close
⇨ Termination power from adapter to external devices enabled	Y50	Close
Termination power from adapter to external devices disabled	Y50	Open

SCSI BIOS ADDRESS SELECTION		
Address	**Y36**	**Y37**
⇨ C800h	Close	Close
D800h	Close	Open
DC00h	Open	Close
Disabled	Open	Open

I/O ADDRESS SELECTION		
Address	**Y33**	**Y35**
⇨ 170h	Open	Close
1F0h	Close	Close
230h	Open	Open
330h	Close	Open

Continued on next page. . .

DISTRIBUTED PROCESSING TECHNOLOGY
PM3021

. . .continued from previous page

INTERRUPT SELECTION		
IRQ	Y29	Y30
IRQ14	Close	Close
IRQ12	Open	Close
⇨ IRQ15	Close	Open
Disabled	Open	Open

SCSI ID SELECTION			
SCSI ID	Y18	Y25	Y26
0	Open	Open	Open
1	Open	Close	Open
2	Close	Open	Open
3	Close	Close	Open
4	Open	Open	Close
5	Open	Close	Close
6	Close	Open	Close
⇨ 7	Close	Close	Close

DMA SELECTION		
Channel	Y31	Y32
⇨ 5	Close	Close
6	Close	Open
7	Open	Close
0	Open	Open

DMA SPEED SELECTION			
Transfer Rate (MB/s)	Y12	Y13	Y14
3.0	Close	Close	Close
4.0	Open	Close	Close
4.4	Close	Open	Close
⇨ 5.0	Open	Open	Close
5.7	Close	Close	Open
6.667	Open	Close	Open
8	Close	Open	Open
10	Open	Open	Open

Continued on next page. . .

DISTRIBUTED PROCESSING TECHNOLOGY
PM3021

. . .continued from previous page

DRAM CONFIGURATION				
Size	Bank 0	Bank 1	Bank 2	Bank 3
1MB	(1) 256K x 36	None	None	None
1MB	None	(1) 256K x 36	None	None
1MB	None	None	(1) 256K x 36	None
1MB	None	None	None	(1) 256K x 36
2MB	(1) 256K x 36	(1) 256K x 36	None	None
2MB	None	(1) 256K x 36	(1) 256K x 36	None
2MB	None	None	(1) 256K x 36	(1) 256K x 36
3MB	(1) 256K x 36	(1) 256K x 36	(1) 256K x 36	None
3MB	None	(1) 256K x 36	(1) 256K x 36	(1) 256K x 36
3MB	(1) 256K x 36	None	(1) 256K x 36	(1) 256K x 36
3MB	(1) 256K x 36	(1) 256K x 36	None	(1) 256K x 36
4MB	(1) 256K x 36	(1) 256K x 36	(1) 256K x 36	(1) 256K x 36
4MB	(1) 1M x 36	None	None	None
4MB	None	(1) 1M x 36	None	None
4MB	None	None	(1) 1M x 36	None
4MB	None	None	None	(1) 1M x 36
8MB	(1) 1M x 36	(1) 1M x 36	None	None
8MB	None	(1) 1M x 36	(1) 1M x 36	None
8MB	None	None	(1) 1M x 36	(1) 1M x 36
12MB	(1) 1M x 36	(1) 1M x 36	(1) 1M x 36	None
12MB	None	(1) 1M x 36	(1) 1M x 36	(1) 1M x 36
12MB	(1) 1M x 36	None	(1) 1M x 36	(1) 1M x 36
12MB	(1) 1M x 36	(1) 1M x 36	None	(1) 1M x 36
16MB	(1) 1M x 36	(1) 1M x 36	(1) 1M x 36	(1) 1M x 36
16MB	(1) 4M x 36	None	None	None
16MB	None	(1) 4M x 36	None	None
16MB	None	None	(1) 4M x 36	None
16MB	None	None	None	(1) 4M x 36
32MB	(1) 4M x 36	(1) 4M x 36	None	None
32MB	None	(1) 4M x 36	(1) 4M x 36	None
32MB	None	None	(1) 4M x 36	(1) 4M x 36
48MB	(1) 4M x 36	(1) 4M x 36	(1) 4M x 36	None
48MB	None	(1) 4M x 36	(1) 4M x 36	(1) 4M x 36
48MB	(1) 4M x 36	None	(1) 4M x 36	(1) 4M x 36
48MB	(1) 4M x 36	(1) 4M x 36	None	(1) 4M x 36
64MB	(1) 4M x 36	(1) 4M x 36	(1) 4M x 36	(1) 4M x 36

Notes: Although not shown above, 1MB, 4MB and 16MB SIMMs can be combined and DPT ECC SIMMs
       can replace parity SIMMs of 4MB or 16MB. Single sided SIMMs are preferred, but low-profile
       double sided 2M and 8MB increments are supported.

DTK COMPUTER, INC.
PTI-255W (VER. 1.01)

Data bus:	32-bit VL-bus
Size:	Three-quarter length, half-height card
Hard drive supported:	Four IDE(AT) drives
Floppy drives supported:	Two 360KB, 720KB, 1.2MB, or 1.44MB drives

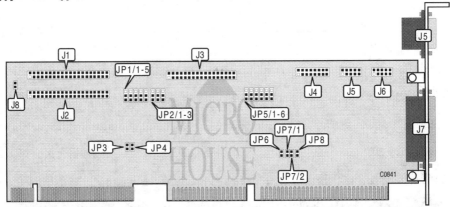

CONNECTIONS	
Function	**Location**
40-pin primary IDE(AT) connector	J1
40-pin secondary IDE(AT) connector	J2
34-pin cable connector - floppy drive	J3
16-pin game port	J4
10-pin serial port 1 - internal, 9-pin serial port 1 - external	J5
10-pin serial port 2 - internall	J6
25-pin Parallel port	J7
2-pin connector - drive active LED	J8

DRIVE SPEED CONFIGURATION		
Speed	**JP1/4**	**JP1/5**
⇨ 600ns	pins 1 & 2 closed	pins 1 & 2 closed
500ns	pins 2 & 3 closed	pins 1 & 2 closed
400ns	pins 1 & 2 closed	pins 2 & 3 closed
240ns	pins 2 & 3 closed	pins 2 & 3 closed

USER CONFIGURABLE SETTINGS		
Function	**Location**	**Setting**
⇨ Secondary IDE(AT) IOCHRDY signal disabled	JP3	open
Secondary IDE(AT) IOCHRDY signal enabled	JP3	closed
⇨ Primary IDE(AT) IOCHRDY signal enabled	JP4	closed
Primary IDE(AT) IOCHRDY signal disabled	JP4	open
⇨ Parallel port is unidirectional	JP6	closed
Parallel port is bi-directional	JP6	open
⇨ Game port enabled	JP8	closed

Continued on next page. . .

DTK COMPUTER, INC.
PTI-255W (VER. 1.01)

. . .continued from previous page

USER CONFIGURABLE SETTINGS CONTINUED		
Function	**Location**	**Setting**
Game port disabled	JP8	open
➪ IDE(AT) interface enabled	JP1/1	pins 1 & 2 closed
IDE(AT) interface disabled	JP1/1	pins 2 & 3 closed
➪ IDE(AT) address is 170h & 1F0h	JP1/2	pins 1 & 2 closed
IDE(AT) address is 1F0h	JP1/2	pins 2 & 3 closed
➪ CPU speed is 50MHz	JP1/3	pins 1 & 2 closed
CPU speed is 33MHz	JP1/3	pins 2 & 3 closed
➪ Floppy drive order is normal (A:, B:)	JP2/1	pins 1 & 2 closed
Floppy drive order is reversed (B:, A:)	JP2/1	pins 2 & 3 closed
➪ Floppy drive address is 3F0h	JP2/2	pins 1 & 2 closed
Floppy drive address is 370h	JP2/2	pins 2 & 3 closed
➪ Floppy drive interface enabled	JP2/3	pins 1 & 2 closed
Floppy drive interface disabled	JP2/3	pins 2 & 3 closed

SERIAL PORT 1 ADDRESS SELECTION		
COM	**JP5/1**	**JP5/2**
➪ COM1 (3F8h)	pins 1 & 2 closed	pins 1 & 2 closed
COM3 (3E8h)	pins 2 & 3 closed	pins 2 & 3 closed
COM4 (2E8h)	pins 2 & 3 closed	pins 2 & 3 closed
Disabled	pins 2 & 3 closed	pins 1 & 2 closed

SERIAL PORT 2 ADDRESS SELECTION		
COM	**JP5/3**	**JP5/4**
➪ COM2 (2F8h)	pins 1 & 2 closed	pins 1 & 2 closed
COM3 (3E8h)	pins 1 & 2 closed	pins 2 & 3 closed
COM4 (2E8h)	pins 2 & 3 closed	pins 2 & 3 closed
Disabled	pins 2 & 3 closed	pins 1 & 2 closed

PARALLEL PORT ADDRESS SELECTION		
LPT	**JP5/5**	**JP6/6**
➪ LPT1 (378h)	pins 1 & 2 closed	pins 1 & 2 closed
LPT2 (278h)	pins 2 & 3 closed	pins 2 & 3 closed
LPT3 (3BCh)	pins 2 & 3 closed	pins 1 & 2 closed
Disabled	pins 1 & 2 closed	pins 2 & 3 closed

PARALLEL PORT INTERRUPT SELECTION		
IRQ	**JP7/1**	**JP7/1**
➪ 7	closed	open
5	open	closed

FUTURE DOMAIN CORPORATION
TMC-1795

Data bus: 32-bit EISA
Size: Three-quarter length, Full-height card
Hard drive supported: Up to fourteen SCSI devices
Floppy drives supported: 360KB, 720KB, 1.2MB, 1.44MB

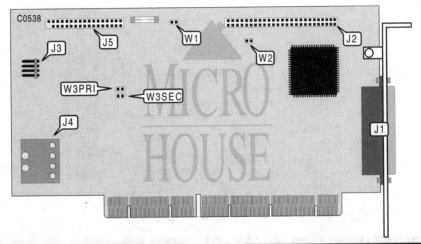

CONNECTIONS	
Function	**Location**
50-pin SCSI connector - external	J1
50-pin SCSI connector - internal	J2
4-pin connector - drive active LED	J3
Optional power connector	J4
34-pin control cable connector - floppy drive	J5

USER CONFIGURABLE SETTINGS		
Function	**Location**	**Setting**
TERMPWR disabled	W1	open
TERMPWR enabled	W1	closed
Host adapter TERMPWR enabled	W2	closed
Host adapter TERMPWR disabled	W2	open

ADDRESS SELECT				
Address	**DMA**	**IRQ**	**W3PRI**	**W3SEC**
⇨ 3F2 - 3F7h	2	IRQ6	closed	open
372 - 377h	3	IRQ5	open	closed

LAVA COMPUTER MANUFACTURING, INC.
LAVA COMPLETE

Data bus:	16-bit ISA
Size:	Half-length, full-height card
Hard drive supported:	Two IDE(AT) interface drives
Floppy drives supported:	Two 360KB, 720KB, 1.2MB, or 1.44MB drives

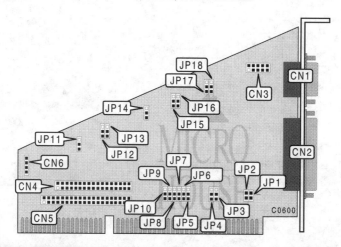

CONNECTIONS	
Function	**Location**
9-pin serial port 1 - external	CN1
25-pin parallel port - external	CN2
10-pin serial port 2 - internal	CN3
34-pin cable connector - floppy drive	CN4
40-pin primary IDE(AT) connector	CN5
4-pin connector - drive active LED	CN6

USER CONFIGURABLE SETTINGS		
Function	**Location**	**Setting**
Floppy drive controller enabled	JP11	pins 2 & 3 closed
Floppy drive controller disabled	JP11	pins 1 & 2 closed
Parallel port LPT2	JP12	pins 1 & 2 closed
Parallel port LPT1	JP12	pins 2 & 3 closed
Parallel port enabled	JP13	pins 2 & 3 closed
Parallel port disabled	JP13	pins 1 & 2 closed
IDE(AT) interface enabled	JP14	pins 2 & 3 closed
IDE(AT) interface disabled	JP14	pins 1 & 2 closed
Serial port 1 COM3 select	JP15	pins 1 & 2 closed
Serial port 1 COM1 select	JP15	pins 2 & 3 closed

Continued on next page. . .

LAVA COMPUTER MANUFACTURING, INC.
LAVA COMPLETE

. . .continued from previous page

USER CONFIGURABLE SETTINGS (CONTINUED)		
Function	**Location**	**Setting**
Serial port 1 enabled	JP16	pins 2 & 3 closed
Serial port 1 disabled	JP16	pins 1 & 2 closed
Serial port 2 COM4	JP17	pins 1 & 2 closed
Serial port 2 COM2	JP17	pins 2 & 3 closed
Serial port 2 enabled	JP18	pins 2 & 3 closed
Serial port 2 disabled	JP18	pins 1 & 2 closed

PARALLEL PORT INTERRUPT SELECTION		
IRQ	**JP1**	**JP2**
IRQ7	closed	open
IRQ5	open	closed

SERIAL PORT 1 INTERRUPT SELECTION				
IRQ	**JP3**	**JP4**	**JP5**	**JP6**
IRQ2	open	open	pins 1 & 2 closed	open
IRQ3	pins 1 & 2 closed	open	open	open
IRQ4	open	pins 1 & 2 closed	open	open
IRQ5	open	open	open	pins 1 & 2 closed

SERIAL PORT 1 INTERRUPT SELECTION (CONTINUED)				
IRQ	**JP7**	**JP8**	**JP9**	**JP10**
IRQ10	pins 1 & 2 closed	open	open	open
IRQ11	open	pins 1 & 2 closed	open	open
IRQ12	open	open	pins 1 & 2 closed	open
IRQ13	open	open	open	pins 1 & 2 closed

SERIAL PORT 2 INTERRUPT SELECTION				
IRQ	**JP3**	**JP4**	**JP5**	**JP6**
IRQ2	open	open	pins 2 & 3 closed	open
IRQ3	pins 2 & 3 closed	open	open	open
IRQ4	open	pins 2 & 3 closed	open	open
IRQ5	open	open	open	pins 2 & 3 closed

SERIAL PORT 2 INTERRUPT SELECTION (CONTINUED)				
IRQ	**JP7**	**JP8**	**JP9**	**JP10**
IRQ10	pins 2 & 3 closed	open	open	open
IRQ11	open	pins 2 & 3 closed	open	open
IRQ12	open	open	pins 2 & 3 closed	open
IRQ13	open	open	open	pins 2 & 3 closed

LONGSHINE MICROSYSTEM, INC.
LCS-6633, LCS-6633(F)

Data bus:	16-bit, ISA
Size:	Three/quarter-length, full-height card
Hard drive supported:	Two IDE (AT) Interface drives
Hard drive supported:	Up to seven SCSI devices
Floppy drives supported:	LCS-6633: None
	LCS-6633(F): Two 360KB, 720KB, 1.2MB, or 1.44MB drives

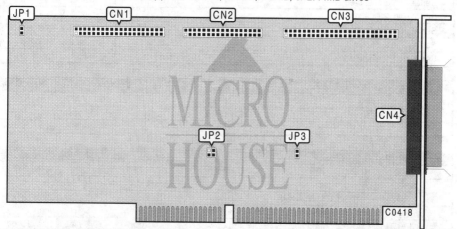

CONNECTIONS	
Function	**Location**
40-pin IDE(AT) Interface connector	CN1
34-pin control cable connector - floppy drive	CN2
50-pin SCSI connector - internal	CN3
25-pin SCSI connector - external	CN4
2-pin connector - Drive active LED	JP1

BIOS ADDRESS		
Address	**JP2/jumper 1**	**JP2/jumper 2**
⇨ D000h	closed	closed
D400h	closed	open
D800h	open	closed
Disabled	open	open

USER CONFIGURABLE SETTINGS		
Function	**Location**	**Setting**
⇨ Floppy drive enabled	JP3	open
Floppy drive disabled	JP3	closed

MODULAR CIRCUIT TECHNOLOGY
MCT-IDEIO+

Data bus: 16-bit ISA
Size: Three–quarter length, full-height card
Hard drive supported: Two IDE (AT) interface drives
Floppy drives supported: Two 360KB, 720KB, 1.2MB, or 1.44MB drives

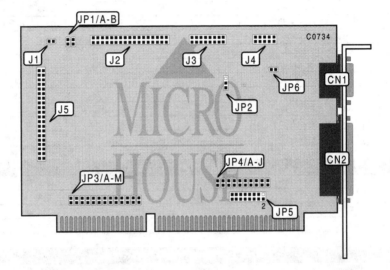

CONNECTIONS	
Function	**Location**
9-pin connector - serial port 1 - external	CN1
25-pin connector - parallel port	CN2
2-pin connector - drive active LED	J1
34-pin connector - floppy drive interface	J2
16-pin connector - game port	J3
10-pin connector - serial port 2 - internal	J4
40-pin connector - IDE(AT) interface	J5

Continued on next page. . .

MODULAR CIRCUIT TECHNOLOGY
MCT-IDEIO+

. . .continued from previous page

USER CONFIGURABLE SETTINGS		
Function	**Location**	**Setting**
⇨ UART clock speed 1.8432MHZ select	JP2	pins 2 & 3 closed
UART clock speed 7.3728MHz select	JP2	pins 1 & 2 closed
⇨ IDE(AT) interface enabled	JP3/A	closed
IDE(AT) interface disabled	JP3/A	open
⇨ Floppy drive interface enabled	JP3/B	closed
Floppy drive interface disabled	JP3/B	open
⇨ Game port enabled	JP3/C	closed
Game port disabled	JP3/C	open
⇨ Parallel port is uni-directional	JP6	closed
Parallel port is bi-directional	JP6	open

PARALLEL PORT CONFIGURATION		
LPT	**JP3/D**	**JP3/E**
⇨ LPT1	closed	open
LPT2	open	closed
Disabled	open	open

PARALLEL PORT INTERRUPT SELECTION		
IRQ	**JP4/A**	**JP4/B**
⇨ IRQ7	closed	open
IRQ5	open	closed

PRIMARY SERIAL PORT CONFIGURATION				
COM	**JP3/J**	**JP3/K**	**JP3/L**	**JP3/M**
⇨ COM1	closed	open	open	open
COM2	open	open	closed	open
COM3	open	closed	open	open
COM4	open	open	open	closed

SECONDARY SERIAL PORT CONFIGURATION				
COM	**JP3/F**	**JP3/G**	**JP3/H**	**JP3/I**
⇨ COM2	open	open	closed	open
COM1	closed	open	open	open
COM3	open	closed	open	open
COM4	open	open	open	closed

Continued on next page. . .

MODULAR CIRCUIT TECHNOLOGY
MCT-IDEIO+

. . .continued from previous page

PRIMARY SERIAL PORT INTERRUPT SELECTION				
IRQ	**JP4/G**	**JP4/H**	**JP4/I**	**JP4/J**
⇨ IRQ4	open	closed	open	open
IRQ2	open	open	open	closed
IRQ3	closed	open	open	open
IRQ5	open	open	closed	open

SECONDARY SERIAL PORT INTERRUPT SELECTION				
IRQ	**JP4/C**	**JP4/D**	**JP4/E**	**JP4/F**
⇨ IRQ3	closed	open	open	open
IRQ2	open	open	open	closed
IRQ4	open	closed	open	open
IRQ5	open	open	closed	open

SERIAL PORT DMA CONFIGURATION		
Setting	**JP1/A**	**JP1/B**
⇨ DMA disabled	open	open
Primary port DMA enabled	closed	open
Secondary port DMA enabled	open	closed
Both ports DMA enabled	closed	closed

PRIMARY SERIAL PORT DMA SELECTION		
DMA	**Mode**	**JP5**
⇨ 1	Receive	pins 3 & 4, 7 & 8 closed
3	Transmit	pins 1 & 2, 5 & 6 closed

SECONDARY SERIAL PORT DMA SELECTION		
DMA	**Mode**	**JP5**
⇨ 3	Receive	pins 10 & 12, 13 & 14 closed
1	Transmit	pins 9 & 11, 15 & 16 closed

MODULAR CIRCUIT TECHNOLOGY
MCT-IMS+

Data bus: 16-bit ISA
Size: Full-length, full-height card
Hard drive supported: Two IDE (AT) Interface drives
Floppy drives supported: Four 360KB, 720KB, 1.2MB, or 1.44MB drives

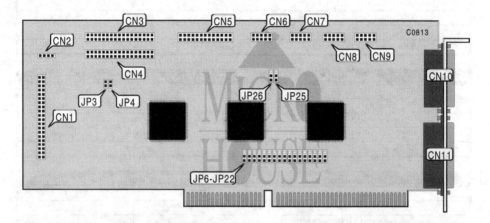

CONNECTIONS	
Function	**Location**
40 pin connector-IDE(AT) interface	CN1
4 pin connector-drive active LED	CN2
34 pin connector-floppy drive interface	CN3
34 pin connector-floppy drive interface	CN4
26 pin connector-parallel port(internal)	CN5
10 pin connector-serial port 1	CN6
10 pin connector-serial port 2	CN7
10 pin connector-serial port 3	CN8
10 pin connector-serial port 4	CN9
15 pin connector-game port(external)	CN10
25 pin connector-parallel port(external)	CN11

Continued on next page. . .

MODULAR CIRCUIT TECHNOLOGY
MCT-IMS+

. . .continued from previous page

Function	Location	Setting
USER CONFIGURABLE SETTINGS CONTINUED		
⇨ Floppy drive interface enabled	JP3	closed
Floppy drive interface disabled	JP3	open
⇨ On-card floppy drive interface is primary	JP4	open
On-card floppy drive interface is secondary	JP4	closed
⇨ Serial port 1 address COM1 select	JP6	pins 2 & 3 closed
Serial port 1 address COM2 select	JP6	pins 1 & 2 closed
Serial port 1 disabled	JP6	all open
⇨ Serial port 2 address COM2 select	JP7	pins 1 & 2 closed
Serial port 2 address COM1 select	JP7	pins 2 & 3 closed
Serial port 2 disabled	JP7	all open
⇨ Serial port 3 address COM3 select	JP8	pins 2 & 3 closed
Serial port 3 address COM4 select	JP8	pins 1 & 2 closed
Serial port 3 disabled	JP8	all open
⇨ Serial port 4 address COM4 select	JP9	pins 1 & 2 closed
Serial port 4 address COM3 select	JP9	pins 2 & 3 closed
Serial port 4 disabled	JP9	all open
⇨ Parallel port 1 address select LPT1	JP10	pins 2 & 3 closed
Parallel port 1 address select LPT2	JP10	pins 1 & 2 closed
Parallel port 1 disabled	JP10	all open
⇨ Parallel port 2 address select LPT2	JP11	pins 1 & 2 closed
Parallel port 2 address select LPT1	JP11	pins 2 & 3 closed
Parallel port 2 disabled	JP11	all open
⇨ Serial port 1 interrupt IRQ4 enabled	JP12	pins 2 & 3 closed
Serial port 1 interrupt IRQ3 enabled	JP12	pins 1 & 2 closed
Serial port 1 disabled	JP12	all open
⇨ Serial port 2 interrupt IRQ3 enabled	JP13	pins 1 & 2 closed
Serial port 2 interrupt IRQ4 enabled	JP13	pins 2 & 3 closed
Serial port 2 disabled	JP13	all open
⇨ Serial port 3 interrupt IRQ4 enabled	JP14	pins 2 & 3 closed
Serial port 3 interrupt IRQ3 enabled	JP14	pins 1 & 2 closed
Serial port 3 interrupts IRQ3 & IRQ4 disabled	JP14	all open
⇨ Serial port 4 interrupt IRQ3 enabled	JP15	pins 1 & 2 closed
Serial port 4 interrupt IRQ4 enabled	JP15	pins 2 & 3 closed
⇨ Serial port 3 interrupts IRQ5 & IRQ9 disabled	JP16	all open
Serial port 3 interrupt IRQ5 enabled	JP16	pins 2 & 3 closed
Serial port 3 interrupt IRQ9 enabled	JP16	pins 1 & 2 closed

Continued on next page. . .

MODULAR CIRCUIT TECHNOLOGY
MCT-IMS+

. . .continued from previous page

Function	Location	Setting
USER CONFIGURABLE SETTINGS CONTINUED		
⇨ Serial port 4 interrupts IRQ5 & IRQ9 disabled	JP17	all open
Serial port 4 interrupt IRQ9 enabled	JP17	pins 1 & 2 closed
Serial port 4 interrupt IRQ5 enabled	JP17	pins 2 & 3 closed
⇨ Parallel port 1 interrupt IRQ7 enabled	JP18	pins 1 & 2 closed
Parallel port 1 interrupt IRQ5 enabled	JP18	pins 2 & 3 closed
Parallel port 1 interrupts disabled	JP18	all open
⇨ Parallel port 2 interrupt IRQ5 enabled	JP19	pins 2 & 3 closed
Parallel port 2 interrupt IRQ7 enabled	JP19	pins 1 & 2 closed
Parallel port 2 interrupts disabled	JP19	all open
⇨ IDE(AT) interface enabled	JP20	closed
IDE(AT) interface disabled	JP20	open
⇨ Serial port 3 interrupts IRQ10 & IRQ11 disabled	JP21	all open
Serial port 3 interrupt IRQ11 enabled	JP21	pins 1 & 2 closed
Serial port 3 interrupt IRQ10 enabled	JP21	pins 2 & 3 closed
⇨ Serial port 4 interrupts IRQ12 & IRQ15 disabled	JP22	all open
Serial port 4 interrupt IRQ15 enabled	JP22	pins 1 & 2 closed
Serial port 4 interrupt IRQ12 enabled	JP22	pins 2 & 3 closed
⇨ Parallel port 1 bi-directional mode enabled	JP25	pins 2 & 3 closed
Parallel port 1 bi-directional mode disabled	JP25	pins 1 & 2 closed
⇨ Parallel port 2 bi-directional mode enabled	JP26	pins 2 & 3 closed
Parallel port 2 bi-directional mode disabled	JP26	pins 1 & 2 closed
⇨ IDE interface enabled	JP20	closed
IDE interface disabled	JP20	open
⇨ Serial port 3 interrupt IRQ10 & IRQ11 disabled	JP21	all open
Serial port 3 interrupt IRQ11 enabled	JP21	pins 1 & 2 closed
Serial port 3 interrupt IRQ10 enabled	JP21	pins 2 & 3 closed

NEXSTOR, INC.
NXT-93

Data bus: 32-bit PCI
Size: Half-length, full-height card
Hard drive supported: Up to seven SCSI-1 & SCSI-2 devices
Floppy drives supported: None

CONNECTIONS	
Function	**Location**
50-pin SCSI-2 connector - external	CN1
50-pin SCSI connector - internal	CN2

USER CONFIGURABLE SETTINGS		
Function	**Location**	**Setting**
On board BIOS enabled	JP1	open
On board BIOS disabled	JP1	closed
Supports hard drive >1GB	JP2	closed
Supports hard drive <=1GB	JP2	open
Host adapter termination enabled	JP4	open
Host adapter termination disabled	JP4	closed

BASE I/O ADDRESS			
Address	**JP3/jumper 1**	**JP3/jumper 2**	**JP3/jumper 3**
⇨ DC000h	open	open	open
CC000h	open	open	closed
D4000h	open	closed	open

PINE TECHNOLOGY
PT-627

Data bus: 32-bit, VL-bus
Size: Three/quarter-length, half-height card
Hard drive supported: Four IDE (AT) interface drives
Floppy drives supported: Two 360KB, 720KB, 1.2MB, 1.44MB, or 2.88MB drives

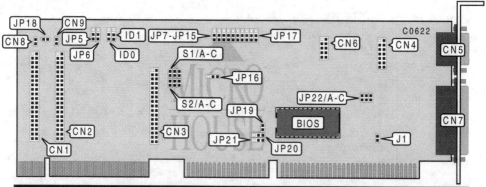

CONNECTIONS	
Function	**Location**
40-pin IDE (AT) interface connector - port 1	CN1
40-pin IDE (AT) interface connector - port 2	CN2
34-pin control cable connector - floppy drive	CN3
Game port	CN4
Serial port 1 - external	CN5
Serial port 2 - internal	CN6
Parallel port	CN7
2-pin connector - primary drive port active LED	CN8
2-pin connector - secondary drive port active LED	CN9

USER CONFIGURABLE SETTINGS		
Function	**Location**	**Setting**
IOCHRDY enabled	J1	Closed
IOCHRDY disabled	J1	Open
Primary IDE port enabled	JP5	Pins 1 & 2 closed
Primary IDE port disabled	JP5	Pins 2 & 3 closed
Secondary IDE port disabled	JP6	Pins 2 & 3 closed
Secondary IDE port enabled	JP6	Pins 1 & 2 closed
Floppy drive enabled	JP7	Pins 1 & 2 closed
Floppy drive disabled	JP7	Pins 2 & 3 closed
Game port enabled	JP8	Pins 1 & 2 closed
Game port disabled	JP8	Pins 2 & 3 closed
ECP enabled	JP16	Pins 1 & 2 closed
ECP disabled	JP16	Pins 2 & 3 closed

USER CONFIGURABLE SETTINGS		
Function	**Location**	**Setting**
CN8 and CN9 enabled for both primary and secondary IDE ports	JP18	Closed
CN8 used for primary IDE port/CN9 used for secondary IDE port	JP18	Open

Continued on next page . . .

PINE TECHNOLOGY
PT-627

. . . continued from previous page

PARALLEL PORT CONFIGURATION		
LPT	**JP9**	**JP11**
LPT2	Pins 1 & 2 closed	Pins 1 & 2 closed
LPT3	Pins 2 & 3 closed	Pins 1 & 2 closed
Disabled	N/A	Pins 2 & 3 closed

ENHANCED PARALLEL PORT CONFIGURATION		
Setting	**JP10**	**JP11**
Standard parallel port enabled	Pins 1 & 2 closed	Pins 2 & 3 closed
EPP enabled	Pins 2 & 3 closed	Pins 1 & 2 closed
ECP enabled	Pins 1 & 2 closed	Pins 1 & 2 closed

SERIAL PORT 1 CONFIGURATION		
COM/Address	**JP12**	**JP13**
COM1/3F8h	Pins 1 & 2 closed	Pins 1 & 2 closed
COM3/3E8h	Pins 1& 2 closed	Pins 1 & 2 closed
Disabled	Pins 2 & 3 closed	N/A

SERIAL PORT 2 CONFIGURATION		
COM	**JP14**	**JP15**
COM2/2F8h	Pins 1 & 2 closed	Pins 1 & 2 closed
COM4/2E8h	Pins 2 & 3 closed	Pins 1 & 2 closed
Disabled	N/A	Pins 2 & 3 closed

SERIAL PORTS 1 & 2 INTERRUPT SELECT		
IRQ	**JP20**	**JP21**
IRQ3	Pins 2 & 3 closed	N/A
IRQ4	N/A	Pins 2 & 3 closed
IRQ5	Pins 1 & 2 closed	N/A
IRQ9	N/A	Pins 1 & 2 closed

HARD DRIVE SPEED		
Setting	**ID0**	**ID1**
Speed 0 (HDD < 40MB)	Pins 2 & 3 closed	Pins 2 & 3 closed
Speed 1 (40/50Mhz CPU)	Pins 1 & 2 closed	Pins 1 & 2 closed
Speed 2 (25/33Mhz CPU)	Pins 1 & 2 closed	Pins 2 & 3 closed
Speed 3 (<20Mhz CPU)	Pins 2 & 3 closed	Pins 1 & 2 closed

DRQ SELECT - S1			
DRQ	**Jumper A**	**Jumper B**	**Jumper C**
DRQ1	Closed	Open	Open
DRQ3	Open	Closed	Open
Disabled	Open	Open	Closed

DACK SELECT - S2			
DACK	**Jumper A**	**Jumper B**	**Jumper C**
DACK1	Closed	Open	Open
DACK3	Open	Closed	Open
Disabled	Open	Open	Closed

PROCOMP USA, INC.
PI-350 PC

Data bus: 32-bit PCI
Size: Half-length, full-height card
Hard drive supported: Up to seven normal SCSI-2 or fifteen SCSI-3 Wide devices
Floppy drives supported: None

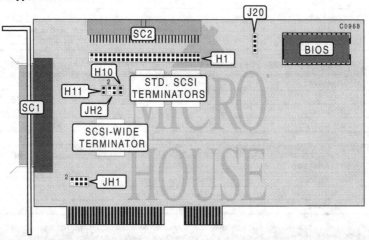

CONNECTIONS	
Function	**Location**
50-pin SCSI connector - internal	H1
4-pin connector - drive active LED	J20
50-pin SCSI connector - external	SC1
68-pin SCSI Wide connector - internal	SC2

USER CONFIGURABLE SETTINGS		
Function	**Location**	**Setting**
⇨ PCI INT A select	JH1	Pins 1 & 2 closed
PCI INT B select	JH1	Pins 3 & 4 closed
PCI INT C select	JH1	Pins 5 & 6 closed
PCI INT D select	JH1	Pins 7 & 8 closed

Continued on next page. . .

PROCOMP USA, INC.
PI-350 PC

. . .continued from previous page

TERMINATION SELECTION			
Standard SCSI Terminators	**Wide SCSI Terminator**	**H10**	**H11**
Software configured	Software configured	Closed	Closed
Software configured	Hardware configured	Closed	Open
Hardware configured	Software configured	Open	Closed
Hardware configured	Hardware configured	Open	Open

TERMINATION CONFIGURATION			
SCSI Configuration		**JH2/pins 1 & 2**	**JH2/pins 3 & 4**
External Devices	**Internal Devices**		
None	Standard	Open	Closed
None	Wide	Open	Open
Standard	None	Open	Closed
Standard	Standard	Closed	Closed
None	Standard & Wide	Closed	Open
Standard	Wide	Closed	Open

Note: Opening JH2/pins 1 & 2 enables standard SCSI terminators. Opening JH2/pins 3 & 4 enables SCSI-Wide terminator. Please see Miscellaneous Technical Notes.

MISCELLANEOUS TECHNICAL NOTES

The standard SCSI terminators terminate data bits 0-7 on the SCSI bus. The SCSI-wide terminator terminates data bits 8-15 (wide portion) on the bus.

Maximum use of two SCSI connectors is recommended. This means devices should be chained off connectors SC1 & H1, SC1 & SC2 *or* SC2 & H1, but not all three.

PROMISE TECHNOLOGY, INC.
DC2040

Data bus:	16-bit, ISA
Size:	Full-length, full-height card
Hard drives supported:	Seven SCSI hard drives
Floppy drives supported:	Two 360KB, 720KB, 1.2MB, or 1.44MB drives
	One floppy tape drive

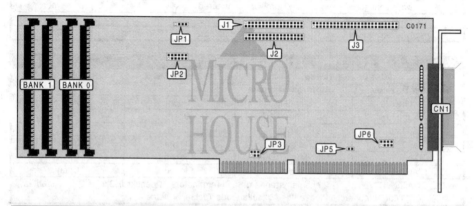

CONNECTIONS	
Function	**Location**
DB-25 SCSI control cable connector-external	CN1
34-pin control cable connector-floppy drive	J1
34-pin control cable connector-floppy tape drive	J2
50-pin SCSI control cable connector-internal	J3
4-pin connector-drive active LED	JP1

USER CONFIGURABLE SETTINGS		
Function	**Location**	**Setting**
▷ Factory configured - do not alter	JP2/jumper 1	open
▷ Floppy and tape drive enabled	JP5	closed
Floppy and tape drive disabled	JP5	open

INTERRUPT REQUEST					
IRQ	**JP2/2**	**JP2/3**	**JP3/1**	**JP3/2**	**JP3/3**
IRQ12	closed	open	closed	open	open
▷ IRQ14	open	open	open	closed	open
IRQ15	open	closed	open	open	closed

Continued on next page . . .

PROMISE TECHNOLOGY, INC.
DC2040

. . . continued from previous page

SCSI ADDRESS			
Address	**JP2/jumper 4**	**JP2/jumper 5**	**JP2/jumper 6**
0	open	open	open
1	closed	open	open
2	open	closed	open
3	closed	closed	open
4	open	open	closed
5	closed	open	closed
6	open	closed	closed
⇨ 7	closed	closed	closed

BIOS ADDRESS				
Address	**JP6/jumper 1**	**JP6/jumper 2**	**JP6/jumper 3**	**JP6/jumper 4**
C800h	closed	open	closed	closed
CA00h	closed	open	closed	open
CC00h	closed	open	open	closed
CE00h	closed	open	open	open
D000h	open	closed	closed	closed
D200h	open	closed	closed	open
D400h*	open	closed	open	closed
D600h	open	closed	open	open
⇨ D800h	open	open	closed	closed
DA00h	open	open	closed	open
DC00h	open	open	open	closed
DE00h	open	open	open	open

ON-BOARD CACHE CONFIGURATION		
Size	**Bank 0**	**Bank 1**
512KB	(2) 256KB x 9	NONE
1MB	(2) 256KB x 9	(2) 256KB x 9
2MB	(2) 1MB x 9	NONE
2.5MB	(2) 256KB x 9	(2) 1MB x 9
4MB	(2) 1MB x 9	(2) 1MB x 9
8MB	(2) 4MB x 9	NONE
8.5MB	(2) 256KB x 9	(2) 4MB x 9
10MB	(2) 1MB x 9	(2) 4MB x 9
16MB	(2) 4MB x 9	(2) 4MB x 9
Note:	Uses only 80nsec or faster SIMM's; 256K, 1M, or 4M (either x8 or x9).	

PROMISE TECHNOLOGY, INC.
DC-440

Data bus: 32-bit, VL-bus
Size: Three/quarter-length, full-height card
Hard drive supported: Up to seven SCSI devices, and two IDE (AT) interface drives
Floppy drives supported: Two 360KB, 720KB, 1.2MB or 1.44MB drives

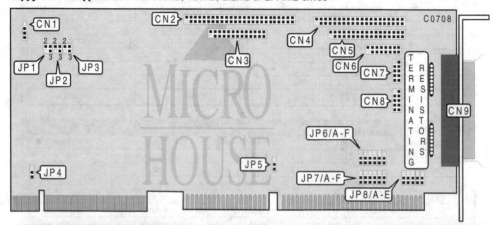

CONNECTIONS	
Function	**Location**
4-pin connector - drive active LED	CN1
50-pin SCSI connector - internal	CN2
26-pin parallel port connector	CN3
40-pin IDE (AT) interface connector - port 1	CN4
34-pin control cabled connector - floppy drive	CN5
Game port	CN6
10-pin serial port 2	CN7
10-pin serial port 1	CN8
50-pin SCSI connector - external	CN9

USER CONFIGURABLE SETTINGS		
Function	**Location**	**Setting**
Factory configured - do not alter	JP1	Pins 1 & 3 closed
Factory configured - do not alter	JP2	Pins 1 & 2, 3 & 4 closed
Factory configured - do not alter	JP3	Pins 1 & 2, 3 & 4 closed
Factory configured - do not alter	JP4	Pins 1 & 2 closed
CPU speed ≥ 33MHz	JP5	Pins 1 & 2 closed
CPU speed < 33MHz	JP5	Pins 2 & 3 closed
Floppy drive enabled	JP6/jumper A	Pins 1 & 2 closed
Floppy drive disabled	JP6/jumper A	Pins 2 & 3 closed
Game port enabled	JP6/jumper B	Pins 1 & 2 closed
Game port disabled	JP6/jumper B	Pins 2 & 3 closed

Continued on next page . . .

PROMISE TECHNOLOGY, INC.
DC-440

. . . continued from previous page

USER CONFIGURABLE SETTINGS		
Function	**Location**	**Setting**
Parallel port is output only	JP6/jumper C	Pins 2 & 3 closed
Parallel port is input/output	JP6/jumper C	Pins 1 & 2 closed
IDE port disabled	JP8/jumper E	Pins 2 & 3 closed
IDE port enabled	JP8/jumper E	Pins 1 & 2 closed

SCSI I/O ADDRESS - JP7			
Address	**Jumper A**	**Jumper B**	**Jumper C**
330h	Pins 1 & 2 closed	Pins 2 & 3 closed	Pins 2 & 3 closed
130h	Pins 1 & 2 closed	Pins 2 & 3 closed	Pins 1 & 2 closed
134h	Pins 2 & 3 closed	Pins 2 & 3 closed	Pins 1 & 2 closed
230h	Pins 1 & 2 closed	Pins 1 & 2 closed	Pins 2 & 3 closed
234h	Pins 2 & 3 closed	Pins 1 & 2 closed	Pins 2 & 3 closed
334h	Pins 2 & 3 closed	Pins 2 & 3 closed	Pins 2 & 3 closed

BIOS ADDRESS - JP7			
Address	**Jumper D**	**Jumper E**	**Jumper F**
C8000h	Pins 1 & 2 closed	Pins 2 & 3 closed	Pins 1 & 2 closed
CC000h	Pins 2 & 3 closed	Pins 2 & 3 closed	Pins 1 & 2 closed
D0000h	Pins 1 & 2 closed	Pins 1 & 2 closed	Pins 2 & 3 closed
D4000h	Pins 2 & 3 closed	Pins 1 & 2 closed	Pins 2 & 3 closed
D8000h	Pins 1 & 2 closed	Pins 2 & 3 closed	Pins 2 & 3 closed
DC000h	Pins 2 & 3 closed	Pins 2 & 3 closed	Pins 2 &3 closed

SERIAL PORT 1 CONFIGURATION - JP8		
COM/Address	**Jumper C**	**Jumper D**
COM1/3F8h	Pins 2 & 3 closed	Pins 1 & 2 closed
COM3/3E8h	Pins 1 & 2 closed	Pins 2 & 3 closed
Disabled	Pins 2 & 3 closed	Pins 2 & 3 closed

SERIAL PORT 2 CONFIGURATION - JP8		
COM/Address	**Jumper A**	**Jumper B**
COM2/2F8h	Pins 2 & 3 closed	Pins 1 & 2 closed
COM4/2E8h	Pins 1 & 2 closed	Pins 2 & 3 closed
Disabled	Pins 2 & 3 closed	Pins 2 & 3 closed

PARALLEL PORT CONFIGURATION - JP6			
Address/IRQ	**Jumper D**	**Jumper E**	**Jumper F**
3BCh/IRQ7	Pins 2 & 3 closed	Pins 1 & 2 closed	Pins 1 & 2 closed
278h/IRQ5	Pins 1 & 2 closed	Pins 1 & 2 closed	Pins 2 & 3 closed
378h/IRQ7	Pins 2 & 3 closed	Pins 2 & 3 closed	Pins 1 & 2 closed
Disabled	All pins open	Pins 2 & 3 closed	Pins 2 & 3 closed

PROMISE TECHNOLOGY, INC.
DC5030

Data bus: 32-bit PCI
Size: Half-length, full-height card
Hard drive supported: Four IDE (AT) interface drives
Floppy drives supported: None

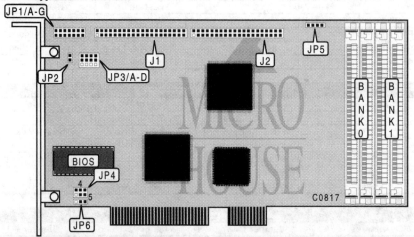

CONNECTIONS	
Function	**Location**
40-pin primary IDE (AT) interface connector	J1
40-pin secondary IDE (AT) interface connector	J2
4-pin connector - drive active LED	JP5

USER CONFIGURABLE SETTINGS		
Function	**Location**	**Setting**
▷ Factory configured - do not alter	JP1/A	N/A
▷ Factory configured - do not alter	JP1/D	N/A
▷ Factory configured - do not alter	JP1/E	N/A
▷ Factory configured - do not alter	JP1/F	N/A
▷ Factory configured - do not alter	JP1/G	N/A
▷ INTX# enabled	JP2	closed
INTX# disabled	JP2	open
▷ Relocatable I/O address disabled	JP3/A pins 1 & 2	closed
Relocatable I/O address enabled	JP3/A pins 2 & 3	closed
▷ BIOS address is D8000h	JP3/B pins 1 & 2	closed
BIOS address is DC000h	JP3/B pins 2 & 3	closed
▷ Primary IDE (AT) interface enabled	JP3/C pins 2 & 3	closed
Secondary IDE (AT) interface enabled	JP3/C pins 1 & 2	closed
*IRQ14 connect to ISA	JP3/D pins 1 & 2	closed
*IRQ15 connect to ISA	JP3/D pins 2 & 3	closed
▷ PCI configuration register enabled	JP6/pins 2 & 3	closed
PCI configuration register disabled	JP6/pins 1 & 2	closed
Note: If any PCI INT# is used, do not connect IRQ14 & IRQ15.		

Continued on next page. . .

PROMISE TECHNOLOGY, INC.
DC5030

. . .continued from previous page

INTERRUPT SELECTION		
IRQ	**JP1/B**	**JP1/C**
14	closed	open
15	open	closed

PCI INT CONFIGURATION	
INT	**JP4**
A	pins 1 & 3 closed
B	pins 3 & 5 closed
C	pins 2 & 4 closed
D	pins 4 & 6 closed

CACHE MEMORY CONFIGURATION		
Size	**Bank 0**	**Bank 1**
512KB	(2) 256K x 9	NONE
1MB	(2) 256K x 9	(2) 256K x 9
2MB	(2) 1MB x 9	NONE
2.5MB	(2) 1MB x 9	(2) 256K x 9
4MB	(2) 1MB x 9	(2) 1MB x 9
8MB	(2) 4MB x 9	NONE
8.5MB	(2) 4MB x 9	(2) 256K x 9
10MB	(2) 4MB x 9	(2) 1MB x 9
16MB	(2) 4MB x 9	(2) 4MB x 9

PROMISE TECHNOLOGY, INC.
EIDE 4030 PLUS

Data bus: 32-bit VESA local bus
Size: Three/quarter-length, full-height card
Hard drive supported: Four IDE (AT) Interface drives
Floppy drives supported: Two 360KB, 720KB, 1.2MB, 1.44MB drives

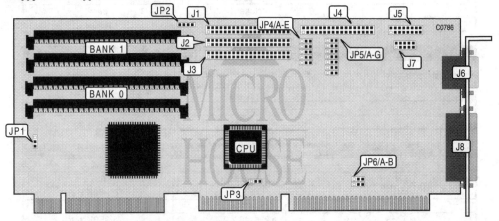

CONNECTIONS	
Function	**Location**
40-pin primary VESA IDE(AT) interface connector	J1
40-pin secondary VESA IDE(AT) interface connector	J2
40-pin ISA ATAPI IDE(AT) interface connector	J3
34-pin connector - floppy drive interface	J4
16-pin connector - game port (external)	J5
9-pin connector - serial port 1 (external)	J6
10-pin connector - serial port 2 (internal)	J7
25-pin parallel port (external)	J8
4-pin connector - drive active LED	JP2
Note: Connector J3 is used for IDE CD-ROM (ATAPI) and tape drives.	

USER CONFIGURABLE SETTINGS		
Function	**Location**	**Setting**
▷ VESA IDE is primary channel	JP1	pins 1 & 2 closed
VESA IDE is secondary channel	JP1	pins 2 & 3 closed
VESA IDE channel is disabled	JP1	all open
▷ ISA IDE(AT) interrupt IRQ15 select	JP3	pins 1 & 2 closed
ISA IDE(AT) interrupt IRQ14 select	JP3	pins 2 & 3 closed
▷ Game port enabled	JP4/A	pins 1 & 2 closed
Game port disabled	JP4/A	pins 2 & 3 closed
▷ Factory configured - do not alter	JP4/B	pins 1 & 2 closed
▷ Floppy drive interface enabled	JP4/C	pins 1 & 2 closed
Floppy drive interface disabled	JP4/C	pins 2 & 3 closed
▷ Parallel port interrupt select IRQ7	JP5/A	pins 1 & 2 closed
Parallel port interrupt select IRQ5	JP5/A	pins 2 & 3 closed

Continued on next page. . .

PROMISE TECHNOLOGY, INC.
EIDE 4030 PLUS

. . .continued from previous page

PARALLEL PORT ADDRESS SELECTION		
Address	JP5/B	JP5/C
⇨ 378h	pins 2 & 3 closed	pins 1 & 2 closed
278h	pins 1 & 2 closed	pins 1 & 2 closed
3BCh	pins 1 & 2 closed	pins 2 & 3 closed
Disabled	pins 2 & 3 closed	pins 2 & 3 closed

PRIMARY SERIAL PORT ADDRESS SELECTION		
Address	JP5/F	JP5/G
⇨ 3F8h (COM1)	pins 1 & 2 closed	pins 1 & 2 closed
2F8h (COM2)	pins 2 & 3 closed	pins 1 & 2 closed
3E8h (COM3)	pins 1 & 2 closed	pins 2 & 3 closed
Disabled	pins 2 & 3 closed	pins 2 & 3 closed

SECONDARY SERIAL PORT ADDRESS SELECTION		
Address	JP5/D	JP5/E
⇨ 2F8h (COM2)	pins 1 & 2 closed	pins 1 & 2 closed
3F8h (COM1)	pins 2 & 3 closed	pins 1 & 2 closed
2E8h (COM3)	pins 1 & 2 closed	pins 2 & 3 closed
Disabled	pins 2 & 3 closed	pins 2 & 3 closed

ISA IDE CONFIGURATION		
Setting	JP4/D	JP4/E
⇨ ISA IDE(AT) interface is secondary interface	pins 1 & 2 closed	pins 1 & 2 closed
ISA IDE(AT) interface is primary interface	pins 1 & 2 closed	pins 2 & 3 closed
ISA IDE(AT) interface is disabled	pins 2 & 3 closed	pins 2 & 3 closed

DMA CHANNEL CONFIGURATION		
DMA	JP6/A	JP6/B
⇨ 3	pins 2 & 3 closed	pins 2 & 3 closed
1	pins 1 & 2 closed	pins 1 & 2 closed

DRAM CONFIGURATION		
Size	Bank 0	Bank 1
512KB	(2) 256K x 9	NONE
1MB	(2) 256K x 9	(2) 256K x 9
2MB	(2) 1M x 9	NONE
4MB	(2) 1M x 9	(2) 1M x 9
8MB	(2) 4M x 9	NONE
16MB	(2) 4M x 9	(2) 4M x 9

Note: The EIDE 4030 PLUS must have at least 512KB installed in order to function. Optimum operation is achieved using 4 identical SIMM modules.

PROMISE TECHNOLOGY, INC.
EIDEMAX

Data bus: 16-bit, ISA
Size: Half-length, half-height card
Hard drive supported: Two IDE (AT) Interface drives
Floppy drives supported: None

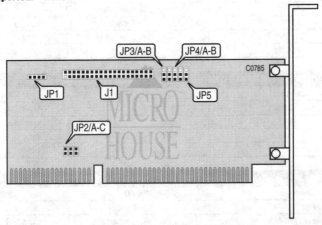

CONNECTIONS	
Function	**Location**
40-pin IDE(AT) interface connector	J1
4-pin connector - drive active LED	JP1

USER CONFIGURABLE SETTINGS		
Function	**Location**	**Setting**
⇨ IDE(AT) interface enabled	JP3/A	pins 1 & 2 closed
IDE(AT) interface disabled	JP3/A	pins 2 & 3 closed
⇨ EIDEMAX is primary IDE(AT) interface in system	JP3/B	pins 1 & 2 closed
EIDEMAX is secondary IDE(AT) interface in system	JP3/B	pins 2 & 3 closed
⇨ On-board BIOS enabled	JP5	pins 1 & 2 closed
On-board BIOS disabled	JP5	pins 2 & 3 closed

INTERRUPT SELECTION			
IRQ	**JP2/A**	**JP2/B**	**JP2/C**
⇨ IRQ15	closed	open	open
IRQ12	open	open	closed
IRQ14	open	closed	open

BASE MEMORY ADDRESS SELECTION		
Address	**JP4/A**	**JP4/B**
⇨ D0000h	pins 2 & 3 closed	pins 2 & 3 closed
D4000h	pins 2 & 3 closed	pins 1 & 2 closed
D8000h	pins 1 & 2 closed	pins 2 & 3 closed
DC000h	pins 1 & 2 closed	pins 1 & 2 closed

SIIG, INC.
SCSI CONTROLLER SCSI-PRO

Data bus: 16-bit ISA
Size: Half-length, full-height card
Hard drive supported: Up to seven SCSI devices
Floppy drives supported: None

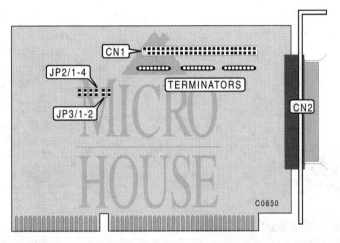

CONNECTIONS	
Function	**Location**
50-pin SCSI connector - internal	CN1
50-pin SCSI connector - external	CN2

BIOS ADDRESS SELECTION		
Address	**JP3/1**	**JP3/2**
⇨ C800h	open	open
CC00h	open	closed
D800h	closed	open
DC00h	closed	closed

INTERRUPT SELECTION				
IRQ	**JP2/1**	**JP2/2**	**JP2/3**	**JP2/4**
⇨ 11	open	closed	open	open
10	closed	open	open	open
12	open	open	closed	open
15	open	open	open	closed

MISCELLANEOUS TECHNICAL NOTES
Remove terminators only when connecting both internal & external devices to host adapter.

SUNIX CO., LTD.
SUN-5249P (EX-3220)

Data Bus	32-bit PCI
Card Size	Three-quarter length, full-height card
Hard Drives supported	Four IDE (AT) drives
Floppy drives supported	Two 360KB, 720KB, 1.2MB, 1.44MB or 2.88 MB drives

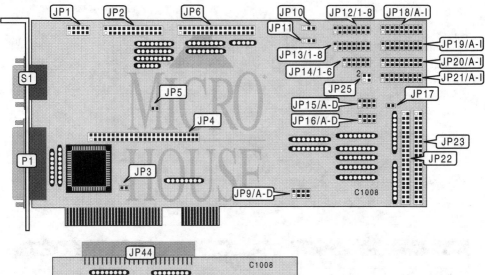

AT BUS EXPANSION CARD

CONNECTIONS	
Function	**Location**
10-pin serial port 2 - internal	JP1
26-pin parallel port 2 - internal	JP2
Proprietary expansion card connector	JP4
2-pin connector - drive active LED	JP5
34-pin cable connector - floppy drive	JP6
2-pin connector - drive active LED	JP17
40-pin IDE(AT) secondary connector	JP22
40-pin IDE(AT) primary connector	JP23
25-pin parallel port 1 - external	P1
9-pin serial port 1 - external	S1
Proprietary expansion card connector	JP44

Continued on next page. . .

SUNIX CO., LTD.
SUN-5249P (EX-3220)

. . .continued from previous page

USER CONFIGURABLE SETTINGS		
Function	**Location**	**Setting**
▷ Floppy drive primary address select	JP10	Pins 1 & 2 closed
Floppy drive secondary address select	JP10	Pins 3 & 4 closed
▷ Floppy drive interface enabled	JP11	Pins 1 & 2 closed
Floppy drive interface disabled	JP11	Pins 2 & 3 closed
▷ Factory configured - do not alter	JP3	Open
▷ Factory configured - do not alter	JP9/A	Open
▷ Factory configured - do not alter	JP9/B	Closed
▷ Factory configured - do not alter	JP9/C	Open
▷ Factory configured - do not alter	JP9/D	Open

SERIAL PORT 1 ADDRESS SELECTION				
COM	**JP12/1**	**JP12/2**	**JP12/3**	**JP12/4**
▷ COM1(3F8h)	Closed	Open	Open	Open
COM2(2F8h)	Open	Closed	Open	Open
COM3(3E8h)	Open	Open	Closed	Open
COM4(2E8h)	Open	Open	Open	Closed
COM5(3F0h)	Open	Open	Open	Open
COM6(3E0h)	Open	Open	Open	Open
COM7(2E0h)	Open	Open	Open	Open
COM8(260h)	Open	Open	Open	Open

SERIAL PORT 1 ADDRESS SELECTION (CONTINUED)				
COM	**JP12/5**	**JP12/6**	**JP12/7**	**JP12/8**
▷ COM1(3F8h)	Open	Open	Open	Open
COM2(2F8h)	Open	Open	Open	Open
COM3(3E8h)	Open	Open	Open	Open
COM4(2E8h)	Open	Open	Open	Open
COM5(3F0h)	Closed	Open	Open	Open
COM6(3E0h)	Open	Closed	Open	Open
COM7(2E0h)	Open	Open	Closed	Open
COM8(260h)	Open	Open	Open	Closed

SERIAL PORT 2 ADDRESS SELECTION				
COM	**JP13/1**	**JP13/2**	**JP13/3**	**JP13/4**
COM1(3F8h)	Closed	Open	Open	Open
▷ COM2(2F8h)	Open	Closed	Open	Open
COM3(3E8h)	Open	Open	Closed	Open
COM4(2E8h)	Open	Open	Open	Closed
COM5(3F0h)	Open	Open	Open	Open
COM6(3E0h)	Open	Open	Open	Open
COM7(2E0h)	Open	Open	Open	Open
COM8(260h)	Open	Open	Open	Open

Continued on next page. . .

SUNIX CO., LTD.
SUN-5249P (EX-3220)

. . .continued from previous page

SERIAL PORT 2 ADDRESS SELECTION (CONTINUED)				
COM	JP13/5	JP13/6	JP13/7	JP13/8
COM1(3F8h)	Open	Open	Open	Open
⇨ COM2(2F8h)	Open	Open	Open	Open
COM3(3E8h)	Open	Open	Open	Open
COM4(2E8h)	Open	Open	Open	Open
COM5(3F0h)	Closed	Open	Open	Open
COM6(3E0h)	Open	Closed	Open	Open
COM7(2E0h)	Open	Open	Closed	Open
COM8(260h)	Open	Open	Open	Closed

PARALLEL PORT 1 ADDRESS SELECTION						
LPT	JP14/1	JP14/2	JP14/3	JP14/4	JP14/5	JP14/6
⇨ LPT1(3BCh)	Closed	Open	Open	Open	Open	Open
LPT2(378h)	Open	Closed	Open	Open	Open	Open
LPT3(278h)	Open	Open	Closed	Open	Open	Open
LPT4(268h)	Open	Open	Open	Closed	Open	Open
LPT5(27Ch)	Open	Open	Open	Open	Closed	Open
LPT6(26Ch)	Open	Open	Open	Open	Open	Closed

PARALLEL PORT 2 ADDRESS SELECTION		
LPT	JP25/pins 1 & 2	JP25/pins 3 & 4
LPT2(378h)	Closed	Open
⇨ LPT3(278h)	Open	Closed

SERIAL PORT 1 INTERRUPT SELECTION				
IRQ	JP18/A	JP18/B	JP18/C	JP18/D
IRQ3	Closed	Open	Open	Open
⇨ IRQ4	Open	Closed	Open	Open
IRQ5	Open	Open	Closed	Open
IRQ7	Open	Open	Open	Closed
IRQ9	Open	Open	Open	Open
IRQ10	Open	Open	Open	Open
IRQ11	Open	Open	Open	Open
IRQ12	Open	Open	Open	Open
IRQ15	Open	Open	Open	Open

SERIAL PORT 1 INTERRUPT SELECTION (CONTINUED)					
IRQ	JP18/E	JP18/F	JP18/G	JP18/H	JP18/I
IRQ3	Open	Open	Open	Open	Open
⇨ IRQ4	Open	Open	Open	Open	Open
IRQ5	Open	Open	Open	Open	Open
IRQ7	Open	Open	Open	Open	Open
IRQ9	Closed	Open	Open	Open	Open
IRQ10	Open	Closed	Open	Open	Open
IRQ11	Open	Open	Closed	Open	Open
IRQ12	Open	Open	Open	Closed	Open
IRQ15	Open	Open	Open	Open	Closed

Continued on next page. . .

SUNIX CO., LTD.
SUN-5249P (EX-3220)

. . .continued from previous page

| SERIAL PORT 2 INTERRUPT SELECTION					
IRQ	**JP19/A**	**JP19/B**	**JP19/C**	**JP19/D**	**JP19/E**
⇨ IRQ3	Closed	Open	Open	Open	Open
IRQ4	Open	Closed	Open	Open	Open
IRQ5	Open	Open	Closed	Open	Open
IRQ7	Open	Open	Open	Closed	Open
IRQ9	Open	Open	Open	Open	Closed
IRQ10	Open	Open	Open	Open	Open
IRQ11	Open	Open	Open	Open	Open
IRQ12	Open	Open	Open	Open	Open
IRQ15	Open	Open	Open	Open	Open

SERIAL PORT 2 INTERRUPT SELECTION (CONTINUED)				
IRQ	**JP19/F**	**JP19/G**	**JP19/H**	**JP19/I**
⇨ IRQ3	Open	Open	Open	Open
IRQ4	Open	Open	Open	Open
IRQ5	Open	Open	Open	Open
IRQ7	Open	Open	Open	Open
IRQ9	Open	Open	Open	Open
IRQ10	Closed	Open	Open	Open
IRQ11	Open	Closed	Open	Open
IRQ12	Open	Open	Closed	Open
IRQ15	Open	Open	Open	Closed

PARALLEL PORT 1 INTERRUPT SELECTION				
IRQ	**JP20/A**	**JP20/B**	**JP20/C**	**JP20/D**
IRQ3	Closed	Open	Open	Open
IRQ4	Open	Closed	Open	Open
IRQ5	Open	Open	Closed	Open
⇨ IRQ7	Open	Open	Open	Closed
IRQ9	Open	Open	Open	Open
IRQ10	Open	Open	Open	Open
IRQ11	Open	Open	Open	Open
IRQ12	Open	Open	Open	Open
IRQ15	Open	Open	Open	Open

PARALLEL PORT 1 INTERRUPT SELECTION (CONTINUED)				
IRQ	**JP20/E**	**JP20/F**	**JP20/G**	**JP20/H**	**JP20/I**
IRQ3	Open	Open	Open	Open	Open
IRQ4	Open	Open	Open	Open	Open
IRQ5	Open	Open	Open	Open	Open
⇨ IRQ7	Open	Open	Open	Open	Open
IRQ9	Closed	Open	Open	Open	Open
IRQ10	Open	Closed	Open	Open	Open
IRQ11	Open	Open	Closed	Open	Open
IRQ12	Open	Open	Open	Closed	Open
IRQ15	Open	Open	Open	Open	Closed

Continued on next page. . .

SUNIX CO., LTD.
SUN-5249P (EX-3220)

. . .continued from previous page

PARALLEL PORT 2 INTERRUPT SELECTION					
IRQ	J21/A	J21/B	J21/C	J21/D	J21/E
IRQ3	Closed	Open	Open	Open	Open
IRQ4	Open	Closed	Open	Open	Open
⇨ IRQ5	Open	Open	Closed	Open	Open
IRQ7	Open	Open	Open	Closed	Open
IRQ9	Open	Open	Open	Open	Closed
IRQ10	Open	Open	Open	Open	Open
IRQ11	Open	Open	Open	Open	Open
IRQ12	Open	Open	Open	Open	Open
IRQ15	Open	Open	Open	Open	Open

PARALLEL PORT 2 INTERRUPT SELECTION (CONTINUED)				
IRQ	J21/F	J21/G	J21/H	J21/I
IRQ3	Open	Open	Open	Open
IRQ4	Open	Open	Open	Open
⇨ IRQ5	Open	Open	Open	Open
IRQ7	Open	Open	Open	Open
IRQ9	Open	Open	Open	Open
IRQ10	Closed	Open	Open	Open
IRQ11	Open	Closed	Open	Open
IRQ12	Open	Open	Closed	Open
IRQ15	Open	Open	Open	Closed

PRIMARY IDE INTERRUPT SELECTION				
Setting	JP15/A	JP15/B	JP15/C	JP15/D
⇨ INTA	Closed	Open	Open	Open
INTB	Open	Closed	Open	Open
INTC	Open	Open	Closed	Open
INTD	Open	Open	Open	Closed

SECONDARY IDE INTERRUPT SELECTION				
Setting	JP16/A	JP16/B	JP16/C	JP16/D
⇨ INTA	Closed	Open	Open	Open
INTB	Open	Closed	Open	Open
INTC	Open	Open	Closed	Open
INTD	Open	Open	Open	Closed

TEKRAM TECHNOLOGY CO., LTD.

DC-690C

Data bus: 32-bit PCI
Size: Half-length, full-height card
Hard drive supported: Four IDE(AT) drives
Floppy drives supported: None

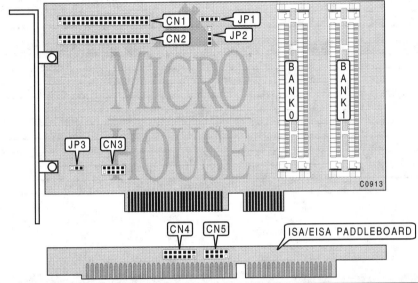

CONNECTIONS	
Function	**Location**
40-pin primary IDE(AT) connector	CN1
40-pin secondary IDE(AT) connector	CN2
10-pin legacy header connector to CN5 on paddleboard	CN3
4-pin connector - drive active LED	JP1
4-pin speaker connector	JP2

PADDLEBOARD CONNECTIONS	
Function	**Location**
10-pin legacy header connector to CN3 on mainboard	CN5
14-pin legacy header connector to another PCI control card	CN4

Continued on next page. . .

TEKRAM TECHNOLOGY CO., LTD.
DC-690C

Continued on next page. .

USER CONFIGURABLE SETTINGS		
Function	**Location**	**Setting**
PCI configuration space enabled	JP3	pins 2 & 3 closed
PCI configuration space disabled	JP3	pins 1 & 2 closed

DRAM CONFIGURATION		
Size	**Bank 0**	**Bank 1**
512K	(2) 256K x 9	none
1MB	(2) 256K x 9	(2) 256K x 9
2MB	(2) 1MB x 9	none
2.5MB	(2) 1MB x 9	(2) 256K x 9
4MB	(2) 1MB x 9	(2) 1MB x 9
8MB	(2) 4MB x 9	none
8.5MB	(2) 4MB x 9	(2) 256K x 9
10MB	(2) 4MB x 9	(2) 1MB x 9
16MB	(2) 4MB x 9	(2) 4MB x 9

TYAN COMPUTER CORPORATION
S1365 (Rev. 1.1)

Data bus: 32-bit PCI
Size: Half-length, Full-height card
Hard drive supported: Up to fifteen SCSI drives
Floppy drives supported: None

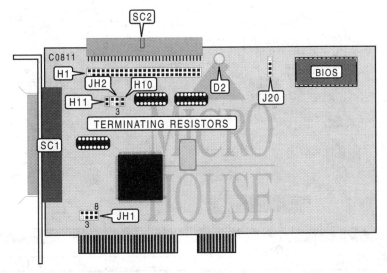

CONNECTIONS	
Function	**Location**
50-pin SCSI connector - internal	H1
4-pin connector - drive active LED	J20
50-pin SCSI connector - external	SC1
68-pin SCSI connector - internal	SC2

USER CONFIGURABLE SETTINGS		
Function	**Location**	**Setting**
SCSI active terminator enable/disable through software	H10	closed
SCSI active terminator not enabled/disabled through software	H10	open
Wide portion of terminator enable/disable through software	H11	closed
Wide portion of terminator not enabled/disabled through software	H11	open
Manual active on-board terminator disabled	JH2/pins 1 & 2	closed
Manual active on-board terminator enabled	JH2/pins 1 & 2	open
Manual active on-board wide portion terminator disabled	JH2/pins 3 & 4	closed
Manual active on-board wide portion terminator enabled	JH2/pins 3 & 4	open

PCI INTERRUPT LINE SELECTION	
INT	**JH1**
⇨ A	pins 1 & 2 closed
B	pins 3 & 4 closed
C	pins 5 & 6 closed
D	pins 7 & 8 closed

TYAN COMPUTER
S1366

Data bus: 32-bit PCI
Size: Half-length, full-height card
Hard drive supported: Two IDE (AT) Interface drives
Floppy drives supported: Two 360KB, 720KB, 1.2MB, or 1.44MB drives

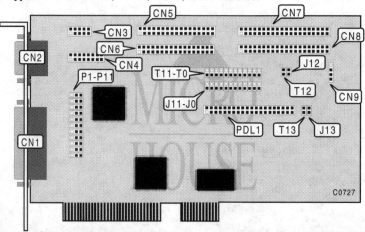

CONNECTIONS	
Function	**Location**
25 pin parallel port - external	CN1
9 pin serial port - external	CN2
10 pin serial port - internal	CN3
16 pin game port - internal	CN4
34 pin data cable connector - primary floppy drive interface	CN5
34 pin data cable connector - secondary floppy drive interface	CN6
40 pin connector - primary IDE(AT) interface	CN7
40 pin connector - secondary IDE(AT) interface	CN8
4 pin connector - drive active LED	CN9
S136x paddle card daughterboard connector	PDL1

USER CONFIGURABLE SETTINGS		
Function	**Location**	**Setting**
⇨ Factory configured - do not alter	J0	N/A
⇨ Floppy drive interface DSKCHG signal not intercepted	J1	open
Floppy drive interface DSKCHG signal intercepted	J1	closed
⇨ I/O address fixed	J2	closed
I/O address relocatable	J2	open
⇨ Primary IDE(AT) channel legacy IRQ tied to IRQ14	J5	closed
No primary IDE(AT) channel legacy IRQ tied to IRQ14	J5	open
⇨ Primary IDE(AT) legacy ISA IRQ14 not buffered	J6	open
Primary IDE(AT) legacy ISA IRQ14 buffered	J6	closed
⇨ Secondary IDE(AT) channel legacy IRQ tied to IRQ15	J7	closed
No secondary IDE(AT) channel legacy IRQ tied to IRQ15	J7	open
⇨ Secondary IDE(AT) legacy ISA IRQ15 not buffered	J8	open
Secondary IDE(AT) legacy ISA IRQ15 buffered	J8	closed

Continued on next page . . .

TYAN COMPUTER
S1366

. . . continued from previous page

USER CONFIGURABLE SETTINGS CONTINUED		
Function	**Location**	**Setting**
➪ IDE(AT) interrupt native mode not utilized	J9	open
IDE(AT) interrupt native mode utilized to PCI INTA	J9	closed
➪ Factory configured - do not alter	J10	N/A
➪ AT printer mode(ISA) enabled	J11	open
Normal mode enabled, floppy interface pin 29 grounded	J11	closed
➪ Floppy drive interface normal DRATE out mode select	P1	pins 2 & 3 closed
Floppy drive interface media ID input OS2 enhanced mode	P1	pins 1 & 2 closed
➪ Floppy drive interface I/O address 3F0h select	P2	pins 2 & 3 closed
Floppy drive interface I/O address 370h select	P2	pins 1 & 2 closed
➪ Floppy drive interface enabled	P3	pins 2 & 3 closed
Floppy drive interface disabled	P3	pins 1 & 2 closed
➪ Factory configured - do not alter	T0	N/A
➪ ISA AT printer mode enabled	T1	open
PS/2 bi-directional printer mode enabled	T1	closed
➪ Parallel port interrupt IRQ7 select	T2	closed
Parallel port interrupt disabled	T2	open
➪ Serial port 1 interrupt IRQ4 select	T4	closed
Serial port 1 interrupt disabled	T4	open
➪ Serial port 2 interrupt IRQ3 select	T5	closed
Serial port 2 interrupt disabled	T5	open
➪ Game port enabled	T6	closed
Game port disabled	T6	open

PCI IDE CONFIGURATION		
Setting	**J3**	**J4**
➪ PCI IDE channels enabled	closed	open
PCI IDE channels disabled	open	closed

SECONDARY IDE PCI INTERRUPT CONFIGURATION		
Setting	**J12**	**J13**
➪ Secondary IDE interrupt not inverted(PCI bus INTB#)	open	N/A
Secondary IDE interrupt inverted(PCI bus INTB#)	N/A	closed

PRIMARY IDE PCI INTERRUPT CONFIGURATION		
Setting	**T12**	**T13**
➪ Primary IDE interrupt not inverted(PCI bus INTA#)	open	N/A
Primary IDE interrupt inverted(PCI bus INTA#)	N/A	closed

PARALLEL PORT I/O ADRESS SELECT		
Address	**P8**	**P9**
➪ 378-37Fh	pins 2 & 3 closed	pins 2 & 3 closed
278-27Fh	pins 2 & 3 closed	pins 1 & 2 closed
3BC-3BEh	pins 1 & 2 closed	pins 1 & 2 closed
Disabled	pins 1 & 2 closed	pins 2 & 3 closed

Continued on next page . . .

TYAN COMPUTER
S1366

. . . continued from previous page

PRIMARY SERIAL PORT I/O ADRESS SELECT		
Address	**P4**	**P5**
⇨ 3F8h (COM1)	pins 2 & 3 closed	pins 2 & 3 closed
2F8h (COM2)	pins 2 & 3 closed	pins 1 & 2 closed
3E8h (COM3)	pins 1 & 2 closed	pins 2 & 3 closed
Disabled	pins 1 & 2 closed	pins 1 & 2 closed

SECONDARY SERIAL PORT I/O ADRESS SELECT		
Address	**P6**	**P7**
⇨ 2F8h (COM2)	pins 2 & 3 closed	pins 2 & 3 closed
2E8h (COM4)	pins 1 & 2 closed	pins 2 & 3 closed
3F8h (COM1)	pins 2 & 3 closed	pins 1 & 2 closed
Disabled	pins 1 & 2 closed	pins 1 & 2 closed

PARALLEL PORT INTERRUPT SELECT		
IRQ	**T2**	**T3**
⇨ IRQ7	closed	open
IRQ5	open	closed
Disabled	open	open

ENHANCED PARALLEL PORT MODE CONFIGURATION		
Modes Supported	**P10**	**P11**
⇨ PRN	pins 2 & 3 closed	pins 2 & 3 closed
PRN, EPP	pins 1 & 2 closed	pins 2 & 3 closed
PRN, ECP	pins 2 & 3 closed	pins 1 & 2 closed
PRN, ECP, EPP	pins 1 & 2 closed	pins 1 & 2 closed

ECP MODE CONFIGURATION					
Setting	**T7**	**T8**	**T9**	**T10**	**T11**
⇨ ECP mode disabled	open	open	open	open	open
ECP mode w/DMA1	closed	open	closed	open	closed
ECP mode w/DMA3	open	closed	open	closed	closed

SERIAL PORT INTERRUPT SELECT				
Port 1	**Port 2**	**T3**	**T4**	**T5**
IRQ4	IRQ3	open	closed	closed
IRQ4	Disabled	open	closed	open
Disabled	IRQ3	open	open	closed
IRQ3	IRQ4	open	T4 pin 1 to T5 pin 1 T4 pin 2 to T5 pin 2	
IRQ5	IRQ3	open	T4 pin 1 to T5 pin 1	
Disabled	IRQ4	open	T4 pin 2 to T5 pin 2	
IRQ4	IRQ5	T3 pin 2 to T4 pin 2		closed
Disabled	IRQ5	T3 pin 2 to T4 pin 2		open

MISCELLANEOUS TECHNICAL NOTES
Note: In order to utilize the S1366's IDE and I/O functions, the S136x paddle card must be installed on connector PDL1

ULTRASTOR CORPORATION
ULTRA 34C

Data bus: 32-bit VL-Bus
Size: Full-length, half-height card
Hard drive supported: Up to seven SCSI drives
Floppy drives supported: Two 360KB, 720KB, 1.2MB, or 1.44MB, or 2.88MB drives

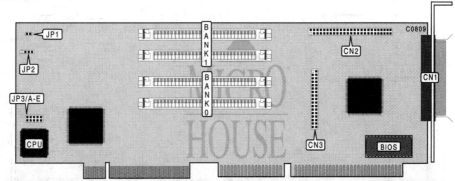

CONNECTIONS	
Function	**Location**
50-pin SCSI connector - external	CN1
50-pin SCSI connector - internal	CN2
34-pin cable connector - floppy drive	CN3
2-pin connector - drive active LED	JP1
4-pin connector - speaker	JP2

USER CONFIGURABLE SETTINGS		
Function	**Location**	**Setting**
⮕ Floppy drive enabled	JP3/A	closed
Floppy drive disabled	JP3/A	open
⮕ Factory configured - do not alter	JP3/E	open

BASE I/O ADDRESS			
Address	**JP3/B**	**JP3/C**	**JP3/D**
⮕ 330h	closed	closed	closed
130h	open	open	closed
134h	open	open	open
230h	open	closed	closed
234h	open	closed	open
334h	closed	open	closed

CACHE MEMORY CONFIGURATION		
Size	**Bank 0**	**Bank 1**
512KB	(2) 256K x 9	NONE
1MB	(2) 256K x 9	(2) 256K x 9
2MB	(2) 1MB x 9	NONE
2.5MB	(2) 1MB x 9	(2) 256K x 9
4MB	(2) 1MB x 9	(2) 1MB x 9
8MB	(2) 4MB x 9	NONE
8.5MB	(2) 4MB x 9	(2) 256K x 9
10MB	(2) 4MB x 9	(2) 1MB x 9
16MB	(2) 4MB x 9	(2) 4MB x 9

WESTERN DIGITAL CORPORATION
PARADISE ACCELERATOR/PORTS O' CALL

Data bus: 32-bit, VL bus
Size: Three/quarter-length, full-height card
Hard drive supported: Two IDE (AT) Interface drives
Floppy drives supported: Four 360KB, 720KB, 1.2MB, 1.44MB, or 2.88MB drives

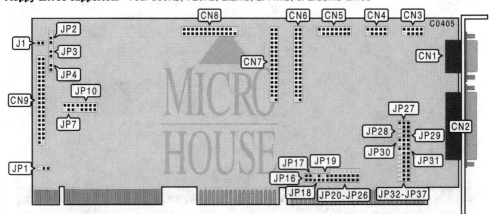

CONNECTIONS	
Function	**Location**
15-pin VGA analog video port - external	CN1
25-pin parallel port (LPT1/2/3) - external	CN2
10-pin serial port 1 (COM1/2/3) - internal	CN3
10-pin serial port 2 (COM1/2/4) - internal	CN4
15-pin game port - internal	CN5
34-pin control cable connector - floppy drive 0	CN6
34-pin control cable connector - floppy drive 1	CN7
26-pin VESA feature connector - internal	CN8
40-pin IDE(AT) Interface connector	CN9
2-pin connector - Drive active LED	J1

USER CONFIGURABLE SETTINGS		
Function	**Location**	**Setting**
⇨ VL-bus IDE enabled	JP1	pins 1 & 2 closed
VL-bus IDE disabled	JP1	pins 2 & 3 closed
⇨ 60Hz refresh rate in mode 3, 12, 5E, 5F	JP7/jumper 1	open
72Hz refresh rate in mode 3, 12, 5E, 5F	JP7/jumper 1	closed
⇨ 0 wait state enabled	JP7/jumper 2	closed
1 wait state enabled	JP7/jumper 2	open
⇨ Hardware configuration by JP10 enabled	JP7/jumper 3	open
EEPROM configuration enabled	JP7/jumper 3	closed

Continued on next page . . .

WESTERN DIGITAL CORPORATION
PARADISE ACCELERATOR/PORTS O' CALL

. . . continued from previous page

USER CONFIGURABLE SETTINGS		
Function	**Location**	**Setting**
⇨ Standard fonts enabled	JP10/jumper 5	open
TUV fonts enabled (German standard)	JP10/jumper 5	closed
⇨ Serial Port Interrupt Request IRQ3 enabled	JP19/jumper 1 or 2	closed
Serial Port Interrupt Request disabled	JP19/jumper 1 and 2	open
⇨ Parallel Port Interrupt Request IRQ7 enabled	JP21	pins 1 & 2 closed
Parallel Port Interrupt Request IRQ5 enabled	JP21	pins 2 & 3 closed
⇨ Printer Data Request is DREQ3	JP24	pins 1 & 2 closed
Printer Data Request is DREQ3	JP24	pins 2 & 3 closed
⇨ Printer Data Acknowledge Is DACK3	JP26	pins 1 & 2 closed
Printer Data Acknowledge is DACK4	JP26	pins 2 & 3 closed
⇨ Floppy drive enabled	JP28	pins 1 & 2 closed
Floppy drive disabled	JP28	pins 2 & 3 closed
⇨ Hard drive enabled	JP29	pins 1 & 2 closed
Hard drive disabled	JP29	pins 2 & 3 closed
⇨ Game Port (CN5) enabled	JP32	pins 1 & 2 closed
Game Port (CN5) disabled	JP32	open
⇨ Hard drive port address is 1F0-1F7h	JP34	pins 1 & 2 closed
Hard drive port address is 170-177h	JP34	pins 2 & 3 closed
⇨ Floppy drive port address is 3F0-3F7h	JP35	pins 1 & 2 closed
Floppy drive port address is 370-377h	JP35	pins 2 & 3 closed

800 X 600 X 16 MODE/256 COLOR MODE REFRESH RATE		
Function	**JP10/jumper 1**	**JP10/jumper 2**
⇨ 56Hz vertical/<=35.3KHz horizontal/non-interlaced	open	open
56Hz vertical/<=35.3KHz horizontal/non-interlaced	closed	closed
72Hz vertical/>=48.2KHz horizontal/non-interlaced	closed	open
60Hz vertical/>=38.0KHz horizontal/non-interlaced	open	closed

1024 X 768 MODE REFRESH RATE		
Function	**JP10/jumper 3**	**JP10/jumper 4**
⇨ 86.7Hz vertical/>=35.4KHz horizontal/interlaced	open	open
72Hz vertical/<=59.7KHz horizontal/non-interlaced	closed	closed
70Hz vertical/<=56.6KHz horizontal/non-interlaced	closed	open
60Hz vertical/<=48.5KHz horizontal/non-interlaced	open	closed

Continued on next page . . .

WESTERN DIGITAL CORPORATION
PARADISE ACCELERATOR/PORTS O' CALL

. . . continued from previous page

SERIAL PORT 1 (CN3) CONFIGURATION		
COM	JP27/jumper 1	JP27/jumper 2
⇨ COM1	pins 1 & 2 closed	pins 1 & 2 closed
COM2	pins 1 & 2 closed	pins 2 & 3 closed
COM3	pins 2 & 3 closed	pins 1 & 2 closed
Disabled	pins 2 & 3 closed	pins 2 & 3 closed

SERIAL PORT 2 (CN4) CONFIGURATION		
COM	JP30/jumper 1	JP30/jumper 2
COM1	pins 1 & 2 closed	pins 2 & 3 closed
⇨ COM2	pins 1 & 2 closed	pins 1 & 2 closed
COM4	pins 2 & 3 closed	pins 1 & 2 closed
Disabled	pins 2 & 3 closed	pins 2 & 3 closed

PARALLEL PORT (CN2) CONFIGURATION		
LPT	JP31/jumper 1	JP31/j umper 2
⇨ LPT1	pins 1 & 2 closed	pins 2 & 3 closed
LPT2	pins 1 & 2 closed	pins 1 & 2 closed
LPT3	pins 2 & 3 closed	pins 1 & 2 closed
Disabled	pins 2 & 3 closed	pins 2 & 3 closed

MISCELLANEOUS TECHNICAL NOTES
Jumpers JP2, JP3, JP5, JP6, JP8, JP9, JP11, JP12, JP13, JP14, JP15, JP16, JP17, JP18, JP20, JP22, JP23, and JP25 are factory configured - do not alter. Jumper JP4 is factory configured to pins 2 & 3 closed - do not alter.

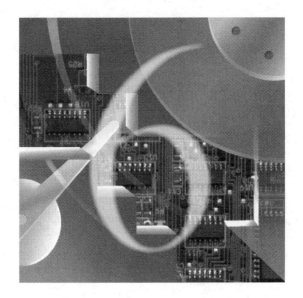

Drive Settings

Chapter Six Contents:

General Hard Drive Information

Interface Connections

Please consult Chapter Three for specific details on connectors for IDE, SCSI, ESDI, and ST-506/412 interfaces.

Default Jumper Settings

The default or most common jumper positions are indicated by the ⇨ symbol. Pin-1 and jumper 1 are indicated by the **Δ** symbol.

Jumper Types

See the diagram below for examples of common devices used to change the hardware configuration of hard drives.

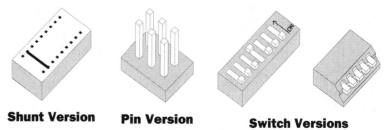

Shunt Version   **Pin Version**   **Switch Versions**

Figure 6-1: Common Jumper Types

Undocumented Jumpers

Some jumper settings are specified as "unidentified," "factory configured – do not alter," or may have a dash. Information was not available on these jumpers or settings. These jumpers may be used by the factory for diagnostic or low-level purposes, and should be left as received out of the box. Also, some connection points for test equipment look like jumpers. In most cases, the diagrams do not show these test points.

Typical Jumpered Options

Most of the jumper settings in this chapter are self-explanatory. The most important hardware option to set will be Drive Select (SCSI, ESDI, ST-506/412), or Master/Slave (IDE). Please see the appropriate sections in Chapters Three and Four for more information on typical jumpered options.

Selected Drive Settings

Jumper settings and diagrams for the industry's most popular hard drives are provided in this chapter. The drives are listed in alphabetical order by manufacturer.

The diagrams only reflect the important access points and are not shown in fine detail. Some terminator resistor packs and jumper block locations change from one Printed Circuit Board (PCB) revision to another, but the functions of each remain the same.

CONNER PERIPHERALS, INC.
CFA-1080A, CFA-170A, CFA-270A, CFA-340A, CFA-540A
CFA-810A, CFS-210A, CFS-420A, CP30174, CP-30344

Interface: IDE(AT)
Size: 3.5 in. third height
View: Bottom

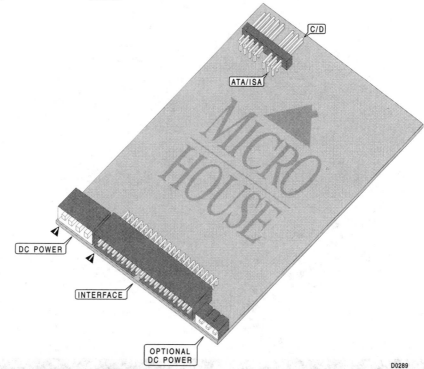

D0289

DRIVE CONFIGURATION	
Selection	**C/D**
⇨ Single drive only	closed
Master drive in a two drive system	closed
Slave drive in a two drive system	open

USER CONFIGURABLE SETTINGS		
Function	**Location**	**Setting**
Conner master/slave mode is used	ATA/ISA	open
ATA/CAM master/slave mode is used	ATA/ISA	closed
⇨ Factory configured - do not alter	all other jumpers	N/A

CONNER PERIPHERALS, INC.
CFL350A, CFL420A

Interface: EIDE
Size: 2.5 in. fifth height
View: Bottom

D0452

DRIVE SELECTION			
Selection	**C/D**	**A/C**	**CS**
Single CAM drive in a system	closed	open	open
CAM master in a two drive system	closed	open	open
Single ISA drive in a system	closed	closed	open
ISA master in a two drive system	closed	closed	open
CAM slave in a two drive system	open	open	open
ISA slave in a two drive system	open	closed	open
CAM cable select (master or slave) enabled	open	open	closed
ISA cable select (master or slave) enabled	open	closed	closed

CONNER PERIPHERALS, INC.
CFP-1060S, CFP-1060B, CFP-1060W, CFP-1060E

Interface: SCSI
Size: 3.5 in. Third Height
View: Bottom

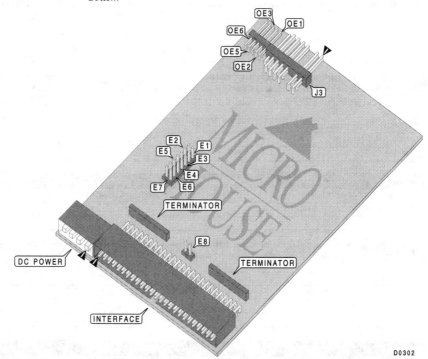

DRIVE CONFIGURATION			
Drive number	Jumper E1 or OE1	Jumper E2 or OE2	Jumper E3 or OE3
⇨ 0	open	open	open
1	closed	open	open
2	open	closed	open
3	closed	closed	open
4	open	open	closed
5	closed	open	closed
6	open	closed	closed
7	closed	closed	closed
Note: Use either E1, E2, and E3 or EO1, EO2, and EO3, but not both to set drive number. Jumpers EO1, EO2, and EO3 are not present on drive configurations with an LED on the circuit board.			

Continued on next page . . .

CONNER PERIPHERALS, INC.
CFP-1060S, CFP-1060B, CFP-1060W, CFP-1060E

. . . continued from previous page

SPINDLE MOTOR OPTION SETTINGS		
Function	**E5 or OE5**	**E6**
⇨ Spindle motor starts on power-up	open	open
Spindle motor starts on command only	closed	open
Spindle motor starts delayed (13 sec. x Drive I.D. #)	open	closed

USER CONFIGURABLE SETTINGS		
Function	**Location**	**Setting**
⇨ SCSI parity check enabled	E7	open
SCSI parity check disabled	E7	closed
⇨ TERMPWR supplied by drive	E8	closed
TERMPWR supplied by the SCSI Interface pin 26	E8	open

CONNECTIONS	
Function	**Location**
External spindle synchronization signal	J3/jumper 1
External LED	J3/jumper 2 and/or OE6

MODEL DESCRIPTIONS	
Model	**Description**
CFP-1060S	50-pin SCSI-2
CFP-1060D	Differential 50-pin SCSI-2
CFP-1060W	68-pin SCSI-3
CFP-1060E	80-pin single power/SCSI connector

MISCELLANEOUS TECHNICAL NOTES
Jumper E4 and J3/jumpers 3-7 are factory configured - do not alter.

CONNER PERIPHERALS, INC.
CFP2107E, CFP4207E

Interface: SCSI Fast wide
Size: 3.5 in. third height
View: Bottom

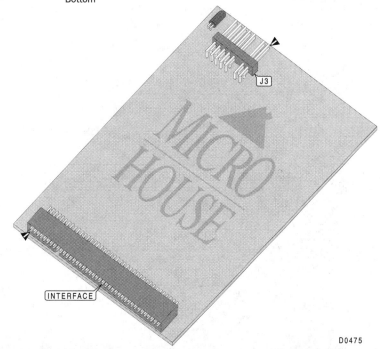

D0475

CONNECTIONS	
Purpose	**Location**
Spindle synch option connector	J3/jumper 1
LED connector	J3/jumper 2

CONNER PERIPHERALS, INC.
CFP2107S, CFP4207S

Interface: SCSI 2 Fast
Size: 3.5 in. third height
View: Bottom

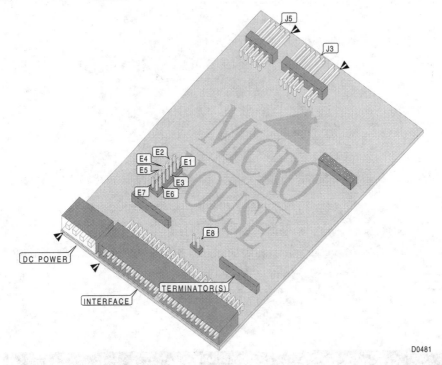

D0481

DRIVE SELECTION			
Drive Number	E1	E2	E3
0	open	open	open
1	closed	open	open
2	open	closed	open
3	closed	closed	open
4	open	open	closed
5	closed	open	closed
6	open	closed	closed
7	closed	closed	closed

Continued on next page. . .

CONNER PERIPHERALS, INC.
CFP2107S, CFP4207S

. . .continued from previous page

USER CONFIGURABLE SETTINGS		
Function	**Location**	**Setting**
⇨ Factory configured - do not alter	E4	open
⇨ Spindle motor starts on power-up	E5	open
Spindle motor starts on command only	E5	closed
⇨ Spindle motor delayed (Drive ID x 4 sec.)	E6	closed
Spindle motor not delayed	E6	open
⇨ SCSI parity check enabled	E7	open
SCSI parity check disabled	E7	closed
⇨ TERMPWR enabled	E8	closed
TERMPWR disabled	E8	open

CONNECTIONS	
Purpose	**Location**
Spindle Synch connector	J3/jumper 1
External LED	J3/jumper 2

MISCELLANEOUS TECHNICAL NOTE
Note: Jumpers E1-E3 and the first three jumpers of J5 are mutually exclusive. Do not set both. All other jumpers and settings are undocumented.

CONNER PERIPHERALS, INC.
CFP2107W, CFP4207W

Interface: SCSI 2 Fast/Wide
Size: 3.5 in. third height
View: Bottom

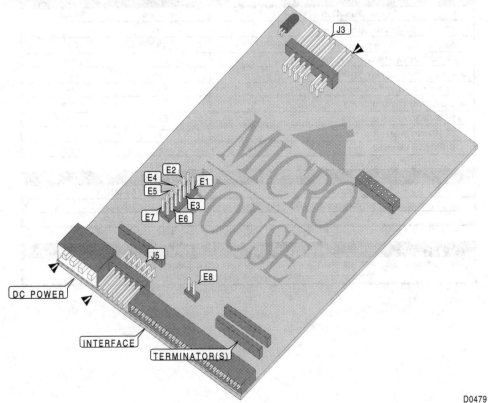

D0479

Continued on next page. . .

CONNER PERIPHERALS, INC.
CFP2107W, CFP4207W

. . .continued from previous page

DRIVE SELECTION				
Drive Number	**E1**	**E2**	**E3**	**E4**
0	open	open	open	open
1	closed	open	open	open
2	open	closed	open	open
3	closed	closed	open	open
4	open	open	closed	open
5	closed	open	closed	open
6	open	closed	closed	open
7	closed	closed	closed	open
8	open	open	open	closed
9	closed	open	open	closed
10	open	closed	open	closed
11	closed	closed	open	closed
12	open	open	closed	closed
13	closed	open	closed	closed
14	open	closed	closed	closed
15	closed	closed	closed	closed

USER CONFIGURABLE SETTINGS		
Function	**Location**	**Setting**
⇨ Spindle motor starts on power-up	E5	open
Spindle motor starts on command only	E5	closed
⇨ Spindle motor delayed (Drive ID x 4 sec.)	E6	closed
Spindle motor not delayed	E6	open
⇨ SCSI parity check enabled	E7	open
SCSI parity check disabled	E7	closed
⇨ TERMPWR enabled	E8	closed
TERMPWR disabled	E8	open

CONNECTIONS	
Purpose	**Location**
Spindle Synch connector	J3/jumper 1
External LED	J3/jumper 2

MISCELLANEOUS TECHNICAL NOTE
Note: Jumper E1-E4 and the first four jumper of J5 are mutually exclusive. Do not alter both.

CONNER PERIPHERALS, INC.
CP3304, CP3364, CP3504, CP3544

Interface: IDE(AT)
Size: 3.5 in. half height
View: Bottom

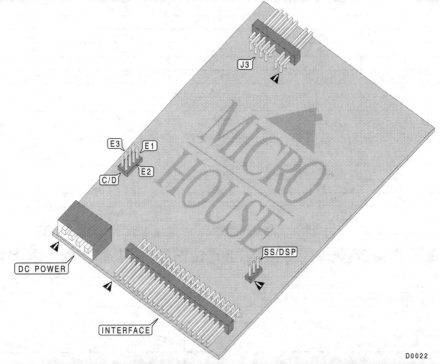

D0022

DRIVE CONFIGURATION	
Selection	**Jumper C/D**
⇨ Single drive only	closed
Master drive in a two drive system	closed
Slave drive in a two drive system	open

USER CONFIGURABLE SETTINGS		
Function	**Location**	**Setting**
⇨ Spindle motor starts on power-up	E1	open
Spindle motor starts on command only	E1	closed
⇨ Not used	E2	open
⇨ Not used	E3	open

Continued on next page . . .

CONNER PERIPHERALS, INC.
CP3304, CP3364, CP3504, CP3544

. . . continued from previous page

CONNECTIONS	
Function	**Location**
External Spindle Sync.	J3/jumper 1
External LED	J3/jumper 2
Serial I/O connector	J3/jumper 3 - 7

INTERFACE PIN 39 CONFIGURATION - SS/DSP		
Function	**Pins 1 & 2**	**Pins 2 & 3**
⇨ Drive Active LED signal output on interface pin 39	closed	open
SPSYNC signal enabled on interface pin 39	open	closed
⇨ Interface pin 39 is not used	open	open

HEWLETT-PACKARD COMPANY
HP C3323A, HP C3724D, HP C3724S
HP C3725D, HP C3725S

Interface:	SCSI-2 ("D" models are differential)
Size:	3.5 in. third height
View:	Bottom

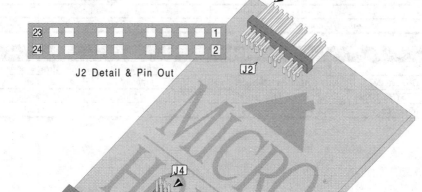

J2 Detail & Pin Out

D0556

DRIVE CONFIGURATION - J2			
Drive Number	**Jumper 10**	**Jumper 11**	**Jumper 12**
0	open	open	open
1	open	open	closed
2	open	closed	open
3	open	closed	closed
4	closed	open	open
5	closed	open	closed
6	closed	closed	open
7	closed	closed	closed

Continued on next page . . .

HEWLETT-PACKARD COMPANY
HP C3323A, HP C3724D, HP C3724S
HP C3725D, HP C3725S

. . . continued from previous page

USER CONFIGURABLE SETTINGS		
Function	**Location**	**Setting**
◇ Write protect disabled	J2/jumper 1	open
Write protect enabled	J2/jumper 1	closed
◇ SCSI mode is SCSI-2 (if SCSI1/2 pin is active)	J2/pins 1 & 3	open
SCSI mode is SCSI-1 (if SCSI1/2 pin is active)	J2/pins 1 & 3	closed
SDTR message disabled (if SDTR function is active)	J2/jumper 3	open
SDTR message enabled (if SDTR function is active)	J2/jumper 3	closed
Unit attention enabled (if U/A function is active)	J2/jumper 3	open
Unit attention disabled (if U/A function is active)	J2/jumper 3	closed
Spindle motor starts on power-up	J2/jumper 5	closed
Spindle motor starts on command only	J2/jumper 5	open
◇ Active termination enabled	J4/jumper 1	closed
Active termination disabled	J4/jumper 1	open
◇ Factory configured - do not alter	J4/jumper 2	N/A
TERMPWR supplied by drive to drive	J4/jumper 3	open
TERMPWR supplied by drive to drive and SCSI interface pin 26	J4/jumper 3	closed

SPINDLE SYNC SIGNAL ROUTING		
Route	**J2/jumper 7**	**J2/jumper 8**
SCSI interface pin 29 connected to ground	closed	open
Spindle sync signal routed to interface pin 29	open	closed
Not connected	open	open
Not connected	closed	closed

Note: If spindle sync mode is disabled the above settings are not valid.

CONNECTIONS	
Purpose	**Location**
LED	J2/jumper 4

MISCELLANEOUS TECHNICAL NOTES
On HP C3323A option 011 active termination is not available.

HEWLETT-PACKARD COMPANY
HP C3724SC, HP C3724TC, HP C3724WC
HP C3725SC, HP C3725TC, HP C3725WC

Interface: SCA SCSI-2 single ended ("SC" models)
    SCA SCSI-2 single ended wide ("TC" models)"
    SCA SCSI-2 differential wide ("WC" models")
Size: 3.5 in. third height
View: Bottom

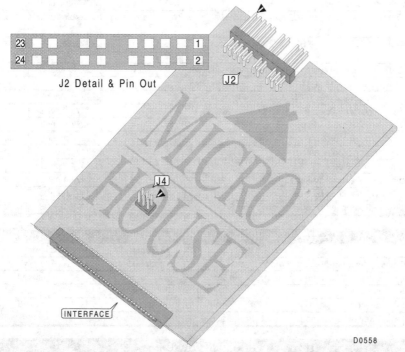

J2 Detail & Pin Out

D0558

DRIVE CONFIGURATION - J2			
Drive Number	Jumper 10	Jumper 11	Jumper 12
0	open	open	open
1	open	open	closed
2	open	closed	open
3	open	closed	closed
4	closed	open	open
5	closed	open	closed
6	closed	closed	open
7	closed	closed	closed

Continued on next page . . .

HEWLETT-PACKARD COMPANY
HP C3724SC, HP C3724TC, HP C3724WC
HP C3725SC, HP C3725TC, HP C3725WC

. . . continued from previous page

USER CONFIGURABLE SETTINGS		
Function	Location	Setting
⇨ Write protect disabled	J2/jumper 1	open
Write protect enabled	J2/jumper 1	closed
⇨ SCSI mode is SCSI-2 (if SCSI1/2 pin is active)	J2/pins 1 & 3	open
SCSI mode is SCSI-1 (if SCSI1/2 pin is active)	J2/pins 1 & 3	closed
SDTR message disabled (if SDTR function is active)	J2/jumper 3	open
SDTR message enabled (if SDTR function is active)	J2/jumper 3	closed
Unit attention enabled (if U/A function is active)	J2/jumper 3	open
Unit attention disabled (if U/A function is active)	J2/jumper 3	closed
Spindle motor starts on power-up	J2/jumper 5	closed
Spindle motor starts on command only	J2/jumper 5	open
⇨ Factory configured - do not alter	J4/jumper 1	N/A
⇨ Factory configured - do not alter	J4/jumper 2	N/A
⇨ Factory configured - do not alter	J4/jumper 3	N/A

SPINDLE SYNC SIGNAL ROUTING		
Route	J2/jumper 7	J2/jumper 8
SCSI interface pin 29 connected to ground	closed	open
Spindle sync signal routed to interface pin 29	open	closed
Not connected	open	open
Not connected	closed	closed
Note: If spindle sync mode is disabled the above settings are not valid.		

CONNECTIONS	
Purpose	Location
LED	J2/jumper 4

MISCELLANEOUS TECHNICAL NOTES
On all models with SCA connector only passive termination is available.

MAXTOR CORPORATION
71050A, 71084A, 71084AP, 71260A, 71260AP, 71626A, 71626AP, 7541A, 7541AP

Interface: IDE(AT)
Size: 3.5 in. third height
View: Bottom

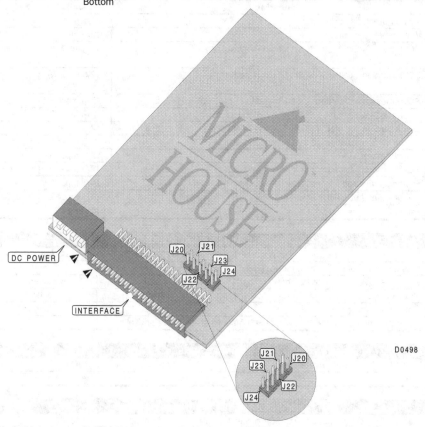

In some PCB versions the orientation of the
jumper block is as shown above

D0498

DRIVE CONFIGURATION	
Setting	**J20**
⇨ Single drive in a system	closed
Master drive in a two drive system	closed
Slave drive in a two drive system	open

Continued on next page. . .

MAXTOR CORPORATION
71050A, 71084A, 71084AP, 71260A, 71260AP, 71626A, 71626AP, 7541A, 7541AP

. . .continued from previous page

USER CONFIGURABLE SETTINGS		
Function	**Location**	**Setting**
⇨ Factory configured-do not alter	J21	open
⇨ Factory configured-do not alter	J22	open
⇨ Factory configured-do not alter	J23	open
⇨ Factory configured-do not alter	J24	open

MISCELLANEOUS TECHNICAL NOTE
A spare shunt, which is placed horizontally over J23 and J24 is shipped with the drives.

MAXTOR CORPORATION
7405AV, 7540AV, 7420AV, 7270AV, 7135AV

Interface:	IDE(AT)
Size:	3.5 in. half height
View:	Bottom

D0463

DRIVE SELECTION		
Function	**Location**	**Setting**
⇨ Single drive only	J20	closed
Master in a two drive system	J20	closed
Slave in a two drive system	J20	open

USER CONFIGURABLE SETTINGS		
Function	**Location**	**Setting**
⇨ Factory configured - do not alter	J21	open
Logical translation is 1046 x 16 x 63 (7540AV Only)	J22	Open
Logical translation is 1024 x 16 x 63	J22	Closed
⇨ Write cache enabled	J23	open
Write cache disabled	J23	closed
⇨ Cable select disabled	J24	open
Cable select enabled	J24	closed
⇨ Factory configured - do not alter	J25	open

MISCELLANEOUS TECHNICAL NOTE
Note: The logical translation of 1046 x 16 x 63 is used as a default for the 7540AV, under 6.2 or earlier DOS the maximum number of Cylinders is 1024.

MAXTOR CORPORATION
LXT-200A, LXT-213A, LXT-340A, LXT-437A, LXT-535A

Interface:	IDE(AT)
Size:	3.5 in. half height
View:	Bottom

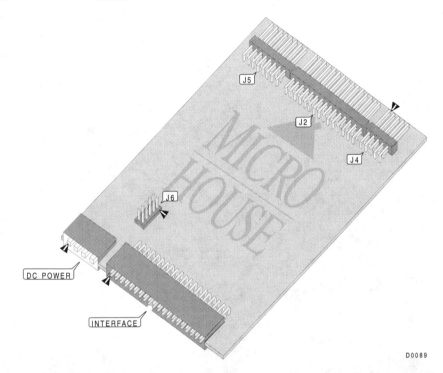

D0089

DRIVE CONFIGURATION			
Selection	**J6/jumper 1**	**J6/jumper 3**	**J6/jumper 4**
⇨ Single drive system	open	open	open
Master drive in a two drive system	open	open	closed
Slave drive in a two drive system	closed	open	open

CONNECTIONS	
Function	**Location**
External LED	J6/jumper 2
External LED	J4/pins 9 & 10
HDA connector	J2

MISCELLANEOUS TECHNICAL NOTES
All other jumpers are Factory configured - do not alter

MAXTOR CORPORATION
LXT-200S, LXT-213S, LXT-340S, LXT-437S, LXT-535S (OPTION A)

Interface: SCSI
Size: 3.5 in. half height
View: Bottom

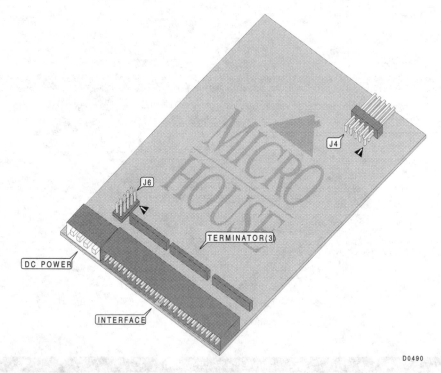

D0490

DRIVE SELECTION - J6			
Drive Number	**Jumper 1**	**Jumper 2**	**Jumper 3**
0	open	open	open
1	closed	open	open
2	open	closed	open
3	closed	closed	open
4	open	open	closed
5	closed	open	closed
6	open	closed	closed
7	closed	closed	closed

Continued on next page . . .

MAXTOR CORPORATION
LXT-200S, LXT-213S, LXT-340S, LXT-437S, LXT-535S (OPTION A)

. . . continued from previous page

USER CONFIGURABLE SETTINGS		
Function	**Location**	**Setting**
⇨ SCSI parity check enabled	J6/jumper 4	closed
SCSI parity check disabled	J6/jumper 4	open
⇨ Spindle motor starts on power-up	J6/jumper 5	closed
Spindle motor starts on command only	J6/jumper 5	open

J4 PIN ASSIGNMENT	
Pin	**Function**
1	Ground
2	CNMI
3	CTDX
4	CRDX
5	Ground
6	Ground
7	N/C
8	SPDL Pulse Ref.
9	+5 V DC
10	-LED DRV

MAXTOR CORPORATION
MXT-540SL, MXT-1240S

Interface:	SCSI
Size:	3.5 in. third height
View:	Bottom

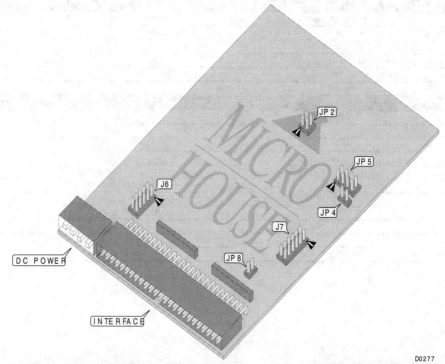

D0277

DRIVE SELECTION - J6			
Drive Number	**Jumper 1**	**Jumper 2**	**Jumper 3**
0	open	open	open
1	open	open	closed
2	open	closed	open
3	open	closed	closed
4	closed	open	open
5	closed	open	closed
⇨ 6	closed	closed	open
7	closed	closed	closed

Continued on next page . . .

MAXTOR CORPORATION
MXT-540SL, MXT-1240S

. . . continued from previous page

USER CONFIGURABLE SETTINGS		
Function	**Location**	**Setting**
⇨ SCSI parity check enabled	J6/jumper 4	closed
SCSI parity check disabled	J6/jumper 4	open
⇨ Spindle motor starts on power-up	J6/jumper 5	closed
Spindle motor starts on command only	J6/jumper 5	open
Factory configured - do not alter	JP2	-
⇨ Write protect disabled	JP4	closed
Write protect enabled	JP4	open
Factory configured - do not alter	JP5/jumpers 1-4	-
⇨ Drive supplies TERMPWR to SCSI Interface pin 26	JP8	closed
TERMPWR not supplied to SCSI Interface pin 26	JP8	open

SINGLE-ENDED/DIFFERENTIAL OPERATION - J7		
Function	**Jumper 1, jumpers 3-7**	**Jumper 2**
⇨ Single ended operation enabled	open	closed
Differential operation enabled	closed	open

QUANTUM CORPORATION
420AT, 635AT, 850AT (TRAILBLAZER)
540AT, 640AT, 1080AT, 1280AT (FIREBALL)

Interface: IDE(AT)
Size: 3.5 in. third height
View: Bottom

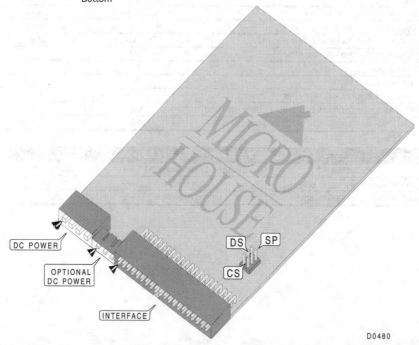

D0480

DRIVE CONFIGURATION				
Selection	CS	DS	SP	Pin 28
▷ Drive is master	open	closed	open	N/A
Slave drive in a two drive system	open	open	open	N/A
Master drive when non-CAM drive is slave	open	closed	closed	N/A
Drive is master (cable select enabled)	closed	N/A	open	grnd
Slave in a two drive system (cable select enabled)	closed	N/A	open	open
Master drive when non-CAM drive is slave (cable select enabled)	closed	N/A	closed	grnd
Note: When configuring master/slave with the Cable Select jumper (CS), a cable that provides the correct signal to pin 28 needs to be used.				

QUANTUM CORPORATION
ATLAS XP SERIES: XP31070S, XP32150S, XP34300S
ATLAS II SERIES: XP32181S, XP34361S, XP39100S

Interface: SCSI-2 Fast (ATLAS XP)
    SCSI-3 (ATLAS II)
Size: 3.5 in. half height
View: Bottom

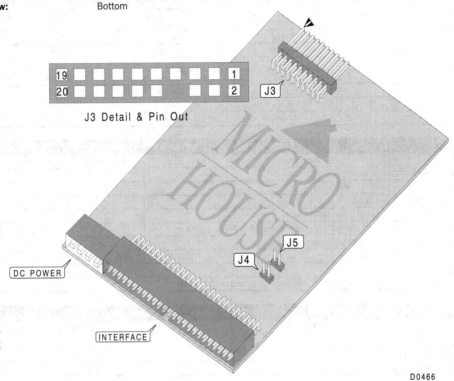

J3 Detail & Pin Out

D0466
Continued on next page . . .

QUANTUM CORPORATION
ATLAS XP SERIES: XP31070S, XP32150S, XP34300S
ATLAS II SERIES: XP32181S, XP34361S, XP39100S

. . . continued from previous page

DRIVE SELECTION - J3			
Drive ID	**Jumper 1**	**Jumper 2**	**Jumper 3**
0	open	open	open
1	closed	open	open
2	open	closed	open
3	closed	closed	open
4	open	open	closed
5	closed	open	closed
6	open	closed	closed
7	closed	closed	closed

USER CONFIGURABLE SETTINGS		
Function	**Location**	**Setting**
Active termination enabled	J4	closed
Active termination disabled	J4	open
TRMPWR supplied to SCSI bus	J5	closed
TRMPWR is not supplied to SCSI bus	J5	open
Spindle motor starts on power-up with delay of SCSI ID x 12 sec.	J3/jumper 7	closed
Spindle motor starts on command only	J3/jumper 7	open
Write protect enabled	J3/jumper 9	closed
Write protect disabled	J3/jumper 9	open
Note: Jumpers not mentioned in this document are unidentified.		

CONNECTIONS	
Function	**Location**
Spindle sync	J3/pins 10 & 19
Remote Busy LED	J3/pins 11 & 9
Remote Fault LED	J3/pins 11 & 7

QUANTUM CORPORATION
ATLAS WIDE SCSI SERIES: XP31070W/WD, XP32150W/WD, XP34300W/WD
ATLAS II SERIES: XP32181W/WD, XP34361W/WD, XP39100W/WD

Interface:	SCSI-2 Fast/Wide (ATLAS "W" models)
	SCSI-2 Fast/Wide/Differential (ATLAS WD models)
	SCSI-3 Wide (ATLAS II "W" models)
	SCSI-3 Wide/Differential (ATLAS II "WD" models)
Size:	3.5 in. third height (XP34300W/WD is half height)
View:	Bottom

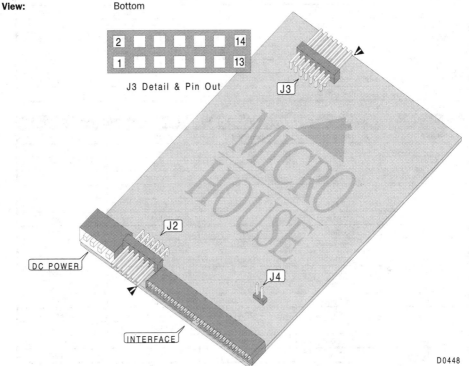

J3 Detail & Pin Out

D0448

USER CONFIGURABLE SETTINGS	
Function	**Location**
Remote Busy LED	J3/pins 11 & 13
Remote Fault LED	J3/pins 13 & 14
Spindle sync connection	J3/pins 5 & 6

Continued on next page . . .

QUANTUM CORPORATION
ATLAS WIDE SCSI SERIES: XP31070W/WD, XP32150W/WD, XP34300W/WD
ATLAS II SERIES: XP32181W/WD, XP34361W/WD, XP39100

. . . continued from previous page

USER CONFIGURABLE SETTINGS		
Function	**Location**	**Setting**
Active termination enabled	J2/jumper 5	closed
Active termination disabled	J2/jumper 5	open
Spindle motor starts on power-up	J3/jumper 1	closed
Spindle motor starts on command only	J3/jumper 1	open
Write protect enabled	J3/jumper 4	closed
Write protect disabled	J3/jumper 4	open
TRMPWR supplied to SCSI bus	J4	closed
TRMPWR is not supplied to SCSI bus	J4	open

DRIVE SELECTION - J2				
Drive ID	**Jumper 1**	**Jumper 2**	**Jumper 3**	**Jumper 4**
0	open	open	open	open
1	closed	open	open	open
2	open	closed	open	open
3	closed	closed	open	open
4	open	open	closed	open
5	closed	open	closed	open
6	open	closed	closed	open
7	closed	closed	closed	open
8	open	open	open	closed
9	closed	open	open	closed
10	open	closed	open	closed
11	closed	closed	open	closed
12	open	open	closed	closed
13	closed	open	closed	closed
14	open	closed	closed	closed
15	closed	closed	closed	closed

MISCELLANEOUS TECHNICAL NOTES
The wide differential drives (WD) do not provide active termination.
TERMPWR jumper (J4) is oriented differently on wide differential drives.
Busy LED & Fault LED can also be connected in J2 jumper block.
All other jumpers and their function are unidentified.

QUANTUM CORPORATION
DSP3053L/LD, 3107L/LD, 3133L/LD, DSP3160, DSP3210

Interface: SCSI-2
Size: 3.5 in. Half/Third Height
View: Bottom

D0491

DRIVE SELECTION - J3			
Drive Number	**Jumper 1**	**Jumper 2**	**Jumper 3**
0	open	open	open
1	closed	open	open
2	open	closed	open
3	closed	closed	open
4	open	open	closed
5	closed	open	closed
6	open	closed	closed
7	closed	closed	closed

Continued on next page . . .

QUANTUM CORPORATION
DSP3053L/LD, 3107L/LD, 3133L/LD, DSP3160, DSP3210

. . . continued from previous page

USER CONFIGURABLE SETTINGS		
Function	**Location**	**Setting**
Spindle motor starts on power-up	J3/Jumper 7	closed
Spindle motor starts on command only	J3/Jumper 7	open
Write protection enabled	J3/Jumper 7	closed
Write protection disabled	J3/Jumper 7	open
Note: Write protection and spindle motor options are not supported simultaneously.		

TERMINATION POWER - J4			
Setting	**Jumper 1**	**Jumper 2**	**Jumper 3**
TERMPWR supplied by drive to SCSI bus, active termination is disabled.	closed	open	open
TERMPWR supplied SCSI bus, active termination is enabled	open	open	closed
TERMPWR supplied by drive to SCSI bus, active termination is enabled.	closed	open	closed
TERMPWR disabled	open	open	open
Note: LD models do not support active termination.			

MISCELLANEOUS TECHNICAL NOTES
(1) Models DSP3160 and DSP3210 are half-height, all other models are third-height.
(2) J4 may be installed as 2, 4, or 6 pin jumper.
(3) All other jumpers and their significance are unidentified.

QUANTUM CORPORATION
DSP3085, DSP3105, DSP3105D

Interface: SCSI-2
Size: 3.5 in. Half Height
View: Bottom

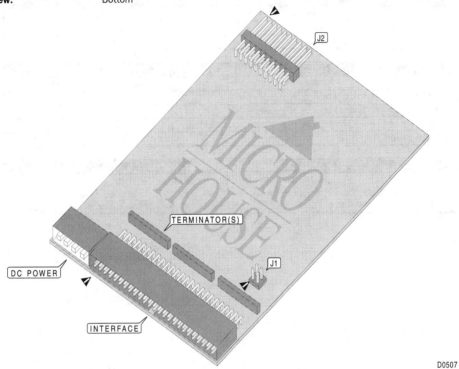

D0507

DRIVE SELECTION - J2			
Drive Number	Jumper 1	Jumper 2	Jumper 3
0	open	open	open
1	closed	open	open
2	open	closed	open
3	closed	closed	open
4	open	open	closed
5	closed	open	closed
6	open	closed	closed
7	closed	closed	closed

Continued on next page . . .

QUANTUM CORPORATION
DSP3085, DSP3105, DSP3105D

. . . continued from previous page

USER CONFIGURABLE SETTINGS		
Function	**Location**	**Setting**
Spindle motor starts on power-up	J2/Jumper 7	closed
Spindle motor starts on command only	J2/Jumper 7	open

TERMINATION POWER		
Setting	**J1/Jumper 1**	**J1/Jumper 2**
TERMPWR supplied by SCSI bus to drive terminators	closed	open
TERMPWR supplied by drive to drive terminators	open	closed
TERMPWR supplied by drive to drive terminators and SCSI bus	closed	closed
TERMPWR disabled	open	open

MISCELLANEOUS TECHNICAL NOTES
All other jumpers and their significance are unidentified.
Jumper block J1 may be a 2-pin jumper on some versions of model DSP 3105D. Closing this jumper will provide TERMPWR to the SCSI bus. Terminating resistors are not present on the DSP 3105D.

QUANTUM CORPORATION
EUROPA 540AT, 810AT, 1080AT

Interface: Fast ATA-2
Size: 2.5 in. forth height (810AT, 1080AT)
     2.5 in. fifth height (540AT)
View: Bottom

D0520

DRIVE CONFIGURATION			
Selection	**CS**	**DS**	**SP**
Single drive in a system	open	closed	open
Master drive when slave does not support PDIAG/DASP	open	closed	closed
Slave drive in a system	open	open	open
Master/slave is configured by cable select	closed	open	open

QUANTUM CORPORATION
LIGHTNING 365AT, 540AT, 730AT
MAVERICK 270AT, 540AT
PRODRIVE ELS 42AT, 85AT, 127AT, 170AT
PRODRIVE LPS 120AT, 127AT, 170AT, 210AT, 240AT, 270AT, 340AT, 420AT, 540AT

Interface:	IDE(AT)
Size:	3.5 in. half height
	3.5 in. third height (LPS)
View:	Bottom

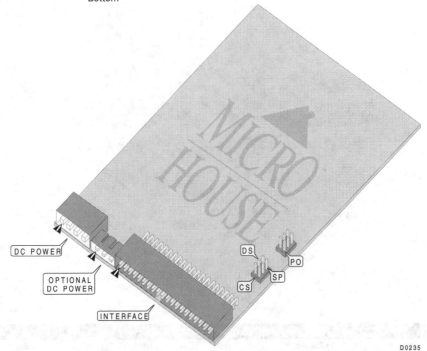

D0235

DRIVE CONFIGURATION		
Selection	**DS**	**SP**
⇨ Single drive only	closed	open
Master drive in a two drive system	closed	closed
Slave drive in a two drive system	open	open
Note:When Jumper SP is "closed" in Slave mode the drive will perform a selftest in seek mode.		

USER CONFIGURABLE SETTINGS		
Function	**Location**	**Setting**
⇨ Drive order is set by jumpers DS & SP.	CS	open
Drive order is set by pin 28 of the AT interface.	CS	closed

MISCELLANEOUS TECHNICAL NOTES
Note: PO is a product options set of jumpers and are not used. ELS drives do not have this jumper.

QUANTUM CORPORATION
PRODRIVE 40S, 52S, 80S, 105S, 120S, 170S, 210S, 330S, 425S, 425IS
PRODRIVE LPS 52S, 80S, 105S, 120S, 240S
PRODRIVE LIGHTNING 365S, 540S, 730S

Interface: 40, 52, 80, and 105S are SCSI-1 hard drives
120, 170, 210, 330, 425S, 425iS and LPS models are SCSI-2 hard drives

Size: 3.5 in. half height
3.5 in. third height (LPS)

View: Bottom

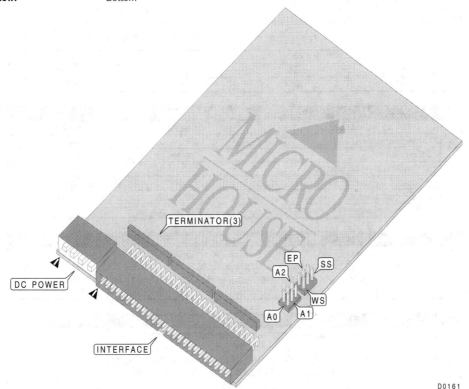

D0161

Continued on next page . . .

QUANTUM CORPORATION
PRODRIVE 40S, 52S, 80S, 105S, 120S, 170S, 210S, 330S, 425S, 425IS
PRODRIVE LPS 52S, 80S, 105S, 120S, 240S
PRODRIVE LIGHTNING 365S, 540S, 730S

. . . continued from previous page

DRIVE SELECTION			
Drive Number	**Jumper A0**	**Jumper A1**	**Jumper A2**
◇ 6	open	closed	closed
0	open	open	open
1	closed	open	open
2	open	closed	open
3	closed	closed	open
4	open	open	closed
5	closed	open	closed
7	closed	closed	closed

USER CONFIGURABLE SETTINGS		
Function	**Location**	**Setting**
◇ SCSI parity check enabled	Jumper EP	closed
SCSI parity check disabled	Jumper EP	open
◇ Normal operation mode enabled	Jumper SS	open
Self Seek Test mode enabled	Jumper SS	closed
◇ Spindle motor starts on power-up	Jumper WS	open
Spindle motor starts on command only	Jumper WS	closed

MISCELLANEOUS TECHNICAL NOTES	
Note:	When you enable the Self Seek Test and Drive #6 is selected a random seek pattern will be performed until power is removed. If any other SCSI ID # is selected, the drive will perform a butterfly seek pattern with a single track seek at the middle cylinder and extend out to a full stroke seek.

MISCELLANEOUS TECHNICAL NOTES(CONTINUED)	
Note:	The following models have jumper A0-A2 oriented toward the front of the drive: ProDrive LPS 120S, LPS 240S.
Note:	The following models have jumper A0-A2 oriented toward the back of the drive: ProDrive 40S, LPS 52S, 80S, LPS 80S, LPS 105S, 120S, 170S, 210S, 425S, 425iS.
Note:	The following models may have jumper WS labeled as "PO"–setting this jumper in the closed positon enables the functions of the EP and SS jumpers. Leaving the "PO" jumper in the open position disables the functions of these jumpers: ProDrive LPS 270S, 540S, Lightning 365S, 540S, and 730S.

QUANTUM CORPORATION
VP31110W/WD, VP32210W/WD
(CAPELLA WIDE SCSI SERIES)

Interface: SCSI-2 F/W/D
Size: 3.5 in. third height
View: Bottom

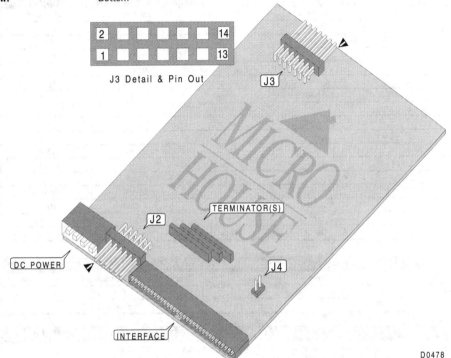

J3 Detail & Pin Out

D0478

USER CONFIGURABLE SETTINGS		
Function	**Location**	**Setting**
Active termination enabled	J2/jumper 5	closed
Active termination disabled	J2/jumper 5	open
Spindle motor starts on power-up	J3/jumper 1	closed
Spindle motor starts on command only	J3/jumper 1	open
TRMPWR supplied to SCSI bus	J4	closed
TRMPWR is not supplied to SCSI bus	J4	open
Drive is first or last drive in chain	terminators	installed
Drive is not first or last drive in chain	terminators	removed

Continued on next page . . .

QUANTUM CORPORATION
VP3111OW/WD, VP32210W/WD
(CAPELLA WIDE SCSI SERIES)

. . . continued from previous page

DRIVE SELECTION - J2				
Drive ID	Jumper 1	Jumper 2	Jumper 3	Jumper 4
0	open	open	open	open
1	closed	open	open	open
2	open	closed	open	open
3	closed	closed	open	open
4	open	open	closed	open
5	closed	open	closed	open
6	open	closed	closed	open
7	closed	closed	closed	open
8	open	open	open	closed
9	closed	open	open	closed
10	open	closed	open	closed
11	closed	closed	open	closed
12	open	open	closed	closed
13	closed	open	closed	closed
14	open	closed	closed	closed
15	closed	closed	closed	closed

USER CONFIGURABLE SETTINGS	
Function	Location
Remote Busy LED	J3/pins 11 & 13
Remote Fault LED	J3/pins 13 & 14

MISCELLANEOUS TECHNICAL NOTES
The wide differential drives (WD) do not provide active termination.
Busy LED & Fault LED can also be connected in J2 jumper block.
All other jumpers and their function are unidentified.

SAMSUNG ELECTRONICS, INC.
PLS-30854A, PLS-31084A, PLS-31274A

Interface: EIDE
Size: 3.5 in. third height
View: Bottom

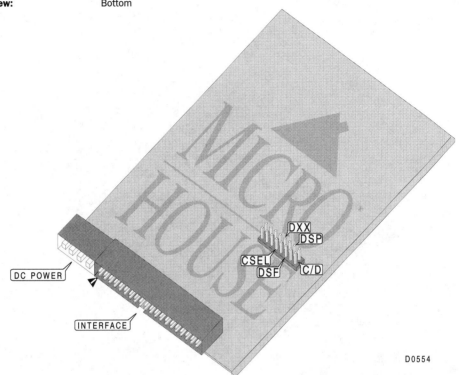

D0554

DRIVE CONFIGURATION	
Selection	**C/D**
⇨ Single drive only	closed
Master drive in a two drive system	closed
Slave drive in a two drive system	open
Note: The rest of the jumpers are factory configured - do not alter.	

SAMSUNG ELECTRONICS, INC.
PLS-30854S, PLS-31084S, PLS-31274S

Interface:	SCSI-2 , Fast SCSI-2 (PLS-30854S)
Size:	3.5 in. third height
View:	Bottom

D0555

DRIVE CONFIGURATION	
Selection	**C/D**
⇨ Single drive only	closed
Master drive in a two drive system	closed
Slave drive in a two drive system	open
Note: The rest of the jumpers are factory configured - do not alter.	

SAMSUNG ELECTRONICS, INC.

SHD-30280A, SHD-30420A, SHD-30560A, SHD-3171A, SHD-3171A1, SHD-3172A, SHD-3172A1, SHD-3211A, SHD-3212A

Interface:	IDE (AT)
Size:	3.5 in. Third Height
View:	Bottom

D0330

DRIVE CONFIGURATION		
Selection	**C/D**	**DSP**
⇨ Single drive only	closed	open
Master drive in a two drive system	closed	closed
Slave drive in a two drive system	open	open

FACTORY CONFIGURED - DO NOT ALTER	
Jumper	**Setting**
RES1	open
RES2	open

SAMSUNG ELECTRONICS, INC.
STG-31271A, STG-31601A

Interface: IDE (AT)
Size: 3.5 in. Third Height
View: Bottom

D0590

DRIVE CONFIGURATION		
Setting	**JP1/Jumper 1**	**JP1/Jumper 2**
Single drive only	Closed	Open
Drive is slave in a two drive system	Open	Open
Master/Slave determined by Cable Select	Open	Closed

USER CONFIGURABLE SETTINGS		
Function	**Label**	**Position**
Jumper information not available	JP1/jumper 3	Unidentified
Jumper information not available	JP1/jumper 4	Unidentified

SAMSUNG ELECTRONICS, INC.
TBR-31081A

Interface:	IDE (AT)
Size:	3.5 in. Third Height
View:	Bottom

D0589

DRIVE CONFIGURATION		
Setting	**JP1/Jumper 1**	**JP1/Jumper 2**
Single drive only	Closed	Open
Drive is master when slave uses DASP signal	Closed	Open
Drive is master when slave does not use DASP signal	Closed	Closed
Drive is slave in a two drive system	Open	Open

USER CONFIGURABLE SETTINGS		
Function	**Label**	**Position**
Jumper information not available	JP1/jumper 3	Unidentified
Jumper information not available	JP1/jumper 4	Unidentified

SEAGATE TECHNOLOGY, INC.

ST11200N, ST11200ND, ST11201N, ST11201ND, ST11700N, ST11700ND, ST11900N, ST11900ND, ST12400N, ST12400ND, ST1830N, ST1950N, ST1980N, ST1980ND, ST3500N, ST3600N, ST3600ND, ST3610N, ST3610ND

Interface:	SCSI-2
Size:	3.5 in. half height (ST1xxxN)
	3.5 in. third height (ST3xxxN)
View:	Bottom

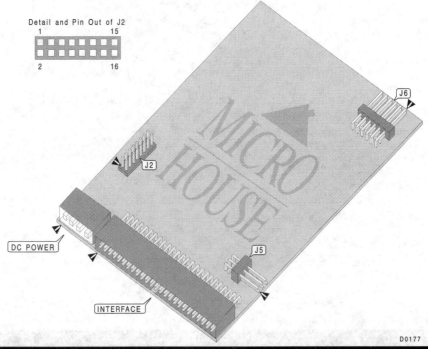

D0177

DRIVE SELECTION - J5			
Drive Number	**Jumper 1**	**Jumper 2**	**Jumper 3**
0	open	open	open
1	closed	open	open
2	open	closed	open
3	closed	closed	open
4	open	open	closed
5	closed	open	closed
6	open	closed	closed
7	closed	closed	closed

CONNECTIONS	
Purpose	**Location**
External Spindle Sync	J6/pins 5 & 6
Hard drive active LED	J6/pins 3 & 4

Continued on next page . . .

SEAGATE TECHNOLOGY, INC.
ST11200N, ST11200ND, ST11201N, ST11201ND, ST11700N, ST11700ND, ST11900N, ST11900ND, ST12400N, ST12400ND, ST1830N, ST1950N, ST1980N, ST1980ND, ST3500N, ST3600N, ST3600ND, ST3610N, ST3610ND

. . . continued from previous page

DRIVE SELECTION - J5			
Drive Number	Jumper 1	Jumper 2	Jumper 3
0	open	open	open
1	open	open	closed
2	open	closed	open
3	open	closed	closed
4	closed	open	open
5	closed	open	closed
6	closed	closed	open
7	closed	closed	closed

Note: This table applies to ST1980N, ST11200N, and ST3500N/ST3600N with PCB# 75782480 only. Use the table on the previous page for any other PCB#.

USER CONFIGURABLE SETTINGS		
Function	Location	Setting
⇨ Drive termination enabled	J2/jumper 3	closed
Drive termination disabled	J2/jumper 3	open
⇨ SCSI parity check disabled	J2/jumper 4	open
SCSI parity check enabled	J2/jumper 4	closed
⇨ Write protect disabled	J2/jumper 5	open
Write protect enabled	J2/jumper 5	closed
⇨ Spindle motor starts on power-up	J2/jumper 6	open
Spindle motor starts on command only	J2/jumper 6	closed
⇨ Spindle motor delay disabled	J2/jumper 7	open
Spindle motor delay enabled (ID x 12 sec.)	J2/jumper 7	closed
⇨ Factory configured-do not alter	J2/jumper 8	open

TERMINATION POWER SETTINGS			
Function	J2/jumper 1	J2/jumper 2	J2/pins 2 & 4
⇨ TERMPWR supplied by drive to drive	open	closed	N/A
TERMPWR supplied by drive to SCSI pin 26	closed	open	N/A
TERMPWR supplied by drive to drive and SCSI pin 26	closed	closed	N/A
TERMPWR is not connected to drive or SCSI bus	open	open	N/A
TERMPWR supplied by SCSI pin 26 to drive	N/A	N/A	closed

MISCELLANEOUS TECHNICAL NOTES
Spindle motor starts on power-up and Spindle motor start delay enabled are mutually exclusive. SCSI I.D. may also be set using J6/jumpers 4, 5, and 6. These Jumpers perform the same function and are mutually exclusive with J5/jumpers 1, 2, and 3.

SEAGATE TECHNOLOGY, INC.
ST11950N, ST11950ND, ST12550N, ST12550ND

Interface: SCSI-2
Size: 3.5 in. Half Height
View: Bottom

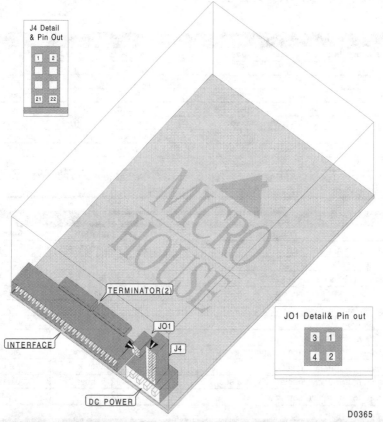

D0365

DRIVE CONFIGURATION - J4			
Drive Number	**Jumper 9**	**Jumper 10**	**Jumper 11**
0	open	open	open
1	closed	open	open
2	open	closed	open
3	closed	closed	open
4	open	open	closed
5	closed	open	closed

Continued on next page . . .

SEAGATE TECHNOLOGY, INC.
ST11950N, ST11950ND, ST12550N, ST12550ND

... continued from previous page

DRIVE CONFIGURATION - J4			
Drive Number	Jumper 9	Jumper 10	Jumper 11
6	open	closed	closed
7	closed	closed	closed

TERMINATION POWER SETTINGS	
Function	J01
⇨ TERMPWR supplied by drive *	pins 1 & 2 closed
TERMPWR supplied by SCSI bus *	pins 2 & 4 closed
TERMPWR supplied to SCSI bus	pins 1 & 3 closed
TERMPWR supplied to SCSI bus and drive *	pins 1 & 3, 2 & 4 closed

Note: * These settings are valid for single-ended (N-type) drives only. Settings without an asterisk apply to ND-type drives.

USER CONFIGURABLE SETTINGS		
Function	Location	Setting
⇨ Factory configured - do not alter	J4/jumper 2	closed
⇨ Write protection disabled	J4/jumper 4	open
Write protection enabled	J4/jumper 4	closed
⇨ Delay motor start disabled	J4/jumper 5	open
Delay motor start enabled (target ID x 10sec.)	J4/jumper 5	closed
⇨ Spindle motor starts on power-up	J4/jumper 6	open
Spindle motor starts on command only	J4/jumper 6	closed
⇨ Parity check enabled	J4/jumper 7	open
Parity check disabled	J4/jumper 7	closed
⇨ Factory configured - do not alter	J4/jumper 8	closed

CONNECTIONS	
Function	Location
Remote LED connector	J4/jumper 3
Spindle sync	J4/jumper 1

SEAGATE TECHNOLOGY, INC.
ST11950W, ST11950WD, ST12550W, ST12550WD

Interface: SCSI-2
Size: 3.5 in. Half Height
View: Top

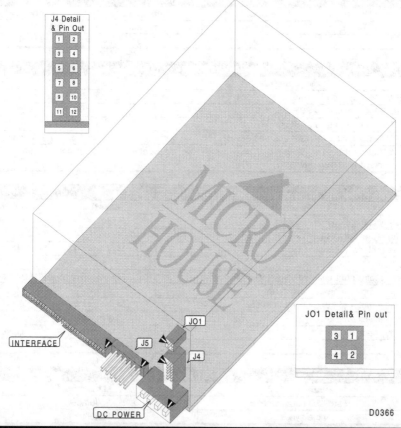

D0366

DRIVE CONFIGURATION - J5				
Drive Number	Jumper 1	Jumper 2	Jumper 3	Jumper 4
0	open	open	open	open
1	closed	open	open	open
2	open	closed	open	open
3	closed	closed	open	open
4	open	open	closed	open
5	closed	open	closed	open

Continued on next page . . .

SEAGATE TECHNOLOGY, INC.
ST11950W, ST11950WD, ST12550W, ST12550WD

. . . continued from previous page

DRIVE CONFIGURATION - J4				
Drive Number	**Jumper 1**	**Jumper 2**	**Jumper 3**	**Jumper 4**
6	open	closed	closed	open
7	closed	closed	closed	open
8	open	open	open	closed
9	closed	open	open	closed
10	open	closed	open	closed
11	closed	closed	open	closed
12	open	open	closed	closed
13	closed	open	closed	closed
14	open	closed	closed	closed
15	closed	closed	closed	closed

TERMINATION POWER SETTINGS	
Function	**J01**
⇨ TERMPWR supplied by drive *	pins 1 & 2 closed
TERMPWR supplied by SCSI bus	pins 2 & 4 closed
TERMPWR supplied to SCSI bus *	pins 1 & 3 closed
TERMPWR supplied to SCSI bus and drive *	pins 1 & 3, 2 & 4 closed

Note: * These settings are valid for single-ended drives only (W models).

USER CONFIGURABLE SETTINGS		
Function	**Location**	**Setting**
⇨ Write protection disabled	J4/jumper 1	open
Write protection enabled	J4/jumper 1	closed
⇨ Delay motor start disabled	J4/jumper 2	open
Delay motor start enabled (target ID x 10sec.)	J4/jumper 2	closed
⇨ Spindle motor starts on power-up	J4/jumper 3	open
Target waits for Start Unit command from SCSI host	J4/jumper 3	closed
⇨ Parity check enabled	J4/jumper 4	open
Parity check disabled	J4/jumper 4	closed
⇨ Factory configured - do not alter	J4/jumper 5	closed
⇨ Drive terminators disabled*	J4/jumper 6	open
Drive terminators enabled*	J4/jumper 6	closed

Note: * These settings are valid for single-ended drives only (W models).

CONNECTIONS	
Function	**Location**
Remote LED connector	J5/jumper 5
Spindle sync	J5/jumper 6

SEAGATE TECHNOLOGY, INC.
ST1400A, ST1401A, ST1480A
4-PIN J6 VERSION

Interface: IDE(AT)
Size: 3.5 in. half height
View: Bottom

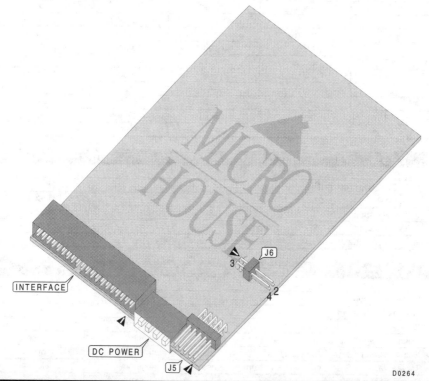

D0264

DRIVE CONFIGURATION - J5		
Selection	**Jumper 3**	**Jumper 4**
⇨ Single drive only	closed	open
Master drive in a two drive system	closed	closed
Slave drive in a two drive system	open	open

USER CONFIGURABLE SETTINGS		
Function	**Location**	**Setting**
Host/Slave Present signal output on interface pin 39	J5/jumper 2	closed
⇨ Drive Active signal output on interface pin 39	J5/jumper 5	closed
⇨ Factory configured - do not alter	J6	pins 1 & 2 open
Note:J5, Jumper 2 and Jumper 5 are mutually exclusive.		

CONNECTIONS	
Function	**Location**
External Spindle Sync	J5/jumper 1
Hard drive active LED	J6/pins 3 & 4

SEAGATE TECHNOLOGY INC.
ST1400A, ST1401A, ST1480A, ST3500A, ST3600A
6-PIN J6 VERSION

Interface: IDE(AT)
Size: 3.5 in. half height (ST14xxA)
3.5 in. third height (ST3xxxA)
View: Bottom

DRIVE CONFIGURATION - J5		
Selection	**Pins 8 & 10**	**Pins 9 & 10**
➪ Single drive only	open	closed
Master drive in a two drive system	closed	open
Slave drive in a two drive system	open	open

CONNECTIONS	
Function	**Location**
External Spindle Sync	J5/pins 3 & 4
Hard drive active LED	J6/Jumper 3

USER CONFIGURABLE SETTINGS		
Function	**Location**	**Setting**
SPSYNC signal enabled on interface pin 28	J5	pins 1 & 3 closed
SPSYNC signal enabled on interface pin 39	J5	pins 3 & 5 closed
➪ Drive Active Signal output on interface pin 39	J5	pins 5 & 6 closed
Host/Slave Present signal output on interface pin 39	J5	pins 5 & 7 closed
➪ Factory configured - do not alter	J6/Jumper 1	open
➪ I/O Channel Ready signal disabled	J6/Jumper 2	open
I/O Channel Ready signal enabled	J6/Jumper 2	closed

SEAGATE TECHNOLOGY, INC.

ST1400N, ST1401N, ST1480N, ST1480NV, ST1481N, ST1581N

Interface: SCSI
Size: 3.5 in. half height
View: Top

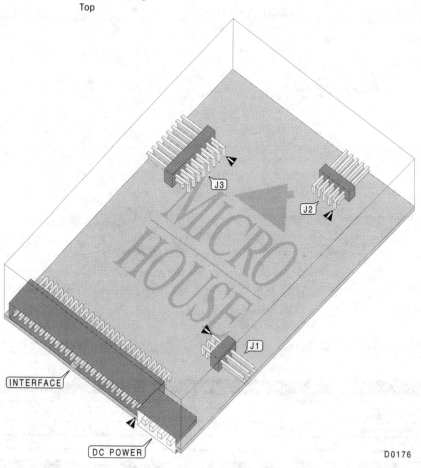

D0176

Continued on next page . . .

SEAGATE TECHNOLOGY, INC.
ST1400N, ST1401N, ST1480N, ST1480NV, ST1481N, ST1581N

. . . continued from previous page

DRIVE SELECTION - J1			
Drive Number	Jumper 1	Jumper 2	Jumper 3
0	open	open	open
1	closed	open	open
2	open	closed	open
3	closed	closed	open
4	open	open	closed
5	closed	open	closed
6	open	closed	closed

DRIVE SELECTION - J1			
Drive Number	Jumper 1	Jumper 2	Jumper 3
7	closed	closed	closed
Note: J2/jumpers 1, 2 & 3 perform the same function and are mutually exclusive with this table.			

USER CONFIGURABLE SETTINGS		
Function	Location	Setting
⇨ SPSYNC signal disabled	J2/jumper 4	open
SPSYNC signal enabled on interface pin 28	J2/jumper 4	closed
⇨ Write protect disabled	J3/jumper 4	open
Write protect enabled	J3/jumper 4	closed
⇨ SCSI parity check disabled	J3/jumper 5	open
SCSI parity check enabled	J3/jumper 5	closed

SPINDLE MOTOR OPTION SETTINGS		
Function	J3/jumper 2	J3/jumper 3
⇨ Spindle motor starts on power-up	open	open
Spindle motor starts on command only	closed	open
Spindle motor starts delayed (16 sec. x Drive I.D. #)	open	closed

TERMINATION POWER SETTINGS	
Function	J3
TERMPWR supplied by drive to SCSI Interface pin 26	pins 13 & 14 closed
TERMPWR supplied by drive	pins 15 & 16 closed
TERMPWR supplied by the SCSI Interface pin 26	pins 14 & 16 closed

CONNECTIONS	
Function	Location
External LED	J2/jumper 5

MISCELLANEOUS TECHNICAL NOTES
J3/jumper 1 and 6 are reserved for Factory tests and should remain "open".

SEAGATE TECHNOLOGY, INC.
ST15230W/WD, ST31230W/WD, ST32430W/WD

Interface: SCSI-2 Fast Wide
Size: 3.5 in. third height
View: Bottom

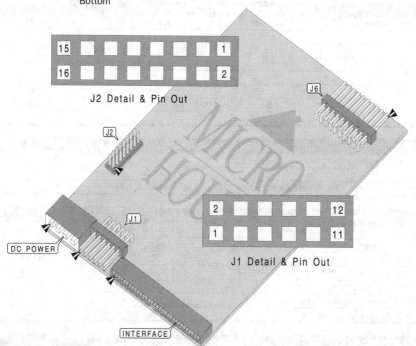

J2 Detail & Pin Out

J1 Detail & Pin Out

D0443

DRIVE SELECTION - J1				
SCSI ID Number	**Jumper 1**	**Jumper 2**	**Jumper 3**	**Jumper 4**
0	open	open	open	open
1	closed	open	open	open
2	open	closed	open	open
3	closed	closed	open	open
4	open	open	closed	open
5	closed	open	closed	open
6	open	closed	closed	open
7	closed	closed	closed	open
8	open	open	open	closed

Continued on next page . . .

SEAGATE TECHNOLOGY, INC.
ST15230W/WD, ST31230W/WD, ST32430W/WD

. . . continued from previous page

DRIVE SELECTION - J1 (CONTINUED)				
SCSI ID Number	Jumper 1	Jumper 2	Jumper 3	Jumper 4
9	closed	open	open	closed
10	open	closed	open	closed
11	closed	closed	open	closed
12	open	open	closed	closed
13	closed	open	closed	closed
14	open	closed	closed	closed
15	closed	closed	closed	closed

USER CONFIGURABLE SETTINGS		
Function	Location	Setting
⇨ Factory configured - do not alter	J1/Jumper 5	open
⇨ Factory configured - do not alter	J1/Jumper 6	open
⇨ Factory configured - do not alter	J2/Jumper 3	open
⇨ SCSI parity check enabled	J2/Jumper 4	closed
SCSI parity check disabled	J2/Jumper 4	open
⇨ Write protect disabled	J2/Jumper 5	open
Write protect enabled	J2/Jumper 5	closed
⇨ Terminating resistors enabled ("W" models only)	J2/Jumper 8	closed
Terminating resistors disabled ("W" models only)	J2/Jumper 8	open
⇨ Factory configured - do not alter ("WD" models only)	J2/Jumper 8	N/A

SPINDLE MOTOR OPTIONS - J2		
Function	Jumper 6	Jumper 7
⇨ Spindle motor starts on power up	open	open
Spindle motor starts on command only	closed	open
Spindle motor delay enabled (SCSI ID x 12 sec.)	open	closed
Spindle motor delay disabled	closed	closed

TERMINATION POWER - J2		
Setting	Jumper 1	Jumper 2
⇨ TERMPWR supplied by drive to drive	open	closed
TERMPWR supplied by drive to SCSI pin 26	closed	open
TERMPWR supplied by drive to drive and to SCSI pin 26	closed	closed
TERMPWR not connected to drive or SCSI pin 26	open	open
TERMPWR supplied by SCSI bus pin 26 to drive ("W" models only)	pins 2 & 4 closed	
Note: For 15230W/WD the SCSI bus TERMPWR pins are 17, 18, 51 & 52.		

CONNECTIONS	
Function	Location
Remote LED connection	J1/pins 8 & 11

MISCELLANEOUS TECHNICAL NOTES
J1 & J6 are mutually exclusive. When configuring the drive with J1, do not alter J6. Same settings and pin-out apply for both jumpers.
J6 jumpers 7-10 are shipped with cover installed. Do not remove cover or install jumpers.11

SEAGATE TECHNOLOGY, INC.
ST31051N, ST31055N, ST32151N, ST32155N

Interface:	SCSI-2 (Ultra/ASA II)
Size:	3.5 in. third height
View:	Bottom

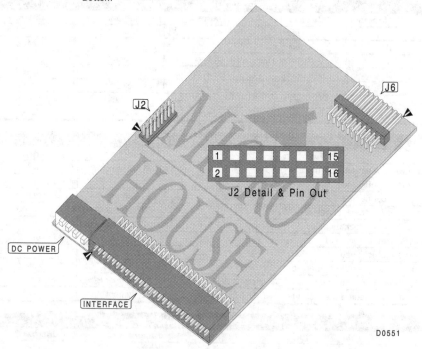

J2 Detail & Pin Out

D0551

DRIVE CONFIGURATION -J6			
Drive Number	**Jumper 1**	**Jumper 2**	**Jumper 3**
0	open	open	open
1	closed	open	open
2	open	closed	open
3	closed	closed	open
4	open	open	closed
5	closed	open	closed
6	open	closed	closed
7	closed	closed	closed

Continued on next page . . .

SEAGATE TECHNOLOGY, INC.
ST31051N, ST31055N, ST32151N, ST32155N

. . . continued from previous page

USER CONFIGURABLE SETTINGS		
Function	**Location**	**Setting**
➪ Factory configured - do not alter	J2/jumper 3	N/A
➪ SCSI parity check disabled	J2/jumper 4	closed
SCSI parity check enabled	J2/jumper 4	open
➪ Write protect disabled	J2/jumper 5	open
Write protect enabled	J2/jumper 5	closed
➪ Spindle motor starts on power-up	J2/jumper 6	open
Spindle motor starts on command only	J2/jumper 6	closed
➪ Spindle motor start delay disabled	J2/jumper 7	open
Spindle motor start delay enabled (12sec x SCSI ID)	J2/jumper 7	closed
➪ Termination power enabled	J2/jumper 8	closed
Termination power disabled	J2/jumper 8	open
➪ Factory configured - do not alter	J6/jumper 4	N/A
➪ Factory configured - do not alter	J6/jumper 5	N/A
➪ Factory configured - do not alter	J6/jumpers 7-10	N/A

TERMINATION POWER SETTINGS - J2		
Function	**Jumper 1**	**Jumper 2**
➪ TERMPWR supplied by drive	open	closed
TERMPWR supplied by drive to SCSI interface	closed	open
TERMPWR supplied by SCSI interface	pins 2 & 4 closed	

CONNECTIONS	
Function	**Location**
Remote LED	J6/jumper 6

SEAGATE TECHNOLOGY, INC.
ST31200N/ND

Interface: SCSI-2
Size: 3.5 in. third height
View: Bottom

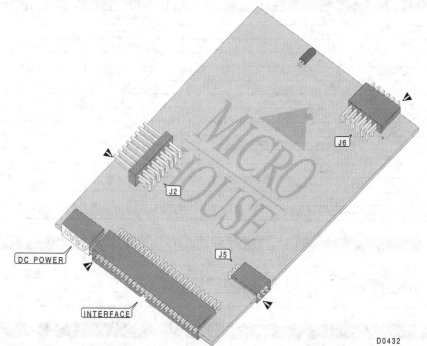

D0432

DRIVE SELECTION - J6			
SCSI ID Number	**Jumper 4**	**Jumper 5**	**Jumper 6**
0	open	open	open
1	closed	open	open
2	open	closed	open
4	open	open	closed

USER CONFIGURABLE SETTINGS		
Function	**Location**	**Setting**
▷ Terminating resistor enabled	J2/Jumper 3	closed
Terminating resistor disabled	J2/Jumper 3	open

Continued on next page . . .

SEAGATE TECHNOLOGY, INC.
ST31200N/ND

. . . continued from previous page

USER CONFIGURABLE SETTINGS		
Function	**Location**	**Setting**
⇨ SCSI parity check enabled	J2/Jumper 4	closed
SCSI parity check disabled	J2/Jumper 4	open
⇨ Write protect enabled	J2/Jumper 5	closed
Write protect disabled	J2/Jumper 5	open
⇨ Factory configured - do not alter	J2/Jumper 8	N/A
⇨ Factory configured - do not alter	J6/Jumper 1	N/A

SPINDLE MOTOR OPTION SETTINGS		
Function	**J2/Jumper 6**	**J2/Jumper 7**
⇨ Spindle motor starts on power-up	open	N/A
Spindle motor starts on command only	closed	N/A
Spindle motor start delayed (12 sec. x Drive I.D. #)	N/A	open
Spindle motor start delayed disabled	N/A	closed

TERMINATION POWER SETTINGS - J2		
Function	**Jumper 1**	**Jumper 2**
⇨ TERMPWR supplied by drive	open	closed
TERMPWR supplied by bus	closed	open
TERMPWR supplied by bus to drive	bottom pins closed horizontally	

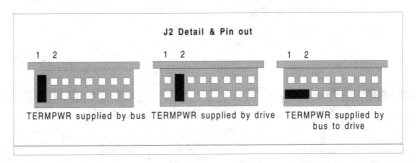

J2 Detail & Pin out

TERMPWR supplied by bus   TERMPWR supplied by drive   TERMPWR supplied by bus to drive

MISCELLANEOUS TECHNICAL NOTES
Note: J5 & J6 are mutually exclusive. When configuring the drive with J6, do not alter J5.

SEAGATE TECHNOLOGY, INC.
ST31220A (VERSION 2), ST3780A

Interface: IDE (AT)
Size: 3.5 in. third height
View: Bottom

D0503

DRIVE CONFIGURATION - J8			
Setting	**Jumper 1**	**Jumper 2**	**Jumper 3**
▷ Single drive system	open	open	open
Drive is master in a two drive system	open	closed	open
Drive is slave in a two drive system	closed	open	open
Drive is slave in a two-drive system when drive is not ST3780A or 31220A	closed	open	closed

Continued on next page . . .

SEAGATE TECHNOLOGY, INC.
ST31220A (VERSION 2), ST3780A

. . . continued from previous page

USER CONFIGURABLE SETTINGS		
Function	**Location**	**Setting**
⇨ Cable select disabled	J8/jumpers 1 & 2	open
Cable select enabled	J8/jumpers 1 & 2	closed
⇨ Dual drive emulation mode disabled	J8/jumpers 3 & 6	open
Dual drive emulation mode enabled	J8/jumpers 3 & 6	closed
⇨ Factory configured - do not alter	J8/jumper 4	open
⇨ Factory configured - do not alter	J8/jumper 5	open

CONNECTIONS	
Function	**Location**
Remote LED connection	J8/jumper 7

MISCELLANEOUS TECHNICAL NOTES
(1) When the drive is configured to support dual-drive emulation, both emulated drives respond as one to any power-management command.
(2) Dual drive emulation and cable select cannot be enabled simultaneously.
(3) Dual drive emulation cannot be enabled with a second, physical drive.

SEAGATE TECHNOLOGY, INC.
ST31230N/ND, ST31231N, ST32430N/ND

Interface: SCSI-2 Fast ("ND" models are Differential)
Size: 3.5 in. third height
View: Bottom

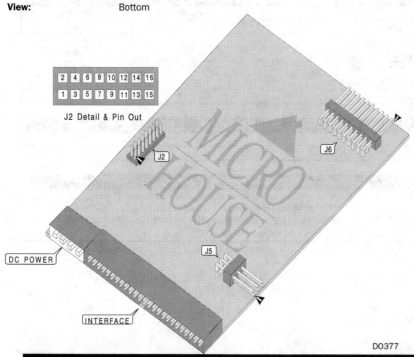

J2 Detail & Pin Out

DC POWER

INTERFACE

DO377

DRIVE ID SELECTION			
SCSI ID	J6/Jumper 4	J6/Jumper 5	J6/Jumper 6
0	open	open	open
1	closed	open	open
2	open	closed	open
3	closed	closed	open
4	open	open	closed
5	closed	open	closed
6	open	closed	closed
7	closed	closed	closed

Note: J5 can be used for drive selection as well. J5/jumper 1 takes the same settings as J6/jumper 6, J5/jumper 2 is same as J6/jumper 5 and J5/jumper 3 is same as J6/jumper 4. Do not use both J6 & J5 at the same time.

Continued on next page. . .

SAMSUNG ELECTRONICS, INC.
ST31230N/ND, ST31231N, ST32430N/ND

. . .continued from previous page

USER CONFIGURABLE SETTINGS		
Function	**Location**	**Setting**
⇨ Factory configured - do not alter	J2/jumper 3	open
⇨ SCSI parity check enabled	J2/jumper 4	closed
SCSI parity check disabled	J2/jumper 4	open
⇨ Write protection disabled	J2/Jumper 5	open
Write protection enabled	J2/jumper 5	closed
⇨ Drive termination enabled ("N" models only)	J2/jumper 8	closed
Drive termination disabled ("N" models only)	J2/jumper 8	open
⇨ Factory configured - do not alter	J6/jumper 1	unidentified
⇨ Factory configured - do not alter	J6/jumper 3	unidentified
⇨ Factory configured - do not alter	J6/jumper 7	open
⇨ Factory configured - do not alter	J6/jumper 8	open
⇨ Factory configured - do not alter	J6/jumper 9	open
⇨ Factory configured - do not alter	J6/jumper 10	open
Note: J6/jumpers 7-10 come from the factory with a cover installed - do not remove.		

SPINDLE MOTOR CONFIGURATION		
Function	**J2/Jumper 6**	**J2/Jumper 7**
⇨ Spindle motor starts on power-up	open	open
Spindle motor starts on command only	closed	open
Spindle startup is delayed by SCSI ID x 12 sec	open	closed
Spindle starts on command without delay	closed	closed

TERMINATION POWER ("N" MODELS ONLY)		
Setting	**J2/Jumper 1**	**J2/Jumper 2**
⇨ TERMPWR supplied by drive to drive	open	closed
TERMPWR supplied by drive to SCSI pin 26	closed	open
TERMPWR supplied to drive by drive and to SCSI pin 26	closed	closed
TERMPWR not connected to drive or SCSI pin 26	open	open
TERMPWR supplied by SCSI bus pin 26	pins 2 & 4 closed	
Note: For differential models, J2/jumper 1 may need to be installed to enable external termination.		

CONNECTIONS	
Function	**Location**
Hard drive active LED	J6/jumper 2

SEAGATE TECHNOLOGY, INC.
ST31250DC/WC, ST32550DC/WC

Interface: SCSI-2 Fast
Size: 3.5 in. third height
View: Bottom

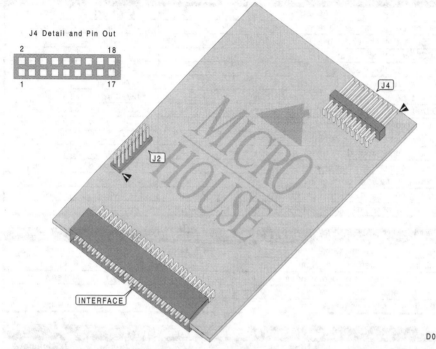

J4 Detail and Pin Out

D0497

DRIVE SELECTION - J4				
SCSI ID Number	**Jumper 1**	**Jumper 2**	**Jumper 3**	**Jumper 4**
⇨ 0	open	open	open	open
1	closed	open	open	open
2	open	closed	open	open
3	closed	closed	open	open
4	open	open	closed	open
5	closed	open	closed	open
6	open	closed	closed	open
7	closed	closed	closed	open
8	open	open	open	closed

Continued on next page. . .

SEAGATE TECHNOLOGY, INC.
ST31250DC/WC, ST32550DC/WC

. . .continued from previous page

DRIVE SELECTION - J4 (CONTINUED)				
SCSI ID Number	Jumper 1	Jumper 2	Jumper 3	Jumper 4
9	closed	open	open	closed
10	open	closed	open	closed
11	closed	closed	open	closed
12	open	open	closed	closed
13	closed	open	closed	closed
14	open	closed	closed	closed
15	closed	closed	closed	closed

USER CONFIGURABLE SETTINGS		
Function	Location	Setting
⇨ Factory configured-do not alter	J2/jumper 1	N/A
⇨ Factory configured-do not alter	J2/jumper 2	N/A
⇨ SCSI parity check enabled	J2/jumper 3	open
SCSI parity check disabled	J2/jumper 3	closed
⇨ Write protect disabled	J2/jumper 4	open
Write protect enabled	J2/jumper 4	closed
⇨ Spindle motor starts on power-up	J2/jumper 5	open
Spindle motor starts on command only	J2/jumper 5	closed
⇨ Spindle motor delay disabled	J2/jumper 6	open
Spindle motor delay enabled (10 sec. X SCSI ID)	J2/jumper 6	closed
⇨ Factory configured-do not alter	J2/jumper 7	N/A
⇨ Factory configured-do not alter	J2/jumper 9	N/A
⇨ Factory configured-do not alter	J2/jumper 8	N/A
⇨ Factory configured-do not alter	J4/jumper 5	N/A
⇨ Factory configured-do not alter	J4/jumper 6	N/A
⇨ Factory configured-do not alter	J4/jumper 7	N/A
⇨ Factory configured-do not alter	J4/jumper 8	N/A
⇨ Factory configured-do not alter	J4/jumper 9	N/A
⇨ Factory configured-do not alter	J4/jumper 10	N/A

CONNECTIONS	
Function	Location
Remote LED connection	J4/pins 8 & 11

SEAGATE TECHNOLOGY, INC.
ST31270A

Interface:	IDE AT)
Size:	3.5 in. third height
View:	Bottom

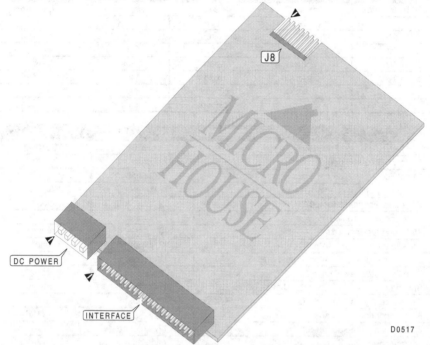

D0517

DRIVE CONFIGURATION J8		
Selection	**Jumper 1**	**Jumper 2**
Single drive in a system	open	open
Drive is master in a two drive system	open	closed
Drive is slave in a two drive system	closed	open

CONNECTIONS	
Function	**Location**
Remote LED connection	J8/jumper 7

Continued on next page . . .

SEAGATE TECHNOLOGY, INC.
ST31270A

. . . continued from previous page

USER CONFIGURABLE SETTINGS		
Function	**Location**	**Setting**
Cable select enabled	J8/jumper 1 & 2	closed
Cable select disabled	J8/jumper 1 & 2	open
Dual drive emulation mode enabled	J8/jumper 3 & 6	closed
Dual drive emulation mode disabled	J8/jumper 3 & 6	open
⇨ Factory configured - do not alter	J8/jumper 4	N/A
⇨ Factory configured - do not alter	J8/jumper 5	N/A
Master/slave timing protocol enabled	J8/jumper 1 & 3	closed
Master/slave timing protocol disabled	J8/jumper 1 & 3	open
Note: Dual-drive mode cannot be used with cable select option or with another physical drive.		

MISCELLANEOUS TECHNICAL NOTES
Shunts installed across jumpers 1 & 2 and 3 & 4 are spares.

SEAGATE TECHNOLOGY, INC.
ST31640A, ST32140A

Interface:	IDE AT)
Size:	3.5 in. third height
View:	Bottom

D0548

DRIVE CONFIGURATION J8		
Selection	**Jumper 1**	**Jumper 2**
Single drive in a system	open	open
Drive is master in a two drive system	open	closed
Drive is slave in a two drive system	closed	open

USER CONFIGURABLE SETTINGS		
Function	**Location**	**Setting**
⇨ Slave's ready signal response timing is 5 seconds	J8/jumper 3	open
Slave's ready signal response timing is 30 seconds	J8/jumper 3	closed
⇨ Factory configured - do not alter	J8/jumper 4	N/A
Cable select enabled	J8/jumper 5	closed
Cable select disabled	J8/jumper 5	open

CONNECTIONS	
Function	**Location**
Remote LED connection	J8/jumper 6

MISCELLANEOUS TECHNICAL NOTES
A shunt installed across jumper 1 & 2 is a spare.

SEAGATE TECHNOLOGY, INC.
ST3250A, ST3291A, ST3391A, ST3491A

Interface: IDE (AT)
Size: 3.5 in. Third Height
View: Bottom

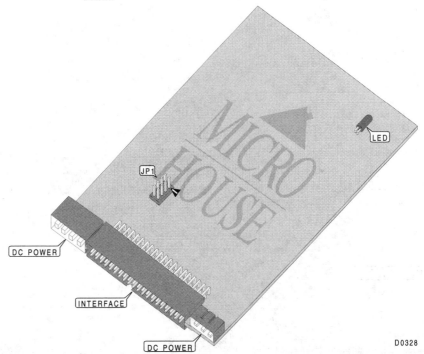

D0328

DRIVE CONFIGURATION -		
Selection	**JP1/jumper 3**	**JP1/jumper 4**
⇨ Single drive only	open	open
Master drive in a two drive system	closed	open
Slave drive in a two drive system	open	closed

USER CONFIGURABLE SETTINGS		
Function	**Location**	**Setting**
⇨ Cable select enabled*	JP1/jumper 2	open
Cable select disabled*	JP1/jumper 2	closed
⇨ Master drive assumes slave is always present	JP1/jumper 1	open
Master drive uses DASP to determine slave presence	JP1/jumper 1	closed
*Cable select option allows "master/slave" configuration to be determined by the cabling of the host system. If pin 28 on the interface is tied to the ground, drive is considered a master, if pin 28 is not grounded, drive is considered a slave. Both of the drives must have a Cable Select option and pin 28 must not be used for any other signal in order for this option to function. This feature is useful when drive is used in a removable subsystem.		

SEAGATE TECHNOLOGY, INC.
ST3283N (PCB Rev. > 260035), ST3285N, ST3390N, ST3550N, ST3655N

Interface: SCSI
Size: 3.5 in. third height
View: Bottom

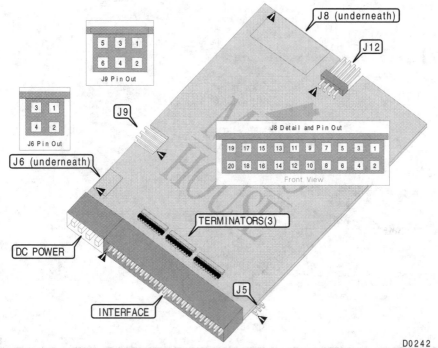

D0242

DRIVE SELECTION - J5			
Drive Number	Jumper 1	Jumper 2	Jumper3
0	open	open	open
1	open	open	closed
2	open	closed	open
3	open	closed	closed
4	closed	open	open
5	closed	open	closed
6	closed	closed	open
7	closed	closed	closed
Note: J8, Jumper 1, 2, & 3 perform the same function and are mutually exclusive with this table.			

Continued on next page . . .

SEAGATE TECHNOLOGY, INC.
ST3283N (PCB Rev. > 260035), ST3285N, ST3390N, ST3550N, ST3655N

. . . continued from previous page

CONNECTIONS	
Purpose	**Location**
External Spindle Sync	J8/pins 7 & 8 or J12/jumper 3
Hard drive active LED	J8/pins 9 & 10 or J12/jumper 4

USER CONFIGURABLE SETTINGS		
Function	**Location**	**Setting**
⇨ Factory configured - do not alter	J8/pins 11 - 20	open
⇨ SCSI parity check enabled	J12/jumper 1	closed
SCSI parity check disabled	J12/jumper 1	open
⇨ Spindle motor starts on power-up	J12/jumper 2	open
Spindle motor starts on command only	J12/jumper 2	closed

TERMINATION POWER SETTINGS - J6	
Function	**J6**
TERMPWR supplied by the SCSI interface pin 26	pins 1 & 2 closed
TERMPWR supplied by drive	pins 1 & 3 closed
TERMPWR not present	pins 2 & 4 closed
TERMPWR supplied to SCSI interface only	pins 3 & 4 closed
TERMPWR supplied by drive to SCSI interface pin 26	pins 1 & 2 and 3 & 4 closed

ACTIVE/PASSIVE TERMINATION SETTINGS	
Function	**J9**
Active termination enabled (110Ω for Fast SCSI-2)	pins 1 & 2 closed
Passive termination enabled (220/330Ω for SCSI-1(CCS))	pins 2 & 4 and 5 & 6

SEAGATE TECHNOLOGY, INC.
ST3295A, ST3630A, ST3660A

Interface: IDE(AT)
Size: 3.5 in. third height
View: Bottom

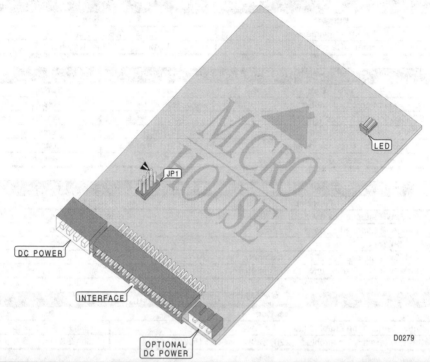

D0279

DRIVE CONFIGURATION - JP1			
Selection	**Jumper 1**	**Jumper 3**	**Jumper 4**
⇨ Master drive with a Medalist family slave or an ATA slave	open	open	open
Master drive with a non-ATA slave	open	closed	open
Master drive with a slave that uses PDIAG signal (no DASP signal)	closed	open	open
Slave drive to an ATA-compatible master	open	open	closed

USER CONFIGURABLE SETTINGS		
Function	**Location**	**Setting**
⇨ Cable select enabled	JP1/jumper 2	closed
Cable select disabled	JP1/jumper 2	open

MISCELLANEOUS TECHNICAL NOTE
Note: Do not install jumpers on jumper 3 and 4 at the same time. The heads will continuously seek back and forth across the media and the drive ignores all signals sent by the interface.

SEAGATE TECHNOLOGY, INC.
ST3620N, ST3620ND

Interface:	SCSI/SCSI-2
Size:	3.5 in. third height
View:	Bottom

D0482

DRIVE SELECTION - J6			
Drive Number	**Jumper 4**	**Jumper 5**	**Jumper 6**
0	open	open	open
1	closed	open	open
2	open	closed	open
3	closed	closed	open
4	open	open	closed
5	closed	open	closed
6	open	closed	closed
7	closed	closed	closed

Continued on next page . . .

SEAGATE TECHNOLOGY, INC.
ST3620N, ST3620ND

. . . continued from previous page

USER CONFIGURABLE SETTINGS		
Function	**Location**	**Setting**
⇨ On-board SCSI Terminators enabled	J2/jumper 3	closed
On-board SCSI Terminators disabled	J2/jumper 3	open
SCSI parity check enabled	J2/jumper 4	closed
SCSI-parity check disabled	J2/jumper 4	open
⇨ Write protection enabled	J2/jumper 5	closed
Write protection disabled	J2/jumper 5	open
⇨ Spindle motor starts on power-up	J2/jumper 6	open
Spindle motor starts on command only	J2/jumper 6	closed
⇨ Motor delay start disabled	J2/jumper 7	open
Motor delay start enabled (12 sec X SCSI ID#)	J2/jumper 7	closed
⇨ Factory configured - do not alter	J2/jumper 8	open
⇨ Factory configured - do not alter	J6/jumper 1	open
⇨ Sync Spindle enabled	J6/jumper 3	closed
Sync Spindle disabled	J6/jumper 3	open

TERMINATION POWER - J2		
Setting	**Location**	**Setting**
TERMPWR supplied by drive	J2/jumper 2	closed
TERMPWR supplied by SCSI bus	J2/pins 2 & 4	closed
TERMPWR supplied to SCSI bus	J2/jumper 1	closed

CONNECTIONS	
Function	**Location**
External LED	J6/jumper 2

MISCELLANEOUS TECHNICAL NOTE
Note: J5 and J2/jumpers 4, 5, and 6 are mutually exclusive. When configuring the drive with J2, do not alter J5.

SEAGATE TECHNOLOGY, INC.
ST3780A, ST31220A

Interface: IDE (AT)
Size: 3.5 in. third height
View: Bottom

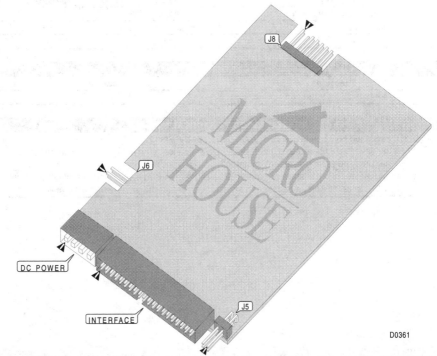

D0361

DRIVE CONFIGURATION J5		
Selection	**Jumper 1**	**Jumper 2**
⇨ Single drive system	open	open
Drive is slave in a two drive system	closed	open
Drive is master in a two drive system	open	closed
Cable select *	closed	closed
Note:The * indicates you must also install a jumper on pins 6 & 8 of J8.		

Continued on next page . . .

SEAGATE TECHNOLOGY, INC.
ST3780A, ST31220A

. . . continued from previous page

USER CONFIGURABLE SETTINGS		
Function	**Location**	**Setting**
Dual drive emulation mode enabled	J6/jumper 1 & 2	closed
Dual drive emulation mode disabled	J6/jumper 1 & 2	open
Cable select enabled	J8/pins 6 & 8	closed

CONNECTIONS	
Function	**Location**
Remote LED connection	J8/jumper 7

MISCELLANEOUS TECHNICAL NOTES
Note:Shunts installed on J5/pins 1 & 3, J8/pins 1 & 2, and J6/pins 1 & 3 are spares. When the drive is configured to support dual-drive emulation, both emulated drives respond as one to any power-management command. If both the master and the slave are of the ST31220 family drives, you need not install a jumper on J5/jumper 2. This is because the master can detect the presence of a slave with DASP.

SEAGATE TECHNOLOGY INC.
ST41200N, ST41200ND, ST41200NM, ST41200NV, ST41650N, ST41650ND, ST41651N, ST41651ND, ST42100N, ST42101N

Interface:	SCSI
Size:	5.25 in. full height
View:	Bottom

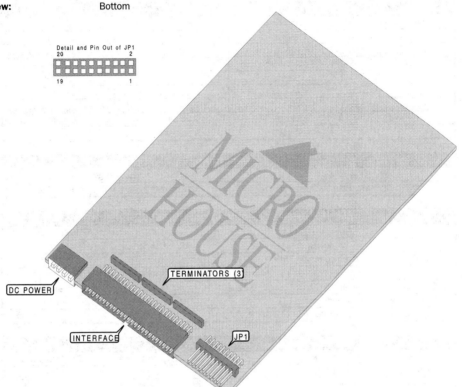

D0257

Continued on next page . . .

SEAGATE TECHNOLOGY INC.
ST41200N, ST41200ND, ST41200NM, ST41200NV, ST41650N,
ST41650ND, ST41651N, ST41651ND, ST42100N, ST42101N

. . . continued from previous page

DRIVE SELECTION - JP1			
Drive Number	Jumper 3	Jumper 4	Jumper 5
0	open	open	open
1	open	open	closed
2	open	closed	open
3	open	closed	closed
4	closed	open	open
5	closed	open	closed
6	closed	closed	open
7	closed	closed	closed

CONNECTIONS	
Function	Location
External Spindle Sync	JP1/jumpers 9 & 10

USER CONFIGURABLE SETTINGS		
Function	Location	Setting
➪ Spindle motor starts on power-up	JP1/jumper 6	open
Spindle motor starts on command only	JP1/jumper 6	closed
➪ SCSI parity check enabled	JP1/jumper 7	open
SCSI parity check disabled	JP1/jumper 7	closed
➪ Motor delay start disabled	JP1/jumper 8	open
Motor delay start enabled (16 sec x SCSI I.D.#)	JP1/jumper 8	closed

TERMINATION POWER SETTINGS		
Function	JP1/jumper 1	JP2/jumper 2
TERMPWR supplied to SCSI pin 26	open	closed
TERMPWR supplied by drive	closed	open
TERMPWR supplied by SCSI pin 26	JP1/pins 1 & 3 closed	

SEAGATE TECHNOLOGY, INC.
ST41600N/ND, ST41601N/ND, ST42000N/ND
ST42400N/ND, ST43400N/ND

Interface: SCSI
Size: 5.25 in. full height
View: Bottom

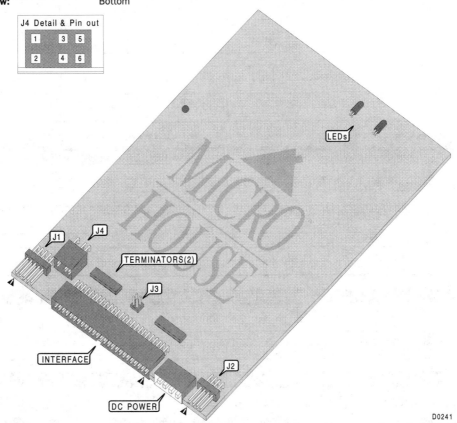

D0241

SPINDLE MOTOR OPTION SETTINGS		
Function	J2/jumper 1	J2/jumper 2
⇨ Spindle motor starts on power-up	open	open
Spindle motor starts on command only	open	closed
Spindle motor starts delayed (13 sec. x Drive I.D. #)	closed	open

Continued on next page . . .

SEAGATE TECHNOLOGY, INC.
ST41600N/ND, ST41601N/ND, ST42000N/ND, ST42400N/ND, ST43400N/ND

. . . continued from previous page

DRIVE SELECTION - J1			
Drive Number	**Jumper 1**	**Jumper 2**	**Jumper 3**
0	open	open	open
1	open	open	closed
2	open	closed	open
3	open	closed	closed
4	closed	open	open
5	closed	open	closed
6	closed	closed	open
7	closed	closed	closed

USER CONFIGURABLE SETTINGS		
Function	**Location**	**Setting**
⇨ Write protect disabled	J1/jumper 4	open
Write protect enabled	J1/jumper 4	closed
⇨ Spindle Sync. Master mode enabled	J1/jumper 5	open
Spindle Sync. Slave mode enabled	J1/jumper 5	closed
⇨ SCSI parity check enabled	J2/jumper 3	open
SCSI parity check disabled	J2/jumper 3	closed
⇨ Sweep Cycle disabled	J2/jumper 4	open
Sweep Cycle enabled	J2/jumper 4	closed

TERMINATION POWER SETTINGS	
Function	**Jumper J3**
TERMPWR supplied by drive to SCSI Interface pin 26	pins 1 & 2 and 3 & 4 closed
TERMPWR supplied by drive	pins 1 & 2 closed
TERMPWR supplied by the SCSI Interface pin 26	pins 2 & 4 closed

J4 PIN ASSIGNMENTS			
This connector allows the spindle rotation of multiple drives to be synchronized. The drives are daisy-chained be connector J4, which consists of two parallel, 3-pin connectors. The chain must be terminated at each end with a Spindle Sync. Terminator (PN 70574221). Sync. Reference Source may be set by an external source (Host Adapter); or by one of the drives on the chain by making that drive Master (J1/jumper 5, open) and all other drives on the a chain Slave (J1/jumper 5, closed). The location of the Master drive on the chain is not significant.			
Pin	**Function/Signal**	**Pin**	**Function/Signal**
1	Ground	2	Ground
3	Negative (-) Sync. Ref	4	Negative (-) Sync. Ref
5	Positive (+) Sync. Ref	6	Positive (+) Sync. Ref

SEAGATE TECHNOLOGY, INC.
ST51080A, ST51270A, ST5540A, ST5851A

Interface: ATA-2
Size: 3.5 in. fourth height
View: Bottom

D0504

DRIVE CONFIGURATION - J8			
Setting	**Jumper 1**	**Jumper 2**	**Jumper 3**
⇨ Single drive in a system	open	open	open
Drive is master in a two drive system	open	closed	open
Drive is slave in a two drive system	closed	open	open
Master/slave timing protocol enabled	open	closed	closed
Note: The timing protocol function allows the master drive to wait for up to 30 seconds for the slave drive to respond. Without this function enabled the timing is 5 seconds.			

USER CONFIGURABLE SETTINGS		
Function	**Location**	**Setting**
⇨ Factory configured - do not alter	J8/jumper 4	open
⇨ Cable select disabled	J8/jumper 5	open
Cable select enabled	J8/jumper 5	closed
Note: Shunt installed between jumpers 1 & 2 is a spare.		

CONNECTIONS	
Function	**Location**
Remote LED connection	J8/jumper 6

TOSHIBA
MK-1122FC, MK-1824FCV, MK-1924FCV, MK-1926FCV, MK-2024FC, MK-2124FC, MK-2526FC, MK-2528FC, MK-2628FC

Interface:	IDE (44-pin)
Size:	2.5 in. quarter height
View:	Bottom

D0217

DRIVE CONFIGURATION	
Selection	**Jumper J2**
⇨ Single drive only	open
Master drive in a two drive system	open
Slave drive in a two drive system	closed

MISCELLANEOUS TECHNICAL NOTES
Jumper J1 is reserved for future use.

TOSHIBA
MK-2224FC, MK-2326FC, MK-2428FC

Interface: IDE (44PIN)
Size: 2.5 in. Quarter Height
View: Bottom

D0318

DRIVE CONFIGURATION	
Selection	**J2**
⇨ Single drive only/Master drive in a two drive system	open
Slave drive in a two drive system	closed

MISCELLANEOUS TECHNICAL NOTES
Jumper J1 is factory configured - do not alter

WESTERN DIGITAL CORPORATION
WDAC1170, WDAC1210, WDAC1270, WDAC1365, WDAC140,WDAC1425, WDAC160, WDAC21000, WDAC2120, WDAC21200, WDAC21600, WDAC2170, WDAC2200, WDAC2250, WDAC2340, WDAC2420, WDAC2540, WDAC2635, WDAC2700, WDAC280, WDAC2850, WDAC31000, WDAC31200, WDAC31600, WDAC32100, WDAC33100

Interface:	IDE(AT)
	EIDE (Models 21000, 21200, 21600, 2850, 31000, 31600, 32100, 33100)
Size:	3.5 in. third height
View:	Top

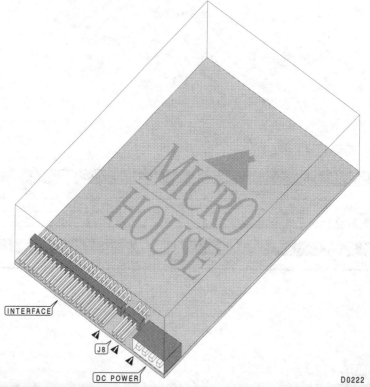

D0222

DRIVE CONFIGURATION		
Selection	**J8/Jumper 2**	**J8/Jumper 3**
⇨ Single drive only	open	open
Master drive in a two drive system	open	closed
Slave drive in a two drive system	closed	open

MISCELLANEOUS TECHNICAL NOTES
On older versions of some Caviar drives J8/jumper 1 must be closed to make it slave to a Conner Peripherals CP3022 or CP342. On newer versions leave J8/jumper 1 open. Caviar drives are shipped with a spare shunt jumpered across J8/jumpers 2 & 3.

WESTERN DIGITAL CORPORATION
WDAC32500

Interface: ATA-2
Size: 3.5 in. third height
View: Top

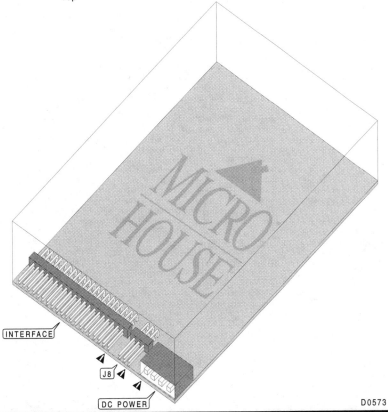

D0573

DRIVE CONFIGURATION		
Selection	**J8/Jumper 2**	**J8/Jumper 3**
⇨ Single drive only	open	open
Master drive in a two drive system	open	closed
Slave drive in a two drive system	closed	open

ALTERNATE DRIVE CONFIGURATION			
Selection	**J8/Jumper 1**	**J8/Jumper 2**	**J8/Jumper 3**
⇨ Single drive only	open	closed	closed
Master drive in a two drive system	closed	open	closed
Slave drive in a two drive system	closed	closed	open

MISCELLANEOUS TECHNICAL NOTES
The alternate drive configuration is for system BIOS that don't accept drives that have more than 4095 cylinders. In the first drive configuration J8/jumper 1 is reserved - leave open. Caviar drives are shipped with a spare shunt jumpered across J8/jumpers 2 & 3.

WESTERN DIGITAL CORPORATION
WDSC8320, WDSC8400

Interface: SCSI
Size: 5.25 in. full height
View: Bottom

D0224

USER CONFIGURABLE SETTINGS		
Function	**Location**	**Setting**
⇨ Spindle motor starts on power-up	J1/jumper 5	closed
Spindle motor starts on command only	J1/jumper 5	open

DRIVE SELECTION - J1			
Drive Number	**Jumper 1**	**Jumper 2**	**Jumper 3**
0	open	open	open
1	closed	open	open
2	open	closed	open
3	closed	closed	open
4	open	open	closed
5	closed	open	closed
6	open	closed	closed
7	closed	closed	closed

Care, Prevention, and Improving Drive Performance

Chapter Seven Contents:

Care And Prevention

Every hard drive will eventually fail. Fortunately, there are steps that can be taken to lessen the likelihood of a spontaneous, catastrophic failure, and to soften the impact when the inevitable occurs. Although hard drive failure is an inescapable eventuality, proper care will allow the drive to fulfill its manufacturer's promise of long life. More importantly, it will allow the drive to give the warnings of normal wear, rather than experience a sudden failure that will leave you stranded with lots of unrecoverable data.

Hard drives are factory-sealed, therefore there is little the end-user can do as far as mechanical maintenance and repair. However, there are steps that can be taken to maximize the life of a hard drive and help prevent a sudden catastrophic failure.

Hard drives operate under very tight tolerances. Exposure to high temperatures could result in a shorter life-span. Because of this, try to install the drive away from components that give off large amounts of heat. Also, be sure that there is adequate air circulation inside the computer by checking the cooling fan for dust and obstructions.

Shield the computer from power spikes and surges with a high quality surge suppressor. An erratic power supply could result in corrupt data, and even lead to component damage. Although costly, an uninterruptible power supply would be an even better solution because, in addition to shielding the computer from power surges, it allows for at least an orderly shut down in the case of a general power-outage.

Although modern hard drives are built to withstand minor jolts, it is best to isolate them from shock as much as possible. Because data heads float mere microns from platters spinning at several thousand rpms, an impact sustained during a read/write operation could cause a head "slap," resulting in lost data or even physical damage. Placing the computer on the floor may save desk space, but may leave it vulnerable to the occasional kick or collision with a chair leg.

Warning signs of drive failure

Hard drives sometimes give warning signs when they are about to experience a failure. When these indicators begin to appear, it is best to back up all data on the drive and attempt to determine the cause of any problems through a diagnostic utility.

During the boot sequence, the system BIOS performs a **Power-On Self-Test (POST)**. If any errors are detected during the POST, it will report the error with a **POST Code**.

Watch for disk accessing problems, such as files that are corrupt or missing, which seem to appear with greater frequency as time goes by. These are signs of widespread media failure which will eventually become fatal. Also, run one of the DOS utilities **ScanDisk** or **CHKDSK** often. Do not depend on a drive that shows any sign of unreliability. This does not mean you should throw away drives that exhibit such problems right away. They can still be used for games and files that you do not access very often – just remember to keep a current backup.

Not all apparent problems are symptoms of impending failure. Slowing access times are not usually an indicator of impending drive failure – your drive may simply be filling up with so many **fragmented** files that the data heads have to make several jumps to retrieve/write a single file. See the section in this chapter on improving drive performance.

On some older drives, periodic low-level formatting is recommended in order to "refresh" the sector header information. The sector header information is read repeatedly, but never altered during normal read/write operations. On older drives the sector headers tend to degrade over time. Performing a low-level format renews the sector header information, usually fixing apparent media problems. If your drive is an ST-506/412 or ESDI model, this may be the case.

> Most IDE drives are factory low-level formatted with special equipment. These drives cannot be formatted using over-the-counter methods, and attempting to do so may render the drive inoperable. Consult the user's manual for your drive model prior to attempting a low-level format on it.

Computer Viruses

Some hard drive problems aren't caused by defects or acts of God, but by high-tech vandals. Computer viruses have in recent years been getting lots of press. The importance of guarding against computer viruses has become greater with the proliferation of effective entry level home computers and increased use of on-line services.

One method of guarding your data is to install a program that automatically detects the presence of computer viruses. For example, a **boot-sector virus** attaches itself to the hidden boot files on your drive, waiting to cause all sorts of damage, such as wrecking the **FAT**, making file access erratic or impossible. Some anti-virus programs are called up during the boot process and can automatically notify the user when a boot-sector virus is detected.

Not all computer viruses hide in the boot sector, however. Consider virus checks as a routine part of your computer maintenance tasks. There are many anti-virus utilities available, and many are shareware. Newer versions of MS-DOS and Windows include easy-to-use anti-virus utilities. Because new viruses are constantly being created, it is important that you are using an anti-virus program with a recently updated database. A good practice is to run a virus check prior to performing a system back up. This incorporates virus checks into your routine, as well as preventing possible infection of crucial back-up data.

When Disaster Strikes

When your drive's time is up, hopefully you have taken the appropriate steps necessary to keep down-time at a minimum – the most important being a regular back-up routine.   Keep an emergency boot disk on hand. Drive failures are not always fatal. Booting the computer with the emergency disk will allow you to run a diagnostic program, such as **CHKDSK** and **ScanDisk** in DOS. If the problem is a head malfunction or similarly unrecoverable ailment, getting your system back up to speed means installing a new drive and restoring all necessary files from a back up. The following sections will help you diagnose and recover from common hard drive problems which may arise.

Backing Up Data

Modern hard drives are extremely reliable devices which will probably out-last the time it takes for your system to become obsolete. Does this mean that you should have complete confidence in your hardware and that backing-up data on a regular basis is only for the paranoid? The question can only be answered by you. How valuable is your data?

Let's face it: your data is probably much more valuable than the equipment it's stored on. Keeping in mind that all hard drives will eventually fail, investing in a data back up system is cheap insurance. If you do not already practice backing up your data routinely, we strongly recommend you do so.

Besides eventual hard-drive failure, there are many reasons to be prepared for data loss. Events beyond your control, anything from lightning strikes to accidents and theft could result in losing valuable information. In addition, the inadvertent over-writing of important files is a common occurrence. Having a recent copy of important data will save untold time and effort in reconstructing lost or damaged files.

Back Up Device Types

There are many back up methods available today. Again, you will have to balance your needs against what you can afford. It is important to be realistic when choosing a back up method. On the lowest level, you may opt to simply use floppy disks and a data compression program. This will work, but do you really want to be tied to your desk, switching floppies while backing up hundreds of megabytes worth of data? Chances are, this will quickly grow tiresome and seem like it's not worth the effort, which in turn will lead to complacency and an eventual tragic episode.

A back up device should have:

1. Removable media to store back up data away from the computer and allow data transfer between computers.
2. Adequate storage capacity when compared to the total capacity of the system hard drive.
3. A common standard followed by all manufacturers of the device. This allows reliable data transfers among different computers if needed.

The following are some popular methods available for data back up:

Floppy Disks

Floppy disks are by far the most popular removable-media storage devices. 3.5 in. drives are the most common today, although 5.25 in. drives are still widely available.

Advantages: Drives are inexpensive. Floppy drives generally come as standard equipment on desk-top PCs. Back up software with a data compression feature is included in the newest versions of DOS and Windows. Shareware such as PKZIP is also readily available. Floppy drives are adequate for small back up tasks. Floppy disks are available just about anywhere.

Disadvantages: Small capacity (up to 2.88MB uncompressed capacity per disk) means that many disks must be used for larger back up tasks. This means that the user must switch disks as they fill up. The problem is compounded by relatively slow data transfer rates, making back up tasks extremely tedious. Multiple disks are cumbersome, having to be labeled in the proper order and physically stored. The costs can add up rapidly, as a megabyte of storage on a floppy disk can run several times that of tape cartridge, depending on quality. Also, floppy disks are relatively delicate and more susceptible to data loss than other mass storage formats. Several manufacturers are pushing to replace the archaic floppy format with newer versions that exceed 120MB per cartridge. Iomega's popular Zip™ drive is also being pushed for this purpose.

Tape Drives

Tape drives are dedicated back-up devices of various standards, which when considered as a group are the most popular method of backing up data. Tape drives are considered dedicated back up devices because data cannot be accessed randomly with the speed of disk storage formats. The tape must be positioned at the location of the desired data before access can be accomplished. The reason tape drives are so popular is that they use proven, reliable technology to simply guard against data loss. There are several tape drive formats available today, basically being separated, once again, by performance versus cost. The following are some of the most popular:

- **Quarter-Inch Cartridge (QIC) Tape Drives**

  QIC is overwhelmingly the most popular format for tape drives. Although the standard has been around for some time, the recent proliferation of large capacity hard drives has caused its popularity to soar.

Advantages: Relatively inexpensive. Newer QIC format tape drives can be purchased for under $200, depending on capacity. 120MB (uncompressed) tape cartridges are generally under $15 each, making the dollar/MB figure much less expensive than an equivalent amount of floppy disks. Tape cartridges are readily available in the local discount store. Also, the cost of individual tapes is low enough to use for small volumes when it is not necessary to back up an entire hard drive. Back up duties take relatively little overseeing unless multiple tapes are required. Installation is very simple, requiring no special adapter − most attach to the floppy drive cable or parallel port, and IDE (ATA) tape drives are also available. The QIC format is very reliable and rugged, due to the simplicity of the design.

Disadvantages: Larger drives require multiple tapes for a complete back up, depending on hard drive and tape drive capacity. Selective restoration of sub-directories and individual files is time consuming due to the nature of storage on a linear tape. Back up time can be relatively long, depending on tape drive performance and amount of data being copied (up to one hour for 250MB).

- **Digital Audio Tape (DAT) Drives**

  DAT drives are ideal for storing massive amounts of data (several gigabytes per DAT cartridge). DAT is similar to CD-ROM in that it uses technology developed for audio recording applications. The difference is its ability to write to the recording media more than one time. DAT is gaining popularity for high-performance applications, such as backing-up network servers.

  Advantages: Large data capacity (multi-gigabytes) on a small cartridge. DAT cartridges are smaller than audio tape cassettes. Also the cartridges are a very good value − the cost for a megabyte of storage is less than a penny. DAT drives are very fast, with data transfer rates that are several times faster than QIC-format tape drives.

Disadvantages: Expensive drive unit. DAT drives are getting cheaper, but are generally still in the $1000 range. However, keep in mind that DAT cartridges are relatively inexpensive, being listed at under $10/cartridge by some mail-order companies. IDE-interface DAT drives were not available at the time this text went to press. DAT drives commonly use the SCSI interface.

- **8mm Tape Drives:**

8mm tape drives, like DAT, take advantage of technology developed for the home-electronics industry. 8mm tapes are the same cartridges used by home video cameras. The high density of the magnetic particles on the tapes allow an enormous amount of data to be packed on them.

Advantages: Huge data capacity (up to 10GB compressed) on a small cartridge. Very fast – several times faster than even DAT drives. Cartridges are comparable in price to other tape formats: around $10 each.

Disadvantages: Expensive drive unit. Lower-capacity models start at over $1000. Being the least popular of the tape drive formats listed here, incompatibility problems are more likely when transferring data among systems.

Removable Media Drives

Removable media drives are, in theory, a blend of the best features of hard drives and floppy drives – large capacity, high speed, and transferable media. Although not generally used as back up devices, their flexibility and additional features make them an attractive choice over tape drives. The capacity of removable media drives is in theory unlimited – simply add more cartridges for additional capacity. In some cases, the performance of removable media drives is close enough to fixed media drives that they can be considered a viable alternative. There are several types of removable media drives on the market today. The following are some of the most popular:

- **Bernoulli Drives**

  Bernoulli drives, introduced by the Iomega Corporation, use a flexible disk enclosed in a rigid case, similar to floppy disks. Instead of a read/write head that contacts the magnetic media, as in floppy drives, Bernoulli drive heads float a microscopic distance above the media, like hard drives. Bernoulli drives achieve hard-drive-like seek times because the flexible disk is spinning at speeds of several thousand rpms. Unlike floppy drives, this high rotation speed is safe for the disk and data heads because the flexible disk is made stable by a rigid plate in the drive unit. High-speed air flow is caused by the rotation of the flexible disk. This air flow between the disk and plate causes them to be sucked closer to each other, while never touching. These drives derive their name from this feature, taking advantage of the Bernoulli principle of the relationship between fluid speed and pressure. The maximum uncompressed capacity of a cartridge is 230MB at the present time.

  Advantages: Seek times and data throughput are moderately fast, although slower than modern fixed-media drives. Cartridges are rugged and can be reliably transported without fear of damage. Available in IDE and SCSI interfaces.

  Disadvantages: Small capacity per cartridge. Large back up tasks can require several cartridges, which, in addition to requiring more attendance by the user, can become very expensive. Although the price of the drive unit is moderate, roughly equal to that of high-end fixed-media drives, cartridges are relatively expensive. Expect to pay around $100, more or less, depending on capacity.

- **Syquest Drives**

  Syquest drives are similar to fixed-media drives in that they use a rigid disk. However, the disk is housed in a hard case, comprising a cartridge that can be removed and transferred just like a floppy disk. The rigid media allows the disk to spin at high rpms which results in performance similar to modern fixed-media drives. The maximum uncompressed capacity of a cartridge is 1.3GB at the present time.

Advantages: Fast – seek times and data throughput approaches fixed-media drives. Moderate price. Comparable in price to high-end fixed-media drives, and cartridges range in cost from $20-$100, depending on capacity. Very popular data transfer method for the print industry. Available in IDE and SCSI interfaces.

Disadvantages: Limited capacity per cartridge. Large back up tasks can require several cartridges, which, in addition to requiring more user attendance, can become expensive. The disks in Syquest cartridges are rigid plastic, and tend to be less impact-resistant than other transferable media.

- **Magnetic Optical Drives**

Magnetic Optical, or Magneto Optical (MO) drives are outwardly similar to CD-ROM drives, with the important distinction that the cartridges can be written to more than once. Rather than burning "dark" spots into the disk which prevent light from being reflected back to the optical receiver, the MO disk uses weak magnetic fields to bend the polarized light being reflected from the disk media. The reflective media on MO drives must be excited by heat, applied by a laser beam, before it can receive a magnetic signal. Because a laser can focus the heat on a very tight area, an individual magnetic flux placed on MO media can be much smaller than on "plain" magnetic media. The result of the ability to tightly localize magnetic fields on the MO disk is that it allows information to be packed more densely than on a straight magnetic disk.

Advantages: Large capacity – 230MB to over 1GB per cartridge. 230MB cartridges currently go for about $40, making storage of large volumes of readily-accessible data economical.

Disadvantages: Drives are moderately expensive – around $600 and steeply upwards depending on capacity and options. Relatively slow compared to other removable media drives. Large back up tasks can require several cartridges.

Back up methods are as varied as the people who use them. The back up routine you follow should depend most on how much you value your data.

As a minimum, you should keep a complete system back up and perform daily back ups of work and changed files. Using the same tape over and over will eventually wear out the media, breaking down the integrity of the stored data. Use multiple tape sets and have a rotation strategy to maximize both economy and reliability. It is also recommended that you keep a copy of the comprehensive back up off the work site. Be sure to update the remote copies on a regular basis. Lastly, check that the backups are reliable by restoring the data every once in a while.

Making an Emergency Boot Disk

When your hard drive does experience a failure, you will need to boot the computer by floppy in order to attempt repairs and/or data recovery. An emergency boot disk should contain all the files necessary to boot the computer as well as additional files that contain your system's parameters. To make an emergency boot disk, begin by formatting a clean floppy with the **FORMAT /S** command. If you are using Windows, bring up the **File Manager**, pull down the **Disk** menu, and choose **Make System Disk**. The **COMMAND.COM** and some hidden system files are now transferred to the disk.

Although you can now boot with this disk, you will need additional files for a custom configuration. Copy the **CONFIG.SYS** and **AUTOEXEC.BAT** files to the floppy. Using the **EDIT** command, modify the CONFIG.SYS and AUTOEXEC.BAT files **on the floppy disk** to streamline the files, eliminating any non-essential instructions. Make sure that any device drivers or other files referred to in CONFIG.SYS and AUTOEXEC.BAT are on the disk and that all paths are changed to work from C: drive to A: drive.

You should also add some files on the disk, which will save some time getting your system back to its pre-failure configuration. Among the files you should copy to the emergency disk are the DOS files **FDISK** and **FORMAT**, as well as the diagnostic utilities **CHKDSK** and **ScanDisk**. Losing the **Master Boot Record (MBR)**, the partition table, **DOS Boot Record (DBR)**, the **File Allocation Table (FAT)**, or the **CMOS** drive settings will cause the system to be unable to access the drive correctly.

ON THE CD

> ***DrivePro*** contains valuable utilities that will help bring you back from potential disaster. These programs allow you to save and quickly restore system parameters and important hard drive areas. Run the DrivePro demonstration on the CD-ROM for more information. Other valuable utilities are also included on the disk. Please see **Appendix E** for more information on these utilities.

DrivePro features an Important Info Back up function which allows the user to save the vital disk information to a file for later retrieval in case of disaster. If you are a technician that installs many systems, we suggest that you use this option on every system you set up; that is, save the important system info for every machine to a diskette that will remain with the machine. If any of the mentioned information is lost from the system, as long as the drive can still be written to, running Restore System Info will restore the state of the system at the time of the last system save. This can save a great deal of time with the newer systems that have many settings, and with IDE drives that must use a user-definable drive type. Specifically, with the IDE translated parameters, if you don't use the original specifications (heads, cylinders and sectors) when resetting this, the IDE drive will not work properly. Note that if determining the drive's original parameters is your primary task, this is best accomplished through Get Lost Parameters in Basic Mode or Drive Boot Fixer, Retrieve Drive Specs From MBR in Enhanced Mode, and entering the parameters into CMOS.

Data Recovery

As much as most computer publications stress the importance of making regular back ups, there will be those who get complacent and end up between a rock and a hard place. It is these people who keep data-recovery services in business. Although there are some cases in which data-recovery software may be used to retrieve most "lost" files, in the more severe failures, dedicated tools and special skills will be necessary. There are a number of these services available across the country. Look in the advertising section in the back of a major computer publication, such as *PC Magazine* or *Computer Shopper* for listings of companies providing data-recovery services. Shop around by comparing success rates and references. Be prepared to let them know as much as you can about the nature of the failure.

Special skills and tools come at a cost, and if you're in need of the services of a data-recovery company, you probably aren't in a position to complain about high prices. Remember, the fastest, most economical way to recover from media failure is to be prepared through regular back up.

Getting Around Capacity Barriers

This section is limited to a discussion of getting around IDE capacity barriers. There are basically three capacity barriers of current concern:

1. 528MB BIOS/ATA-1 capacity limit
2. 4,096 BIOS cylinder limit
3. 2.1GB DOS partition limit
4. 8.4GB BIOS capacity limit

IDE Capacity Barriers

The 8.4GB barrier will not be discussed here, since there is no solution that doesn't involve redefining the BIOS and/or IDE.

Remember to perform a backup prior to any operation that will change the configuration of the system.

Solutions to the 528MB limit are well documented, and the barrier no longer exists for systems currently on the market. This problem may still be encountered when attempting to upgrade an older system with a new >528MB drive. If the drive cannot be translated to less than 1,024 cylinders, you must:

1. Truncate the drive at 1,024 cylinders in CMOS setup (resulting in the loss of drive capacity).
2. Use the >1,024 cylinder support from a third-party software package, such as **EZ- Drive** or **DrivePro**.
3. Upgrade to a CHS-translating BIOS.

Some of the newer BIOSes can only handle 4,096 cylinders, effectively limiting drive capacity to 2.1GB. As with the 528MB barrier, there are hardware and software solutions to this problem. If the drive cannot be translated to less than 4,096 cylinders, you will need to:

1. Truncate the drive at 4,095 cylinders in CMOS setup (resulting in the loss of drive capacity).
2. Use the >4,096 cylinder support from a third-party software package, such as **EZ- Drive** or **DrivePro**.
3. Upgrade the system BIOS to one that is clearly stated to translate up to 8.4GB BIOS theoretical limit.

See page 60 for more details on this topic.

2.1GB DOS Partition Limit

Current 16-bit file systems limit the size of a single partition to 2.1GB. See page 25 for details on DOS partition limits. Partition size limits are not so much a problem as they are a hassle. The obvious solution is to back up everything and divide the drive into multiple partitions of less than 2.1GB. This can either be done manually through the DOS FDISK, or more easily through a third-party utility such as **EZ-Drive**. Smaller partitions actually have the added benefit of more efficient use of drive space through smaller cluster sizes (see Table 1-3). Newer operating systems that use more advanced (32-bit) file systems do not have this limit.

Improving Drive Performance

Simply purchasing a faster drive does not necessarily result in improved performance. The system must mesh together to take advantage of all the features of which the drive is capable. In the case of Enhanced IDE/ATA-2, advanced PIO and DMA modes require additional BIOS support as well as local bus attachment.

Sometimes it is neither necessary nor desirable to invest in new hardware to get improved performance out of your system's hard drive. Some tools are available and waiting for you to take advantage of them at no extra cost.

Caching

Caching is the process where the system loads data from the hard disk to the **RAM** set aside as **cache memory**. As long as the same file is being accessed, the system may refer to the **cache memory** for information instead of going back to the hard disk, thereby increasing the processing speed. Caching does not really increase data throughput, but makes the drive appear faster by eliminating repetitious access.

Read-through caching facilitates read operations by making an educated guess as to which piece of information will be requested next, and holding it in cache memory. When an application wants data from the drive, the cache program intercepts the request and tries to find the data in the cache memory. If the requested data is in the cache memory, a cache **hit** is said to have occurred. If the requested data is not found in the cache memory, a cache **miss** has occurred, and the cache program sends the request to the hard drive. There are different types of caching algorithms that vary in sophistication as to how they anticipate what information will be requested in the near future. System performance can be greatly improved depending on the percentage of cache hits to misses a cache program can produce.

Write-back caching is used to store information on its way to being written to disk. System resources are freed because the cache memory holds the data until the drive is ready to accept it.

> Be aware of the possible dangers of using a write-back cache. Depending on the type of cache being used, it could take up to several seconds for the drive to actually perform a write process after being instructed to do so. If anything inopportune should occur (power outage, system crash) between the time the cache intercepts the data and before the cache can send the data to the drive, the data will be permanently lost.

Caching is an effective way to improve data transfer performance, but it comes at a cost. The question, once again, is how much performance are you willing to pay for? The data throughput of today's IDE drives is adequate for most, but multi-media applications are making even the casual computer-user look for ways to increase system performance.

There are two types of caches – **dedicated cache memory** and **system memory cache**:

- Dedicated cache memory is (usually) the higher performing and subsequently more expensive option. The cache RAM is installed on the controller in this case. Caching controllers are more costly to begin with, and optional RAM additions can drive up the price substantially.

- System memory cache serves the same purpose, but does not require additional hardware. A portion of system RAM is set aside as the drive cache. Microsoft calls the caching program it includes with DOS **SmartDrive**. Use **SMARTDRV** in the AUTOEXEC.BAT file to create a cache during the boot sequence. Look in the DOS user's guide or use the command HELP SMARTDRV for more information on the proper syntax.

Data Compression

Data compression is an encoding process where data strings that are repeated often are cut out when written to disk, then replaced before being used by an application. Some programs, such as the popular PKZIP, compress individual files as designated by the user. Others compress a portion of the entire disk drive and require no intervention by the user after the compression program is installed. These programs are the cheapest way to roughly double storage space. **DriveSpace** comes with latest versions of DOS and Windows. The cost of increasing capacity in this manner is slower file transfers because of the extra steps involved in compressing and uncompressing data. To maximize the drive's performance, you may want to use compression only on files that you do not use very often.

Data Transfer Modes

Newer IDE drives support additional data transfer modes that dramatically increase performance. These drives usually require support by the controller and system BIOS in order to take advantage of the new modes. Please see the IDE section in Chapter Three for more information on advanced **PIO** and **DMA** modes.

Defragmenting Files

If your drive seems to be slowing down as time goes by, you should start by checking to see how "**fragmented**" your drive is. File fragmentation occurs because DOS assigns disk space as it is available. Files do not always fit in the available space. In these cases DOS fragments the files to different locations on the disk, which means that the heads must be repositioned to retrieve the complete file. As the drive fills up, more files become increasingly fragmented, resulting in a degradation of performance.

The solution is to **defragment** the drive on a regular basis. Newer versions of DOS include a defragmentation program. Simply use the command **DEFRAG** to run the program and choose from among the options presented.

Sleep Modes

One of the current fads in the computer industry is to make hardware more "green," or environmentally friendly, through the addition of energy-saving "**sleep**" modes. Some drives can have this feature enabled through on-board jumpers. There are also utilities available that enable the spindle motor to power down after the program detects a lack of usage, then start it back up on demand. Although commendable in intent, there are some drawbacks to this feature. The drive uses the most power and its components are under the most stress during the power-up sequence because of the torque required to quickly get the disk spinning at operating rpm. The life of the drive may be shortened due to the increase in spin-up sequences. The sleep function has more practical value in secondary drives which see little use, and in laptops to prolong battery life.

Windows 3.1x 32-Bit Access

32-Bit Disk and File Access are Windows 3.1x features that speed up data transfers. **32-Bit Disk Access**, also called **FastDisk**, is a feature which is intended to speed up data transfers. FastDisk is a device driver which effectively replaces the system BIOS for data transfers. By doing so, Windows does not have to switch from protected mode to real mode in order to handle requests by a non-Windows application for disk access. Overall access times appear faster because Windows is not switching back and forth between protected and real modes.

There are potential compatibility problems with using FastDisk. The FastDisk originally bundled with Windows 3.1x will not work with Large IDE drives (see Chapter Three). If you encounter this problem, *EZ-Drive* contains a replacement FastDisk driver that overcomes this compatibility problem. Even if you do not wish to use *EZ-Drive*, you may still install the Custom FastDisk driver. To do this, enter Windows and run the SETUP program that comes with *EZ-Drive*.

32-Bit File Access has more of an effect on overall drive performance because it is intended more for Windows-specific programs. It is actually a caching program that replaces the 16-bit DOS **SmartDrive** cache and creates a Windows-specific cache. Like 32-Bit Disk Access, it allows file transfers to be accomplished in protected mode. 32-Bit File Access also allows the File Allocation Tables to be altered in protected mode, rather than switching to real mode. Cutting out the extra mode switches speeds up overall system performance.

The default mode for both 32-Bit Disk and File Access is disabled. To enable these functions, go into the Windows Control Panel and double-click on the 386 Enhanced Icon. Choose the Virtual Memory option and subsequently click on the Change button. At the bottom of the box will appear "Use 32-Bit Disk Access" and "Use 32-Bit File Access." Enable both of these and exit the utility.

Some programs conflict with the use of 32-Bit Disk and File Access. If this appears to be a problem, you will have to disable these functions while using the application.

Chapter Review:

- Use common sense to prevent damage to the drive that will result in data loss. Place the system in a stable location and isolate it from electrical spikes with a UPS.

- All drives will eventually fail. The best protection against data loss is an effective back-up system.

- Minimize down-time by keeping an emergency boot disk handy.

- 528MB and 2.1GB IDE drive barriers can be overcome. See page 368 for further information.

- Maximize drive performance and storage capacity by taking the time to find out about the capabilities of the equipment.

Diagnostics and Troubleshooting

Chapter Eight Contents:

Diagnostics

If you are experiencing some problems with your hard drive, the first step is to back up your drive completely in preparation for the worst. You should then attempt to narrow down the cause of the problem (if it is not already obvious) to determine the reliability of the drive for future use. DOS contains some basic diagnostic utilities, **CHKDSK** (DOS only) and **ScanDisk** (DOS and Windows), which you should run periodically to get an idea of the overall health of your drive(s).

DrivePro contains powerful and easy to use diagnostics that will give you a precise report on the condition of your drive. Please run the *DrivePro* demonstration that is included on the CD-ROM provided with this text for a hands-on introduction to these features.

The following text is excerpted from the *DrivePro* User's Manual as an illustration of hard drive diagnostics:

This menu option leads to several diagnostic test selections. An option is toggled for selection/de-selection by pressing ↵ while on an item. The tests toggled for execution will have a small filled-in box to the left of them. Selecting **ESC** exits the window and executes the tests selected.

```
┌─ SELECT TESTS ══════════════╗
║                             ║
║   Controller/Disk Electronics
║   Linear Read Diagnostics   ║
║   Butterfly Read Diagnostics║
║   Random Read Diagnostics   ║
║                             ║
║   Esc, ↑↓, or ◄─┘           ║
╚═════════════════════════════╝
```

Figure 8-1: DrivePro Diagnostics Menu

Controller/Disk Electronics

This option checks the integrity of the controller and disk drive electronics. Since these tests are dependent on the controller and drive, some will not support all commands sent to them. If this is the case with your controller and drive, then messages such as "Can't test controller RAM" (meaning that the controller does not support the controller RAM test) will appear in the **RESULTS** window. This is perfectly normal and does not mean that there is a problem with your controller or drive.

Linear, Butterfly and Random Read Tests

These diagnostics test the drive's ability to read data from the drive. These are all **non-destructive** tests. Most diagnostic programs also give the user the option of choosing the level of testing thoroughness.

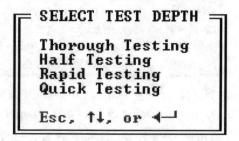

```
┌─ SELECT TEST DEPTH ─┐
│                      │
│   Thorough Testing   │
│   Half Testing       │
│   Rapid Testing      │
│   Quick Testing      │
│                      │
│   Esc, ↑↓, or ←┘     │
│                      │
└──────────────────────┘
```

Figure 8-2: DrivePro Test Depth Menu

After selecting the test depth, the test will be run and the results placed into the **RESULTS** window.

Surface Scan

Surface scan tests give the user various levels of testing to perform on the drive media and report back any defective sectors. Typically, the higher levels will find any bad sectors, but you can run the longer and more thorough tests to be absolutely sure.

Performance

The most comprehensive measure of a drive's performance is its **data transfer rate**, or **throughput**. Checking seek times and interleave may help diagnose why a drive is not performing up to specifications.

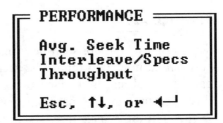

Figure 8-3: DrivePro Performance Tests Menu

Seek Times

These tests check the drive for average, track-to-track and full-stroke seek times. The seek times are obtained as follows:

Average Seek

Seeks are performed within the highest and lowest cylinders for all possible seek lengths. **DrivePro** performs the number of cylinders minus 1 seek. This is a more exact measure of average seek time than doing a 1/3-stroke seek as some other programs do.

Track-to-Track Seek

The time it takes the drive to seek between adjacent tracks.

Full-Stroke Seek

The time it takes the drive to seek from the lowest cylinder to the highest cylinder.

These tests are usually accurate but certain variables such as system timing, BIOS type, and transfer rate might cause this figure to deviate slightly. **DrivePro**'s figures will usually not exactly match the manufacturer's due to the fact that their tests usually do not take into account system and controller overhead, and are measured in an idealized way.

Average seek times are most accurate on non-translated drives. Average seek time for SCSI drives may not be a valid test because SCSI drives always perform an addressing translation (see Chapter Three). Average seek times on translated ESDI and IDE drives may deviate from manufacturer's specifications because the seek time between logical tracks may differ from physical tracks, but still can be useful in comparisons.

Throughput

The most widely-published performance rating is **seek** time. Most software utilities will report the **seek** time of the drive. While this can be useful and is, in fact, one of the most critical aspects of a drive's performance, a more practical measure of drive performance is **throughput**. **Seek** time is a rating of the time involved when moving the drive heads across the platters. In addition to seek time, however, there are additional factors such as **Latency**, which is the time involved in spinning the platter around so that the desired data is below the heads; **Head Switch Time**, which is the time involved in switching to a different head of the head assembly; and Controller, BIOS, and System Bus-to-Memory overhead. These factors all affect the speed at which desired information can be retrieved and made available to applications. By performing data transfers from the drive, all of these factors can be measured together as overall system throughput.

Dramatic performance (throughput) increases can be realized by such innovations as track buffers, caching, and local bus controllers. Please note: manufacturers of controller cards and drives often publish throughput ratings for their products, but these figures are based on ideal conditions, and for that device only, rather than the whole system, and so may differ from the actual overall system throughput achieved, and measured by *DrivePro*. Note also that performance can be affected by the type and manner of hard drive access of a particular application. An application that does more random access of information will perform more poorly than one that confines its accesses mainly to a particular area of the drive.

Interleave/Specs

Checks the drive for its current interleave and determines the optimum interleave. The optimum interleave given is only valid for the system in which the drive is currently installed. Interleave testing is usually only needed for ST-506/412 drives.

Most newer drives <u>only</u> use an interleave of 1:1, as they have a full track buffer. Interleave optimization is not required on these drives.

If you want to permanently adjust the interleave on an ST-506/412 drive, re-do the low-level format. Although this can be done non-destructively, remember to perform a backup first.

POST Error Codes

The BIOS performs a Power On Self Test (POST) during the boot process. If an error is detected, the POST will halt the boot process and return an error code corresponding to the problem encountered. No real standard has existed since the original IBM BIOS. Modern error codes are particular to individual BIOS manufacturers.

The table on the following page is only useful for older systems which may use older IBM conventions. If your system is fairly current (80486 and above), you should refer to the BIOS manufacturer's documentation for information. Only the codes pertaining to hard and floppy disks are contained here.

Table 8-1: IBM BIOS Error Codes

Code	Description	Code	Description
01x	Undetermined problem errors	1702	Fixed disk adapter error
6xx	Floppy drive/adapter errors	1703	Fixed disk drive error
601	Floppy drive/adapter POST failure	1704	Fixed disk adapter or drive error
602	Drive test failure; disk boot record	1780	Fixed disk 0 failure
606	Disk change line function failure; drive error	1781	Fixed disk 1 failure
607	Disk is write protected; drive error	1782	Fixed disk controller failure
608	Bad command; drive error	1790	Fixed disk 0 error
01x	Undetermined problem errors	1791	Fixed disk 1 error
6xx	Floppy drive/adapter errors	7306	Disk change line function failure; drive error
601	Floppy drive/adapter POST failure	7307	Disk is write protected; drive error
602	Drive test failure; disk boot record	7308	Bad command; drive error
606	Disk change line function failure; drive error	7310	Disk initialization failure; track 0 bad
607	Disk is write protected; drive error	7311	Time-out; drive error
608	Bad command; drive error	7312	Bad Controller chi
610	Disk initialization failure; track 0 bad	7313	Bad Direct Memory Access; drive error
611	Time-out; drive error	7314	Bad Direct Memory Access; boundary overrun
612	Bad Controller chip	7315	Bad index timing; drive error
613	Bad Direct Memory Access; drive error	7316	Drive speed error
614	Bad Direct Memory Access; boundary overrun	7321	Bad seek; drive error
615	Bad index timing; drive error	7323	Record not found; drive error
616	Drive speed error	7324	Bad address mark; drive error
621	Bad seek; drive error	7325	Bad Controller chip; seek error
622	Bad Cyclic Redundancy Check; drive error	104xx	PS/2 ESDI Fixed disk errors
623	Record not found; drive error	10480	PS/2 ESDI Fixed disk 0 failure
624	Bad address mark; drive error	10481	PS/2 ESSI Fixed disk 1 failure
625	Bad Controller chip; seek error	10482	PS/2 ESDI Fixed disk controller failure
17xx	Fixed disk errors	10483	PS/2 ESDI Fixed disk controller failure
1701	Fixed disk POST error	10490	PS/2 ESDI Fixed disk 0 error
		10491	PS/2 ESDI Fixed disk 1 error

Troubleshooting Frequently Asked Questions (FAQs)

This section answers some questions that are commonly asked concerning hard drive set-up and operation.

FAQ Index

All Drives

SCSI Drives

FAQ	PAGE
• What CMOS Drive Type is used for SCSI drives?	392

ESDI Drives

FAQ	PAGE
• What CMOS Drive Type is used for ESDI drives?	392
• ESDI drive shows less capacity than it actually has when in FDISK.	393

ST-506/412 Drives

FAQ	PAGE
• No response from MFM/RLL (ST-506/412) hard drive after installing.	393
• "Nothing done exit" appears when doing a low-level format with a Western Digital Controller.	393
• Getting a "recal error" or a "no drive attached" error.	393

All Drives

Are the cables installed correctly?

Ensure that you are using the correct type of cable according to your system configuration on ST-506/412 or ESDI drives. See Chapter 4 for information on matching cables to the system.

Ensure that the red or blue wire on all cables is plugged into pin 1 of the interface. Ensure that the red or blue wire also matches pin-1 on the controller card.

A common symptom of an incorrectly installed IDE cable is floppy drives that don't work correctly or don't work at all.

Drive doesn't spin.

1. Check that drive has power supplied to it. Ensure that the power cable connector is firmly seated to the receptacle on the drive.

2. Some of the older hard drives have a problem with the media becoming sticky after years of use. The heads get stuck to the platter and prevent it from spinning. To get them spinning again, make sure you touch a good ground (like bare metal on the case of your computer if it is plugged into a good 3-prong outlet), remove the drive from the case, turn the drive over and slightly turn the spindle (be careful!) to loosen it. It should then work long enough to make a backup. Get your data off quickly and replace the drive!

CMOS shows drives capacity as less than it should be.

CMOS and FDISK calculate drive capacity by the formula HEADS x CYLINDERS x SECTORS / 2,048. DIR, CHKDSK, and **DrivePro** use the formula HEADS x CYLINDERS x SECTORS x 512. CxHxSx512 yields decimal number of bytes, which when divided by 1,000,000 gives you decimal million bytes (MB). CxHxS/2,048 yields binary *megabytes*. There are 1,000,000 bytes in each decimal million byte. There are 1,048,576 bytes in a binary megabyte. Therefore, if the CMOS value for the capacity of the drive is less than some other indicator by around 5%, the difference is due to different calculation methods.

"C: Drive Failure. F1 to continue" message

If after pressing F1 your drive goes on to boot, the parameters set in CMOS are not supported by the drive (for some Conner, Maxtor, and a few other older drive models not supporting translation) or are too large for the drive (on a Compaq system). If a **DrivePro** or **EZ-Drive** Custom Drive Type is installed, merely set the CMOS for type 1. If not, check the jumper settings and manufacturer's recommended parameters for the hard drive. Correct the CMOS setup and try again. If no matching CMOS drive type can be found and the BIOS does not have a user-definable drive type or automatic selection, **DrivePro** lets you define a Custom Drive Type.

"Hard Drive Controller Failure" message

Most likely your controller is not functioning. Try switching controllers, cables, and drives, and make sure that the cables are attached correctly, that the jumpers are set correctly, and try different bus slot locations. On IDE drives, the "controller" is contained on the drive itself, therefore this message could be due to a bad or incorrectly installed drive. Also check the section above on "C: Drive Failure, Press F1 to Continue."

"Error Reading Fixed Disk" or similar message

If this message appears when booting from the hard drive, but you can boot from a floppy and then access the hard drive, it is most likely that the parameters used to configure the IDE drive slightly exceeded the drive's capacity. Use slightly lower parameters, then re-partition and re-format the drive. Reboot for the changes to take effect.

The error message "1790" appears at boot-up.

A 1790 error is normal for an unformatted drive. Simply do the low-level if this is a new ESDI or ST-506/412 installation. If this is an existing installation then the drive has probably lost its format and cannot be salvaged by normal means. If the data has been backed-up, you can try redoing the low-level format, followed by the normal partitioning and high-level (DOS) format, finally restoring your backup to the drive. If this works, the drive may still be close to total failure, so it is wise to not place any important information on it.

Unable to delete a Novell or other non-DOS partition or unable to DOS format such a partition.

This is particularly troublesome with IDE and SCSI drives due to the fact that they usually cannot simply be low-level formatted. If you own a copy of *DrivePro*, select **Format Operations** from the main menu, then select **Erase First Ten Cylinders**. *DrivePro*'s **Partition/MBR Editor** will also allow you to edit or delete a non-DOS partition table entry, so you can also use that option, or the **Super Sector Editor,** to remove the Novell or non-DOS partition. Also, more recent versions of the DOS command **FDISK** allow the removal of non-DOS partitions.

Need to use only the floppy section of an 80x86-type hard/floppy controller card but no jumper is provided to disable. How do I disable the hard drive from the controller?

In most cases you can disable the hard drive section of the controller by setting the hard drive port address to the secondary setting (170h-177h) . You must also move the controller to an 8-bit slot (ISA bus only).

Long boot time after installing a drive into an 80x86-type machine.

Some 80x86 systems may continue to retry booting from the newly installed disk several times, even though it has not even been formatted. You will have to wait until the computer is done with the retry process before the system will boot to the floppy drive. Then you can proceed to do the hard drive setup. If you obtain an error message after the wait period, then the drive in not installed correctly.

Drive Active LED always stays lit.

8086/8088 installations: Check cable connections. Try to reverse or replace the cables. If this doesn't correct the problem, then the drive is probably bad. AT installation: This is not a problem. On 80x86 systems the drive is always selected and therefore the LED is always lit. Also, you can try turning off all power to the system, waiting 10-15 seconds, and then turning the system back on.

"Hard disk drive not ready" or 01 error code when booting.

Possibly one of two problems: 1) System BIOS drive table doesn't support the controller and drive or 2) the power supply is overloaded – replace it with one of a higher wattage or remove or replace some of the cards with lower-power ones to reduce the load. Check the manufacturer's documentation for electrical specifications.

Error code 80 while doing a low-level format.

Drive select jumper is incorrectly set on the hard drive or the cables are on backwards. Possibly could be bad cables, no power to drive, or simply a bad drive.

Error codes 20 or 40 while doing a low-level format.

Check cable connections. Try to reverse or replace the cables. Could also be a bad drive.

After DOS format, message "Insert disk and press ENTER" appears.

Motherboard switches are set for the incorrect number of floppy drives (PC or XT). Check to see if RAM disk drivers are present; if so, then set the motherboard switches to include the RAM drives.

"Bad track 0" using DOS 3.1

Make sure the line, "BUFFERS=99" is in the CONFIG.SYS file.

"Bad track 0" using DOS 2.1

DOS 2.1 cannot support a drive that has bad tracks above 16.7MB. Upgrade the system's DOS to 3.1 or better.

Getting intermittent operation errors or read/write errors at random.

Ensure that the termination resistors on the hard drive(s) are properly placed. Also ensure that the power supply can support the added hard drive, and that voltages from the power supply are within range.

IDE Drives

Check the drive's jumper settings.

You must set the jumpers on the hard drive(s) correctly. Most drives come from the factory in the "Master" or "Only Drive" configuration. Do you have these jumpers set correctly? The jumper settings on both the existing drive and the new drive must be changed if you are installing a second drive into the same system. See Chapter Six or check with the manufacturer if you are having difficulties with the drive(s) and are unsure of these settings.

Two IDE drives will not work together even though I have the Master/Slave settings set correctly.

Check or switch out the cabling. Re-check the **I/O Channel Ready** and **Drive Slave Present** jumpers (contact the drive or controller manufacturer's Technical Support for more information). In some cases both IDE drives must be of the same make in order to work together. If the two IDE drives work independently of each other, try switching the drives in terms of Master and Slave. If the two drives work independently, but not together, then the solutions are to use two drives of the same make, or to use a secondary adapter and put one on the primary adapter and the other on the secondary adapter. In the case of non-Enhanced IDE systems *EZ-Drive* should be used.

Installed an IDE hard drive; now the floppy drives don't work.

If you have installed an IDE drive and now the floppy drives don't work or even light up during boot, then you have hooked-up the IDE cables backwards.

Most IDE drives do not show the location of pin-1. If you can't locate pin-1, then a good rule-of-thumb is to assume pin-1 is the closest pin to the DC power connector.

The manufacturer gave me specifications that don't match your book!

Who's right?

Well, believe it or not, we're both right. **Appendix A** contains (where possible) *physical* specifications (the actual number of heads, cylinders, and sectors).

What was given to you by the manufacturer are the *logical* (translated) specifications (so that the hard drive will get along with your BIOS and DOS). Note, however, that the logical parameters that the manufacturer supplied you with are not the only parameters you may use. Just remember the rule:

*Choose a drive type that is equal to or less than, **but never more than,** the size of the hard drive in megabytes.*

The IDE drive will take it from there.

Here is an example to help demonstrate:

Let's take one of the more popular IDE drives, the Maxtor 7213AT. This is a 212MB drive with 4 heads, 1,690 cylinders and variable sectors per track (See ZBR in the glossary). Here are the specifications, both PHYSICAL and LOGICAL:

Table 8-1: Physical vs. Logical Specifications Example					
PHYSICAL (Actual)			LOGICAL (Translation)		
Heads	Cylinders	SPT	Heads	Cylinders	SPT
4	1,690	48-72	16	683	38
= 212.78 MB formatted			= 212.61 MB formatted		

This drive suffers from having a sector per track (SPT) value not supported by the BIOS, and too many cylinders for DOS. That's where the LOGICAL (translation) specifications come in.

The 7213A also serves as a good example of how to recognize logical parameters. This drive, like most manufactured today, is only an inch high. Many times we are told the book is wrong because we say it has 4 heads and the manufacturer says it has 16. It would be quite impractical, if not impossible, to put 8 platters (16 heads) into a drive with a one-inch height. With this in mind it is often easy to distinguish logical and physical specifications.

No matching type in BIOS for IDE drive.

If the BIOS does not have a user-definable drive type, or the cylinders of the drive are over 1024 (or other DOS limitations are exceeded), you may select the closest fitting table entry that does not use the entire disk. *EZ-Drive* allows you to create a **Custom Drive Type**. Note that you must not set the number of cylinders greater than 1,024 with any version of DOS, unless you use the *EZ-Drive* 512MB-2GB Drive Type, or a replacement block device driver for DOS that supports over 1,024 cylinders. To exceed these limitations without one of these installed may result in loss of all data on the drive! In addition, you cannot use more than 63 sectors or 16 heads, unless your controller has an on-board BIOS that allows for a greater number than that, because of AT-standard BIOS limitations. You must use a translated set of parameters that equal the same capacity without exceeding these limitations. To use the best matching BIOS entry, choose the entry that is equal to or less than, but never more than, the drive's capacity in megabytes.

Other options are hardware ones, including upgrading your system's BIOS and purchasing a controller with an on-board BIOS.

IDE drive was moved to another system or computer lost its CMOS setup. Now the IDE drive won't work properly. (Need to determine drive's original parameters.)

The parameters for the IDE drive must be set *identically* as when the computer was initially set up. Note that different parameters can yield the same capacity, so using just any parameters that yield the correct capacity does not necessarily mean you are using the correct parameters. If you own a copy of **DrivePro**, you can determine from the drive's partition table the original parameters used to setup the drive, using **DrivePro**'s **Get Lost Parameters** feature. Upon determining the correct parameters, either: match them to a drive type in the CMOS, or; configure the CMOS user-definable. Alternatively, you may run **DrivePro** /MBR to set up a **DrivePro** Custom Drive Type with the correct parameters without erasing the partition table. The drive may then be used in any machine as long as the CMOS is set to a value besides 0, or is not installed.

Drive won't boot after FDISK and DOS format, but Norton Disk Doctor corrects this. Why?

This is a problem that usually arises with some older IDE drives. DOS appears to have some problems marking the first partition of a drive "active." The first partition must be marked "active" for it to boot. FDISK is supposed to do this for you on the first partition, but it sometimes fails to do so. The most problematic DOS version is 3.3. Norton Disk Doctor fixes this because this simply marks the first partition as "active." You can also fix this by running FDISK and setting the first partition to "active", or by using **DrivePro**'s Partition Table/MBR editor and marking the first partition BOOTABLE – "YES."

"Hard drive controller failure" after installing a second IDE drive.

You should carefully check and reconfirm the jumper settings and check or switch out the cabling, and try changing such jumpers as I/O Channel Ready and the Drive Slave Present jumpers (consult the drive manufacturer's Technical Support for additional help with this). You can also try switching the two hard drives around, setting the jumpers on the Master drive to be the Slave, and on the Slave drive to be the Master. Also, due to the proprietary beginnings of the IDE interface, two IDE drives that are not from the manufacturer are very frequently incompatible. This is especially true of some older Conner and Seagate drives. The solution to this problem when adding a second IDE drive is to use drives of the same make, or alternatively, use *EZ-Drive* to allow the second drive to be used on a secondary adapter.

Ran FDISK or Partition Table/MBR on an IDE drive several times, but it won't save the partition tables.

Translation values used in the CMOS setup that are greater than the capacity of the IDE drive or parameters that the IDE drive does not support can cause this problem. Try another set of heads, cylinders and sectors. Be sure that you don't go over the drive's total capacity in megabytes. You should also recheck jumper settings and check or switch out the cabling.

SCSI Drives

What CMOS Drive Type is used for SCSI drives?

In most installations set the type to "0" or "none," and the SCSI controller and drive will take it from there.

ESDI Drives

What CMOS Drive Type is used for ESDI drives?

In most installations set the type to "1," and the ESDI controller and drive will take it from there.

ESDI drive shows less capacity than it actually has when in FDISK.

If using a Western Digital ESDI controller or compatible: when in debug (G=xxxx:5) you must select menu item 7, **Change drive type and exit**. Then use the +/- keys to select a set of parameters that is equal to your drive's capacity. These parameters need not match the actual physical parameters of the drive. These are the parameter's logical translation that DOS will refer to. If you are not using a Western Digital controller, then refer to your controller manual for information on the above.

ST-506/412 Drives

No response from MFM/RLL (ST-506/412) hard drive after installing.

Change the cables. Note: Do not use a floppy cable on a hard drive if you are performing an ST-506/412 installation. They both use a 34-pin control cable, but floppy drive cables are not compatible with hard drive cables. Floppy cables use a larger twist. Check to make sure that the drive has power and is spinning. Also, re-check the jumper settings.

"Nothing done exit" appears when doing a low-level format with a Western Digital Controller.

You didn't press the <Y> key when prompted. Restart the low-level format.

Getting a "recal error" or a "no drive attached" error.

Check the drive select jumpers for proper installation. On MFM/RLL (ST-506/412) or ESDI drives, ensure that the data cables are attached to the proper drives. Also ensure that pin-1 on the controller is attached to pin-1 on the drive.

Chapter Review:

- Upon receiving <u>any</u> indication that there is a problem with a drive, immediately back up all data on it.

- Run the DOS/Windows utilities CHKDSK and ScanDisk periodically to get an idea of drive health.

- Programs such as **DrivePro** contain in-depth diagnostic routines that will help analyze the source of a drive's problem.

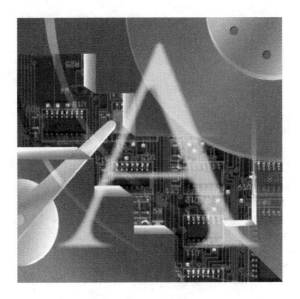

Drive Specifications

Appendix A Contents:

Introduction

This appendix contains the specifications required when setting up a hard drive. It is alphabetically sorted by manufacturer. It contains the actual physical specifications. The IDE manufacturers' recommended parameter table, or the IDE quick reference table, should be used in most cases to locate parameters for IDE hard drives.

Categories and Abbreviations

The following table defines the abbreviations used in this chapter. See Chapters One and Two for complete information on terms contained in this section.

CAP: Capacity in megabytes

HDS: Number of **PHYSICAL** data heads. Servo heads are not included in this figure.

CYL: Number of **PHYSICAL** user-accessible cylinders. **If the drive is an IDE drive and this number exceeds 1,024, a translation must be used.**

SPT: Number of **PHYSICAL** sectors per track.

SEEK: Average track seek time in milliseconds.

FF: Form Factor denotes the diameter of the drive platter(s) in inches.

HGT: The drive's height. FH=Full, HH=Half, 3H=1", and 4H=less than 1".

INT: Interface type.

ENCODE: Encoding scheme.

LZ: Landing zone (or parking, shipping) cylinder. Not used on most of the newer drives.

WP: Write Precompensation cylinder. Not used on most of the newer drives.

RWC: Reduced Write Current cylinder. Not used on most of the newer drives.

MTBF: Mean Time Between Failures, in number of hours.

Where possible, actual (physical) heads, cylinders and sectors are provided. For a complete description, please see the explanation of *logical* and *physical* specifications in the IDE section of Chapter Three.

About MTBF Values

In recent years as technology advanced, MTBF values increased on many of the hard drives that are still in production. For example, Seagate Technologies has increased some of their MTBF values from 20,000 power-on hours to 1,000,000 and more. All MTBF values expressed in these tables represent (where possible) current values.

Changes in Make and Model

Several companies have changed names or have been bought out by other companies. If you can't find the model you are looking for, look through the other manufacturers to see if it is under another brand name. The model numbers usually stay unchanged when the drive changes to another manufacturer.

The following is a list of some brand names to cross reference when looking for a drive model:

- ATASI and PRIAM may be the same
- CDC, CONNER, IMPRIMIS and SEAGATE may be the same (see Seagate in this chapter for the conversion chart)
- MAXTOR and MINISCRIBE may be the same
- OTARI and DISCTRON may be the same
- PRIAM and VERTEX may be the same
- YE DATA and C.ITOH may be the same
- BRAND and NCL may be the same

There may be others not listed here so look thoroughly through all brands to locate your drive.

Manufacturers' Recommended Parameters

Older BIOSes can only access 1,024 cylinders, and most IDE drives now use more. If this is the case, an IDE drive's physical parameters cannot be used to achieve a safe setup with full capacity. Most IDE drives manufactured after 1990 support a logical translation to alleviate this problem. Please see the IDE section of Chapter Three for a more detailed explanation of IDE/BIOS limits.

The following is a list of some of the most popular IDE drives and the translations recommended by their makers.

ALPS ELECTRIC				
Model	Cap	Hds	Cyl	SPT
DR311C901	105	16	759	17
DR311C901A	105	16	759	17
DR311C911	105	16	759	17
DR312C012A	211	16	992	26
DR312C901	211	16	992	26
DR312C911	211	16	992	26

BRAND TECHNOLOGY				
Model	Cap	Hds	Cyl	SPT
BT9121A	107	10	583	36
BT9170A	150	14	583	36
BT9220A	200	16	401	61
BT9400S	400	16	801	61
BT9650A	650	16	1024	63

CONNER PERIPHERALS				
Model	Cap	Hds	Cyl	SPT
CFA-1080A	1080	16	2097	63
CFA-1275A	1278	16	2479	63
CFA-170A	171	16	332	63
CFA-270A	270	16	524	63
CFA-340A	343	16	665	63
CFA-425A	426	16	826	63
CFA-540A	541	16	1048	63
CFA-810A	810	16	1572	63
CFA-850A	852	16	1652	63
CFL-350A	350	12	905	63
CFL-425A	426	16	826	63
CFN-170A	168	16	326	63
CFN-250A	252	16	489	63
CFN-340A	344	16	667	63
CFS-1275A	1278	16	2479	63
CFS-210A	213	16	685	38
CFS-270A	270	16	525	63

CONNER PERIPHERALS				
Model	Cap	Hds	Cyl	SPT
CFS-420A	426	16	826	63
CFS-425A	425	16	826	63
CFS-540A	540	16	1050	63
CP-2022	21	2	653	32
CP-2024	21	2	653	32
CP-2034	32	2	823	38
CP-2044PK	42	4	552	38
CP-2064	64	4	823	38
CP-2084	85	8	548	38
CP-2088	85	8	548	38
CP-2124	126	8	900	33
CP-2254	253	16	489	63
CP-3000	42	5	980	17
CP-30061	60	4	762	39
CP-30061G	60	4	762	39
CP-30064	60	4	762	39
CP-30064H	60	4	762	39
CP-30081	84	8	526	39
CP-30081E	85	8	526	39
CP-30084	84	8	526	39
CP-30084E	85	4	903	46
CP-30101	121	8	762	39
CP-30101Gi	121	8	762	39
CP-30104	121	8	762	39
CP-30104H	121	8	762	39
CP-30124	125	5	895	55
CP-30174E	170	8	903	46
CP-30204	212	16	683	38
CP-3022	21	2	636	33
CP-3024	21	2	636	33
CP-30254	251	10	895	55
CP-30344	343	16	665	63
CP-3041	42	5	980	17
CP-3044	42	5	980	17

CONNER PERIPHERALS				
Model	Cap	Hds	Cyl	SPT
CP-30544	545	16	1057	63
CP-3102	104	8	776	33
CP-3104	104	8	776	33
CP-3111	112	8	832	33
CP-3114	112	8	832	33
CP-3181	84	6	832	33
CP-3184	84	6	832	33
CP-3201i	215	16	683	38
CP-3204	215	16	683	38
CP-3204F	212	16	683	38
CP-3304	340	16	659	63
CP-3364	362	16	702	63
CP-341	42	4	805	26
CP-341i	42	4	805	26
CP-342	42	4	805	26
CP-344	42	4	805	26
CP-346	42	4	805	26
CP-3501	510	16	989	63
CP-3504	510	16	989	63
CP-3544	543	16	1024	63
CP-4024	21	2	620	34
CP-4041	42	5	980	17
CP-4044	42	5	980	17

CONTROL DATA CORPORATION				
Model	Cap	Hds	Cyl	SPT
94204-074	53	5	948	26
94204-081	71	10	516	27
94244-274	232	10	873	54
94244-383	338	14	873	54
94354-090	79	16	335	29
94354-111	98	10	536	36
94354-126	111	16	469	29
94354-133	117	10	636	36
94354-155	138	14	596	36
94354-160	143	16	603	29
94354-186	164	14	636	36
94354-200	177	12	804	36
94354-239	211	14	817	36

CORE INTERNATIONAL				
Model	Cap	Hds	Cyl	SPT
HC200	200	12	986	33

DAEYOUNG ELECTRONICS				
Model	Cap	Hds	Cyl	SPT
DX-3130A	42	8	866	34

FUJITSU AMERICA				
Model	Cap	Hds	Cyl	SPT
M2611ET	45	4	667	33
M2611T	45	4	667	33
M2612ET	90	8	667	33
M2612T	90	8	667	33
M2613ET	135	12	667	33
M2613T	135	12	667	33
M2614ET	180	16	667	33
M2614T	180	16	667	33
M2616ET	104	8	771	33
M2616T	104	8	771	33
M2622T	327	10	1013	63
M2623T	421	13	1002	63
M2624T	515	16	995	63
M2635T	160	8	620	63
M2637T	240	8	930	63
M2681T	264	11	977	48
M2682T	352	11	992	63
M2684T	528	16	1024	63

HEWLETT PACKARD				
Model	Cap	Hds	Cyl	SPT
D1697A	240	8	930	63
HP C2233	238	16	462	63
HP C2234	334	16	647	63
HP C2235	429	16	832	63
HP C3013A	21	4	615	17
HP C3014A	42	6	820	17

IBM CORPORATION				
Model	Cap	Hds	Cyl	SPT
0662A10	1052	16	2038	63
DHA-2270	270	16	524	63
DHA-2405	405	16	785	63
DHA-2540	540	16	1047	63
DSAA-3270	281	16	954	36
DSAA-3360	365	16	929	48
DSAA-3540	540	16	1062	63
DSAA-3540	528	16	1024	63
DSAA-3720	730	16	1416	63
H2172-A2	172	10	989	34
H2258-A3	258	15	989	34
H2344-A4	344	15	915	49
H3133-A2	133	15	1023	17
H3171-A2	171	10	984	34
H3256-A3	257	16	872	36
H3342-A4	342	16	872	48
TYPE 0662	1051	16	2038	63
WDA-2120	126	15	969	17

IBM CORPORATION				
Model	Cap	Hds	Cyl	SPT
WDA-240	43	8	619	17
WDA-280	86	10	989	17
WDA-L160	171	10	984	34
WDA-L80	85	10	984	17
WDA-S260	63	8	909	17

KALOK				
Model	Cap	Hds	Cyl	SPT
KL 3100	105	6	979	35
KL 3120	120	6	981	40
KL 383	84	6	815	33

KYOCERA				
Model	Cap	Hds	Cyl	SPT
KC 40GA	39	4	577	33
KC 80GA	78	8	577	33

MAXTOR				
Model	Cap	Hds	Cyl	SPT
25084A	84	16	569	18
25125A	128	14	1024	17
25128A	128	14	1024	17
25125A	128	14	1024	17
25252A	230	16	1024	30
2585A	85	10	981	17
7040A	43	5	981	17
7060A	65	7	1024	17
7080A	85	10	981	17
7120A	130	14	1024	17
7131A	130	8	1002	32
7135AV	135	13	966	21
7170A	170	16	683	38
7171A	171	15	866	26
7213A	212	16	683	38
7270AV	270	11	959	50
7245A	245	16	967	31
7273AT	275	16	967	31
7290A	290	9	998	63
7345A	345	15	790	57
7405A	405	16	989	50
7405AV	405	16	989	50
7540AV	540	16	1046	63
7546AT	528	16	1024	63
8051A	42	4	745	28
LXT-200A	207	15	816	32
LXT-213A	212	16	683	38
LXT-340A	340	16	654	63
LXT-437A	437	16	842	63

MAXTOR				
Model	Cap	Hds	Cyl	SPT
LXT-535A	528	16	1024	63
MXT-540A	528	16	1046	63

MICROPOLIS				
Model	Cap	Hds	Cyl	SPT
2105(A)	560	16	1084	63
2112(A)	528	16	1024	63
2205A	528	16	1024	63
2210A	976	16	1891	63
2217(A)	1626	16	3152	63
4110(A)	1057	16	2048	63

MINISCRIBE				
Model	Cap	Hds	Cyl	SPT
7040A	42	5	981	17
7060A	65	7	1024	17
7080A	85	10	981	17
7120A	130	14	1024	17
8051A	42	4	745	28

NCL AMERICA				
Model	Cap	Hds	Cyl	SPT
9220A	200	16	401	61
NDC 5125	150	10	583	36

NEC				
Model	Cap	Hds	Cyl	SPT
D3735	45	4	542	41
D3741	45	7	733	17
D3755	104	8	625	41
D3756	104	8	625	41
D3761	118	7	915	35
D3781	425	9	1464	63

PLUS DEVELOPMENT				
Model	Cap	Hds	Cyl	SPT
105AT/LP	105	16	755	17
120AT	120	9	814	32
170AT	169	10	966	34
210AT	210	13	873	36
40AT	41	5	968	17
52AT/LP	52	8	751	17
80AT	83	6	611	17
80AT/LP	85	6	611	17

QUANTUM				
Model	**Cap**	**Hds**	**Cyl**	**SPT**
DAYTONA 127AT	127	9	677	41
DAYTONA 170AT	170	10	538	62
DAYTONA 256AT	256	11	723	63
DAYTONA 341AT	341	15	1011	44
GD 60AT	63	7	1024	17
GD 80AT	82	9	1024	17
GD 120AT	126	13	731	26
GD GLS 40AT	41	6	820	17
GD GLS 60AT	63	7	1024	17
GD GLS 80AT	82	9	1024	17
GD GLS 85AT	85	10	722	23
GD GLS 120AT	126	13	731	26
GD-GLS 127AT	127	9	677	41
GD-GLS 160AT	170	9	1024	36
GD-GLS 170AT	171	10	538	62
GD-GLS 256AT	256	11	723	63
GD-GRS 160AT	169	9	1024	36
GD-GRS 80AT	84	5	966	34
L. 365AT	365	12	976	61
L. 540AT	541	16	1120	59
L. 730AT	730	16	1416	63
PD 105AT	105	16	755	17
PD 120AT	120	9	814	32
M. 270AT	270	14	944	40
M. 540AT	541	16	1048	63
PD 170AT	168	10	968	34
PD 210AT	209	13	873	36
PD 40AT	42	5	968	17
PD 425AT	426	16	1021	51
PD 80AT	84	16	611	17
PD ELS 127AT	127	16	919	17
PD ELS 170AT	170	15	1011	22
PD ELS 42AT	42	5	968	17
PD ELS 85AT	85	10	977	17
PD LPS 105AT	104	16	755	17
PD LPS 120AT	122	5	901	53
PD LPS 127AT	127	16	919	17
PD LPS 170AT	426	16	1021	51
PD LPS 210AT	211	15	723	38
PD LPS 240AT	245	13	723	51
PD LPS 270AT	271	14	944	40
PD LPS 340AT	340	15	1011	44
PD LPS 420AT	421	16	1021	51
PD LPS 52AT	52	8	751	17
PD LPS 525AT	527	16	1017	63
PD LPS 540AT	541	16	1048	63
PD LPS 80AT	85	16	611	17

RODIME				
Model	**Cap**	**Hds**	**Cyl**	**SPT**
RO3058A	45	3	868	34
RO3058A	45	3	868	34
RO3088A	75	5	868	34
RO3095A	80	5	923	34
RO3099A	80	15	614	17
RO3099AP	80	15	614	17
RO3135A	112	7	923	34
RO3139A	50	15	861	17
RO3139AP	112	15	861	17
RO3259A	209	15	976	28
RO3259AP	212	15	990	28

SAMSUNG				
Model	**Cap**	**Hds**	**Cyl**	**SPT**
RO3058A	45	3	868	34
RO3058A	45	3	868	34
RO3088A	75	5	868	34
RO3095A	80	5	923	34
RO3099A	80	15	614	17
RO3099AP	80	15	614	17
RO3135A	112	7	923	34
RO3139A	50	15	861	17
RO3139AP	112	15	861	17
RO3259A	209	15	976	28
RO3259AP	212	15	990	28

SEAGATE TECHNOLOGY				
Model	**Cap**	**Hds**	**Cyl**	**SPT**
ST1057A	53	6	1024	17
ST1090A	79	16	335	29
ST1102A	89	10	1024	17
ST1111A	98	10	536	36
ST1126A	111	16	469	29
ST1133A	117	10	636	36
ST1144A	130	15	1001	17
ST1156A	138	14	536	36
ST1162A	143	16	603	29
ST1186A	164	14	636	36
ST1201A	177	12	804	36
ST1239A	211	14	814	36
ST125A	21	4	404	26
ST125A-1	21	4	404	26
ST1274A	21	4	407	26
ST138A	32	4	604	26
ST138A-1	32	4	604	26
ST1400A	331	12	1018	53
ST1401A	340	15	726	61

SEAGATE TECHNOLOGY			
Model	**Cap**	**Hds**	**Cyl**	**SPT**
ST1480A	426	15	895	62
ST157A	44	6	560	26
ST157A-1	44	6	560	26
ST2274A	241	10	873	54
ST2383A	338	14	873	54
ST274A	63	5	948	26
ST280A	71	10	516	27
ST3025A	21	2	808	26
ST3051A	43	6	820	17
ST3096A	89	10	1024	17
ST3120A	106	12	1024	17
ST3144A	130	15	1001	17
ST3145A	130	15	1001	17
ST3195A	170	10	981	34
ST3243A	213	12	1024	34
ST3250A	214	12	1024	34
ST325A/X	21	2	697	30
ST3283A	245	14	978	35
ST3290A	261	15	1001	34
ST3291A	272	14	761	50
ST3295A	272	14	761	50
ST3385A	340	14	768	62
ST3390A	341	14	768	62
ST3391A	341	14	768	62
ST3491A	428	15	899	62
ST3500A	426	15	895	62
ST351A\X	42	6	820	17
ST3550A	452	14	1018	62
ST3600A	540	16	1024	63
ST3655A	528	16	1024	63
ST3660A	545	16	1024	63
ST5660A	545	16	1024	63
ST9025A	21	4	615	17
ST9051A	42	6	820	17
ST9052A	42	5	980	17
ST9077A	64	11	669	17
ST9080A	64	4	823	38
ST9096A	85	10	980	17
ST9100AG	85	14	748	16
ST9140AG	128	15	980	17
ST9144A	130	15	980	17
ST9145AG	128	15	980	17
ST9150AG	131	13	419	47
ST9190AG	172	16	873	24
ST9235A	209	13	985	32
ST9235AG	209	13	985	32
ST9240AG	210	8	988	52

SEAGATE TECHNOLOGY			
Model	**Cap**	**Hds**	**Cyl**	**SPT**
ST9300AG	262	15	569	60
ST9385AG	340	14	934	51
ST9550AG	455	16	942	59
ST9655AG	524	16	1016	63

TALON			
Model	**Cap**	**Hds**	**Cyl**	**SPT**
TA3020A	121	8	739	40
TA3101A	105	8	641	40

TEAC			
Model	**Cap**	**Hds**	**Cyl**	**SPT**
SD-3105(A)	105	8	641	40
SD-3210	209	8	847	62
SD-3210(A)	215	8	847	62
SD-3240	245	8	965	62
SD-340A	43	4	525	40
SD-380	86	8	965	62

TOSHIBA			
Model	**Cap**	**Hds**	**Cyl**	**SPT**
MK-1034FC	107	8	664	39
MK-1122FC	43	5	988	17
MK-1422FCV	86	10	988	17
MK-2024FC	86	10	988	17
MK-2124FC	130	16	934	17
MK-2224FC	213	16	684	38
MK-2326FC	340	14	969	49
MK-234FC	110	7	845	35
MK-234FCH-I	107	7	845	35
MK-2428FC	524	16	1016	63

WESTERN DIGITAL			
Model	**Cap**	**Hds**	**Cyl**	**SPT**
93024-A	21	4	615	17
93028-AD	21	4	615	17
93044-A	43	5	977	17
95024-A	21	4	615	17
95044-A	43	5	977	17
95048-AD	43	5	977	17
WDAB130	31	4	916	17
WDAC1170	170	6	1010	55
WDAC1210	212	12	989	35
WDAC1270	270	12	917	48
WDAC1365	365	16	708	63
WDAC140	42	5	980	17
WDAC1425	426	16	827	63

WESTERN DIGITAL				
Model	**Cap**	**Hds**	**Cyl**	**SPT**
WDAC160	63	7	1024	17
WDAC2120	126	8	872	35
WDAC2170	170	6	1010	55
WDAC2200	212	12	989	35
WDAC2250	256	9	1010	55
WDAC2340	341	12	1010	55
WDAC2420	425	15	989	56
WDAC2540	540	16	1048	63
WDAC2700	696	16	1416	63
WDAC280	85	10	980	17
WDAC2850	853	16	1654	63
WDAC3100	1084	16	2100	63
WDAH260	63	7	1024	17
WDAL2120	126	8	872	35
WDAL2170	170	6	1010	55
WDAP4200	214	12	987	35

Physical Specifications

The following is a list of the some of the most popular drives of the four major interface types and their physical specifications.

Legend:

*	= Variable sectors per track.
**	= 256 bytes per sector.
***	= 1,024 bytes per sector.

Note: Capacity in these tables is specified in MB.

ALPS ELECTRIC (USA), INC.

MODEL	CAP	HDS	CYL	SPT	SEEK	FF	HGT	INT	ENCODE	LZ	WP	RWC	MTBF
DR312C901	211.54	4	2105	*	13	3.50	3H	IDE(AT)	RLL 1,7	AUTO	N/A	N/A	150
DR312C911	211.5	4	2108	*	13	3.50	3H	IDE(AT)	RLL 1,7	AUTO	N/A	N/A	150
DR312D	211.50	4	2108	*	13	3.50	3H	SCSI-2	RLL 1,7	AUTO	N/A	N/A	150
DR312D911A	211.5	4	2108	*	13	3.50	3H	SCSI-2	RLL 1,7	AUTO	N/A	N/A	150
DRPO-20A	16.37	2	615	26	60	3.50	HH	ST-506/412	RLL 2,7	—	616	616	
DRPO-20D	16.37	2	615	26	60	3.50	HH	ST-506/412	RLL 2,7	—	616	616	

AMPEX CORPORATION

MODEL	CAP	HDS	CYL	SPT	SEEK	FF	HGT	INT	ENCODE	LZ	WP	RWC	MTBF
PYXIS-07	5.57	2	320	17	90	5.25	FH	ST-506/412	MFM	–	132	132	
PYXIS-13	11.14	4	320	17	90	5.25	FH	ST-506/412	MFM	–	132	132	
PYXIS-20	16.71	6	320	17	90	5.25	FH	ST-506/412	MFM	–	132	132	
PYXIS-27	22.28	8	320	17	90	5.25	FH	ST-506/412	MFM	–	132	132	

AREAL TECHNOLOGY, INC.

MODEL	CAP	HDS	CYL	SPT	SEEK	FF	HGT	INT	ENCODE	LZ	WP	RWC	MTBF
A120	136.9	4	1070	250	15	2.50	5H	IDE(44PIN)	RLL 2,7	AUTO	N/A	N/A	100
A130	131.48	2	1438	*	15	2.50	4H	IDE(44PIN)	RLL 1,7	AUTO	N/A	N/A	150
A170	172.03	4	1344	*	15	2.50	4H	IDE(44PIN)	RLL 2,7	AUTO	N/A	N/A	100
A175L	166.99	2			13	2.50	4H	IDE(44PIN)	RLL 1,7	AUTO	N/A	N/A	250
A180	182.7	4	1430	250	15	2.50	5H	IDE(44PIN)	RLL 2,7	AUTO	N/A	N/A	100
A260	262.96	4	1438	*	15	2.50	4H	IDE(44PIN)	RLL 1,7	AUTO	N/A	N/A	150
A265	262.969	4			13	2.50	4H	IDE(44PIN)	RLL 1,7	AUTO	N/A	N/A	150
A340	394.81	6	1501	*	15	2.50	4H	IDE(44PIN)	RLL 1,7	AUTO	N/A	N/A	100
A345L	333.99	4			13	2.50	4H	IDE(44PIN)	RLL 1,7	AUTO	N/A	N/A	250
A520L	502.03	6			13	2.50	4H	IDE(44PIN)	RLL 1,7	AUTO	N/A	N/A	250
A525	526.41	8	1501	*	15	2.50	4H	IDE(44PIN)	RLL 1,7	AUTO	N/A	N/A	100
A700L	700.88	8			13	2.50	4H	IDE(44PIN)	RLL 1,7	AUTO	N/A	N/A	250
A85	86.01	2	1344	*	15	2.50	4H	IDE(44PIN)	RLL 2,7	AUTO	N/A	N/A	100
A90	90.78	2	1430	62	15	2.50	4H	IDE(XT/AT)	RLL 2,7	AUTO	N/A	N/A	100
MD-2050	50.31	2	819	60	28	2.50	4H	SCSI	RLL 2,7	AUTO	N/A	N/A	45
MD-2060	62.4	2	1024	119	19	2.50	4H	IDE(44PIN)	RLL 2,7	AUTO	N/A	N/A	100
MD-2080	80.35	2	1330	59	<19	2.50	4H	IDE(44PIN)	RLL 2,7	AUTO	N/A	N/A	100
MD-2080	81	2	1330	119	19	2.50	4H	IDE(44PIN)	RLL 2,7	AUTO	N/A	N/A	100
MD-2085	85.90	2	1410	59	<19	2.50	4H	IDE(44PIN)	RLL 2,7	AUTO	N/A	N/A	100
MD-2085	85.90	14	705	238	16	2.50	5H	IDE(44PIN)	RLL 2,7	AUTO	N/A	N/A	100

ATASI TECHNOLOGY, INC.

MODEL	CAP	HDS	CYL	SPT	SEEK	FF	HGT	INT	ENCODE	LZ	WP	RWC	MTBF
3020	16.84	3	645	17	38	5.25	FH	ST-506/412	MFM	–	320	320	0
3033	28.07	5	645	17	33	5.25	FH	ST-506/412	MFM	–	320	320	40
3046	39.29	7	645	17	28	5.25	FH	ST-506/412	MFM	644	320	320	0
3051	42.89	7	704	17	33	5.25	FH	ST-506/412	MFM	–	350	359	0
3051+	44.66	7	733	17	33	5.25	FH	ST-506/412	MFM	732	350	359	0
3053	44.66	7	733	17	33	5.25	FH	ST-506/412	MFM	–	368	350	0
3075	71.30	8	1024	17	28	5.25	FH	ST-506/412	MFM	–	1,025	1,025	40
3085	71.30	8	1024	17	28	5.25	FH	ST-506/412	MFM	1024	512	–	40
519	159.80	15	1224	17	22	5.25	FH	ST-506/412	MFM	–	N/A	N/A	40
519R	244.40	15	1224	26	22	5.25	FH	ST-506/412	RLL 2,7	–	N/A	N/A	40

ATASI TECHNOLOGY, INC.

MODEL	CAP	HDS	CYL	SPT	SEEK	FF	HGT	INT	ENCODE	LZ	WP	RWC	MTBF
638	338.68	15	1225	35	18	5.25	FH	ESDI-10MHZ	RLL	AUTO	N/A	N/A	40
676	676.82	15	1632	54	16	5.25	FH	ESDI-15MHZ	RLL	AUTO	N/A	N/A	150
7120	1046.39	15	1919	71	14	5.25	FH	SCSI	RLL	AUTO	N/A	N/A	150
738	338.68	15	1225	35	18	5.25	FH	SCSI	RLL	AUTO	N/A	N/A	40
776	676.82	15	1632	54	16	5.25	FH	SCSI	RLL	AUTO	N/A	N/A	150

AURA ASSOCIATES

MODEL	CAP	HDS	CYL	SPT	SEEK	FF	HGT	INT	ENCODE	LZ	WP	RWC	MTBF
AU63	63.92	2	—	*	17	—	—	PCMCIA	RLL 1,7	AUTO	—	—	100
AU 126	125.85	4	—	*	17	—	—	PCMCIA	RLL 1,7	AUTO	—	—	100

BASF

MODEL	CAP	HDS	CYL	SPT	SEEK	FF	HGT	INT	ENCODE	LZ	WP	RWC	MTBF
6185	22.97	6	440	17	99	5.25	FH	ST-506/412	MFM	—	220	220	0
6186	15.31	4	440	17	70	5.25	FH	ST-506/412	MFM	—	220	220	0
6187	7.65	2	440	17	70	5.25	FH	ST-506/412	MFM	—	220	220	0
6188-R1	10.65	2	612	17	70	5.25	FH	ST-506/412	MFM	—	—	—	0
6188-R3	21.30	4	612	17	70	5.25	FH	ST-506/412	MFM	—	—	—	0

BRAND TECHNOLOGIES

MODEL	CAP	HDS	CYL	SPT	SEEK	FF	HGT	INT	ENCODE	LZ	WP	RWC	MTBF
BT8085	71.30	8	1024	17	25	5.25	FH	ST-506/412	MFM	AUTO	N/A	N/A	50
BT8128	109.05	8	1024	26	25	5.25	FH	ST-506/412	RLL	AUTO	N/A	N/A	50
BT8170E	142.60	8	1024	34	25	5.25	FH	ESDI-10MHZ	RLL 2,7	AUTO	N/A	N/A	50
BT8170S	142.60	8	1024	34	25	5.25	FH	SCSI	RLL 2,7	AUTO	N/A	N/A	50
BT9121A	107.45	5	1166	36	16.5	3.50	HH	IDE(AT)	RLL 2,7	AUTO	N/A	N/A	50
BT9121E	107.45	5	1166	36	16.5	3.50	HH	ESDI-10MHZ	RLL 2,7	AUTO	N/A	N/A	50
BT9121S	107.45	5	1166	36	16.5	3.50	HH	SCSI	RLL 2,7	AUTO	N/A	N/A	50
BT9170A	150.44	7	1166	36	16.5	3.50	HH	IDE(AT)	RLL 2,7	AUTO	N/A	N/A	50
BT9170E	150.44	7	1166	36	16.5	3.50	HH	ESDI-10MHZ	RLL 2,7	AUTO	N/A	N/A	50
BT9170S	150.44	7	1166	36	16.5	3.50	HH	SCSI	RLL 2,7	AUTO	N/A	N/A	50
BT9220A	200.39	9	1208	36	16.5	3.50	HH	IDE(AT)	RLL 2,7	AUTO	N/A	N/A	50
BT9220E	200.39	9	1208	36	16.5	3.50	HH	ESDI-10MHZ	RLL 2,7	AUTO	N/A	N/A	50
BT9220S	200.39	9	1208	36	16.5	3.50	HH	SCSI	RLL 2,7	AUTO	N/A	N/A	50
BT9400S	400.00	6	1800	*	12	3.50	FH	IDE(AT)	RLL 1,7	AUTO	N/A	N/A	100
BT9650A	650.00	6	1800	*	12	3.50	FH	IDE(AT)	RLL 1,7	AUTO	N/A	N/A	100

BULL HN INFORMATION SYSTEMS, INC.

MODEL	CAP	HDS	CYL	SPT	SEEK	FF	HGT	INT	ENCODE	LZ	WP	RWC	MTBF
D-530	25.77	3	987	17	65	5.25	FH	ST-506/412	MFM	987	988	988	0
D-550	42.95	5	987	17	65	5.25	FH	ST-506/412	MFM	987	988	988	0
D-570	60.13	7	987	17	65	5.25	FH	ST-506/412	MFM	987	988	988	0
D-585	71.04	7	1166	17	65	5.25	FH	ST-506/412	RLL	1166	1,166	1,166	0

C.ITOH ELECTRONICS

MODEL	CAP	HDS	CYL	SPT	SEEK	FF	HGT	INT	ENCODE	LZ	WP	RWC	MTBF
YD-3042	43.57	4	788	–	28	3.50	HH	SCSI	RLL	AUTO	N/A	N/A	40
YD-3081B	45.45	2	1057	–	28	3.50	HH	SCSI	RLL 2,7	AUTO	N/A	N/A	30
YD-3082	87.14	8	788	–	28	3.50	3H	SCSI	RLL	AUTO	N/A	N/A	40
YD-3082B	90.91	4	1057	–	28	3.50	HH	SCSI	RLL 2,7	AUTO	N/A	N/A	30
YD-3083B	136.37	6	1057	–	28	3.50	HH	SCSI	RLL 2,7	AUTO	N/A	N/A	30
YD-3084B	181.83	8	1057	–	28	3.50	HH	SCSI	RLL 2,7	AUTO	N/A	N/A	30
YD-3161B	45.45	2	1057	–	19	3.50	3H	IDE(AT)	RLL 2,7	AUTO	N/A	N/A	40
YD-3162B	90.91	4	1057	–	19	3.50	3H	IDE(AT)	RLL 2,7	AUTO	N/A	N/A	40
YD-3181B	45.45	2	1057	–	19	3.50	3H	SCSI	RLL 2,7	AUTO	N/A	N/A	40
YD-3182B	90.91	4	1057	–	19	3.50	3H	SCSI	RLL 2,7	AUTO	N/A	N/A	40
YD-3530	31.81	5	731	17	–	–	–	ST-506/412	MFM	–	732	732	0
YD-3540	44.53	7	731	–	26	5.25	HH	ST-506/412	MFM	–	732	732	0

CARDIFF PERIPHERALS CORPORATION

MODEL	CAP	HDS	CYL	SPT	SEEK	FF	HGT	INT	ENCODE	LZ	WP	RWC	MTBF
F-3053	44.56	5	1024	17	20	3.50	HH	ST-506/412	MFM	–	–	–	0
F-3080E	68.15	5	1024	26	20	3.50	HH	ST-506/412	RLL 2,7	AUTO	N/A	N/A	0
F-3080S	68.15	5	1024	26	20	3.50	HH	SCSI	RLL 2,7	AUTO	N/A	N/A	0
F-3127E	91.75	5	1024	35	20	3.50	HH	ESDI-10MHZ	RLL 2,7	AUTO	N/A	N/A	0
F-3127S	91.75	5	1024	35	20	3.50	HH	SCSI	RLL 2,7	AUTO	N/A	N/A	0

CENTURY DATA, INC.

MODEL	CAP	HDS	CYL	SPT	SEEK	FF	HGT	INT	ENCODE	LZ	WP	RWC	MTBF
CAST-10203(E)	56.44	3	1050	35	28	5.25	FH	ESDI-10MHZ	RLL 2,7	AUTO	N/A	N/A	0
CAST-10203(S)	56.44	3	1050	35	28	5.25	FH	SCSI	RLL 2,7	AUTO	N/A	N/A	0
CAST-10304(E)	75.26	4	1050	35	28	5.25	FH	ESDI-10MHZ	RLL 2,7	AUTO	N/A	N/A	0
CAST-10304(S)	75.26	4	1050	35	28	5.25	FH	SCSI	RLL 2,7	AUTO	N/A	N/A	0
CAST-10305(E)	94.08	5	1050	35	28	5.25	FH	ESDI-10MHZ	RLL 2,7	AUTO	N/A	N/A	0
CAST-10305(S)	94.08	5	1050	35	28	5.25	FH	SCSI	RLL 2,7	AUTO	N/A	N/A	0
CAST-14404(E)	113.97	4	1590	35	25	5.25	HH	ESDI-10MHZ	RLL 2,7	AUTO	N/A	N/A	0
CAST-14404(S)	113.97	4	1590	35	25	5.25	HH	SCSI	RLL 2,7	AUTO	N/A	N/A	0
CAST-14405(E)	142.46	5	1590	35	25	5.25	HH	ESDI-10MHZ	RLL 2,7	AUTO	N/A	N/A	0

CENTURY DATA, INC.

MODEL	CAP	HDS	CYL	SPT	SEEK	FF	HGT	INT	ENCODE	LZ	WP	RWC	MTBF
CAST-14405(S)	142.46	5	1590	35	25	5.25	HH	SCSI	RLL 2,7	AUTO	N/A	N/A	0
CAST-14406(E)	170.95	6	1590	35	25	5.25	HH	ESDI-10MHZ	RLL 2,7	AUTO	N/A	N/A	0
CAST-14406(S)	170.95	6	1590	35	25	5.25	HH	SCSI	RLL 2,7	AUTO	N/A	N/A	0
CAST-24509(E)	257.88	9	1599	35	18	5.25	FH	ESDI-10MHZ	RLL 2,7	AUTO	N/A	N/A	0
CAST-24509(S)	257.88	9	1599	35	18	5.25	FH	SCSI	RLL 2,7	AUTO	N/A	N/A	0
CAST-24611 (E)	315.19	11	1599	35	18	5.25	FH	ESDI-10MHZ	RLL 2,7	AUTO	N/A	N/A	0
CAST-24611(S)	315.19	11	1599	35	18	5.25	FH	SCSI	RLL 2,7	AUTO	N/A	N/A	0
CAST-24713 (E)	372.50	13	1599	35	18	5.25	FH	ESDI-10MHZ	RLL 2,7	AUTO	N/A	N/A	0
CAST-24713(S)	372.50	13	1599	35	18	5.25	FH	SCSI	RLL 2,7	AUTO	N/A	N/A	0

CMS ENHANCEMENTS, INC.

CMS Enhancements drives are manufactured by other companies and labeled with a CMS model number. The CMS model number may not always apply to the same OEM drive. For this reason, we do not list the CMS model numbers. Often, the OEM's model number is visible on the drive and may be used. In the case of IDE Interface drives, a drive inquiry may be performed using one of the Micro House utilities: MH-IDE.EXE or *DrivePro*™. MH-IDE is included on the CD-ROM bundled with this text. Other utilites may be obtained from our BBS at 303-443-9957.

COGITO

MODEL	CAP	HDS	CYL	SPT	SEEK	FF	HGT	INT	ENCODE	LZ	WP	RWC	MTBF
CG-906	5.32	2	306	17	—	5.25	HH	ST-506/412	MFM	—	128	128	0
CG-912	10.65	4	306	17	—	5.25	HH	ST-506/412	MFM	—	128	128	0
CG-925	21.30	4	612	17	—	5.25	HH	ST-506/412	MFM	—	307	307	0
PT-912	10.65	2	612	17	—	5.25	HH	ST-506/412	MFM	—	307	307	0
PT-925	21.30	4	612	17	—	5.25	HH	ST-506/412	MFM	—	307	307	0

COMPAQ COMPUTER CORPORATION

MODEL	CAP	HDS	CYL	SPT	SEEK	FF	HGT	INT	ENCODE	LZ	WP	RWC	MTBF
113640-001	43.13	2	1053	40	29	3.50	HH	IDE-COMPAQ	RLL	AUTO	N/A	N/A	40
113641-001	112.45	8	832	33	25	3.50	HH	IDE-COMPAQ	RLL	AUTO	N/A	N/A	40
115145-001	84.34	6	832	33	25	3.50	HH	IDE-COMPAQ	RLL	AUTO	N/A	N/A	40
115147-001	325.02	7	1744	52	19	5.25	HH	ESDI-15MHZ	RLL	AUTO	N/A	N/A	60
115158-001	651.35	15	1631	52	19	5.25	FH	ESDI-15MHZ	RLL	AUTO	N/A	N/A	40
115627-001	112.45	8	832	33	25	3.50	HH	IDE-COMPAQ	RLL	AUTO	N/A	N/A	40
115830-001	318.56	15	1220	34	18	5.25	FH	ESDI-10MHZ	RLL	AUTO	N/A	N/A	40
116562-001	123.96	4	1552	39	19	3.50	HH	IDE-COMPAQ	RLL	AUTO	N/A	N/A	40
116565-001	207.94	8	1336	38	19	3.50	HH	IDE-COMPAQ	RLL	AUTO	N/A	N/A	40
122136-001	60.70	2	1520	39	19	3.50	HH	IDE-COMPAQ	RLL	AUTO	N/A	N/A	40
131067-001	510.41	12	1806	46	—	3.50	HH	IDE-COMPAQ	RLL	AUTO	N/A	N/A	150
131362-001	325.02	7	1744	52	18	5.25	HH	ESDI-15MHZ	RLL	AUTO	N/A	N/A	60
CFA-170A	171.60	—	—	*	13	3.50	3H	IDE(AT)	RLL 1,7	AUTO	N/A	N/A	250
CP-2088	85.00	4	—	—	19	2.50	3H	IDE(AT)	RLL 1,7	AUTO	N/A	N/A	150

COMPAQ COMPUTER CORPORATION

MODEL	CAP	HDS	CYL	SPT	SEEK	FF	HGT	INT	ENCODE	LZ	WP	RWC	MTBF
CP-30061	60.86	2	1524	39	<19	3.50	3H	IDE(AT)	RLL 1,7	AUTO	N/A	N/A	150
CP-30061G	60.86	2	1524	39	<19	3.50	3H	IDE(AT)	RLL 1,7	AUTO	N/A	N/A	150
CP-30081 I	84.50	4	1058	39	<19	3.50	3H	IDE(AT)	RLL 2,7	AUTO	N/A	N/A	150
CP-30081E	85.06	2	1806	46	17	3.50	3H	IDE(AT)	RLL 1,7	AUTO	N/A	N/A	150
CP-30101	121.72	4	1524	39	<19	3.50	3H	IDE(AT)	RLL 1,7	AUTO	N/A	N/A	150
CP-30101G	121.72	4	1524	39	<19	3.50	3H	IDE(AT)	RLL 1,7	AUTO	N/A	N/A	150
CP-30171E	170.13	4	1806	46	17	3.50	3H	IDE(AT)	RLL 1,7	AUTO	N/A	N/A	150
CP-3041	42.88	2	1047	40	25	3.50	3H	IDE(AT)	RLL 2,7	AUTO	N/A	N/A	150
CP-3111	112.45	8	832	33	–	3.50	HH	IDE(AT)	RLL	AUTO	N/A	N/A	0
CP-3181	84.34	6	832	33	25	3.50	HH	IDE(AT)	RLL 2,7	AUTO	N/A	N/A	150
CP-3201I	215.33	8	1348	39	19	3.50	HH	IDE(AT)	RLL 2,7	AUTO	N/A	N/A	150
CP-341	42.86	4	805	26	29	3.50	HH	IDE(AT)	RLL 2,7	AUTO	N/A	N/A	20
CP-341I	42.86	4	805	26	29	3.50	HH	IDE(AT)	RLL 2,7	AUTO	N/A	N/A	20
CP-3501	510.41	12	1806	46	12	3.50	HH	IDE(AT)	RLL 2,7	AUTO	N/A	N/A	150
CP-4041	42.64	2	1096	38	29	3.50	4H	IDE-COMPAQ	RLL 2,7	AUTO	N/A	N/A	150

COMPUTER MEMORIES, INC.

MODEL	CAP	HDS	CYL	SPT	SEEK	FF	HGT	INT	ENCODE	LZ	WP	RWC	MTBF
5018H	15.00	2	–	17	85	5.25	FH	ST-506/412	MFM	–	–	–	0
514	58.55	7	961	17	–	–	–	ST-506/412	MFM	–	1,225	1,225	0
7660	50.13	6	960	17	28	5.25	FH	ST-506/412	MFM	–	450	961	0
CM 3206	10.65	4	306	17	–	5.25	FH	ST-506/412	MFM	–	–	–	0
CM 3412	10.65	4	306	17	–	5.25	FH	ST-506/412	MFM	–	256	306	0
CM 3426	21.41	4	615	17	–	5.25	FH	ST-506/412	MFM	–	256	616	0
CM 5205	4.45	2	256	17	–	5.25	FH	ST-506/412	MFM	–	128	128	0
CM 5206	5.32	2	306	32**	80	5.25	FH	ST-506/412	MFM	–	256	307	0
CM 5410	8.91	4	256	17	–	5.25	FH	ST-506/412	MFM	–	128	128	0
CM 5412	10.65	4	306	32**	85	5.25	FH	ST-506/412	MFM	–	128	307	0
CM 5616	13.36	6	256	17	–	5.25	FH	ST-506/412	MFM	–	257	257	0
CM 5619	15.98	6	306	32**	85	5.25	FH	ST-506/412	MFM	–	128	307	0
CM 5826	21.30	8	306	17	–	5.25	FH	ST-506/412	MFM	–	–	–	0
CM 6213	11.14	2	640	17	–	5.25	FH	ST-506/412	MFM	–	256	641	0
CM 6413	10.70	2	615	17	39	5.25	FH	ST-506/412	MFM	–	256	615	0
CM 6426	22.28	4	640	17	39	5.25	FH	ST-506/412	MFM	–	256	641	0
CM 6426S	22.28	4	640	17	–	5.25	FH	ST-506/412	MFM	–	256	256	0
CM 6640	32.11	6	615	17	–	5.25	FH	ST-506/412	MFM	–	256	616	0
CM 7000	44.66	7	733	17	–	5.25	FH	ST-506/412	MFM	–	512	733	0
CM 7030	25.52	4	733	17	–	5.25	FH	ST-506/412	MFM	–	512	733	0
CM 7038	31.90	5	733	17	–	5.25	FH	ST-506/412	MFM	–	512	733	0
CM 7053	44.66	7	733	17	–	5.25	FH	ST-506/412	MFM	–	512	733	0
CM 7085	71.30	8	1024	17	–	5.25	FH	ST-506/412	MFM	–	512	1,024	0
CM 7660	50.13	6	960	17	–	5.25	FH	ST-506/412	MFM	–	512	961	0
CM 7880	66.84	8	960	17	–	5.25	FH	ST-506/412	MFM	–	450	961	0

CONNER PERIPHERALS, INC. (also see SEAGATE TECHNOLOGY, INC.)

MODEL	CAP	HDS	CYL	SPT	SEEK	FF	HGT	INT	ENCODE	LZ	WP	RWC	MTBF
CFA-1080A	1000	–	–	–	13	3.50	3H	IDE(AT)	RLL 1,7	AUTO	N/A	N/A	250
CFA-1275A	1278	6	2479	*	11.25	3.50	3H	IDE(AT)	UNIDENT	2480	N/A	N/A	300
CFA-1275S	1278	6	–	*	12	3.50	3H	SCSI-2	RLL 1,7	AUTO	N/A	N/A	300
CFA-170A	163.4	–	–	–	13	3.50	3H	IDE(AT)	RLL 1,7	AUTO	N/A	N/A	
CFA-170S	170.13	4	1806	46	17	3.50	3H	SCSI	RLL 1,7	AUTO	N/A	N/A	150
CFA-2161A	2147	8	4474	*	10	3.50	3H	IDE(AT)	RLL 1,7	AUTO	N/A	N/A	500
CFA-270A	270.50	2	2805	*	12	3.50	3H	IDE(AT)	RLL 1,7	AUTO	–	–	0
CFA-270S	270.50	2	2805	*	12	3.50	3H	SCSI-2	RLL 1,7	AUTO	–	–	0
CFA-340A	343.00	4	2111	*	13	3.50	3H	IDE(AT)	RLL 1,7	AUTO	N/A	N/A	250
CFA-340S	343.00	4	–	–	13	3.50	3H	SCSI-2	RLL 1,7	AUTO	N/A	N/A	250
CFA-425A	426	2	862	*	11.25	3.50	3H	IDE(AT)	UNIDENT	863	N/A	N/A	300
CFA-540A	540.86	4	2111	*	13	3.50	3H	IDE(AT)	RLL 1,7	AUTO	N/A	N/A	250
CFA-540S	541	4	2805	*	12	3.50	3H	SCSI-2	RLL 1,7	AUTO	N/A	N/A	300
CFA-810A	810	–	–	–	12	3.50	3H	IDE(AT)	RLL 1,7	1572	N/A	N/A	300
CFA-850A	850	4	3640	111	14	3.50	3H	IDE(AT)	RLL 1,7	N/A	N/A	N/A	250
CFA-850S	852	4	–	*	12	3.50	3H	SCSI-2	RLL 1,7	AUTO	N/A	N/A	300
CFL-350A	350	4	2225	*	12.0	2.50	FH	IDE(AT)	RLL 1,7	905	N/A	N/A	300
CFL-420A	422	4	2393	*	12	2.50	5H	IDE(AT)	RLL 1,7	818	N/A	N/A	300
CFN-170A	168.20	4	1339	*	12	2.50	4H	IDE(AT)	RLL 1,7	AUTO	N/A	N/A	250
CFN-170S	168.20	4	1339	*	12	2.50	4H	SCSI-2	RLL 1,7	AUTO	N/A	N/A	250
CFN-250A	252.70	6	1339	*	12	2.50	4H	IDE(AT)	RLL 1,7	AUTO	–	–	0
CFN-250S	252.70	6	1339	*	12	2.50	4H	SCSI-2	RLL 1,7	AUTO	–	–	0
CFN-340A	344.50	6	1598	*	13	2.50	4H	IDE(AT)	RLL 1,7	AUTO	N/A	N/A	250
CFN-340S	344.50	6	1598	*	13	2.50	4H	SCSI-2	RLL 1,7	AUTO	N/A	N/A	250
CFP-1060B	1062.44	8	2757	*	9	3.50	3H	SCSI-2DIFF	RLL 1,7	–	–	–	500
CFP-1060E	1062.44	8	2757	*	9	3.50	3H	SCSI	RLL 1,7	–	–	–	500
CFP-1060S	1062.44	8	2757	*	9	3.50	3H	SCSI-2	RLL 1,7	–	–	–	500
CFP-1060W	1062.44	8	2757	*	9	3.50	3H	SCSI-2 W	RLL 1,7	–	–	–	500
CFP-1080S	1080	6	–	*	11	3.50	3H	SCSI-2F	RLL 1,7	AUTO	N/A	N/A	500
CFP-2105S	2147	10	3892	*	8.75	3.50	3H	SCSI-2 W	UNIDENT	AUTO	N/A	N/A	999
CFP-2105W	2147	10	3892	*	8.75	3.50	3H	SCSI-2	UNIDENT	AUTO	N/A	N/A	999
CFP-2107E	2110	10	3924	91	8.5	3.50	3H	SCSI-2 F/W	RLL 1,7	AUTO	N/A	N/A	999
CFP-2107S	2110	10	3924	91	8.5	3.50	3H	SCSI-2F	RLL 1,7	AUTO	N/A	N/A	999
CFP-2107W	2110	10	3924	91	8.5	3.50	3H	SCSI-2 F/W	RLL 1,7	AUTO	N/A	N/A	999
CFP-4207E	4295	20	3924	96	9.0	3.50	3H	SCSI-2 F/W	RLL 1,7	AUTO	N/A	N/A	999
CFP-4207S	4295	20	3924	96	9.0	3.50	3H	SCSI-2 W	RLL 1,7	AUTO	N/A	N/A	999
CFP-4207W	4295	20	3924	96	9.0	3.50	3H	SCSI-2 F/W	RLL 1,7	–	N/A	N/A	999
CFS-1081A	1080	4	3924	*	14	3.50	3H	IDE(AT)	UNIDENT	2097	N/A	N/A	300
CFS-1275A	1278	–	–	–	15	3.50	HH	IDE(AT)	RLL 1,7	2479	0	–	250
CFS-1275A -A	1275	6	3640		15	3.50	HH	IDE(AT)	RLL 1,7	AUTO	N/A	N/A	250
CFS-1621A	1620	6	3924	*	14	3.50	3H	IDE(AT)	UNIDENT	3146	N/A	N/A	300
CFS-210A	213.23	–	–	–	13	3.50	3H	IDE(AT)	RLL 1,7	AUTO	N/A	N/A	250

CONNER PERIPHERALS, INC.

MODEL	CAP	HDS	CYL	SPT	SEEK	FF	HGT	INT	ENCODE	LZ	WP	RWC	MTBF
CFS-270A	270.9	2	—	*	—	3.50	3H	IDE(AT)	RLL 1,7	AUTO	N/A	N/A	250
CFS-420A	426.80	4	2388	*	14	3.50	3H	IDE(AT)	RLL 1,7	AUTO	—	—	250
CFS-425A	425	2	—	*	14	3.50	3H	IDE(AT)	RLL 1,7	AUTO	N/A	N/A	250
CFS-540A	540	4	—	*	14	3.50	3H	IDE(AT)	RLL 1,7	AUTO	N/A	N/A	250
CFS-541A	540	2	3924	*	14	3.50	3H	IDE(AT)	RLL 1,7	1048	N/A	N/A	300
CFS-635A	635	3	3640	*	14	3.50	3H	IDE(AT)	RLL 1,7	AUTO	N/A	N/A	300
CFS-850A	850	4	3640	*	14	3.50	3H	IDE(AT)	RLL 1,7	AUTO	N/A	N/A	300
CP-2020 KATO	21.39	2	653	32	23	2.50	4H	SCSI	RLL 2,7	AUTO	N/A	N/A	150
CP-2022	21.39	2	653	32	—	2.50	4H	IDE(AT)	RLL 2,7	AUTO	N/A	N/A	0
CP-2024	21.39	2	653	32	23	2.50	4H	IDE(XT/AT)	RLL 2,7	AUTO	N/A	N/A	150
CP-2034	32.02	2	823	38	19	2.50	4H	IDE(AT)	RLL 2,7	AUTO	N/A	N/A	150
CP-2044	42.6	4	548	38	15	2.50	4H	IDE(44PIN)	RLL 2,7	980	N/A	N/A	150
CP-2044PK	42.6	4	548	38	15	2.50	4H	IDE(44PIN)	RLL 2,7	980	N/A	N/A	150
CP-2064	64.04	4	823	38	19	2.50	4H	IDE(AT)	RLL 2,7	AUTO	N/A	N/A	150
CP-2084	85.37	4	1097	38	19	2.50	4H	IDE(AT)	RLL 1,7	AUTO	N/A	N/A	150
CP-2088	85	4		38	19	2.50	4H	IDE(44PIN)	RLL 1,7	548	0	N/A	100
CP-2124	121.6	4	—	53	16	2.50	4H	IDE(AT)	RLL 1,7	762	0	—	150
CP-2304	215.33	8	1348	39	19	3.50	4H	IDE(AT)	RLL	AUTO	N/A	N/A	0
CP-3000	42.80	2	1045	40	28	3.50	3H	IDE(AT)	RLL 2,7	AUTO	N/A	N/A	150
CP-30060	60.86	2	1524	39	<19	3.50	3H	SCSI	RLL 1,7	AUTO	N/A	N/A	150
CP-30064	60.86	2	1524	39	<19	3.50	3H	IDE(AT)	RLL 1,7	AUTO	N/A	N/A	150
CP-30064H	60.86	2	1524	39	<19	3.50	3H	IDE(AT)	RLL 1,7	AUTO	N/A	N/A	150
CP-30069	60.86	2	1524	39	<19	3.50	3H	MCA	RLL 1,7	AUTO	N/A	N/A	150
CP-30080	84.50	4	1058	39	<19	3.50	3H	SCSI	RLL 2,7	AUTO	N/A	N/A	150
CP-30080E	85.06	2	1806	46	17	3.50	4H	SCSI	RLL 1,7	AUTO	N/A	N/A	150
CP-30084	84.50	4	1058	39	<19	3.50	3H	IDE(AT)	RLL 2,7	AUTO	N/A	N/A	150
CP-30084E	85.06	2	1806	46	17	3.50	3H	IDE(AT)	RLL 1,7	AUTO	N/A	N/A	150
CP-30100	121.72	4	1524	39	<19	3.50	3H	SCSI	RLL 1,7	AUTO	N/A	N/A	150
CP-30104	121.56	4	1522	39	19	3.50	3H	IDE(AT)	RLL 1,7	AUTO	N/A	N/A	150
CP-30104H	121.56	4	1522	39	19	3.50	3H	IDE(AT)	RLL 1,7	AUTO	N/A	N/A	150
CP-30109	121.56	4	1522	39	19	3.50	3H	MCA	RLL 1,7	AUTO	N/A	N/A	150
CP-30124	125.02	2	1985	62	14	3.50	3H	IDE(AT)	RLL 1,7	AUTO	N/A	N/A	250
CP-30170	170.13	4	1806	46	17	3.50	3H	SCSI	RLL 1,7	AUTO	N/A	N/A	150
CP-30170E	170	4	1806	46	17	3.50	3H	SCSI	RLL 1,7	AUTO	N/A	N/A	150
CP-30174	171.6				13	3.50	3H	IDE(AT)	RLL 1,7	AUTO	N/A	N/A	250
CP-30174E	170.13	4	1806	46	17	3.50	3H	IDE(AT)	RLL 1,7	AUTO	N/A	N/A	150
CP-3020	21.01	2	622	33	27	3.50	3H	SCSI	RLL 2,7	AUTO	N/A	N/A	150
CP-30200	212.64	4	2119	49	12	3.50	3H	SCSI-2	RLL 2,7	AUTO	N/A	N/A	150
CP-30204	212.64	4	2119	49	12	3.50	3H	IDE(AT)	RLL 2,7	AUTO	N/A	N/A	150
CP-3022	21.49	2	636	33	27	3.50	3H	IDE(AT)	RLL 2,7	AUTO	N/A	N/A	150
CP-3024	21.49	2	636	33	27	3.50	3H	IDE(AT)	RLL 2,7	AUTO	N/A	N/A	150
CP-30254	251	—	—	—	14	3.50	3H	IDE(AT)	RLL 1,7	895	N/A	N/A	250
CP-30254H	251	—	—	—	14	3.50	3H	IDE(AT)	RLL 1,7	895	N/A	N/A	250
CP-30340	343.00	4	—	—	13	3.50	3H	SCSI-2	RLL 1,7	AUTO	N/A	N/A	250

CONNER PERIPHERALS, INC.

MODEL	CAP	HDS	CYL	SPT	SEEK	FF	HGT	INT	ENCODE	LZ	WP	RWC	MTBF
CP-30344	343	—	—	—	17	3.50	3H	IDE(AT)	RLL 1,7	665	N/A	N/A	300
CP-3040	42.02	2	1026	40	25	3.50	3H	SCSI	RLL 2,7	AUTO	N/A	N/A	150
CP-3044	42.88	2	1047	40	25	3.50	3H	IDE(AT)	RLL 2,7	AUTO	N/A	N/A	150
CP-3046F	42.8	2	1045	40	19	3.50	3H	IDE(AT)	UNIDENT	977	300	N/A	100
CP-30540	—	—	—	—	—	3.50	3H	SCSI	RLL 1,7	—	—	—	0
CP-30544	545.51	12	1806	49	10	3.50	3H	IDE(AT)	RLL 2,7	AUTO	N/A	N/A	150
CP-3100	104.89	8	776	33	25	3.50	3H	SCSI	RLL 2,7	AUTO	N/A	N/A	150
CP-3102	104.89	8	776	33	25	3.50	HH	IDE(AT)	RLL 2,7	AUTO	N/A	N/A	150
CP-3104	104.89	8	776	33	25	3.50	HH	IDE(AT)	RLL 2,7	AUTO	N/A	N/A	150
CP-3114	112.45	8	832	33	—	3.50	HH	IDE(AT)	RLL	AUTO	N/A	N/A	0
CP-31370	1300.00	14	2386	*	10	3.50	3H	SCSI-2	RLL	AUTO	N/A	N/A	0
CP-3150	52.44	4	776	33	25	3.50	HH	SCSI	RLL 2,7	AUTO	N/A	N/A	150
CP-3180	84.34	6	832	33	25	3.50	HH	SCSI	RLL 2,7	AUTO	N/A	N/A	150
CP-3184	84.34	6	832	33	25	3.50	HH	IDE(AT)	RLL 2,7	AUTO	N/A	N/A	150
CP-3200	212.61	8	1366	38	16	3.50	HH	SCSI	RLL	AUTO	N/A	N/A	150
CP-3200F	212.61	8	1366	38	16	3.50	HH	SCSI	RLL 2,7	AUTO	N/A	N/A	150
CP-3204	215.33	8	1348	39	19	3.50	HH	IDE(AT)	RLL 2,7	AUTO	N/A	N/A	150
CP-3204F	212.61	8	1366	38	16	3.50	HH	IDE(AT)	RLL 2,7	AUTO	N/A	N/A	50
CP-3209F	212.61	8	1366	38	16	3.50	HH	MCA	RLL 2,7	AUTO	N/A	N/A	50
CP-3304	340.27	8	1806	46	—	3.50	HH	IDE(AT)	RLL 1,7	AUTO	N/A	N/A	150
CP-3360	362.47	8	1806	49	12	3.50	3H	SCSI-2	RLL 2,7	AUTO	N/A	N/A	150
CP-3364	362.47	8	1806	49	12	3.50	3H	IDE(AT)	RLL 2,7	AUTO	N/A	N/A	150
CP-340	41.95	4	788	26	29	3.50	HH	SCSI	RLL 2,7	AUTO	N/A	N/A	20
CP-342	42.86	4	805	26	29	3.50	HH	IDE(AT)	RLL 2,7	AUTO	N/A	N/A	0
CP-344	42.86	4	805	26	29	3.50	HH	IDE(AT)	RLL 2,7	AUTO	N/A	N/A	20
CP-346	42.86	4	805	26	29	3.50	HH	IDE(AT)	RLL 2,7	AUTO	N/A	N/A	20
CP-3500	510.41	12	1806	46	12	3.50	HH	SCSI-2	RLL 2,7	AUTO	N/A	N/A	150
CP-3504	509.38	12	1806	46	12	3.50	HH	IDE(AT)	RLL 2,7	AUTO	N/A	N/A	150
CP-3540	543.70	12	1806	49	12	3.50	3H	SCSI-2	RLL 2,7	AUTO	N/A	N/A	150
CP-3544	544.3	12	1808	49	49	3.50	HH	IDE(AT)	RLL 2,7	AUTO	N/A	N/A	150
CP-4024	21.58	2	620	34	29	3.50	4H	IDE(XT/AT)	RLL 2,7	AUTO	N/A	N/A	150
CP-4044	42.64	2	1096	38	29	3.50	4H	IDE(XT/AT)	RLL 2,7	AUTO	N/A	N/A	150

CONTROL DATA CORPORATION

MODEL	CAP	HDS	CYL	SPT	SEEK	FF	HGT	INT	ENCODE	LZ	WP	RWC	MTBF
9415-5 21	18.20	3	697	17	—	5.25	FH	ST-506/412	MFM	698	0	0	30
9415-5 25	24.26	4	697	17	—	5.25	FH	ST-506/412	MFM	698	0	0	30
9415-5 28	24.26	4	697	17	—	5.25	FH	ST-506/412	MFM	698	0	0	30
9415-5 36	30.33	5	697	17	—	5.25	FH	ST-506/412	MFM	698	0	0	30
9415-5 38 I	31.91	5	977	17	—	5.25	FH	ST-506/412	MFM	698	0	0	30
94155-021	18.20	3	697	17	18	5.25	FH	ST-506/412	MFM	—	697	697	0

CONTROL DATA CORPORATION

MODEL	CAP	HDS	CYL	SPT	SEEK	FF	HGT	INT	ENCODE	LZ	WP	RWC	MTBF
94155-025	24.26	4	697	17	24	5.25	FH	ST-506/412	MFM	–	128	697	0
94155-036	31.90	5	733	17	28	5.25	FH	ST-506/412	MFM	–	128	697	0
94155-038	31.90	5	733	17	28	5.25	FH	ST-506/412	MFM	–	0	734	0
94155-048	40.25	5	925	17	28	5.25	FH	ST-506/412	MFM	AUTO	128	926	40
94155-051	43.04	5	989	17	28	5.25	FH	ST-506/412	MFM	–	128	990	0
94155-057	48.30	6	925	17	28	5.25	FH	ST-506/412	MFM	AUTO	128	926	40
94155-067	56.35	7	925	17	28	5.25	FH	ST-506/412	MFM	AUTO	128	926	40
94155-077	64.40	8	925	17	28	5.25	FH	ST-506/412	MFM	AUTO	128	926	40
94155-085	71.30	8	1024	17	28	5.25	FH	ST-506/412	MFM	AUTO	128	1,025	40
94155-085P	71.30	8	1024	17	28	5.25	FH	ST-506/412	MFM	AUTO	128	1,025	40
94155-086	72.46	9	925	17	28	5.25	FH	ST-506/412	MFM	AUTO	128	926	40
94155-096	80.21	9	1024	17	28	5.25	FH	ST-506/412	MFM	AUTO	–	–	40
94155-135	115.01	9	960	26	28	5.25	FH	ST-506/412	RLL 2,7	AUTO	128	961	40
94156-048	80.51	5	925	34	28	5.25	FH	ESDI-10MHZ	RLL 2,7	AUTO	N/A	N/A	40
94156-48	80.51	5	925	34	28	5.25	FH	ESDI-10MHZ	RLL 2,7	AUTO	N/A	N/A	40
94156-67	112.71	7	925	34	28	5.25	FH	ESDI-10MHZ	RLL 2,7	AUTO	N/A	N/A	40
94156-86	144.92	9	925	34	28	5.25	FH	ESDI-10MHZ	RLL 2,7	AUTO	N/A	N/A	40
94161-086	86.82	5	969	35	16.5	5.25	FH	SCSI	RLL 2,7	AUTO	N/A	N/A	100
94161-101	84.34	5	969	34	16.5	5.25	FH	SCSI	RLL 2,7	AUTO	N/A	N/A	100
94161-103	104.18	6	969	35	16.5	5.25	FH	SCSI	RLL 2,7	AUTO	N/A	N/A	100
94161-121	121.55	7	969	35	16.5	5.25	FH	SCSI	RLL 2,7	AUTO	N/A	N/A	100
94161-138	138.91	8	969	35	16.5	5.25	FH	SCSI	RLL 2,7	AUTO	N/A	N/A	100
9461-141	121.5	7	969	35	16.5	5.25	FH	SCSI	RLL 2,7	AUTO	N/A	N/A	100
94161-151	156.28	9	969	35	16.5	5.25	FH	SCSI	RLL 2,7	AUTO	N/A	N/A	100
94161-155	151.81	9	969	34	16.5	5.25	FH	SCSI	RLL 2,7	AUTO	N/A	N/A	100
94161-182	156.28	9	969	35	16.5	5.25	FH	SCSI	RLL 2,7	AUTO	N/A	N/A	100
94166-101	89.30	5	969	35	16.5	5.25	FH	ESDI-10MHZ	RLL 2,7	AUTO	N/A	N/A	100
94166-121	107.16	7	969	36	16.5	5.25	FH	ESDI-10MHZ	RLL 2,7	AUTO	N/A	N/A	100
94166-141	125.02	7	969	36	16.5	5.25	FH	ESDI-10MHZ	RLL 2,7	AUTO	N/A	N/A	100
94166-161	142.88	8	969	36	16.5	5.25	FH	ESDI-10MHZ	RLL 2,7	AUTO	N/A	N/A	100
94166-161 COMPAQ	160.74	9	969	36	16.5	5.25	FH	ESDI-10MHZ	RLL 2,7	AUTO	N/A	N/A	100
94166-182	160.74	9	969	36	16.5	5.25	FH	ESDI-10MHZ	RLL 2,7	AUTO	N/A	N/A	100
94171-300	300.42	9	1412	*	17	5.25	FH	SCSI	RLL 2,7	AUTO	N/A	N/A	0
94171-307	300.42	9	1412	*	17	5.25	FH	SCSI	RLL 2,7	AUTO	N/A	N/A	0
94171-327	300.42	9	1412	*	17	5.25	FH	SCSI	RLL 2,7	AUTO	N/A	N/A	0
94171-344	323.08	9	1549	*	18	5.25	FH	SCSI	RLL 2,7	AUTO	N/A	N/A	0
94171-350	307.00	9	1412	*	16.5	5.25	FH	SCSI	RLL 2,7	AUTO	N/A	N/A	100
94171-375	330.00	9	1549	*	16	5.25	FH	SCSI	RLL 2,7	AUTO	N/A	N/A	0
94171-376	323.00	9	1549	*	17.5	5.25	FH	SCSI	RLL 2,7	AUTO	N/A	N/A	100
94171-376D	323.00	9	1549	*	17.5	5.25	FH	SCSI	RLL 2,7	AUTO	N/A	N/A	100
94181-385D	337.00	15	791	*	10.7	5.25	FH	SCSI	RLL 2,7	AUTO	N/A	N/A	100
94181-385H	337.00	15	791	*	10.7	5.25	FH	SCSI	RLL 2,7	AUTO	N/A	N/A	100
94181-574	574.00	15	1549	*	16	5.25	FH	SCSI	RLL 2,7	AUTO	N/A	N/A	100

CONTROL DATA CORPORATION

MODEL	CAP	HDS	CYL	SPT	SEEK	FF	HGT	INT	ENCODE	LZ	WP	RWC	MTBF
94181-702	601.00	15	1546	*	16.5	5.25	FH	SCSI	RLL 2,7	AUTO	N/A	N/A	100
94181-702D	601.00	15	1546	*	16.5	5.25	FH	SCSI	RLL 2,7	AUTO	N/A	N/A	100
94186-265	227.72	9	1412	35	–	5.25	FH	ESDI-10MHZ	RLL 2,7	AUTO	N/A	N/A	100
94186-324	278.33	11	1412	35	–	5.25	FH	ESDI-10MHZ	RLL 2,7	AUTO	N/A	N/A	0
94186-383	338.10	13	1412	36	18	5.25	FH	ESDI-10MHZ	RLL 2,7	AUTO	N/A	N/A	100
94186-383H	338.10	15	1224	36	14.5	5.25	FH	ESDI-10MHZ	RLL 2,7	AUTO	N/A	N/A	100
94186-442	379.54	15	1412	35	16	5.25	FH	ESDI-10MHZ	RLL 2,7	AUTO	N/A	N/A	100
94191-766	676.82	15	1632	54	15.5	5.25	FH	SCSI	RLL 2,7	AUTO	N/A	N/A	100
94191-766D	676.82	15	1632	54	15.5	5.25	FH	SCSI	RLL 2,7	AUTO	N/A	N/A	100
94196-383	338.10	7	1747	54	16.5	5.25	FH	ESDI-10MHZ	RLL 2,7	AUTO	N/A	N/A	100
94196-766	676.82	15	1632	54	16.5	5.25	FH	ESDI-10MHZ	RLL 2,7	AUTO	N/A	N/A	100
94204-051	43.04	5	989	26	28	5.25	HH	IDE(AT)	RLL 2,7	AUTO	N/A	N/A	40
94204-065	63.09	5	948	26	28	5.25	HH	IDE(AT)	RLL 2,7	AUTO	N/A	N/A	40
94204-071	63.09	5	1032	27	28	5.25	HH	IDE(AT)	RLL 2,7	AUTO	N/A	N/A	40
94204-074	63.09	5	948	26	28	5.25	HH	IDE(AT)	RLL 2,7	AUTO	N/A	N/A	40
94204-081	71.33	5	1032	27	28	5.25	HH	IDE(AT)	RLL 2,7	AUTO	N/A	N/A	40
94205-030	25.82	3	989	17	–	5.25	FH	ST-506/412	MFM	AUTO	–	989	40
94205-041	43.04	4	989	17	28	5.25	HH	ST-506/412	MFM	AUTO	128	990	40
94205-051	43.04	5	989	17	28	5.25	HH	ST-506/412	MFM	AUTO	128	990	40
94205-053	43.04	5	1024	17	28	5.25	HH	ST-506/412	MFM	AUTO	128	990	40
94205-071	43.04	5	989	26	28	5.25	HH	ST-506/412	RLL	AUTO	128	990	40
94205-075	61.82	5	966	25	28	5.25	HH	ST-506/412	RLL	AUTO	128	966	40
94205-077	65.82	5	989	26	28	5.25	HH	ST-506/412	RLL 2,7	AUTO	–	–	40
94208-051	42.82	5	966	25	–	5.25	HH	IDE(AT)	MFM	AUTO	128	N/A	40
94208-062	61.82	5	966	25	–	5.25	HH	IDE(SDI)	RLL	AUTO	128	N/A	40
94208-075	65.82	5	989	26	30	5.25	HH	IDE(AT)	RLL 2,7	AUTO	N/A	N/A	0
94211-091	91.75	5	992	35	18	5.25	HH	SCSI	RLL 2,7	AUTO	N/A	N/A	100
94211-106	91.75	5	1024	35	18	5.25	HH	SCSI	RLL 2,7	AUTO	N/A	N/A	100
94211-106M	91.75	5	1024	35	28	5.25	HH	SCSI	RLL 2,7	AUTO	N/A	N/A	40
94216-106	89.12	5	1024	34	18	5.25	HH	ESDI-10MHZ	RLL 2,7	AUTO	N/A	N/A	100
94221-125	107.00	3	1544	*	18	5.25	HH	SCSI	RLL 2,7	AUTO	N/A	N/A	100
94221-169	158.99	5	1310	*	18	5.25	HH	SCSI	RLL 2,7	AUTO	N/A	N/A	100
94221-184	158.99	5	1310	*	18	5.25	HH	SCSI	RLL 2,7	AUTO	N/A	N/A	100
94221-209	179.00	5	1544	*	18	5.25	HH	SCSI	RLL 2,7	AUTO	N/A	N/A	100
94241-383	331.00	7	1261	*	14	5.25	HH	SCSI	RLL 2,7	AUTO	N/A	N/A	100
94241-502	435.00	7	1765	*	16	5.25	HH	SCSI	RLL 2,7	AUTO	N/A	N/A	100
94241-502M	440.00	7	1765	*	16	5.25	HH	SCSI-MAC	RLL 2,7	AUTO	N/A	N/A	100
94244-274	232.56	5	1747	52	16	5.25	HH	IDE(AT)	RLL 2,7	AUTO	N/A	N/A	100
94244-383	338.10	7	1747	54	16	5.25	HH	IDE(AT)	RLL 2,7	AUTO	N/A	N/A	100
94246-182	160.69	4	1453	54	15	5.25	HH	ESDI-15MHZ	RLL 2,7	AUTO	N/A	N/A	100
94246-383	338.10	7	1747	54	16	5.25	HH	ESDI-15MHZ	RLL 2,7	AUTO	N/A	N/A	100
94311-136	120.00	5	–	–	15	3.50	3H	SCSI	RLL 2,7	AUTO	N/A	N/A	70
94311-136S	114.92	5	1247	36	15	3.50	3H	SCSI-2	RLL 2,7	AUTO	N/A	N/A	70

CONTROL DATA CORPORATION

MODEL	CAP	HDS	CYL	SPT	SEEK	FF	HGT	INT	ENCODE	LZ	WP	RWC	MTBF
94314-136	120.00	5	—	—	15	3.50	3H	IDE(AT)	RLL 2,7	AUTO	N/A	N/A	70
94316-111	98.00	5	—	—	23	3.50	HH	ESDI-10MHZ	RLL 2,7	AUTO	N/A	N/A	70
94316-136	120.00	5	—	—	15	3.50	HH	ESDI-10MHZ	RLL 2,7	AUTO	N/A	N/A	70
94316-155	138.31	7	1072	36	15	3.50	HH	ESDI-10MHZ	RLL 2,7	AUTO	N/A	N/A	70
94316-200	177.00	5	—	—	15	3.50	HH	ESDI-10MHZ	RLL 2,7	AUTO	N/A	N/A	70
94351-090	79.28	5	1068	29	15	3.50	HH	SCSI	RLL 2,7	AUTO	N/A	N/A	150
94351-111	98.42	5	1068	36	15	3.50	HH	SCSI	RLL 2,7	AUTO	N/A	N/A	70
94351-126	111.00	7	1068	29	15	3.50	HH	SCSI	RLL 2,7	AUTO	N/A	N/A	70
94351-128	111.00	7	1068	29	15	3.50	HH	SCSI	RLL 2,7	AUTO	N/A	N/A	70
94351-133S	116.85	5	1268	36	15	3.50	HH	SCSI-2	RLL 2,7	AUTO	N/A	N/A	70
94351-155	137.79	7	1068	36	15	3.50	HH	SCSI	RLL 2,7	AUTO	N/A	N/A	70
94351-155S	137.79	7	1068	36	15	3.50	HH	SCSI-2	RLL 2,7	AUTO	N/A	N/A	70
94351-160	142.71	9	1068	29	15	3.50	HH	SCSI	RLL 2,7	AUTO	N/A	N/A	150
94351-172	177.16	9	1068	36	15	3.50	HH	SCSI	RLL 2,7	AUTO	N/A	N/A	70
94351-186S	163.60	7	1268	36	15	3.50	HH	SCSI-2	RLL 2,7	AUTO	N/A	N/A	150
94351-200	177.16	9	1068	36	15	3.50	HH	SCSI	RLL 2,7	AUTO	N/A	N/A	150
94351-200S	177.16	9	1068	36	15	3.50	HH	SCSI-2	RLL 2,7	AUTO	N/A	N/A	150
94351-230	210.34	9	1268	36	15	3.50	HH	SCSI	RLL 2,7	AUTO	N/A	N/A	70
94351-230S	210.34	9	1268	36	15	3.50	HH	SCSI-2	RLL 2,7	AUTO	N/A	N/A	70
94354-090	79.58	5	1072	29	15	3.50	HH	IDE(AT)	RLL 2,7	AUTO	N/A	N/A	150
94354-111	98.79	5	1072	36	15	3.50	HH	IDE(AT)	RLL 2,7	AUTO	N/A	N/A	70
94354-126	111.41	7	1072	29	15	3.50	HH	IDE(AT)	RLL 2,7	AUTO	N/A	N/A	150
94354-133	117.22	5	1272	36	15	3.50	HH	IDE(AT)	RLL 2,7	AUTO	N/A	N/A	70
94354-155	138.31	7	1072	36	15	3.50	HH	IDE(AT)	RLL 2,7	AUTO	N/A	N/A	70
94354-160	143.25	9	1072	29	15	3.50	HH	IDE(AT)	RLL 2,7	AUTO	N/A	N/A	150
94354-186	164.11	7	1272	36	15	3.50	HH	IDE(AT)	RLL 2,7	AUTO	N/A	N/A	150
94354-200	177.83	9	1072	36	15	3.50	HH	IDE(AT)	RLL 2,7	AUTO	N/A	N/A	150
94354-239	211.00	9	1272	36	15	3.50	HH	IDE(AT)	RLL 2,7	AUTO	N/A	N/A	70
94355-055	46.00	5	—	17	25	3.50	HH	ST-506/412	MFM	AUTO	—	—	70
94355-100	83.97	9	1072	17	15	3.50	HH	ST-506/412	MFM	AUTO	300	1,073	150
94355-150	128.43	9	1072	26	15	3.50	HH	ST-506/412	RLL 2,7	AUTO	300	1,073	150
94356-111	98.79	5	1072	36	15	3.50	HH	ESDI-10MHZ	RLL 2,7	AUTO	N/A	N/A	150
94356-155	138.31	7	1072	36	15	3.50	HH	ESDI-10MHZ	RLL 2,7	AUTO	N/A	N/A	70
94356-200	177.83	9	1072	36	15	3.50	HH	ESDI-10MHZ	RLL 2,7	AUTO	N/A	N/A	70
94601-12D	1035.00	15	1931	*	15	5.25	FH	SCSI-DIFF	RLL 2,7	AUTO	N/A	N/A	150
94601-12G	1035.00	15	1931	*	15	5.25	FH	SCSI	RLL 2,7	AUTO	N/A	N/A	150
94601-12GM	1035.00	15	1931	*	15	5.25	FH	SCSI-MAC	RLL 2,7	AUTO	N/A	N/A	150
94601-767H	676.00	15	1356	*	11.9	5.25	FH	SCSI-MAC	RLL 2,7	AUTO	N/A	N/A	100
97155-036	30.00	—	—	17	—	8.00	FH	ST-506/412	MFM	—	—	—	70
97501-15G	1500.00	17	—		12	5.25	FH	SCSI-2	RLL 2,7	AUTO	N/A	N/A	100
BJ7D5A/ 77731600	18.20	3	697	17	—	5.25	FH	ST-506/412	MFM	—	128	—	0

CONTROL DATA CORPORATION

MODEL	CAP	HDS	CYL	SPT	SEEK	FF	HGT	INT	ENCODE	LZ	WP	RWC	MTBF
BJ7D5A/ 77731601	18.20	3	697	17	–	5.25	FH	ST-506/412	MFM	–	128	–	0
BJ7D5A/ 77731602	30.33	5	697	17	–	5.25	FH	ST-506/412	MFM	–	128	–	0
BJ7D5A/ 77731603	30.33	5	697	17	–	5.25	FH	ST-506/412	MFM	–	128	–	0
BJ7D5A/ 77731604	36.00	5	697	–	–	5.25	FH	ST-506/412	MFM	–	128	–	0
BJ7D5A/ 77731605	30.33	5	697	17	–	5.25	FH	ST-506/412	MFM	–	128	–	0
BJ7D5A/ 77731606	27.00	–	–	17	–	5.25	FH	ST-506/412	MFM	–	128	–	0
BJ7D5A/ 77731607	18.20	3	697	17	–	5.25	FH	ST-506/412	MFM	–	128	–	0
BJ7D5A/ 77731608	30.33	5	697	17	–	5.25	FH	ST-506/412	MFM	–	128	–	0
BJ7D5A/ 77731609	30.33	5	697	17	–	5.25	FH	ST-506/412	MFM	–	128	–	0
BJ7D5A/ 77731610	18.20	3	697	17	–	5.25	FH	ST-506/412	MFM	–	128	–	0
BJ7D5A/ 77731611	30.33	5	697	17	–	5.25	FH	ST-506/412	MFM	–	128	–	0
BJ7D5A/ 77731612	24.26	4	697	17	–	5.25	FH	ST-506/412	MFM	–	128	–	0
BJ7D5A/ 77731613	31.90	5	733	17	–	5.25	FH	ST-506/412	MFM	–	128	–	0
BJ7D5A/ 77731614	24.26	4	697	17	–	5.25	FH	ST-506/412	MFM	–	128	–	0
BJ7D5A/ 77731615	24.26	4	697	17	–	5.25	FH	ST-506/412	MFM	–	128	–	0
BJ7D5A/ 777316160	31.90	5	733	17	–	5.25	FH	ST-506/412	MFM	–	128	–	
BJ7D5A/ 77731617	30.33	5	697	17	–	5.25	FH	ST-506/412	MFM	–	128	–	0
BJ7D5A/ 77731618	30.33	5	697	17	–	5.25	FH	ST-506/412	MFM	–	128	–	0
BJ7D5A/ 77731619	30.33	5	697	17	–	5.25	FH	ST-506/412	MFM	–	128	–	0
BJ7D5A/ 77731620	30.33	5	697	17	–	5.25	FH	ST-506/412	MFM	–	128	–	0

CONTROL DATA CORPORATION

The first two digits denote where the drive was manufactured:
94 - Oklahoma City
97 - Minneapolis/St. Paul

The fifth digit indicates the Interface:
0 - SMD
1 - SCSI/SASI
2 - LDI
3 - FDI
4 - IDE(AT)
5 - ST506/412
6 - ESDI
8 – 20286(Compaq)

The alpha suffix denotes Special Features:
P - Precompensation
M - MacWren
H - High Performance
D – Differential
S - Sync Spindle (Wren)
   Synchronous SCSI (Swift)
G - Gigabyte

94 18 1 - 702 H

The next two digits indicate Series & Form Factor:

15 - Wren I/FH	**20** - Wren II/HH
15 - Wren II/FH	**21** - Wren III/HH
16 - Wren III/FH	**22** - Wren V/HH
17 - Wren IV/FH	**24** - Wren VI/HH
18 - Wren V/FH	**35** - Swift/HH
19 - Wren VII/FH	**60** - Wren VII/HH

The numbers after the dash represent the Unformatted Capacity

CORE INTERNATIONAL, INC.

MODEL	CAP	HDS	CYL	SPT	SEEK	FF	HGT	INT	ENCODE	LZ	WP	RWC	MTBF
3SHC230	230.00	5	–	–	13	3.50	FH	SCSI	RLL	AUTO	N/A	N/A	150
AT-115F	160.74	9	969	54	–	5.25	FH	ESDI-10MHZ	RLL 2,7	AUTO	N/A	N/A	0
AT-145	58.97	7	968	17	–	5.25	FH	ST-506/412	MFM	–	–	–	0
AT-150	156.28	9	969	35	16	5.25	FH	ESDI-10MHZ	RLL 2,7	AUTO	N/A	N/A	99
AT-30	31.90	5	733	17	26	5.25	FH	ST-506/412	MFM	–	–	–	0
AT-30R	48.78	5	733	26	26	5.25	FH	ST-506/412	RLL 2,7	–	–	–	0
AT-32	31.90	5	733	17	21	5.25	HH	ST-506/412	MFM	–	–	–	0
AT-32R	48.78	5	733	26	21	5.25	HH	ST-506/412	RLL 2,7	–	–	–	0
AT-40	40.21	5	924	17	26	5.25	FH	ST-506/412	MFM	–	–	–	0
AT-40R	61.50	5	924	26	26	5.25	FH	ST-506/412	RLL 2,7	–	–	–	0
ATPLUS-20	21.41	4	615	17	26	5.25	HH	ST-506/412	MFM	–	–	–	50
ATPLUS-43	42.99	5	988	17	26	5.25	HH	ST-506/412	MFM	–	–	–	50
ATPLUS-43R	65.76	5	988	26	26	5.25	HH	ST-506/412	RLL 2,7	–	–	–	50
ATPLUS-44	44.66	7	733	17	26	3.50	HH	ST-506/412	MFM	–	–	–	50
ATPLUS-44R	68.30	7	733	26	26	3.50	HH	ST-506/412	RLL 2,7	–	–	–	50
ATPLUS-72	72.38	9	924	17	26	5.25	FH	ST-506/412	MFM	–	–	–	50
ATPLUS-72R	110.70	9	924	26	26	5.25	FH	ST-506/412	RLL 2,7	–	–	–	50
ATPLUS-80	80.21	9	1024	17	15	3.50	HH	ST-506/412	MFM	–	–	–	50
ATPLUS-80R	122.68	9	1024	26	15	3.50	HH	ST-506/412	RLL 2,7	–	–	–	50
HC1000-FH (SCSI)	1005.58	16	1918	64	15	5.25	FH	SCSI	RLL 2,7	AUTO	N/A	N/A	150
HC1000-FH (ESDI)	1056.76	15	1787	77	14	5.25	FH	ESDI-24MHZ	RLL 2,7	AUTO	N/A	N/A	99
HC150-FH	151.81	9	969	34	16.5	5.25	FH	ESDI-10MHZ	RLL 2,7	AUTO	N/A	N/A	100

CORE INTERNATIONAL, INC.

MODEL	CAP	HDS	CYL	SPT	SEEK	FF	HGT	INT	ENCODE	LZ	WP	RWC	MTBF
HC150-FH (SCSI)	156.28	9	969	35	16.5	5.25	FH	SCSI	RLL 2,7	AUTO	N/A	N/A	150
HC150-HH	156.80	7	1250	35	17	5.25	HH	ESDI-10MHZ	RLL 2,7	AUTO	N/A	N/A	100
HC175-FH	172.89	9	1072	35	16	5.25	FH	ESDI-10MHZ	RLL 2,7	AUTO	N/A	N/A	150
HC200	200.00	8	–	–	16	5.25	FH	IDE(AT)	RLL	AUTO	N/A	N/A	150
HC260-FH	260.62	12	1212	35	16	5.25	FH	ESDI-10MHZ	RLL 2,7	AUTO	N/A	N/A	0
HC310-5FH -V1	338.41	15	1224	36	18	5.25	FH	ESDI-10MHZ	RLL 2,7	AUTO	N/A	N/A	150
HC310-5FH -V2	319.54	13	1412	34	18	5.25	FH	ESDI-10MHZ	RLL 2,7	AUTO	N/A	N/A	100
HC310-5FH -V3	319.54	13	1412	34	18	5.25	FH	ESDI-10MHZ	RLL 2,7	AUTO	N/A	N/A	100
HC310-FH (SCSI)	331.90	8	1447	56	16.5	5.25	FH	SCSI	RLL 2,7	AUTO	N/A	N/A	150
HC310-HH	325.58	7	1747	52	18	5.25	HH	ESDI-15MHZ	RLL 2,7	AUTO	N/A	N/A	100
HC315-FH	337.83	8	1447	57	17	5.25	FH	ESDI-15MHZ	RLL 2,7	AUTO	N/A	N/A	150
HC380-FH	379.54	15	1412	35	16	5.25	FH	ESDI-10MHZ	RLL 2,7	AUTO	N/A	N/A	150
HC40-FH	40.42	4	564	35	10	5.25	FH	ESDI-10MHZ	RLL 2,7	AUTO	N/A	N/A	150
HC650-FH (SCSI)	666.73	14	1661	56	16.5	5.25	FH	SCSI	RLL 2,7	AUTO	N/A	N/A	150
HC650-FH -V1	679.09	15	1661	53	17	5.25	FH	ESDI-15MHZ	RLL 2,7	AUTO	N/A	N/A	100
HC650-FH -V2	676.09	15	1661	53	17	5.25	FH	ESDI-15MHZ	RLL 2,7	AUTO	N/A	N/A	100
HC650-FH -V3	676.82	15	1632	54	16	5.25	FH	ESDI-15MHZ	RLL 2,7	AUTO	N/A	N/A	150
HC655-FH	675.66	16	1447	57	16	5.25	FH	ESDI-15MHZ	RLL 2,7	AUTO	N/A	N/A	150
HC90	86.82	5	969	35	16	5.25	HH	ESDI-10MHZ	RLL 2,7	AUTO	N/A	N/A	0
MC120	120.58	8	920	32	23	5.25	FH	MCA	RLL	AUTO	N/A	N/A	45
MC60	60.81	4	928	32	23	5.25	FH	MCA	RLL	AUTO	N/A	N/A	45
OPTIMA 30	31.90	5	733	17	21	5.25	HH	ST-506/412	MFM	–	–	–	0
OPTIMA 30R	48.78	5	733	26	21	5.25	HH	ST-506/412	RLL 2,7	–	–	–	0
OPTIMA 40	41.90	5	963	17	26	5.25	HH	ST-506/412	MFM	–	–	–	35
OPTIMA 40R	64.09	5	963	26	26	5.25	HH	ST-506/412	RLL 2,7	–	–	–	35
OPTIMA 70	71.91	9	918	17	26	5.25	FH	ST-506/412	MFM	–	–	–	35
OPTIMA 70R	109.98	9	918	26	26	5.25	FH	ST-506/412	RLL 2,7	–	–	–	35
OPTIMA 80	80.21	9	1024	17	15	3.50	HH	ST-506/412	MFM	–	–	–	35
OPTIMA 80R	122.68	9	1024	26	15	3.50	HH	ST-506/412	RLL 2,7	–	–	–	35

DAEYOUNG ELECTRONICS

MODEL	CAP	HDS	CYL	SPT	SEEK	FF	HGT	INT	ENCODE	LZ	WP	RWC	MTBF
DX-3120A	120	3	1040	27	25	3.50	3H	IDE(AT)	RLL 2,7	AUTO	N/A	N/A	50

DIGITAL EQUIPMENT CORPORATION

MODEL	CAP	HDS	CYL	SPT	SEEK	FF	HGT	INT	ENCODE	LZ	WP	RWC	MTBF
DP3055	551	4	3115	*	9.5	3.50	3H	SCSI-2	RLL 1,7	AUTO	N/A	N/A	700
DP3055W	551	4	3115	*	9.5	3.50	3H	SCSI-2 W	RLL 1,7	AUTO	N/A	N/A	700
DP3110	1103	8	3115	*	9.5	3.50	3H	SCSI-2	RLL 1,7	AUTO	N/A	N/A	700
DP3110W	1103	8	3115	*	9.5	3.50	3H	SCSI-2 W	RLL 1,7	AUTO	N/A	N/A	700

DIGITAL EQUIPMENT CORPORATION

MODEL	CAP	HDS	CYL	SPT	SEEK	FF	HGT	INT	ENCODE	LZ	WP	RWC	MTBF
DSP3053L	535	4	3117	*	9.5	3.50	3H	SCSI-2 W	RLL 1,7	AUTO	N/A	N/A	500
DSP3053LD	535	4	3117	*	9.5	3.50	3H	SCSI-2DIFF	RLL 1,7	AUTO	N/A	N/A	500
DSP3053LR	535	4	3117	*	9.5	3.50	3H	SCSI-2/D80	RLL 1,7	AUTO	N/A	N/A	500
DSP3053LW	535	4	3117	*	9.5	3.50	3H	SCSI-2 W	RLL 1,7	AUTO	N/A	N/A	500
DSP3053LWD	535	4	3117	*	9.5	3.50	3H	SCSI-2 W/D	RLL 1,7	AUTO	N/A	N/A	500
DSP3085	852	14	—	57	9.5	3.50	HH	SCSI-2	NONE	AUTO	N/A	N/A	0
DSP3105	1050	14	—	57	9.5	3.50	HH	SCSI-2	NONE	AUTO	N/A	N/A	250
DSP3105D	1050	14	—	57	9.5	3.50	HH	SCSI-2DIFF	NONE	AUTO	N/A	N/A	250
DSP3107L	1070	8	3117	*	9.5	3.50	3H	SCSI-2DIFF	RLL 1,7	AUTO	N/A	N/A	500
DSP3107LD	1070	8	3117	*	9.5	3.50	3H	SCSI-2DIFF	RLL 1,7	AUTO	N/A	N/A	500
DSP3107LR	1070	8	3117	*	9.5	3.50	3H	SCSI-2/D80	RLL 1,7	AUTO	N/A	N/A	500
DSP3107LW	1070	8	3117	*	9.5	3.50	3H	SCSI-2 W	RLL 1,7	AUTO	N/A	N/A	500
DSP3107LWD	1070	8	3117	*	9.5	3.50	3H	SCSI-2 W/D	RLL 1,7	AUTO	N/A	N/A	500
DSP3133L	1338	10	3117	*	9.5	3.50	3H	SCSI-2	RLL 1,7	AUTO	N/A	N/A	500
DSP3133LD	1338	10	3117	*	9.5	3.50	3H	SCSI-2DIFF	RLL 1,7	AUTO	N/A	N/A	500
DSP3133LR	1337.5	10	3117	*	9.5	3.50	3H	SCSI-2F	RLL 1,7	N/A	N/A	N/A	500
DSP3133LW	1338	10	3117	*	9.	3.50	3H	SCSI-2 W/D	RLL 1,7	AUTO	N/A	N/A	500
DSP3133LWD	1338	10	3117	*	9.5	3.50	3H	SCSI-2 W	RLL 1,7	AUTO	N/A	N/A	500
DSP3160	1600	16	2599	*	9.7	3.50	3H	SCSI-2	RLL 1,7	AUTO	N/A	N/A	350
DSP3160W	1600	16	2599	*	9.7	3.50	3H	SCSI-2 W	RLL 1,7	AUTO	N/A	N/A	350
DSP3210	2148	16	3045	*	9.5	3.50	3H	SCSI-2	RLL 1,7	AUTO	N/A	N/A	500
DSP3210W	2148	16	3045	*	9.5	3.50	3H	SCSI-2 W	RLL 1,7	AUTO	N/A	N/A	500
DSP3210WD	2148	16	3045	*	9.5	3.50	3H	SCSI-2 W/D	RLL 1,7	AUTO	N/A	N/A	500
RZ55	—	—	—	—	—	—	—	SCSI	RLL	AUTO	N/A	N/A	0
RZ55E	—	—	—	—	—	—	—	SCSI	RLL	AUTO	N/A	N/A	0

DISCTEC

MODEL	CAP	HDS	CYL	SPT	SEEK	FF	HGT	INT	ENCODE	LZ	WP	RWC	MTBF
RHD-120	129.80	—	—	—	17	3.50	3H	IDE(AT)	RLL	AUTO	N/A	N/A	100
RHD-180	183.00	—	—	—	15	3.50	3H	IDE(AT)	RLL	AUTO	N/A	N/A	100
RHD-20	21.41	—	—	—	23	3.50	3H	IDE(AT)	RLL	AUTO	N/A	N/A	50
RHD-210	209.70	—	—	—	19	3.50	3H	IDE(AT)	RLL	AUTO	N/A	N/A	150
RHD-60	62.91	—	—	—	22	3.50	3H	IDE(AT)	RLL	AUTO	N/A	N/A	100
RHD-80	81.33	—	—	—	16	3.50	3H	IDE(AT)	RLL	AUTO	N/A	N/A	150

DISCTRON, INC.

MODEL	CAP	HDS	CYL	SPT	SEEK	FF	HGT	INT	ENCODE	LZ	WP	RWC	MTBF
D-503	2.66	2	153	17	85	5.25	FH	ST-506/412	MFM	—	—	—	0
D-504	3.74	2	215	17	85	5.25	FH	ST-506/412	MFM	—	—	—	0
D-506	5.32	4	153	17	85	5.25	FH	ST-506/412	MFM	—	—	—	0
D-507	5.32	2	306	17	85	5.25	FH	ST-506/412	MFM	—	128	128	0

DISCTRON, INC.

MODEL	CAP	HDS	CYL	SPT	SEEK	FF	HGT	INT	ENCODE	LZ	WP	RWC	MTBF
D-509	7.48	4	215	17	85	5.25	FH	ST-506/412	MFM	—	128	128	0
D-512	10.65	8	153	17	85	5.25	FH	ST-506/412	MFM	—	—	—	0
D-513	11.22	6	215	17	85	5.25	FH	ST-506/412	MFM	—	128	128	0
D-514	10.65	4	306	17	85	5.25	FH	ST-506/412	MFM	—	128	128	0
D-518	14.97	8	215	17	85	5.25	FH	ST-506/412	MFM	—	128	128	0
D-519	15.98	6	306	17	85	5.25	FH	ST-506/412	MFM	—	128	128	0
D-526	21.30	8	306	17	85	5.25	FH	ST-506/412	MFM	—	128	128	0

DMA SYSTEMS

MODEL	CAP	HDS	CYL	SPT	SEEK	FF	HGT	INT	ENCODE	LZ	WP	RWC	MTBF
306	10.65	2	612	17	85	5.25	HH	ST-506/412	MFM	—	400	612	0

ELCOH

MODEL	CAP	HDS	CYL	SPT	SEEK	FF	HGT	INT	ENCODE	LZ	WP	RWC	MTBF
DISCACHE10	11.14	4	320	17	65	5.25	FH	ST-506/412	MFM	—	321	321	0
DISCACHE20	22.28	8	320	17	65	5.25	FH	ST-506/412	MFM	—	321	321	0

EPSON, INC.

MODEL	CAP	HDS	CYL	SPT	SEEK	FF	HGT	INT	ENCODE	LZ	WP	RWC	MTBF
HD-560	21.41	4	615	17	78	5.25	HH	ST-506/412	MFM	—	300	615	0
HD-830	10.65	2	612	17	93	5.25	HH	ST-506/412	MFM	—	—	—	0
HD-850	10.65	4	306	17	93	5.25	HH	ST-506/412	MFM	—	—	—	0
HD-860	21.30	4	612	17	93	5.25	HH	ST-506/412	MFM	—	—	—	0
HMD-710	10.70	2	612	32**	80	5.25	HH	ST-506/412	MFM	—	—	—	20
HMD-720	21.41	4	612	32**	80	5.25	HH	ST-506/412	MFM	—	—	—	20
HMD-726A	20.78	4	615	33**	80	3.50	HH	SCSI	RLL 2,7	AUTO	—	—	20
HMD-755	21.41	2	615	34	80	5.25	HH	ST-506/412	RLL 2,7	—	—	—	20
HMD-765	41.82	4	615	34	80	5.25	HH	ST-506/412	RLL 2,7	—	—	—	20

FUJI ELECTRIC CORPORATION

MODEL	CAP	HDS	CYL	SPT	SEEK	FF	HGT	INT	ENCODE	LZ	WP	RWC	MTBF
FK301-13	10.65	4	306	17	65	3.50	HH	ST-506/412	MFM	—	—	—	45
FK302-13	10.65	2	612	17	65	3.50	HH	ST-506/412	MFM	—	307	613	0
FK302-26	21.30	4	612	17	65	3.50	HH	ST-506/412	MFM	—	307	613	0
FK302-39	31.96	6	612	17	65	3.50	HH	ST-506/412	MFM	—	307	613	0
FK303-52	42.82	8	615	17	40	3.50	HH	ST-506/412	MFM	—	—	—	20
FK305-26	21.41	4	615	17	65	3.50	HH	ST-506/412	MFM	—	616	—	0

FUJI ELECTRIC CORPORATION

MODEL	CAP	HDS	CYL	SPT	SEEK	FF	HGT	INT	ENCODE	LZ	WP	RWC	MTBF
FK305-39	32.11	6	615	17	65	3.50	HH	ST-506/412	MFM	–	616	–	20
FK305-58	32.11	6	615	17	65	3.50	HH	ST-506/412	MFM	–	616	–	20
FK305-58R	49.12	6	615	26	65	3.50	HH	ST-506/412	RLL 2,7	–	616	–	20
FK308S-39R	32.74	4	615	26	65	3.50	HH	SCSI	RLL 2,7	AUTO	N/A	N/A	20
FK308S-58R	49.12	6	615	26	65	3.50	HH	SCSI	RLL 2,7	AUTO	N/A	N/A	0
FK309-26	21.41	4	615	17	65	3.50	HH	ST-506/412	MFM	–	616	–	20
FK309-39R	32.74	4	615	26	65	3.50	HH	ST-506/412	RLL 2,7	–	616	–	20
FK309S-50R	41.56	4	615	33	47	3.50	HH	SCSI	RLL 2,7	AUTO	N/A	N/A	20

FUJITSU CORPORATION

MODEL	CAP	HDS	CYL	SPT	SEEK	FF	HGT	INT	ENCODE	LZ	WP	RWC	MTBF
M1603S	540	3	3457	94	10	3.50	3H	SCSI-2	RLL 1,7	AUTO	N/A	N/A	800
M1603TA	544	3	3457		12	3.50	3H	IDE(AT)	RLL 1,7	AUTO	N/A	N/A	250
M1606S	1080	6	3457	94	10	3.50	3H	SCSI-2	RLL 1,7	AUTO	N/A	N/A	800
M1606TA	1089	6	3457		12	3.50	3H	IDE(AT)	RLL 1,7	AUTO	N/A	N/A	250
M1612TAU	546.68	2	4133	*	12	3.50	3H	IDE(AT)	PRML	AUTO	N/A	N/A	300
M1614TAU	1091	4	4133	*	12	3.50	3H	IDE(AT)	PRML	AUTO	N/A	N/A	300
M1623TAU	1702	3	2491	63	10	3.50	3H	IDE(AT)	PRML	N/A		N/A	
M1624TAU	2269	4			10	3.50	3H	IDE(AT)	PRML	N/A	N/A	N/A	
M1636TAU	1286				10	3.50	3H	IDE(AT)	PRML	N/A	N/A	N/A	
M1638TAU	2571				10	3.50	3H	IDE(AT)	PRML	N/A	N/A	N/A	
M2225D	20.15	4	615	32**	40	3.50	HH	ST-506/412	MFM	–	–	–	30
M2225D2	20.15	4	615	32**	35	3.50	HH	ST-506/412	MFM	–	–	–	30
M2225DR	32.74	4	615	26	35	3.50	HH	ST-506/412	RLL 2,7	–	–	–	30
M2226D	30.22	6	615	32**	40	3.50	HH	ST-506/412	MFM	–	–	–	30
M2226D2	30.22	6	615	32**	35	3.50	HH	ST-506/412	MFM	–	–	–	30
M2226DR	49.12	6	615	26	35	3.50	HH	ST-506/412	RLL 2,7	–	–	–	30
M2227D	40.30	8	615	32**	40	3.50	HH	ST-506/412	MFM	–	–	–	30
M2227D2	40.30	8	615	32**	35	3.50	HH	ST-506/412	MFM	–	–	–	30
M2227DR	65.49	8	615	26	35	3.50	HH	ST-506/412	RLL 2,7	–	–	–	30
M2230	5.24	2	320	*	85	5.25	FH	ST-506/412	MFM	–	128	320	0
M2230AS	5.57	2	320	17	85	5.25	FH	ST-506/412	MFM	–	128	320	0
M2230AT	5.57	2	320	32	85	5.25	HH	ST-506/412	MFM	–	128	320	0
M2231	5.32	2	306	17	85	5.25	FH	ST-506/412	MFM	–	–	–	0
M2233	10.48	4	320	*	80	5.25	FH	ST-506/412	MFM	–	128	320	0
M2233AS	11.14	4	320	17	80	5.25	FH	ST-506/412	MFM	–	128	320	0
M2233AT	20.97	4	320	32**	95	5.25	HH	ST-506/412	MFM	–	18	320	0
M2234	15.73	6	320	*	85	5.25	FH	ST-506/412	MFM	–	128	320	0
M2234AS	16.71	6	320	17	85	5.25	FH	ST-506/412	MFM	–	128	320	0
M2235	22.28	8	320	*	85	5.25	FH	ST-506/412	MFM	–	128	320	0
M2235AS	22.28	8	320	17	85	5.25	FH	ST-506/412	MFM	–	128	320	0
M2241AS	24.70	4	754	16	33	5.25	FH	ST-506/412	MFM	–	375	–	20
M2241AS2	24.70	4	754	32**	30	5.25	FH	ST-506/412	MFM	–	375	–	20

FUJITSU CORPORATION

MODEL	CAP	HDS	CYL	SPT	SEEK	FF	HGT	INT	ENCODE	LZ	WP	RWC	MTBF
M2242AS	43.23	7	754	16	33	5.25	FH	ST-506/412	MFM	–	754	754	30
M2242AS2	43.23	7	754	32**	30	5.25	FH	ST-506/412	MFM	–	–	–	30
M2243AS	67.94	11	754	16	33	5.25	FH	ST-506/412	MFM	–	754	754	30
M2243AS2	67.94	11	754	32**	30	5.25	FH	ST-506/412	MFM	–	–	–	0
M2243R	110.51	7	1186	26	25	5.25	HH	ST-506/412	RLL 2,7	–	–	–	0
M2243T	72.26	7	1186	17	25	5.25	HH	ST-506/412	MFM	–	–	–	0
M2244E	134.84	5	823	64**	25	5.25	FH	ESDI-10MHZ	RLL 2,7	AUTO	N/A	N/A	30
M2244S	73.74	5	823	65	25	5.25	FH	SCSI	RLL 2,7	AUTO	N/A	N/A	35
M2244SA	73.74	5	823	35	25	5.25	FH	SCSI	RLL 2,7	AUTO	N/A	N/A	35
M2244SB	73.74	5	823	19	25	5.25	FH	SCSI	RLL 2,7	AUTO	N/A	N/A	35
M2245E	188.77	7	823	64**	25	5.25	FH	ESDI-10MHZ	RLL 2,7	AUTO	N/A	N/A	30
M2245S	103.23	7	823	64	25	5.25	FH	SCSI	RLL 2,7	AUTO	N/A	N/A	35
M2245SA	103.23	7	823	35	25	5.25	FH	SCSI	RLL 2,7	AUTO	N/A	N/A	35
M2245SB	103.23	7	823	19	25	5.25	FH	SCSI	RLL 2,7	AUTO	N/A	N/A	35
M2246E	147.48	10	823	*	25	5.25	FH	ESDI-10MHZ	RLL 2,7	AUTO	N/A	N/A	30
M2246S	147.48	10	823	65	25	5.25	FH	SCSI	RLL 2,7	AUTO	N/A	N/A	35
M2246SA	147.48	10	823	35	25	5.25	FH	SCSI	RLL 2,7	AUTO	N/A	N/A	35
M2246SB	147.48	10	823	19	25	5.25	FH	SCSI	RLL 2,7	AUTO	N/A	N/A	35
M2247E	142.5	7	1243	64**	18	5.25	FH	ESDI-10MHZ	RLL 1,7	AUTO	N/A	N/A	30
M2247S	289.56	7	1243	65**	18	5.25	FH	SCSI	RLL 1,7	AUTO	N/A	N/A	30
M2247SA	155.92	7	1243	35	18	5.25	FH	SCSI	RLL 1,7	AUTO	N/A	N/A	30
M2247SB	84.64	7	1243	19***	18	5.25	FH	SCSI	RLL 1,7	AUTO	N/A	N/A	30
M2248E	224	11	1243	64**	18	5.25	FH	ESDI-10MHZ	RLL 1,7	AUTO	N/A	N/A	30
M2248S	455.03	11	1243	65**	18	5.25	FH	SCSI	RLL 1,7	AUTO	N/A	N/A	30
M2248SA	245.02	11	1243	35	18	5.25	FH	SCSI	RLL 1,7	AUTO	N/A	N/A	30
M2248SB	133.01	11	1243	19***	18	5.25	FH	SCSI	RLL 1,7	AUTO	N/A	N/A	30
M2249E	305.5	15	1243	64**	18	5.25	FH	ESDI-10MHZ	RLL 1,7	AUTO	N/A	N/A	30
M2249S	620.50	15	1243	65**	18	5.25	FH	SCSI	RLL 1,7	AUTO	N/A	N/A	30
M2249SA	334.11	15	1243	35	18	5.25	FH	SCSI	RLL 1,7	AUTO	N/A	N/A	30
M2249SB	181.37	15	1243	19***	18	5.25	FH	SCSI	RLL 1,7	AUTO	N/A	N/A	30
M2261E	366.72	8	1658	54	16	5.25	FH	ESDI-15MHZ	RLL 1,7	AUTO	N/A	N/A	200
M2261H	346.34	8	1658	94	16	5.25	FH	SCSI	RLL 1,7	AUTO	N/A	N/A	200
M2261HA	346.34	8	1658	51	16	5.25	FH	SCSI	RLL 1,7	AUTO	N/A	N/A	200
M2261HB	346.34	8	1658	27	16	5.25	FH	SCSI	RLL 1,7	AUTO	N/A	N/A	200
M2261S	346.34	8	1658	94	16	5.25	FH	SCSI	RLL 1,7	AUTO	N/A	N/A	200
M2261SA	346.34	8	1658	51	16	5.25	FH	SCSI	RLL 1,7	AUTO	N/A	N/A	200
M2261SB	346.34	8	1658	27	16	5.25	FH	SCSI	RLL 1,7	AUTO	N/A	N/A	200
M2262E	504.24	11	1658	54	16	5.25	FH	ESDI-15MHZ	RLL 1,7	AUTO	N/A	N/A	200
M2262H	476.23	11	1658	94	16	5.25	FH	SCSI	RLL 1,7	AUTO	N/A	N/A	200
M2262HA	476.23	11	1658	51	16	5.25	FH	SCSI	RLL 1,7	AUTO	N/A	N/A	200
M2262HB	476.23	11	1658	27	16	5.25	FH	SCSI	RLL 1,7	AUTO	N/A	N/A	200
M2262S	476.23	11	1658	94	16	5.25	FH	SCSI	RLL 1,7	AUTO	N/A	N/A	200
M2262SA	476.23	11	1658	51	16	5.25	FH	SCSI	RLL 1,7	AUTO	N/A	N/A	200
M2262SB	476.23	11	1658	27	16	5.25	FH	SCSI	RLL 1,7	AUTO	N/A	N/A	200

FUJITSU CORPORATION

MODEL	CAP	HDS	CYL	SPT	SEEK	FF	HGT	INT	ENCODE	LZ	WP	RWC	MTBF
M2263E	687.60	15	1658	54	16	5.25	FH	ESDI-15MHZ	RLL 1,7	AUTO	N/A	N/A	200
M2263H	674.87	15	1658	94	16	5.25	FH	SCSI	RLL 1,7	AUTO	N/A	N/A	200
M2263HA	674.87	15	1658	53	16	5.25	FH	SCSI	RLL 1,7	AUTO	N/A	N/A	200
M2263HB	674.87	15	1658	27	16	5.25	FH	SCSI	RLL 1,7	AUTO	N/A	N/A	200
M2263S	674.87	15	1658	53	16	5.25	FH	SCSI	RLL 1,7	AUTO	N/A	N/A	200
M2263SA	674.87	15	1658	53	16	5.25	FH	SCSI	RLL 1,7	AUTO	N/A	N/A	200
M2263SB	674.87	15	1658	53	16	5.25	FH	SCSI	RLL 1,7	AUTO	N/A	N/A	200
M2266E	674.87	15	1658	53	16	5.25	FH	ESDI-15MHZ	RLL 1,7	AUTO	N/A	N/A	200
M2266H	953.10	15	1658	—	14.5	5.25	FH	SCSI	RLL 1,7	AUTO	N/A	N/A	200
M2266HA	1079.10	15	1658	—	14.5	5.25	FH	SCSI	RLL 1,7	AUTO	N/A	N/A	200
M2266HB	1140.20	15	1658	—	14.5	5.25	FH	SCSI	RLL 1,7	AUTO	N/A	N/A	200
M2266S	953.10	15	1658	—	14.5	5.25	FH	SCSI	RLL 1,7	AUTO	N/A	N/A	200
M2266SA	1079.10	15	1658	—	14.5	5.25	FH	SCSI	RLL 1,7	AUTO	N/A	N/A	200
M2266SB	1140.24	15	1658	—	14.5	5.25	FH	SCSI	RLL 1,7	AUTO	N/A	N/A	200
M2611ES	46.44	2	1334	68**	25	3.50	HH	SCSI	RLL 1,7	AUTO	N/A	N/A	50
M2611ESA	46.44	2	1334	34	25	3.50	HH	SCSI	RLL 1,7	AUTO	N/A	N/A	50
M2611ESB	46.44	2	1334	17***	25	3.50	HH	SCSI	RLL 1,7	AUTO	N/A	N/A	50
M2611ET	45.07	2	1334	33	25	3.50	HH	IDE(AT)	RLL 1,7	AUTO	N/A	N/A	50
M2611H	46.44	2	1334	34	25	3.50	HH	SCSI	RLL 1,7	AUTO	N/A	N/A	50
M2611S	46.44	2	1334	68**	25	3.50	HH	SCSI	RLL 1,7	AUTO	N/A	N/A	50
M2611SA	46.44	2	1334	34	25	3.50	HH	SCSI	RLL 1,7	AUTO	N/A	N/A	50
M2611SB	46.44	2	1334	17***	25	3.50	HH	SCSI	RLL 1,7	AUTO	N/A	N/A	50
M2611T	45.07	2	1334	33	33	3.50	HH	IDE(AT)	RLL 1,7	AUTO	N/A	N/A	50
M2612ES	92.88	4	1334	68**	20	3.50	HH	SCSI	RLL 1,7	AUTO	N/A	N/A	50
M2612ESA	92.88	4	1334	34	20	3.50	HH	SCSI	RLL 1,7	AUTO	N/A	N/A	50
M2612ESB	92.88	4	1334	17***	20	3.50	HH	SCSI	RLL 1,7	AUTO	N/A	N/A	50
M2612ET	90.15	4	1334	33	20	3.50	HH	IDE(AT)	RLL 1,7	AUTO	N/A	N/A	50
M2612S	92.88	4	1334	68**	20	3.50	HH	SCSI	RLL 1,7	AUTO	N/A	N/A	50
M2612SA	92.88	4	1334	34	20	3.50	HH	SCSI	RLL 1,7	AUTO	N/A	N/A	50
M2612SB	92.88	4	1334	17***	20	3.50	HH	SCSI	RLL 1,7	AUTO	N/A	N/A	50
M2612T	90.15	4	1334	33	20	3.50	HH	IDE(AT)	RLL 1,7	AUTO	N/A	N/A	50
M2613ES	139.33	6	1334	68**	20	3.50	HH	SCSI	RLL 1,7	AUTO	N/A	N/A	50
M2613ESA	139.33	6	1334	34	20	3.50	HH	SCSI	RLL 1,7	AUTO	N/A	N/A	50
M2613ESB	139.33	6	1334	17***	20	3.50	HH	SCSI	RLL 1,7	AUTO	N/A	N/A	50
M2613ET	135.23	6	1334	33	20	3.50	HH	IDE(AT)	RLL 1,7	AUTO	N/A	N/A	50
M2613S	139.33	6	1334	68**	20	3.50	HH	SCSI	RLL 1,7	AUTO	N/A	N/A	50
M2613SA	139.33	6	1334	34	20	3.50	HH	SCSI	RLL 1,7	AUTO	N/A	RWC	50
M2613SB	139.33	6	1334	17***	20	3.50	HH	SCSI	RLL 1,7	AUTO	N/A	N/A	50
M2613T	135.23	6	1334	33	20	3.50	HH	IDE(AT)	RLL 1,7	AUTO	N/A	N/A	50
M2614ES	185.77	8	1334	68**	20	3.50	HH	SCSI	RLL 1,7	AUTO	N/A	N/A	50
M2614ESA	185.77	8	1334	34	20	3.50	HH	SCSI	RLL 1,7	AUTO	N/A	N/A	50
M2614ESB	185.77	8	1334	17***	20	3.50	HH	SCSI	RLL 1,7	AUTO	N/A	N/A	50
M2614ET	180.31	8	1334	33	20	3.50	HH	IDE(AT)	RLL 1,7	AUTO	N/A	N/A	50
M2614S	185.77	8	1334	68**	20	3.50	HH	SCSI	RLL 1,7	AUTO	N/A	N/A	50

FUJITSU CORPORATION

MODEL	CAP	HDS	CYL	SPT	SEEK	FF	HGT	INT	ENCODE	LZ	WP	RWC	MTBF
M2614SA	185.77	8	1334	34	20	3.50	HH	SCSI	RLL 1,7	AUTO	N/A	N/A	50
M2614SB	185.77	8	1334	17***	20	3.50	HH	SCSI	RLL 1,7	AUTO	N/A	N/A	50
M2614T	180.31	8	1334	33	20	3.50	HH	IDE(AT)	RLL 1,7	AUTO	N/A	N/A	50
M2616ET	104.21	4	1542	33	20	3.50	HH	IDE(AT)	RLL 1,7	AUTO	N/A	N/A	50
M2616SA	104.21	4	1542	33	20	3.50	HH	SCSI	RLL 1,7	AUTO	N/A	N/A	50
M2616T	104.21	4	1542	33	20	3.50	HH	IDE(AT)	RLL 1,7	AUTO	N/A	N/A	50
M2621S	234.12	5	1429	64	12	3.50	HH	SCSI-2	RLL 1,7	AUTO	N/A	N/A	200
M2622F	330.17	7	1429	*	12	3.50	HH	SCSI-2	RLL 1,7	AUTO	N/A	N/A	200
M2622FA	330.17	7	1429	*	12	3.50	HH	SCSI-2	RLL 1,7	AUTO	N/A	N/A	200
M2622FB	330.17	7	1429	*	12	3.50	HH	SCSI-2	RLL 1,7	AUTO	N/A	N/A	200
M2622HA	330	7	1429	*		3.50	–	SCSI	UNIDENT				
M2622S	327.77	7	1429	64	12	3.50	HH	SCSI-2	RLL 1,7	AUTO	N/A	N/A	200
M2622SA	327.77	7	1429	64	12	3.50	HH	SCSI-2	RLL 1,7	AUTO	N/A	N/A	200
M2622T	327.77	7	1429	64	12	3.50	HH	IDE(AT)	RLL 1,7	AUTO	N/A	N/A	200
M2623F	425.13	9	1429	*	12	3.50	HH	SCSI-2	RLL 1,7	AUTO	N/A	N/A	200
M2623FA	425.13	9	1429	*	12	3.50	HH	SCSI-2	RLL 1,7	AUTO	N/A	N/A	200
M2623FB	425.13	9	1429	*	12	3.50	HH	SCSI-2	RLL 1,7	AUTO	N/A	N/A	200
M2623HA	425	9	1429	*		3.50	–	SCSI	UNIDENT				
M2623S	421.42	9	1429	64	12	3.50	HH	SCSI-2	RLL 1,7	AUTO	N/A	N/A	200
M2623SA	421.42	9	1429	64	12	3.50	HH	SCSI-2	RLL 1,7	AUTO	N/A	N/A	200
M2623T	421.42	9	1429	63	12	3.50	HH	IDE(AT)	RLL 1,7	AUTO	N/A	N/A	200
M2624F	520.10	11	1429	*	12	3.50	HH	SCSI-2	RLL 1,7	AUTO	N/A	N/A	200
M2624FA	520.10	11	1429	*	12	3.50	HH	SCSI-2	RLL 1,7	AUTO	N/A	N/A	200
M2624FB	520.10	11	1429	*	12	3.50	HH	SCSI-2	RLL 1,7	AUTO	N/A	N/A	200
M2624HA	520.1	7	1429	*		3.50	–	SCSI	UNIDENT				
M2624S	515.08	11	1429	64	12	3.50	HH	SCSI-2	RLL 1,7	AUTO	N/A	N/A	200
M2624SA	515.08	11	1429	64	12	3.50	HH	SCSI-2	RLL 1,7	AUTO	N/A	N/A	200
M2624T	515.08	11	1429	64	12	3.50	HH	IDE(AT)	RLL 1,7	AUTO	N/A	N/A	200
M2635S	160.00	4	1569	*	14.5	2.50	4H	SCSI-2	RLL	AUTO	N/A	N/A	150
M2635T	160.00	4	1569	*	14.5	2.50	4H	IDE(AT)	RLL	AUTO	N/A	N/A	150
M2637S	240.00	6	1569	*	14.5	2.50	4H	SCSI-2	RLL	AUTO	N/A	N/A	150
M2637SA	240.1	–	–	–	14.5	3.50	3H	SCSI-2	RLL 1,7	AUTO	N/A	N/A	0
M2637T	240.00	6	1569	*	14.5	2.50	4H	IDE(AT)	RLL	AUTO	N/A	N/A	150
M2651HA	1313	15	1944	88	11	5.25	FH	SCSI-2	RLL 1,7	AUTO	N/A	N/A	200
M2651SA	1313	15	1944	88	11	5.25	FH	SCSI-2	RLL 1,7	AUTO	N/A	N/A	200
M2652HA	1628.28	20	1893	84	11	5.25	FH	SCSI-2	RLL 1,7	AUTO	N/A	N/A	200
M2652SA	1628.28	20	1893	84	11	5.25	FH	SCSI-2	RLL 1,7	AUTO	N/A	N/A	200
M2653HA	1404.39	15	2078	88	12	5.25	FH	SCSI-2DIFF	RLL	AUTO	N/A	N/A	300
M2653SA	1404.39	15	2078	88	12	5.25	FH	SCSI-2	RLL	AUTO	N/A	N/A	300
M2654HA	2061.71	21	2179	88	12	5.25	FH	SCSI-2DIFF	RLL	AUTO	N/A	N/A	300
M2654SA	2061.71	21	2179	88	12	5.25	FH	SCSI-2DIFF	RLL	AUTO	N/A	N/A	300
M2681S	264.24	3	2378	*	14	3.50	HH	SCSI	RLL	AUTO	N/A	N/A	300
M2681T	264	–	–	–	14	3.50	HH	IDE(AT)	RLL	AUTO	N/A	N/A	300
M2681TA (IDE)	260	3			12	3.50	–	IDE(AT)	UNIDENT	AUTO	N/A	N/A	250

FUJITSU CORPORATION

MODEL	CAP	HDS	CYL	SPT	SEEK	FF	HGT	INT	ENCODE	LZ	WP	RWC	MTBF
M2681TA (SCSI)	525	6			12	3.50	–	SCSI	UNIDENT	AUTO	N/A	N/A	250K
M2682S	353.54	4	2378	*	14	3.50	HH	SCSI	RLL	AUTO	N/A	N/A	300
M2682T	352	–	–	–	14	3.50	HH	IDE(AT)	RLL	AUTO	N/A	N/A	300
M2682TA (IDE)	350	4			12	3.50	–	IDE(AT)	UNIDENT	AUTO	N/A	N/A	250K
M2682TA (SCSI)	350	4			12	3.50	–	SCSI	UNIDENT	AUTO	N/A	N/A	250K
M2684S	532.14	6	2378	*	14	3.50	HH	SCSI	RLL	AUTO	N/A	N/A	300
M2684T	528	–	–	–	14	3.50	HH	IDE(AT)	RLL	AUTO	N/A	N/A	300
M2684TA (IDE)		6			12	3.50	–	IDE(AT)	UNIDENT	AUTO	N/A	N/A	250K
M2684TA (SCSI)	525	6			12	3.50	–	SCSI	UNIDENT	AUTO	N/A	N/A	250K
M2691EH	756				9.5	3.50	HH	SCSI	RLL 1,7	AUTO	N/A	N/A	
M2691EHA	648.00	9	1818	*	<10	3.50	HH	SCSI-2DIFF	RLL 1,7	AUTO	N/A	N/A	300
M2691EQ	756.44	9	1819	*	9.5	3.50	HH	SCSI	RLL 1,7	AUTO		N/A	0
M2691ER	756.44	9	1819	*	9.5	3.50	HH	SCSI-DIFF	RLL 1,7	AUTO	N/A	N/A	0
M2691ES	756				9	3.50	HH	SCSI	RLL 1,7	AUTO	N/A	N/A	
M2691ESA	648.00	9	1818	*	<10	3.50	HH	SCSI-2	RLL 1,7	AUTO	N/A	N/A	300
M2692EH	924				9	3.50	HH	SCSI	RLL 1,7	AUTO	N/A	N/A	
M2692EHA	793.00	11	1818	*	<10	3.50	HH	SCSI-2DIFF	RLL 1,7	AUTO	N/A	N/A	300
M2692EQ	924.54	11	1819	*	9.5	3.50	HH	SCSI	RLL 1,7	AUTO	N/A	N/A	0
M2692ER	924.54	11	1819	*	9.5	3.50	HH	SCSI-DIFF	RLL 1,7	AUTO	N/A	N/A	0
M2692ES	924				9	3.50	HH	SCSI	RLL 1,7	AUTO	N/A	N/A	
M2692ESA	793.00	11	1818	*	<10	3.50	HH	SCSI-2	RLL 1,7	AUTO	N/A	N/A	300
M2693EH	1092				9	3.50	HH	SCSI	RLL 1,7	AUTO	N/A	N/A	
M2693EHA	938.00	13	1818	*	<10	3.50	HH	SCSI-2DIFF	RLL 1,7	AUTO	N/A	N/A	300
M2693EQ	1092.64	13	1819	*	9.5	3.50	HH	SCSI	RLL 1,7	AUTO	N/A	N/A	0
M2693ER	1092.64	13	1819	*	9.5	3.50	HH	SCSI-DIFF	RLL 1,7	AUTO	N/A	N/A	0
M2693ES	1092				9	3.50	HH	SCSI	RLL 1,7	AUTO	N/A	N/A	
M2693ESA	938.00	13	1818	*	<10	3.50	HH	SCSI-2	RLL 1,7	AUTO	N/A	N/A	300
M2694EH	1260					3.50	HH	SCSI	RLL 1,7				
M2694EHA	1083.00	15	1818	*	<10	3.50	HH	SCSI-2DIFF	RLL 1,7	AUTO	N/A	N/A	300
M2694EQ	1260.74	15	1819	*	9.5	3.50	HH	SCSI	RLL 1,7	AUTO	N/A	N/A	0
M2694ER	1260.74	15	1819	*	9.5	3.50	HH	SCSI-DIFF	RLL 1,7	AUTO	N/A	N/A	0
M2694ES	1083.9	15	1819	*	<10	3.50	HH	SCSI-2	RLL 1,7	AUTO	N/A	N/A	300
M2694ESA	1083.00	15	1818	*	<10	3.50	HH	SCSI-2	RLL 1,7	AUTO	N/A	N/A	300
M2694HA	1083	15	1819	*		3.50	–	SCSI	UNIDENT				
M2694SA	1083	15	1819	*		3.50	–	SCSI	UNIDENT				
M2706SA	532	6	2306	*	12	2.50	5H	SCSI-2	PRML	AUTO	N/A	AUTO	300
M2915QA	2176	15	3012	*	11	3.50	HH	SCSI-2 W	PRML	AUTO	N/A	N/A	500
M2915SA	2176.	15	3184	89	11	3.50	HH	SCSI-2	RLL	AUTO	N/A	N/A	500
M2932QA	2177	9	3422	*	11	3.50	HH	SCSI-2 W	PRML	AUTO	N/A	AUTO	800
M2932RA	2177	9	3422	*	11	3.50	HH	SCSI-2 W/D	PRML	AUTO	N/A	AUTO	800
M2932SA	2177	9	3422	*	11	3.50	HH	SCSI-2	PRML	AUTO	N/A	AUTO	800
M2934QA	4355	18	3422	*	11	3.50	HH	SCSI-2 W/D	PRML	AUTO	N/A	AUTO	800
M2934RA	4355	18	3422	*	11	3.50	HH	SCSI-2	PRML	AUTO	N/A	AUTO	800
M2934SA	4355	18	3422	*	11	3.50	HH	SCSI-2	PRML	AUTO	N/A	AUTO	800

HEWLETT-PACKARD COMPANY

MODEL	CAP	HDS	CYL	SPT	SEEK	FF	HGT	INT	ENCODE	LZ	WP	RWC	MTBF
D1296A	21.41	4	615	17	65	5.25	HH	ST-506/412	MFM	670	300	N/A	100
D1297A	42.82	6	820	17H	40	5.25	HH	ST-506/412	MFM	AUTO	N/A	N/A	100
D1660A	330	8	1457	57	16	5.25	FH	ESDI-15MHZ	RLL 2,7	AUTO	N/A	N/A	150
D1661A	670	16	1457	57	16	5.25	FH	ESDI-15MHZ	RLL 2,7	AUTO	N/A	N/A	150
D1674A	103					5.25	FH	ESDI-15MHZ	RLL 2,7				0
D1675A	155					5.25	FH	ESDI-15MHZ	RLL 2,7				0
D1676A	310					5.25	FH	ESDI-15MHZ	RLL 2,7				0
D1697A	240	4	1800	*	17	3.50	3H	IDE(AT)	RLL 1,7	722	-1	N/A	250
HP 97501A	10.00	2	698	28	75	3.50	HH	–	MFM	–	–	–	0
HP 97501B	20.02	2	1400	28	–	3.50	HH	–	MFM	–	–	–	0
HP 97530S	204.00	6	–	–	18	5.25	FH	SCSI	RLL 2,7	AUTO	N/A	N/A	0
HP 97532D	107.67	4	1643	64**	17	5.25	FH	SCSI-DIFF	RLL 2,7	AUTO	N/A	N/A	99
HP 97532E	107.67	4	1643	64**	17	5.25	FH	ESDI-10MHZ	RLL 2,7	AUTO	N/A	N/A	99
HP 97532S	107.67	4	1643	64**	17	5.25	FH	SCSI	RLL 2,7	AUTO	N/A	N/A	99
HP 97532T	107.67	4	1643	64**	17	5.25	FH	SCSI-2	RLL 2,7	AUTO	N/A	N/A	99
HP 97533D	161.51	6	1643	64**	17	5.25	FH	SCSI-DIFF	RLL 2,7	AUTO	N/A	N/A	99
HP 97533E	161.51	6	1643	64**	17	5.25	FH	ESDI-10MHZ	RLL 2,7	AUTO	N/A	N/A	99
HP 97533S	161.51	6	1643	64**	17	5.25	FH	SCSI	RLL 2,7	AUTO	N/A	N/A	99
HP 97533T	161.51	6	1643	64**	17	5.25	FH	SCSI-2	RLL 2,7	AUTO	N/A	N/A	99
HP 97536D	323.02	12	1643	64**	17	5.25	FH	SCSI-DIFF	RLL 2,7	AUTO	N/A	N/A	99
HP 97536E	323.02	12	1643	64**	17	5.25	FH	ESDI-10MHZ	RLL 2,7	AUTO	N/A	N/A	99
HP 97536S	323.02	12	1643	64**	17	5.25	FH	SCSI	RLL 2,7	AUTO	N/A	N/A	99
HP 97536T	323.02	12	1643	64**	17	5.25	FH	SCSI-2	RLL 2,7	AUTO	N/A	N/A	99
HP 97544D	331.90	8	1447	56	16.5	5.25	HH	SCSI-DIFF	RLL 2,7	AUTO	N/A	N/A	150
HP 97544E	337.83	8	1447	57	17	5.25	FH	ESDI-15MHZ	RLL 2,7	AUTO	N/A	N/A	150
HP 97544P	331.90	8	1447	56	17	5.25	FH	SCSI-2	RLL 2,7	AUTO	N/A	N/A	150
HP 97544S	331.90	8	1447	56	16.5	5.25	HH	SCSI	RLL 2,7	AUTO	N/A	N/A	150
HP 97544T	331.90	8	1447	56	17	5.25	FH	SCSI-2	RLL 2,7	AUTO	N/A	N/A	150
HP 97548D	663.81	16	1447	56	16.5	5.25	HH	SCSI-DIFF	RLL 2,7	AUTO	N/A	N/A	150
HP 97548E	675.66	16	1447	57	17	5.25	FH	ESDI-15MHZ	RLL 2,7	AUTO	N/A	N/A	150
HP 97548P	663.81	16	1447	56	17	5.25	FH	SCSI-2	RLL 2,7	AUTO	N/A	N/A	150
HP 97548S	663.81	16	1447	56	16.5	5.25	HH	SCSI	RLL 2,7	AUTO	N/A	N/A	150
HP 97548T	663.81	16	1447	56	17	5.25	FH	SCSI-2	RLL 2,7	AUTO	N/A	N/A	150
HP 97549P	1001.91	16	1911	64	17.5	5.25	FH	SCSI-2	RLL 2,7	AUTO	N/A	N/A	150
HP 97549T	1001.91	16	1911	64	17.5	5.25	FH	SCSI-2	RLL 2,7	AUTO	N/A	N/A	150
HP 97556E	688.14	11	1697	72	14	5.25	FH	ESDI-24MHZ	RLL 2,7	AUTO	N/A	N/A	150
HP 97556P	677.19	11	–	72	14	5.25	FH	SCSI-2	RLL 2,7	AUTO	N/A	N/A	150
HP 97556S	677.19	11	1670	72	14	5.25	FH	SCSI-2	RLL 2,7	AUTO	N/A	N/A	150
HP 97556T	677.19	11	1670	72	14	5.25	FH	SCSI-2	RLL 2,7	AUTO	N/A	N/A	150
HP 97558E	1084.90	15	1962	72	14	5.25	FH	ESDI-24MHZ	RLL 2,7	AUTO	N/A	N/A	150
HP 97558P	1069.97	15	1935	72	14	5.25	FH	SCSI-2	RLL 2,7	AUTO	N/A	N/A	150
HP 97558S	1069.97	15	1935	72	14	5.25	FH	SCSI-2	RLL 2,7	AUTO	N/A	N/A	150
HP 97558T	1069.97	15	1935	72	14	5.25	FH	SCSI-2	RLL 2,7	AUTO	N/A	N/A	150
HP 97560E	1374.21	19	1962	72	14	5.25	FH	ESDI-24MHZ	RLL 2,7	AUTO	N/A	N/A	150

HEWLETT-PACKARD COMPANY

MODEL	CAP	HDS	CYL	SPT	SEEK	FF	HGT	INT	ENCODE	LZ	WP	RWC	MTBF
HP 97560P	1355.30	19	1935	72	14	5.25	FH	SCSI-2	RLL 2,7	AUTO	N/A	N/A	150
HP 97560S	1355.30	19	1935	72	14	5.25	FH	SCSI-2	RLL 2,7	AUTO	N/A	N/A	150
HP 97560T	1355.30	19	1935	72	14	5.25	FH	SCSI-2	RLL 2,7	AUTO	N/A	N/A	150
HP C2233	234.67	5	1546	*	13	3.50	HH	SCSI-2	RLL 1,7	AUTO	N/A	N/A	150
HP C2233-060	238.68	5	1546	*	12.6	3.50	HH	IDE(AT)	RLL 1,7	AUTO	N/A	N/A	150
HP C2234	328.53	7	1546	*	13	3.50	HH	SCSI-2	RLL 1,7	AUTO	N/A	N/A	150
HP C2234-060	334.16	7	1546	*	12.6	3.50	HH	IDE(AT)	RLL 1,7	AUTO	N/A	N/A	150
HP C2235	422.40	9	1546	*	13	3.50	HH	SCSI-2	RLL 1,7	AUTO	N/A	N/A	150
HP C2235-060	429.64	9	1546	*	13	3.50	HH	IDE(AT)	RLL 1,7	AUTO	N/A	N/A	150
HP C2244	566	7	2051	79	10.2	3.50	HH	SCSI-2	RLL 1,7	AUTO	N/A	N/A	300
HP C2245	728	9	2051	79	10.2	3.50	HH	SCSI-2	RLL 1,7	AUTO	N/A	N/A	300
HP C2246	890	11	2051	79	10.2	3.50	HH	SCSI-2	RLL 1,7	AUTO	N/A	N/A	300
HP C2247	1052.09	13	1981	*	10.5	3.50	HH	SCSI-2	RLL 1,7	AUTO	N/A	N/A	150
HP C2490A	2100	18	2630	90	8.75	3.50	HH	SCSI-2	RLL 1,7	AUTO	N/.A	N/A	500
HP C3013A-001	21.42	3	700	*	15	1.30	4H	IDE(AT)	RLL	AUTO	N/A	N/A	300
HP C3013A-003	21.42	3	700	*	15	1.30	4H	PCMCIA	RLL	AUTO	N/A	N/A	300
HP C3014A-001	42.83	4	786	*	15	1.30	4H	IDE(AT)	RLL	AUTO	N/A	N/A	300
HP C3014A-003	42.83	4	786	*	15	1.30	4H	PCMCIA	RLL	AUTO	N/A	N/A	300
HP C3323A	1050	7	2982	100	9.5	3.50	3H	SCSI-2	RLL 1,7	AUTO	N/A	N/A	500
HP C3724D	1200	5	3610	*	9.5	3.50	3H	SCSI-2DIFF	PRML	AUTO	N/A	N/A	800
HP C3724S	1200	5	3610	*	9.5	3.50	3H	SCSI-2	PRML	AUTO	N/A	N/A	800
HP C3724SC	1200	5	3610	*	9.5	3.50	3H	SCSI SCA	PRML	AUTO	N/A	N/A	800
HP C3724TC	1200	5	3610	*	9.5	3.50	3H	SCSI SCA	PRML	AUTO	N/A	N/A	800
HP C3724W	1200	5	3610	*	9.5	3.50	3H	SCSI-2 W/D	PRML	AUTO	N/A	N/A	800
HP C3724WC	1200	5	3610	*	9.5	3.50	3H	SCSI SCA	PRML	AUTO	N/A	N/A	800
HP C3725D	2170	9	3610	*	9.5	3.50	3H	SCSI-2DIFF	PRML	AUTO	N/A	N/A	800
HP C3725S	2170	9	3610	*	9.5	3.50	3H	SCSI-2	PRML	AUTO	N/A	N/A	800
HP C3725SC	2170	9	3610	*	9.5	3.50	3H	SCSI SCA	PRML	AUTO	N/A	N/A	800
HP C3725TC	2170	9	3610	*	9.5	3.50	3H	SCSI SCA	PRML	AUTO	N/A	N/A	800
HP C3725W	2170	9	3610	*	9.5	3.50	3H	SCSI-2 W/D	PRML	AUTO	N/A	N/A	800
HP C3725WC	2170	9	3610	*	9.5	3.50	3H	SCSI SCA	PRML	AUTO	N/A	N/A	800
HP C5435A	1336	4		*	12	3.50	3H	IDE(AT)	RLL 1,7				
HP C5436A	2004	6		*	12	3.50	3H	IDE(AT)	RLL 1,7	N/A			

HITACHI CORPORATION

MODEL	CAP	HDS	CYL	SPT	SEEK	FF	HGT	INT	ENCODE	LZ	WP	RWC	MTBF
DK 211A-51	510	6	2244		12	2.50	4H	IDE(AT)	RLL 1,7	AUTO	N/A	N/A	300
DK 211A-54	680	6	2244		12	2.50	4H	IDE(AT)	RLL 1,7	AUTO	N/A	N/A	300
DK 211A-68	680	8	2094		12	2.50	4H	IDE(AT)	RLL 1,7	AUTO	N/A	N/A	300
DK 212A-10	1080	8	2602		12	2.50	4H	IDE(AT)	RLL 1,7	AUTO	N/A	N/A	300
DK 212A-81	810	6	2602		12	2.50	4H	IDE(AT)	RLL 1,7	AUTO	N/A	N/A	300
DK 221A-34	340	4	2094		12	2.50	5H	IDE(AT)	RLL 1,7	AUTO	N/A	N/A	300

HITACHI CORPORATION

MODEL	CAP	HDS	CYL	SPT	SEEK	FF	HGT	INT	ENCODE	LZ	WP	RWC	MTBF
DK 222A-27	540	2	2602		12	2.50	5H	IDE(AT)	RLL 1,7	AUTO	N/A	N/A	300
DK 222A-54	540	4	2602		12	2.50	5H	IDE(AT)	RLL 1,7	AUTO	N/A	N/A	300
DK 301-1	10.65	4	306	17	85	3.50	HH	ST-506/412	MFM	–	–	–	0
DK 301-2	15.98	6	306	17	85	3.50	HH	ST-506/412	MFM	–	–	–	0
DK 312C-20	209.34	10	1076	38	16.8	3.50	HH	SCSI	RLL 2,7	AUTO	N/A	N/A	150
DK 312C-25	251.21	12	1076	38	16.8	3.50	HH	SCSI	RLL 2,7	AUTO	N/A	N/A	100
DK 314C-41	418.96	14	1169	50	17	3.50	HH	SCSI	RLL 2,7	AUTO	N/A	N/A	150
DK 315C-10	1054	11	2469	59	11.8	3.50	HH	SCSI	RLL 1,7	AUTO	N/A	N/A	200
DK 315C-10D	1054	11	2469	59	11.8	3.50	HH	SCSI	RLL 1,7	AUTO	N/A	N/A	200
DK 315C-10M	10.70	2	615	17	60	3.50	HH	SCSI	MFM	–	616	616	0
DK 315C-11	1105	15	2480	58	11.8	3.50	HH	SCSI	RLL 1,7	AUTO	N/A	N/A	200
DK 315C-11	1105	15	2480	58	11.8	3.50	HH	SCSI	RLL 1,7	AUTO	N/A	N/A	200
DK 315C-14	1437	15	2464	57	11.8	3.50	HH	SCSI	RLL 1,7	AUTO	N/A	N/A	200
DK 315C-14	1437	15	2464	57	11.8	3.50	HH	SCSI	RLL 1,7	AUTO	N/A	N/A	200
DK 315C-14D	1437	15	2464	57	11.8	3.50	HH	SCSI	RLL 1,7	AUTO	N/A	N/A	200
DK 325C	573	6	2458	57	12.4	3.50	3H	SCSI	RLL 1,7	AUTO	N/A	N/A	200
DK 325C-57	573	6	2458	57	12.4	3.50	3H	SCSI	RLL 1,7	AUTO	N/A	N/A	200
DK 326C-10	1052	7	3320	*	9.8	3.50	3H	SCSI-2	RLL 1,7	AUTO	NA	N/A	400
DK 326C-10WD	1052	7	3320	*	9.8	3.50	3H	SCSI-2	RLL 1,7	AUTO	N/A	N/A	400
DK 326C-6	601	4	3315	*	9.8	3.50	3H	SCSI-2	RLL 1,7	AUTO	NA	N/A	400
DK 326C-6WD	601	5	3202	*	9.8	3.50	HH	SCSI-2	RLL 1,7	N/A	N/A	N/A	400K
DK 328C-10	1050	3			9.8	3.50	3H	SCSI-2	RLL 1,7	AUTO	N/A	N/A	800
DK 328C-10WD	1050	3			9.8	3.50	3H	SCSI-2 W/D	RLL 1,7	AUTO	N/A	N/A	800
DK 328C-10WS	1050	3			9.8	3.50	3H	SCSI-2 W	RLL 1,7	AUTO	N/A	N/A	800
DK 328C-21	2100	5			9.8	3.50	3H	SCSI-2	RLL 1,7	AUTO	N/A	N/A	800
DK 328C-21WD	2100	5			9.8	3.50	3H	SCSI-2 W/D	RLL 1,7	AUTO	N/A	N/A	800
DK 328C-21WS	2100	5			9.8	3.50	3H	SCSI-2 W	RLL 1,7	AUTO	N/A	N/A	800
DK 328C-43	4300	10			9.8	3.50	3H	SCSI-2	RLL 1,7	AUTO	N/A	N/A	800
DK 328C-43WD	4300	10			9.8	3.50	3H	SCSI-2 W/D	RLL 1,7	AUTO	N/A	N/A	800
DK 328C-43WS	4300	10			9.8	3.50	3H	SCSI-2 W	RLL 1,7	AUTO	N/A	N/A	800
DK 505-2	23.04	4	615	32**	85	5.25	HH	ST-506/412	MFM	–	–	–	20
DK 511-3	28.63	5	699	32**	30	5.25	FH	ST-506/412	MFM	–	128	–	20
DK 511-5	40.08	7	699	32**	30	5.25	FH	ST-506/412	MFM	–	128	–	20
DK 511-8	134.84	10	823	32**	23	5.25	FH	ST-506/412	MFM	–	–	–	20
DK 512-12	94.4	7	823	*	23	5.25	FH	ESDI-10MHZ	RLL 2,7	AUTO	N/A	N/A	20
DK 512-17	134.8	10	823	*	23	5.25	FH	ESDI-10MHZ	RLL 2,7	AUTO	N/A	N/A	20
DK 512-8	67.4	5	823	*	23	5.25	FH	ESDI-10MHZ	RLL 2,7	AUTO	N/A	N/A	20
DK 512C-12	188.77	7	823	64**	23	5.25	FH	SCSI	RLL 2,7	AUTO	N/A	N/A	20
DK 512C-17	269.68	10	823	64**	23	5.25	FH	SCSI	RLL 2,7	AUTO	N/A	N/A	20
DK 512C-8	134.84	5	823	64**	23	5.25	FH	SCSI	RLL 2,7	AUTO	N/A	N/A	20
DK 514-38	330.10	14	903	51	16	5.25	FH	ESDI-15MHZ	RLL 2,7	AUTO	N/A	N/A	30
DK 514C-38 +A/D2	330.10	14	903	51	16	5.25	FH	SCSI	RLL 2,7	AUTO	N/A	N/A	30

HITACHI CORPORATION

MODEL	CAP	HDS	CYL	SPT	SEEK	FF	HGT	INT	ENCODE	LZ	WP	RWC	MTBF
DK514C-38 -A/D1	330.10	14	903	51	16	5.25	FH	SCSI	RLL 2,7	AUTO	N/A	N/A	30
DK 514C-38 A/D2	321.8	14	898	50	16	5.25	FH	SCSI	RLL 2,7	AUTO	N/A	N/A	30
DK 515-12	1229.00	15	—	69	14	5.25	FH	ESDI-20MHZ	RLL 2,7	AUTO	N/A	N/A	150
DK 515-78	673.13	14	1361	69	16	5.25	FH	ESDI-20MHZ	RLL 2,7	AUTO	N/A	N/A	150
DK 515C-78	673.13	14	1361	69	16	5.25	FH	SCSI	RLL 2,7	AUTO	N/A	N/A	150
DK 515C-78D	673.13	14	1361	69	16	5.25	FH	SCSI	RLL 2,7	AUTO	N/A	N/A	150
DK 516-12	1056.76	15	1787	77	14	5.25	FH	ESDI-24MHZ	RLL 2,7	AUTO	N/A	N/A	100
DK 516-15	1321.68	15	2235	77	14	5.25	FH	ESDI-24MHZ	RLL 2,7	AUTO	N/A	N/A	150
DK 516C-16	1351.15	15	2172	81	14	5.25	FH	SCSI-2	RLL 2,7	AUTO	N/A	N/A	100
DK 516C-16D	1342	15	2172	81	13.5	5.25	FH	SCSI-2	RLL 2,7	AUTO	N/A	N/A	150
DK 517C-26	—	—	—	*	—	5.25	FH	SCSI	NONE	—	—	—	0
DK 517C-37	2873	21	3299	*	12.8	5.25	FH	SCSI-2	RLL	AUTO	N/A	N/A	200
DK 517C-37D	2873	21	3299	81	12.8	5.25	FH	SCSI-2	RLL 1,7	AUTO	N/A	N/A	400
DK 521-5	42.98	6	823	17	25	5.25	HH	ST-506/412	MFM	—	—	—	0
DK 522-10	91.01	6	823	36	25	5.25	HH	ESDI-10MHZ	RLL 2,7	AUTO	N/A	N/A	30
DK 522C-10	88.05	6	819	35	25	5.25	HH	SCSI	RLL 2,7	AUTO	N/A	N/A	30
DK 524C-20	168.90	6	1100	50	25	5.25	HH	SCSI	RLL 2,7	AUTO	N/A	N/A	40
DR 311D	105.80	2	2108	*	13	3.50	3H	SCSI-2	RLL 1,7	AUTO	N/A	N/A	150

Capacity:
This nuber is the first two digits of the unformatted capacity

Winchester Drive

DK515C-78D

Form Factors:
3.50 in.
5.25 in.

Interface:
None - ST506,
ESDI
or IPI
C - SCSI
S - SMD

Soecial Features:
D - Differential (SCSI)
Dual Port (SMD)
S - Single Port (SMD)
P - Parallel Head
A - HDA Revision

HYOSUNG COMPUTER

MODEL	CAP	HDS	CYL	SPT	SEEK	FF	HGT	INT	ENCODE	LZ	WP	RWC	MTBF
HC 8085	71.30	8	1024	17	25	5.25	FH	ST-506/412	RLL	AUTO	N/A	N/A	28
HC 8128	109.05	8	1024	26	25	5.25	FH	ST-506/412	RLL	AUTO	N/A	N/A	28
HC 8170E	150.99	8	1024	36	25	5.25	FH	ESDI-10MHZ	RLL	AUTO	N/A	N/A	28

IBM CORPORATION

MODEL	CAP	HDS	CYL	SPT	SEEK	FF	HGT	INT	ENCODE	LZ	WP	RWC	MTBF
115	118.05	7	915	36	28	5.25	–	ESDI-10MHZ	RLL	AUTO	–	–	0
120	120.58	8	920	32	23	5.25	FH	ST-506/412	MFM	–	–	–	0
20	21.30	4	612	17	–	5.25	FH	ST-506/412	MFM	663	306	–	0
20 PS/2	21.30	4	612	17	80	3.50	HH	ST-506/412	MFM	–	128	–	0
30	31.48	4	615	25	–	5.25	FH	ST-506/412	MFM	663	300	–	0
314	319.87	15	1225	34	23	5.25	FH	ESDI-10MHZ	RLL	AUTO	N/A	N/A	0
44	44.66	7	733	17	–	5.25	FH	ST-506/412	MFM	733	300	–	0
60	60.86	6	762	26	27	5.25	FH	ST-506/412	MFM	–	–	–	0
70	75.22	7	583	36	30	5.25	FH	ESDI-10MHZ	RLL	AUTO	N/A	N/A	0
DESKSTAR 540 (06H8558,9)	540	2	4899	*	12.3	3.50	3H	SCSI-2F	PRML	AUTO	N/A	N/A	350
DHA-2270	270.43	–	–	–	–	2.50	4H	IDE(44PIN)	–	AUTO	N/A	N/A	300
DHA-2405	405.13	–	–	–	–	2.50	4H	IDE(44PIN)	–	AUTO	N/A	N/A	300
DHA-2540	540.35	–	–	–	–	2.50	4H	IDE(44PIN)	–	AUTO	N/A	N/A	300
DPES-30540	540	2			10.5	3.50	3H	SCSI-2F	UNIDENT	AUTO	N/A	N/A	0
DPES-30810	810	3			10.5	3.50	3H	SCSI-2F	UNIDENT	AUTO	N/A	N/A	0
DPES-31080	1080	4			10.5	3.50	3H	SCSI-2F	UNIDENT	AUTO	N/A	N/A	0
DSAA-3270	281.34	–	–	–	12	3.50	3H	IDE(AT)	–	AUTO	N/A	N/A	300
DSAA-3360	365.29	–	–	–	12	3.50	3H	IDE(AT)	–	AUTO	N/A	N/A	300
DSAA-3540 -V1	548.09	–	–	–	12	3.50	3H	IDE(AT)	–	AUTO	N/A	N/A	300
DSAA-3540 -V2	528.48	–	–	–	12	3.50	3H	IDE(AT)	–	AUTO	N/A	N/A	300
DSAA-3720	730.79	–	–	–	12	3.50	3H	IDE(AT)	–	AUTO	N/A	N/A	300
H2172-A2	172.16	–	–	–	–	2.50	4H	IDE(44PIN)	–	AUTO	N/A	N/A	0
H2172-S2	172.00	–	–	–	–	2.50	3H	SCSI-2	–	AUTO	N/A	N/A	300
H2258-A3	258.24	–	–	–	–	2.50	4H	IDE(44PIN)	–	AUTO	N/A	N/A	0
H2258-S3	258.00	–	–	–	–	2.50	3H	SCSI-2	–	AUTO	N/A	N/A	300
H2344-A4	344.33	–	–	–	–	2.50	4H	IDE(44PIN)	–	AUTO	N/A	N/A	0
H2344-S4	344.00	–	–	–	–	2.50	3H	SCSI-2	–	AUTO	N/A	N/A	300
H3133-A2	133.56	–	–	–	14	3.50	3H	IDE(AT)	–	AUTO	N/A	N/A	250
H3171-A2	171.29	–	–	–	14	3.50	3H	IDE(AT)	–	AUTO	N/A	N/A	250
H3256-A3	257.16	–	–	–	14	3.50	3H	IDE(AT)	–	AUTO	N/A	N/A	250
H3342-A4	342.88	–	–	–	14	3.50	3H	IDE(AT)	–	AUTO	N/A	N/A	250
PS/2 MODEL 25 20	20.00	–	–	–	–	5.25	–	ST-506/412	–	–	–	–	0
TYPE 0661 MODEL 371	326.51	14	949	48	12.5	3.50	HH	SCSI-2	RLL	AUTO	N/A	N/A	300
TYPE 0661 MODEL 467	412.53	14	1199	48	11.5	3.50	HH	SCSI-2	RLL	AUTO	N/A	N/A	300
TYPE 0662 MODEL A10	1051.80	–	–	–	9	3.50	3H	IDE(AT)	–	AUTO	N/A	N/A	500
TYPE 0662 MODEL S12	1050	16	2038	63	9	3.50	FH	SCSI-2F	UNIDENT	AUTO	N/A	N/A	800
TYPE 0662 MODEL S1D	1050	16	2038	63	9	3.50	FH	SCSI-2F	UNIDENT	AUTO	N/A	N/A	800
TYPE 0662 MODEL SW1	1050	16	2038	63	9	3.50	FH	SCSI-2 W	UNIDENT	AUTO	N/A	N/A	800

IBM CORPORATION

MODEL	CAP	HDS	CYL	SPT	SEEK	FF	HGT	INT	ENCODE	LZ	WP	RWC	MTBF
TYPE 0662 MODEL SWD	1050	16	2038	63	9	3.50	FH	SCSI-2 W	UNIDENT	AUTO	N/A	N/A	800
TYPE 0663 MODEL E12	1044.00	13	2469	*	11.4	3.50	HH	SCSI-2	RLL	AUTO	N/A	N/A	500
TYPE 0663 MODEL E15	1206.00	15	2469	*	11.4	3.50	HH	SCSI-2	RLL	AUTO	N/A	N/A	500
TYPE 0663 MODEL H12	1039.61	15	2051	66	9.8	3.50	HH	SCSI-2	RLL	AUTO	N/A	N/A	400
TYPE 0663 MODEL L08	623.76	9	2051	66	9.8	3.50	HH	SCSI-2	RLL	AUTO	N/A	N/A	400
TYPE 0663 MODEL L11	900.99	13	2051	66	11	3.50	HH	SCSI-2	RLL	AUTO	N/A	N/A	400
TYPE 0663 MODEL L12	1039.61	15	2051	66	11	3.50	HH	SCSI-2	RLL	AUTO	N/A	N/A	880
TYPE 0664 CSH/ESH	4000	2	2857	–	9.5	5.25	FH	SCSI	RLL	AUTO	N/A	N/A	375
TYPE 0665 MODEL 38	31.90	5	733	17	40	5.25	FH	ST-506/412	MFM	AUTO	N/A	N/A	0
TYPE 0665 MODEL 53	44.66	7	733	17	40	5.25	FH	ST-506/412	MFM	AUTO	N/A	N/A	0
TYPE 0667 MODEL 61	52.14	5	582	35	30	5.25	FH	ESDI-10MHZ	RLL	AUTO	N/A	N/A	0
TYPE 0667 MODEL 85	73.00	7	582	64	30	5.25	FH	ESDI-10MHZ	RLL	AUTO	N/A	N/A	0
TYPE 0669 MODEL 61	48.42	5	582	35	30	5.25	FH	ESDI-10MHZ	RLL	AUTO	N/A	N/A	0
TYPE 0669 MODEL 85	67.79	7	582	64	30	5.25	FH	ESDI-10MHZ	RLL	AUTO	N/A	N/A	0
TYPE 0671 MODEL S11	234.38	11	1224	34	21.5	5.25	FH	SCSI	RLL	AUTO	N/A	N/A	0
TYPE 0671 MODEL S11	231	11	1225	34	21.5	5.25	FH	SCSI-2F	UNIDENT	AUTO	N/A	N/A	0
TYPE 0671 MODEL S15	319.61	15	1224	34	21.5	5.25	FH	SCSI	RLL	AUTO	N/A	N/A	0
TYPE 0681 MODEL 500	476.26	11	1458	58	<13	5.25	FH	SCSI	RLL	AUTO	N/A	N/A	150
TYPE 0681 MODEL1000	865.93	20	1458	58	<13	5.25	FH	SCSI	RLL	AUTO	N/A	N/A	150
WD-12	10.00	4	306	17	–	5.25	FH	ST-506/412	MFM	–	296	296	0
WD-2120	127.28	4	1243	50	16.5	3.50	3H	MCA	RLL	AUTO	N/A	N/A	150
WD-240	43.65	2	1122	38	19	2.50	4H	MCA	RLL	AUTO	N/A	N/A	150
WD-25	20.00	–	–	17	–	5.25	FH	ST-506/412	MFM	–	296	296	0
WD-3158	120.58	8	920	32	23	3.50	FH	MCA	RLL	AUTO	N/A	N/A	45
WD-3160	163.09	8	1021	39	16	3.50	HH	MCA	RLL	AUTO	N/A	N/A	110
WD-380	81.54	4	1021	39	16	3.50	HH	MCA	RLL	AUTO	N/A	N/A	110
WD-387	60.81	4	928	32	23	3.50	HH	MCA	RLL	AUTO	N/A	N/A	45
WD-L40	41.45	2	1038	39	17	3.50	HH	MCA	RLL	AUTO	N/A	N/A	90
WD-L40S	41.45	2	1038	39	17	3.50	HH	MCA	RLL	AUTO	N/A	N/A	90
WDA-2120	126.51	4	1243	50	16.5	3.50	3H	IDE(AT)	RLL 1,7	AUTO	N/A	N/A	150
WDA-240	43.10	2	1122	38	18.5	2.50	4H	IDE(AT)	RLL 1,7	AUTO	N/A	N/A	150

IBM CORPORATION

MODEL	CAP	HDS	CYL	SPT	SEEK	FF	HGT	INT	ENCODE	LZ	WP	RWC	MTBF
WDA-260	63.64	2	1243	50	16.5	3.50	3H	IDE(AT)	RLL	AUTO	N/A	N/A	150
WDA-280	86.08	4	1122	38	16.5	2.50	3H	IDE(AT)	RLL 1,7	AUTO	N/A	N/A	150
WDA-3160	81.54	4	1021	39	16	3.50	HH	IDE(AT)	RLL	AUTO	N/A	N/A	110
WDA-380	81.54	4	1021	39	16	3.50	HH	IDE(AT)	RLL	AUTO	N/A	N/A	110
WDA-L160	171.29	4	1923	44	16	3.50	3H	IDE(AT)	RLL 1,2	AUTO	N/A	N/A	150
WDA-L40	41.53	2	1040	39	17	3.50	3H	IDE(AT)	RLL 2,7	AUTO	N/A	N/A	90
WDA-L42	42.61	2	1067	39	17	3.50	3H	IDE(AT)	RLL 2,7	AUTO	N/A	N/A	90
WDA-L80	85.64	2	1923	44	16	3.50	3H	IDE(AT)	RLL 1,2	AUTO	N/A	N/A	150
WDA-S260	63.30	2	1243	50	18.5	3.50	4H	IDE(AT)	RLL 1,7	AUTO	N/A	N/A	150
WDS-240	43.65	2	1122	38	19	3.50	4H	SCSI-2	RLL	AUTO	N/A	N/A	150
WDS-3100	108.27	2	2009	*	12	3.50	4H	SCSI-2	RLL	AUTO	N/A	N/A	150
WDS-3160	163.09	8	1021	39	16	3.50	HH	SCSI-2	RLL	AUTO	N/A	N/A	110
WDS-3200	216.53	4	2009	*	12	3.50	4H	SCSI-2	RLL	AUTO	N/A	N/A	150
WDS-380	81.54	4	1021	39	16	3.50	HH	SCSI-2	RLL	AUTO	N/A	N/A	110
WDS-L160	171.40	4	1923	44	16	3.50	3H	SCSI-2	RLL 1,2	AUTO	N/A	N/A	150
WDS-L40	41.45	2	1038	39	17	3.50	FH	SCSI-2	RLL	AUTO	N/A	N/A	90
WDS-L42	42.57	2	1066	39	17	3.50	3H	SCSI-2	RLL 1,2	AUTO	N/A	N/A	80
WDS-L80	85.60	2	1923	44	17	3.50	3H	SCSI-2	RLL 1,2	AUTO	N/A	N/A	150

IMPRIMIS (SEE SEAGATE TECHNOLOGY, INC.)

INTEGRAL PERIPHERALS

MODEL	CAP	HDS	CYL	SPT	SEEK	FF	HGT	INT	ENCODE	LZ	WP	RWC	MTBF
1820 MUSTANG	21.41	2	—	*	18	1.80	5H	IDE(44PIN)	RLL 1,7	AUTO	N/A	N/A	100
1820 MUSTANG-B	21.4	2		*	18	1.80	5H	IDE(44PIN)	RLL 1,7	AUTO	N/A	N/A	100
1842 STINGRAY	42.51	3	—	*	18	1.80	5H	IDE(AT)	RLL 1,7	AUTO	N/A	N/A	100
1862 MAVERICK	64.04	3	—	*	18	1.80	4H	IDE(AT)	RLL 1,7	AUTO	N/A	N/A	100
8105PA	105.4	4		*	15	1.80	5H	PCMCIA	RLL 1,7	AUTO	N/A	N/A	250
8170PA	170.8	4		*	12	1.80	5H	PCMCIA	RLL 1,7	AUTO	N/A	N/A	250
8105PA	105.4	4		*	15	1.80	5H	PCMCIA	RLL 1,7	AUTO	N/A	N/A	250
8260PA	260.7	4		*	12	1.80	5H	PCMCIA	PRML	AUTO	N/A	N/A	250
8340PA	341.1	4		*	12	1.80	5H	PCMCIA	PRML	AUTO	N/A	N/A	250

INTERNATIONAL MEMORIES, INC. (IMI)

MODEL	CAP	HDS	CYL	SPT	SEEK	FF	HGT	INT	ENCODE	LZ	WP	RWC	MTBF
5006	5.32	2	306	17	85	5.25	FH	ST-506/412	MFM	—	214	307	0
5006H	5	2		32	99	5.25	FH	ST-506/412	MFM				10K
5007	5.32	2	306	17	85	5.25	FH	ST-506/412	MFM	—	—	—	0
5012	10.65	4	306	17	85	5.25	FH	ST-506/412	MFM	—	214	307	0
5012H	15.00	—	—	17	85	5.25	FH	ST-506/412	MFM	—	—	—	0

INTERNATIONAL MEMORIES, INC. (IMI)

MODEL	CAP	HDS	CYL	SPT	SEEK	FF	HGT	INT	ENCODE	LZ	WP	RWC	MTBF
5018	15.98	6	306	17	85	5.25	FH	ST-506/412	MFM	–	214	307	0
5018H	15	6		32	99	5.25	FH	ST-506/412	MFM				
7720	20.00	–	–	17	85	8.00	FH	ST-506/412	MFM	–	–	–	0
7740	40.00	–	–	17	85	8.00	FH	ST-506/412	MFM	–	–	–	0

IOMEGA CORPORATION

MODEL	CAP	HDS	CYL	SPT	SEEK	FF	HGT	INT	ENCODE	LZ	WP	RWC	MTBF
BETA 20I	–	–	–	–	–	5.25	HH	SCSI	–	–	–	–	0
BETA 20L	–	–	–	–	–	–	–	SCSI	–	–	–	–	0
BETA 44	–	–	–	–	–	–	–	SCSI	–	–	–	–	0

J&A COMPUTER CO., LTD.

MODEL	CAP	HDS	CYL	SPT	SEEK	FF	HGT	INT	ENCODE	LZ	WP	RWC	MTBF
D5882	675	15	1633	53	16	5.25	FH	SCSI	RLL 1,7				50

JCT

MODEL	CAP	HDS	CYL	SPT	SEEK	FF	HGT	INT	ENCODE	LZ	WP	RWC	MTBF
100	3.93	2	226	17	110	5.25	HH	ST-506/412	MFM	–	–	–	0
1000	5.00	–	–	17	–	5.25	HH	COMMODORE	MFM	–	–	–	0
1005	7.00	–	–	17	–	5.25	HH	COMMODORE	MFM	–	–	–	0
1010	14.00	–	–	17	–	5.25	HH	COMMODORE	MFM	–	–	–	0
105	5.32	2	306	17	110	5.25	HH	ST-506/412	MFM	–	–	–	0
110	14.00	–	–	17	130	5.25	HH	ST-506/412	MFM	–	–	–	0
120	20.00	–	–	17	100	5.25	HH	ST-506/412	MFM	–	–	–	0

JTS CORPORATION

MODEL	CAP	HDS	CYL	SPT	SEEK	FF	HGT	INT	ENCODE	LZ	WP	RWC	MTBF
P1000-2AF	1000				14	3.50	5H	IDE(AT)	RLL 1,7	AUTO	N/A	N/A	250
P1200-2AF	1200	4			14	3.50	5H	IDE(AT)	RLL 1,7	AUTO	N/A	N/A	250
P1600-3AF	1600				14	3.50	5H	IDE(AT)	RLL 1,7	AUTO	N/A	N/A	250
P3540AF	540.5				14	3.50	5H	IDE(AT)	RLL 1,7	AUTO		N/A	250
P3850AF	850.5				14	3.50	5H	IDE(AT)	RLL 1,7	AUTO		N/A	250

JVC

MODEL	CAP	HDS	CYL	SPT	SEEK	FF	HGT	INT	ENCODE	LZ	WP	RWC	MTBF
JD-3812MOZA	10.61	2	610	17	28	3.50	HH	JVC(26PIN)	MFM	N/A	N/A	N/A	30
JD-3824TA	21.43	2	436	48	28	3.50	HH	JVC(26PIN)	RLL 2,7	N/A	N/A	N/A	30
JD-3848HA	42.76	4	436	48	28	3.50	HH	JVC(26PIN)	RLL 2,7	N/A	N/A	N/A	30

JVC

MODEL	CAP	HDS	CYL	SPT	SEEK	FF	HGT	INT	ENCODE	LZ	WP	RWC	MTBF
JD-E2042M	42.84	2	973	43	16	2.50	4H	IDE(AT)	RLL 1,7	AUTO	N/A	N/A	130
JD-E2085M	85.68	4	973	43	16	2.50	4H	IDE(AT)	RLL 1,7	AUTO	N/A	N/A	130
JD-E2825P(A)	21.41	2	581	36	23	2.50	4H	IDE(AT)	RLL 2,7	AUTO	N/A	N/A	30
JD-E2825P(S)	21.41	2	581	36	23	2.50	4H	SCSI	RLL 2,7	AUTO	N/A	N/A	30
JD-E2825P(X)	21.41	2	581	36	23	2.50	4H	IDE(XT)	RLL 2,7	AUTO	N/A	N/A	30
JD-E2850P(A)	42.52	3	791	35	25	2.50	4H	IDE(AT)	RLL 2,7	AUTO	N/A	N/A	130
JD-E2850P(S)	42.52	3	—	35	25	2.50	4H	SCSI	RLL 2,7	AUTO	N/A	N/A	130
JD-E3896V(A)	84.73	4	862	48	25	3.50	3H	IDE(AT)	RLL 2,7	AUTO	N/A	N/A	30
JD-E3896V(S)	84.73	4	862	48	25	3.50	3H	SCSI	RLL 2,7	AUTO	N/A	N/A	30
JD-E3896V(X)	84.73	4	862	48	25	3.50	3H	IDE(XT)	RLL 2,7	AUTO	N/A	N/A	30

KALOK CORPORATION

MODEL	CAP	HDS	CYL	SPT	SEEK	FF	HGT	INT	ENCODE	LZ	WP	RWC	MTBF
KL 3100	105.20	6	820	*	25	3.50	HH	IDE(AT)	RLL 2,7	AUTO	N/A	N/A	100
KL 3120	120.60	6	820	*	19	3.50	HH	IDE(AT)	RLL 2,7	AUTO	N/A	N/A	100
KL 320	21.41	4	615	17	40	3.50	HH	ST-506/412	MFM	—	—	—	43
KL 330	32.74	4	615	26	40	3.50	HH	ST-506/412	RLL 2,7	—	—	—	43
KL 332	32.74	4	615	26	48	3.50	HH	MCA	RLL	—	—	—	0
KL 340	42.82	6	820	17	25	3.50	HH	ST-506/412	MFM	—	—	—	50
KL 341	42.91	4	676	31	33	3.50	HH	SCSI	RLL 2,7	AUTO	N/A	N/A	40
KL 342	42.91	4	676	31	30	3.50	HH	MCA	RLL 2,7	AUTO	N/A	N/A	40
KL 343	42.91	4	676	31	28	3.50	HH	IDE(AT)	RLL 2,7	AUTO	N/A	N/A	100
KL 360	65.49	6	820	26	25	3.50	HH	ST-506/412	RLL 2,7	—	—	—	50
KL 381	84.00	6	815	—	25	3.50	HH	SCSI	RLL 2,7	AUTO	N/A	N/A	50
KL 383	84.00	6	815	—	25	3.50	HH	IDE(AT)	RLL 2,7	AUTO	N/A	N/A	50
P5-125(A)	125.80	2	2048	*	<17	3.50	5H	IDE(AT)	RLL 1,7	AUTO	N/A	N/A	100
P5-125(S)	125.80	2	2048	*	<17	3.50	5H	SCSI-2	RLL 1,7	AUTO	N/A	N/A	100
P5-250(A)	251.90	4	2048	*	<17	3.50	5H	IDE(AT)	RLL 1,7	AUTO	N/A	N/A	100
P5-250(S)	251.90	4	2048	*	<17	3.50	5H	SCSI-2	RLL 1,7	AUTO	N/A	N/A	100

KINGSTON TECHNOLOGY CORPORATION

MODEL	CAP	HDS	CYL	SPT	SEEK	FF	HGT	INT	ENCODE	LZ	WP	RWC	MTBF
KTM-DC16/127	127				16	CARD	NO	IDE(AT)	RLL 1,7	AUTO	N/A	N/A	0
KTM-DC16/209	209				16	CARD	NO	IDE(AT)	RLL 2,7	AUTO	N/A	N/A	0
KTM-DC16/260	260				16	CARD	NO	IDE(AT)	RLL 1,7	AUTO	N/A	N/A	0
KTM-DC16/340	340				16	CARD	NO	IDE(AT)	RLL 1,7	AUTO	N/A	N/A	0
KTM-DC32/127	127				16	CARD	NO	IDE(AT)	RLL 1,7	AUTO	N/A	N/A	0
KTM-DC32/209	209				16	CARD	NO	IDE(AT)	RLL 1,7	AUTO	N/A	N/A	0
KTM-DC32/260	260				16	CARD	NO	IDE(AT)	RLL 1,7	AUTO	N/A	N/A	0
KTM-DC32/340	340				16	CARD	NO	IDE(AT)	RLL 1,7	AUTO	N/A	N/A	0

KYOCERA ELECTRONICS, INC.

MODEL	CAP	HDS	CYL	SPT	SEEK	FF	HGT	INT	ENCODE	LZ	WP	RWC	MTBF
KC 20A	21.44	4	616	17	65	3.50	HH	ST-506/412	MFM	644	0	N/A	40
KC 20B	21.41	4	615	17	62	3.50	HH	ST-506/412	MFM	664	0	N/A	40
KC 30A	32.80	4	616	26	62	3.50	HH	ST-506/412	RLL 2,7	664	0	N/A	40
KC 30B	32.74	4	615	26	62	3.50	HH	ST-506/412	RLL 2,7	664	0	N/A	40
KC 40GA	39.55	2	1073	*	28	3.50	HH	IDE(AT)	RLL 2,7	AUTO	N/A	N/A	40
KC 80GA	78.81	4	1069	*	23	3.50	HH	IDE(AT)	RLL 2,7	AUTO	N/A	N/A	40

LAPINE

MODEL	CAP	HDS	CYL	SPT	SEEK	FF	HGT	INT	ENCODE	LZ	WP	RWC	MTBF
3522	10.65	4	306	17	65	3.50	HH	ST-506/412	MFM	–	–	307	0
LT 10	10.70	2	615	17	65	3.50	HH	ST-506/412	MFM	–	–	616	0
LT 20	21.41	4	615	17	65	3.50	HH	ST-506/412	MFM	–	–	616	0
LT 200	21.37	4	614	17	65	3.50	HH	ST-506/412	MFM	–	–	615	0
LT 2000	21.37	4	614	17	65	3.50	HH	ST-506/412	MFM	–	–	615	0
LT 300	32.69	4	614	26	65	3.50	HH	ST-506/412	RLL 2,7	–	–	615	0
LT 3065	10.65	4	306	17	65	3.50	HH	ST-506/412	RLL 2,7	–	128	306	0
LT 3512	10.65	4	306	17	65	3.50	HH	ST-506/412	RLL 2,7	–	128	306	0
LT 3522	10.65	4	306	17	65	3.50	HH	ST-506/412	RLL 2,7	–	128	306	0
LT 3532	32.69	4	614	26	65	3.50	HH	ST-506/412	RLL 2,7	–	–	615	0
TITAN 20	21.41	4	615	17	65	3.50	HH	ST-506/412	MFM	–	–	–	0
TITAN 30	32.74	4	615	26	65	3.50	HH	ST-506/412	RLL	–	–	–	0

MAXTOR CORPORATION

Note: Maxtor purchased Miniscribe. They still distribute the Miniscribe drives with the same model numbers but with the Maxtor name. Look under Miniscribe if you can't locate the drive here.

MODEL	CAP	HDS	CYL	SPT	SEEK	FF	HGT	INT	ENCODE	LZ	WP	RWC	MTBF
250837	837	5	3196	*	14	2.50	5H	IDE(44PIN)	RLL 1,7	AUTO	N/A	N/A	300
25084A	84	–	–	–	12	2.50	3H	IDE(AT)	RLL	AUTO	N/A	N/A	150
251005	11005	6	3196	*	14	2.50	5H	IDE(44PIN)	RLL 1,7	AUTO	N/A	N/A	300
25125S	128.20	4	1092	*	15	2.50	4H	SCSI	RLL 1,7	AUTO	N/A	N/A	150
25128A	128.2	4	1092	*	15	2.50	4H	IDE(AT)	RLL 1,7	AUTO	N/A	N/A	150
251340	1340	8	3196	*	14	2.50	5H	IDE(44PIN)	RLL 1,7	AUTO	N/A	N/A	300
25252A	252	–	–	–	12	2.50	3H	IDE(AT)	RLL	AUTO	N/A	N/A	150
25252S	252	6	1418	*	12	2.50	4H	SCSI	UNIDENT	AUTO	N/A	N/A	0
2585A	85.41	4	1092	*	15	2.50	4H	IDE(AT)	RLL 1,7	AUTO	N/A	N/A	150
2585S	85.41	4	1092	*	15	2.50	4H	SCSI	RLL 1,7	AUTO	N/A	N/A	150
7040A	43.13	2	1170	36	17	3.50	3H	IDE(AT)	RLL 1,7	AUTO	N/A	N/A	150
7040S	42.57	2	1155	36	19	3.50	3H	SCSI	RLL 1,7	AUTO	N/A	N/A	40
7060A	65.20	2	1516	42	15	3.50	3H	IDE(AT)	RLL 1,7	AUTO	N/A	N/A	150
7060S	64.42	2	1498	42	15	3.50	3H	SCSI	RLL 1,7	AUTO	N/A	N/A	150
7080A	85.15	4	1155	36	17	3.50	3H	IDE(AT)	RLL 1,7	AUTO	N/A	N/A	150

MAXTOR CORPORATION

MODEL	CAP	HDS	CYL	SPT	SEEK	FF	HGT	INT	ENCODE	LZ	WP	RWC	MTBF
7080S	85.15	4	1155	36	19	3.50	3H	SCSI	RLL 1,7	AUTO	N/A	N/A	150
71000A	1002	3			12	3.50	3H	IDE(AT)	RLL 1,7	AUTO	N/A	N/A	300K
71050A	1050					3.50	3H	IDE(AT)	UNIDENT	AUTO	N/A	N/A	0
71084A	1,08	4	3,721	*	12	3.50	4H	IDE(AT)	RLL 1,7	AUTO	N/A	N/A	300
71084AP	1,08	4	3,721	*	12	3.50	4H	IDE(AT)	RLL 1,7	AUTO	N/A	N/A	300
7120A	130.40	4	1516	42	15	3.50	3H	IDE(AT)	RLL 1,7	AUTO	N/A	N/A	150
7120S	128.85	4	1498	42	15	3.50	3H	SCSI	RLL 1,7	AUTO	N/A	N/A	150
71260A	1260					3.50	3H	IDE(AT)	UNIDENT	AUTO	N/A	N/A	0
71260AP	1260					3.50	3H	IDE(AT)	UNIDENT	AUTO	N/A	N/A	0
7131A	130.00	—	—	*	15	3.50	3H	IDE(AT)	RLL 1,7	AUTO	N/A	N/A	150
71336A	1336	4	4702	*	12	3.50	3H	IDE(AT)	RLL 1,7	AUTO	N/A	N/A	300
71336AP	1336	4	4702	*	12	3.50	3H	IDE(AT)	RLL 1,7	AUTO	N/A	N/A	300
7135AV	135	-	-	-	—	3.50	HH	IDE(AT)	UNIDENT	—	N/A	N/A	0
71626A	1626	6	3721	*	12	3.50	3H	IDE(AT)	RLL 1,7	AUTO	N/A	N/A	300
71626AP	1,626	6	3,721	*	12	3.50	3H	IDE(AT)	RLL 1,7	AUTO	N/A	N/A	300
71670A	1670	5	4702	*	12	3.50	3H	IDE(AT)	RLL 1,7	AUTO	N/A	N/A	300
71670AP	1670	5	4702	*	12	3.50	3H	IDE(AT)	RLL 1,7	AUTO	N/A	N/A	300
7170A	170.00	—	—	*	15	3.50	3H	IDE(AT)	RLL 1,7	AUTO	N/A	N/A	150
7171A	171	—	—	—	15	3.50	3H	IDE(AT)	RLL 1,7	AUTO	N/A	N/A	150
72004A	2004	6	4702	*	12	3.50	3H	IDE(AT)	RLL 1,7	AUTO	N/A	N/A	300
72004AP	2004	6	4702	*	12	3.50	3H	IDE(AT)	RLL 1,7	AUTO	N/A	N/A	300
7213A	212.78	4	1690	*	15	3.50	3H	IDE(AT)	RLL 1,7	AUTO	N/A	N/A	150
7213S	212.78	4	1690	*	15	3.50	3H	SCSI	RLL 1,7	AUTO	N/A	N/A	150
7245A	245.57	4	1944	*	15	3.50	3H	IDE(AT)	RLL 1,7	AUTO	N/A	N/A	150
7245S	245	4	1944	*	15	3.50	3H	SCSI	RLL 1,7	AUTO	N/A	N/A	150
7270AV	270	-	-	-	—	3.50	HH	IDE(AT)	UNIDENT	—	N/A	N/A	0
7270S	270	4	1629	*	14	3.50	3H	SCSI	RLL 1,7	AUTO	N/A	N/A	300
7273A	275.39	2	2771	*	12	3.50	3H	IDE(AT)	RLL 1,7	AUTO	N/A	N/A	150
7273A (NEW)	273	2	2793	*	12	3.50	3H	IDE(AT)	RLL 1,7	AUTO	N/A	N/A	300
7290A	290	—	—	—	15	3.50	HH	IDE(AT)	RLL 1,7	AUTO	N/A	N/A	150
7290S	290	4	1765	*	—	3.50	3H	SCSI	RLL 1,7	AUTO	N/A	N/A	0
7345A	345.00	4	—	*	15	3.50	3H	IDE(AT)	RLL 1,7	AUTO	N/A	N/A	150
7345S	345	4	2219	*	14	—	—	SCSI	RLL 1,7	AUTO	N/A	N/A	0
7405A	405	—	—	—	—	3.50	3H	IDE(AT)	UNIDENT	AUTO	N/A	N/A	150
7405AV	405	-	-	-	—	3.50	HH	IDE(AT)	UNIDENT	—	N/A	N/A	0
7420AV	420	-	-	-	—	3.50	HH	IDE(AT)	UNIDENT	—	N/A	N/A	0
7425AV	425					3.50	3H	IDE(AT)	UNIDENT	AUTO	N/A	N/A	0
7540A	528.4	4	2771	*	12	3.50	3H	IDE(AT)	RLL 1,7	AUTO	N/A	N/A	150
7540AV	540	-	-	-	—	3.50	HH	IDE(AT)	UNIDENT	—	N/A	N/A	0
7541A	541	2	3,721	*	12	3.50	4H	IDE(AT)	RLL 1,7	AUTO	N/A	N/A	300
7541AP	541	2	3,721	*	12	3.50	4H	IDE(AT)	RLL 1,7	AUTO	N/A	N/A	300
7546A	528.48	4	2771	*	12	3.50	3H	IDE(AT)	RLL 1,7	AUTO	N/A	N/A	150
7546A (NEW)	547	4	2793	*	12	3.50	3H	IDE(AT)	RLL 1,7	AUTO	N/A	N/A	300

MAXTOR CORPORATION

MODEL	CAP	HDS	CYL	SPT	SEEK	FF	HGT	INT	ENCODE	LZ	WP	RWC	MTBF
7668A	668	2	4702	*	12	3.50	3H	IDE(AT)	RLL 1,7	AUTO	N/A	N/A	300
7668AP	668	2	4702	*	12	3.50	3H	IDE(AT)	RLL 1,7	AUTO	N/A	N/A	300
7850AV	850					3.50	3H	IDE(AT)	UNIDENT	AUTO	N/A	N/A	0
8050S	50	4	809	26	66	3.50	HH	SCSI	RLL 2,7	AUTO	N/A	N/A	30
8051A	42.72	4	745	28	28	3.50	HH	IDE(AT)	RLL 2,7	AUTO	N/A	N/A	150
8051S	44.90	4	783	–	28	3.50	HH	SCSI	RLL 2,7	AUTO	N/A	N/A	150
DR311C901	105.8	2	2106	*	13	3.50	3H	IDE(AT)	RLL 1,7	AUTO	N/A	N/A	150
DR311C901A	105.8	2	2106	*	13	3.50	3H	IDE(AT)	RLL 1,7	AUTO	N/A	N/A	150
DR311D911A	105.8	2	2108	*	13	3.50	3H	SCSI-2	RLL 1,7	AUTO	N/A	N/A	150
EXT-4175	149.15	7	1224	34	27	5.25	FH	ESDI-10MHZ	–	–	–	–	20
EXT-4280	149.1	11	1224	34	27	5.25	FH	ESDI-10MHZ	–	–	–	–	20
EXT-4380	319.61	15	1224	34	27	5.25	FH	ESDI-10MHZ	RLL	AUTO	N/A	N/A	20
LXT-100S	93.07	8	733	31	27	3.50	HH	SCSI	RLL 1,7	AUTO	N/A	N/A	150
LXT-200A	207.00	7	1320	*	15	3.50	HH	IDE(AT)	RLL 1,7	AUTO	N/A	N/A	150
LXT-200S	207.00	7	1320	*	15	3.50	HH	SCSI	RLL 2,7	AUTO	N/A	N/A	150
LXT-213A	212.00	7	1320	*	15	3.50	HH	IDE(AT)	RLL 1,7	AUTO	N/A	N/A	150
LXT-213S	212.00	7	1320	*	15	3.50	HH	SCSI	RLL 1,7	AUTO	N/A	N/A	150
LXT-340A	340.00	7	1560	*	13	3.50	HH	IDE(AT)	RLL 2,7	AUTO	N/A	N/A	150
LXT-340S	340	7	1560	*		3.50	HH	SCSI	RLL 2,7	AUTO	N/A	N/A	150
LXT-437A	437.00	9	1560	*	13	3.50	HH	IDE(AT)	RLL 2,7	AUTO	N/A	N/A	150
LXT-437S	437.00	9	1560	*	13	3.50	HH	SCSI	RLL 2,7	AUTO	N/A	N/A	150
LXT-50S	46.53	4	733	31	27	3.50	HH	SCSI	RLL 1,7	AUTO	N/A	N/A	40
LXT-535A	528.48	11	1560	*	12	3.50	HH	IDE(AT)	RLL 2,7	AUTO	N/A	N/A	150
LXT-535S	535.00	11	1560	*	12	3.50	HH	SCSI	RLL 2,7	AUTO	N/A	N/A	150
MX9217SDN	2170	9	3703	*	10	3.50	3H	SCSI-2DIFF	PRML	AUTO	N/A	N/A	800
MX9217SDW	2170	9	3703	*	10	3.50	3H	SCSI-2 W/D	PRML	AUTO	N/A	N/A	800
MX9217SSN	2170	9	3703	*	10	3.50	3H	SCSI-2	PRML	AUTO	N/A	N/A	800
MX9217SSW	2170	9	3703	*	10	3.50	3H	SCSI SCA	PRML	AUTO	N/A	N/A	800
MXT-1240S	1240.00	–	–	*	9	3.50	3H	SCSI-2	RLL 1,7	AUTO	N/A	N/A	300
MXT-540A	528.48	–	–	*	9	3.50	3H	IDE(AT)	RLL 1,7	AUTO	N/A	N/A	300
MXT-540AL	528.5	7	2234	*	9	3.50	3H	IDE(AT)	RLL 1,7	AUTO	N/A	N/A	300
MXT-540SL	540.00	–	–	*	9	3.50	3H	SCSI-2	RLL 1,7	AUTO	N/A	N/A	300
P0-12S	1051.00	15	1795	*	13	5.25	FH	SCSI-2	RLL	AUTO	N/A	N/A	100
P0-12S	1051.00	15	1795	*	13	5.25	FH	SCSI-2	RLL	AUTO	N/A	N/A	100
P1-08E	696.40	9	1778	85	12	5.25	FH	ESDI-24MHZ	RLL	AUTO	N/A	N/A	100
P1-08S	696.40	9	1778	85	12	5.25	FH	SCSI-2	RLL	AUTO	N/A	N/A	100
P1-12E	1051.43	15	1778	77	13	5.25	FH	ESDI-24MHZ	AUTO	N/A	N/A	100K	0
P1-12S	1005.48	19	1216	85	11	5.25	FH	SCSI-2	RLL	AUTO	N/A	N/A	100
P1-13E	1160.67	15	1778	85	13	5.25	FH	ESDI-24MHZ	AUTO	N/A	N/A	N/A	100
P1-16E	1331.82	19	1778	77	13	5.25	FH	ESDI-24MHZ	RLL	AUTO	N/A	N/A	100
P1-17E	1470.19	19	1778	85	13	5.25	FH	ESDI-24MHZ	RLL	AUTO	N/A	N/A	100
P1-17S	1470.19	19	1778	85	13	5.25	FH	SCSI-2	RLL	AUTO	N/A	N/A	100
P1-17S	1470.19	19	1778	85	13	5.25	FH	SCSI-2	RLL	AUTO	N/A	N/A	100

MAXTOR CORPORATION

MODEL	CAP	HDS	CYL	SPT	SEEK	FF	HGT	INT	ENCODE	LZ	WP	RWC	MTBF
RXT-800 SERIES	–	–	–	–	–	–	–	SCSI	RLL	–	–	–	0
XT 8800E	694.68	15	1274	71	14	5.25	FH	ESDI-10MHZ	RLL 1,7	AUTO	N/A	N/A	150
XT-1050	39.25	5	902	17	30	5.25	FH	ST-506/412	MFM	–	–	–	150
XT-1065	55.93	7	918	17	30	5.25	FH	ST-506/412	MFM	–	919	919	150
XT-1085	71.30	8	1024	17	27	5.25	FH	ST-506/412	MFM	–	N/A	N/A	150
XT-1105	87.89	11	918	17	27	5.25	FH	ST-506/412	MFM	–	919	919	150
XT-1120R	104.85	8	1024	25	27	5.25	FH	ST-506/412	RLL 2,7	–	N/A	N/A	70
XT-1140	119.85	15	918	17	27	5.25	FH	ST-506/412	MFM	–	N/A	N/A	150
XT-1240R	196.60	15	1024	25	27	5.25	FH	ST-506/412	RLL 2,7	–	N/A	N/A	150
XT-2085	74.57	7	1224	17	30	5.25	FH	ST-506/412	MFM	–	1,225	1,225	150
XT-2140	117.19	11	1224	17	30	5.25	FH	ST-506/412	MFM	–	1,225	1,225	150
XT-2190	159.80	15	1224	17	29	5.25	FH	ST-506/412	MFM	–	N/A	N/A	150
XT-3170 NONSHROUDED	141.00	9	1224	25	30	5.25	FH	SCSI	RLL	AUTO	N/A	N/A	20
XT-3170 SHROUDED	141.00	9	1224	25	30	5.25	FH	SCSI	RLL	AUTO	N/A	N/A	20
XT-3280	235.00	15	1224	25	30	5.25	FH	SCSI	RLL	AUTO	N/A	N/A	20
XT-3380	319.61	15	1224	34	27	5.25	FH	SCSI	RLL	AUTO	N/A	N/A	20
XT-4170E	153.53	7	1224	36	16	5.25	FH	ESDI-10MHZ	RLL 1,7	AUTO	N/A	N/A	30
XT-4170S PCB	157.92	7	1224	36	14	5.25	FH	SCSI	RLL 1,7	AUTO	N/A	N/A	150
XT-4230E	197.40	9	1224	36	16	5.25	FH	ESDI-10MHZ	RLL 1,7	AUTO	N/A	N/A	150
XT-4280E	241.27	11	1224	35	18	5.25	FH	ESDI-10MHZ	RLL	AUTO	N/A	N/A	30
XT-4280S	248.16	11	1224	36	16	5.25	FH	SCSI	RLL	AUTO	N/A	N/A	30
XT-4380E	329.01	15	1224	36	18	5.25	FH	ESDI-10MHZ	RLL 1,7	AUTO	N/A	N/A	30
XT-4380EF	329.01	15	1224	36	18	5.25	FH	ESDI-10MHZ	RLL 1,7	AUTO	N/A	N/A	30
XT-4380F PCB	338.41	15	1224	36	16	5.25	FH	SCSI	RLL 1,7	AUTO	N/A	N/A	150
XT-4380S PCB	338.41	15	1224	36	16	5.25	FH	SCSI	RLL 1,7	AUTO	N/A	N/A	150
XT-8380DS	360	8	1632	–	–	5.25	FH	SCSI	UNIDENT	AUTO	N/A	N/A	150
XT-8380E	360.97	8	1632	54	16	5.25	FH	ESDI-15MHZ	RLL 1,7	AUTO	N/A	N/A	150
XT-8380EH -V1	360.97	8	1632	54	13.5	5.25	FH	ESDI-15MHZ	RLL 1,7	AUTO	N/A	N/A	150
XT-8380EH -V2	360.97	8	1632	54	15	5.25	FH	ESDI-15MHZ	RLL 1,7	AUTO	N/A	N/A	150
XT-8380EH -V3	360.97	8	1632	54	15	5.25	FH	ESDI-15MHZ	RLL 1,7	AUTO	N/A	N/A	150
XT-8380EH -V4	360.97	8	1632	54	15	5.25	FH	ESDI-15MHZ	RLL 1,7	AUTO	N/A	N/A	150
XT-8380EH -V5	360.97	8	1632	54	15	5.25	FH	ESDI-15MHZ	RLL 1,7	AUTO	N/A	N/A	150
XT-8380EH -V6	360.97	8	1632	54	15	5.25	FH	ESDI-15MHZ	RLL 1,7	AUTO	N/A	N/A	150
XT-8380S	360.97	8	1632	54	15	5.25	FH	SCSI	RLL 1,7	AUTO	N/A	N/A	150
XT-8380SH	360.3	8	1632	54	14.5	5.25	FH	SCSI	RLL 1,7	AUTO	N/A	N/A	150
XT-8380SH	360	8	1632	*	–	5.25	–	SCSI	UNIDENT	AUTO	N/A	N/A	150
XT-8610E -V1	541.45	12	1632	54	54	5.25	FH	ESDI-15MHZ	RLL 1,7	AUTO	N/A	N/A	150
XT-8610E -V2	541.45	12	1632	54	18	5.25	FH	ESDI-15MHZ	RLL 1,7	AUTO	N/A	N/A	150
XT-8610E -V3	541.45	12	1632	54	18	5.25	FH	ESDI-15MHZ	RLL 1,7	AUTO	N/A	N/A	150
XT-8610E -V4	541.45	12	1632	54	18	5.25	FH	ESDI-15MHZ	RLL 1,7	AUTO	N/A	N/A	150
XT-8610E -V5	541.45	12	1632	54	18	5.25	FH	ESDI-15MHZ	RLL 1,7	AUTO	N/A	N/A	150

MAXTOR CORPORATION

MODEL	CAP	HDS	CYL	SPT	SEEK	FF	HGT	INT	ENCODE	LZ	WP	RWC	MTBF
XT-8610E -V6	541.45	12	1632	54	18	5.25	FH	ESDI-15MHZ	RLL 1,7	AUTO	N/A	N/A	150
XT-8702S	616.68	15	1487	54	17	5.25	FH	SCSI	RLL 1,7	AUTO	N/A	N/A	150
XT-8760DS	676	15	1632	—	—	5.25	FH	SCSI	UNIDENT	AUTO	N/A	N/A	150
XT-8760E -V1	676.82	15	1632	54	16.5	5.25	FH	ESDI-15MHZ	RLL 1,7	AUTO	N/A	N/A	150
XT-8760E -V2	676.82	15	1632	54	18	5.25	FH	ESDI-15MHZ	RLL 1,7	AUTO	N/A	N/A	150
XT-8760E -V3	676.82	15	1632	54	18	5.25	FH	ESDI-15MHZ	RLL 1,7	AUTO	N/A	N/A	150
XT-8760E -V4	676.82	15	1632	54	18	5.25	FH	ESDI-15MHZ	RLL 1,7	AUTO	N/A	N/A	150
XT-8760E -V5	676.82	15	1632	54	18	5.25	FH	ESDI-15MHZ	RLL 1,7	AUTO	N/A	N/A	150
XT-8760E -V6	676.82	15	1632	54	18	5.25	FH	ESDI-15MHZ	RLL 1,7	AUTO	N/A	N/A	150
XT-8760EH -V1	676.82	15	1632	54	15.5	5.25	FH	ESDI-15MHZ	RLL 1,7	AUTO	N/A	N/A	150
XT-8760EH -V2	676.82	15	1632	54	15.5	5.25	FH	ESDI-15MHZ	RLL 1,7	AUTO	N/A	N/A	150
XT-8760EH -V3	676.82	15	1632	54	15.5	5.25	FH	ESDI-15MHZ	RLL 1,7	AUTO	N/A	N/A	150
XT-8760EH -V4	676.82	15	1632	54	15.5	5.25	FH	ESDI-15MHZ	RLL 1,7	AUTO	N/A	N/A	150
XT-8760EH -V5	676.82	15	1632	54	18	5.25	FH	ESDI-15MHZ	RLL 1,7	AUTO	N/A	N/A	150
XT-8760EH -V6	676.82	15	1632	54	15.5	5.25	FH	ESDI-15MHZ	RLL 1,7	AUTO	N/A	N/A	150
XT-8760S	676.82	15	1632	54	17	5.25	FH	SCSI	RLL 1,7	AUTO	N/A	N/A	150
XT-8760SH	675.6	15	1632	54	15.5`	5.25	FH	SCSI	RLL 1,7	AUTO	N/A	N/A	150
XT-8760SH	676	15	1632	*	—	5.25	–	SCSI	UNIDENT	AUTO	N/A	N/A	150
XT-8800E	694	15	1274	71	14	5.25	FH	ESDI-24MHZ	RLL 1,7	AUTO	N/A	N/A	150
XT81000E	889.89	15	1632	71	16	5.25	FH	ESDI-24MHZ	RLL 1,7	AUTO	N/A	N/A	150

MEGA DRIVE SYSTEMS

MODEL	CAP	HDS	CYL	SPT	SEEK	FF	HGT	INT	ENCODE	LZ	WP	RWC	MTBF
P105	103.30	6	1019	33	19	3.50	HH	SCSI	RLL 2,7	AUTO	N/A	N/A	50
P120	120.00	5	1123	—	14	3.50	HH	SCSI	RLL 1,7	AUTO	N/A	N/A	50
P170	168.00	7	1123	—	14	3.50	HH	SCSI	RLL 1,7	AUTO	N/A	N/A	50
P210	210.00	7	1156	—	14	3.50	HH	SCSI	RLL 1,7	AUTO	N/A	N/A	50
P320	320.00	15	886	—	12.5	3.50	HH	SCSI	RLL 1,7	AUTO	N/A	N/A	150
P42	42.27	3	834	33	19	3.50	HH	SCSI	RLL 2,7	AUTO	N/A	N/A	50
P425	426.00	9	1512	—	12	3.50	HH	SCSI	RLL 1,7	AUTO	N/A	N/A	75
P84	84.54	6	834	33	19	3.50	HH	SCSI	RLL 2,7	AUTO	N/A	N/A	50

MEMOREX TELEX CORPORATION

MODEL	CAP	HDS	CYL	SPT	SEEK	FF	HGT	INT	ENCODE	LZ	WP	RWC	MTBF
321	5.57	2	320	17	90	5.25	FH	ST-506/412	MFM	—	128	321	0
322	11.14	4	320	17	90	5.25	FH	ST-506/412	MFM	—	128	321	0
323	16.71	6	320	17	90	5.25	FH	ST-506/412	MFM	—	128	321	0
324	22.28	8	320	17	90	5.25	FH	ST-506/412	MFM	—	128	321	0
450	10.65	2	612	17	90	5.25	FH	ST-506/412	MFM	—	350	321	0
512	25.09	3	961	17	90	5.25	FH	ST-506/412	MFM	—	480	321	0
513	41.82	5	961	17	90	5.25	FH	ST-506/412	MFM	—	480	321	0
514	58.55	7	961	—	90	5.25	FH	ST-506/412	MFM	—	480	961	0

MICROPOLIS CORPORATION

MODEL	CAP	HDS	CYL	SPT	SEEK	FF	HGT	INT	ENCODE	LZ	WP	RWC	MTBF
1302	20.4	3	830	17	30	5.25	FH	ST-506/412	MFM	830	N/A	N/A	20
1303	34.0	5	830	17	30	5.25	FH	ST-506/412	MFM	830	N/A	N/A	20
1304	40.8	6	830	17	30	5.25	FH	ST-506/412	MFM	830	N/A	N/A	20
1323	35.6	4	1024	17	28	5.25	FH	ST-506/412	MFM	AUTO	N/A	N/A	35
1323A	44.5	5	1024	17	28	5.25	FH	ST-506/412	MFM	AUTO	N/A	N/A	35
1324	53.4	6	1024	17	28	5.25	FH	ST-506/412	MFM	1024	N/A	N/A	35
1324A	62.3	7	1024	17	28	5.25	FH	ST-506/412	MFM	1024	N/A	N/A	35
1325	71.30	8	1024	17	28	5.25	FH	ST-506/412	MFM	1024	N/A	N/A	35
1333	35.6	4	1024	17	28	5.25	FH	ST-506/412	MFM	1024	N/A	N/A	25
1333A	44.5	5	1024	17	28	5.25	FH	ST-506/412	MFM	1024	N/A	N/A	25
1334	53.4	6	1024	17	28	5.25	FH	ST-506/412	MFM	1024	N/A	N/A	25
1334A	62.3	7	1024	17	28	5.25	FH	ST-506/412	MFM	1024	N/A	N/A	25
1335	71.3	8	1024	17	28	5.25	FH	ST-506/412	MFM	1024	N/A	N/A	25
1352	37.74	2	1024	36	23	5.25	FH	ESDI-10MHZ	RLL 2,7	AUTO	N/A	N/A	0
1352A	56.62	3	1024	36	23	5.25	FH	ESDI-10MHZ	RLL 2,7	AUTO	N/A	N/A	0
1353	75.49	4	1024	36	23	5.25	FH	ESDI-10MHZ	RLL 2,7	AUTO	N/A	N/A	150
1353A	94.37	5	1024	36	23	5.25	FH	ESDI-10MHZ	RLL 2,7	AUTO	N/A	N/A	150
1354	113.24	6	1024	36	23	5.25	FH	ESDI-10MHZ	RLL 2,7	AUTO	N/A	N/A	150
1354A	132.12	7	1024	36	23	5.25	FH	ESDI-10MHZ	RLL 2,7	AUTO	N/A	N/A	150
1355	150.99	8	1024	36	23	5.25	FH	ESDI-10MHZ	RLL 2,7	AUTO	N/A	N/A	150
1373	72.97	4	1018	35	23	5.25	FH	SCSI	RLL 2,7	AUTO	N/A	N/A	30
1373A	91.21	5	1018	35	23	5.25	FH	SCSI	RLL 2,7	AUTO	N/A	N/A	30
1374	109.45	6	1018	35	23	5.25	FH	SCSI	RLL 2,7	AUTO	N/A	N/A	30
1374A	127.69	7	1018	35	23	5.25	FH	SCSI	RLL 2,7	AUTO	N/A	N/A	30
1375	145.94	8	1018	35	23	5.25	FH	SCSI	RLL 2,7	AUTO	N/A	N/A	30
1516-10S	678.29	10	1840	72	14	5.25	FH	ESDI-24MHZ	RLL 2,7	AUTO	N/A	N/A	0
1517-13	922.52	13	1925	72	14	5.25	FH	ESDI-24MHZ	RLL 2,7	AUTO	N/A	N/A	0
1518-14	993.48	14	1925	72	14	5.25	FH	ESDI-24MHZ	RLL 1,7	AUTO	N/A	N/A	0
1518-15	1354.75	15	2100	84	14	5.25	FH	ESDI-24MHZ	RLL 1,7	AUTO	N/A	N/A	150
1528-15	1354.75	15	2100	84	14	5.25	FH	SCSI-2	RLL 1,7	AUTO	N/A	N/A	150
1538-15	871.61	15	1669	68	14	5.25	FH	ESDI-20MHZ	RLL 1,7	AUTO	N/A	N/A	150
1548	1748.00	15	2089	*	14	5.25	FH	SCSI-2	RLL 1,7	AUTO	N/A	N/A	150
1548-15	1748.00	15	2089	*	14	5.25	FH	SCSI-2	RLL 1,7	AUTO	N/A	N/A	150
1554-07	157.92	7	1224	36	18	5.25	FH	ESDI-10MHZ	RLL 2,7	AUTO	N/A	N/A	150
1555-08	180.48	8	1224	36	18	5.25	FH	ESDI-10MHZ	RLL 2,7	AUTO	N/A	N/A	150
1555-09	203.04	9	1224	36	18	5.25	FH	ESDI-10MHZ	RLL 2,7	AUTO	N/A	N/A	150
1556-10	225.60	10	1224	36	18	5.25	FH	ESDI-10MHZ	RLL 2,7	AUTO	N/A	N/A	150
1556-11	248.16	11	1224	36	18	5.25	FH	ESDI-10MHZ	RLL 2,7	AUTO	N/A	N/A	150
1557-12	270.72	12	1224	36	18	5.25	FH	ESDI-10MHZ	RLL 2,7	AUTO	N/A	N/A	150
1557-13	293.28	13	1224	36	18	5.25	FH	ESDI-10MHZ	RLL 2,7	AUTO	N/A	N/A	150
1558	338.41	15	1224	36	18	5.25	FH	ESDI-10MHZ	RLL 2,7	AUTO	N/A	N/A	150
1558-14	315.85	12	1224	36	18	5.25	FH	ESDI-10MHZ	RLL 2,7	AUTO	N/A	N/A	150
1558-15	338.41	15	1224	36	18	5.25	FH	ESDI-10MHZ	RLL 2,7	AUTO	N/A	N/A	150

MICROPOLIS CORPORATION

MODEL	CAP	HDS	CYL	SPT	SEEK	FF	HGT	INT	ENCODE	LZ	WP	RWC	MTBF
1564-07	315.85	7	1632	54	16	5.25	FH	ESDI-15MHZ	RLL 2,7	AUTO	N/A	N/A	150
1565-08	360.97	8	1632	54	16	5.25	FH	ESDI-15MHZ	RLL 2,7	AUTO	N/A	N/A	150
1565-09	406.09	9	1632	54	16	5.25	FH	ESDI-15MHZ	RLL 2,7	AUTO	N/A	N/A	150
1566-10	451.21	10	1632	54	16	5.25	FH	ESDI-15MHZ	RLL 2,7	AUTO	N/A	N/A	150
1566-11	496.33	11	1632	54	16	5.25	FH	ESDI-15MHZ	RLL 2,7	AUTO	N/A	N/A	150
1567-12	541.45	12	1632	54	16	5.25	FH	ESDI-15MHZ	RLL 2,7	AUTO	N/A	N/A	150
1567-13	586.57	13	1632	54	16	5.25	FH	ESDI-15MHZ	RLL 2,7	AUTO	N/A	N/A	150
1568-14	631.70	14	1632	54	16	5.25	FH	ESDI-15MHZ	RLL 2,7	AUTO	N/A	N/A	150
1568-15	676.82	15	1632	54	16	5.25	FH	ESDI-15MHZ	RLL 2,7	AUTO	N/A	N/A	150
1574-07	157.92	7	1224	36	16	5.25	FH	SCSI	RLL 2,7	AUTO	N/A	N/A	150
1575-08	180.48	8	1224	36	16	5.25	FH	SCSI	RLL 2,7	AUTO	N/A	N/A	150
1575-09	203.04	9	1224	36	16	5.25	FH	SCSI	RLL 2,7	AUTO	N/A	N/A	150
1576-10	225.60	10	1224	36	16	5.25	FH	SCSI	RLL 2,7	AUTO	N/A	N/A	150
1576-11	248.16	11	1224	36	16	5.25	FH	SCSI	RLL 2,7	AUTO	N/A	N/A	150
1577-12	270.72	12	1224	36	16	5.25	FH	SCSI	RLL 2,7	AUTO	N/A	N/A	150
1577-13	293.28	13	1224	36	16	5.25	FH	SCSI	RLL 2,7	AUTO	N/A	N/A	150
1578-14	315.85	14	1224	36	16	5.25	FH	SCSI	RLL 2,7	AUTO	N/A	N/A	150
1578-15	338.41	15	1224	36	16	5.25	FH	SCSI	RLL 2,7	AUTO	N/A	N/A	150
1586-11	495.12	11	1628	54	16	5.25	FH	SCSI	RLL 2,7	AUTO	N/A	N/A	150
1587-12	540.13	12	1628	54	16	5.25	FH	SCSI	RLL 2,7	AUTO	N/A	N/A	150
1587-13	585.14	13	1628	54	16	5.25	FH	SCSI	RLL 2,7	AUTO	N/A	N/A	150
1588-14	630.15	14	1628	54	16	5.25	FH	SCSI	RLL 2,7	AUTO	N/A	N/A	150
1588-15	676.82	15	1632	54	16	5.25	FH	SCSI	RLL 2,7	AUTO	N/A	N/A	150
1588T-15	676.82	15	1632	54	16	5.25	FH	SCSI	RLL 2,7	AUTO	N/A	N/A	150
1596-10S	676.08	10	1834	72	14	5.25	FH	SCSI	RLL 2,7	AUTO	N/A	N/A	150
1597-13	919.64	13	1919	72	14	5.25	FH	SCSI	RLL 2,7	AUTO	N/A	N/A	150
1598-14	976.63	14	1919	71	14	5.25	FH	SCSI	RLL 2,7	AUTO	N/A	N/A	150
1598-15	1051.29	15	1928	71	14	5.25	FH	SCSI-2	RLL 2,7	AUTO	N/A	N/A	150
1624	668	7	2089	*	15	5.25	FH	SCSI	UNIDENT	AUTO	N/A	N/A	150
1624-07	667.00	7	2099	*	15	5.25	FH	SCSI-2	RLL	AUTO	N/A	N/A	150
1653-04	92.08	4	1249	36	16	5.25	HH	ESDI-10MHZ	RLL 2,7	AUTO	N/A	N/A	150
1653-05	115.10	5	1249	36	16	5.25	HH	ESDI-10MHZ	RLL 2,7	AUTO	N/A	N/A	150
1654-06	138.12	6	1249	36	16	5.25	HH	ESDI-10MHZ	RLL 2,7	AUTO	N/A	N/A	150
1654-07	161.15	7	1249	36	16	5.25	HH	ESDI-10MHZ	RLL 2,7	AUTO	N/A	N/A	150
1663-04	196.85	4	1780	54	14	5.25	HH	ESDI-15MHZ	RLL 2,7	AUTO	N/A	N/A	150
1663-05	246.06	5	1780	54	14	5.25	HH	ESDI-15MHZ	RLL 2,7	AUTO	N/A	N/A	150
1664-06	295.28	6	1780	54	14	5.25	HH	ESDI-15MHZ	RLL 2,7	AUTO	N/A	N/A	150
1664-07	344.49	7	1780	54	15	5.25	HH	ESDI-15MHZ	RLL 2,7	AUTO	N/A	N/A	150
1673-04	92.08	4	1249	36	16	5.25	HH	SCSI	RLL 2,7	AUTO	N/A	N/A	150
1673-05	115.10	5	1249	36	16	5.25	HH	SCSI	RLL 2,7	AUTO	N/A	N/A	150
1673-05 MAC	114.73	5	1245	36	16	5.25	HH	SCSI-MAC	RLL	AUTO	N/A	N/A	150
1674-06	138.12	6	1249	36	16	5.25	HH	SCSI	RLL 2,7	AUTO	N/A	N/A	150
1674-07	161.15	7	1249	36	16	5.25	HH	SCSI	RLL 2,7	AUTO	N/A	N/A	150

MICROPOLIS CORPORATION

MODEL	CAP	HDS	CYL	SPT	SEEK	FF	HGT	INT	ENCODE	LZ	WP	RWC	MTBF
1674-07 MAC	160.63	7	1245	36	16	5.25	HH	SCSI-MAC	RLL	AUTO	N/A	N/A	150
1683-04	196.41	4	1776	54	14	5.25	HH	SCSI	RLL 2,7	AUTO	N/A	N/A	150
1683-04 MAC	196.41	4	1776	54	16	5.25	HH	SCSI-MAC	RLL	AUTO	N/A	N/A	150
1683-05	245.51	5	1776	54	14	5.25	HH	SCSI	RLL 2,7	AUTO	N/A	N/A	150
1684	340	7	1774	54	15	5.25	FH	SCSI	UNIDENT	AUTO	N/A	N/A	150
1684-06	294.61	6	1776	54	14	5.25	HH	SCSI	RLL 2,7	AUTO	N/A	N/A	150
1684-07	343.33	7	1774	54	15	5.25	HH	SCSI	RLL 2,7	AUTO	N/A	N/A	150
1684-07 MAC	343.71	7	1776	54	16	5.25	HH	SCSI-MAC	RLL	AUTO	N/A	N/A	150
1743-05	81.71	5	1140	*	15	3.50	HH	IDE(AT)	RLL 2,7	AUTO	N/A	N/A	0
1744-06	98.05	6	1140	*	15	3.50	HH	IDE(AT)	RLL 2,7	AUTO	N/A	N/A	0
1744-07	114.40	7	1140	*	15	3.50	HH	IDE(AT)	RLL 2,7	AUTO	N/A	N/A	0
1745-08	130.74	8	1140	*	15	3.50	HH	IDE(AT)	RLL 2,7	AUTO	N/A	N/A	0
1745-09	147.08	9	1140	*	15	3.50	HH	IDE(AT)	RLL 2,7	AUTO	N/A	N/A	0
1773-05	81.71	5	1140	*	15	3.50	HH	SCSI	RLL 2,7	AUTO	N/A	N/A	0
1774-06	98.05	6	1140	*	15	3.50	HH	SCSI	RLL 2,7	AUTO	N/A	N/A	0
1774-07	114.40	7	1140	*	15	3.50	HH	SCSI	RLL 2,7	AUTO	N/A	N/A	0
1775-08	130.74	8	1140	*	15	3.50	HH	SCSI	RLL 2,7	AUTO	N/A	N/A	0
1775-09	147.08	9	1140	*	15	3.50	HH	SCSI	RLL 2,7	AUTO	N/A	N/A	0
1908	1408	15	2100	*	10	5.25	HH	SCSI-2	UNIDENT	AUTO	N/A	N/A	150
1908-15	1408.00	15	2089	*	11.5	5.25	FH	SCSI-2	RLL	AUTO	N/A	N/A	150
1924	2100	21	2267	*	12	5.25	HH	SCSI-2F	UNIDENT	AUTO	N/A	N/A	250
1924 DIFFERENTIAL	2100	21	2267	*	12	5.25	HH	SCSI-2DIFF	UNIDENT	AUTO	N/A	N/A	250
1924-21	2100.00	21	2280	*	11.5	5.25	FH	SCSI-2	RLL	AUTO	N/A	N/A	250
1926	2158	15	2772	*	13	5.25	–	SCSI-2	NONE	AUTO	N/A	N/A	300
1926-15	2158	15	2772	*	13	5.25	–	SCSI-2	NONE	AUTO	N/A	N/A	300
1936	3000	21	2772	*	10	3.50	HH	SCSI-2	UNIDENT	AUTO	N/A	N/A	250
1936-21	3022	21	2772	*	11.5	5.25	–	SCSI-2	RLL 2,7	AUTO	N/A	N/A	300
1936AV	3000	21	2772	*	10	3.50	HH	SCSI-2	UNIDENT	AUTO	N/A	N/A	250
1936D	3000	21	2772	*	10	3.50	HH	SCSI-2DIFF	UNIDENT	AUTO	N/A	N.A	250
1991	9091	21	4446	*	12	5.25	FH	SCSI-2F	RLL 1,7	AUTO	N/A	N/A	650
1991AV	9091	21	4446	*	12	5.25	FH	SCSI-2F	RLL 1,7	AUTO	N/A	N/A	650
1991W	9091	21	4477	*	12	5.25	FH	SCSI-2 F/W	UNIDENT	AUTO	N/A	N/A	650
1991WAV	9091	21	4477	*	12	5.25	FH	SCSI-2 F/W	UNIDENT	AUTO	N/A	N/A	650
2105	560	8	1744	*	10	3.50	HH	SCSI	UNIDENT	AUTO	N/A	N/A	300
2105-8	560.00	8	1760	*	10	3.50	HH	SCSI-2	RLL 1,7	AUTO	N/A	N/A	300
2105A	650	8	1760	*	10	3.50	HH	IDE(AT)	RLL	AUTO	N/A	N/A	300
2108	693	10	1744	*	10	3.50	HH	SCSI	UNIDENT	AUTO	N/A	N/A	300
2108-6	666.00	10	1745	*	10	3.50	HH	SCSI-2	RLL 1,7	AUTO	N/A	N/A	300
2112	1050	15	1744	*	10	3.50	HH	SCSI	UNIDENT	AUTO	N/A	N/A	300
2112-15-1	1050	15	1747	*	10	3.50	HH	SCSI-2F	RLL 1,7	AUTO	–	–	300
2112-15-2	1050	15	1747	*	10	3.50	FH	SCSI-2	RLL 1,7	AUTO	N/A	N/A	300
2112A	1050	15	1760	*	10	3.50	HH	IDE(AT)	RLL	AUTO	N/A	N/A	300

MICROPOLIS CORPORATION

MODEL	CAP	HDS	CYL	SPT	SEEK	FF	HGT	INT	ENCODE	LZ	WP	RWC	MTBF
2112D	1050 10	15	1744	*	10	3.50	HH	SCSI-2DIFF	UNIDENT	AUTO	N/A	N/A	300
2205-15	528.48	5	2372	*	10	3.50	HH	IDE(AT)	NONE	AUTO	N/A	N/A	300
2205-5	584.0	5	2372	*	10	3.50	HH	SCSI-2	RLL 1,7	AUTO	N/A	N/A	300
2205A	528.48	5	2372	*	10	3.50	HH	IDE(AT)	NONE	AUTO	N/A	N/A	300
2207-6	700	6	2372	*	10	3.50	HH	SCSI-2	RLL 1,7	AUTO	N/A	N/A	300
2210-9	1050	9	2372	*	10	3.50	HH	SCSI-2	RLL 1,7	AUTO	N/A	N/A	300
2210A	976	9	2372	*	10	3.50	HH	IDE(AT)	AUTO	AUTO	N/A	N/A	300
2210AV	1000	15	2360	*	10	3.50	HH	SCSI-2	UNIDENT	AUTO	N/A	N/A	300
2217-15	1765	15	2372	*	10	3.50	FH	SCSI-2	RLL 1,7	AUTO	N/A	N/A	300
2217-AV	1700	15	2372	*	10	3.50	HH	SCSI-2	NONE	AUTO	N/A	N/A	300
2217A	1626	15	2372	*	10	3.50	–	IDE(AT)	NONE	AUTO	N/A	N/A	300
3221	2050		3,956	*	8.9	3.50	HH	SCSI-2F	– NEW	AUTO	N/A	N/A	650K
3243	4294	10	3957	*	8.5	3.50	HH	SCSI-2F	RLL 1,7	4125	–	–	650
3243AV	4294	10	3957	*	8.5	3.50	HH	SCSI-2F	RLL 1,7	4125	–	–	650
3243S	4294		3957	*	8.9	3.50	HH	SCSI	UNIDENT	AUTO	N/A	N/A	650
3243W	4294	10	3957	*	8.5	3.50	HH	SCSI-2 F/W	RLL 1,7	AUTO	N/A	N/A	650
3243WAV	4294	10	3957	*	8.9	3.50	HH	SCSI-2 F/W	UNIDENT	AUTO	N/A	N/A	650
3243WD	4294	10	3957	*	8.9	3.50	FH	SCSI-2 FWD	UNIDENT	AUTO	N/A	N/A	650
3243WDAV	4294	10	3957	*	8.9	3.50	FH	SCSI-2 FWD	UNIDENT	AUTO	N/A	N/A	650
4110-A	1050.00	9	2372	*	10	3.50	HH	SCSI-2	RLL	AUTO	N/A	N/A	300
4110-B	1056	16	2048	*	8.5	3.50	3H	SCSI-2F	UNIDENT	AUTO	N/A	N/A	500
4110A	1057	–	–	–	8.5	3.50	3H	IDE(AT)	UNIDENT	AUTO	N/A	N/A	500
4110AV	1000	16	2048	*	8.5	3.50	3H	SCSI-2F	UNIDENT	AUTO	N/A	N/A	500
4210W	1,060	10	4,150	*	8.9	3.50	HH	SCSI-2 F/W	UNIDENT	AUTO	N/A	N/A	650
4210WAV	1060	10	4150	*	8.9	3.50	HH	SCSI-2 F/W	UNIDENT	AUTO	N/A	N/A	650
4221	2.05GB	10	4150	*	8.9	3.50	3H	SCSI-2F	UNIDENT	AUTO	N/A	N/A	650
4221AV	2.05G	10	4150	*	8.9	3.50	3H	SCSI-2F	UNIDENT	AUTO	N/A	N/A	650
4221W	2,050	10	4150	*	8.9	3.50	HH	SCSI-2 F/W	UNIDENT	AUTO	N/A	N/A	650
4221WAV	2050	10	4150	*	8.9	3.50	HH	SCSI-2 F/W	UNIDENT	AUTO	N/A	N/A	650
4221WD	2050	10	4150	*	8.9	3.50	HH	SCSI-2 FWD	UNIDENT	AUTO	N/A	N/A	650
4221WDAV	2050	10	4150	*	8.9	3.50	HH	SCSI-2 FWD	UNIDENT	AUTO	N/A	N/A	650
4421 (TZ0030-01-7)	2147	7	4050	*	9.75	3.50	3H	SCSI-2F	UNIDENT	AUTO	N/A	N/A	650
4421 (TZ0030-02-5)	2147	7	4050	*	8.8	3.50	3H	SCSI-2F	UNIDENT	AUTO	N/A	N/A	650

MICROSCIENCE INTERNATIONAL CORPORATION

MODEL	CAP	HDS	CYL	SPT	SEEK	FF	HGT	INT	ENCODE	LZ	WP	RWC	MTBF
FH-21200	1062.23	15	1921	72	14	5.25	FH	ESDI-24MHZ	RLL 2,7	AUTO	N/A	N/A	100
FH-21600	1418.05	15	2147	86	14	5.25	FH	ESDI-24MHZ	RLL 2,7	AUTO	N/A	N/A	100
FH-2414	366.72	8	1658	54	14	5.25	FH	ESDI-15MHZ	RLL 2,7	AUTO	N/A	N/A	100
FH-2777	687.60	15	1658	54	14	5.25	FH	ESDI-15MHZ	RLL 2,7	AUTO	N/A	N/A	100

MICROSCIENCE INTERNATIONAL CORPORATION

MODEL	CAP	HDS	CYL	SPT	SEEK	FF	HGT	INT	ENCODE	LZ	WP	RWC	MTBF
FH-31200	1062.23	15	1921	72	14	5.25	FH	SCSI	RLL 2,7	AUTO	N/A	N/A	100
FH-31600	1418.05	15	2147	86	14	5.25	FH	SCSI	RLL 2,7	AUTO	N/A	N/A	100
FH-3414	366.72	8	1658	54	14	5.25	FH	SCSI	RLL 2,7	AUTO	N/A	N/A	100
FH-3777	687.60	15	1658	54	14	5.25	FH	SCSI	RLL 2,7	AUTO	N/A	N/A	100
HH-1050	44.56	5	1024	17	28	5.25	HH	ST-506/412	MFM	–	1,025	1,025	140
HH-1060	65.53	5	1024	25	28	5.25	HH	ST-506/412	RLL 2,7	–	1,025	1,025	140
HH-1075	62.39	7	1024	17	28	5.25	HH	ST-506/412	MFM	–	1,025	1,025	0
HH-1080	68.15	5	1024	26	28	5.25	HH	ST-506/412	RLL 2,7	–	–	–	50
HH-1090	80.05	7	1314	17	28	5.25	HH	ST-506/412	MFM	–	1,315	1,315	40
HH-1095	95.42	7	1024	26	28	5.25	HH	ST-506/412	RLL 2,7	–	1,025	1,025	0
HH-1120	122.44	7	1314	26	28	5.25	HH	ST-506/412	RLL 2,7	–	1,315	1,315	40
HH-21200	128.45	7	1024	35	28	5.25	HH	ESDI-10MHZ	RLL 2,7	AUTO	N/A	N/A	40
HH-21600	160.06	7	1276	35	28	5.25	HH	ESDI-10MHZ	RLL 2,7	AUTO	N/A	N/A	40
HH-2414	366.72	8	1658	54	14	5.25	HH	ESDI-15MHZ	RLL 2,7	AUTO	N/A	N/A	100
HH-2777	687.60	15	1658	54	14	5.25	HH	ESDI-15MHZ	RLL 2,7	AUTO	N/A	N/A	100
HH-312	10.65	4	306	17	65	5.25	HH	ST-506/412	MFM	–	307	307	0
HH-3120	121.09	5	1314	36	28	5.25	HH	SCSI	RLL 2,7	AUTO	N/A	N/A	40
HH-315	10.65	4	306	17	65	5.25	HH	ST-506/412	MFM	–	307	307	0
HH-3160	169.53	7	1314	36	28	5.25	HH	SCSI	RLL 2,7	AUTO	N/A	N/A	40
HH-325	21.30	4	612	17	80	5.25	HH	ST-506/412	MFM	–	613	613	0
HH-330	32.58	4	612	26	105	5.25	HH	ST-506/412	RLL 2,7	–	613	613	0
HH-4050	44.56	5	1024	17	18	3.50	HH	ST-506/412	MFM	–	1,025	1,025	36
HH-4060	68.15	5	1024	26	18	3.50	HH	ST-506/412	RLL 2,7	–	–	–	36
HH-4070	62.39	7	1024	17	18	3.50	HH	ST-506/412	MFM	–	–	–	36
HH-4090	95.42	7	1024	26	18	3.50	HH	ST-506/412	RLL 2,7	–	–	–	36
HH-5040	45.96	3	855	35	18	3.50	HH	ESDI-10MHZ	RLL 2,7	AUTO	N/A	N/A	36
HH-5070	76.60	5	855	35	18	3.50	HH	ESDI-10MHZ	RLL 2,7	AUTO	N/A	N/A	36
HH-5070-20	86.01	5	960	35	18	3.50	HH	ESDI-10MHZ	RLL 2,7	AUTO	N/A	N/A	36
HH-5100	107.25	7	855	35	18	3.50	HH	ESDI-10MHZ	RLL 2,7	AUTO	N/A	N/A	60
HH-5100-20	120.42	7	960	35	18	3.50	HH	ESDI-10MHZ	RLL 2,7	AUTO	N/A	N/A	60
HH-5160	159.43	7	1271	35	18	3.50	HH	ESDI-10MHZ	RLL 2,7	AUTO	N/A	N/A	36
HH-6100	110.31	7	855	36	18	3.50	HH	SCSI	RLL 2,7	AUTO	N/A	N/A	36
HH-612	10.65	4	306	17	85	5.25	HH	ST-506/412	MFM	–	307	307	0
HH-625	21.30	4	612	17	65	5.25	HH	ST-506/412	MFM	–	613	613	0
HH-7040	47.27	3	855	36	18	3.50	HH	IDE(AT)	RLL 2,7	AUTO	N/A	N/A	36
HH-7070-20	86.01	5	960	35	18	3.50	HH	IDE(AT)	RLL 2,7	960	960	N/A	36
HH-7100-00	107.25	7	855	35	18	3.50	HH	IDE(AT)	RLL 2,7	855	855	N/A	36
HH-7100-20	120.42	7	960	35	18	3.50	HH	IDE(AT)	RLL 2,7	960	960	N/A	60
HH-7100-21	121.31	5	1077	44	18	3.50	HH	IDE(AT)	RLL 2,7	992	992	N/A	60
HH-712	10.65	2	612	17	105	5.25	HH	ST-506/412	MFM	–	613	613	0
HH-712A	10.65	2	612	17	75	5.25	HH	ST-506/412	MFM	–	–	–	0
HH-7200	201.37	7	1277	44	18	3.50	HH	IDE(AT)	RLL 2,7	977	977	N/A	60
HH-725	21.30	4	612	17	105	5.25	HH	ST-506/412	MFM	–	613	613	0

MICROSCIENCE INTERNATIONAL CORPORATION

MODEL	CAP	HDS	CYL	SPT	SEEK	FF	HGT	INT	ENCODE	LZ	WP	RWC	MTBF
HH-738	32.58	4	612	26	105	5.25	HH	ST-506/412	RLL 2,7	–	613	613	0
HH-7400	420.00	8	1904	*	15	3.50	HH	IDE(AT)	RLL	AUTO	N/A	N/A	100
HH-8040	42.88	2	1047	40	25	3.50	3H	IDE(AT)	RLL 2,7	AUTO	N/A	N/A	36
HH-8040/ MLC 48-000	41.94	2	1024	40	25	3.50	3H	IDE(AT)	RLL 2,7	AUTO	N/A	N/A	36
HH-8080	85.09	2	1768	47	17	3.50	3H	IDE(AT)	RLL	AUTO	N/A	N/A	100
HH-8200	210.00	4	1904	*	16	3.50	3H	IDE(AT)	RLL	AUTO	N/A	N/A	100
HH-825	21.41	4	615	17	65	5.25	HH	ST-506/412	MFM	–	616	616	0
HH-830	32.74	4	615	26	65	5.25	HH	ST-506/412	RLL 2,7	–	616	616	0

MINISCRIBE (ALSO SEE MAXTOR)

MODEL	CAP	HDS	CYL	SPT	SEEK	FF	HGT	INT	ENCODE	LZ	WP	RWC	MTBF
1012	10.65	4	306	17	179	5.25	FH	ST-506/412	MFM	10	128	307	8
2006	5.32	2	306	17	93	5.25	FH	ST-506/412	MFM	336	128	307	10
2012	10.65	4	306	17	85	5.25	FH	ST-506/412	MFM	336	128	307	10
3006	5.32	2	306	17	–	5.25	HH	ST-506/412	MFM	306	128	307	10
3012	10.65	2	612	17	155	5.25	HH	ST-506/412	MFM	656	128	613	10
3053	44.56	5	1024	–	25	5.25	HH	ST-506/412	MFM	AUTO	512	1,024	30
3085	71.28	7	1170	–	22	5.25	HH	ST-506/412	MFM	AUTO	512	1,170	35
3085E	70.22	3	1270	36	17	5.25	HH	ESDI-10MHZ	RLL	AUTO	N/A	N/A	0
3085S	69.39	3	1255	36	17	5.25	HH	SCSI	RLL	AUTO	N/A	N/A	0
3130E	115.20	5	1250	36	17	5.25	HH	ESDI-10MHZ	RLL 2,7	AUTO	512	1,251	35
3130S	115.66	5	1255	36	17	5.25	HH	SCSI	RLL	AUTO	512	1,256	0
3180E	156.80	7	1250	35	17	5.25	HH	ESDI-10MHZ	RLL 2,7	AUTO	512	1,251	35
3180S	161.28	7	1250	36	17	5.25	HH	SCSI	RLL 2,7	AUTO	512	1,256	35
3180SM	161.28	7	1250	36	17	5.25	HH	SCSI-MAC	RLL	AUTO	N/A	N/A	35
3212	10.65	2	612	17	85	5.25	HH	ST-506/412	MFM	656	128	613	11
3212P (PLUS)	10.65	2	612	17	53	5.25	HH	ST-506/412	MFM	656	128	613	0
3412	10.65	4	306	17	60	5.25	HH	ST-506/412	MFM	336	128	307	11
3425	21.41	4	615	17	85	5.25	HH	ST-506/412	MFM	656	128	616	20
3425P (PLUS)	21.41	4	615	17	53	5.25	HH	ST-506/412	MFM	656	128	616	20
3425S	21.30	4	612	17	68	5.25	HH	SCSI	RLL	656	N/A	N/A	20
3438	32.74	4	615	26	85	5.25	HH	ST-506/412	RLL 2,7	656	128	616	20
3438P (PLUS)	32.74	4	615	26	53	5.25	HH	ST-506/412	RLL 2,7	656	128	616	20
3650	42.24	6	809	17	61	5.25	HH	ST-506/412	MFM	852	128	809	25
3650F	42.24	6	809	17	46	5.25	HH	ST-506/412	MFM	852	128	810	0
3650R	64.61	6	809	26	61	5.25	HH	ST-506/412	RLL 2,7	852	128	809	25
3675	64.61	6	809	26	61	5.25	HH	ST-506/412	RLL 2,7	852	128	809	25
4010	8.35	2	480	17	133	5.25	FH	ST-506/412	MFM	520	128	480	10
4020	16.71	4	480	17	133	5.25	FH	ST-506/412	MFM	520	128	480	10
5330	25.06	6	480	17	–	5.25	FH	ST-506/412	MFM	–	128	481	0
5338	31.96	6	612	17	–	5.25	FH	ST-506/412	MFM	–	128	613	0

MINISCRIBE

MODEL	CAP	HDS	CYL	SPT	SEEK	FF	HGT	INT	ENCODE	LZ	WP	RWC	MTBF
5440	33.42	8	480	17	–	5.25	FH	ST-506/412	MFM	–	128	481	0
5451	42.61	8	612	17	–	5.25	FH	ST-506/412	MFM	–	128	613	0
6032	26.73	3	1024	17	28	5.25	FH	ST-506/412	MFM	AUTO	512	1,024	25
6053	44.56	5	1024	17	28	5.25	FH	ST-506/412	MFM	AUTO	512	1,024	25
6074	62.39	7	1024	17	28	5.25	FH	ST-506/412	MFM	–	512	1,025	0
6079	68.15	5	1024	26	28	5.25	FH	ST-506/412	RLL 2,7	AUTO	551	102	25
6085	71.30	8	1024	17	28	5.25	FH	ST-506/412	MFM	AUTO	512	1,024	25
6128	109.05	8	1024	26	28	5.25	FH	ST-506/412	RLL 2,7	AUTO	512	1,024	25
6170E	142.60	8	1024	34	28	5.25	FH	ESDI-10MHZ	RLL	AUTO	N/A	N/A	0
6212	10.65	2	612	17	–	5.25	FH	ST-506/412	MFM	–	128	613	0
7040A	42.57	2	1155	–	19	3.50	3H	IDE(AT)	RLL 1,7	AUTO	N/A	N/A	150
7040S	42.57	2	1155	–	19	3.50	3H	SCSI	RLL 1,7	AUTO	N/A	N/A	40
7060A	65.20	2	1516	–	15	3.50	3H	IDE(AT)	RLL 1,7	AUTO	N/A	N/A	150
7060S	65.20	2	1516	–	15	3.50	3H	SCSI	RLL 1,7	AUTO	N/A	N/A	150
7080A	85.15	4	1155	–	19	3.50	3H	IDE(AT)	RLL 1,7	AUTO	N/A	N/A	150
7080S	85.15	4	1155	–	19	3.50	3H	SCSI	RLL 1,7	AUTO	N/A	N/A	150
7120A	130.40	4	1516	–	15	3.50	3H	IDE(AT)	RLL 1,7	AUTO	N/A	N/A	150
7120S	130.40	4	1516	–	15	3.50	3H	SCSI	RLL 1,7	AUTO	N/A	N/A	150
7426	21.30	4	612	17	–	3.50	HH	ST-506/412	MFM	–	128	613	0
8051A	42.72	4	745	–	28	3.50	HH	IDE(AT)	RLL 2,7	AUTO	N/A	N/A	150
8051S	42.72	4	745	28	28	3.50	HH	SCSI	RLL	AUTO	N/A	N/A	150
8212	10.70	2	615	17	68	3.50	HH	ST-506/412	MFM	664	128	616	20
8225	20.52	2	771	26	45	3.50	HH	ST-506/412	RLL 2,7	810	128	772	20
8225AT	20.52	2	771	26	40	3.50	HH	IDE(AT)	RLL 2,7	820	N/A	N/A	30
8225S	20.52	2	771	26	68	3.50	HH	SCSI	RLL 2,7	820	N/A	N/A	30
8225XT	20.52	2	771	26	68	3.50	HH	IDE(XT)	RLL 2,7	820	N/A	N/A	30
8412	10.72	4	308	17	50	3.50	HH	ST-506/412	MFM	336	128	616	20
8425	21.41	4	615	17	68	3.50	HH	ST-506/412	MFM	664	128	616	20
8425F	21.41	4	615	17	40	3.50	HH	ST-506/412	MFM	664	128	616	20
8425S	21.41	4	615	17	68	3.50	HH	SCSI	RLL	664	N/A	N/A	20
8425XT	21.41	4	615	17	68	3.50	HH	IDE(XT)	RLL	664	N/A	N/A	20
8434F	32.74	4	615	26	40	3.50	HH	ST-506/412	RLL	–	128	616	0
8438	32.74	4	615	26	68	3.50	HH	ST-506/412	RLL 2,7	664	128	616	20
8438F	32.74	4	615	26	40	3.50	HH	ST-506/412	RLL 2,7	664	128	616	20
8438P (PLUS)	32.74	4	615	26	55	3.50	HH	ST-506/412	RLL 2,7	664	128	615	20
8438XT	32.74	4	615	26	68	3.50	HH	IDE(XT)	RLL	664	N/A	N/A	0
8450	41.05	4	771	26	45	3.50	HH	ST-506/412	RLL 2,7	810	128	772	20
8450AT	42.72	4	745	28	40	3.50	HH	IDE(AT)	RLL 2,7	820	N/A	N/A	30
8450XT	42.86	4	805	26	68	3.50	HH	IDE(XT)	RLL 2,7	820	N/A	N/A	30
9000E	338.41	15	1224	36	16	5.25	FH	ESDI-10MHZ	RLL	AUTO	N/A	N/A	30
9000S	347.00	15	1224	–	16	5.25	FH	SCSI	RLL	AUTO	N/A	N/A	30
9230E	203.04	9	1224	36	16	5.25	FH	ESDI-10MHZ	RLL	AUTO	N/A	N/A	0
9230S	203.04	9	1224	36	16	5.25	FH	SCSI	RLL	AUTO	N/A	N/A	50

MINISCRIBE

MODEL	CAP	HDS	CYL	SPT	SEEK	FF	HGT	INT	ENCODE	LZ	WP	RWC	MTBF
9380E	329.01	15	1224	35	16	5.25	FH	ESDI-10MHZ	RLL 2,7	AUTO	N/A	N/A	50
9380S	327.39	15	1218	35	16	5.25	FH	SCSI	RLL 2,7	AUTO	N/A	N/A	50
9380SM	319.00	15	1218	—	16	5.25	FH	SCSI-MAC	RLL	AUTO	N/A	N/A	50
9424E	360.00	8	1661	53	17	5.25	FH	ESDI-15MHZ	RLL	AUTO	N/A	N/A	0
9424S	355.00	8	1661	—	17	5.25	FH	SCSI	RLL	AUTO	N/A	N/A	0
9780E	676.09	15	1661	53	17	5.25	FH	ESDI-15MHZ	RLL 1,7	AUTO	N/A	N/A	50
9780S	676.09	15	1661	53	17	5.25	FH	SCSI	RLL	AUTO	N/A	N/A	50

MITSUBISHI ELECTRONICS

MODEL	CAP	HDS	CYL	SPT	SEEK	FF	HGT	INT	ENCODE	LZ	WP	RWC	MTBF
M2860-2	50.00	—	—	17	—	8.00	FH	ST-506/412	MFM	—	—	—	0
M2860-3	85.00	—	—	17	—	8.00	FH	ST-506/412	MFM	—	—	—	0
MF504B	21.00	—	—	17	—	8.00	FH	ST-506/412	MFM	—	—	—	0
MR521	10.65	2	612	17	85	5.25	HH	ST-506/412	MFM	—	—	—	0
MR522	21.30	4	612	17	85	5.25	HH	ST-506/412	MFM	—	—	—	0

MITSUBISHI ELECTRONICS

MODEL	CAP	HDS	CYL	SPT	SEEK	FF	HGT	INT	ENCODE	LZ	WP	RWC	MTBF
MR533	25.35	3	971	17	—	5.25	HH	ST-506/412	MFM	971	—	—	0
MR535	42.51	5	977	17	28	5.25	HH	ST-506/412	MFM	—	300	300	30
MR535-V00	42.51	5	977	17	28	5.25	HH	ST-506/412	MFM	—	300	300	30
MR535R	65.02	5	977	26	28	5.25	HH	ST-506/412	RLL 2,7	—	—	—	30

MMI

MODEL	CAP	HDS	CYL	SPT	SEEK	FF	HGT	INT	ENCODE	LZ	WP	RWC	MTBF
M 106	5.32	2	306	17	75	3.50	HH	ST-506/412	MFM	—	128	—	0
M 112	10.65	4	306	17	75	3.50	HH	ST-506/412	MFM	—	128	—	0
M 125	21.30	8	306	17	75	3.50	HH	ST-506/412	MFM	—	128	—	0
M 212	10.65	4	306	17	75	5.25	HH	ST-506/412	MFM	—	128	—	0
M 225	21.30	8	306	17	75	5.25	HH	ST-506/412	MFM	—	128	—	0
M 306	5.32	2	306	17	75	5.25	HH	ST-506/412	MFM	—	128	—	0
M 312	10.65	4	306	17	75	5.25	HH	ST-506/412	MFM	—	128	—	0
M 325	21.30	8	306	17	75	5.25	HH	ST-506/412	MFM	—	128	—	0

NCL AMERICA (ALSO SEE QUANTUM CORPORATION)

MODEL	CAP	HDS	CYL	SPT	SEEK	FF	HGT	INT	ENCODE	LZ	WP	RWC	MTBF
9170E	150.44	7	1166	36	16.5	3.50	HH	ESDI-10MHZ	RLL 2,7	AUTO	–	–	50
9170S	150.44	7	1166	36	16.5	3.50	HH	SCSI	RLL 2,7	AUTO	–	–	50
9220A	200.55	9	1209	36	16.5	3.50	HH	IDE(AT)	RLL 2,7	AUTO	–	–	50
9220E	200.72	9	1210	36	16.5	3.50	HH	ESDI-10MHZ	RLL 2,7	AUTO	–	–	50
9220S	200.72	9	1210	36	16.5	3.50	HH	SCSI	RLL 2,7	AUTO	–	–	50
NDC 5125	150.31	7	1165	36	16.5	3.50	HH	IDE(AT)	RLL 2,7	AUTO	–	–	50

NCR CORPORATION

MODEL	CAP	HDS	CYL	SPT	SEEK	FF	HGT	INT	ENCODE	LZ	WP	RWC	MTBF
6091-5101	323.00	9	–	–	27	5.25	–	SCSI	RLL 2,7	AUTO	N/A	N/A	0
6091-5301	675.00	15	–	–	25	5.25	–	SCSI	RLL 2,7	AUTO	N/A	N/A	0
H6801-STD1-03-17	53.12	7	872	17	28	3.50	HH	ST-506/412	MFM	–	650	–	20
H6801-STD1-07-17	45.33	3	868	34	18	3.50	HH	IDE(AT)	RLL 2,7	AUTO	N/A	N/A	20
H6801-STD1-10-17	104.89	8	776	33	25	3.50	HH	IDE(AT)	RLL 2,7	AUTO	N/A	N/A	150
H6801-STD1-12-17	42.88	2	1047	40	25	3.50	3H	IDE(AT)	RLL 2,7	AUTO	N/A	N/A	150
H6801-STD1-46-46	21.41	4	615	17	68	3.50	HH	ST-506/412	MFM	664	128	616	20
H6801-STD1-47-46	71.30	8	1024	17	28	5.25	FH	ST-506/412	MFM	AUTO	128	1,025	40
H6801-STD1-49-46	121.55	7	969	35	16.5	5.25	FH	ESDI-10MHZ	RLL 2,7	AUTO	N/A	N/A	100

NEC TECHNOLOGIES, INC.

MODEL	CAP	HDS	CYL	SPT	SEEK	FF	HGT	INT	ENCODE	LZ	WP	RWC	MTBF
D3126	21.41	4	615	17	85	3.50	HH	ST-506/412	MFM	–	256	616	20
D3142	44.70	8	642	17	28	3.50	HH	ST-506/412	MFM	–	N/A	N/A	30
D3146H	42.82	8	615	17	35	3.50	HH	ST-506/412	MFM	–	–	–	20
D3661	118.05	7	915	36	20	3.50	HH	ESDI-10MHZ	RLL 2,7	AUTO	N/A	N/A	30
D3711	172.8				12	3.50	3H	IDE(AT)	RLL 1,7	AUTO	N/A	N/A	250
D3713	345.6				12	3.50	3H	IDE(AT)	RLL 1,7	AUTO	N/A	N/A	250
D3715	270		2924		12	3.50	3H	IDE(AT)	RLL 1,7	AUTO	N/A	N/A	250
D3717	540				12	3.50	3H	IDE(AT)	RLL 1,7	AUTO	N/A	N/A	250
D3723	365				11	3.50	3H	IDE(AT)	RLL 1,7	AUTO	N/A	N/A	300
D3724	426.8	2	3493	*	14	3.50	3H	IDE(AT)	PRML	AUTO	N/A	N/A	300
D3725	730				11	3.50	3H	IDE(AT)	RLL 1,7	AUTO	N/A	N/A	300
D3726	853.6	4	3493	*	14	3.50	3H	IDE(AT)	PRML	AUTO	N/A	N/A	300
D3727	1083				11	3.50	3H	IDE(AT)	RLL 1,7	AUTO	N/A	N/A	300

NEC TECHNOLOGIES, INC.

MODEL	CAP	HDS	CYL	SPT	SEEK	FF	HGT	INT	ENCODE	LZ	WP	RWC	MTBF
D3735	45.51	2	1084	41	20	3.50	3H	IDE(AT)	RLL 1,7	AUTO	N/A	N/A	30
D3741	45.04	8	423	26	–	3.50	HH	IDE(AT)	RLL	AUTO	N/A	N/A	0
D3743	540	2	3678	*	11	3.50	3H	IDE(AT)	PRML	AUTO	N/A	N/A	300
D3745	1080	4	3678	*	11	3.50	3H	IDE(AT)	PRML	AUTO	N/A	N/A	300
D3747	1620	6	3678	*	11	3.50	3H	IDE(AT)	PRML	AUTO	N/A	N/A	300
D3755	104.96	4	1250	41	20	3.50	3H	IDE(AT)	RLL 1,7	AUTO	N/A	N/A	30
D3756	104.96	4	1250	41	19	3.50	HH	IDE(AT)	RLL 1,7	AUTO	N/A	N/A	50
D3761	118.05	7	915	36	20	3.50	HH	IDE(AT)	RLL 2,7	AUTO	N/A	N/A	30
D3781	425.00	9	1464	63	15	3.50	HH	IDE(AT)	RLL 1,7	AUTO	N/A	N/A	50
D3815	270.4		2924		12	3.50	3H	SCSI-2	RLL 1,7	AUTO	N/A	N/A	0
D3817	540.8		2924		12	3.50	3H	SCSI-2	RLL 1,7	AUTO	N/A	N/A	0
D3823	365				11	3.50	3H	SCSI-2	RLL 1,7	AUTO	N/A	N/A	300
D3825	730				11	3.50	3H	SCSI-2	RLL 1,7	AUTO	N/A	N/A	300
D3827	1083				11	3.50	3H	SCSI-2	RLL 1,7	AUTO	N/A	N/A	300
D3835	45.09	2	1074	41	20	3.50	3H	SCSI	RLL 1,7	AUTO	N/A	N/A	30
D3843	540				11	3.50	3H	SCSI-2	PRML	AUTO	N/A	N/A	300
D3845	1080	4	3678	*	11	3.50	3H	SCSI-2	PRML	AUTO	N/A	N/A	300
D3847	1620	6	3678	*	11	3.50	3H	SCSI-2	PRML	AUTO	N/A	N/A	300
D3855	104.96	4	1250	41	20	3.50	3H	SCSI	RLL 1,7	AUTO	N/A	N/A	30
D3861	114.77	7	915	35	20	3.50	HH	SCSI	RLL 2,7	AUTO	N/A	N/A	30
D3881	425.00	9	1464	63	15	3.50	HH	SCSI	RLL 1,7	AUTO	N/A	N/A	50
D3896	2160	9	3928	*	9	3.50	3H	SCSI-2	RLL 1,7	AUTO	N/A	N/A	800
D5114	5.32	2	306	17	–	5.25	–	ST-506/412	MFM	–	–	–	0
D5124	10.75	4	309	17	85	5.25	HH	ST-506/412	MFM	–	310	310	0
D5126	21.30	4	612	17	85	5.25	HH	ST-506/412	MFM	–	–	613	0
D5126H	21.30	4	612	17	40	5.25	HH	ST-506/412	MFM	–	–	613	0
D5127	60.45	4	615	17	85	5.25	HH	ST-506/412	RLL 2,7	AUTO	N/A	616	0
D5146	42.82	8	615	17	85	5.25	HH	ST-506/412	MFM	–	–	616	0
D5146H	42.82	8	615	17	40	5.25	HH	ST-506/412	MFM	–	–	616	0
D5452	67.42	10	823	34	23	5.25	HH	ESDI-10MHZ	RLL 2,7	AUTO	N/A	N/A	0
D5652	143.26	10	823	34	23	5.25	HH	ESDI-10MHZ	RLL 2,7	AUTO	N/A	N/A	0
D5655	153.53	7	1224	35	18	5.25	HH	ESDI-10MHZ	RLL 2,7	AUTO	N/A	N/A	30
D5662	329.01	15	1224	35	18	5.25	FH	ESDI-10MHZ	RLL 2,7	AUTO	N/A	N/A	45
D5682	664.69	15	1633	53	16	5.25	FH	ESDI-15MHZ	RLL 1,7	AUTO	N/A	N/A	50
D5862	328.20	15	1221	35	18	5.25	FH	SCSI	RLL 1,7	AUTO	N/A	N/A	50
D5882	664.69	15	1633	53	16	5.25	FH	SCSI	RLL 1,7	AUTO	N/A	N/A	50
D5892	1403.82	19	1678	86	14	5.25	FH	SCSI	RLL 1,7	AUTO	N/A	N/A	100
DSE1340A	1340	4	4323	*	11	3.50	3H	IDE(AT)	PRML	AUTO	N/A	N/A	300
DSE2010A	2010	6	4323	*	11	3.50	3H	IDE(AT)	PRML	AUTO	N/A	N/A	300

NEI

MODEL	CAP	HDS	CYL	SPT	SEEK	FF	HGT	INT	ENCODE	LZ	WP	RWC	MTBF
RD 3127	10.65	2	612	17	–	5.25	HH	ST-506/412	MFM	–	–	–	0
RD 3255	21.30	4	612	17	–	5.25	HH	ST-506/412	MFM	–	–	–	0
RD 4127	10.65	4	306	17	–	5.25	FH	ST-506/412	MFM	–	–	–	0
RD 4255	21.30	8	306	17	–	5.25	FH	ST-506/412	MFM	–	–	–	0

NEWBURY DATA

MODEL	CAP	HDS	CYL	SPT	SEEK	FF	HGT	INT	ENCODE	LZ	WP	RWC	MTBF
NDR 1065	55.93	7	918	17	25	5.25	FH	ST-506/412	MFM	–	–	–	0
NDR 1085	71.30	8	1024	17	26	5.25	FH	ST-506/412	MFM	–	–	–	0
NDR 1105	87.89	11	918	17	25	5.25	FH	ST-506/412	MFM	–	–	–	0
NDR 1140	119.85	15	918	17	25	5.25	FH	ST-506/412	MFM	–	–	–	0
NDR 2085	74.57	7	1224	17	–	5.25	FH	ST-506/412	MFM	–	1,224	1,224	0
NDR 2140	117.19	11	1224	17	–	5.25	FH	ST-506/412	MFM	–	1,224	1,224	0
NDR 2190	119.85	15	918	17	28	5.25	FH	ST-506/412	MFM	–	1,224	1,224	0
NDR 3170S	146.64	9	1224	26	28	5.25	FH	SCSI	RLL 2,7	AUTO	N/A	N/A	0
NDR 320	21.41	4	615	17	–	5.25	FH	ST-506/412	MFM	615	–	–	0
NDR 3280S	244.40	15	1224	26	28	5.25	FH	SCSI	RLL 2,7	AUTO	N/A	N/A	0
NDR 3380S	319.61	15	1224	34	28	5.25	FH	SCSI	RLL 2,7	AUTO	N/A	N/A	50
NDR 340	42.82	8	615	17	40	3.50	HH	ST-506/412	MFM	–	–	–	0
NDR 4175	157.92	7	1224	36	28	5.25	FH	ESDI-10MHZ	RLL 2,7	AUTO	N/A	N/A	0
NDR 4380	338.41	15	1224	36	28	5.25	FH	ESDI-10MHZ	RLL 2,7	AUTO	N/A	N/A	0
NDR 4380S	319.61	15	1224	34	28	5.25	FH	SCSI	RLL	AUTO	N/A	N/A	0
PENNY 340	42.82	8	615	17	–	5.25	HH	ST-506/412	MFM	–	615	615	0

NPL

MODEL	CAP	HDS	CYL	SPT	SEEK	FF	HGT	INT	ENCODE	LZ	WP	RWC	MTBF
4064	5.00	–	–	17	–	5.25	FH	ST-506/412	MFM	–	–	–	0
4127	10.00	–	–	17	–	5.25	FH	ST-506/412	MFM	–	–	–	0
4191S	15.00	–	–	17	–	5.25	FH	ST-506/412	MFM	–	–	–	0
4255	20.00	–	–	17	–	5.25	FH	ST-506/412	MFM	–	–	–	0
NP 02-13	11.14	4	320	17	95	5.25	HH	ST-506/412	MFM	320	0	N/A	0
NP 02-26A/26S	22.28	4	640	17	40	5.25	HH	ST-506/412	MFM	640	0	N/A	0
NP 02-52A	44.56	8	640	17	40	5.25	HH	ST-506/412	MFM	640	640	N/A	0
NP 03-20	15.98	6	306	17	85	3.50	HH	ST-506/412	MFM	306	0	N/A	0
NP 03-6	5.32	2	306	17	–	5.25	–	ST-506/412	MFM	–	–	–	0
NP 04-13T	10.00	–	–	17	85	5.25	FH	ST-506/412	MFM	–	–	–	0
NP 04-55	45.93	7	754	17	35	5.25	HH	ST-506/412	MFM	754	0	N/A	0
NP 04-85	72.19	11	754	17	35	5.25	HH	ST-506/412	MFM	754	0	N/A	0

OKIDATA

MODEL	CAP	HDS	CYL	SPT	SEEK	FF	HGT	INT	ENCODE	LZ	WP	RWC	MTBF
OD 526	22.28	4	640	17	–	5.25	HH	ST-506/412	RLL 2,7	–	–	–	0
OD 540	33.42	6	640	17	–	5.25	HH	ST-506/412	RLL 2,7	–	–	–	0

OLIVETTI

MODEL	CAP	HDS	CYL	SPT	SEEK	FF	HGT	INT	ENCODE	LZ	WP	RWC	MTBF
HD 662/11	10.65	2	612	17	65	5.25	HH	ST-506/412	MFM	–	–	–	0
HD 662/12	21.30	4	612	17	65	5.25	HH	ST-506/412	MFM	–	–	–	0
XM 3220	21.30	4	612	17	85	3.50	HH	ST-506/412	MFM	656	128	N/A	0
XM 5210	10.00	–	–	17	65	5.25	HH	ST-506/412	MFM	–	–	–	0
XM 5220/2	21.30	4	612	17	85	5.25	FH	ST-506/412	MFM	656	128	–	0
XM 5221	21.41	4	615	17	40	5.25	HH	ST-506/412	MFM	700	256	N/A	0
XM 5340	42.82	6	820	17	40	5.25	HH	ST-506/412	MFM	819	256	256	0
XM 5360	42.82	6	820	17	40	5.25	HH	ST-506/412	RLL	819	128	128	0

OPTIMA TECHNOLOGY

MODEL	CAP	HDS	CYL	SPT	SEEK	FF	HGT	INT	ENCODE	LZ	WP	RWC	MTBF
CONCORDE 1050	1050.00	15	–	–	15	5.25	–	SCSI	RLL 2,7	AUTO	N/A	N/A	50
CONCORDE 635	640.00	14	–	–	16	5.25	–	SCSI	RLL 2,7	AUTO	N/A	N/A	150
DISKOVERY 420	416.00	8	–	–	16	5.25	–	SCSI	RLL 2,7	AUTO	N/A	N/A	100
MINIPAK 100	104.00	4	–	–	25	3.50	HH	SCSI	RLL 2,7	AUTO	N/A	N/A	30
MINIPAK 200	209.00	8	–	–	20	3.50	HH	SCSI	RLL 2,7	AUTO	N/A	N/A	40
MINIPAK 300	320.00	–	–	–	13	3.50	HH	SCSI	RLL 2,7	AUTO	N/A	N/A	150

ORCA TECHNOLOGY

MODEL	CAP	HDS	CYL	SPT	SEEK	FF	HGT	INT	ENCODE	LZ	WP	RWC	MTBF
320A	370.00	9	–	–	12	3.50	HH	IDE(AT)	RLL 2,7	AUTO	N/A	N/A	100
320S	370.00	9	–	–	12	3.50	HH	SCSI	RLL 2,7	AUTO	N/A	N/A	100
400A	470.00	9	–	–	12	3.50	HH	IDE(AT)	RLL 2,7	AUTO	N/A	N/A	100
400S	470.00	9	–	–	12	3.50	HH	SCSI	RLL 2,7	AUTO	N/A	N/A	100
760E	760.00	15	–	–	14	5.25	–	ESDI-15MHZ	RLL 2,7	AUTO	N/A	N/A	50
760S	760.00	15	–	–	14	5.25	–	SCSI	RLL 2,7	AUTO	N/A	N/A	50
OT5H 53-MFM	44.56	5	1024	17	23	5.25	HH	ST-506/412	MFM	1024	–	–	40

OTARI

MODEL	CAP	HDS	CYL	SPT	SEEK	FF	HGT	INT	ENCODE	LZ	WP	RWC	MTBF
C-214	10.65	4	306	17	—	5.25	FH	ST-506/412	MFM	—	128	128	0
C-507	5.32	2	306	17	79	5.25	FH	ST-506/412	MFM	—	128	128	0
C-514	10.65	4	306	17	79	5.25	FH	ST-506/412	MFM	—	128	128	0
C-519	15.98	6	306	17	79	5.25	FH	ST-506/412	MFM	—	128	128	0
C-526	21.30	8	306	17	—	5.25	FH	ST-506/412	MFM	—	128	128	0

PANASONIC INDUSTRIAL COMPANY

MODEL	CAP	HDS	CYL	SPT	SEEK	FF	HGT	INT	ENCODE	LZ	WP	RWC	MTBF
JU-116	21.41	4	615	17	85	3.50	HH	ST-506/412	MFM	—	616	616	0
JU-128	44.66	7	733	17	35	3.50	HH	ST-506/412	MFM	—	734	734	0

PERIPHERALS ENTERPRISE CO., LTD.

MODEL	CAP	HDS	CYL	SPT	SEEK	FF	HGT	INT	ENCODE	LZ	WP	RWC	MTBF
PL-100 TURBO	105.00	4	—	—	19	3.50	HH	SCSI	RLL 2,7	AUTO	N/A	N/A	60
PL-200 TURBO	210.00	7	—	—	19	3.50	HH	SCSI	RLL 2,7	AUTO	N/A	N/A	50
PL-320 TURBO	320.00	14	—	—	12	3.50	HH	SCSI	RLL 2,7	AUTO	N/A	N/A	100
PT-225	21.41	4	615	17	35	3.50	HH	ST-506/412	MFM	—	—	—	0
PT-234	28.54	4	820	17	35	3.50	HH	ST-506/412	MFM	—	—	—	0
PT-238A	32.74	4	615	26	35	3.50	HH	IDE(AT)	RLL 2,7	AUTO	N/A	N/A	0
PT-238R	32.74	4	615	26	35	3.50	HH	ST-506/412	RLL 2,7	—	—	—	0
PT-238S	32.74	4	615	26	35	3.50	HH	SCSI	RLL 2,7	AUTO	N/A	N/A	0
PT-251A	43.66	4	820	26	35	3.50	HH	IDE(AT)	RLL 2,7	AUTO	N/A	N/A	0
PT-251R	43.66	4	820	26	35	3.50	HH	ST-506/412	RLL 2,7	—	—	—	0
PT-251S	43.66	4	820	26	35	3.50	HH	SCSI	RLL 2,7	AUTO	N/A	N/A	0
PT-338	32.11	6	615	17	35	3.50	HH	ST-506/412	MFM	—	—	—	0
PT-351	42.82	6	820	17	35	3.50	HH	ST-506/412	MFM	—	—	—	0
PT-357A	49.12	6	615	26	35	3.50	HH	IDE(AT)	RLL 2,7	AUTO	N/A	N/A	0
PT-357R	49.12	6	615	26	35	3.50	HH	ST-506/412	RLL 2,7	—	—	—	0
PT-357S	49.12	6	615	26	35	3.50	HH	SCSI	RLL 2,7	AUTO	N/A	N/A	0
PT-376A	65.49	6	820	26	35	3.50	HH	IDE(AT)	RLL 2,7	AUTO	N/A	N/A	0
PT-376R	65.49	6	820	26	35	3.50	HH	ST-506/412	RLL 2,7	—	—	—	0
PT-376S	65.49	6	820	26	35	3.50	HH	SCSI	RLL 2,7	AUTO	N/A	N/A	0
PT-4102A	87.32	8	820	26	35	3.50	HH	IDE(AT)	RLL 2,7	AUTO	N/A	N/A	80
PT-4102R	87.32	8	820	26	35	3.50	HH	ST-506/412	RLL 2,7	AUTO	—	—	80

PLUS DEVELOPMENT CORPORATION (SEE QUANTUM CORPORATION)

MODEL	CAP	HDS	CYL	SPT	SEEK	FF	HGT	INT	ENCODE	LZ	WP	RWC	MTBF
HARDCARD 20	21.41	4	615	17	40	CARD	3H	IDE(AT)	RLL 2,7	AUTO	N/A	N/A	60
HARDCARD 40	42.61	8	612	17	40	CARD	3H	IDE(AT)	RLL 2,7	AUTO	N/A	N/A	60
HARDCARD II-80	80.51	10	925	17	25	CARD	3H	IDE(AT)	RLL 2,7	AUTO	N/A	N/A	0
HARDCARD II-XL105	105.23	15	806	17	17	CARD	3H	IDE(AT)	RLL 2,7	AUTO	N/A	N/A	0
HARDCARD II-XL50	52.31	10	601	17	17	CARD	3H	IDE(AT)	RLL 2,7	AUTO	N/A	N/A	0
IMPULSE 105AT/LP	105.24	4	1219	*	17	3.50	3H	IDE(AT)	RLL 2,7	AUTO	—	—	60
IMPULSE 105S	105.24	4	1219	*	19	3.50	HH	SCSI-2	RLL 2,7	AUTO	—	—	50
IMPULSE 105S/LP	104.85	4	1219	*	17	3.50	3H	SCSI-2	RLL 2,7	AUTO	—	—	60
IMPULSE 120AT	120.74	5	1123	42	15	3.50	HH	IDE(AT)	RLL 1,7	AUTO	—	—	50
IMPULSE 120S	120.74	5	1123	42	15	3.50	HH	SCSI-2	RLL 1,7	AUTO	—	—	50
IMPULSE 170AT	169.04	7	1123	42	15	3.50	HH	IDE(AT)	RLL 1,7	AUTO	—	—	50
IMPULSE 170S	169.04	7	1123	42	15	3.50	HH	SCSI-2	RLL 1,7	AUTO	—	—	50
IMPULSE 210AT	210.00	7	1156	*	15	3.50	HH	IDE(AT)	RLL 1,7	AUTO	—	—	50
IMPULSE 210S	210.00	7	1156	*	15	3.50	HH	SCSI-2	RLL 1,7	AUTO	—	—	50
IMPULSE 330AT	331.20	7	1512	*	14	3.50	HH	IDE(AT)	RLL 1,7	AUTO	—	—	75
IMPULSE 330S	331.20	7	1512	*	14	3.50	HH	SCSI-2	RLL 1,7	AUTO	—	—	75
IMPULSE 40AT	41.99	5	965	17	19	3.50	HH	IDE(AT)	RLL 2,7	AUTO	N/A	N/A	50
IMPULSE 40S	42.00	3	—	—	19	3.50	HH	SCSI-2	RLL 2,7	AUTO	—	—	50
IMPULSE 425AT	425.80	—	—	—	14	3.50	HH	SCSI-2	RLL 1,7	AUTO	—	—	75
IMPULSE 425S	425.80	—	—	—	14	3.50	HH	SCSI-2	RLL 1,7	AUTO	—	—	75
IMPULSE 52AT/LP	52.29	8	751	17	17	3.50	3H	IDE(AT)	RLL 2,7	AUTO	—	—	60
IMPULSE 52S/LP	52.20	2	—	—	17	3.50	3H	SCSI-2	RLL 2,7	AUTO	—	—	60
IMPULSE 80AT	83.99	10	965	17	19	3.50	HH	IDE(AT)	RLL 2,7	AUTO	N/A	N/A	50
IMPULSE 80AT/LP	85.78	16	616	17	17	3.50	3H	IDE(AT)	RLL 2,7	AUTO	—	—	60
IMPULSE 80S	84.00	6	—	—	19	3.50	HH	SCSI-2	RLL 2,7	AUTO	—	—	50
IMPULSE 80S/LP	85.70	4	—	—	17	3.50	3H	SCSI-2	RLL 2,7	AUTO	—	—	60

PRAIRIETEK

MODEL	CAP	HDS	CYL	SPT	SEEK	FF	HGT	INT	ENCODE	LZ	WP	RWC	MTBF
PRAIRIE 120	21.41	2	615	34	23	2.50	4H	IDE(XT/AT)	RLL 2,7	AUTO	N/A	N/A	20
PRAIRIE 140	42.82	4	615	34	23	2.50	4H	IDE(XT/AT)	RLL 2,7	AUTO	N/A	N/A	20
PRAIRIE 220A	21.30	2	612	34	28	2.50	3H	IDE(AT)	RLL 2,7	AUTO	N/A	N/A	20
PRAIRIE 220S	21.30	2	612	34	28	2.50	3H	SCSI	RLL 2,7	AUTO	N/A	N/A	20
PRAIRIE 240	42.82	4	615	34	28	2.50	3H	IDE(XT/AT)	RLL 2,7	AUTO	N/A	N/A	20
PRAIRIE 242A	42.82	4	615	34	23	2.50	3H	IDE(XT/AT)	RLL 2,7	AUTO	N/A	N/A	20
PRAIRIE 242S	42.82	4	615	34	23	2.50	3H	SCSI	RLL 2,7	AUTO	N/A	N/A	20
PRAIRIE 282A	82.00	4	—	34	28	2.50	3H	IDE(XT/AT)	RLL 2,7	AUTO	N/A	N/A	20
PRAIRIE 282S	82.00	4	—	34	23	2.50	3H	SCSI	RLL 2,7	AUTO	N/A	N/A	20

PRIAM CORPORATION

MODEL	CAP	HDS	CYL	SPT	SEEK	FF	HGT	INT	ENCODE	LZ	WP	RWC	MTBF
502	46.00	7	755	17	22	5.25	FH	ST-506/412	MFM	—	756	756	0
504	46.00	7	755	17	22	5.25	FH	ST-506/412	MFM	—	756	756	0
514	117.19	11	1224	—	22	5.25	FH	ST-506/412	MFM	—	—	—	0
519	159.80	15	1224	—	22	5.25	FH	ST-506/412	MFM	—	1,225	1,225	0
617	153.66	7	1225	35	20	5.25	FH	ESDI-10MHZ	RLL 2,7	AUTO	N/A	N/A	0
628	241.47	11	1225	35	20	5.25	FH	ESDI-10MHZ	RLL 2,7	AUTO	N/A	N/A	0
638	329.28	15	1225	35	20	5.25	FH	ESDI-10MHZ	RLL 2,7	AUTO	N/A	N/A	0
717	153.66	7	1225	35	20	5.25	FH	SCSI	RLL 2,7	AUTO	N/A	N/A	0
728	241.47	11	1225	35	20	5.25	FH	SCSI	RLL 2,7	AUTO	N/A	N/A	0
738	329.28	15	1225	—	20	5.25	FH	SCSI	RLL 2,7	AUTO	N/A	N/A	0
ID 120-E	121.11	7	1024	33	28	5.25	HH	ESDI-10MHZ	RLL 2,7	AUTO	N/A	N/A	0
ID 130-PS041	133.69	15	1024	17	13	5.25	FH	ST-506/412	MFM	—	—	—	40
ID 150	160.06	7	1276	35	28	5.25	HH	ESDI-10MHZ	RLL 2,7	AUTO	N/A	N/A	0
ID 160-E	158.05	7	1225	36	18	5.25	FH	ESDI-10MHZ	RLL 2,7	AUTO	N/A	N/A	0
ID 160-PS071	158.05	7	1225	36	18	5.25	FH	ESDI-10MHZ	RLL 2,7	AUTO	N/A	N/A	0
ID 160-PSCSI	159.55	7	1225	36	18	5.25	FH	SCSI	RLL 2,7	AUTO	N/A	N/A	0
ID 160-S	159.55	7	1225	36	18	5.25	FH	SCSI	RLL 2,7	AUTO	N/A	N/A	0
ID 20	25.61	3	981	17	23	5.25	FH	ST-506/412	MFM	—	—	—	40
ID 200L	201.00	7	1318	*	—	3.50	HH	IDE(AT)	RLL 1,7	AUTO	N/A	N/A	100
ID 250-E	248.37	11	1225	36	18	5.25	FH	ESDI-10MHZ	RLL	AUTO	N/A	N/A	0
ID 250-PS071	248.37	11	1225	36	18	5.25	FH	ESDI-10MHZ	RLL	AUTO	N/A	N/A	0
ID 330-PS071	330.39	15	1195	36	18	5.25	FH	ESDI-10MHZ	RLL 2,7	AUTO	N/A	N/A	0
ID 340H	344.49	7	1780	54	14	5.25	HH	SCSI	RLL 2,7	AUTO	N/A	N/A	150
ID 45H-AT	44.56	5	1018	17	23	5.25	HH	ST-506/412	MFM	—	—	—	40
ID 60AT	59	5	1018	—	23	5.25	FH	ST-506/412	MFM	AUTO	N/A	N/A	150
ID 62-PS041	62.39	7	1024	17	23	5.25	FH	ST-506/412	MFM	—	—	—	40
ID 75-Q	73.98	5	1156	25	23	5.25	FH	ST-506/412	RLL	AUTO	—	—	40
ID/ED40	42.69	5	981	17	23	5.25	FH	ST-506/412	MFM	981	—	—	40
ID/ED45-AT-D2	44.30	5	1018	17	23	5.25	FH	ST-506/412	MFM	—	—	—	40
ID/ED60	59.77	7	981	17	23	5.25	FH	ST-506/412	MFM	981	—	—	150

PRIAM CORPORATION

MODEL	CAP	HDS	CYL	SPT	SEEK	FF	HGT	INT	ENCODE	LZ	WP	RWC	MTBF
ID/ED62-AT-D2	62.02	7	1018	17	23	5.25	FH	ST-506/412	MFM	—	—	—	40
ID/ED 100-Q	108.65	7	1166	26	15	5.25	HH	ST-506/412	RLL 2,7	AUTO	N/A	N/A	40
ID/ED 130-AT-D2	159.80	15	1224	17	28	5.25	FH	ST-506/412	MFM	AUTO	N/A	N/A	0
ID/ED 230-Q	233.08	15	1214	25	11	5.25	FH	ST-506/412	RLL	—	—	—	40
ID/ED 240	243.60	15	1220	26	28	5.25	FH	ST-506/412	RLL 2,7	AUTO	—	—	40
ID/ED 250-PSCSI	248.37	11	1225	36	18	5.25	FH	SCSI	RLL	AUTO	N/A	N/A	0
ID/ED 250-S	248.37	11	1225	36	18	5.25	FH	SCSI	RLL	AUTO	N/A	N/A	0
ID/ED 330-E	338.68	15	1225	36	18	5.25	FH	ESDI-10MHZ	RLL 2,7	AUTO	N/A	N/A	0
ID/ED 330-PSCSI	338.68	15	1225	36	18	5.25	FH	SCSI	RLL 2,7	AUTO	N/A	N/A	0
ID/ED 330-S	338.68	15	1225	36	18	5.25	FH	SCSI	RLL 2,7	AUTO	N/A	N/A	0
ID/ED 660	675.16	15	1628	54	16	5.25	FH	SCSI	RLL	AUTO	N/A	N/A	150
ID/ED1000	1046.39	15	1919	71	14	5.25	FH	SCSI	RLL	AUTO	N/A	N/A	150
INNERSPACE INTERNAL DISK SYSTEM	32.74	4	820	26	27	3.50	HH	ST-506/412	RLL 2,7	—	—	—	0
S14	117.19	11	1224	17	—	5.25	–	ST-506/412	MFM	—	1,224	1,224	0
S15	159.80	15	1224	17	—	5.25	–	ST-506/412	MFM	—	1,224	1,224	0
TYPE A	—	—	—	—	—	5.25	HH	ST-506/412	–	—	—	—	0
V130	25.77	3	987	17	28	5.25	FH	ST-506/412	MFM	—	988	988	0
V150	42.95	5	987	17	28	5.25	FH	ST-506/412	MFM	—	988	988	0
V160	50.74	5	1166	17	28	5.25	FH	ST-506/412	MFM	—	1,167	1,167	0
V170	60.13	7	987	17	28	5.25	FH	ST-506/412	MFM	—	988	988	0
V170R	91.97	7	987	26	—	5.25	FH	ST-506/412	RLL 2,7	—	—	—	0
V185	71.04	7	1166	17	28	5.25	FH	ST-506/412	MFM	—	1,167	1,167	0
V519	159.80	15	1224	17	—	5.25	FH	ST-506/412	MFM	1223	—	—	0

QUANTUM CORPORATION

MODEL	CAP	HDS	CYL	SPT	SEEK	FF	HGT	INT	ENCODE	LZ	WP	RWC	MTBF
ATLAS II XP32181R	2180	6	5952	*	8	3.50	3H	SCSI 3 80W	RLL 1,7	AUTO	N/A	N/A	1000
ATLAS II XP32181S	2180	6	5952	*	8	3.50	3H	SCSI-3	RLL 1,7	AUTO	N/A	N/A	1000
ATLAS II XP32181W	2180	6	5952	*	8	3.50	3H	SCSI 3W	RLL 1,7	AUTO	N/A	N/A	1000
ATLAS II XP32181WD	2180	6	5952	*	8	3.50	3H	SCSI 3WD	RLL 1,7	AUTO	N/A	N/A	1000
ATLAS II XP34361R	4360	10	5952	*	8	3.50	3H	SCSI 3 80W	RLL 1,7	AUTO	N/A	N/A	1000
ATLAS II XP34361S	4360	10	5952	*	8	3.50	3H	SCSI-3	RLL 1,7	AUTO	N/A	N/A	1000
ATLAS II XP34361W	4360	10	5952	*	8	3.50	3H	SCSI 3W	RLL 1,7	AUTO	N/A	N/A	1000
ATLAS II XP34361WD	4360	10	5952	*	8	3.50	3H	SCSI 3WD	RLL 1,7	AUTO	N/A	N/A	1000

QUANTUM CORPORATION

MODEL	CAP	HDS	CYL	SPT	SEEK	FF	HGT	INT	ENCODE	LZ	WP	RWC	MTBF
ATLAS II XP39100R	8678	20	5952	*	8	3.50	FH	SCSI 3 80W	RLL 1,7	AUTO	N/A	N/A	1000
ATLAS II XP39100S	8678	20	5952	*	8	3.50	HH	SCSI-3	RLL 1,7	AUTO	N/A	N/A	1000
ATLAS II XP39100W	8678	20	5952	*	8	3.50	HH	SCSI 3W	RLL 1,7	AUTO	N/A	N/A	1000
ATLAS II XP39100WD	8678	20	5952	*	8	3.50	HH	SCSI 3WD	RLL 1,7	AUTO	N/A	N/A	1000
ATLAS XP31070R	1075	5	3832	*	8.5	3.50	3H	SCSI SCA	UNIDENT				
ATLAS XP31070S	1075	5	3832	*	8.5	3.50	3H	SCSI-2F	RLL 1,7	AUTO	N/A	N/A	800
ATLAS XP31070S	1075	5	3832	*	8.5	3.50	3H	SCSI-2F	RLL 1,7	AUTO	N/A	N/A	800
ATLAS XP31070W	1075	5	3832	*	8.5	3.50	3H	SCSI-2 F/W	RLL 1,7	AUTO	N/A	N/A	800
ATLAS XP31070WD	1075	5	3832	*	8.5	3.50	3H	SCSI-2 FWD	RLL 1,7	AUTO	N/A	N/A	800
ATLAS XP32150S	2150	10	3832	*	8.5	3.50	3H	SCSI-2F	RLL 1,7	AUTO	N/A	N/A	800
ATLAS XP32150W	2150	10	3832	*	8.5	3.50	3H	SCSI-2 F/W	RLL 1,7	AUTO	N/A	N/A	800
ATLAS XP32150WD	2150	10	3832	*	8.5	3.50	3H	SCSI-2 FWD	RLL 1,7	AUTO	N/A	N/A	800
ATLAS XP34300S	4300	20	3832	*	8.5	3.50	HH	SCSI-2F	RLL 1,7	AUTO	N/A	N/A	800
ATLAS XP34300W	4300	20	3832	*	8.5	3.50	HH	SCSI-2 F/W	RLL 1,7	AUTO	N/A	N/A	800
ATLAS XP34300WD	4300	20	3832	*	8.5	3.50	HH	SCSI-2 FWD	RLL 1,7	AUTO	N/A	N/A	800
BIGFOOT 1275	1275	2	5738	*	15.5	5.25	4H	IDE(AT)	PRML	2492	N/A	N/A	
BIGFOOT 1275AT	1275	2	5738	*	15.5	5.25	4H	IDE(AT)	PRML	2492	N/A	N/A	
BIGFOOT 2550	4994	4	5738	*	15.5	5.25	4H	IDE(AT)	PRML	4994	N/A	N/A	
BIGFOOT 2550AT	4994	4	5738	*	15.5	5.25	4H	IDE(AT)	PRML	4994	N/A	N/A	
CAPELLA VP31110	1108	4	4165	*	9	3.50	3H	SCSI-2F	RLL 1,7	AUTO	N/A	N/A	800
CAPELLA VP31110W	1108	4	4165	*	9	3.50	3H	SCSI-2 F/W	RLL 1,7	AUTO	N/A	N/A	800
CAPELLA VP31110WD	1108	4	4165	*	9	3.50	3H	SCSI-2 FWD	RLL 1,7	AUTO	N/A	N/A	800
CAPELLA VP32210	2216	8	4165	*	9	3.50	3H	SCSI-2F	RLL 1,7	AUTO	N/A	N/A	800
CAPELLA VP32210W	2216	8	4165	*	9	3.50	3H	SCSI-2 F/W	RLL 1,7	AUTO	N/A	N/A	800
CAPELLA VP32210WD	2216	8	4165	*	9	3.50	3H	SCSI-2 FWD	RLL 1,7	AUTO	N/A	N/A	800
DAYTONA 127AT	127	—	—	—	17	2.50	3H	IDE(AT)	RLL 1,7	AUTO	N/A	N/A	350
DAYTONA 127S	127	2	—	*	17	2.50	5H	SCSI	RLL 1,7	AUTO	N/A	N/A	350
DAYTONA 170AT	170	—	—	—	17	2.50	3H	IDE(AT)	RLL 1,7	AUTO	N/A	N/A	350
DAYTONA 170S	170	3	—	*	17	2.50	5H	SCSI	RLL 1,7	AUTO	N/A	N/A	350

QUANTUM CORPORATION

MODEL	CAP	HDS	CYL	SPT	SEEK	FF	HGT	INT	ENCODE	LZ	WP	RWC	MTBF
DAYTONA 256AT	256	–	–	–	17	2.50	3H	IDE(AT)	RLL 1,7	AUTO	N/A	N/A	350
DAYTONA 256S	256	4	–	*	17	2.50	5H	SCSI	RLL 1,7	AUTO	N/A	N/A	350
DAYTONA 341AT	341	–	–	–	17	2.50	3H	IDE(AT)	RLL 1,7	AUTO	N/A	N/A	350
DAYTONA 341S	341	6	–	*	17	2.50	4H	SCSI	RLL 1,7	AUTO	N/A	N/A	350
DAYTONA 514AT	514	–	–	–	17	2.50	3H	IDE(AT)	RLL 1,7	AUTO	N/A	N/A	350
DAYTONA 514S	514	8	–	*	17	2.50	4H	SCSI	RLL 1,7	AUTO	N/A	N/A	350
DSP3053L	535	4	3117	*	9.5	3.50	3H	SCSI-2 W	RLL 1,7	AUTO	N/A	N/A	500
DSP3053LD	535	4	3117	*	9.5	3.50	3H	SCSI-2DIFF	RLL 1,7	AUTO	N/A	N/A	500
DSP3085	852	14	–	57	9.5	3.50	HH	SCSI-2	NONE	AUTO	N/A	N/A	0
DSP3105	1050	14	–	57	9.5	3.50	HH	SCSI-2	NONE	AUTO	N/A	N/A	250
DSP3105D	1050	14	–	57	9.5	3.50	HH	SCSI-2	NONE	AUTO	N/A	N/A	250
DSP3107L	1070	8	3117	*	9.5	3.50	3H	SCSI-2DIFF	RLL 1,7	AUTO	N/A	N/A	500
DSP3107LD	1070	8	3117	*	9.5	3.50	3H	SCSI-2DIFF	RLL 1,7	AUTO	N/A	N/A	500
DSP3133L	1338	10	3117	*	9.5	3.50	3H	SCSI-2	RLL 1,7	AUTO	N/A	N/A	500
DSP3133LD	1338	10	3117	*	9.5	3.50	3H	SCSI-2DIFF	RLL 1,7	AUTO	N/A	N/A	500
DSP3160	1600	16	2599	*	9.7	3.50	3H	SCSI-2	RLL 1,7	AUTO	N/A	N/A	350
DSP3210	2148	16	3045	*	9.5	3.50	3H	SCSI-2	RLL 1,7	AUTO	N/A	N/A	500
EMPIRE 1080S	1232.00	8	2874	*	10	3.50	HH	SCSI-3	RLL 1,7	AUTO	N/A	N/A	500
EMPIRE 1400S	1400	8	3115	*	10	3.50	HH	SCSI-3	PRML	AUTO	N/A	N/A	500
EMPIRE 1440S	1440	8	–	*	11	3.50	HH	SCSI-3	RLL 1,7	AUTO	N/A	N/A	500
EMPIRE 2100S	2100	12	3115	*	10	3.50	HH	SCSI-3	PRML	AUTO	N/A	N/A	500
EMPIRE 2160S	2160	12	–	*	11	3.50	HH	SCSI-3	RLL 1,7	AUTO	N/A	N/A	500
EMPIRE 540S	540.00	4	2874	*	10	3.50	HH	SCSI-3	RLL 1,7	AUTO	N/A	N/A	500
EPS 510	107					5.25	FH	SCSI-2F	UNIDENT				
EPS 530	267					5.25	FH	SCSI-2F	UNIDENT				
EPS 540	428					5.25	FH	SCSI-2F	UNIDENT				
EPS 580	856					5.25	FH	SCSI-2F	UNIDENT				
EUROPA 1080AT	1.08G	8	2,925	*	14	2.50	4H	IDE(AT)	PRML	AUTO	N/A	N/A	350
EUROPA 540AT	540	4	2,925	*	14	2.50	5H	IDE(AT)	PRML	AUTO	N/A	N/A	350
EUROPA 810AT	810	6	2,925	*	14	2.50	4H	IDE(AT)	PRML	AUTO	N/A	N/A	350
FIREBALL 1080AT	1089	4	3835	*	12	3.50	3H	IDE(AT)	PRML	2112	N/A	N/A	500
FIREBALL 1080S	1092.7	4	3835	*	12	3.50	3H	SCSI-3	PRML	AUTO	N/A	N/A	500
FIREBALL 1280AT	1282	4	4142	*	12	3.50	3H	IDE(AT)	PRML	AUTO	N/A	N/A	500
FIREBALL 540AT	544	2	3835	*	12	3.50	3H	IDE(AT)	PRML	1056	N/A	N/A	500
FIREBALL 540S	545.4	2	3835	*	12	3.50	3H	SCSI-3	PRML	AUTO	N/A	N/A	500
FIREBALL 640AT	642	2	4142	*	12	3.50	3H	IDE(AT)	PRML	AUTO	N/A	N/A	500
FIREBALL TM 1.0AT	1080	2	6825	*	12	3.50	3H	IDE(AT)	PRML	AUTO	N/A	N/A	400K
FIREBALL TM 2.1AT	2168	4	6825	*	10.5	3.50	3H	IDE(AT)	PRML	AUTO	N/A	N/A	400
FIREBALL TM 3.2AT	3254	6	6825	*	10.5	3.50	3H	IDE(AT)	PRML	AUTO	N/A	N/A	400K

QUANTUM CORPORATION

MODEL	CAP	HDS	CYL	SPT	SEEK	FF	HGT	INT	ENCODE	LZ	WP	RWC	MTBF
GODRIVE 120AT	126.62	4	1097	*	19	2.50	3H	IDE(AT)	RLL 1,7	AUTO	N/A	N/A	150
GODRIVE 120S	126.62	4	1097	*	19	2.50	3H	SCSI	RLL 1,7	AUTO	N/A	N/A	150
GODRIVE 120S	126.6	4	*	*	17	2.50	4H	SCSI	RLL 1,7	AUTO	N/A	N/A	150
GODRIVE 40AT	41.15	2	957	42	19	2.50	3H	IDE(AT)	RLL 1,7	AUTO	N/A	N/A	80
GODRIVE 40S	42.90	2	870	*	19	2.50	3H	SCSI	RLL 1,7	AUTO	N/A	N/A	80
GODRIVE 60AT	63.03	2	1097	*	19	2.50	3H	IDE(AT)	RLL 1,7	AUTO	N/A	N/A	150
GODRIVE 60S	63	2	*	*	17	2.50	5H	SCSI	RLL 1,7	AUTO	N/A	N/A	150
GODRIVE 80AT	82.31	4	957	42	19	2.50	3H	IDE(AT)	RLL 1,7	AUTO	N/A	N/A	80
GODRIVE 80S	86.30	4	870	*	19	2.50	3H	SCSI	RLL 1,7	AUTO	N/A	N/A	80
GODRIVE GLS 127AT	127.90	3	1395	*	17	2.50	3H	IDE(AT)	RLL 1,7	AUTO	N/A	N/A	350
GODRIVE GLS 127S	127.91	3	1395	*	17	2.50	3H	SCSI	RLL 1,7	AUTO	N/A	N/A	350
GODRIVE GLS 170AT	170.78	4	1395	*	17	2.50	3H	IDE(AT)	RLL 1,7	AUTO	N/A	N/A	350
GODRIVE GLS 170S	170.78	4	1395	*	17	2.50	3H	SCSI	RLL 1,7	AUTO	N/A	N/A	350
GODRIVE GLS 256AT	256.53	6	1395	*	17	2.50	3H	IDE(AT)	RLL 1,7	AUTO	N/A	N/A	350
GODRIVE GLS 256S	256.53	6	1395	*	17	2.50	3H	SCSI	RLL 1,7	AUTO	N/A	N/A	350
GODRIVE GLS 85AT	85.02	2	1395	*	17	2.50	3H	IDE(AT)	RLL 1,7	AUTO	N/A	N/A	350
GODRIVE GLS 85S	85.03	2	1395	*	17	2.50	3H	SCSI	RLL 1,7	AUTO	N/A	N/A	350
GODRIVE GRS 160AT	169.87	4	1376	*	17	2.50	3H	IDE(AT)	RLL 1,7	AUTO	N/A	N/A	150
GODRIVE GRS 160S	168.16	4	1376	*	17	2.50	3H	SCSI-2	RLL 1,7	AUTO	N/A	N/A	150
GODRIVE GRS 80AT	84.08	2	1376	*	17	2.50	3H	IDE(AT)	RLL 1,7	AUTO	N/A	N/A	150
GODRIVE GRS 80S	84.10	2	1376	*	17	2.50	3H	SCSI-2	RLL 1,7	AUTO	N/A	N/A	150
GRAND PRIX XP32151S	2152	10	—	*	9.6	3.50	HH	SCSI	UNIDENT	AUTO	N/A	N/A	800
GRAND PRIX XP34301S	4306	20	—	*	9.6	3.50	HH	SCSI	UNIDENT	AUTO	N/A	N/A	800
LIGHTNING 365AT	365.7	—	—	—	13	3.50	HH	IDE(AT)	RLL 1,7	AUTO	N/A	N/A	300
LIGHTNING 365S	366.5	2	—	*	13	3.50	HH	SCSI-2	RLL 1,7	AUTO	N/A	N/A	300
LIGHTNING 540AT	541.3	—	—	—	13.5	3.50	HH	IDE(AT)	RLL 1,7	AUTO	N/A	N/A	300
LIGHTNING 540S	550.7	2	—	*	12.5	3.50	HH	SCSI-2	RLL 1,7	AUTO	N/A	N/A	300
LIGHTNING 730AT	730.8	—	—	—	13.5	3.50	HH	IDE(AT)	RLL 1,7	AUTO	N/A	N/A	300

QUANTUM CORPORATION

MODEL	CAP	HDS	CYL	SPT	SEEK	FF	HGT	INT	ENCODE	LZ	WP	RWC	MTBF
LIGHTNING 730S	733.1	4	–	*	13.5	3.50	HH	SCSI-2	RLL 1,7	AUTO	N/A	N/A	300
MAVERICK 270AT	270.66	2	2740	*	12	3.50	3H	IDE(AT)	RLL 1,7	944	N/A	N/A	300
MAVERICK 270S	270.7	2	–	*	14	3.50	3H	SCSI	RLL 1,7	AUTO	N/A	N/A	300
MAVERICK 540AT	541.32	4	2740	*	12	3.50	3H	IDE(AT)	RLL 1,7	1120	N/A	N/A	300
MAVERICK 540S	541.5	4	–	*	14	3.50	3H	SCSI	RLL 1,7	AUTO	N/A	N/A	300
PRODRIVE 1050S	1054.71	12	2448	*	11	3.50	HH	SCSI	RLL 1,7	AUTO	N/A	N/A	150
PRODRIVE 105AT	105.24	4	1219	*	17	3.50	HH	IDE(AT)	RLL 2,7	AUTO	N/A	N/A	60
PRODRIVE 105S	104.99	6	1019	*	19	3.50	HH	SCSI	RLL 2,7	AUTO	N/A	N/A	50
PRODRIVE 1080S	1232.00	8	2874	*	10	3.50	HH	SCSI-3	RLL 1,7	AUTO	N/A	N/A	500
PRODRIVE 120AT	120.04	5	1123	*	15	3.50	HH	IDE(AT)	RLL 1,7	AUTO	N/A	N/A	50
PRODRIVE 120S	120.04	5	1123	*	15	3.50	HH	SCSI	RLL 1,7	AUTO	N/A	N/A	50
PRODRIVE 1225S	1230.50	14	2448	*	11	3.50	HH	SCSI	RLL 1,7	AUTO	N/A	N/A	150
PRODRIVE 160AT	168.39	4	839	*	19	3.50	HH	IDE(AT)	RLL 1,7	AUTO	N/A	N/A	80
PRODRIVE 170AT	168.52	7	1123	*	15	3.50	HH	IDE(AT)	RLL 1,7	AUTO	N/A	N/A	50
PRODRIVE 170S	169.52	7	1123	*	15	3.50	HH	SCSI	RLL 1,7	AUTO	N/A	N/A	50
PRODRIVE 1800S	1800.00	14	2959	*	12	3.50	HH	SCSI-2	RLL 1,7	AUTO	N/A	N/A	350
PRODRIVE 210AT	209.19	7	1156	*	15	3.50	HH	IDE(AT)	RLL 1,7	AUTO	N/A	N/A	50
PRODRIVE 210S	209.19	7	1156	*	15	3.50	HH	SCSI	RLL 1,7	AUTO	N/A	N/A	50
PRODRIVE 40AT	42.27	3	834	*	19	3.50	HH	IDE(AT)	RLL 2,7	AUTO	N/A	N/A	50
PRODRIVE 40S	42.27	3	834	*	19	3.50	HH	SCSI	RLL 2,7	AUTO	N/A	N/A	50
PRODRIVE 425	426.57	9	1512	*	14	3.50	HH	IDE(AT)	RLL 1,7	AUTO	N/A	N/A	150
PRODRIVE 425AT	426	9	1520	44-78	14	3.50	HH	IDE(AT)	RLL 1,7	N/A	N/A	N/A	150
PRODRIVE 425IAT	426.57	9	1512	*	14	3.50	HH	IDE(AT)	RLL 1,7	AUTO	N/A	N/A	150
PRODRIVE 425IS	426.57	9	1512	*	14	3.50	HH	SCSI	RLL 1,7	AUTO	N/A	N/A	150
PRODRIVE 425S	426.57	9	1512	*	14	3.50	HH	SCSI	RLL 1,7	AUTO	N/A	N/A	150
PRODRIVE 525S	525.00	6	2448	*	11	3.50	3H	SCSI-2	RLL 1,7	AUTO	N/A	N/A	350
PRODRIVE 52S	52.42	2	1219	*	17	3.50	HH	SCSI	RLL 2,7	AUTO	N/A	N/A	60

QUANTUM CORPORATION

MODEL	CAP	HDS	CYL	SPT	SEEK	FF	HGT	INT	ENCODE	LZ	WP	RWC	MTBF
PRODRIVE 700S	703.14	8	2448	*	11	3.50	HH	SCSI	RLL 1,7	AUTO	N/A	N/A	150
PRODRIVE 80AT	84.54	6	834	*	19	3.50	HH	IDE(AT)	RLL 2,7	AUTO	N/A	N/A	50
PRODRIVE 80S	84.54	6	834	*	19	3.50	HH	SCSI	RLL 2,7	AUTO	N/A	N/A	50
PRODRIVE ELS 127AT	127.98	2	1536	*	17	3.50	3H	IDE(AT)	RLL 1,7	AUTO	N/A	N/A	250
PRODRIVE ELS 127S	127.98	2	1536	*	17	3.50	3H	SCSI	RLL 1,7	AUTO	N/A	N/A	250
PRODRIVE ELS 170AT	170.81	4	1536	*	17	3.50	3H	IDE(AT)	RLL 1,7	AUTO	N/A	N/A	250
PRODRIVE ELS 170S	170.81	4	1536	*	17	3.50	3H	SCSI	RLL 1,7	AUTO	N/A	N/A	250
PRODRIVE ELS 42AT	42.12	1	1536	*	19	3.50	3H	IDE(AT)	RLL 2,7	AUTO	N/A	N/A	250
PRODRIVE ELS 42S	42.12	1	1536	*	19	3.50	3H	SCSI	RLL 2,7	AUTO	N/A	N/A	250
PRODRIVE ELS 85AT	85.03	2	1536	*	17	3.50	3H	IDE(AT)	RLL 2,7	AUTO	N/A	N/A	250
PRODRIVE ELS 85S	85.03	2	1536	*	17	3.50	3H	SCSI	RLL 2,7	AUTO	N/A	N/A	250
PRODRIVE LPS 105AT	104.85	4	1219	*	17	3.50	3H	IDE(AT)	RLL 2,7	AUTO	N/A	N/A	60
PRODRIVE LPS 105S	104.85	4	1219	*	17	3.50	3H	SCSI	RLL 2,7	AUTO	N/A	N/A	60
PRODRIVE LPS 120AT	122.24	2	1800	*	17	3.50	3H	IDE(AT)	RLL 2,7	AUTO	N/A	N/A	250
PRODRIVE LPS 120S	122.00	2	1800	*	17	3.50	3H	SCSI	RLL 1,7	AUTO	N/A	N/A	250
PRODRIVE LPS 127AT	127.9	–	–	–	14	3.50	3H	IDE(AT)	RLL	AUTO	N/A	N/A	300
PRODRIVE LPS 127S	128.31	2	1745	*	5	3.50	3H	SCSI-2	RLL 1,7	AUTO	N/A	N/A	300
PRODRIVE LPS 170AT	426.57	9	1520	*	14	3.50	HH	IDE(AT)	RLL 1,7	AUTO	N/A	N/A	150
PRODRIVE LPS 170S	171.65	2	2337	*	5	3.50	3H	SCSI-2	RLL 1,7	AUTO	N/A	N/A	300
PRODRIVE LPS 210AT	211	2	–	–	14	3.50	3H	IDE(AT)	RLL 1,7	AUTO	N/A	N/A	300
PRODRIVE LPS 240AT	245.42	4	1800	*	17	3.50	3H	IDE(AT)	RLL 1,7	AUTO	N/A	N/A	250
PRODRIVE LPS 240S	245.00	4	1800	*	17	3.50	3H	SCSI	RLL 1,7	AUTO	N/A	N/A	250
PRODRIVE LPS 270AT	270.66	2	2740	*	12	3.50	3H	IDE(AT)	RLL 1,7	944	N/A	N/A	300
PRODRIVE LPS 270S	270.66	2	2740	*	12	3.50	3H	SCSI-2	RLL 1,7	AUTO	N/A	N/A	300
PRODRIVE LPS 340AT	340.	4	1800	*	17	3.50	3H	IDE(AT)	RLL 1,7	AUTO	N/A	N/A	250

QUANTUM CORPORATION

MODEL	CAP	HDS	CYL	SPT	SEEK	FF	HGT	INT	ENCODE	LZ	WP	RWC	MTBF
PRODRIVE LPS 340S	342.63	4	2337	*	12	3.50	3H	SCSI-2	RLL 1,7	AUTO	N/A	N/A	300
PRODRIVE LPS 420AT	421.9	–	–	–	12	3.50	3H	IDE(AT)	RLL	AUTO	N/A	N/A	300
PRODRIVE LPS 525AT	524.86	6	2448	*	11	3.50	HH	IDE(AT)	RLL 1,7	AUTO	N/A	N/A	250
PRODRIVE LPS 525S	525	6	–	*	12	3.50	HH	SCSI-2	RLL 1,7	AUTO	N/A	N/A	250
PRODRIVE LPS 52AT	52.42	2	1219	*	17	3.50	3H	IDE(AT)	RLL 2,7	AUTO	N/A	N/A	60
PRODRIVE LPS 52S	52.42	2	1219	*	17	3.50	3H	SCSI	RLL 2,7	AUTO	N/A	N/A	60
PRODRIVE LPS 540AT	541.32	4	2740	*	12	3.50	3H	IDE(AT)	RLL 1,7	1120	N/A	N/A	300
PRODRIVE LPS 540S	541.33	4	2740	*	12	3.50	3H	SCSI-2	RLL 1,7	AUTO	N/A	N/A	300
PRODRIVE LPS 80AT	85	–	–	–	19	3.50	3H	IDE(AT)	RLL 2,7	AUTO	N/A	N/A	60
PRODRIVE LPS 80S	85	4	-	*	19	3.50	3H	SCSI	RLL 2,7	AUTO	N/A	N/A	60
Q-160	200.00	12	1800	–	26	5.25	HH	SCSI	RLL 1,7	AUTO	N/A	N/A	0
Q-2010	16.77	2	512	32	55	8.00	FH	SA1000	MFM	–	256	256	12
Q-2020	33.55	4	512	32	60	8.00	FH	SA1000	MFM	–	256	256	12
Q-2030	50.33	6	512	32	60	8.00	FH	SA1000	MFM	–	256	256	12
Q-2040	67.10	8	512	32	65	8.00	FH	SA1000	MFM	–	256	256	12
Q-2080	134.41	7	1172	32	40	8.00	FH	SA1000	MFM	–	256	256	8
Q-250	53.93	4	823	32	26	5.25	HH	SCSI	RLL 1,7	AUTO	256	256	25
Q-280	80.90	6	823	32	26	5.25	HH	SCSI	RLL 1,7	AUTO	256	256	25
Q-510	8.91	2	512	17	30	5.25	HH	ST-506/412	MFM	–	256	256	0
Q-520	17.82	4	512	17	–	5.25	HH	ST-506/412	MFM	–	256	256	0
Q-540	35.65	8	512	17	45	5.25	FH	ST-506/412	MFM	–	256	256	15
SATURN VP31080	1085				8.5	3.50	3H	SCSI-2F	UNIDENT	N/A	N/A	N/A	800K
SATURN SCSI-2 VP31080S	1080	5			8.5	3.50	3H	SCSI-2	RLL 1,7				
SATURN VP32170	2170				8.5	3.50	3H	SCSI-2F	UNIDENT	N/A	N/A	N/A	800K
SATURN SCSI-2 VP32170S	2170				8.5	3.50	3H	SCSI-2	RLL 1,7	AUTO	N/A	N/A	
SIROCCO 1700AT	1700	4			11	3.50	3H	IDE(AT)	UNIDENT	AUTO	N/A	N/A	400
SIROCCO 2550AT	2250	6			11	3.50	3H	IDE(AT)	UNIDENT	AUTO	N/A	N/A	400
TRAILBLAZER 420AT	421.97	2	3653	*	14	3.50	3H	IDE(AT)	RLL 1,7	AUTO	N/A	N/A	300
TRAILBLAZER 420S	425	2	3653	*	14	3.50	3H	SCSI-2	RLL 1,7	AUTO	N/A	N/A	300

QUANTUM CORPORATION

MODEL	CAP	HDS	CYL	SPT	SEEK	FF	HGT	INT	ENCODE	LZ	WP	RWC	MTBF
TRAILBLAZER 635AT	636.86	3	3653	*	14	3.50	3H	IDE(AT)	RLL 1,7	AUTO	N/A	N/A	300
TRAILBLAZER 840S	852	3	3653	*	14	3.50	3H	SCSI-2	RLL 1,7	AUTO	N/A	N/A	300
TRAILBLAZER 850AT	850	4	3653	*	14	3.50	3H	IDE(AT)	RLL 1,7	AUTO	N/A	N/A	300
TRAILBLAZER 850S	852	4	3653	*	14	3.50	3H	SCSI-2	RLL 1,7	AUTO	N/A	N/A	300

RICOH CORPORATION

MODEL	CAP	HDS	CYL	SPT	SEEK	FF	HGT	INT	ENCODE	LZ	WP	RWC	MTBF
RH-5130	10.65	2	612	17	85	5.25	HH	ST-506/412	MFM	—	400	613	0
RH-5260	10.70	2	615	17	85	5.25	HH	ST-506/412	MFM	—	—	—	0
RH-5261	10.65	2	612	17	85	5.25	HH	SCSI	RLL	AUTO	N/A	N/A	0
RH-5500	100.00	2	1285	76	25	5.25	HH	SCSI	RLL 2,7	AUTO	N/A	N/A	20
RS-9150AR	100.00	2	1285	76	25	5.25	HH	SCSI	RLL 2,7	AUTO	N/A	N/A	20

RMS

MODEL	CAP	HDS	CYL	SPT	SEEK	FF	HGT	INT	ENCODE	LZ	WP	RWC	MTBF
RMS 506	5.32	4	153	17	—	5.25	FH	ST-506/412	MFM	—	77	77	0
RMS 509	7.99	6	153	17	—	5.25	FH	ST-506/412	MFM	—	77	77	0
RMS 512	10.65	8	153	17	—	5.25	FH	ST-506/412	MFM	—	77	77	0

RODIME, INC.

MODEL	CAP	HDS	CYL	SPT	SEEK	FF	HGT	INT	ENCODE	LZ	WP	RWC	MTBF
COBRA 110AT	110.00	4	—	—	20	3.50	HH	IDE(AT)	RLL 2,7	AUTO	N/A	N/A	40
COBRA 210AT	210.00	5	—	—	20	3.50	HH	IDE(AT)	RLL 2,7	AUTO	N/A	N/A	40
COBRA 40AT	40.00	—	—	—	<20	3.50	HH	IDE(AT)	RLL 2,7	AUTO	N/A	N/A	40
COBRA 80AT	80.00	—	—	—	<20	3.50	HH	IDE(AT)	RLL 2,7	AUTO	N/A	N/A	40
RO101	3.34	2	192	17	55	5.25	FH	ST-506/412	MFM	—	192	96	0
RO102	6.68	4	192	17	55	5.25	FH	ST-506/412	MFM	—	192	96	0
RO103	10.02	6	192	17	55	5.25	FH	ST-506/412	MFM	—	192	96	0
RO104	13.36	8	192	17	55	5.25	FH	ST-506/412	MFM	—	192	96	0
RO200	11.14	4	320	17	—	5.25	FH	ST-506/412	MFM	—	132	—	0
RO201	5.57	2	320	17	85	5.25	FH	ST-506/412	MFM	—	0	132	0
RO201E	11.14	2	640	17	55	5.25	FH	ST-506/412	MFM	—	300	264	0
RO202	11.14	4	320	17	85	5.25	HH	ST-506/412	MFM	—	300	132	0
RO202E	22.28	4	640	17	55	5.25	FH	ST-506/412	MFM	—	300	264	0
RO203	16.71	6	320	17	85	5.25	HH	ST-506/412	MFM	—	300	132	0
RO203E	33.42	6	640	17	55	5.25	FH	ST-506/412	MFM	—	300	264	0

RODIME, INC.

MODEL	CAP	HDS	CYL	SPT	SEEK	FF	HGT	INT	ENCODE	LZ	WP	RWC	MTBF
RO204	22.28	8	320	17	85	5.25	FH	ST-506/412	MFM	–	300	132	0
RO204E	44.56	8	640	17	55	5.25	FH	ST-506/412	MFM	–	300	264	0
RO251	5.32	2	306	17	85	5.25	HH	ST-506/412	MFM	–	307	307	0
RO252	10.65	4	306	17	85	5.25	HH	ST-506/412	MFM	–	128	64	0
RO3045	37.94	5	872	17	28	3.50	HH	ST-506/412	MFM	–	–	873	0
RO3055	45.53	6	872	17	28	3.50	HH	ST-506/412	MFM	–	–	873	0
RO3055T	45.28	3	1053	28	–	3.50	HH	SCSI	RLL	AUTO	N/A	N/A	0
RO3057S	62.04	3	1224	33	28	3.50	HH	SCSI	RLL 2,7	AUTO	N/A	N/A	0
RO3058A	45.33	3	868	34	18	3.50	HH	IDE(AT)	RLL 2,7	AUTO	N/A	N/A	20
RO3058T	45.33	3	868	34	18	3.50	HH	SCSI	RLL 2,7	AUTO	N/A	N/A	20
RO3059A	46.00	2	1216	–	18	3.50	HH	IDE(AT)	RLL 2,7	AUTO	N/A	N/A	20
RO3059T	42.33	2	1216	34	18	3.50	HH	SCSI	RLL 2,7	AUTO	N/A	N/A	20
RO3060R	49.92	5	750	26	28	3.50	HH	ST-506/412	RLL 2,7	–	600	–	20
RO3065	53.12	7	872	17	28	3.50	HH	ST-506/412	MFM	–	650	–	20
RO3070S	71.00	–	–	–	28	3.50	HH	SCSI	RLL 2,7	AUTO	N/A	N/A	0
RO3075R	59.90	6	750	26	28	3.50	HH	ST-506/412	RLL 2,7	–	650	–	20
RO3085R	69.88	7	750	26	28	3.50	HH	ST-506/412	RLL 2,7	–	650	–	20
RO3085S	69.88	7	750	26	28	3.50	HH	SCSI	RLL 2,7	AUTO	N/A	N/A	0
RO3088A	75.55	5	868	34	18	3.50	HH	IDE(AT)	RLL 2,7	AUTO	N/A	N/A	20
RO3088T	75.55	5	868	34	18	3.50	HH	SCSI	RLL 2,7	AUTO	N/A	N/A	20
RO3089A	63.50	3	1216	34	18	3.50	HH	IDE(AT)	RLL 2,7	AUTO	N/A	N/A	20
RO3089T	63.50	3	1216	34	18	3.50	HH	SCSI	RLL 2,7	AUTO	N/A	N/A	20
RO3090T	75.47	5	1053	28	–	3.50	HH	SCSI	RLL 2,7	AUTO	N/A	N/A	0
RO3095A	80.33	5	923	34	18	3.50	HH	IDE(AT)	RLL 2,7	AUTO	N/A	N/A	20
RO3099A	80.20	4	1030	*	–	3.50	HH	IDE(AT)	RLL 2,7	AUTO	N/A	N/A	0
RO3099AP	80.20	4	1030	*	–	3.50	HH	IDE(AT)	RLL 2,7	AUTO	N/A	N/A	0
RO3128A	105.77	7	868	34	18	3.50	HH	IDE(AT)	RLL 2,7	AUTO	N/A	N/A	20
RO3128T	105.77	7	868	34	18	3.50	HH	SCSI	RLL 2,7	AUTO	N/A	N/A	20
RO3129A	47.43	5	1090	17	18	3.50	HH	IDE(AT)	RLL 2,7	AUTO	N/A	N/A	20
RO3129T	47.43	5	1090	17	18	3.50	HH	SCSI	RLL 2,7	AUTO	N/A	N/A	20
RO3130S	112.57	7	1047	30	22	5.25	HH	SCSI	RLL 2,7	AUTO	N/A	N/A	20
RO3130T	105.67	7	1053	28	–	3.50	HH	SCSI	RLL 2,7	AUTO	N/A	N/A	0
RO3135A	112.47	7	923	34	19	3.50	HH	IDE(AT)	RLL 2,7	AUTO	N/A	N/A	20
RO3139A	50.83	5	1168	*	18	3.50	HH	IDE(AT)	RLL 2,7	AUTO	N/A	N/A	20
RO3139AP	112.46	5	1168	*	–	3.50	HH	IDE(AT)	RLL 2,7	AUTO	N/A	N/A	0
RO3139TP	112.85	5	1148	*	–	3.50	HH	SCSI	RLL 2,7	AUTO	N/A	N/A	0
RO3258T	210.00	–	–	–	18	3.50	HH	SCSI	RLL 2,7	AUTO	N/A	N/A	32
RO3259A	209.87	9	1235	*	18	3.50	HH	IDE(AT)	RLL 2,7	AUTO	N/A	N/A	0
RO3259AP	212.88	9	1235	*	–	3.50	HH	IDE(AT)	RLL 2,7	AUTO	N/A	N/A	0
RO3259T	210.00	9	1216	–	18	3.50	HH	SCSI	RLL 2,7	AUTO	N/A	N/A	0
RO3259TP	210.54	9	1148	*	–	3.50	HH	SCSI	RLL 2,7	AUTO	N/A	N/A	0
RO351	5.32	2	306	17	85	3.50	HH	ST-506/412	MFM	–	307	307	0

RODIME, INC.

MODEL	CAP	HDS	CYL	SPT	SEEK	FF	HGT	INT	ENCODE	LZ	WP	RWC	MTBF
RO352	10.65	4	306	17	85	3.50	HH	ST-506/412	MFM	—	128	64	0
RO365	21.30	4	612	17	—	3.50	HH	ST-506/412	MFM	—	613	613	0
RO5040S	38.00	3	—	17	28	5.25	HH	SCSI	RLL	AUTO	N/A	N/A	0
RO5065	53.26	5	1224	17	28	5.25	HH	ST-506/412	MFM	—	N/A	N/A	0
RO5075E	65.80	3	1224	35	—	5.25	HH	ESDI-10MHZ	RLL 2,7	—	N/A	N/A	0
RO5075S	62.04	3	1224	33	28	5.25	HH	SCSI	RLL 2,7	AUTO	N/A	N/A	0
RO5078S	62.04	3	1224	33	—	5.25	HH	SCSI	RLL 2,7	AUTO	N/A	N/A	0
RO5090	74.57	7	1224	17	28	5.25	HH	ST-506/412	MFM	—	600	—	0
RO5095R	81.46	5	1224	26	—	5.25	HH	ST-506/412	RLL 2,7	AUTO	N/A	N/A	0
RO5125-1F2	106.10	5	1219	34	18	5.25	HH	SCSI	RLL 2,7	AUTO	N/A	N/A	20
RO5125E	109.67	5	1224	35	18	5.25	HH	ESDI-10MHZ	RLL 2,7	AUTO	N/A	N/A	25
RO5125S	103.40	5	1224	33	28	5.25	HH	SCSI	RLL 2,7	AUTO	N/A	N/A	0
RO5128S	103.40	5	1224	33	—	5.25	HH	SCSI	RLL 2,7	AUTO	N/A	N/A	0
RO5130R	114.05	7	1224	26	28	5.25	HH	ST-506/412	RLL 2,7	—	N/A	N/A	20
RO5178S	144.76	7	1224	33	19	5.25	HH	SCSI	RLL 2,7	AUTO	N/A	N/A	0
RO5180-1F2	148.54	7	1219	34	19	5.25	HH	SCSI	RLL 2,7	AUTO	N/A	N/A	20
RO5180E	153.53	7	1224	35	18	5.25	HH	ESDI-10MHZ	RLL 2,7	AUTO	N/A	N/A	25
RO5180S	144.76	7	1224	33	28	5.25	HH	SCSI	RLL 2,7	AUTO	N/A	N/A	0
RO652	20.68	4	306	33	85	3.50	HH	SCSI	RLL 2,7	AUTO	N/A	N/A	0
RO752	20.68	4	306	33	85	5.25	HH	SCSI	RLL 2,7	AUTO	N/A	N/A	0

SAMSUNG ELECTRONICS, INC.

MODEL	CAP	HDS	CYL	SPT	SEEK	FF	HGT	INT	ENCODE	LZ	WP	RWC	MTBF
PLS-30544A	540	2	3952	*	11	3.50	3H	IDE(AT)	RLL 1,7				300,0
PLS-30854A	850	4	3858	*	11	3.50	3H	IDE(AT)	RLL 1,7	1647	0	N/A	300
PLS-30854S	850	4	3858	*	11	3.50	3H	SCSI-2F	RLL 1,7	1647	0	N/A	300
PLS-31084A	1080	5	3840	*	11	3.50	3H	IDE(AT)	RLL 1,7	2055	0	N/A	300
PLS-31084S	1080	5	3840	*	11	3.50	3H	SCSI-2	RLL 1,7	2055	0	N/A	300
PLS-31274A	1272.6	5	3844	*	11	3.50	3H	IDE(AT)	RLL 1,7	2466	0	N/A	300
PLS-31274S	1272.6	5	3844	*	11	3.50	3H	SCSI-2	RLL 1,7	2466	0	N/A	300
SHD-2040N	43.66	4	820	26	—	3.50	HH	ST-506/412	RLL 2,7	—	544	—	0
SHD-2041B	47.02	4	820	28	25	3.50	HH	IDE(AT)	RLL 2,7	AUTO	N/A	N/A	0
SHD-30280A	280.3	2	2668	*	12	3.50	3H	IDE(AT)	RLL 1,7	AUTO	N/A	N/A	250
SHD-30420A	420.7	3	2668	*	12	3.50	3H	IDE(AT)	RLL 1,7	AUTO	N/A	N/A	250
SHD-30560A	560.9	4	2668	*	12	3.50	3H	IDE(AT)	RLL 1,7	AUTO	N/A	N/A	250
SHD-3061A	60.53	2	1478	40	16	3.50	3H	IDE(AT)	RLL 1,7	AUTO	N/A	N/A	200
SHD-3062A	121.07	4	1478	40	16	3.50	3H	IDE(AT)	RLL 1,7	AUTO	N/A	N/A	200
SHD-3101A	105.02	4	1282	40	16	3.50	3H	IDE(AT)	RLL 1,7	AUTO	N/A	N/A	200
SHD-3121A	125.90	2	1956	*	16	3.50	3H	IDE(AT)	RLL 2,7	AUTO	N/A	N/A	250
SHD-3122A	251.90	4	1956	*	16	3.50	3H	IDE(AT)	RLL 2,7	AUTO	N/A	N/A	250
SHD-3171A	178.42	2	2227	*	13	3.50	3H	IDE(AT)	RLL	AUTO	N/A	N/A	250

SAMSUNG ELECTRONICS, INC.

MODEL	CAP	HDS	CYL	SPT	SEEK	FF	HGT	INT	ENCODE	LZ	WP	RWC	MTBF
SHD-3171A1	178	2	2210	*	13	3.50	3H	IDE(AT)	RLL 1,7	AUTO	N/A	N/A	250
SHD-3172A	356.84	4	2227	*	13	3.50	3H	IDE(AT)	RLL	AUTO	N/A	N/A	250
SHD-3172A1	356	4	2210	*	13	3.50	3H	IDE(AT)	RLL 1,7	AUTO	N/A	N/A	250
SHD-3202S	212.05	7	1376	43	16	3.50	HH	SCSI	RLL 1,7	AUTO	N/A	N/A	50
SHD-3210S	212.05	7	1376	43	16	3.50	HH	SCSI	RLL 1,7	AUTO	N/A	N/A	50
SHD-3211A	213.4	2	2570	*	13	3.50	3H	IDE(AT)	RLL 1,7	AUTO	N/A	N/A	250
SHD-3212A	426.8	4	2570	*	13	3.50	3H	IDE(AT)	RLL 1,7	AUTO	N/A	N/A	250
STG-31271A	1281	4		*	12	3.50	3H	IDE(AT)	UNIDENT	AUTO	N/A	N/A	300
STG-31601A	1601	4		*	12	3.50	3H	IDE(AT)	UNIDENT	AUTO	N/A	N/A	300
TBR-31081A	1080	4		*	9	3.50	3H	IDE(AT)	RLL 1,7	AUTO	N/A	N/A	500

SEAGATE TECHNOLOGY, INC.

MODEL	CAP	HDS	CYL	SPT	SEEK	FF	HGT	INT	ENCODE	LZ	WP	RWC	MTBF
ST1057A	53.47	6	1024	17	18	3.50	HH	IDE(AT)	RLL	AUTO	N/A	N/A	150
ST1057N	49.09	3	940	34	18	3.50	HH	SCSI-2	RLL 2,7	AUTO	N/A	N/A	150
ST1090A	79.58	5	1072	29	15	3.50	HH	IDE(AT)	RLL 2,7	AUTO	N/A	N/A	150
ST1090N	79.28	5	1068	29	15	3.50	HH	SCSI	RLL 2,7	AUTO	N/A	N/A	150
ST1096N	84.42	7	906	26	24	3.50	HH	SCSI	RLL 2,7	AUTO	N/A	N/A	150
ST1100	83.97	9	1072	17	15	3.50	HH	ST-506/412	MFM	AUTO	1,073	1,073	150
ST1102A	89.12	10	1024	17	18	3.50	HH	IDE(AT)	RLL	AUTO	N/A	N/A	50
ST1102N	83.99	5	965	*	20	3.50	HH	SCSI-2	RLL	AUTO	N/A	N/A	50
ST1106R	91.04	7	977	26	24	3.50	HH	ST-506/412	RLL 2,7	–	978	978	50
ST1111A	98.79	5	1072	36	15	3.50	HH	IDE(AT)	RLL 2,7	AUTO	N/A	N/A	70
ST1111E	98.79	5	1072	36	15	3.50	HH	ESDI-10MHZ	RLL 2,7	AUTO	N/A	N/A	150
ST1111N	98.42	5	1068	36	15	3.50	HH	SCSI	RLL 2,7	AUTO	N/A	N/A	70
ST11200N	1054.00	15	1872	*	11.2	3.50	HH	SCSI-2	RLL 1,7	AUTO	N/A	N/A	200
ST11200NC	1050.00	15	1877	*	12	3.50	HH	SCSI SCA	RLL 1,7	AUTO	N/A	N/A	200
ST11200ND	1050.00	15	1877	*	12	3.50	HH	SCSI-2DIFF	RLL 1,7	AUTO	N/A	N/A	200
ST11201N	1050.00	15	1877	*	12	3.50	HH	SCSI-2	RLL 1,7	AUTO	N/A	N/A	200
ST11201ND	1050.00	15	1877	*	12	3.50	HH	SCSI-2DIFF	RLL 1,7	AUTO	N/A	N/A	500
ST1126A	111.41	7	1072	29	15	3.50	HH	IDE(AT)	RLL 2,7	AUTO	N/A	N/A	150
ST1126N	111.00	7	1068	29	15	3.50	HH	SCSI	RLL 2,7	AUTO	N/A	N/A	150
ST1133A	117.22	5	1272	36	15	3.50	HH	IDE(AT)	RLL 2,7	AUTO	N/A	N/A	150
ST1133N	116.85	5	1268	36	15	3.50	HH	SCSI-2	RLL 2,7	AUTO	N/A	N/A	150
ST1144A	130.69	7	–	*	18	3.50	HH	IDE(AT)	RLL	AUTO	N/A	N/A	150
ST1144N	125.00	7	–	*	20	3.50	HH	SCSI-2	RLL	AUTO	N/A	N/A	50
ST1150R	128.43	9	1072	26	15	3.50	HH	ST-506/412	RLL 2,7	AUTO	300	1,073	150
ST1156A	138.31	7	1072	36	15	3.50	HH	IDE(AT)	RLL 2,7	AUTO	N/A	N/A	150
ST1156E	138.31	7	1072	36	15	3.50	HH	ESDI-10MHZ	RLL 2,7	AUTO	N/A	N/A	70
ST1156N	137.79	7	1068	36	15	3.50	HH	SCSI	RLL 2,7	AUTO	N/A	N/A	70
ST1156NS	137.79	7	1068	36	15	3.50	HH	SCSI-2	RLL 2,7	AUTO	N/A	N/A	70

SEAGATE TECHNOLOGY, INC.

MODEL	CAP	HDS	CYL	SPT	SEEK	FF	HGT	INT	ENCODE	LZ	WP	RWC	MTBF
ST1162A	143.25	9	1072	29	15	3.50	HH	IDE(AT)	RLL 2,7	AUTO	N/A	N/A	150
ST1162N	142.71	9	1068	29	15	3.50	HH	SCSI	RLL 2,7	AUTO	N/A	N/A	70
ST11700N	1430.0	13	2626	*	10.5	3.50	HH	SCSI-2	RLL 1,7	AUTO	N/A	N/A	500
ST11700ND	1430.0	13	2626	*	10.5	3.50	HH	SCSI-2DIFF	RLL 1,7	AUTO	N/A	N/A	500
ST1186A	164.11	7	1272	36	15	3.50	HH	IDE(AT)	RLL 2,7	AUTO	N/A	N/A	150
ST1186N	163.60	7	1268	36	15	3.50	HH	SCSI-2	RLL 2,7	AUTO	N/A	N/A	150
ST11900N	1700.00	15	2621	*	10.5	3.50	HH	SCSI-2	RLL 1,7	AUTO	N/A	N/A	500
ST11900NC	1700.00	15	2621	*	10.5	3.50	HH	SCSI SCA	RLL 1,7	AUTO	N/A	N/A	500
ST11900ND	1700.00	15	2621	*	10.5	3.50	HH	SCSI-2	RLL 1,7	AUTO	N/A	N/A	500
ST11900W	1430.00	13	2626	*	10.5	3.50	HH	SCSI-2 F/W	RLL 1,7	AUTO	N/A	N/A	500
ST11900WC	1700	15	2621	83	10	3.50	HH	SCSI-2 F/W	RLL 1,7	AUTO	N/A	N/A	500
ST11900WD	1430.00	13	2626	*	10.5	3.50	HH	SCSI-2 F/W	RLL 1,7	AUTO	N/A	N/A	500
ST11950N	1690	15	2706	*	9	3.50	HH	SCSI-2	RLL 1,7	AUTO	N/A	N/A	500
ST11950ND	1690	15	2706	*	9	3.50	HH	SCSI-2	RLL 1,7	AUTO	N/A	N/A	500
ST11950W	1690	15	2706	*	9	3.50	HH	SCSI-2 W	RLL 1,7	AUTO	N/A	N/A	500
ST11950WD	1690	15	2706	*	9	3.50	HH	SCSI-2 W/D	RLL 1,7	AUTO	N/A	N/A	500
ST1201A	177.83	9	1072	36	15	3.50	HH	IDE(AT)	RLL 2,7	AUTO	N/A	N/A	150
ST1201E	177.83	9	1072	36	15	3.50	HH	ESDI-10MHZ	RLL 2,7	AUTO	N/A	N/A	150
ST1201N	177.16	9	1068	36	15	3.50	HH	SCSI	RLL 2,7	AUTO	N/A	N/A	150
ST1201NS	177.16	9	1068	36	15	3.50	HH	SCSI-2	RLL 2,7	AUTO	N/A	N/A	150
ST1239A	211.00	9	1272	—	15	3.50	HH	IDE(AT)	RLL 2,7	AUTO	N/A	N/A	150
ST1239N	210.34	9	1268	36	15	3.50	HH	SCSI-2	RLL 2,7	AUTO	N/A	N/A	150
ST124	21.41	4	615	17	40	3.50	HH	ST-506/412	MFM	670	616	616	150
ST12400N	2148.00	19	2621	*	10.5	3.50	HH	SCSI-2	RLL 1,7	AUTO	N/A	N/A	500
ST12400NC	2100.0	19`	2626	*	10.5	3.50	HH	SCSI SCA	RLL 1,7	AUTO	N/A	N/A	500
ST12400ND	2148.00	19	2621	*	10.5	3.50	HH	SCSI-2DIFF	RLL 1,7	AUTO	N/A	N/A	500
ST12400W	21.00	19	2626	*	10	3.50	HH	SCSI-2 W	RLL 1,7	AUTO	N/A	N/A	500
ST12400WC	2148	19	2621	*	10	3.50	HH	SCSI-2 W	RLL 1,7	AUTO	N/A	N/A	500
ST12400WD	21.00	19	2626	*	10	3.50	HH	SCSI-2 W/D	RLL 1,7	AUTO	N/A	N/A	500
ST12401N	21.00	19	2626	*	10.5	3.50	HH	SCSI-2	RLL 1,7	AUTO	N/A	N/A	500
ST12401ND	21.00	19	2626	*	10.5	3.50	HH	SCSI-2DIFF	RLL 1,7	AUTO	N/A	N/A	500
ST12450W	2134	18	2710	*	9	3.50	HH	SCSI-2 F/W	RLL 1,7	AUTO	N/A	N/A	500
ST12450WD	2134	18	2710	*	9	3.50	HH	SCSI-2 F/W	RLL 1,7	AUTO	N/A	N/A	500
ST125	21.41	4	615	17	40	3.50	HH	ST-506/412	MFM	AUTO	616	616	150
ST125-1	21.41	4	615	17	28	3.50	HH	ST-506/412	MFM	AUTO	616	616	150
ST12550N	2139	19	2707	*	9	3.50	HH	SCSI-2	RLL 1,7	AUTO	N/A	N/A	500
ST12550ND	2139	19	2707	*	9	3.50	HH	SCSI-2	RLL 1,7	AUTO	N/A	N/A	500
ST12550W	2139	19	2707	*	9	3.50	HH	SCSI-2 W	RLL 1,7	AUTO	N/A	N/A	500
ST12550WD	2139	19	2707	*	9	3.50	HH	SCSI-2 W/D	RLL 1,7	AUTO	N/A	N/A	500
ST12551N	2100.00	19	2756	*	9	3.50	HH	SCSI-2	RLL 1,7	AUTO	N/A	N/A	500
ST12551ND	2100.00	19	2756	*	9	3.50	HH	SCSI-2DIFF	RLL 1,7	AUTO	N/A	N/A	500
ST125A	21.51	4	404	26	40	3.50	HH	IDE(AT)	RLL 2,7	AUTO	N/A	N/A	70

SEAGATE TECHNOLOGY, INC.

MODEL	CAP	HDS	CYL	SPT	SEEK	FF	HGT	INT	ENCODE	LZ	WP	RWC	MTBF
T125A-1	21.51	4	404	26	28	3.50	HH	IDE(AT)	RLL 2,7	AUTO	N/A	N/A	70
ST125N	21.67	4	407	26	40	3.50	HH	SCSI	RLL 2,7	AUTO	N/A	N/A	70
ST125N-1	21.67	4	407	26	28	3.50	HH	SCSI	RLL 2,7	AUTO	N/A	N/A	70
ST125R	21.51	4	404	26	80	3.50	HH	ST-506/412	RLL 2,7	404	N/A	N/A	150
ST1274A	21.67	4	407	26	18	3.50	HH	IDE(AT)	RLL 2,7	AUTO	N/A	N/A	70
ST137R	32.74	4	615	26	40	3.50	HH	ST-506/412	RLL 2,7	AUTO	–	–	70
ST138	32.11	6	615	17	40	3.50	HH	ST-506/412	MFM	AUTO	616	616	150
ST138-1	32.11	6	615	17	28	3.50	HH	ST-506/412	MFM	AUTO	616	616	150
ST138A	32.16	4	604	26	40	3.50	HH	IDE(AT)	RLL 2,7	AUTO	N/A	N/A	150
ST138A-1	32.16	4	604	26	28	3.50	HH	IDE(AT)	RLL 2,7	AUTO	N/A	N/A	150
ST138N	32.74	4	615	26	40	3.50	HH	SCSI	RLL 2,7	AUTO	N/A	N/A	150
ST138N-1	32.74	4	615	26	28	3.50	HH	SCSI	RLL 2,7	AUTO	N/A	N/A	150
ST138R	32.74	4	615	26	40	3.50	HH	ST-506/412	RLL 2,7	AUTO	616	616	150
ST138R-1	32.74	4	615	26	28	3.50	HH	ST-506/412	RLL 2,7	AUTO	616	616	150
ST1400A	331.00	7	1478	*	14	3.50	HH	IDE(AT)	RLL	AUTO	N/A	N/A	150
ST1400N	331.00	7	1476	*	14	3.50	HH	SCSI-2	RLL	AUTO	N/A	N/A	150
ST1401A	340.00	9	1100	*	12	3.50	HH	IDE(AT)	RLL	AUTO	N/A	N/A	150
ST1401N	340.00	9	1100	*	12	3.50	HH	SCSI-2	RLL	AUTO	N/A	N/A	150
ST1480A	426.00	9	1478	*	14	3.50	HH	IDE(AT)	RLL	AUTO	N/A	N/A	150
ST1480N	426.00	9	1476	*	14	3.50	HH	SCSI-2	RLL	AUTO	N/A	N/A	150
ST1480NV	426.00	9	1478	*	14	3.50	HH	SCSI-2	RLL 1,7	AUTO	N/A	N/A	150
ST1481N	426.00	9	1476	*	14	3.50	HH	SCSI-2	RLL	AUTO	N/A	N/A	150
ST151	42.51	5	977	17	24	3.50	HH	ST-506/412	MFM	AUTO	978	978	150
ST15150DC	4294	21	3711	*	8.5	3.50	HH	SCSI-2 F/W	RLL 1,7	AUTO	N/A	N/A	800
ST15150N	4297	21	3711	*	9	3.50	HH	SCSI-2 W	RLL 1,7	AUTO	N/A	N/A	800
ST15150ND	4294	21	3711	*	9	3.50	HH	SCSI-2 W	RLL 1,7	AUTO	N/A	N/A	800
ST15150W	4294	21	3711	*	9	3.50	HH	SCSI-2 F/W	RLL 1,7	AUTO	N/A	N/A	800
ST15150WC	4294	21	3711	*	8.5	3.50	HH	SCSI-2 F/W	RLL 1,7	AUTO	N/A	N/A	800
ST15150WD	4294	21	3711	*	9	3.50	HH	SCSI-2 F/W	RLL 1,7	AUTO	N/A	N/A	800
ST15230DC	4,294	19	3992		16.84	3.50	HH	SCSI SCA	UNIDENT	AUTO	N/A	N/A	800
ST15230N	4294	19	3992	110	10.5	3.50	HH	SCSI-2F	RLL 1,7	AUTO	N/A	N/A	800
ST15230NC	4294	19	3992	110	10.5	3.50	HH	SCSI-2F	RLL 1,7	AUTO	N/A	N/A	800
ST15230ND	4596	19	3992	110	10.5	3.50	HH	SCSI-2F	RLL 1,7	AUTO	N/A	N/A	800
ST15230W	4294	19	3992	110	10.9	3.50	3H	SCSI-2 F/W	RLL 1,7	AUTO	N/A	N/A	800
ST15230WC	4294	19	3992	110	10.9	3.50	3H	SCSI-2 F/W	RLL 1,7	AUTO	N/A	N/A	800
ST15230WD	4294	19	3992	*	10.9	3.50	HH	SCSI-2 F/W	RLL 1,7	AUTO	N/A	N/A	800
ST157A	44.72	6	560	26	40	3.50	HH	IDE(AT)	RLL 2,7	AUTO	N/A	N/A	150
ST157A-1	44.72	6	560	26	28	3.50	HH	IDE(AT)	RLL 2,7	AUTO	N/A	N/A	150
ST157N	48.96	6	613	26	40	3.50	HH	SCSI	RLL 2,7	AUTO	N/A	N/A	150
ST157N-1	48.96	6	613	26	28	3.50	HH	SCSI	RLL 2,7	AUTO	N/A	N/A	150
ST157R	49.12	6	615	26	40	3.50	HH	ST-506/412	RLL 2,7	AUTO	616	616	150
ST157R-1	49.12	6	615	26	28	3.50	HH	ST-506/412	RLL 2,7	AUTO	616	616	150

SEAGATE TECHNOLOGY, INC.

MODEL	CAP	HDS	CYL	SPT	SEEK	FF	HGT	INT	ENCODE	LZ	WP	RWC	MTBF
ST1581N	525.00	9	1476	*	14	3.50	HH	SCSI-2	RLL	AUTO	N/A	N/A	150
ST177N	61.30	5	921	26	24	3.50	HH	SCSI	RLL 2,7	AUTO	N/A	N/A	150
ST1830N	702.00	–	–	–	–	3.50	HH	SCSI-2F	RLL	AUTO	N/A	N/A	0
ST1950N	803.00	13	1575	*	–	3.50	HH	SCSI-2F	RLL	AUTO	N/A	N/A	0
ST1980N	860.00	13	1730	*	11.4	3.50	HH	SCSI-2	RLL 1,7	AUTO	N/A	N/A	200
ST1980NC	860.00	13	1730	*	9	3.50	HH	SCSI SCA	RLL 1,7	AUTO	N/A	N/A	200
ST1980ND	860.00	13	1730	*	9	3.50	HH	SCSI-2DIFF	RLL 1,7	AUTO	N/A	N/A	200
ST206	5.32	2	306	17	–	5.25	HH	ST-506/412	MFM	–	128	307	0
ST2106E	94.37	5	1024	36	18	5.25	HH	ESDI-10MHZ	RLL 2,7	AUTO	N/A	N/A	100
ST2106N	94.18	5	1022	36	18	5.25	HH	SCSI	RLL 2,7	AUTO	N/A	N/A	100
ST2106NM	94.18	5	1022	36	18	5.25	HH	SCSI	RLL 2,7	AUTO	N/A	N/A	100
ST212 -V1	10.65	4	306	17	–	5.25	HH	ST-506/412	MFM	319	128	307	11
ST212 -V2	10.65	4	306	17	–	5.25	HH	ST-506/412	MFM	319	128	307	11
ST212 -V3	10.65	4	306	17	–	5.25	HH	ST-506/412	MFM	319	128	307	11
ST2125N	107.00	3	1544	*	18	5.25	HH	SCSI	RLL	AUTO	N/A	N/A	100
ST2125NM	107.00	3	1544	*	18	5.25	HH	SCSI	RLL	AUTO	N/A	N/A	100
ST2125NV	107.00	3	1544	*	18	5.25	HH	SCSI	RLL	AUTO	N/A	N/A	100
ST213	10.70	2	615	17	65	5.25	HH	ST-506/412	MFM	670	300	N/A	20
ST2182E	160.69	4	1453	54	16	5.25	HH	ESDI-15MHZ	RLL 2,7	AUTO	N/A	N/A	100
ST2209N	183.00	5	1544	*	18	5.25	HH	SCSI	RLL	AUTO	N/A	N/A	100
ST2209NM	183.00	5	1544	*	18	5.25	HH	SCSI	RLL	AUTO	N/A	N/A	100
ST2209NV	183.00	5	1544	*	18	5.25	HH	SCSI	RLL	AUTO	N/A	N/A	100
ST224N	21.41	4	615	17	70	5.25	HH	SCSI	RLL 2,7	AUTO	N/A	N/A	100
ST225	21.41	4	615	17	65	5.25	HH	ST-506/412	MFM	670	300	N/A	100
ST225N	21.41	4	615	17	65	5.25	HH	SCSI	RLL	670	N/A	N/A	100
ST225R	21.17	2	667	31	70	5.25	HH	ST-506/412	RLL 2,7	667	–	–	100
ST2274A	241.50	5	1747	54	16	5.25	HH	IDE(AT)	RLL 2,7	AUTO	N/A	N/A	100
ST238	32.74	4	615	26	65	5.25	HH	ST-506/412	RLL 2,7	615	–	–	100
ST2383A	338.10	7	1747	54	16	5.25	HH	IDE(AT)	RLL 2,7	AUTO	N/A	N/A	100
ST2383E	338.10	7	1747	54	16	5.25	HH	ESDI-15MHZ	RLL 2,7	AUTO	N/A	N/A	100
ST2383N	332.00	7	1261	*	14	5.25	HH	SCSI	RLL	AUTO	N/A	N/A	100
ST2383NM	332.00	7	1261	*	14	5.25	HH	SCSI	RLL	AUTO	N/A	N/A	100
ST238R	32.74	4	615	26	65	5.25	HH	ST-506/412	RLL 2,7	615	–	–	100
ST2502N	442.00	7	1755	*	16	5.25	HH	SCSI	RLL	AUTO	N/A	N/A	100
ST2502NM	442.00	7	1755	*	16	5.25	HH	SCSI	RLL	AUTO	N/A	N/A	100
ST2502NV	442.00	7	1755	*	16	5.25	HH	SCSI	RLL	AUTO	N/A	N/A	100
ST250N	42.34	4	667	31	70	5.25	HH	SCSI	RLL 2,7	AUTO	N/A	N/A	100
ST250R	42.34	4	667	31	70	5.25	HH	ST-506/412	RLL 2,7	670	–	–	100
ST251	42.82	6	820	17	40	5.25	HH	ST-506/412	MFM	AUTO	–	–	100
ST251-1	42.82	6	820	17	28	5.25	HH	ST-506/412	MFM	AUTO	821	821	100
ST251N	43.66	4	820	26	40	5.25	HH	SCSI	RLL 2,7	AUTO	N/A	N/A	70
ST251N-1	43.86	4	630	34	28	5.25	HH	SCSI	RLL 2,7	AUTO	N/A	N/A	70

SEAGATE TECHNOLOGY, INC.

MODEL	CAP	HDS	CYL	SPT	SEEK	FF	HGT	INT	ENCODE	LZ	WP	RWC	MTBF
ST251R	43.66	4	820	26	40	5.25	HH	ST-506/412	RLL 2,7	–	–	–	100
ST252	42.82	6	820	17	40	5.25	HH	ST-506/412	MFM	AUTO	–	–	100
ST253	43.04	5	989	17	28	5.25	HH	ST-506/412	MFM	AUTO	–	–	40
ST274A	63.09	5	948	26	28	5.25	HH	IDE(AT)	RLL 2,7	AUTO	N/A	N/A	40
ST277N	65.49	6	820	26	40	5.25	HH	SCSI	RLL 2,7	AUTO	N/A	N/A	70
ST277N-1	65.59	6	628	34	28	5.25	HH	SCSI	RLL 2,7	AUTO	N/A	N/A	70
ST277R	65.49	6	820	26	40	5.25	HH	ST-506/412	RLL 2,7	AUTO	–	–	70
ST277R-1	65.49	6	820	26	28	5.25	HH	ST-506/412	RLL 2,7	AUTO	–	–	70
ST278R	65.49	6	820	26	40	5.25	HH	ST-506/412	RLL 2,7	AUTO	–	–	70
ST279R	65.82	5	989	26	28	5.25	HH	ST-506/412	RLL 2,7	AUTO	–	–	40
ST280A	71.33	5	1032	27	28	5.25	HH	IDE(AT)	RLL 2,7	AUTO	N/A	N/A	40
ST296N	85.64	6	820	34	28	5.25	HH	SCSI	RLL 2,7	AUTO	N/A	N/A	70
ST3025A	21.51	1	1616	26	20	3.50	3H	IDE(AT)	RLL 2,7	AUTO	N/A	N/A	50
ST3025N	21.51	1	1616	26	20	3.50	3H	SCSI-2	RLL 2,7	AUTO	N/A	N/A	50
ST3051A	43.10	–	–	–	16	3.50	3H	IDE(AT)	RLL 2,7	AUTO	N/A	N/A	150
ST3057N	49.09	3	940	34	20	3.50	3H	SCSI-2	RLL 2,7	AUTO	N/A	N/A	50
ST3096A	89.12	10	1024	17	<15	3.50	3H	IDE(AT)	RLL 2,7	AUTO	N/A	N/A	50
ST3096N	89.12	10	1024	17	<15	3.50	3H	SCSI-2	RLL 2,7	AUTO	N/A	N/A	50
ST31051N	1050	4	4569	*		3.50	3H	SCSI-2F	RLL	AUTO	N/A	N/A	800
ST31051W	1050	4	4569	*		3.50	3H	SCSI-2 F/W	RLL	AUTO	N/A	N/A	800
ST31051WC	1050	4	4569	*		3.50	4H	SCSI SCA	RLL	AUTO	N/A	N/A	800
ST31055N	1060	4	4176	*	10.9	3.50	3H	SCSI-2	RLL	AUTO	N/A	N/A	800
ST31055W	1060	4	4176	123	10.9	3.50	3H	SCSI-2 W	RLL	AUTO	N/A	N/A	800
ST31055WC	1060	4	4176	*	10.9	3.50	3H	SCSI-2 W	RLL	AUTO	N/A	N/A	800
ST31200N	1052.40	9	2700	*	10.5	3.50	3H	SCSI-2	RLL 1,7	AUTO	N/A	N/A	200
ST31200NC	1052	9	2700	84	9.3	3.50	3H	SCSI SCA	RLL 1,7	AUTO	N/A	N/A	500
ST31200ND	1052.4	9	2700	*	10.5	3.50	3H	SCSI-2	RLL 1,7	AUTO	N/A	N/A	200
ST31200W	1052	9	2700	84	9.3	3.50	3H	SCSI-2 F/W	RLL 1,7	AUTO	N/A	N/A	500
ST31200WC	1052	9	2700	84	9.3	3.50	3H	SCSI-2 F/W	RLL 1,7	AUTO	N/A	N/A	500
ST31200WD	1052	9	2700	84	9.3	3.50	3H	SCSI-2 F/W	RLL 1,7	AUTO	N/A	N/A	500
ST3120A	106.9	–	–	–	15	3.50	3H	IDE(AT)	RLL 2,7	AUTO	N/A	N/A	150
ST31220A	1083.2	6	–	–	12	3.50	3H	IDE(AT)	RLL 1,7	AUTO	N/A	N/A	300
ST31220A -V2	1088	6			13	3.50	3H	IDE(AT)	RLL 1,7	AUTO	N/A	N/A	300
ST31230DC	1060	5	3992		10.9	3.50	3H	SCSI-2 W/DUNIDENT		AUTO	N/A	N/A	800
ST31230N	1060	5	3992	103	11	3.50	3H	SCSI-2F	RLL 1,7	AUTO	N/A	N/A	800
ST31230NC	1060	5	3992	103	11	3.50	3H	SCSI SCA	RLL 1,7	AUTO	N/A	N/A	800
ST31230ND	1060	5	3992	103	11	3.50	3H	SCSI-2DIFF	RLL 1,7	AUTO	N/A	N/A	800
ST31230W	1060	5	3992		10.9	3.50	3H	SCSI-2 W	RLL	AUTO	N/A	N/A	800
ST31230WC	1060	5	3992	*	10.9	3.50	3H	SCSI-2 F/W	RLL 1,7	AUTO	N/A	N/A	800
ST31230WD	1060	5	3992		10.9	3.50	3H	SCSI-2 F/W	RLL	AUTO	N/A	N/A	800
ST31231N	1060	5	3992	103	10.9	3.50	3H	SCSI-2F	RLL 1,7	AUTO	N/A	N/A	800
ST3123A	106.6	–	–	–	16	3.50	3H	IDE(AT)	RLL 1,7	AUTO	N/A	N/A	250

SEAGATE TECHNOLOGY, INC.

MODEL	CAP	HDS	CYL	SPT	SEEK	FF	HGT	INT	ENCODE	LZ	WP	RWC	MTBF
ST31250DC	1020.9	5	3711	*	8.5	3.50	3H	SCSI SCA	RLL 1,7	AUTO	N/A	N/A	800
ST31250N	1020.9	5	3711	*	8.5	3.50	3H	SCSI-2F	RLL 1,7	AUTO	N/A	N/A	800
ST31250ND	1020.9	5	3711	*	8.5	3.50	3H	SCSI-2F	RLL 1,7	AUTO	N/A	N/A	800
ST31250W	1020.9	5	3711	*	8.5	3.50	3H	SCSI-2F	RLL 1,7	AUTO	N/A	N/A	800
ST31250WC	1020.9	5	3711	*	8.5	3.50	3H	SCSI SCA	RLL 1,7	AUTO	N/A	N/A	800
ST31250WD	1020.9	5	3711	*	8.5	3.50	3H	SCSI-2F	RLL 1,7	AUTO	N/A	N/A	800
ST31270A	1282.8				12	3.50	3H	IDE(AT)	RLL 1,7	AUTO	N/A	N/A	300
ST3144A	130.69	3	—	*	—	3.50	3H	IDE(AT)	RLL 2,7	AUTO	N/A	N/A	150
ST3145A	130.2	2	—	*	16	3.50	3H	IDE(AT)	RLL 1,7	AUTO	N/A	N/A	250
ST31640A	1625.7	6	4834	*	10	3.50	3H	IDE(AT)	RLL 1,7	AUTO	N/A	N/A	500
ST31930N	1700.00	—	—	—	<10	3.50	3H	SCSI-2	RLL	AUTO	N/A	N/A	0
ST31930ND	1700.00	—	—	—	<10	3.50	3H	SCSI-2	RLL	AUTO	N/A	N/A	0
ST3195A	170.77	4	—	*	16	3.50	3H	IDE(AT)	RLL 2,7	AUTO	N/A	N/A	150
ST32140A	2113.4	8	4726	*	10	3.50	3H	IDE(AT)	RLL 1,7	AUTO	N/A	N/A	500
ST32151N	2147	8	4569	*		3.50	3H	SCSI-2F	RLL	AUTO	N/A	N/A	800
ST32151W	2147	8	4569	*		3.50	3H	SCSI-2 F/W	RLL	AUTO	N/A	N/A	800
ST32151WC	2147	8	4569	*		3.50	4H	SCSI SCA	RLL	AUTO	N/A	N/A	800
ST32155N	2148	8	4176	*	10.9	3.50	3H	SCSI-2	RLL	AUTO	N/A	N/A	800
ST32155W	2148	8	4176	125	10.9	3.50	3H	SCSI-2 W	RLL	AUTO	N/A	N/A	800
ST32155WC	2148	8	4176	*	10.9	3.50	3H	SCSI-2 W	RLL	AUTO	N/A	N/A	800
ST32430DC	2140	9	3992		10.9	3.50	3H	SCSI SCA	UNIDENT	AUTO	N/A	N/A	800
ST32430N	2140	9	3992	116	11	3.50	3H	SCSI-2F	RLL 1,7	AUTO	N/A	N/A	800
ST32430NC	2140	9	3992	116	11	3.50	3H	SCSI SCA	RLL 1,7	AUTO	N/A	N/A	800
ST32430ND	2140	9	3992	116	11	3.50	3H	SCSI-2DIFF	RLL 1,7	AUTO	N/A	N/A	800
ST32430W	2140	9	3892	*	9	3.50	3H	SCSI-2 F/W	RLL 1,7	AUTO	N/A	N/A	800
ST32430WC	2140	9	3992	116	10.9	3.50	3H	SCSI-2 W	RLL 1,7	AUTO	N/A	N/A	800
ST32430WD	2140	9	3992	*	10.9	3.50	3H	SCSI-2 F/W	RLL 1,7	AUTO	N/A	N/A	800
ST3243A	213.90	4	—	*	16	3.50	3H	IDE(AT)	RLL 2,7	AUTO	N/A	N/A	150
ST3250A	213.90	2	—	—	14	3.50	3H	IDE(AT)	RLL 1,7	AUTO	N/A	N/A	300
ST32550DC	2147.8	11	3510	*	8.5	3.50	3H	SCSI SCA	RLL 1,7	AUTO	N/A	N/A	800
ST32550N	2147.8	11	3510	*	8.5	3.50	3H	SCSI-2F	RLL 1,7	AUTO	N/A	N/A	800
ST32550ND	2147.8	11	3510	*	8.5	3.50	3H	SCSI-2F	RLL 1,7	AUTO	N/A	N/A	800
ST32550W	2147.8	11	3510	*	8.5	3.50	3H	SCSI-2F	RLL 1,7	AUTO	N/A	N/A	800
ST32550WC	2147.8	11	3510	*	8.5	3.50	3H	SCSI SCA	RLL 1,7	AUTO	N/A	N/A	800
ST32550WD	2147.8	11	3510	*	8.5	3.50	3H	SCSI-2F	RLL 1,7	AUTO	N/A	N/A	800
ST325A\X	21.41	2	697	30	28	3.50	3H	IDE(XT/AT)	RLL 2,7	AUTO	N/A	N/A	150
ST325N	21.41	2	697	30	45	3.50	3H	SCSI	RLL 2,7	AUTO	N/A	N/A	50
ST3283A	245.36	5	1691	*	16	3.50	3H	IDE(AT)	RLL 2,7	AUTO	N/A	N/A	150
ST3283N	245.36	5	1691	*	16	3.50	3H	SCSI	RLL 2,7	AUTO	N/A	N/A	150
ST3285N	248.62	3	1689	*	12	3.50	3H	SCSI-2F	RLL 1,7	AUTO	N/A	N/A	250

SEAGATE TECHNOLOGY, INC.

MODEL	CAP	HDS	CYL	SPT	SEEK	FF	HGT	INT	ENCODE	LZ	WP	RWC	MTBF
ST3290A	261.38	4	1691	*	16	3.50	3H	IDE(AT)	RLL 1,7	AUTO	N/A	N/A	150
ST3291A	272.74	4	–	–	13	3.50	3H	IDE(AT)	RLL 1,7	AUTO	N/A	N/A	300
ST3295A	272.7	2	–	–	14	3.50	3H	IDE(AT)	RLL 1,7	AUTO	N/A	N/A	300
ST3385A	340.00	5	1691	*	16	3.50	3H	IDE(AT)	RLL 2,7	AUTO	N/A	N/A	150
ST3390A	341.30	3	2676	*	12	3.50	3H	IDE(AT)	RLL 2,7	AUTO	N/A	N/A	250
ST3390N	344.30	3	2676	*	12	3.50	3H	SCSI-2	RLL 2,7	AUTO	N/A	N/A	250
ST3391A	341.31	4	–	–	13	3.50	3H	IDE(AT)	RLL 1,7	AUTO	N/A	N/A	300
ST3491A	428.1	4–	–	–	14	3.50	3H	IDE(AT)	RLL 1,7	AUTO	N/A	N/A	300
ST3500A	426.16	7	1874	*	12	3.50	3H	IDE(AT)	RLL 1,7	AUTO	N/A	N/A	200
ST3500N	525.00	7	1872	*	12	3.50	3H	SCSI-2	RLL 1,7	AUTO	N/A	N/A	200
ST351A\X	42.82	6	820	17	28	3.50	3H	IDE(XT/AT)	RLL 2,7	AUTO	N/A	N/A	150
ST352	42.82	6	820	17	28	3.50	3H	IDE(XT/AT)	RLL 2,7	AUTO	N/A	N/A	150
ST3550A	452.41	5	1691	*	16	3.50	3H	IDE(AT)	RLL 2,7	AUTO	N/A	N/A	150
ST3550N	456.48	5	2128	*	12	3.50	3H	SCSI-2	RLL 1,7	AUTO	N/A	N/A	200
ST3600A -A	528.48	7	1874	*	28.48	3.50	3H	IDE(AT)	RLL 1,7	AUTO	N/A	N/A	200
ST3600A -B	528.48	7	1874	*		3.50	3H	IDE(AT)	RLL 1,7	AUTO	N/A	N/A	200
ST3600N	525.00	7	1872	*	12	3.50	3H	SCSI-2	RLL 1,7	AUTO	N/A	N/A	200
ST3600ND	525.00	7	1872	*	12	3.50	3H	SCSI-2DIFF	RLL 1,7	AUTO	N/A	N/A	200
ST3610N	535.00	7	1872	*	12	3.50	3H	SCSI-2	RLL 1,7	AUTO	N/A	N/A	200
ST3610NC	570	7	1872	*	13	3.50	3H	SCSI SCA	RLL 1,7	AUTO	N/A	N/A	0
ST3610ND	535.00	7	1872	*	12	3.50	3H	SCSI-2DIFF	RLL 1,7	AUTO	N/A	N/A	200
ST3620N	545.9	5	2700	78	11	3.50	3H	SCSI-2F	RLL 1,7	AUTO	N/A	N/A	500
ST3620NC	545.9	5	2700	78	11	3.50	3H	SCSI SCA	RLL 1,7	AUTO	N/A	N/A	500
ST3620ND	545.9	5	2700	78	11	3.50	3H	SCSI-2DIFF	RLL 1,7	AUTO	N/A	N/A	500
ST3620W	545.9					3.50	3H	SCSI-2 W	RLL 1,7	AUTO	NA	N/A	400
ST3630A	631.1	4		*	14	3.50	3H	IDE(AT)	RLL 1,7	AUTO	N/A	N/A	300
ST3655A	528.48	5	–	*	12	3.50	3H	IDE(AT)	RLL 2,7	AUTO	N/A	N/A	200
ST3655N	545.48	5	2676	79	12	3.50	3H	SCSI-2	RLL 1,7	AUTO	N/A	N/A	200
ST3660A	545.00	–	–	–	14	3.50	3H	IDE(AT)	RLL 1,7	AUTO	N/A	N/A	300
ST3780A	722.02	4	–	–	12	3.50	3H	IDE(AT)	RLL 1,7	AUTO	N/A	N/A	300
ST3780A	722	4			12	3.50	3H	IDE(AT)	RLL 1,7	AUTO	N/A	N/A	300
ST4026	21.41	4	615	17	40	5.25	FH	ST-506/412	MFM	AUTO	307	616	15
ST4038	31.90	5	733	17	40	5.25	FH	ST-506/412	MFM	AUTO	734	734	25
ST4038M	31.90	5	733	17	40	5.25	FH	ST-506/412	MFM	AUTO	734	734	25
ST4051	42.51	5	977	17	40	5.25	FH	ST-506/412	MFM	AUTO	978	978	40
ST4053	44.56	5	1024	17	28	5.25	FH	ST-506/412	MFM	AUTO	1,024	1,024	40
ST406	5.32	2	306	17	85	5.25	FH	ST-506/412	MFM	319	128	307	11
ST4077N	68.15	5	1024	26	28	5.25	FH	SCSI	RLL 2,7	AUTO	N/A	N/A	0
ST4077R	68.15	5	1024	26	28	5.25	FH	ST-506/412	RLL 2,7	–	1,025	1,025	0
ST4085	71.30	8	1024	17	28	5.25	FH	ST-506/412	MFM	AUTO	1,025	1,025	40
ST4086	72.46	9	925	17	28	5.25	FH	ST-506/412	MFM	AUTO	926	926	40
ST4096	80.21	9	1024	17	28	5.25	FH	ST-506/412	MFM	AUTO	1,025	1,025	40

SEAGATE TECHNOLOGY, INC.

MODEL	CAP	HDS	CYL	SPT	SEEK	FF	HGT	INT	ENCODE	LZ	WP	RWC	MTBF
ST4096N	80.21	9	1024	17	28	5.25	FH	SCSI	RLL	AUTO	N/A	N/A	40
ST4097	80.21	9	1024	17	28	5.25	FH	ST-506/412	MFM	AUTO	1,024	1,024	40
ST410800N	9090	27	4925	*	13	5.25	FH	SCSI-2 W	RLL 1,7	AUTO	–	–	500
ST410800ND	9080.00	27	4925	*	13	5.25	FH	SCSI-2	RLL 1,7	AUTO	N/A	N/A	500
ST410800W	9090.00	27	4925	*	13	5.25	FH	SCSI-2 F/W	RLL 1,7	AUTO	N/A	N/A	500
ST410800WD	9090.00	27	4925	*	13	5.25	FH	SCSI-2 F/W	RLL 1,7	AUTO	N/A	N/A	500
ST412	10.65	4	306	17	85	5.25	FH	ST-506/412	MFM	319	128	307	11
ST41200N	1037.00	15	1931	*	15	5.25	FH	SCSI	RLL 1,7	AUTO	N/A	N/A	150
ST41200ND	1037.00	15	1931	*	15	5.25	FH	SCSI	RLL 1,7	AUTO	N/A	N/A	150
ST41200NM	1037.00	15	1931	*	15	5.25	FH	SCSI	RLL 1,7	AUTO	N/A	N/A	150
ST41200NV	1037.00	15	1931	*	15	5.25	FH	SCSI	RLL 1,7	AUTO	N/A	N/A	150
ST4135R	115.01	9	960	26	28	5.25	FH	ST-506/412	RLL 2,7	AUTO	128	1,025	40
ST4144N	122.68	9	1024	26	28	5.25	FH	SCSI	RLL 2,7	1023	N/A	N/A	0
ST4144R	122.68	9	1024	26	28	5.25	FH	ST-506/412	RLL 2,7	AUTO	1,025	1,025	40
ST41520N	370.00	17	2101	*	11.5	5.25	FH	SCSI-2	RLL 2,7	AUTO	N/A	N/A	150
ST41520N	1352	17	2101	*	12	5.25	FH	SCSI-2	RLL 2,7	AUTO	N/A	N/A	150
ST41520ND	1370.00	17	2101	*	11.5	5.25	FH	SCSI-2DIFF	RLL 2,7	AUTO	N/A	N/A	150
ST41600N	1370.00	17	2101	*	11.5	5.25	FH	SCSI-2	RLL 2,7	AUTO	N/A	N/A	150
ST41600ND	1370.00	17	2101	*	11.5	5.25	FH	SCSI-2DIFF	RLL 2,7	AUTO	N/A	N/A	150
ST41601N	1370.00	17	2101	*	11.5	5.25	FH	SCSI-2	RLL 2,7	AUTO	N/A	N/A	150
ST41601ND	1370.00	17	2101	*	11.5	5.25	FH	SCSI-2	RLL 2,7	AUTO	N/A	N/A	150
ST41650N	1415.00	15	2107	*	15	5.25	FH	SCSI-2	RLL 1,7	AUTO	N/A	N/A	150
ST41650ND	1415.00	15	2107	*	15	5.25	FH	SCSI-2DIFF	RLL 1,7	AUTO	N/A	N/A	150
ST41651N	1415.00	15	2107	*	15	5.25	FH	SCSI-2	RLL 1,7	AUTO	N/A	N/A	150
ST41651ND	1415.00	15	2107	*	15	5.25	FH	SCSI-2DIFF	RLL 1,7	AUTO	N/A	N/A	150
ST4182E	151.81	9	969	34	16.5	5.25	FH	ESDI-10MHZ	RLL 2,7	AUTO	N/A	N/A	100
ST4182N	160.74	9	969	36	16.5	5.25	FH	SCSI	RLL 2,7	AUTO	N/A	N/A	100
ST4182NM	160.74	9	969	36	16.5	5.25	FH	SCSI	RLL 2,7	AUTO	N/A	N/A	100
ST419	15.98	6	306	17	85	5.25	FH	ST-506/412	MFM	–	128	307	11
ST4192E	169.13	8	1147	36	17	5.25	FH	ESDI-10MHZ	RLL 2,7	AUTO	N/A	N/A	20
ST4192N	169.13	8	1147	36	17	5.25	FH	SCSI	RLL 2,7	AUTO	N/A	N/A	20
ST42000N	1792.00	16	2627	*	11	5.25	FH	SCSI-2	RLL 2,7	AUTO	N/A	N/A	150
ST42000ND	1792.00	16	2627	*	11	5.25	FH	SCSI-2DIFF	RLL 2,7	AUTO	N/A	N/A	150
ST42100N	1900.00	16	2627	*	13	5.25	FH	SCSI-2	RLL 2,7	AUTO	N/A	N/A	150
ST42101N	1900.00	16	2627	*	13	5.25	FH	SCSI-2	RLL 2,7	AUTO	N/A	N/A	150
ST42400N	2129.00	19	2627	*	11	5.25	FH	SCSI-2	RLL 2,7	AUTO	N/A	N/A	150
ST42400ND	2129.00	19	2627	*	11	5.25	FH	SCSI-2	RLL 2,7	AUTO	N/A	N/A	150
ST425	21.30	8	306	17	–	5.25	FH	ST-506/412	MFM	–	128	307	0
ST43400N	2912.00	21	2738	*	11	5.25	FH	SCSI-2	RLL 1,7	AUTO	N/A	N/A	150
ST43400ND	2912.00	21	2738	*	11	5.25	FH	SCSI-2DIFF	RLL 1,7	AUTO	N/A	N/A	150
ST43401N	2912.00	21	2738	*	11	5.25	FH	SCSI-2 F/W	RLL 1,7	AUTO	N/A	N/A	150
ST43401ND	2912.00	21	2738	*	11	5.25	FH	SCSI-2 F/W	RLL 1,7	AUTO	N/A	N/A	150
ST43402ND	2912.00	21	2738	*	11	5.25	FH	SCSI-2 FWD	RLL 1,7	AUTO	N/A	N/A	150

SEAGATE TECHNOLOGY, INC.

MODEL	CAP	HDS	CYL	SPT	SEEK	FF	HGT	INT	ENCODE	LZ	WP	RWC	MTBF
ST4350N	307.00	9	1412	*	16.5	5.25	FH	SCSI	RLL	AUTO	N/A	N/A	100
ST4350NM	307.00	9	1412	*	16.5	5.25	FH	SCSI	RLL	AUTO	N/A	N/A	100
ST4376N	330.00	9	1541	*	16.5	5.25	FH	SCSI	RLL	AUTO	N/A	N/A	100
ST4376NM	330.00	9	1541	*	16.5	5.25	FH	SCSI	RLL	AUTO	N/A	N/A	100
ST4376NV	330.00	9	1541	*	16.5	5.25	FH	SCSI	RLL	AUTO	N/A	N/A	100
ST4383E	319.54	13	1412	34	18	5.25	FH	ESDI-10MHZ	RLL 2,7	AUTO	N/A	N/A	100
ST4384E	319.61	15	1224	34	14.5	5.25	FH	ESDI-10MHZ	RLL 2,7	AUTO	N/A	N/A	100
ST4385N	337.00	15	791	*	10.7	5.25	FH	SCSI	RLL	AUTO	N/A	N/A	100
ST4385NM	337.00	15	791	*	10.7	5.25	FH	SCSI	RLL	AUTO	N/A	N/A	100
ST4385NV	337.00	15	791	*	10.7	5.25	FH	SCSI	RLL	AUTO	N/A	N/A	100
ST4442E	368.70	15	1412	34	16	5.25	FH	ESDI-10MHZ	RLL 2,7	AUTO	N/A	N/A	100
ST4702N	613.00	15	1546	*	16.5	5.25	FH	SCSI	RLL	AUTO	N/A	N/A	100
ST4702NM	613.00	15	1546	*	16.5	5.25	FH	SCSI	RLL	AUTO	N/A	N/A	100
ST4766E	664.28	15	1632	53	15.5	5.25	FH	ST-506/412	RLL 1,7	AUTO	N/A	N/A	150
ST4766N	676.82	15	1632	54	15.5	5.25	FH	SCSI	RLL 2,7	AUTO	N/A	N/A	150
ST4766NM	676.82	15	1632	54	15.5	5.25	FH	SCSI	RLL 2,7	AUTO	N/A	N/A	150
ST4766NV	676.82	15	1632	54	15.5	5.25	FH	SCSI	RLL 2,7	AUTO	N/A	N/A	150
ST4767ES	676.89	15	1399	63	12.9	5.25	FH	ESDI-15MHZ	RLL 1,7	AUTO	N/A	N/A	150
ST4767N	666.50	15	1356	64	11.9	5.25	FH	SCSI-2	RLL 1,7	AUTO	N/A	N/A	150
ST4767ND	666.50	15	1356	64	11.9	5.25	FH	SCSI-2	RLL 1,7	AUTO	N/A	N/A	150
ST4767NM	666.50	15	1356	64	11.9	5.25	FH	SCSI-2	RLL 1,7	AUTO	N/A	N/A	150
ST4767NV	666.50	15	1356	64	11.9	5.25	FH	SCSI-2	RLL 1,7	AUTO	N/A	N/A	150
ST4769ES	631.72	15	1552	53	14.4	5.25	FH	ESDI-15MHZ	RLL 1,7	AUTO	N/A	N/A	150
ST506	5.32	4	153	17	85	5.25	FH	ST-506/412	MFM	157	128	128	11
ST51080A	1083.8	4	4834	*	10.5	3.50	3H	IDE(AT)	RLL 1,7	AUTO	N/A	N/A	300
ST51080N	1080.23	4	4826	*	13	3.50	4H	SCSI-2F	RLL 1,7	AUTO	N/A	N/A	300
ST51270A	1282.4	4	5414	*	10.5	3.50	4H	IDE(AT)	RLL 1,7	AUTO	N/A	AUTO	300
ST5540A	540.1	2	4834	*	10.5	3.50	3H	IDE(AT)	RLL 1,7	AUTO	N/A	N/A	300
ST5660A	545.51	4	3420	*	12	3.50	3H	IDE(AT)	RLL 1,7	AUTO	N/A	N/A	300
ST5660N	545.29	4	3420	77	12	3.50	3H	SCSI-2	RLL 1,7	AUTO	N/A	N/A	0
ST5660NC	545.29	4	3002	*	13	3.50	3H	SCSI SCA	RLL 1,7	AUTO	N/A	N/A	300
ST5850A	854.7	4			12	3.50	3H	IDE(AT)	RLL 1,7	AUTO	N/A	N/A	500
ST5851A	854.7	4	4834	*	10.5	3.50	4H	IDE(AT)	RLL 1,7	AUTO	N/A	AUTO	300
ST7050P	42.00	2	—	*	16	1.80	4H	PCMCIA	RLL 1,7	AUTO	N/A	N/A	250
ST706	5.32	2	306	17	—	5.25	FH	ST-506/412	MFM	—	128	307	0
ST81236N	1056.00	15	1635	—	12	8.00	FH	SCSI	RLL 2,7	AUTO	N/A	N/A	150
ST81236N	1000	15	1371		15	8.00	FH	SCSI	RLL 2,7				0
ST81236ND	1000	15	1371		15	8.00	FH	SCSI-DIFF	RLL 2,7				0
ST82500N	2140.00	19	2611	—	12	8.00	FH	SCSI	RLL 2,7	AUTO	N/A	N/A	150
ST8741N	608	15	1371		15	8.00	FH	SCSI	RLL 2,7				0
ST8741ND	608	15	1371		15	8.00	FH	SCSI-DIFF	RLL 2,7				0
ST8851N	727.00	15	1381	—	12	8.00	FH	SCSI	RLL 2,7	AUTO	N/A	N/A	100
ST8851N -V1	693	15	1371		15	8.00	FH	SCSI	RLL 2,7				0
ST8851N -V2	693	15	1371		15	8.00	FH	SCSI	RLL 2,7				0

SEAGATE TECHNOLOGY, INC.

MODEL	CAP	HDS	CYL	SPT	SEEK	FF	HGT	INT	ENCODE	LZ	WP	RWC	MTBF
ST8851N -V3	693	15	1371		15	8.00	FH	SCSI	RLL 2,7				0
ST8851ND	693	15	1371		15	8.00	FH	SCSI-DIFF	RLL 2,7				0
ST9051A	42.86	4	654	32	20	2.50	4H	IDE(44PIN)	RLL 2,7	AUTO	N/A	N/A	150
ST9052A	42.60	—	—	—	16	2.50	4H	IDE(44PIN)	RLL 2,7	AUTO	N/A	N/A	150
ST9077A	64.05	4	802	39	19	2.50	4H	IDE(44PIN)	RLL 2,7	AUTO	N/A	N/A	150
ST9080A	64.00	—	—	—	16	2.50	4H	IDE(44PIN)	RLL 2,7	AUTO	N/A	N/A	150
ST9096A	85.30	—	—	—	20	2.50	4H	IDE(44PIN)	RLL 2,7	AUTO	N/A	N/A	50
ST9100A	85.8	—	—	—	16	2.50	5H	IDE(44PIN)	RLL 1,7	AUTO	N/A	N/A	300
ST9100AG	85.30	—	—	—	16	2.50	3H	IDE(44PIN)	RLL 1,7	AUTO	N/A	N/A	150
ST9140AG	127.94	4	—	*	16	2.50	4H	IDE(44PIN)	RLL 1,7	AUTO	N/A	N/A	300
ST9144A	130.69	3	—	*	16	2.50	4H	IDE(44PIN)	RLL 2,7	AUTO	N/A	N/A	150
ST9145A	127.94	4	1463	*	16	2.50	4H	IDE(44PIN)	RLL 1,7	AUTO	N/A	N/A	300
ST9145AG	127.94	4	1463	*	16	2.50	4H	IDE(44PIN)	RLL 1,7	AUTO	N/A	N/A	300
ST9150AG	131.07	2	—	*	16	2.50	4H	IDE(44PIN)	RLL 1,7	AUTO	N/A	N/A	300
ST9190AG	171.63	4	—	*	16	2.50	4H	IDE(44PIN)	RLL 1,7	AUTO	N/A	N/A	300
ST9235A	209.7	—	—	—	16	3.50	4H	IDE(AT)	RLL 2,7	AUTO	N/A	N/A	150
ST9235AG	209.70	—	—	—	16	2.50	4H	IDE(44PIN)	RLL 2,7	AUTO	N/A	N/A	150
ST9235N	209.00	—	—	—	16	2.50	4H	SCSI	RLL 2,7	AUTO	N/A	N/A	150
ST9240A	210.43	4	—	*	16	2.50	4H	IDE(44PIN)	RLL 1,7	AUTO	N/A	N/A	300
ST9240AG	210.43	4	—	*	16	2.50	4H	IDE(44PIN)	RLL 1,7	AUTO	N/A	N/A	300
ST9295AG	261.00	—	—	—	16	2.50	4H	IDE(44PIN)	RLL 2,7	AUTO	N/A	N/A	150
ST9295N	250.60	—	—	—	16	2.50	4H	SCSI	RLL 2,7	AUTO	N/A	N/A	150
ST9300AG	262.19	4	—	*	16	2.50	4H	IDE(44PIN)	RLL 1,7	AUTO	N/A	N/A	300
ST9385AG	341.44	6	—	—	27	2.50	4H	IDE(AT)	RLL 1,7	AUTO	N/A	N/A	300
ST9420A	420.8	4		*	16	2.50	5H	IDE(44PIN)	RLL 1,7	AUTO	N/A	N/A	300
ST9420AG	420.8	4	—	*	16	2.50	5H	IDE(44PIN)	RLL 1,7	AUTO	N/A	N/A	300
ST9550AG	455.29	6	—	—	16	2.50	4H	IDE(AT)	RLL 1,7	AUTO	N/A	N/A	300
ST9655AG	524.35	6	—	*	16	2.50	4H	IDE(44PIN)	RLL 1,7	AUTO	N/A	N/A	300
ST9816AG	810	8		*	16	2.50	5H	IDE(44PIN)	RLL 1,7	AUTO	N/A	N/A	300

Seagate Technology   Unformatted Capacity

ST11750ND

Form Factors:
1 - 3.50 HH
2 - 5.25 HH
3 - 3.50 3H
4 - 5.25 FH
7 - 1.80 4H
8 - 8.00 FH
9 - 2.50 3H

Interface:
- ST506/MFM
R - ST506/RLL
E - ESDI
A - IDE (AT)
X - IDE (XT)
N - SCSI
ND - Differential SCSI
NS - Synchronous SCSI
NM - Mac SCSI
NV - Netware Certified SCSI

SEAGATE TECHNOLOGY, INC.

OLD IMPRIMIS & CDC MODEL TO SEAGATE MODEL CONVERSION TABLE

CDC	Seagate	CDC	Seagate	CDC	Seagate	CDC	Seagate
94155-135	ST4135R	94196-766	ST4766E	94246-383	ST2383E	94354-126	ST1126A
94155-85	ST4085	94204-65	ST274A	94351-090	ST1090N	94354-133	ST1133A
94155-86	ST4086	94204-71	ST280A	94351-111	ST1111N	94354-155	ST1156A
94155-96	ST4097	94204-74	ST274A	94351-126	ST1126N	94354-160	ST1162A
94161-182	ST4182N	94204-81	ST280A	94351-133S	ST1133NS	94354-186	ST1186A
94166-182	ST4182E	94205-51	ST253	94351-155	ST1156N	94354-200	ST1201A
94171-350	ST4350N	94205-77	ST279R	94351-155S	ST1156NS	94354-239	ST1239A
94171-376	ST4376N	94211-106	ST2106N	94351-160	ST1162N	94355-100	ST1100
94181-385H	ST4385N	94216-106	ST2106E	94351-186S	ST1186NS	94355-150	ST1150R
94181-702	ST4702N	94221-125	ST2125N	94351-200	ST1201N	94356-155	ST1156E
94186-383	ST4383E	94241-502	ST2502N	94351-200S	ST1201NS	94356-200	ST1201E
94186-383H	ST4384E	94244-274	ST2274A	94351-230S	ST1239NS	94536-111	ST1111E
94186-442	ST4442E	94244-383	ST2383A	94354-090	ST1090A	94601-12G/M	ST41200N
94191-766	ST4766N	94246-182	ST2182E	94354-111	ST1111A	94601-767H	ST4767N

SHUGART CORPORATION

MODEL	CAP	HDS	CYL	SPT	SEEK	FF	HGT	INT	ENCODE	LZ	WP	RWC	MTBF
SA 1002	5.00	–	–	17	–	8.00	FH	ST-506/412	MFM	–	–	–	0
SA 1004	10.00	–	–	17	–	8.00	FH	ST-506/412	MFM	–	–	–	0
SA 1106	30.00	–	–	17	–	8.00	FH	ST-506/412	MFM	–	–	–	0
SA 4004	14.00	–	–	17	–	14.0	FH	ST-506/412	MFM	–	–	–	0
SA 4008	29.00	–	–	17	–	14.0	FH	ST-506/412	MFM	–	–	–	0
SA 4100	56.00	–	–	17	–	14.0	FH	ST-506/412	MFM	–	–	–	0
SA 604	5.57	4	160	17	–	5.25	FH	ST-506/412	MFM	–	128	128	0
SA 606	8.35	6	160	17	–	5.25	FH	ST-506/412	MFM	–	128	128	0
SA 607	5.32	2	306	17	–	5.25	FH	ST-506/412	MFM	–	–	–	0
SA 612	10.65	4	306	17	–	5.25	FH	ST-506/412	MFM	–	128	307	0
SA 706	5.57	2	320	17	–	5.25	FH	ST-506/412	MFM	–	128	321	0
SA 712	11.14	4	320	17	–	5.25	HH	ST-506/412	MFM	–	128	321	0

SIEMENS NIXDORF INFORMATIONSSYSTEME AG

MODEL	CAP	HDS	CYL	SPT	SEEK	FF	HGT	INT	ENCODE	LZ	WP	RWC	MTBF
1200	174.32	8	1216	35	25	5.25	FH	ESDI-10MHZ	RLL 2,7	AUTO	N/A	N/A	0
1300	261.48	12	1216	35	25	5.25	FH	ESDI-10MHZ	RLL 2,7	AUTO	N/A	N/A	0
2200	174.00	8	1216	35	25	5.25	FH	ESDI-10MHZ	RLL 2,7	AUTO	N/A	N/A	0
2300	261.48	12	1216	35	25	5.25	FH	SCSI	RLL 2,7	AUTO	N/A	N/A	0

SIEMENS NIXDORF INFORMATIONSSYSTEME AG

MODEL	CAP	HDS	CYL	SPT	SEEK	FF	HGT	INT	ENCODE	LZ	WP	RWC	MTBF
4410	322.15	11	1100	52	18	5.25	FH	ESDI-15MHZ	RLL 2,7	AUTO	N/A	N/A	30
4420	334.54	11	1100	54	16	5.25	FH	SCSI	RLL 2,7	AUTO	N/A	N/A	40
5710	655.00	15	1224	48	16	5.25	FH	ESDI-15MHZ	RLL 2,7	AUTO	N/A	N/A	0
5720	655.00	15	1224	48	16	5.25	FH	SCSI	RLL	AUTO	N/A	N/A	0
5810	733.45	16	1658	54	18	5.25	FH	ESDI-15MHZ	RLL 2,7	AUTO	N/A	N/A	0
5820	733.45	16	1658	54	18	5.25	FH	SCSI	RLL 2,7	AUTO	N/A	N/A	0
6200	1200.00	–	–	–	14	5.25	–	SCSI	RLL 2,7	AUTO	N/A	N/A	0
7520	655.00	15	–	–	16	5.25	FH	SCSI	RLL 2,7	AUTO	N/A	N/A	0

SIMPLE TECHNOLOGY, INC.

MODEL	CAP	HDS	CYL	SPT	SEEK	FF	HGT	INT	ENCODE	LZ	WP	RWC	MTBF
STI-105HD	105					CARD	NO	PCMCIA	UNIDENT	AUTO	N/A	N/A	0
STI-130HD	130					CARD	NO	PCMCIA	UNIDENT	AUTO	N/A	N/A	0
STI-170HD	170					CARD	NO	PCMCIA	UNIDENT	AUTO	N/A	N/A	0

SONY CORPORATION

MODEL	CAP	HDS	CYL	SPT	SEEK	FF	HGT	INT	ENCODE	LZ	WP	RWC	MTBF
SRD 2040Z	41.92	4	622	33	–	3.50	HH	SCSI	–	–	–	–	0

STORAGE DIMENSIONS

MODEL	CAP	HDS	CYL	SPT	SEEK	FF	HGT	INT	ENCODE	LZ	WP	RWC	MTBF
AT-1000S	1000.00	15	–	–	15	5.25	–	SCSI	RLL	AUTO	N/A	N/A	100
AT-100S	105.00	3	–	–	19	3.50	HH	SCSI	RLL 2,7	AUTO	N/A	N/A	150
AT-120	119.85	15	918	17	27	5.25	FH	ST-506/412	MFM	–	–	–	100
AT-155E	157.92	7	1224	36	14	5.25	FH	ESDI-10MHZ	RLL 2,7	AUTO	N/A	N/A	100
AT-155S	157.92	7	1224	36	14	5.25	FH	SCSI	RLL 2,7	AUTO	N/A	N/A	100
AT-160	159.80	15	1224	17	28	5.25	FH	ST-506/412	MFM	–	–	–	100
AT-200S	204.00	7	–	–	15	3.50	HH	SCSI	RLL 2,7	AUTO	N/A	N/A	150
AT-320S	338.41	15	1224	36	16	5.25	FH	SCSI	RLL 2,7	AUTO	N/A	N/A	100
AT-335E	338.41	15	1224	36	16	5.25	FH	ESDI-10MHZ	RLL 2,7	AUTO	N/A	N/A	100
AT-650E	651.75	15	1632	52	16	5.25	FH	ESDI-15MHZ	RLL 2,7	AUTO	N/A	N/A	70
AT-650S	651.75	15	1632	52	16	5.25	FH	SCSI	RLL 2,7	AUTO	N/A	N/A	100
MAC-195	195.00	7	–	–	15	3.50	HH	SCSI	RLL 2,7	AUTO	N/A	N/A	150
PS-155E	203.04	9	1224	36	14	5.25	FH	ESDI-15MHZ	RLL 2,7	AUTO	N/A	N/A	70
PS-155S	203.04	9	1224	36	14	5.25	FH	SCSI	RLL 2,7	AUTO	N/A	N/A	70
PS-320S	338.41	15	1224	36	16	5.25	FH	SCSI	RLL 2,7	AUTO	N/A	N/A	150
PS-335E	338.41	15	1224	36	16	5.25	FH	ESDI-10MHZ	RLL 2,7	AUTO	N/A	N/A	70
PS-650S	676.82	15	1632	54	16	5.25	FH	SCSI	RLL 2,7	AUTO	N/A	N/A	100

SYQUEST TECHNOLOGY

MODEL	CAP	HDS	CYL	SPT	SEEK	FF	HGT	INT	ENCODE	LZ	WP	RWC	MTBF
SQ306F	5.00	–	–	17	–	5.25	HH	ST-506/412	MFM	–	–	–	0
SQ306R	5.32	2	306	17	–	5.25	HH	ST-506/412	RLL	–	–	–	0
SQ306RD	5.32	2	306	17	–	5.25	HH	ST-506/412	MFM	–	307	307	0
SQ3105A	105				14.5	3.50	3H	IDE(AT)	UNIDENT	AUTO	N/A	N/A	100
SQ3105S	105	*	*	*	14.5	3.50	3H	SCSI	UNIDENT	AUTO	N/A	N/A	100
SQ312	10.70	2	615	17	–	5.25	HH	ST-506/412	MFM	–	–	–	0
SQ312RD	10.70	2	615	17	–	5.25	HH	ST-506/412	MFM	–	616	616	0
SQ319	10.65	2	612	17	–	5.25	HH	ST-506/412	RLL	–	–	–	0
SQ325	21.30	4	612	17	–	5.25	HH	ST-506/412	MFM	–	–	–	0
SQ325F	21.41	4	615	17	–	5.25	HH	ST-506/412	MFM	–	616	616	0
SQ3270A	256				14.5	3.50	3H	IDE(AT)	UNIDENT	AUTO	N/A	N/A	100
SQ3270S	256	*	*	*	14.5	3.50	3H	SCSI	UNIDENT	AUTO	N/A	N/A	100
SQ338F	32.11	6	615	17	–	5.25	HH	ST-506/412	MFM	–	616	616	0
SQ340AF	33.42	6	640	17	–	5.25	HH	ST-506/412	MFM	–	616	616	0
SQ5110	88				20	5.25	HH	SCSI	RLL 2,7	AUTO	N/A	N/A	60
SQ5110C	88				20	5.25	HH	SCSI	RLL 2,7	AUTO	N/A	N/A	60
SQ5200C	200				18	5.25	HH	SCSI	RLL 1,7	AUTO	N/A	N/A	100
SQ555	40.00	–	–	17	20	5.25	HH	SCSI	RLL 2,7	AUTO	N/A	N/A	60

T.S. MICROSYSTEMS, LTD. (SEE XEBEC)

TALON

MODEL	CAP	HDS	CYL	SPT	SEEK	FF	HGT	INT	ENCODE	LZ	WP	RWC	MTBF
TA3020A	121.07	4	1478	40	16	3.50	3H	IDE(AT)	RLL 1,7	AUTO	N/A	N/A	200
TA3101A	105.02	4	1282	40	16	3.50	3H	IDE(AT)	RLL 1,7	AUTO	N/A	N/A	200

TANDON CORPORATION

MODEL	CAP	HDS	CYL	SPT	SEEK	FF	HGT	INT	ENCODE	LZ	WP	RWC	MTBF
TM 2128	120.28	9	1004	26	25	5.25	FH	SCSI	RLL 2,7	AUTO	N/A	N/A	0
TM 2170	161.02	9	1344	26	25	5.25	FH	SCSI	RLL 2,7	AUTO	N/A	N/A	0
TM 244	41.63	4	782	26	37	3.50	HH	ST-506/412	RLL 2,7	–	783	783	0
TM 246	62.45	6	782	26	37	3.50	HH	ST-506/412	RLL 2,7	–	783	783	0
TM 251	5.32	2	306	17	–	5.25	–	ST-506/412	MFM	–	–	–	0
TM 252	10.65	4	306	17	85	5.25	HH	ST-506/412	MFM	–	307	307	0
TM 261	10.70	2	615	17	–	5.25	–	ST-506/412	MFM	–	616	616	0
TM 262	21.41	4	615	17	65	3.50	HH	ST-506/412	MFM	–	616	616	0
TM 262R	20.81	2	782	26	85	3.50	HH	ST-506/412	RLL 2,7	–	783	783	0
TM 264	41.63	4	782	26	85	3.50	HH	ST-506/412	RLL 2,7	–	783	783	0
TM 3085	71.30	8	1024	17	37	5.25	–	ST-506/412	MFM	–	1,024	1,024	0

TANDON CORPORATION

MODEL	CAP	HDS	CYL	SPT	SEEK	FF	HGT	INT	ENCODE	LZ	WP	RWC	MTBF
TM 3085-R	109.05	8	1024	26	37	5.25	–	ST-506/412	RLL	–	–	–	0
TM 344	41.63	4	782	26	37	3.50	HH	ST-506/412	RLL 2,7	–	783	783	0
TM 346	62.45	6	782	26	37	3.50	HH	ST-506/412	RLL 2,7	–	783	783	0
TM 361	10.70	2	615	17	–	5.25	–	ST-506/412	MFM	–	616	616	0
TM 362	21.41	4	615	17	–	5.25	–	ST-506/412	MFM	–	616	616	0
TM 362R	20.81	2	782	26	85	3.50	HH	ST-506/412	RLL 2,7	–	783	783	0
TM 364	41.63	4	782	26	85	3.50	HH	ST-506/412	RLL 2,7	–	783	783	0
TM 501	5.32	2	306	17	–	5.25	FH	ST-506/412	MFM	–	153	128	0
TM 502	10.65	4	306	17	85	5.25	FH	ST-506/412	MFM	–	153	128	0
TM 503	15.98	6	306	17	85	5.25	FH	ST-506/412	MFM	–	153	128	0
TM 602S	5.32	4	153	17	85	5.25	FH	ST-506/412	MFM	–	128	128	0
TM 602SE	12.00	–	–	17	–	5.25	FH	ST-506/412	MFM	–	–	–	0
TM 603S	7.99	6	153	17	–	5.25	FH	ST-506/412	MFM	–	128	128	0
TM 603SE	12.01	6	230	17	–	5.25	FH	ST-506/412	MFM	–	128	128	0
TM 702	32.74	4	615	26	–	5.25	FH	ST-506/412	RLL 2,7	–	616	616	0
TM 702AT	21.41	4	615	17	–	5.25	FH	ST-506/412	MFM	615	615	615	0
TM 703	30.24	5	695	17	–	5.25	FH	ST-506/412	MFM	AUTO	695	695	0
TM 703-C	25.00	5	576	17	–	5.25	FH	ST-506/412	MFM	AUTO	576	576	0
TM 703AT	31.90	5	733	17	40	5.25	FH	ST-506/412	MFM	733	733	733	0
TM 705	41.86	5	962	17	–	5.25	FH	ST-506/412	MFM	962	–	–	0
TM 755	42.69	5	981	17	–	5.25	HH	ST-506/412	MFM	–	982	982	0

TANDY/RADIO SHACK

MODEL	CAP	HDS	CYL	SPT	SEEK	FF	HGT	INT	ENCODE	LZ	WP	RWC	MTBF
25-1045	28.00	–	–	–	–	3.50	HH	IDE(XT)	RLL	AUTO	–	–	0
25-1046	43.24	4	782	27	28	3.50	HH	IDE(XT)	RLL 2,7	AUTO	N/A	N/A	40
25-4130	100.00	4	1219	–	17	3.50	HH	IDE(AT)	RLL 2,7	AUTO	N/A	N/A	0

TEAC CORPORATION

MODEL	CAP	HDS	CYL	SPT	SEEK	FF	HGT	INT	ENCODE	LZ	WP	RWC	MTBF
SD-150	10.65	4	306	17	–	5.25	–	ST-506/412	MFM	–	–	–	0
SD-3105	105.02	4	1282	40	19	3.50	3H	IDE(AT)	RLL 2,7	AUTO	N/A	N/A	30
SD-3105(S)	105.02	4	1282	40	19	3.50	3H	SCSI	RLL 2,7	AUTO	N/A	N/A	30
SD-3210	209.92	–	–	*	–	3.50	3H	IDE(AT)	RLL	AUTO	N/A	N/A	0
SD-3210(S)	215.22	4	1695	62	17	3.50	3H	SCSI	RLL 1,7	AUTO	N/A	N/A	100
SD-3240	245.06	4	1930	*	17	3.50	3H	IDE(AT)	RLL	AUTO	N/A	N/A	100
SD-340	43.00	2	1050	40	23	3.50	3H	IDE(AT)	RLL 2,7	AUTO	N/A	N/A	30
SD-340S	43.00	2	1050	40	23	3.50	3H	SCSI	RLL 2,7	AUTO	N/A	N/A	30
SD-380	86.01	4	1050	40	20	3.50	3H	IDE(AT)	RLL 2,7	AUTO	N/A	N/A	30
SD-380H(A)	86.01	4	1050	40	19	3.50	3H	IDE(AT)	RLL 2,7	AUTO	N/A	N/A	30

TEAC CORPORATION

MODEL	CAP	HDS	CYL	SPT	SEEK	FF	HGT	INT	ENCODE	LZ	WP	RWC	MTBF
SD-380H(S)	86.01	4	1050	40	19	3.50	3H	SCSI	RLL 2,7	AUTO	N/A	N/A	30
SD-380S	86.01	4	1050	40	20	3.50	3H	SCSI	RLL 2,7	AUTO	N/A	N/A	30
SD-510	10.65	4	306	17	—	5.25	FH	ST-506/412	MFM	—	128	128	0
SD-520	21.41	4	615	17	—	5.25	HH	ST-506/412	MFM	—	128	128	0
SD-540	42.82	8	615	17	—	5.25	HH	ST-506/412	MFM	615	125	N/A	0

TEXAS INSTRUMENTS

MODEL	CAP	HDS	CYL	SPT	SEEK	FF	HGT	INT	ENCODE	LZ	WP	RWC	MTBF
DB260	212.60	8	—	—	16	3.50	HH	SCSI-2	RLL	AUTO	N/A	N/A	0
DB380	333.43	15	—	—	16	5.25	FH	SCSI	RLL	AUTO	N/A	N/A	0
DB760	669.77	15	—	—	—	5.25	FH	SCSI	RLL	AUTO	N/A	N/A	0
TI-5	5.32	4	153	17	—	5.25	FH	ST-506/412	MFM	—	64	64	0

TOKICO

MODEL	CAP	HDS	CYL	SPT	SEEK	FF	HGT	INT	ENCODE	LZ	WP	RWC	MTBF
DK 503-2	10.65	4	306	17	—	5.25	FH	ST-506/412	MFM	—	—	—	0

TOSHIBA

MODEL	CAP	HDS	CYL	SPT	SEEK	FF	HGT	INT	ENCODE	LZ	WP	RWC	MTBF
MK-1034FC	107.42	4	1345	39	16	3.50	3H	IDE(AT)	RLL 2,7	AUTO	N/A	N/A	40
MK-1122FC	43.01	2	977	43	23	2.50	4H	IDE(AT)	RLL 2,7	AUTO	N/A	N/A	80
MK-1301MAV	1.35	6	3650		13	2.50	5H	ATA-2	UNIDENT	AUTO		128	300K
MK-134FA	44.66	7	733	17	25	3.50	HH	ST-506/412	MFM	—	512	N/A	30
MK-134FA(R)	68.30	7	733	26	23	3.50	HH	ST-506/412	RLL 2,7	—	—	—	30
MK-1422FC	86	2			15	2.50	–	IDE(AT)	UNIDENT		N/A	N/A	
MK-1422FCV	86.	2	1501	56	15	2.50	3H	IDE(AT)	RLL	AUTO	N/A	N/A	150
MK-1522FCV	126	2			15	2.50	–	IDE(AT)	UNIDENT		N/A	N/A	
MK-153FA	74.36	5	830	35	23	5.25	FH	ESDI-10MHZ	RLL 2,7	AUTO	N/A	N/A	30
MK-153FA-I	74.36	5	830	35	23	5.25	FH	ESDI-10MHZ	RLL 2,7	AUTO	N/A	N/A	30
MK-154FA	104.11	7	830	35	23	5.25	FH	ESDI-10MHZ	RLL 2,7	AUTO	N/A	N/A	30
MK-154FA-I	104.11	7	830	35	23	5.25	FH	ESDI-10MHZ	RLL 2,7	AUTO	N/A	N/A	30
MK-154FB	104.11	7	830	35	23	5.25	FH	ESDI-10MHZ	RLL 2,7	AUTO	N/A	N/A	30
MK-156FA	148.73	10	830	35	23	5.25	FH	ESDI-10MHZ	RLL 2,7	AUTO	N/A	N/A	30
MK-156FB	148.73	10	830	35	23	5.25	FH	ESDI-10MHZ	RLL 2,7	AUTO	N/A	N/A	30
MK-1722FCV	131				13	2.50	–	IDE(AT)	UNIDENT		N/A	N/A	
MK-1724FCV	262				13	2.50	–	IDE(AT)	UNIDENT		N/A	N/A	
MK-1824FCV	352				13	2.50	5H	IDE(44PIN)	RLL 1,7	682	N/A	N/A	300
MK-1924FCV	543				13	2.50	5H	IDE(44PIN)	RLL 1,7	1053	N/A	N/A	300
MK-1926FCV	810				13	2.50	5H	IDE(44PIN)	RLL 1,7	1579	N/A	N/A	300

TOSHIBA

MODEL	CAP	HDS	CYL	SPT	SEEK	FF	HGT	INT	ENCODE	LZ	WP	RWC	MTBF
MK-2024FC	86.03	4	977	43	19	2.50	4H	IDE(AT)	RLL 2,7	AUTO	N/A	N/A	80
MK-2101MAN (HDD 2616)	2.16	10	3650		13	2.50	4H	ATA-2	RLL			128	300K
MK-2124FC	130.09	4	1155	55	17	2.50	4H	IDE(AT)	RLL 2,7	934	N/A	N/A	80
MK-2224FB	213	4	1560	*	12	2.50	4H	SCSI	RLL 1,7		N/A	N/A	
MK-2224FC	213.	4	1560	*	12	2.50	3H	IDE(AT)	RLL	AUTO	N/A	N/A	150
MK-2224FC	213	4	1560	*	12	2.50	4H	IDE(44PIN)	RLL	AUTO	N/A	N/A	150
MK-2326FB	340	6	1830	*	12	2.50	4H	SCSI	RLL 1,7		N/A	N/A	
MK-2326FC	340.34	6	1830	*	12	2.50	4H	IDE(44PIN)	RLL 1,7	AUTO	N/A	N/A	150
MK-2326FCH	340				12	2.50	–	IDE(AT)	UNIDENT		N/A	N/A	
MK-232FB	45.42	3	845	35	25	3.50	HH	SCSI	RLL 2,7	AUTO	N/A	N/A	30
MK-232FBS	45.42	3	845	35	19	3.50	HH	SCSI	RLL 2,7	AUTO	N/A	N/A	30
MK-232FC	45.42	3	845	35	25	3.50	HH	IDE(AT)	RLL 2,7	AUTO	N/A	N/A	30
MK-233FB	75.71	5	845	35	25	3.50	HH	SCSI	RLL 2,7	AUTO	N/A	N/A	30
MK-234FB	105.99	7	845	35	25	3.50	HH	SCSI	RLL 2,7	AUTO	N/A	N/A	30
MK-234FBS	105.99	7	845	35	19	3.50	HH	SCSI	RLL 2,7	AUTO	N/A	N/A	30
MK-234FC	110.44	7	856	36	25	3.50	HH	IDE(AT)	RLL 2,7	AUTO	N/A	N/A	30
MK-234FCH	107.37	7	856	35	25	3.50	HH	IDE(AT)	RLL 2,7	AUTO	N/A	N/A	30
MK-234FCH-I	107.37	7	856	35	25	3.50	HH	IDE(AT)	RLL 2,7	AUTO	N/A	N/A	30
MK-2428FB	524	8	1920	*	12	2.50	4H	SCSI	RLL 1,7		N/A	N/A	
MK-2428FC	524.35	8	1920	*	12	2.50	4H	IDE(44PIN)	RLL 1,7	AUTO	N/A	N/A	150
MK-250FB	219.34	10	1224	35	18	5.25	FH	SCSI	RLL 2,7	AUTO	N/A	N/A	30
MK-2526FB	528	8	1920	*	12	2.50	4H	SCSI-2	RLL 1,7	AUTO			
MK-2526FC	528				13	2.50	5H	IDE(44PIN)	RLL 1,7	1023	N/A	N/A	300
MK-2528FC	704				13	2.50	5H	IDE(44PIN)	RLL 1,7	1365	N/A	N/A	300
MK-253FA	162.80	5	1223	52	18	5.25	FH	ESDI-15MHZ	RLL 1,7	AUTO	N/A	N/A	30
MK-254FA	227.92	7	1223	52	18	5.25	FH	ESDI-15MHZ	RLL 1,7	AUTO	N/A	N/A	30
MK-256FA	325.61	10	1223	52	18	5.25	FH	ESDI-15MHZ	RLL 1,7	AUTO	N/A	N/A	30
MK-2628FB	811	8	2360	*	13	2.50	4H	SCSI-2	RLL 1,7	AUTO			
MK-2628FC	810				13	2.50	5H	IDE(44PIN)	RLL 1,7	1571	N/A	N/A	300
MK-2720FC	1.35	10	2920		13	2.50	4H	IDE(44PIN)	RLL	AUTO	N/A	128	300K
MK-355FA	405.65	9	1661	53	16	5.25	FH	ESDI-15MHZ	RLL 2,7	AUTO	N/A	N/A	30
MK-355FB	405.65	9	1661	53	16	5.25	FH	SCSI-2	RLL 2,7	AUTO	N/A	N/A	30
MK-358FA	676.09	9	1661	53	16	5.25	FH	ESDI-15MHZ	RLL 2,7	AUTO	N/A	N/A	30
MK-358FB	676.09	15	1661	53	16	5.25	FH	SCSI-2	RLL 2,7	AUTO	N/A	N/A	30
MK-438FB ASSY. 0605	877.00	15	1692	–	12.5	3.50	HH	SCSI-2	RLL 1,7	AUTO	N/A	N/A	200
MK-438FB ASSY. 0817	900.00	11	1980	–	12.5	3.50	HH	SCSI-2	RLL 1,7	AUTO	N/A	N/A	200
MK-438FB ASSY. 0834	877.00	11	1980	35	12	5.25	FH	SCSI-2	RLL 1,7	AUTO	N/A	N/A	200
MK-537FB	1064.00	13	1980	–	12	3.50	HH	SCSI-2	RLL 1,7	AUTO	N/A	N/A	200
MK-538FB	1228.00	15	1980	–	12	3.50	HH	SCSI-2	RLL 1,7	AUTO	N/A	N/A	200

TOSHIBA

MODEL	CAP	HDS	CYL	SPT	SEEK	FF	HGT	INT	ENCODE	LZ	WP	RWC	MTBF
MK-53FA	36.12	5	830	17	30	5.25	FH	ST-506/412	MFM	830	512	–	20
MK-53FB	36.12	5	830	17	25	5.25	FH	ST-506/412	MFM	–	512	830	20
MK-53FB(M)	36.12	5	830	17	25	5.25	FH	ST-506/412	MFM	–	512	830	20
MK-53FB(R)	36.12	5	830	17	25	5.25	FH	ST-506/412	RLL	–	512	830	20
MK-53FB-I	36.12	5	830	17	25	5.25	FH	ST-506/412	MFM	–	512	830	20
MK-54FA(M)	50.57	7	830	17	30	5.25	FH	ST-506/412	MFM	830	512	–	20
MK-54FB(M)	50.57	7	830	17	25	5.25	FH	ST-506/412	MFM	830	512	830	20
MK-54FB-I	50.57	7	830	17	25	5.25	FH	ST-506/412	MFM	830	512	830	20
MK-56FA(M)	72.24	10	830	17	30	5.25	FH	ST-506/412	MFM	–	831	831	20
MK-56FA(R)	110.48	10	830	26	30	5.25	FH	ST-506/412	RLL 2,7	830	512	–	20
MK-56FB(M)	72.24	10	830	17	25	5.25	FH	ST-506/412	MFM	830	512	830	20
MK-56FB(R)	110.48	10	830	26	25	5.25	FH	ST-506/412	RLL 2,7	–	831	831	20
MK-56FB-I	72.24	10	830	17	25	5.25	FH	ST-506/412	MFM	830	512	830	20
MK-72PC	72.24	10	830	17	25	5.25	FH	ST-506/412	MFM	–	–	–	20
MK-72PCR	110.48	10	830	26	25	5.25	FH	ST-506/412	RLL 2,7	–	–	–	20
MKM-0351E	36.12	5	830	17	25	5.25	FH	ST-506/412	MFM	830	512	830	20
MKM-0351J	36.12	5	830	17	25	5.25	FH	ST-506/412	MFM	830	512	830	20
MKM-0352E	50.57	7	830	17	30	5.25	FH	ST-506/412	MFM	830	512	–	20
MKM-0352J	50.57	7	830	17	30	5.25	FH	ST-506/412	MFM	830	512	–	20
MKM-0353E	72.24	10	830	17	25	5.25	FH	ST-506/412	MFM	830	512	830	20
MKM-0353J	72.24	10	830	17	25	5.25	FH	ST-506/412	MFM	830	512	830	20
MKM-0363A	74.36	5	830	35	23	5.25	FH	ESDI-10MHZ	RLL 2,7	AUTO	N/A	N/A	30
MKM-0363J	74.36	5	830	35	23	5.25	FH	ESDI-10MHZ	RLL 2,7	AUTO	N/A	N/A	30
MKM-0364A	104.11	7	830	35	23	5.25	FH	ESDI-10MHZ	RLL 2,7	AUTO	N/A	N/A	30
MKM-0364J	104.11	7	830	35	23	5.25	FH	ESDI-10MHZ	RLL 2,7	AUTO	N/A	N/A	30
MKM-0381E	36.12	5	830	17	25	5.25	FH	ST-506/412	MFM	–	512	830	20
MKM-0381J	36.12	5	830	17	25	5.25	FH	ST-506/412	MFM	830	512	830	20
MKM-0382E	50.57	7	830	17	30	5.25	FH	ST-506/412	MFM	830	512	–	20
MKM-0382J	50.57	7	830	17	30	5.25	FH	ST-506/412	MFM	830	512	–	20
MKM-0383E	72.24	10	830	17	25	5.25	FH	ST-506/412	MFM	830	512	830	20
MKM-0383J	72.24	10	830	17	25	5.25	FH	ST-506/412	MFM	830	512	830	20

TULIN

MODEL	CAP	HDS	CYL	SPT	SEEK	FF	HGT	INT	ENCODE	LZ	WP	RWC	MTBF
TL 213	11.14	2	640	17	–	5.25	HH	ST-506/412	MFM	–	656	656	0
TL 226	22.28	4	640	17	–	5.25	HH	ST-506/412	MFM	–	656	656	0
TL 238	22.28	4	640	17	–	5.25	HH	ST-506/412	MFM	640	–	–	0
TL 240	33.42	6	640	17	–	5.25	HH	ST-506/412	MFM	–	656	656	0
TL 258	33.42	6	640	17	–	5.25	HH	ST-506/412	MFM	640	–	–	0
TL 326	22.28	4	640	17	–	5.25	HH	ST-506/412	MFM	–	641	641	0
TL 340	33.42	6	640	17	–	5.25	HH	ST-506/412	MFM	–	641	641	0

UNIDENTIFIED

MODEL	CAP	HDS	CYL	SPT	SEEK	FF	HGT	INT	ENCODE	LZ	WP	RWC	MTBF
HIPER 380	388.00	8	–	–	17	5.25	–	ESDI-15MHZ	RLL	AUTO	N/A	N/A	100
M2637T	240	12	698	56	14.5	3.50	3H	IDE(AT)	RLL 1,7	AUTO	N/A	N/A	0
MT-4115E	114.4	4	1597	34	16	5.25	HH	ESDI-10MHZ	RLL 2,7	AUTO	N/A	N/A	100
MT-4115S	114.47	4	1597	35	16	5.25	HH	SCSI	RLL 2,7	AUTO	N/A	N/A	100
MT-4140E	143.09	5	1597	35	16	5.25	HH	SCSI	RLL 2,7	AUTO	N/A	N/A	100
MT-4140S	143.09	5	1597	35	16	5.25	HH	SCSI	RLL 2,7	AUTO	N/A	N/A	100
MT-4170E	143.09	5	1597	35	16	5.25	HH	ESDI-10MHZ	RLL 2,7	AUTO	N/A	N/A	100
MT-4170S	171.70	6	1597	35	16	5.25	HH	SCSI	RLL 2,7	AUTO	N/A	N/A	100
MT-5760	673.09	15	1623	54	14	5.25	FH	SCSI	RLL 1,7	AUTO	N/A	N/A	150
MT-5760E	676.82	15	1225	54	14	5.25	FH	ESDI-15MHZ	RLL 1,7	AUTO	N/A	N/A	150
MT-6120	1050.75	15	1927	71	14	5.25	FH	SCSI	RLL 1,7	AUTO	N/A	N/A	100
PROPAQ 185-15	189.00	5	–	–	15	3.50	HH	IDE(AT)	RLL	AUTO	N/A	N/A	70
SI 1000/S5	1037.00	8	–	–	15	5.25	–	SCSI	RLL	AUTO	N/A	N/A	40
SI 200/PS3	209.00	4	–	–	18	3.50	HH	SCSI	RLL 2,7	AUTO	N/A	N/A	70
SI 585/S5	601.00	8	–	–	17	5.25	–	SCSI	RLL	AUTO	N/A	N/A	100

VERTEX

MODEL	CAP	HDS	CYL	SPT	SEEK	FF	HGT	INT	ENCODE	LZ	WP	RWC	MTBF
V130	25.77	3	987	–	–	5.25	FH	ST-506/412	MFM	–	988	988	0
V150	42.95	5	987	–	28	5.25	FH	ST-506/412	MFM	–	988	988	0
V160	50.74	5	1166	–	28	5.25	FH	ST-506/412	MFM	–	1,167	1,167	0
V160A	50.74	5	1166	17	28	5.25	FH	ST-506/412	MFM	–	1,167	1,167	0
V170	60.13	7	987	–	28	5.25	FH	ST-506/412	MFM	–	988	988	0
V170R	91.97	7	987	–	–	5.25	FH	ST-506/412	RLL 2,7	–	–	–	0
V185	71.04	7	1166	–	28	5.25	FH	ST-506/412	MFM	–	1,167	1,167	0
V519	159.80	15	1224	–	–	5.25	FH	ST-506/412	MFM	1223	–	–	0

WESTERN DIGITAL CORPORATION

MODEL	CAP	HDS	CYL	SPT	SEEK	FF	HGT	INT	ENCODE	LZ	WP	RWC	MTBF
WD-262	20	4	615	17	80	5.25	HH	ST-506/412	MFM	663			20
WD-344R	41.63	4	782	26	40	3.50	HH	ST-506/412	RLL	–	783	783	0
WD-362	20	4	615	17	80	3.50	HH	ST-506/412	MFM	663			20
WD-382R	20.81	2	782	26	85	3.50	HH	ST-506/412	RLL 2,7	–	783	783	0
WD-383R	32.74	4	615	26	85	3.50	HH	ST-506/412	RLL 2,7	–	616	616	0
WD-384R	41.63	4	782	26	85	3.50	HH	ST-506/412	RLL 2,7	–	783	783	0
WD-544R	41.63	4	782	26	40	3.50	HH	ST-506/412	RLL 2,7	–	783	783	0
WD-562-5	21.41	4	615	17	80	3.50	HH	ST-506/412	MFM	–	–	–	40
WD-582R	20.81	2	782	26	85	3.50	HH	ST-506/412	RLL 2,7	–	783	783	0
WD-583R	32.74	4	615	26	85	3.50	HH	ST-506/412	RLL 2,7	–	616	616	0

WESTERN DIGITAL CORPORATION

MODEL	CAP	HDS	CYL	SPT	SEEK	FF	HGT	INT	ENCODE	LZ	WP	RWC	MTBF
WD-584R	41.63	4	782	26	85	3.50	HH	ST-506/412	RLL 2,7	–	783	783	0
WD-MI130-44	31.08	2	920	33	19	3.50	3H	MCA	RLL 2,7	AUTO	N/A	N/A	45
WD-MI130-72	30.40	2	928	32	19	3.50	3H	MCA	RLL 2,7	AUTO	N/A	N/A	45
WD-MI260-72	63.61	6	767	27	27	3.50	3H	MCA	RLL 2,7	AUTO	N/A	N/A	45
WD-MI4120-72	125.03	8	925	33	23	3.50	3H	MCA	RLL 2,7	AUTO	N/A	N/A	45
WD-TM262R	20.81	2	782	26	85	3.50	HH	ST-506/412	RLL 2,7	–	783	783	0
WD-TM364	41.63	4	782	26	85	3.50	HH	ST-506/412	RLL 2,7	–	783	783	0
WD93024-A	21.62	2	782	27	28	3.50	HH	IDE(AT)	RLL 2,7	862	N/A	N/A	40
WD93024-X	21.62	2	782	27	39	3.50	HH	IDE(XT)	RLL 2,7	862	N/A	N/A	50
WD93028-AD	21.62	2	782	27	69	3.50	HH	IDE(AT)	RLL 2,7	862	N/A	N/A	40
WD93028-X	21.62	2	782	27	70	3.50	HH	IDE(XT)	RLL 2,7	862	N/A	N/A	40
WD93034-X	32.43	3	782	27	39	3.50	HH	IDE(XT)	RLL 2,7	862	N/A	N/A	50
WD93038-X	32.43	3	782	27	70	3.50	HH	IDE(XT)	RLL 2,7	862	N/A	N/A	40
WD93044-A	43.24	4	782	27	28	3.50	HH	IDE(AT)	RLL 2,7	862	N/A	N/A	40
WD93044-X	43.24	4	782	27	39	3.50	HH	IDE(XT)	RLL 2,7	862	N/A	N/A	50
WD93048-AD	43.24	4	782	27	69	3.50	HH	IDE(AT)	RLL 2,7	862	N/A	N/A	40
WD93048-X	43.24	4	782	27	70	3.50	HH	IDE(XT)	RLL 2,7	862	N/A	N/A	40
WD95024-A	21.62	2	782	27	28	3.50	HH	IDE(AT)	RLL 2,7	862	N/A	N/A	40
WD95028-AD	21.62	2	782	27	70	3.50	HH	IDE(AT)	RLL 2,7	862	N/A	N/A	40
WD95028-X	21.62	2	782	27	70	3.50	HH	IDE(XT)	RLL 2,7	862	N/A	N/A	40
WD95038-X	32.43	3	782	27	70	3.50	HH	IDE(XT)	RLL 2,7	862	N/A	N/A	40
WD95044-A	43.24	4	782	27	28	3.50	HH	IDE(AT)	RLL 2,7	862	N/A	N/A	40
WD95048-AD	43.24	4	782	27	70	3.50	HH	IDE(AT)	RLL 2,7	862	N/A	N/A	40
WD95048-X	43.24	4	782	27	70	3.50	HH	IDE(XT)	RLL 2,7	862	N/A	N/A	40
WDAB130	31.90	2	1020	*	16	2.50	4H	IDE(44PIN)	RLL 2,7	AUTO	N/A	N/A	50
WDAB140	42.7	2	1390		16	2.50	5H	IDE(44PIN)	RLL 2,7	AUTO	N/A	N/A	0
WDAC1170	170.64	2	2233	*	<15	3.50	3H	IDE(AT)	RLL 2,7	AUTO	N/A	N/A	100
WDAC1210	212.	–	–	*	<15	3.50	3H	IDE(AT)	RLL 2,7	AUTO	N/A	N/A	100
WDAC1270	270.4	2	2233	*	11	3.50	3H	IDE(AT)	RLL 2,7	AUTO	N/A	N/A	250
WDAC1365	365.4	–	–	–	11	3.50	3H	IDE(AT)	RLL 1,7	AUTO	N/A	N/A	250
WDAC140	42.65	2	1082	39	18	3.50	3H	IDE(AT)	RLL 2,7	AUTO	N/A	N/A	50
WDAC1425	426.8	–	–	–	11	3.50	3H	IDE(AT)	RLL 1,7	AUTO	N/A	N/A	250
WDAC160	63.20	2	1349	*	<15	3.50	3H	IDE(AT)	RLL 2,7	AUTO	N/A	N/A	100
WDAC21000	1083.8	4			11	3.50	3H	IDE(AT)	UNIDENT	AUTO	N/A	N/A	300
WDAC2120	126.40	4	1349	*	<15	3.50	3H	IDE(AT)	RLL 2,7	AUTO	N/A	N/A	100
WDAC21200	1281.9	4		*	12	3.50	3H	IDE(AT)	PRML	AUTO	N/A	N/A	300
WDAC21600	1624.6	4		*	13	3.50	3H	IDE(AT)	PRML	AUTO	N/A	N/A	300
WDAC2170	170.60	4	1584	*	<14	3.50	3H	IDE(AT)	RLL 2,7	AUTO	N/A	N/A	100
WDAC2200	212.67	4	1971	*	<15	3.50	3H	IDE(AT)	RLL 2,7	AUTO	N/A	N/A	100
WDAC2250	256.00	3	2233	*	<13	3.50	3H	IDE(AT)	RLL 2,7	AUTO	N/A	N/A	100
WDAC2340	341.29	4	2233	*	<15	3.50	3H	IDE(AT)	RLL 2,7	AUTO	N/A	N/A	100
WDAC2420	425.30	–	–	*	<13	3.50	3H	IDE(AT)	RLL 2,7	AUTO	N/A	N/A	100

WESTERN DIGITAL CORPORATION

MODEL	CAP	HDS	CYL	SPT	SEEK	FF	HGT	INT	ENCODE	LZ	WP	RWC	MTBF
WDAC2540	540.86	–	–	*	<13	3.50	3H	IDE(AT)	RLL 2,7	AUTO	N/A	N/A	100
WDAC2635	639.9				10	3.50	3H	IDE(AT)	RLL 1,7	AUTO	N/A	N/A	250
WDAC2700	696.6	–	–	*	9	3.50	3H	IDE(AT)	RLL 2,7	AUTO	N/A	N/A	100
WDAC280	85.29	4	1082	39	18	3.50	3H	IDE(AT)	RLL 2,7	AUTO	N/A	N/A	50
WDAC2850	853.6	–	–	–	11	3.50	3H	IDE(AT)	RLL 1,7	AUTO	N/A	N/A	250
WDAC31000	1084	6	–	*	10	3.50	3H	IDE(AT)	RLL 2,7	AUTO	N/A	N/A	250
WDAC31200	1222.6	–	–	*	10	3.50	3H	IDE(AT)	RLL 2,7	AUTO	N/A	N/A	0
WDAC31600	1549				10	3.50	3H	IDE(AT)	RLL 2,7	AUTO	N/A	N/A	250
WDAC32100	2111.8	5		*	13	3.50	3H	IDE(AT)	PRML	AUTO	N/A	N/A	300
WDAC32500	2559.8	6		*	13	3.50	3H	IDE(XT)	PRML	AUTO	N/A	N/A	300
WDAC33100	3166	6		*	12	3.50	3H	IDE(AT)	UNIDENT	AUTO	N/A	N/A	300
WDAH260	63.25	4	1020	*	19	2.50	4H	IDE(44PIN)	RLL 2,7	AUTO	N/A	N/A	50
WDAH280	85.57	4	1390	*	19	2.50	4H	IDE(44PIN)	RLL 2,7	AUTO	N/A	N/A	50
WDAL1100	100.06	2	1900	*	<17	2.50	4H	IDE(44PIN)	RLL 1,7	AUTO	N/A	N/A	100
WDAL2120	126.40	4	1349	*	<16	2.50	3H	IDE(AT)	RLL 2,7	AUTO	N/A	N/A	100
WDAL2170	170.60	4	1584	*	<16	2.50	3H	IDE(AT)	RLL 2,7	AUTO	N/A	N/A	100
WDAL2200	200.12	2	1900	*	<17	2.50	4H	IDE(44PIN)	RLL 1,7	AUTO	N/A	N/A	100
WDAL2540	540.8	4			13	2.50	5H	IDE(44PIN)	UNIDENT	AUTO	N/A	N/A	300
WDAP105	104.00	4	–	–	15	3.50	HH	IDE(AT)	RLL 2,7	AUTO	N/A	N/A	50
WDAP4200	214.95	8	1280	41	14	3.50	HH	IDE(AT)	RLL 2,7	AUTO	N/A	N/A	86
WDCU140	42.65	2	1050	*	<19	2.50	4H	PCMCIA	RLL 1,7	AUTO	N/A	N/A	255
WDSC8320	326.51	14	949	48	12	3.50	HH	SCSI-2	RLL 1,7	AUTO	N/A	N/A	150
WDSC8400	412.53	14	1199	48	12	3.50	HH	SCSI-2	RLL 1,7	AUTO	N/A	N/A	150
WDSP105	104.00	4	–	–	15	3.50	HH	SCSI	RLL 2,7	AUTO	N/A	N/A	50
WDSP2100	106.21	4	1265	41	14.4	3.50	HH	SCSI-2	RLL 2,7	AUTO	N/A	N/A	50
WDSP4200-1	209.71	8	1280	40	15	3.50	HH	SCSI	RLL 2,7	AUTO	N/A	N/A	86
WDSP4200-2	209.71	8	1280	40	15	3.50	3H	SCSI	RLL 2,7	AUTO	N/A	N/A	86
WDUC140	42.65	2	1050	*	18	5.25	FH	PCMCIA	RLL 2,7	AUTO	N/A	N/A	50

XEBEC AMERICA

MODEL	CAP	HDS	CYL	SPT	SEEK	FF	HGT	INT	ENCODE	LZ	WP	RWC	MTBF
OWL I	25.00	4	–	17	55	5.25	HH	ST-506/412	MFM	AUTO	N/A	N/A	0
OWL II	38.00	4	–	17	40	5.25	HH	ST-506/412	MFM	–	–	–	0
OWL III	52.00	4	–	17	38	5.25	HH	SCSI	RLL	AUTO	N/A	N/A	0

Y-E DATA AMERICA, INC.

MODEL	CAP	HDS	CYL	SPT	SEEK	FF	HGT	INT	ENCODE	LZ	WP	RWC	MTBF
YD-3042	43.57	4	788	27	28	3.50	HH	SCSI	RLL	AUTO	N/A	N/A	40
YD-3081B	45.45	2	1057	42	28	3.50	HH	SCSI	RLL 2,7	AUTO	N/A	N/A	30
YD-3082	87.14	8	788	27	28	3.50	3H	SCSI	RLL	AUTO	N/A	N/A	40
YD-3082B	90.91	4	1057	42	28	3.50	HH	SCSI	RLL 2,7	AUTO	N/A	N/A	30
YD-3083B	136.37	6	1057	42	28	3.50	HH	SCSI	RLL 2,7	AUTO	N/A	N/A	30
YD-3084B	181.83	8	1057	42	28	3.50	HH	SCSI	RLL 2,7	AUTO	N/A	N/A	30
YD-3161B	45.45	2	1057	42	19	3.50	3H	IDE(AT)	RLL 2,7	AUTO	N/A	N/A	40
YD-3162B	90.91	4	1057	42	19	3.50	3H	IDE(AT)	RLL 2,7	AUTO	N/A	N/A	40
YD-3181B	45.45	2	1057	42	19	3.50	3H	SCSI	RLL 2,7	AUTO	N/A	N/A	40
YD-3182B	90.91	4	1057	42	19	3.50	3H	SCSI	RLL 2,7	AUTO	N/A	N/A	40
YD-3530	31.81	5	731	–	–	–	–	ST-506/412	MFM	–	732	732	0
YD-3540	44.53	7	731	17	26	5.25	HH	ST-506/412	MFM	–	732	732	0

ZENTEK STORAGE, INC.

MODEL	CAP	HDS	CYL	SPT	SEEK	FF	HGT	INT	ENCODE	LZ	WP	RWC	MTBF
ZH3100(A)	86.00	–	–	–	20	3.50	HH	IDE(AT)	RLL	AUTO	N/A	N/A	50
ZH3100(S)	86.00	–	–	–	20	3.50	HH	SCSI	RLL	AUTO	N/A	N/A	50
ZH3140(A)	121.00	–	–	–	20	3.50	HH	IDE(AT)	RLL	AUTO	N/A	N/A	50
ZH3140(S)	121.00	–	–	–	20	3.50	HH	SCSI	RLL	AUTO	N/A	N/A	50

IDE Drive Type
Quick Reference Table

Appendix B Contents:

About IDE Drive Types

Most newer IDE systems can automatically configure for a BIOS Drive Type. However, there are still many drives and BIOSes in use that do not support the IDE **Identify Drive** command (see the IDE section of Chapter Three for more information). If this is the case and you do not have a drive that fits the parameters of one of the defined drive types for your particular BIOS, then you will have to enter a user-definable drive type. This appendix contains a table that allows you to simply look up the capacity of your particular drive and enter the corresponding parameters into the BIOS **User Definable Drive Type**.

The User Definable Drive Type does not have to use the physical parameters of a particular drive or even match the drive's capacity exactly. This is because most IDE drives do a translation so that they may be used in systems that do not support the drive type needed.

There are two types of specifications that you will encounter with this kind of hard drive. The first type of specifications are the **physical** (actual) specifications. These are the hard drive's real values. If you opened up the hard drive, looked inside and saw 4 heads, you would be looking at the physical (actual) number of heads. These physical specifications are what we supply in Appendix A. In some cases, the physical specifications are not available to us; we then supply you with the logical values.

The second type of specifications are the **logical** (translation) specifications. These are the heads, cylinders, and sectors that both the AT BIOS table and DOS can agree on. Most AT BIOSes have a limit of 16 heads and 1,024 cylinders. And DOS can never use more than 1,024 cylinders (unless special software is used). Most IDE hard drives exceed these limits. The IDE hard drive will do a mathematical conversion from the logical (translation) specifications to the physical (actual) specifications. These specifications are normally supplied by the hard drive manufacturer. The manufacturer may supply you with one set of logical (translation) specifications but by no means are you limited to those. Just remember to choose a drive type that is equal to or less than, but never more than the size of the drive in megabytes. The IDE drive will handle the translation from there.

If you have the physical (actual) specifications and a user-definable drive type in your BIOS, you may enter these in (but don't go over the DOS 1,024 cylinder limit). If you don't have the logical (translation) information, a table has been provided in Appendix A for those BIOS tables with a user definable drive type.

See the IDE section of Chapter Three for information on calculating total drive capacity.

IDE Quick Reference Chart

On the next two pages, look up your drive capacity in column one and enter the specifications into the host system's user-definable drive type section.

This table is only valid when used with IDE-type hard drives.

Remember:

- Do not choose a type that is over the total capacity of your drive!
- Do not low-level format your IDE hard drive

IDE QUICK REFERENCE TABLE

CAP	HDS	SPT	CYL
20	4	17	574
21	4	17	603
22	4	17	631
23	4	17	660
24	4	17	689
25	4	17	718
26	4	17	746
27	4	17	775
28	4	17	804
29	4	17	832
30	4	17	861
31	4	17	890
32	4	17	919
33	4	17	947
34	4	17	976
35	4	17	1005
36	5	17	827
37	5	17	850
38	5	17	873
39	5	17	896
40	5	17	919
41	5	17	942
42	5	17	965
43	5	17	988
44	5	17	1011
45	6	17	861
46	6	17	880
47	6	17	899
48	6	17	919
49	6	17	938
50	6	17	957
51	6	17	976
52	6	17	995
53	6	17	1014
54	7	17	886
55	7	17	902
56	7	17	919
57	7	17	935
58	7	17	951
59	7	17	968
60	7	17	984
61	7	17	1001
62	7	17	1017
63	8	17	904
64	8	17	919

CAP	HDS	SPT	CYL	CAP	HDS	SPT	CYL
65	8	17	933	115	13	17	1016
66	8	17	947	116	14	17	951
67	8	17	962	117	14	17	960
68	8	17	976	118	14	17	968
69	8	17	990	119	14	17	976
70	8	17	1005	120	14	17	984
71	8	17	1019	121	14	17	992
72	9	17	919	122	14	17	1001
73	9	17	931	123	14	17	1009
74	9	17	944	124	14	17	1017
75	9	17	957	125	15	17	957
76	9	17	970	126	15	17	965
77	9	17	982	127	15	17	972
78	9	17	995	128	15	17	980
79	9	17	1008	129	15	17	988
80	9	17	1021	130	15	17	995
81	10	17	930	131	15	17	1003
82	10	17	942	132	15	17	1011
83	10	17	953	133	15	17	1018
84	10	17	965	134	16	17	962
85	10	17	976	135	16	17	969
86	10	17	988	136	16	17	976
87	10	17	999	137	16	17	983
88	10	17	1011	138	16	17	990
89	10	17	1022	139	16	17	998
90	11	17	940	140	16	17	1005
91	11	17	950	141	16	17	1012
92	11	17	960	142	16	17	1019
93	11	17	971	143	9	33	940
94	11	17	981	144	9	33	946
95	11	17	992	145	9	33	953
96	11	17	1002	146	9	33	960
97	11	17	1013	147	9	33	966
98	11	17	1023	148	9	33	973
99	12	17	947	149	9	33	979
100	12	17	957	150	9	33	986
101	12	17	966	151	9	33	993
102	12	17	976	152	9	33	999
103	12	17	986	153	9	33	1006
104	12	17	995	154	9	33	1012
105	12	17	1005	155	9	33	1019
106	12	17	1014	156	10	33	923
107	12	17	1024	157	10	33	929
108	13	17	954	158	10	33	935
109	13	17	963	159	10	33	941
110	13	17	972	160	10	33	946
111	13	17	980	161	10	33	952
112	13	17	989	162	10	33	958
113	13	17	998	163	10	33	964
114	13	17	1007	164	10	33	970

CAP	HDS	SPT	CYL	CAP	HDS	SPT	CYL	CAP	HDS	SPT	CYL
166	10	33	982	217	13	33	987	268	16	33	991
167	10	33	988	218	13	33	992	269	16	33	995
168	10	33	994	219	13	33	997	270	16	33	998
169	10	33	1000	220	13	33	1001	271	16	33	1002
170	10	33	1006	221	13	33	1006	272	16	33	1006
171	10	33	1012	222	13	33	1010	273	16	33	1009
172	10	33	1017	223	13	33	1015	274	16	33	1013
173	10	33	1023	224	13	33	1019	275	16	33	1017
174	11	33	936	225	13	33	1024	276	16	33	1020
175	11	33	941	226	14	33	955	277	16	33	1024
176	11	33	946	227	14	33	959	278	9	63	957
177	11	33	952	228	14	33	963	279	9	63	961
178	11	33	957	229	14	33	968	280	9	63	964
179	11	33	963	230	14	33	972	281	9	63	967
180	11	33	968	231	14	33	976	282	9	63	971
181	11	33	973	232	14	33	980	283	9	63	974
182	11	33	979	233	14	33	985	284	9	63	978
183	11	33	984	234	14	33	989	285	9	63	981
184	11	33	990	235	14	33	993	286	9	63	985
185	11	33	995	236	14	33	997	287	9	63	988
186	11	33	1000	237	14	33	1001	288	9	63	992
187	11	33	1006	238	14	33	1006	289	9	63	995
188	11	33	1011	239	14	33	1010	290	9	63	998
189	11	33	1016	240	14	33	1014	291	9	63	1002
190	11	33	1022	241	14	33	1018	292	9	63	1005
191	12	33	942	242	14	33	1023	293	9	63	1009
192	12	33	946	243	15	33	958	294	9	63	1012
193	12	33	951	244	15	33	962	295	9	63	1016
194	12	33	956	245	15	33	966	296	9	63	1019
195	12	33	961	246	15	33	970	297	9	63	1023
196	12	33	966	247	15	33	974	298	10	63	923
197	12	33	971	248	15	33	978	299	10	63	926
198	12	33	976	249	15	33	982	300	10	63	930
199	12	33	981	250	15	33	986	301	10	63	933
200	12	33	986	251	15	33	990	302	10	63	936
201	12	33	991	252	15	33	994	303	10	63	939
202	12	33	996	253	15	33	998	304	10	63	942
203	12	33	1001	254	15	33	1002	305	10	63	945
204	12	33	1006	255	15	33	1006	306	10	63	948
205	12	33	1011	256	15	33	1010	307	10	63	951
206	12	33	1016	257	15	33	1014	308	10	63	954
207	12	33	1020	258	15	33	1017	309	10	63	957
208	13	33	946	259	15	33	1021	310	10	63	961
209	13	33	951	260	16	33	961	311	10	63	964
210	13	33	956	261	16	33	965	312	10	63	967
211	13	33	960	262	16	33	969	313	10	63	970
212	13	33	965	263	16	33	972	314	10	63	973
213	13	33	969	264	16	33	976	315	10	63	976
214	13	33	974	265	16	33	980	316	10	63	979
215	13	33	978	266	16	33	983	317	10	63	982
216	13	33	983	267	16	33	987	318	10	63	985

CAP	HDS	SPT	CYL	CAP	HDS	SPT	CYL	CAP	HDS	SPT	CYL
362	11	63	1020	414	13	63	987	464	15	63	958
363	11	63	1023	415	13	63	989	465	15	63	961
364	12	63	940	416	13	63	992	466	15	63	963
365	12	63	942	417	13	63	994	467	15	63	965
366	12	63	945	418	13	63	996	468	15	63	967
367	12	63	948	419	13	63	999	469	15	63	969
368	12	63	950	420	13	63	1001	470	15	63	971
369	12	63	953	421	13	63	1003	471	15	63	973
370	12	63	955	422	13	63	1006	472	15	63	975
371	12	63	958	423	13	63	1008	473	15	63	977
372	12	63	961	424	13	63	1011	474	15	63	979
373	12	63	963	425	13	63	1013	475	15	63	981
374	12	63	966	427	13	63	1018	476	15	63	983
375	12	63	968	428	13	63	1020	477	15	63	985
376	12	63	971	427	13	63	1018	478	15	63	987
377	12	63	973	427	13	63	1018	479	15	63	989
378	12	63	976	428	13	63	1020	480	15	63	992
379	12	63	979	429	13	63	1023	481	15	63	994
380	12	63	981	430	14	63	952	482	15	63	996
381	12	63	984	431	14	63	954	483	15	63	998
382	12	63	986	432	14	63	956	484	15	63	1000
383	12	63	989	433	14	63	958	485	15	63	1002
384	12	63	992	434	14	63	961	486	15	63	1004
385	12	63	994	435	14	63	963	487	15	63	1006
386	12	63	997	436	14	63	965	488	15	63	1008
387	12	63	999	437	14	63	967	489	15	63	1010
388	12	63	1002	438	14	63	969	490	15	63	1012
389	12	63	1004	439	14	63	972	491	15	63	1014
390	12	63	1007	440	14	63	974	492	15	63	1016
391	12	63	1010	441	14	63	976	493	15	63	1018
392	12	63	1012	442	14	63	978	494	15	63	1020
393	12	63	1015	443	14	63	980	495	15	63	1023
394	12	63	1017	444	14	63	983	496	16	63	960
395	12	63	1020	445	14	63	985	497	16	63	962
396	12	63	1023	446	14	63	987	498	16	63	964
397	13	63	946	447	14	63	989	499	16	63	966
398	13	63	949	448	14	63	992	500	16	63	968
399	13	63	951	449	14	63	994	501	16	63	970
400	13	63	953	450	14	63	996	502	16	63	972
401	13	63	956	451	14	63	998	503	16	63	974
402	13	63	958	452	14	63	1000	504	16	63	976
403	13	63	961	453	14	63	1003	505	16	63	978
404	13	63	963	454	14	63	1005	506	16	63	980
405	13	63	965	455	14	63	1007	507	16	63	982
406	13	63	968	456	14	63	1009	508	16	63	984
407	13	63	970	457	14	63	1011	509	16	63	986
408	13	63	972	458	14	63	1014	510	16	63	988
409	13	63	975	459	14	63	1016	511	16	63	990
410	13	63	977	460	14	63	1018	512	16	63	992
411	13	63	980	461	14	63	1020	513	16	63	994
412	13	63	982	462	14	63	1023	514	16	63	995
413	13	63	984	463	15	63	956	515	16	63	997

CAP	HDS	SPT	CYL
516	16	63	999
517	16	63	1001
518	16	63	1003
519	16	63	1005
520	16	63	1007
521	16	63	1009
522	16	63	1011
523	16	63	1013
524	16	63	1015
525	16	63	1017
526	16	63	1019
527	16	63	1021
528	16	63	1023

The parameters provided are calculated *not to exceed* the formatted capacity specified. For example:

The parameters' list for 130MBs, 15HDs x 995CYL x 17SPT x 512BPS = 129,907,200 bytes.

If you know the exact capacity of the drive, you may increase the cylinder count to achieve maximum capacity. For example:

If the drive's capacity is 130.76MB, you could increase the cylinder count to 1001 for a capacity of 130,690,560 bytes, thus only forfeiting about 7KB.

You'll notice that the largest drive available with 17 sectors is 142MB. You can still use a drive with a higher capacity by increasing the sectors, such as the 143 to 528MB drives above.

In addition to this table, a list of manufacturers' recommended parameters is provided in Appendix A.

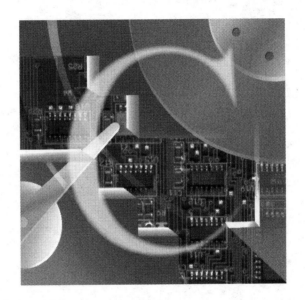

Directory of
Manufacturers

Contact Information

Acculogic, Inc.

Address	7 Whatney	
	Irvine, CA 92718	
Phone	(714) 454-2441	Main
	(714) 454-8527	Fax
	(714) 454-2441	Technical Support
	(800) 234-7811	Toll Free
	(714) 470-1759	BBS
e-mail	techsupport@acctechnology.com	

Acer, Inc.

Address	2641 Orchard Parkway	
	San Jose, CA 95134	
Phone	(408) 432-6200	Main
	(408) 922-2933	Fax
	(800) 873-7255	Technical Support
	(408) 428-0140	BBS
	(800) 554-2494	Fax on Request
Web	www.acer.com/aac/	

Achme Computer, Inc.

Address	4059 Clipper Court	
	Fremont, CA 94538	
Phone	(510) 623-8818	Main
	(510) 623-8585	Fax
	(510) 623-7398	BBS
Web	www.achme.com	
e-mail	support@achme.com	

Actiontec Electronics, Inc.

Address	750 North Mary Avenue	
	Sunnyvale, CA 94086	
Phone	(408) 739-7000	Main
	(408) 739-7001	Fax
	(408) 739-7035	Technical Support
	(800) 797-7001	Toll Free
	(408) 739-7071	BBS
Web	www.actiontec.com	
e-mail	techsupp@actiontec.com	

Actiontec Electronics, Inc.

Address	17702 Mitchell North	
	Irvine, CA 92614	
Phone	(714) 851-8242	Main
	(714) 851-8249	Fax
	(714) 851-8242	Technical Support
	(800) PMC-2277	Toll Free
	(714) 851-1527	BBS
	(888) PMC-8866	Fax on Request

Adaptec, Inc.

Address	691 South Milpitas Blvd.	
	Milpitas, CA 95035	
Phone	(408) 945-8600	Main
	(408) 945-6776	Fax
	(408) 934-7274	Technical Support
	(800) 959-7274	Toll Free
	(408) 945-7727	BBS
	(408) 957-7150	Fax on Request
Web	www.adaptec.com	

ADC Fibermux

Address	21415 Plummer Street	
	Chatsworth, CA 91311	
Phone	(818) 709-6000	Main
	(818) 709-1556	Fax

ADC Kentrox

Address	14375 NW Science Park Drive	
	Portland, OR 97229	
Phone	(503) 643-1681	Main
	(503) 641-3341	Fax
	(800) 733-5511	Toll Free
	(800) 733-5511	Technical Support

ADS International, Inc.

Address	418-B Cloverleaf Drive	
	Baldwin Park, CA 91706-6511	
Phone	(818) 369-2332	Main
	(818) 855-5059	Fax
Web	www.ads.i1.com	

Advanced Digital Information Corporation

Address	10201 Willows Road	
	Redmond, WA 98052	
Phone	(206) 881-8004	Main
	(206) 881-2296	Fax
	(206) 883-4357	Technical Support
	(800) 336-1233	Toll Free
	(206) 883-3211	BBS
Web	www.adic.com	
e-mail	info@adic.com	

Advanced Integration Research, Inc.

Address	2188 Del Franco Street	
	San Jose, CA 95131	
Phone	(408) 428-0800	Main
	(408) 428-0950	Fax
	(408) 428-1547	Technical Support
	(800) 866-1945	Toll Free
	(408) 428-1735	BBS
Web	www.airweb.com	
e-mail	air@ix.netcom.com	

Advanced Logic Research, Inc.

Address	9401 Jeronimo Road	
	Irvine, CA 92618	
Phone	(714) 458-0532	Fax
	(800) 257-1230	Technical Support
	(800) 257-1230	Toll Free
	(714) 458-6834	BBS
	(714) 581-3332	Fax on Request

Advanced Storage Concepts

Address	10713 Ranch Road, 620 North, Suite 305	
	Austin TX 78726	
Phone	(512) 335-1077	Main
	(512) 335-1078	Fax
	(512) 335-3499	BBS
Web	www.eden.com/~asc	
e-mail	asc@eden.com	

Advanced System Products, Inc.

Address	1150 Ringwood Court	
	San Jose, CA 95131	
Phone	(408) 383-5714	Main
	(408) 383-9612	Fax
	(800) 525-7440	Technical Support
	(800) 525-7443	Toll Free
	(408) 383-9540	BBS
	(408) 383-9753	Fax on Request
Web	advansys.com	
e-mail	support@advansys.com	

Advantage Memory Corporation

Address	25-A Technology Drive, Bldg. 1	
	Irvine, CA 92618	
Phone	(714) 453-8111	Main
	(714) 453-8158	Fax
	(714) 453-8111	Technical Support
	(800) 245-5299	Toll Free
e-mail	advantagemem@applelink.apple.com	

Aiwa Data Products, Inc.

Address	19850 E. Business Parkway	
	Walnut, CA 91789-2838	
Phone	(909) 468-5690	Main
	(909) 468-1810	Fax

Aiwa Data Products, Inc.

Address	6500 E Rogers Circle	
	Boca Raton, FL 33487	
Phone	(407) 997-6044	Main
	(407) 997-6202	Fax

Alps Electric (USA), Inc.

Address	3553 North First Street	
	San Jose, CA 95134	
Phone	(408) 432-6000	Main
	(408) 432-6035	Fax
	(800) 449-2577	Technical Support
	(408) 432-6424	BBS
Web	www.alps.com	

American Digicom Corporation

Address	1233 Midas Way	
	Sunnyvale, CA 94086	
Phone	(408) 245-1580	Main
	(408) 245-1584	Fax

**BIOS
Manufacturer**

American Megatrends, Inc.

Address	6145-F Northbelt Parkway	
	Norcross, GA 30071	
Phone	(770) 263-8181	Main
	(770) 246-8791	Fax
	(770) 246-8645	Technical Support
	(800) 828-9264	Toll Free
	(770) 246-8780	BBS
	(770) 246-8787	Fax on Request
Web	www.megatrends.com	

American National Standards Institute

Address	11 West 42nd Street	
	New York, New York 10036	
Phone	(212) 642-4900	Main
	(212) 398-0023	Fax
Web	www.ansi.org	

Ampex Corporation

Address	198 North Nash Street	
	El Segundo, CA 90245	
Phone	(310) 640-0150	Main
	(310) 640-0450	Fax

Andromeda Systems, Inc.

Address	9000 Eton Avenue	
	Canoga Park, CA 91304	
Phone	(818) 709-7600	Main
	(818) 709-7407	Fax
	(818) 709-7600	Technical Support

Aquarius Systems, Inc.

Address	47381 Bayside Parkway	
	Fremont, CA 94538	
Phone	(510) 656-9800	Main
	(510) 656-9876	Fax

Arco Computer Products

Address	2750 N. 29th Avenue, Suite 316	
	Hollywood, FL 33020	
Phone	(305) 925-2688	Main
	(305) 925-2889	Fax
	(800) 458-1666	Toll Free
	(954) 925-2791	BBS
	(954) 925-2889	Fax on Request
Web	www.arcoide.com/adapters	
e-mail	arco@arcoide.com	

Areal Technology, Inc.

Address	2146 Bering Drive	
	San Jose, CA 95131	
Phone	(408) 468-0400	Main
	(408) 468-0410	Fax

Around Technology, Inc.

Address	6777 Engle Road	
	Cleveland, OH 44130	
Phone	(216) 234-6402	Main
	(216) 234-2233	Fax
	(216) 234-6581	BBS
Web	www.aroundtech.com/procomp	

Asicom, Inc.

Address	46716 Fremont Blvd.	
	Fremont, CA 94538	
Phone	(510) 354-0900	Main
	(510) 354-0909	Fax
e-mail	asicom@aol.com	

Asus Computer International

Address	721 Charcot Avenue	
	San Jose, CA 95131	
Phone	(408) 474-0567	Main
	(408) 474-0568	Fax
	(408) 474-0555	BBS
Web	asustek.asus.com.tw	

Atronics International, Inc.

Address	44700-B Industrial Drive	
	Fremont, CA 94538	
Phone	(510) 656-8400	Main
	(510) 656-8560	Fax
	(800) 488-7776	Technical Support
	(510) 226-2671	BBS
Web	atronicsintl.com	
e-mail	info@atronicsintl.com	

Atto Technology, Inc.

Address	40 Hazelwood Drive, Unit 106	
	Amherst, NY 14228	
Phone	(716) 691-1999	Main
	(716) 691-9353	Fax
	(716) 691-9403	BBS
Web	www.attotech.com	

Avatar Systems Corporation

Address	1455 McCarthy Blvd. Milpitas, CA 95035-7433
Phone	(408) 321-0110 Main (408) 321-0115 Fax
Web	www.avatarltd.com

Award Software International, Inc.

BIOS Manufacturer

Address	777 E. Middlefield Road Mountain View, CA 94043
Phone	(415) 968-4433 Main (415) 968-0274 Fax

BASF

Address	3000 Continental Drive - North Mount Olive, NJ 07828-1234
Phone	(201) 426-2600 Main (201) 426-2610 Fax

Baystor, Inc.

Address	6840 Via Del Oro, Suite 275 San Jose, CA 95119
Phone	(408) 578-7760 Main (408) 578-7761 Fax

Behavior Tech Computer Corporation

Address	4180 Business Center Drive Fremont, CA 94538
Phone	(510) 657-3956 Main (510) 657-1859 Fax (510) 249-0342 BBS

Behavior Tech Computer Corporation

Address	6000-F Commerce Parkway Mt. Laurel, NJ 08054
Phone	(609) 273-8500 Main (609) 273-9399 Fax

Behavior Tech Computer Corporation

Address	2001 NW 84th Avenue Miami, FL 33122
Phone	(305) 477-4596 Main (305) 477-9689 Fax

Belfort Memory International
Address   170 Knowles Suite 1
Los Gatos, CA 95030
Phone   (408) 370-5300   Main
(408) 370-3464   Fax

Bering Technology
Address   1357 Dell Avenue
Campbell, CA 95008
Phone   (408) 364-6500   Main
(408) 374-8309   Fax
(800) 237-4641   Technical Support
(800) 237-4641   Toll Free
e-mail   sales@bering.com

Bit 3 computer Corporation
Address   8120 Penn Avenue South
Minneapolis, MN 55431-1393
Phone   (612) 881-6955   Main
(612) 881-9674   Fax

Boca Research, Inc.
Address   1377 Clint Moore Road
Boca Raton, FL 33487-2722
Phone   (407) 997-6227   Main
(407) 994-5848   Fax
(407) 997-5549   Technical Support
Web   www.boca.org

Bull HN Information Systems, Inc.
Address   Technology Park
Billerica, MA 01821-9903
Phone   (508) 294-6000   Main
(508) 294-7411   Fax
(800) 285-5727   Toll Free

Buslogic, Inc.
Address   4151 Burton Drive
Santa Clara, CA 95054
Phone   (408) 492-9090   Main
(408) 492-1542   Fax
(408) 492-1984   BBS
Web   www.buslogic.com

C.Itoh Electronics

Address	2701 Dow Avenue	
	Tustin CA 92780	
Phone	(714) 757-4488	Fax
	(800) 347-2484	Toll Free

Cableflex, Inc.

Address	801-1 E. Frontage Drive	
	Nogales, AR 85621	
Phone	(520) 281-2718	Main
	(520) 281-4073	Fax

Calluna Technology, Inc.

Address	1762 Technology Drive Suite 223	
	San Jose, CA 95110	
Phone	(408) 453-4753	Main
	(408) 453-0427	Fax

Chaintech Computer Company, Ltd

Address	12880 Lakeland Road	
	Santa Fe Springs, CA 90670	
Phone	(310) 906-1698	Main
	(310) 906-1699	Fax

Chicony, Inc.

Address	53 Parker	
	Irvine, CA 92718	
Phone	(714) 380-0928	Main
	(714) 380-9204	Fax

Ciprico, Inc.

Address	2800 Campus Drive, Suite 60	
	Plymouth, MN 55441	
Phone	(612) 551-4000	Main
	(612) 551-4002	Fax

CMD Technology, Inc.

Address	1 Vanderbilt	
	Irvine, CA 92618	
Phone	(714) 454-0800	Main
	(714) 455-1656	Fax
	(800) 426-3832	Toll Free
Web	websvr.cmd.com	

CMS Enhancements, Inc.

Address	Three Imperial Promenade	
	Santa Ana, CA 92707	
Phone	(714) 437-0099	Main
	(714) 513-2465	Fax
	(800) 555-1671	Toll Free
	(714) 871-2023	Fax on Request

Cogent Data Technologies, Inc.

Address	640 Mullis Street	Corporate Office and Support
	Friday Harbor, WA 98250	
Phone	(360) 378-2929	Main
	(360) 378-2882	Fax
	(360) 378-2929	Technical Support
	(800) 426-4368	Toll Free
	(360) 378-5405	BBS
Web	www.cogentdata.com	
e-mail	support@cogentdata.com	

Cogent Data Technologies, Inc.

Address	15375 SE 30th Place, Suite 310	
	Bellevue, WA 98007	
Phone	(206) 603-0333	Main
	(206) 603-9223	Fax
e-mail	sales@cogentdata.com	

Compaq Computer Corporation

Address	20555 State Highway 249 PO Box 692000	
	Houston, TX 77269-2000	
Phone	(713) 370-0670	Main
	(713) 374-1740	Fax
	(800) 652-6672	Technical Support
	(800) 345-1518	Fax on Request
	(713) 378-1418	BBS
	(800) 345-1518	Toll Free
Web	www.compaq.com	

Conner Peripherals, Inc. (see Seagate Technology)

Control Concepts, Inc.

Address	8500 Executive Park Avenue	
	Fairfax, VA 22031-2218	
Phone	(703) 876-6400	Main
	(703) 876-6416	Fax
	(800) 922-9259	Technical Support
	(800) 922-9259	Toll Free
e-mail	taubeg@presearch.com	

Core International, Inc.

Address   6500 East Rogers Circle
                Boca Raton, FL 33487

Phone   (407) 997-6033   Main
                (407) 997-6202   Fax
                (407) 997-6033   Technical Support
                (407) 241-2929   BBS

Corporate Systems Center

Address   1294 Hammerwood Avenue
                Sunnyvale, CA 94089

Phone   (408) 734-3475   Main
                (408) 745-1816   Fax
                (408) 541-8455   BBS

Data Technology Corporation

Address   1515 Centre Pointe Drive
                Milpitas, CA 95035

Phone   (408) 942-4000   Main
                (408) 942-4027   Fax
                (408) 262-7700   Technical Support
                (408) 942-4010   BBS
                (408) 942-4005   Fax on Request

Web   www.datatechnology.com

Dell Computer Corporation

Address   2214 W Breaker Lane Suite D
                Austin TX 78758

Phone   (512) 338-4400   Main
                (512) 728-3653   Fax
                (800) 624-9896   Technical Support
                (800) 624-9897   Toll Free
                (512) 728-8528   BBS
                (800) 950-1329   Fax on Request

Web   www.dell.com

Densitron Corporation

Address   10430 Pioneer Blvd. Suite 2
                Santa Fe Springs, CA 90670

Phone   (310) 941-5000   Main
                (310) 941-5757   Fax

Diamond Flower Inc.
Address	135 Main Avenue	
	Sacramento CA 95838	
Phone	(916) 568-1234	Main
	(916) 568-1233	Fax
	(916) 568-1234	Technical Support
	(800) 808-4334	Toll Free
	(908) 390-4820	BBS
Web	www.dfiusa.com	
e-mail	info@dfiusa.com	

Digital Equipment Corporation
Address	111 Powdermill Road	
	Maynard, MA 01754	
Phone	(508) 493-2211	Main
	(508) 493-8780	Fax
	(800) 354-9000	Technical Support
	(800) 433-4825	Fax on Request
	(508) 264-7227	BBS
	(800) 344-4825	Toll Free
Web	www.digital.com	

Disctec
Address	925 S. Semoran Blvd. Suite 114	
	Winter Park, FL 32792	
Phone	(407) 671-5500	Main
	(407) 671-6606	Fax
	(407) 671-5500	Technical Support
	(800) 553-0337	Toll Free
	(407) 671-6099	BBS
Web	www.distec.com	

Distributed Processing Technology
Address	140 Candace Drive	
	Maitland, FL 32751	
Phone	(407) 830-5522	Main
	(407) 260-5366	Fax
	(407) 830-5522	Technical Support
	(407) 830-1070	BBS
Web	www.dpt.com	

DTK Computer, Inc. – Los Angeles

Address	18645 East Gale Avenue Suite 233	
	City of Industry, CA 91748	
Phone	(818) 810-8880	Main
	(818) 810-5233	Fax
	(800) 289-2385	Toll Free
	(818) 854-0797	BBS
	(800) 806-1385	Fax on Request
Web	www.dtk.com	

DTK Computer, Inc. – Chicago

Address	2375 Estes Avenue	
	Elk Grove Village, IL 60007-5428	
Phone	(847) 593-3080	Main
	(847) 593-3083	Fax
	(847) 593-3080	Technical Support

DTK Computer, Inc. – Miami

Address	8400 NW 17th Street	
	Miami, FL 33126	
Phone	(305) 597-8888	Main
	(305) 477-8322	Fax
	(305) 477-7400	Technical Support

DTK Computer, Inc. – New Jersey

Address	1035 Centennial Avenue	
	Piscataway, NJ 08854-4124	
Phone	(908) 562-8800	Main
	(908) 562-8400	Fax
	(908) 562-8800	Technical Support

DTK Computer, Inc. – Houston

Address	10531 Wilcrest Drive Suite 100	
	Houston, TX 77099-2821	
Phone	(713) 568-6688	Main
	(713) 568-5688	Fax
	(713) 568-6688	Technical Support

Elitegroup Computer Systems, Inc.

Address	45225 Northport Court	
	Fremont, CA 94538	
Phone	(510) 226-7333	Main
	(510) 226-7350	Fax
	(800) 829-8890	Toll Free
Web	www.ecsusa.com	

Emulex Corporation
Address   3535 Harbor Blvd.
Costa Mesa, CA 92626
Phone   (714) 662-5600   Main
(714) 241-0792   Fax
(800) 854-7112   Toll Free
Web   www.emulex.com

Epson, Inc.
Address   20770 Madrona Avenue
Torrance, CA 90503
Phone   (310) 782-0770   Main
(310) 782-5220   Fax
Web   www.epson.com

Epson, Inc.
Address   2833 Junction Avenue Suite 200
San Jose, CA 95134
Phone   (408) 474-0500   Main
(408) 474-0511   Fax

Everex Systems, Inc.
Address   5020 Brandin Court
Fremont, CA 94538
Phone   (510) 498-1111   Main
(510) 683-2186   Fax
(510) 498-4411   Technical Support
(800) 821-0806   Toll Free
(510) 226-9694   BBS
(510) 683-2800   Fax on Request
Web   www.everex.com

Evergreen Systems, Inc.
Address   120 Landing Court
Novato, CA 94945
Phone   (415) 897-8888   Main
(415) 897-6158   Fax
(415) 897-8888   Technical Support
(800) EVERSYS   Toll Free
(415) 898-9398   BBS

Evergreen Technologies, Inc.

Address	806 N.W. Buchanan Street	
	Corvallis, OR 97330-6211	
Phone	(541) 757-0934	Main
	(541) 757-7341	Technical Support
	(800) 733-0934	Toll Free
	(503) 752-9851	BBS

Expert Computer International, Inc.

Address	12951 166th Street	
	Cerritos, CA 90703	
Phone	(310) 407-1740	Main
	(310) 407-1719	Fax
	(310) 407-1721	BBS

Expert Computer International, Inc.

Address	3772 Realty Road	
	Addison TX 75244	
Phone	(214) 484-4744	Main
	(214) 484-3494	Fax

First International Computer, Inc.

Address	980A Mission Court	
	Fremont, CA 94539	
Phone	(510) 252-7777	Main
	(510) 252-8888	Fax
	(510) 252-7758	Technical Support
	(800) 342-2636	Toll Free
	(510) 252-7750	BBS
	(510) 252-8844	Fax on Request
Web	www.fica.com	
e-mail	sales@fica.com	

Fuji Electric Corporation

Address	47520 Westinghouse Drive	
	Fremont, CA 94538	
Phone	(510) 438-9700	Main
	(510) 428-9150	Fax

Fujitsu Corporation

Address	2904 Orchard Parkway	
Phone	San Jose, CA 95134	
	(408) 432-6333	Main
	(408) 894-1709	Fax
	(408) 894-3950	Technical Support
	(800) 626-4686	Toll Free
	(408) 428-0456	Fax on Request
Web	www.fujitsu.com	

Fujitsu Corporation

Address	3545 N. 1st Street	
	San Jose, CA 95134	
Phone	(408) 922-9000	Main

Future Domain Corporation

Address	PO Box 57020	
	Irvine, CA 92619-7020	
Phone	(714) 455-8100	Main
	(714) 253-0913	Fax
	(714) 253-0432	BBS

Giga-Byte Technology Company, Limited

Address	18325 Valley Blvd., Suite E	
	La Puente, CA 91748	
Phone	(818) 854-9338	Main
	(818) 854-9339	Fax
	(818) 369-3985	BBS
e-mail	gigabyte@tpts1.seed.net.tw	

Goldstar Electronics International, Inc.

Address	1000 Sylvan Avenue	
	Englewood Cliffs, NJ 07632	
Phone	(201) 816-2000	Main
	(201) 816-0636	Fax
	(800) 562-0244	Technical Support
	(800) 243-0000	Toll Free

GSI, Inc.

Address	17951-H Skypark Circle	
	Irvine, CA 92614	
Phone	(714) 261-7949	Main
	(714) 757-1778	Fax
	(714) 261-9744	Technical Support
	(800) 486-7800	Toll Free

Hewlett-Packard Company

Address	3000 Hannover Street	
	Palo Alto, CA 94304	
Phone	(800) 752-0900	Main
	(415) 857-5518	Fax
	(208) 323-2551	Technical Support
	(800) 637-7740	Toll Free
	(408) 553-3500	BBS
	(800) 231-9300	Fax on Request
Web	www.corp.hp.com	

Hitachi Corporation

Address	2000 Sierra Point Parkway, MS #500	
	Brisbane, CA 94005-1835	
Phone	(415) 589-8300	Main
	(415) 244-7647	Fax
	(800) 448-2244	Toll Free
	(800) 448-3291	Fax on Request
Web	www.hitachi.com	

Hitachi Corporation

Address	2520 Junction Avenue Bldg. D	
	San Jose, CA 95134	
Phone	(408) 321-5000	Main
	(800) 314-4743	Toll Free

IBM Corporation

Address	Old Orchard Road	
	Armonk, NY 10504	
Phone	(914) 765-1900	Main
	(800) 772-2227	Technical Support
	(800) 426-2255	Toll Free
	(919) 517-0001	BBS
	(800) 426-3395	Fax on Request
Web	www.ibm.com	

IBM Corporation

Address	5600 Cottle Road	
	San Jose, CA 95193	
Phone	(800) 4-IBMSSD	Toll Free
Web	www.ibm.com	

IBM Corporation

Address	Route 100, Box 100	
	Somers, NY 10589	
Phone	(800) IBM-333	Toll Free
Web	www.ibm.com	

Infomatic Power Systems Corporation (IPX)

Address   9945 South Pioneer Blvd.
Santa Fe Springs, CA 90670

Phone   (310) 948-2217   Main
(310) 948-5264   Fax

Initio Corporation

Address   2901 Tasman Drive Suite 201
Santa Clara, CA 95054

Phone   (408) 988-1919   Main
(408) 988-3254   Fax
(408) 988-1919   Technical Support
(800) 99-initio   Toll Free
(408) 988-2054   BBS

Web   www.initio.com

Integral Peripherals

Address   5775 Flatiron Parkway Suite 100
Boulder, CO 80301-5730

Phone   (303) 449-8009   Main
(303) 449-8089   Fax
(303) 449-8009   Technical Support

Interaction Systems, Inc.

Address   10 Commerce Way
Woburn, MA 01801

Phone   (617) 932-0700   Main
(617) 932-3088   Fax

Intergraph Computer Systems

Address   Huntsville, AL 35894-0001

Phone   (205) 730-2000   Main
(205) 730-6445   Fax

Iomega Corporation

Address   1821 West Iomega Way
Roy, Utah 84067

Phone   (801) 778-1000   Main
(801) 778-3748   Fax
(800) 778-0056   Toll Free
(801) 392-9819   BBS

Web   www.iomega.com

JC Information Systems Corporation

Address	4487 Technology Drive	
	Fremont, CA 94538	
Phone	(510) 659-8440	Main
	(510) 659-8449	Fax
	(510) 659-8440	Technical Support
Web	www.jcis.com	
e-mail	info@jcis.com	

JPN Corporation

Address	48006 Fremont Blvd.	
	Fremont, CA 94538	
Phone	(510) 770-3990	Main
	(510) 770-3994	Fax
	(510) 770-3990	Technical Support
	(510) 226-0632	BBS

JTS Corporation

Address	166 Baypointe Parkway	
	San Jose, CA 95134	
Phone	(408) 468-1800	Main
	(408) 468-1801	Fax
	(408) 468-1800	Technical Support
	(408) 435-1741	BBS
e-mail	tech@jtscorp.com	

JVC

Address	17811 Mitchell Avenue	
	Irvine, CA 92614	
Phone	(714) 261-1292	Main
	(714) 261-9690	Fax
Web	www.jvc-us.com	

Kimpsion International

Address	4701 Patrick Henry Drive Suite 401	
	Santa Clara, CA 95054	
Phone	(408) 988-8808	Main
	(408) 988-8809	Fax

Kingston Technology Corporation

Address	17600 Newhope Street	
	Fountain Valley, CA 92708	
Phone	(714) 435-2600	Main
	(714) 438-2699	Fax
	(714) 438-2796	Technical Support
	(800) 435-2620	Toll Free
	(714) 435-2636	BBS
	(714) 435-2677	Fax on Request
Web	www.kingston.com	

Koutech Systems, Inc..

Address	9314 Norwalk Blvd.	
	Santa Fe Springs, CA 90670	
Phone	(310) 699-5340	Main
	(310) 699-0795	Fax
	(310) 692-6798	BBS

Koutech Systems, Inc..

Address	1675 Walsh Avenue Suite A	
	Santa Clara, CA 95050	
Phone	(408) 727-8208	Main
	(408) 727-8440	Fax

Kyocera Electronics, Inc.

Address	8611 Balboa Avenue	
	San Diego, CA 92123	
Phone	(619) 576-2600	Main
	(619) 268-3035	Fax

Kyocera Electronics, Inc.

Address	100 Randolph Road	
	Somerset, NJ 08875	
Phone	(908) 560-3400	Main

Lava Computer Manufacturing, Inc.

Address	PO Box 280 LPO
	Niagara Falls, NY 14304-0280

Linksys

Address 17401 Armstrong Avenue
Irvine, CA 92614

Phone (714) 261-1288   Main
(714) 261-8868   Fax
(714) 261-1288   Technical Support
(800) 546-5797   Toll Free
(714) 222-5111   BBS

Web www.linksys.com

Liuski International, Inc.

Address 10 Hub Drive
Melville, NJ 11747

Phone (516) 454-8220   Main
(516) 454-8266   Fax
(516) 454-8266   Technical Support
(800) 347-5454   Toll Free
(516) 454-8262   BBS

Liuski International, Inc.

Address 6585 Crescent Drive
Norcross, GA 30071

Phone (770) 447-9454   Main
(770) 441-1671   Fax
(800) 347-5454   Technical Support
(800) 454-8754   Toll Free
(770) 447-5454   BBS
(770) 447-9454/4500   Fax on Request

Web www.magitronic.com

Logical Analytical Solutions, Inc.

Address 2391 Zanker Road, Suite 390
San Jose, CA 95131

Phone (408) 383-7420   Main
(408) 383-7429   Fax

Lomas Data Products, Inc.

Address 420 Maple Street Suite 2
Marlboro, MA 01752

Phone (508) 460-0333   Main
(508) 460-0616   Fax
(508) 460-0333   Technical Support

Web www.ourworld.compuserve.com/homepages/Lomasdata

Longshine Microsystems, Inc.

Address	10400-9 Pioneer Blvd.	
	Santa Fe Springs, CA 90670	
Phone	(310) 903-0899	Main
	(310) 944-2201	Fax
	(310) 903-0899	Technical Support
	(310) 903-4590	BBS

Magicram, Inc.

Address	1850 Beverly Blvd.	
	Los Angeles, CA 90057	
Phone	(213) 413-9999	Main
	(213) 413-0828	Fax
	(213) 413-9999	Technical Support
	(800) 272-6242	Toll Free
Web	www.magicram.com	

Magicwand

Address	4487 Technology Drive, Building B	
	Fremont, CA 94538	
Phone	(510) 659-8440	Main
	(510) 659-8449	Fax
Web	www.magicwand.com	
e-mail	infor@magicwand.com	

Magitronics

Address	10 Hub Drive	
	Melville, NJ 11747	
Phone	(800) 347-5454	Technical Support

Magitronics

Address	6585 Crescent Drive	
	Norcross, GA 30071	
Phone	(770) 849-0667	Main
	(770) 447-9928	Fax
	(800) 347-5454	BBS
	(800) 454-8754	Toll Free
	(770) 447-5454	Technical Support

Mass Memory Systems, Inc.

Address	1414 Gay Drive	
	Winter Park, FL 32789	
Phone	(407) 629-1081	Main
	(407) 628-3862	Fax
	(407) 629-1081	Technical Support

Mass Microsystems
Address   6818 Patterson Pass Road Suite G
Livermore, CA 94550
Phone   (510) 294-7900   Main
(510) 294-7909   Fax

Maxtor Corporation
Address   510 Cottonwood Drive
Milpitas, CA 95035
Phone   (408) 432-1700   Main
(408) 432-4510   Fax
(800) 262-9867   Toll Free
(800) 262-9867   Technical Support
(303) 678-2222   BBS
(303) 678-2618   Fax on Request
Web   www.maxtor.com

Maxtor Corporation
Address   2190 Miller Drive
Longmont, CO 80501
Phone   (303) 651-6000   Main
(303) 678-2165   Fax
Web   www.maxtor.com

Mecer Corporation
Address   3217 Whipple Road
Union City, CA 94587
Phone   (510) 475-5730   Main
(510) 475-0982   Fax

Media Vision Technology, Inc.
Web   www.mediavis.com

Mega Drive Systems
Address   489 S. Robertson Blvd.
Beverly Hills, CA 90211
Phone   (310) 247-0006   Main
(310) 247-8118   Fax

Mega Drive Systems
Address   15200 Shady Grove Road Suite 405
Rockville, MD 20850
Phone   (301) 670-6342   Main
(301) 208-2661   Fax

Micro Equipment Corporation
Address	2900 Jones Mill Road	
	Norcross, GA 30071	
Phone	(770) 447-1726	Main
	(770) 449-6103	Fax
	(800) 226-8088	Toll Free

Micro Solutions, Inc.
Address	132 W. Lincoln Highway	
	Dekalb, IL 60115	
Phone	(815) 756-3411	Main
	(815) 756-2928	Fax
	(815) 756-3411	Technical Support
	(800) 890-7227	Toll Free
	(815) 756-9100	BBS

Microid Research, Inc.
BIOS Manufacturer
Address	1538 Turnpike St.	
	North Andover, MA 01845	
Phone	(508) 686-6468	Main
	(508) 683-1630	Fax

Micropolis Corporation
Address	21211 Nordhoff Street	
	Chatsworth, CA 91311	
Phone	(818) 709-3300	Main
	(818) 718-5312	Fax
	(818) 709-3325	Fax on Request
	(800) 395-3748	Toll Free
	(818) 709-3310	BBS
	(818) 709-3325	Fax on Request

Microtech International, Inc.
Address	158 Commerce Street	
	East Haven, CT 06512	
Phone	(203) 468-6223	Main
	(203) 468-6466	Fax
	(800) 666-9689	Technical Support
	(800) 626-4276	Toll Free
	(203) 469-6430	BBS

Mitsubishi Electronics
Address   5665 Plaza Drive
Cypress, CA 90630
Phone   (800) 843-2515   Main
(714) 236-6425   Fax
(800) 344-6352   Technical Support
(714) 236-6286   BBS
(714) 236-6453   Fax on Request
Web   www.mitsubishi-display.com

Monolithic Systems, Inc. (Colorado MSI)
Address   8150 S. Ackron Street Unit 402
Englewood, CO 80112
Phone   (303) 790-0180   Main
(303) 790-0182   Fax

Mylex Corporation
Address   34551 Ardenwood Blvd.
Fremont, CA 94555-3607
Phone   (510) 796-6100   Main
(510) 745-7653   Fax
(800) 776-9539   Technical Support
(800) 776-9539   Toll Free
(510) 793-3491   BBS
Web   www.mylex.com

NCL America
Address   1031 East Duane Avenue Suite H
Sunyvale, CA 94086
Phone   (408) 737-2496   Main
(408) 730-1621   Fax

NCR Corporation
Address   1700 South Patterson Blvd.
Dayton, OH 45479
Phone   (513) 445-5000   Main
(800) 262-7782   Technical Support
(800) 225-5627   Toll Free
Web   www.ncr.com

NCR Corporation
Address   92 Montvale Avenue Suite 3500
Stoneham, MA 02180-3602
Phone   (617) 438-0381   Main
(617) 438-1045   Fax

NCR Corporation

Address	450 East Carpenter Freeway	
	Irving, TX 75062	
Phone	(214) 733-3594	Main
	(214) 713-8121	Fax

NCR Corporation

Address	1731 Technology Drive Suite 610	
	San Jose, CA 95110	
Phone	(408) 453-0303	Main
	(408) 441-7743	Fax

NCR Corporation

Address	3300 Irvine Avenue Suite 255	
	Newport Beach, CA 92660	
Phone	(714) 474-7095	Main
	(714) 474-7264	Fax

NEC Technologies, Inc.

Address	8 Corporate Center Drive	
	Melville, NY 11747	
Phone	(516) 753-7000	Main
	(516) 753-7434	Fax
	(800) 338-7549	Toll Free
Web	www.nec.com	

NEC Technologies, Inc.

Address	1414 Massachusetts Avenue	
	Boxborough, MA 01719-2298	
Phone	(508) 264-8000	Main
	(508) 264-8127	Fax
	(800) 388-8888	Technical Support
	(800) 388-8888	Toll Free
	(508) 635-4706	BBS
	(800) 366-0476	Fax on Request

NEC Technologies, Inc.

Address	265 Santa Ana Court	
	Sunnyvale, CA 94043	
Phone	(415) 528-6000	Main

New Media Corporation

Address	1 Technology, Building A	
	Irvine, CA 92618	
Phone	(714) 453-0100	Main
	(714) 453-0114	Fax
	(714) 453-0314	Technical Support
	(800) 227-3748	Toll Free
	(714) 453-0214	BBS
	(714) 789-5212	Fax on Request
Web	www.newmediacorp.com	

Nexstor, Inc.

Address	631 South Milpitas Blvd.	
	Milpitas, CA 95035	
Phone	(408) 262-1056	Main
	(408) 262-1082	Fax
	(408) 946-6932	BBS

Okidata

Address	532 Fellowship Road	
	Mt. Laurel, NJ 08054	
Phone	(609) 235-2600	Main
	(609) 778-4184	Fax
	(609) 273-0300	Technical Support
	(800) OKI-DATA	Toll Free
	(800) 654-3282	Fax on Request
Web	www.okidata.com	

Olivetti

Address	22425 E. Appleway Avenue	
	Liberty Lake, WA 99019-9534	
Phone	(509) 927-5600	Main
	(509) 927-5774	Fax
	(800) 255-4319	Toll Free

Optima Technology

Address	17062 Murphy Avenue	
	Irvine, CA 92714	
Phone	(714) 476-0515	Main
	(714) 476-0613	Fax
Web	www.optimatech.com	
e-mail	sales@optimatech.com	

Parallel Storage Solutions

Address	116 S. Central Avenue	
	Elmsford, NY 10523	
Phone	(914) 347-7044	Main
	(914) 347-4646	Fax
	(800) 998-7839	Toll Free

Perceptive Solutions, Inc.

Address	2700 Flora Street	
	Dallas, TX 75201	
Phone	(214) 954-1774	Main
	(214) 953-1774	Fax
	(214) 954-1856	BBS

Phoenix Technologies, Ltd.

**BIOS
Manufacturer**

Address	2770 De La Cruz Blvd.	
	Santa Clara, CA 95050	
Phone	(408) 654-9000	Main
	(408) 452-1985	Fax
	(800) 677-7305	Toll Free
	(714) 440-8026	BBS
Web	www.ptltd.com	

Promise Technology, Inc.

Address	1460 Koll Circle	
	San Jose, CA 95112	
Phone	(408) 452-0948	Main
	(408) 452-1534	Fax
	(408) 452-1180	Technical Support
	(800) 888-0245	Toll Free
	(408) 452-1267	BBS
	(408) 452-9160	Fax on Request
Web	www.promise.com	
e-mail	support@promise.com	

Q Logic Corporation

Address	3545 Harbor Blvd.	
	Costa Mesa, CA 92626	
Phone	(714) 668-5090	Fax
	(800) 662-4471	Toll Free
	(714) 708-3170	BBS
Web	www.qlc.com	

QDI Computer, Inc.

Address	11552 East Washington Blvd., Unit D	
	Whittier, CA 90606	
Phone	(310) 908-1029	Main
	(310) 908-1033	Fax

Quantum Corporation

Address	500 McCarthy Blvd.	
	Milpitas, CA 95035	
Phone	(408) 894-4000	Main
	(408) 894-3218	Fax
	(800) 826-8022	Technical Support
	(408) 894-3214	BBS
	(800) 434-7532	Fax on Request
Web	www.quantum.com	

Quick Technology, Inc.

Address	1542 Edinger Avenue, #B	
	Tustin, CA 92680	
Phone	(714) 258-4500	Main
	(714) 258-4508	Fax
	(800) 950-8999	Toll Free

Quickpath Systems, Inc.

Address	46723 Fremont Blvd.	
	Fremont, CA 94538	
Phone	(510) 440-7288	Main
	(510) 440-7289	Fax
	(510) 440-7285	Technical Support
	(800) 995-8828	Toll Free
	(510) 440-7284	BBS
Web	www.quickpath.com	
e-mail	qpinfo@quickpath.com	

Rancho Technology, Inc.

Address	10783 Bell Court	
	Rancho Cucamonga, CA 91730	
Phone	(909) 987-3966	Main
	(909) 989-2365	Fax
	(909) 987-6952	Technical Support
	(909) 980-7699	BBS

Relialogic Corporation Private, Ltd.

Address	48006 Fremont Blvd.	
	Fremont, CA 94538	
Phone	(510) 770-3990	Main
	(510) 770-3994	Fax
	(800) 998-3966	Toll Free
	(800) 998-3966	Technical Support
	(510) 226-0632	BBS
e-mail	rlogic@aol.com	

Samsung Electronics, Inc.

Address	105 Challenger Blvd.	
	Ridgefield Park, NJ 07660	
Phone	(201) 229-7000	Main
	(201) 229-4110	Fax
	(201) 229-4060	Technical Support
	(800) 446-0262	Toll Free
	(201) 691-6238	BBS
	(201) 229-4053	Fax on Request

Samsung Electronics, Inc.

Address	14251 E. Firestone Blvd. Suite 101	
	La Mirada, CA 90638	
Phone	(310) 537-7000	Main
	(310) 802-8820	Fax

Seagate Technology, Inc.

Address	PO Box 66360	
	Scotts Valley, CA 95067-0360	
Phone	(408) 438-6550	Main
	(408) 438-8137	Fax
	(408) 576-5000	Technical Support
	(800) 852-3475	Toll Free
	(408) 438-8771	BBS
	(408) 438-2620	Fax on Request
Web	www.seagate.com	

Siemens Nixdorf Informationssysteme AG

Address	200 Wheeler Road	
	Burlington, MA 01803	
Phone	(617) 273-0480	Main
	(617) 221-0231	Fax

Siig, Inc.

Address	6078 Stewart Avenue	
	Fremont, CA 94538	
Phone	(510) 657-8688	Main
	(510) 657-5962	Fax
	(510) 353-7542	Technical Support
	(510) 353-7532	BBS

Silicon Star International, Inc.

Address	47889 Fremont Blvd.	
	Fremont, CA 94538	
Phone	(510) 623-0500	Main
	(510) 623-1092	Fax

Simple Technology, Inc.

Address	3001 Daimler Street	
	Santa Ana, CA 92705	
Phone	(714) 476-1180	Main
	(714) 476-1209	Fax
	(800) 367-7330	Toll Free
Web	www.simpletech.com	

Sony Corporation

Address	1 Sony Drive	
	Park Ridge, NJ 07656	
Phone	(201) 930-1000	Main
	(201) 573-8608	Fax

Standard Microsystems Corporation

Address	80 Arkay Drive	
	Hauppauge, NY 11788	
Phone	(516) 435-6000	Main
	(516) 273-1803	Fax
	(800) 992-4762	Technical Support
	(800) SMC-4YOU	Toll Free
	(516) 434-3162	BBS
	(800) 762-8329	Fax on Request
Web	www.smc.com	
e-mail	techsupt@ccmail.west.smc.com	

Storage Dimensions

Address	1656 McCarthy Blvd.	
	Milpitas, CA 95035	
Phone	(408) 954-0710	Main
	(408) 944-1203	Fax
Web	www.galahad.xstor.com	

Storage Solutions, Inc.
Address	550 West Avenue	
	Stamford, CT 06902	
Phone	(203) 325-0035	Main
	(203) 327-4675	Fax
e-mail	info@ssi.mhs.compuserve.com	

Symbios Logic
Address	4420 Arrows West Drive	
	Colorado Springs, CO 80907	
Phone	(719) 533-7000	Main
	(719) 533-7244	Fax
Web	www.symbios.com	

Symbios Logic
Address	3718 North Rock Road	
	Wichita, KS 67226-1397	
Phone	(316) 636-8884	Main
	(316) 636-8015	Fax

Syquest Technology
Address	47071 Bayside Parkway	
	Fremont, CA 94538	
Phone	(510) 226-4000	Main
	(510) 226-4102	Fax
	(800) 249-2440	Technical Support
	(800) 245-2278	Toll Free
	(510) 656-0473	BBS
	(510) 226-4120	Fax on Request

Tandon Corporation
Phone	(414) 638-1851	Main
	(414) 638-1852	Fax

Teac Corporation
Address	7733 Telegraph Road	
	Montebello, CA 90640	
Phone	(213) 726-0303	Main
	(213) 727-7672	Fax
	(213) 726-0303	Technical Support
	(213) 727-7660	BBS
	(213) 727-7629	Fax on Request
Web	www.teac.com	

Tekram Technology Company, Ltd.

Address   11500 Metric Blvd. Suite 190
Austin, TX 78758

Phone   (512) 833-6550   Main
(512) 833-7276   Fax
(512) 833-7985   BBS

Web   www.tekram.com/

e-mail   sales@tekram.com.tw

TMC Research Corporation

Address   631 South Milpitas Blvd.
Milpitas, CA 95035

Phone   (408) 262-0888   Main
(408) 262-1082   Fax
(408) 946-6932   BBS

Toshiba

Address   9740 Irvine Blvd. PO Box 19724
Irvine, CA 92713

Phone   (714) 455-0407   Main
(714) 583-3140   Fax
(714) 455-0407   Technical Support
(800) 999-4273   Toll Free
(714) 837-8864   BBS
(714) 455-0407   Fax on Request

Web   www.toshiba.com.

Trantor Systems, Ltd.

Address   691 South Milpitas Blvd.
Milpitas, CA 95035

Phone   (408) 945-8600   Main
(800) 872-6867   Toll Free

Tyan Computer Corporation

Address   1753 S. Main Street
Milpitas, CA 95035

Phone   (408) 956-8000   Main
(408) 956-8044   Fax
(408) 956-8000   Technical Support
(408) 956-8171   BBS

Web   www.tyan.com

Valuestor, Inc.

Address	1609-B Regatta Lane San Jose, CA 95112-116	
Phone	(408) 437-2300	Main
	(408) 437-9333	Fax
	(408) 437-2310	Technical Support
	(800) 873-8258	Toll Free
	(408) 437-1616	BBS

Viva Computer Company

Address	48346 Milmont Drive Fremont, CA 94538	
Phone	(510) 490-4988	Main
	(510) 490-4999	Fax

Western Digital Corporation

Address	8105 Irvine Center Drive Irvine, CA 92718	
Phone	(714) 932-5000	Main
	(714) 932-6294	Fax
	(714) 932-4952	Technical Support
	(800) 832-4778	Toll Free
	(714) 753-1234	BBS
	(714) 932-4300	Fax on Request
Web	www.wdc.com	

WYSE Technology, Inc.

Address	3471 North First Street San Jose, CA 95134-1803	
Phone	(408) 473-1200	Main
	(408) 473-2788	Fax
	(800) 438-9973	Toll Free
	(408) 922-4400	BBS
	(800) 800-9973	Fax on Request
Web	www.wyse.com	

X3 (Accredited Standards Committee)

Address	X3 Secretariat 1250 Eye St. NW Suite 200 Washington, DC 20005-3922	
Phone	(202) 626-5741	Main
	(202) 638-4922	Fax
Web	www.x3.org	
e-mail	x3sec@itic.nw.dc.us	

X3T10 (SCSI Standards)

Address	Submit membership inquiries to the X3 Secretariat (listed above).
Phone	(719) 533-7950 BBS
Web	www.symbios.com/x3t10/
e-mail	john.lohmeyer@symbios.com

X3T13 (ATA Standards)

Address	Submit membership inquiries to the X3 Secretariat (address listed above).
Web	ftp://fission.dt.wdc.com/pub/standards/ x3t13/x3t13.html
e-mail	majordomo@dt.wdc.com (requests for inclusion to ATA e-mail discussion group)

Xirlink, Inc.

Address	2210 O'Toole Avenue San Jose, CA 95131
Phone	(408) 324-2100 Main
	(408) 324-2101 Fax

Y-E Data America, Inc.

Address	2942 MacArthur Blvd. Northbrook, IL 60062
Phone	(847) 291-2340 Main
	(847) 291-4203 Fax

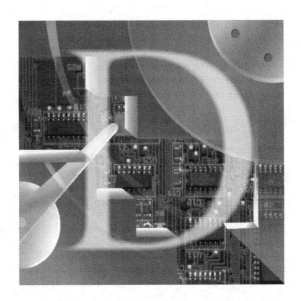

EZ-Drive

Hard Disk Installation & Upgrade Kit

Appendix D Contents:

About *EZ-Drive*

In a hurry? The quick start information on page 537 is usually enough to install your new hard drive.

EZ-Drive is designed to quickly install new IDE hard drives. It will automatically identify the IDE hard drive, set the system's CMOS, partition, DOS (high-level) format, and transfer the operating system to the drive. All this with minimal user intervention!

In addition to one-step installation, *EZ-Drive* enables special features, such as allowing systems with no native support for large drives (>528MBs) to make full use of the drive without expensive hardware upgrades.

EZ-Drive will automatically detect older versions of itself and upgrade the code. In addition, if a drive has been set up with most versions of Disk Manager™, *EZ-Drive* will convert Disk Manager partitions to standard DOS partitions in order to proceed with setup.

Is *EZ-Drive* for me?

EZ-Drive will install IDE (ATA) hard drives only. In addition to hassle-free setup of your drive, *EZ-Drive* can install special code that enables features such as large-drive support. If you have a newer system, you may not need *EZ-Drive* for this purpose. Consult the manufacturer's documentation on your system if you are not sure about what types of drives it will support. Still not sure? Use *EZ-Drive* anyway – it's intelligent enough to know what your system needs.

Your data is safe with us!

EZ-Drive will not overwrite information on hard drives unless directed to by the user. You may safely install your new drive in addition to the existing one. *EZ-Drive* will automatically detect the existing drive and won't overwrite the data on it. Be sure to double-check the jumper settings on all drives before proceeding. It is highly advisable with all new hard drive installations that you back up all data on the existing drives to prevent accidental loss.

Operating System versions

You must have a diskette containing the DOS boot files handy. A good diskette to use is the first diskette in the DOS set. *EZ-Drive* is compatible with the following operating systems and graphical interfaces:

- Microsoft MS-DOS Versions 3.0 and later
- IBM PC-DOS Versions 3.1 and later
- Digital Research DR-DOS Version 6.0
- Novell DOS Version 7.0
- Compaq DOS Version 3.31
- Windows 3.1x, Windows NT, Windows 95, OS/2, and OS/2 Warp.

Hardware Limitations

EZ-Drive will not work on XT, most Toshiba laptops, and Micro Channel computers. *EZ-Drive* will work on most Toshiba laptops that have a BIOS with an automatic detection feature.

Three "EZ"
Steps!

Quick Start

The following information will enable you to get your drive installed as quickly and easily as possible. **EZ-Drive** will assume that you want to use the defaults settings or most common installation methods. See page 538 if you would like to specify the installation options.

1) Physically Install Hard Drive(s)

As with all new hard drive installations, it is highly recommended that you back up all existing data on hard drives already installed.

Install your IDE drive into the system. Ensure that the Master/Slave jumpers are correctly set (see Chapter Four). **EZ-Drive** will set up as many as four IDE drives. If you are adding another drive to your computer, the existing drive may need its jumpers changed from Stand Alone to Master. Secondary drives will need to be set to Slave. If adding a second drive, **EZ-Drive** will not destroy the data on the first drive unless specifically told to. Please refer to page Chapter Four for assistance on physically installing the drive(s).

2) Run *EZ-Drive*

To run the program, change to the floppy drive containing **EZ-Drive** and type: EZ <ENTER>.

Choose "Fully Automatic Installation" from the main menu.

3) Insert a Bootable Diskette

Insert a bootable DOS diskette (the first disk in the DOS set is bootable) when prompted to do so. Such a diskette does not come with **EZ-Drive**.

Problems?

If you come across a question or problem, **EZ-Drive** features extensive on-line information, including jumper settings for many of the most popular hard drives manufactured, context-sensitive help function, and a user's guide. Also see "Before Starting" on page 538, "Troubleshooting" on page 546, and "Support Quick Reference" on page 551.

Using *EZ-DRIVE*

Before Starting

Physically install the new drives. See the IDE section of Chapter Four if you have any questions on controller and drive installation.

Older systems will require a secondary controller if more than two IDE drives will be installed. See the IDE section of Chapter Four for additional information on this topic.

You must have a diskette containing DOS boot files. Use is the first diskette in the DOS set, if available. If you do not have such a diskette, try formatting a floppy using the command FORMAT /S.

Do not write-protect the EZ-Drive floppy diskette!

Do not write protect the *EZ-Drive* floppy diskette! *EZ-Drive* must write important information to the diskette. Per the License Agreement, you may make a back-up copy of the software. If you choose to do so, store the original in a safe place and only use the backup.

Make sure that no other software is running besides the essentials of DOS. The easiest way to do this is to boot from a "clean" floppy.

If *EZ-Drive* is still unable to access a drive that you have installed, it is likely due to a hardware problem. To confirm this, set the Drive Type in the CMOS setup to Type 1. Although the capacity is usually only 10MB, this action will allow the BIOS to perform drive diagnostics. If you get a hardware error while booting up with the drive set in CMOS, this means that there is a hardware problem. You must resolve all hardware problems before attempting to use any software such as *EZ-Drive*. For more help consult the Troubleshooting section on page 546.

Installing a New Drive

Insert the *EZ-Drive* diskette into your floppy drive. If necessary, change the default drive to the floppy containing the *EZ-Drive* diskette, and type EZ <CR> at the DOS prompt.

The **EZ-Drive** Main Menu will give you three installation options:

Figure D-1: EZ-Drive Main Menu

Choose **Installation Help** to bring up the online help function.

1) Fully Automatic Installation

This option will set up the drive as necessary using default settings. Simply follow the prompts presented by the program. If you desire to use other than default installation options, then select **Custom Installation** or **Other Options** from the Main Menu. Selecting this option instructs **EZ-Drive** to install only drives with no data on them. Existing drives with data on them will not be affected.

2) Custom Installation

Warning: incorrect jumper settings may result in setting up the wrong drive!

Select this option if you desire other than the default settings, or if Automatic Installation was not successful. If you specify this option, you will be presented with a list of possible drives to be set up. Custom Installation will allow you to overwrite all information existing on the selected drive(s). Review the list, then select the drive(s) you wish to set up, ensuring that all jumper settings are correct. See "Other Options" below for more information on jumper settings.

After selecting the drive(s), you will be prompted to select the optional features to be installed. These features are described on page 543. You will then be asked how many partitions to use. If you choose Multiple Partitions, you will be asked to specify the size of each partition you desire to set up.

The last thing you will need to do is insert a bootable diskette into the floppy drive when **EZ-Drive** asks for it.

Other Options

Choosing **Other Options** from the Main Menu brings up the Installation Options menu:

Figure D-2: Installation Options

"Change Installed Features" See page 543 for information on this option.

"View Drive Jumpers" Jumper settings for many common drives may be found by selecting this option, as well as in Chapter Six of this text. *If your drive is not covered in these locations, you should consult the owner's manual or contact the manufacturer for setup information. Micro House does not provide additional information concerning hardware installation.*

"Create Recovery Disk" Use this option to create a rescue disk for cases where drive boot information is unintentionally altered or destroyed. The Recovery Disk will allow you to boot the system, access the problem drive, and repair the drive's track 0 boot information . You will need a blank (formatted or unformatted) 1.44M diskette.

Warning: back up all information on system drives before proceeding with this option!

"**Uninstall EZ-Drive**" Use this option to remove the **EZ-Drive** boot code from selected drive(s). **EZ-Drive** will only allow itself to be removed if it can verify that the system BIOS can do an equivalent hard drive translation. If **EZ-Drive** finds that the system BIOS cannot handle the drive's parameters, it will not remove itself. This safeguard prevents data corruption and possible trouble down the road. Read page 544 for more details.

If **EZ-Drive** will not allow itself to be uninstalled and must be removed from the system, boot your system directly from a floppy diskette, then run `FDISK /MBR`. This command will put an ordinary DOS master boot record on the drive.

After Installation

Software Installation Notes

When **EZ-Drive** completes its installation, drive 0 will be bootable and any other drives in the system will be accessible. Please note the following information when installing software for a specific operating system:

All DOS versions

If none of the special features are installed by **EZ-Drive**, there are no special precautions concerning the installation or use of MS-DOS applications.

If special features are installed then you will need to:

Turn on your PC without a floppy in the A: drive (as though you are going to boot from the hard drive).

As soon as you see "**EZ-Drive: Press the Ctrl key to view status screen or to boot from a floppy....**," appear on the screen, hold down the Ctrl key. A status screen will appear. Press **A** and you will be prompted to insert a floppy. Insert a bootable DOS diskette in the A: drive and press any key.

DOS setup will then load and run normally.

Note: Early versions of DriveSpace were not designed to support >528 MB drives, so they will not work on an area of a drive larger than this limit. It is important to note that this is a DriveSpace limitation, not **EZ-Drive**. Stacker™ is completely compatible with large drives.

Windows 3.1x

The installation of Windows is done as usual, no special provisions need to be made

Microsoft Windows 95

Windows 95 is fully compatible with *EZ-Drive* whether Floppy Boot Protection is enabled or disabled (see page 544). Install your hard drive with *EZ-Drive* and then install Windows 95.

Microsoft Windows NT

Windows NT is fully compatible with *EZ-Drive* when Floppy Boot Protection is disabled (see page 544). Install your hard drive with *EZ-Drive* first and then install NT.

IBM OS/2 (Including Warp)

OS/2 is fully compatible with *EZ-Drive* when Floppy Boot Protection is disabled (see page 544). Install your hard drive with *EZ-Drive* first and then install OS/2.

Special *EZ-Drive* Features

When *EZ-Drive* installs special features, a special program (boot code) is placed onto the hard drive that is loaded into memory at boot time. When the *EZ-Drive* program is being loaded you will see a message on the screen at boot time that says: "**EZ-Drive: Initializing...**," and you will see "**EZ-Drive: Press the CTRL key to view status screen or to boot from floppy.**" If you press the CTRL key at this time, you will see a status screen that gives relevant information that will help solve any problems that might possibly occur. Afterwards, you can either continue booting from the C: drive or a floppy diskette.

It is important to note that when your installation does not require special features then the *EZ-Drive* program will not be placed on the drive and the installation will leave the drive in the same state as if it were manually setup without *EZ-Drive*.

Please note that the following features are activated by booting from the hard drive. If you need to boot from a floppy diskette, <u>always</u> follow the procedure described on page 544.

Custom Drive Type: The Custom Drive Type is special program code stored on the drive that supplies parameters for the drive. This is extremely useful for machines that do not have a BIOS with a matching or user-definable drive type. Instead of losing drive capacity, the Custom Drive Type will supply the parameters, allowing you to use all of the drive's capacity. If a machine set up this way ever loses its CMOS settings, you only need to set the Drive Type to 1, and the drive will function correctly. Also, if you ever move a drive with a Custom Drive Type installed to a different machine, you will not have to worry about setting the parameters or even knowing the correct Drive Type in that machine. Merely set the Drive Type to 1 and the drive will be accessible. You will also have to follow the boot instructions on page 544 if this happens.

528+ MB Support: This is support for IDE drives that have a capacity greater than 528 MBs. If your system does not offer native support for large drives, this code allows DOS to support drives of up to 8GB, and up to 2GB per partition. When installing DOS or any other operating system on a drive which is using 528+ MB Support make sure to follow the special boot instructions on page 544.

Changing Installed Features

If the hard drive has already been set up with **EZ-Drive,** you will see the menu option called **Change Installed Features**. This option will also be seen after an **EZ-Drive** installation has occurred, right before rebooting.

All features shown in their DEFAULT mode.

Figure D-3: Change Installed Features

Controlled by EZ-Drive: This option designated whether or not **EZ-Drive** is controlling a particular hard drive. If the drive is not being controlled by **EZ-Drive**, then it is being controlled by the system's BIOS or it is disabled entirely. If you disable **EZ-Drive** and your BIOS is not set to properly control the drive you will be given a warning message to that effect. Disabling **EZ-Drive** when your BIOS is not set properly could cause data corruption.

Floppy Boot Protection Mode: This option will allow the disabling of **EZ-Drive**'s floppy boot protection. (See page 544 for details on properly booting from floppy.) You will need to disable this option in order to install Windows NT or OS /2.

Multiple Sector Transfer: This is a feature of **EZ-Drive** that enables multiple-sectors per interrupt read/write operations. This can speed your drive up significantly. It will only be functional for drives in the system that support it.

32 Bit Transfer: Select this item to enable or disable 32-bit data transfers. This feature requires a local-bus controller, as well as specific hardware support from the drive.

Floppy Boot Delay Time: This option will increase the amount of delay time for **EZ-Drive** boot-up in order to allow the user to boot from a floppy. The message "**EZ-Drive: Press CTRL key to view status screen or to boot from floppy**" will appear on system start-up, allowing you a specified period of time to press the CTRL key if desired. On faster machines, it may be necessary to increase this number in order to properly boot from a floppy diskette.

Save Changes: You must save any changes to installed features before they can be implemented.

Booting From Floppy Disk

Whenever you want to boot from a floppy diskette, turn on your PC **without** a floppy in the A: drive (as though you are going to boot from the hard drive). As soon as you see the prompt: "**EZ-Drive: Press the Ctrl key to view status screen or to boot from a floppy. . .,**" hold down the Ctrl key*, and you will be prompted to insert a floppy. Insert the floppy and press <CR> to boot the computer.

If you get a keyboard error, wait a little bit longer through the boot sequence before holding the Ctrl key. See page 544 for information on increasing the boot delay time to facilitate booting from a floppy diskette.

Removing the *EZ-Drive* Boot Code

Please be sure to back up your data before proceeding with uninstallation.

Prior to removing itself, **EZ-Drive** will check to see if the system can handle the drive without native support. Many older systems use a BIOS which cannot access drive capacity above 528MBs.

READ THIS FIRST! Removing the **EZ-Drive** boot code is a very simple process. However, first ensure that you are aware of the implications.

If **EZ-Drive** is controlling the drive and you do not need it (because your BIOS can handle large drives) you can remove the boot code and continue using your drive without having the data affected in any way. Obviously, back up the hard drive in case you don't actually have your system set-up correctly. If **EZ-Drive** is installed but no longer desired, and your BIOS can't handle the drive's full capacity, the drive must be re-partitioned and formatted within the DOS/BIOS limits of 16 heads, 1,024 cylinders and 63 sectors/track. In this case, you will definitely lose all existing data on the drive.

The easiest way to remove the **EZ-Drive** boot code is to put your **EZ-Drive** diskette into your A: drive, and type EZ. Choose "Other Options," then select the "Uninstall **EZ-Drive**" option.

This option will prompt you through the proper steps required to remove **EZ-Drive**.

Re-installing the *EZ-Drive* Boot Code

Whether or not a drive was originally installed with the **EZ-Drive** boot code, one can usually be installed successfully by running EZ /MBR. This will install a fresh copy of the **EZ-Drive** boot code along with a Custom Drive Type if one was previously installed. If the Large Drive Support is damaged (by virus, FDISK /MBR, SETUP /x /z, sector editor, or other means) the drive can usually be restored by running EZ /MBR.

Troubleshooting

Extensive online help is included in the *EZ-Drive* program is that might be able to help to resolve any problems or questions that you might have.

The following questions are helpful in obtaining the information necessary to diagnose failed installations. Most installations fail due to incorrect jumper settings on the hard drive(s), incompatible master/slave drives, or an unusual non-standard BIOS.

If *EZ-Drive* is having difficulty accessing the hard drive, set the drive in CMOS to type 1 (10MB). If setting the CMOS to type 1 still does not allow your system to boot up properly, try setting the parameters for the drive in the User Definable section of the CMOS Setting a drive in CMOS will have the machine BIOS instruct the drive to perform its self diagnostics. If there is a hardware problem, the BIOS will usually error out with a HDD controller failure or equivalent message. In order for *EZ-Drive* to work successfully, the machine needs to be able to boot with the drive set to a type in CMOS other than 0 without getting a hardware error.

Did *EZ-Drive* appear to go through the installation successfully, or did it encounter problems along the way? If there were no problems encountered, the drive is probably set up correctly with software, so start to look for a hardware incompatibility with the machine's BIOS.

If the problem is getting the drive to boot, what is the exact error message when trying to boot from the hard drive? Is the message in blue and white? (if so, it is from the *EZ-Drive* Boot Code). Try booting from the hard drive and then run the DOS SYS command on the hard drive.

When you boot from the hard drive, do you see an *EZ-Drive* boot notice? If so, the *EZ-Drive* Code is installed. If not, it is not installed. If you used to see the *EZ-Drive* boot notice now no longer do, the *EZ-Drive* code may have been required to use the drive but has been deleted. You may be able to successfully replace the boot code by running EZ /MBR.

If you are unable to boot from the hard drive, can you see the drive if you boot from floppy? If so, back up any critical data and then attempt to make the drive bootable with the DOS SYS command.

If you are having any difficulties with your system or with **EZ-Drive** identifying your hard drive please check the following **before** calling Micro House:

Common Hardware Problems

Is your drive set to a type besides 0 in CMOS?

If not, set it to Type 1. Even though it is usually less than the capacity of the drive, this action will have the machine instruct the drive to perform internal diagnostics. If you get a hardware error when booting to floppy (HDD CONTROLLER FAILURE, HDD FAILURE, etc.) the drive is failing its diagnostics. You **must** resolve this problem **before** attempting to use **EZ-Drive**.

Are the cables installed correctly?

Ensure that the red or blue wire on the IDE cable is plugged into pin 1 of the interface. Ensure that the red or blue wire also matches pin-1 on the controller card.

A common symptom of an incorrectly installed IDE cable is floppy drives that don't work correctly or don't work at all.

Is the power cable pushed in all the way?

Can you hear the drive spinning?

If installing a second or two IDE hard drives:

Are the two IDE drives of the same brand? **Not all IDE drives will work together!** If each drive will work alone in the system but not together, and you know that the jumper settings are correct, then your two drives may not work with each other. Changing the order of the drives (reversing the Master/Slave relationship) sometimes allows the two drives to work together. If this still doesn't work then you will need to use one on a secondary card or replace one of the drives with another model. You might try using two drives from the same manufacturer.

Check the drive's jumper settings:

You must set the jumpers on the hard drive(s) correctly. Most drives come from the factory in the "Master" or "Only Drive" configuration. Do you have these jumpers set correctly? They must be changed if you are installing a second drive into the same system. Complete jumper settings for many hard drives can be found in the section starting in Chapter Six, or the *EZ-Drive* online help section "View Drive Jumpers."

Check with the manufacturer if you are still having difficulties with the drive(s) and are unsure of jumper settings. **Micro House Technical Support does not provide you with these settings.**

Are you using a Toshiba Laptop?

EZ-Drive will not to work with Toshiba laptop computers.

Incompatibility Between Drive and Machine

Some systems may be very particular about the drives installed into them. If a hardware incompatibility exists, *EZ-Drive* will typically appear to go through the installation correctly, but the machine will not reboot from the hard drive. If the *EZ-Drive* boot notice does not get displayed, it indicates that the machine is not getting as far as trying to boot from the hard drive.

Try confirming if an incompatibility exists by moving the drive to a more standard machine and having it boot. If the drive works on the other machine, it indicates an incompatibility rather than a defect. This conflict must be resolved at the hardware level.

Systems with BIOS's dated before 1988 can cause a C: drive error message. Pressing F1 will usually allow the drive to boot and be correctly accessible, but you will have to press F1 with each boot. Additionally, on some Compaq computers the BIOS will return an error message upon boot. Pressing F1 will allow the drive to boot normally.

Common Software Problems

I don't have a User Defined drive type in my CMOS, will *EZ-Drive* work for me?

Yes, just set the CMOS to any drive type that the system will boot off of a floppy diskette to.

I'm installing a second drive – will *EZ-Drive* delete information on my first drive?

Not unless you specifically tell it to. If you select "Install new drives only" *EZ-Drive* will make sure it doesn't write over any drives with data on them.

I setup my drive using *EZ-Drive* and I want to move it to another computer, what do I have to do?

Set your drive type in CMOS to Type 1. Note: if your Type 1 is not smaller than the size of the drive you are installing, set your CMOS to any type that is smaller than your drive.

If you only have "User Defined", "Auto Select", and "None" then select "User Defined" and enter the parameters of your drive.

Will *EZ-Drive* work with Windows NT or OS/2?

In order for *EZ-Drive* to work with Windows NT and OS/2, Floppy Boot Protection must be disabled. See "Change Installed Features," page 543.

Will *EZ-Drive* work with Windows 3.1, Windows for Workgroups 3.11, and Windows 95?

Yes. You should have to do nothing special before installing the operating system.

I have an old drive in my system set up with a previous version of *EZ-Drive*. Do I need to re-install this drive with the new version?

EZ-Drive will automatically detect an older version of itself already installed on the hard drive and allow you to upgrade the old version. By upgrading your version, you will receive many benefits depending on what version you upgraded from. Such benefits include: The ability to swap drives around in the system if needed, full Windows NT, Windows 95, and OS/2 compatibility, and the ability to make multiple partitions of various sizes.

Will *EZ-Drive* work with the drive in my system previously set up with Disk Manager™ 6.03?

EZ-Drive will detect hard drives set up with most versions of Disk Manager™. The partitions on a drive set up with that software will need to be converted to standard DOS partitions in order to set up an additional drive with *EZ-Drive*. This conversion is done without any loss of data. If you choose not to convert these partitions *EZ-Drive* can not continue with the setup of any other drives.

Sometimes Disk Manager(TM) will set up drives with no Primary Partition. These type of drives can not be installed as your C: drive because they will not boot without a Primary Partition. *EZ-Drive* does not change the type of partition when converting these drives therefore you can not boot from these drives as you would if *EZ-Drive* had set them up.

Support Quick Reference

The following items regarding *EZ-Drive* are frequently presented by customers to our support staff:

Removing the *EZ-Drive* **Boot Code**	• Run *EZ-Drive*. • Enter "Installation Options" menu. • Select "Uninstall EZ-Drive." • Follow the prompts. **WARNING!** If the drive was setup needing *EZ-Drive*, you will have to partition and format the drive again. This will be the case when the drive is not supported by the BIOS table of the computer.
To re-establish the *EZ-Drive* **Boot Code**	• Boot from a floppy • Type EZ /MBR • DOS prompt appears • *EZ-Drive* is now placed on the drive(s).
Cannot install OS/2, Warp, or Windows NT	You must go into the Change Installed Features menu and disable Floppy Boot Protection. Turn on your PC without a floppy in the A: drive (as though you are going to boot from the hard drive). As soon as you see "Hold the Ctrl key down to boot from a floppy. . .", hold down the Ctrl key, and you will be prompted to insert a floppy. Insert the first or installation disk for the operating system and press enter to boot the computer and boot off the proper diskette.
Can I use *EZ-Drive* **to install the drive and use a Boot Manager?**	If the Boot Manager re-writes the Master Boot Record, it cannot be done. If, instead, the Boot Manager uses multiple system files, it will work.
How do I install DOS?	Turn on your PC without a floppy in the A: drive (as though you are going to boot from the hard drive). As soon as you see "*EZ-Drive*: Press the CTRL key to view status screen or to boot from floppy..", hold down the Ctrl key, and you will see the **status** screen. Insert the first disk in the DOS set and press enter, then the A key to boot the computer and run DOS setup.
Error message "Unable to load WDCTRL" when booting Windows	Run SETUP on the *EZ-Drive* diskette from within Windows.
Master or Slave not recognized	Not all drives work together, especially drives from different manufacturers. Check and recheck the jumper settings on all drives.

Obtaining Assistance

If *EZ-Drive* is having any difficulties installing your hard drive(s) you may call our Software Support department at 303-443-3389 8am to 5pm MST M-F for assistance. You may also call our computer bulletin board system (BBS) at 303-443-9957 1.2-28.8KBPS and leave questions. You can also contact us via the Internet at WWW.MICROHOUSE.COM.

Be sure to return your registration card! If you need jumper settings for your hard drive please call the manufacturer or the distributor that you purchased the drive from. **Micro House does not provide you with jumper settings for your hard drive.**

Hard Drive Identification Box

Upon completion of the installation, *EZ-Drive* will supply you with the necessary information to fill out these boxes. You will need this information if your system loses its setup information. Keep this manual with your computer to ensure that this data is available if ever needed.

DRIVE ONE		DRIVE TWO	
HEADS	CYLINDERS	HEADS	CYLINDERS
SECTORS	DRIVE TYPE	SECTORS	DRIVE TYPE
DRIVE THREE		**DRIVE FOUR**	
HEADS	CYLINDERS	HEADS	CYLINDERS
SECTORS	DRIVE TYPE	SECTORS	DRIVE TYPE

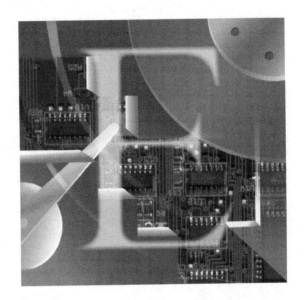

The Micro House
Demos and Utilities

Appendix E Contents:

CD-ROM Contents

CD-ROM includes valuable hard drive utilities as well as demonstrations of Micro House products.

- A brief animated product demonstration of Micro House products can be accessed by running DEMO.EXE in the root directory.

- The directory DEMOS contains demonstration versions of Support On Site for Hardware, the Micro House Technical Library, and DrivePro. Consult the README.TXT file in that directory for directions on running these interactive demos.

- The S.M.A.R.T. application *EZ-SMART™* is located in the EZSMART directory. Run SETUP.EXE to install this

Please note that some of the demos and utilities require Windows 3.1x or greater. Some documents are in Adobe Acrobat™ (.PDF) format. A copy of Acrobat Reader is included in the DEMOS directory for your convenience. Please note that the contents of the CD may have changed since this text went to press. Consult the README.TXT file located in the root directory for the latest information on the contents of the CD.

EZ-SMART

S.M.A.R.T. stands for Self-Monitoring, Analysis, and Reporting Technology. SMART supplements data back-up procedures as a means of protecting against data loss. It does so by constantly monitoring the hardware for any signs of degradation and providing a timely warning if needed.

EZ-SMART is a Windows 95-based program that is useful only for drives that support SMART technology. If you are in doubt, consult the manufacturer's documentation that came with the drive.

A fully operational copy of this utility has been included on the CD-ROM. For information on installing and using EZ-SMART, please read the Acrobat file SMARTMAN.PDF that is also located in the EZSMART directory.

How to Use the Micro House Demos and Utilities

Several Micro House Utilities have been included on the CD-ROM which was packaged with this text. To access the Micro House Utilities, make the CD-ROM drive the active drive, then change the directory to UTILS. Call up the programs using the instructions below

IDECACHE

This utility is used to turn on or off IDE look-ahead sector buffering, for those drives that support that feature.

The proper use of this program is:

`IDECACHE [ON OFF LICENSE]`

on   Enable IDE look-ahead sector buffering.

on   Disable IDE look-ahead sector buffering.

license   View licensing agreement for this software.

MHESDI

This program uses the ESDI Identify Drive command to get information on the drive's manufacturer, model, serial number, firmware revision, logical heads, logical cylinders, logical sectors, as well as various other specifications.

The proper use of this program is:

`MHESDI [/M /C /D /LICENSE]`

`/M`	Force monochrome display mode.
`/C`	Force color display mode.
`/D`	Do not use INT13h BIOS call to get BIOS disk parameters.
`/license`	View licensing agreement for this software.

MHIDE

This program uses the IDE Identify Drive command to get information on the drive's manufacturer, model, serial number, firmware revision, logical heads, logical cylinders, logical sectors, as well as various other specifications.

The proper use of this program is:

`MHIDE [/M /C /D /LICENSE]`

`/M`	Force monochrome display mode.
`/C`	Force color display mode.
`/D`	Do not use INT13h BIOS call to get BIOS disk parameters.
`/license`	View licensing agreement for this software.

MHSYS

MHSYS.EXE is used to copy the system files from one drive to another. MHSYS will transfer from one floppy to another in one pass instead of the multiple passes used by SYS, and can transfer to the same floppy drive. It also does not affect the DOS Boot Record like the DOS SYS utility, and so is also useful in drive recovery. However, MHSYS does not reposition existing files; therefore, it can only be used on blank floppies or floppies that have been formatted with the /B option (leave space for system files).

The proper use of this program is:

```
MHSYS [SourceDrive:] DestinationDrive: [/?]
```

DestinationDrive: The drive to which to copy the DOS system. The colon is necessary and must be used. This parameter must be supplied.

SourceDrive: The drive from which to load the DOS system.

The colon is necessary and must be used. If no drive is specified, then the system is loaded from the current drive. Typical uses are MHSYS A: A: or MHSYS C: A:

Optional command line parameters are:

/?   Displays all command line options.

Glossary of Terms

A

ACTUATOR

The device that moves the read/write heads across the platter surfaces. There are two kinds of actuators that are commonly used, stepper motor actuators and voice-coil actuators. Today all new drives use the voice-coil actuator because it is the faster and sturdier of the two. To give you an idea of the speed difference, a stepper motor drive takes from 65 to 100 milliseconds (65 to 100 thousanths of a second) to move from one track to another, as compared to the voice-coil actuator that usually only requires 15 to 40 milliseconds; more than twice the speed of the stepper motor.

ADDRESS MARK

Two byte address at the beginning of both the ID field and the data field of the track format.

ALTERNATE SECTOR

See sector sparing.

AREAL DENSITY

Areal density tells how densely packed data is on a disk surface. Areal density is the product of bit density (bits per inch, or BPI) multiplied by track density (tracks per inch, or TPI), or bits per square inch of the disk surface.

Also see bit density, track density.

ALLOCATION UNIT

See cluster.

ARLL

Same as RLL 3,9.

See RLL.

AREAL DENSITY

Sometimes called Areal Recording Density. The amount of data that can be packed into a specific area. Areal density can be calculated by multiplying the bits/in by the tracks/in to obtain bits/in^2.

ASYNCHRONOUS DATA

Data sent usually in parallel mode without a clock pulse. Time intervals between transmitted bits may be of unequal lengths.

ATA
AT Attachment interface

See IDE.

ATA-2
Updated AT Attachment interface.

See IDE.

ATA-3

The next major update of the AT Attachment (ATA) interface. This standard has not yet been approved.

Also see IDE.

AT INTERFACE

See IDE.

ATAPI
ATA Packet Interface

ATAPI defines a set of commands supported through the ATA-2 interface that are used for peripherals other than hard drives, such as CD-ROM drives and tape drives.

AVERAGE LATENCY

A measurement of how long a drive must wait before a specified bit of data rotates under the heads. An average figure is one half a platter rotation. Most drives turn at 60 revolutions per second (or 3,600 per minute) making the value the same for most drives: 8.4 milliseconds.

AZIMUTH

The angular distance in the horizontal plane, usually measured as an angle from true track location.

B

BCAI
Byte Count After Index

Used in defect mapping to indicate the position of defects with relation to index.

BFI
Bytes From Index

Used in defect mapping to indicate the position of defects with relation to index.

BIOS
Basic Input/Output System

The **BIOS** is the interpreter that sets up a specific computer to allow the operating system (such as DOS) to communicate with peripherals. The BIOS can be thought of as the "glue" that holds together hardware made by a variety of manufacturers. The BIOS is firmware, that is, the instructions are permanently written on a Read Only Memory (ROM) chip. The BIOS contains the parameters required to initialize (boot) the computer, and performs a Power On Self Test (POST) during the boot sequence.

BIT DENSITY
or Bits Per Inch

Expressed as "BPI" (bits per inch), bit density defines how many bits can be written onto one inch of a track on a disk surface. Bit density is measured around a track (along a constant radius on the disk). It is usually specified for worst case, which is the inner track. Data is the densest in the inner tracks where track circumferences are the smallest.

See track density, areal density.

BLOCK

A group of bytes handled, stored, and accessed as a logical data unit, such as an individual file record. Typically, one block of data is stored as one physical sector of data on a disk drive.

BLOCK PIO

Block PIO (BPIO) uses the advances made possible by local-bus technology to increase data transfer rates by simply multiplying the amount of information sent during a transfer cycle. BPIO counts the 512-byte transfer unit of normal PIO as a portion of a "block" which consists of "n" times 512-bytes.

See PIO.

BPI

Bits Per Inch

See bit density

BUFFER

All modern hard drives have some amount of on-board memory, which is termed the buffer. The buffer is a way-station for requested data after it is read from a location on disk. The advantage to a disk buffer is that it decreases system delays due to the physical limits of the drive speed. Read sequences can be sped up by having the buffer hold information that it anticipates the system will request.

BUFFERED SEEK

A feature of the ST-412 interface. In buffered mode, head motion is postponed until a string of step pulses can be sent to the drive. These pulses represent the number of tracks that the head is to be stepped over and are sent much faster than the heads can move. The pulses are saved or buffered, then the optimum head movement to the correct track is performed.

BURST MODE

A high-speed data transfer mode in which the entire bandwidth of the data transfer channel is used by a single device for a short period of time.

C

CACHE MEMORY/CACHING

Caching is the process where the system loads data from the hard disk to the **RAM** set aside as **cache memory**. As long as the same file is being accessed, the system may refer to the **cache memory** for information instead of going back to the hard disk, thereby increasing the processing speed. Caching does not really increase seek times, but makes the drive appear faster by eliminating repetitious access. Cache memory can either be dedicated or set aside from host RAM. Today's top of the line SCSI and IDE hard disk controllers are equipped with their own cache memory.

CAPACITY

The space in megabytes or million bytes available on a storage device. Unformatted capacity means the total space on the drive before it is organized for use with an operating system. This figure can be found by multiplying the number of physical cylinders, heads, sectors/track, and bytes/sector. The formatted capacity is less because a certain amount of drive space must be dedicated to logically organizing the device.

CARRIAGE ASSEMBLY

Assembly which holds read/write heads and roller bearings. It is used to position the heads radially by the actuator, in order to access a track of data.

CHS
Cylinders, Heads, Sectors per track

The parameters used to determine the capacity of a hard drive. Physical CHS parameters are the actual number of cylinders, heads, and sectors per track under the casing. Logical CHS parameters are translations used to bypass parameter limits imposed by the operating system.

CLUSTER

An operating system term describing the number of sectors that the operating system allocates each time disk space is needed. For example, if the cluster size is 16 (Thirty-two, 512-byte sectors per cluster) then every file will use 16K, even though the actual file size may be less.

CMOS
Ceramic Metal Oxide Semiconductor

See BIOS.

CONTROLLER

A controller is the printed circuit board required to interpret data access commands from host computer (via the bus), and send track seeking, read/write, and other control signals to and from a hard drive.

CPU
Central Processing Unit

CRC
Cyclic-Redundancy-Check

Used to verify data block integrity. In a typical scheme, 2 CRC bytes are added to each user data block. The 2 bytes are computed from the user data by digital logic chips. The mathematical model is polynomials with binary coefficients. When reading back data, the CRC bytes are read and compared to new CRC bytes computed from the read back block to detect a read error. The read back error check process is mathematically equivalent to dividing the read block, including its CRC, by a binomial polynomial. If the division remainder is zero, the data is error free.

CYLINDER

The cylindrical surface formed by identical track numbers on vertically stacked disks. At any location of the head positioning arm, all tracks under all heads are the cylinder. Cylinder number is one of the three address components required to find a specific address, the other two being head number and sector number.

CYLINDER SKEW

See skewing.

D

DAISY CHAIN

A way of connecting multiple drives to one controller. The controller drive select signal is routed serially through the drives, and is intercepted by the drive whose number matches. The disk drives have switches or jumpers on them that allow the user to select the drive number desired. No two devices can have the same number.

DATA COMPRESSION

Data compression is an encoding process where data strings that are repeated often are cut out when written to disk, then replaced before being used by an application.

DMA
Direct Memory Access

A method used to speed up data transfers between peripherals (such as hard drives) and RAM. As the name denotes, DMA avoids the delays imposed by the CPU's data-flow regulation, accessing RAM directly.

DTR
Data Transfer Rate

Speed at which bits are sent: In a disk storage system, the communication is between CPU and controller, plus controller and the disk drive. Typical units are bits per second (BPS) or bytes per second.

DEDICATED SERVO SYSTEM

A complete disk surface and head are dedicated for servo data. Hard drives with an odd (not even) head count will have a dedicated servo.

Also see actuator, embedded servo, servo, servo track.

DISK PLATTER

Hard (rigid) disks use a flat, circular aluminum disk substrate, coated on both sides with a magnetic substance (iron oxide or thin film metal media) for non-volatile data storage. The substrate may consist of metal, plastic, or even glass. Surfaces of disks are usually lubricated to minimize wear during drive start-up or power down.

DRIVE-SELECT JUMPERS

These set the control channel for the hard drive so that the controller knows which drive it's controlling. See the section on hard drive installation and your hard drive manual for the proper setting of these jumpers.

DRIVE TYPE

A number representing a standard configuration of physical parameters: cylinders, heads, and sectors per track of a particular type of disk drive. Each AT system BIOS contains a list of drive types that the system considers "standard types." These types are not necessarily the same from one BIOS to the next. See the chapter on BIOS tables for a listing of these.

DROP-IN/DROP-OUT

Types of disk media defects are usually caused by a pin size hole in the disk coating. If the coating is interrupted, the magnetic flux between medium and head is zero. A large interruption will induce two extraneous pulses, one at the beginning and one at the end of the pin-hole (2 DROP-INs). A small coating interruption will result in no playback from a recorded bit (a DROP-OUT).

E

ECC
Error Correction Code

The ECC hardware in the controller used to interface the drive to the system can typically correct a single burst error of 11 bits or less. This maximum error burst correction length is a function of the controller. With some controllers the user is allowed to select this length. The most common selection is 11.

EIDE
Enhanced Integrated Drive Electronics

See IDE

EMBEDDED SERVO SYSTEM

Servo data is embedded or superimposed along with data on every cylinder as opposed to having a dedicated servo track.

See actuator, dedicated servo, servo, servo track.

ENCODING

The scheme used to write and read data on the recording media.

Also see FM, MFM, RLL.

ESDI

Enhanced Small Device Interface

ESDI is an obsolete peripheral interface standard largely used for hard drives. ESDI was largely derived from the ST506/412 interface, with improvements such as data transfers up to 24 megabits per second and better error checking.

F

FAT

File Allocation Table

The system used by the operating system to keep track of which clusters are allocated to which files, and which are available for use.

FAST ATA

See IDE

FCI

Flux Changes Per Inch

Synonymous with FRPI (flux reversals per inch). In MFM recording 1 FCI equals 1 BPI (bit per inch). In RLL encoding schemes, 1 FCI generally equals 1.5 BPI.

FLUX CHANGE

Location on the data track, where the direction of magnetization reverses in order to define a 1 or 0 bit. See FCI and FRPI for more information.

FM

Frequency Modulation

This is an outdated encoding scheme that is no longer in use. It used up to half of the disk space with timing signals for the encoding process. The technology was refined and replaced with a new standard called MFM encoding.

See encoding, MFM, RLL.

FORMAT

The purpose of a format is to record the "header" data that organize the tracks into sequential sectors on the disk surfaces. This information is never altered during normal read/write operations. Header information identifies the sector number and also contains the head and cylinder address.

FORM FACTOR

This is the hard drive's physical external size and the mounting space it will take up. Usually 3 1/2 inch or 5 1/4 inch for desk-top computers, and 2.5 inch for portables and laptops.

G

"G"

A "G" is a unit of force applied to a mass at rest equal to the force exerted on it by gravity. Hard disk drive shock specifications are usually called out in Gs. A shock specification of 40 Gs non-operating means that a drive will not suffer any permanent damage if subjected to a 40 G shock. This is roughly equivalent to a drop of the drive to a hard surface from a distance of 1 inch.

GIGABYTE

A unit of storage equal to exactly 1,073,741,824 bytes (roughly 1,000 megabytes). Some of the newer hard drives and optical drives are in the gigabyte range.

H

HEAD

Data heads are the component of the hard drive used to write-to and read from the recording media on the disk. There are usually several read/write heads in a hard drive. There are two types of heads commonly used: Inductive and Magnetoresistive.

Also see inductive, MR.

HEAD CRASH

As a normal operation, head landing occurs when the disk drive is turned off. When the heads land, a thin film of lubricant on the disk surface protects the disk from damage. A head crash occurs when the head and disk damage each other during landing because of rough handling, or because a small particle gets between them. Head crash is a catastrophic failure and causes permanent damage and loss of data.

HEAD LANDING AND TAKEOFF

In Winchester drives, the head is in contact with the platter when the drive is not powered. During the power up cycle, the disk begins rotation and an "air bearing" is established as the disk spins up to full RPM. This air bearing prevents any mechanical contact between head and disk.

HEAD PARKING

Parking the heads places them in a safe zone away from data on the platter, usually the highest cylinder on the drive. When a stepper motor drive is turned off, its heads land on the platter wherever it was last doing a read/write. If the drive is jolted, data under the heads can be lost. The stepper motor drive must be parked through software that places the head at a safe zone. Voice-coil drives automatically park themselves due to the design of the solenoid-spring mechanism (see voice-coil actuators). Head parking software is not needed on these drives and should not be used.

HEAD SKEW

See skewing.

HEIGHT

The drive's height.

See form factor.

HOT SWAP

To disconnect a device and replace it with another one without powering down the system.

I

IDE

Integrated Drive Electronics

Also known as the ATA interface, IDE is the most popular hard drive interface on the market today. The hard drives used with this type of interface are "intelligent" devices that have most of the controller functions built into the drive circuitry. These drives link up to the computer via a 40-pin connector (IBM uses a 44-pin or 72-pin connector) and a small paddle card, or directly to the motherboard on newer computers.

The latest version of IDE is sometimes called Enhanced IDE (EIDE), Fast ATA, or ATA-2. Improvements include capacities of up to 8.4GB, increased data transfer rates, an additional channel, and a greater variety of attachable devices.

ID FIELD

See sector header.

INDEX PULSE

The Index Pulse is the starting point for each disk track. The index pulse provides initial synchronization for sector addressing on each individual track.

INDEX TIME

The time interval between similar edges of the index pulse, which measures the time for the disk to take one revolution. This information is used by a disk drive to verify correct rotational speed of the media.

INDUCTIVE

Used to describe data heads that use magnetic inductance to impart and sense magnetic fluxes on the recording media.

Also see heads, MR.

INTERLEAVE

Interleaving means to logically distribute access order in other than a straight sequential fashion. Older hard drives interleaved sectors by renumbering them in order to leave a space between sequential units, effectively skipping a number of sectors during a revolution. In this case, interleaving alleviated the problem of the drive getting ahead of the system by forcing the drive to read the data a little slower.

Also see striping.

IOCHRDY

Input/Output Channel Ready

A signal sent by the CPU to a peripheral to let the peripheral know that more of the CPU's resources are available for data transfer.

Also see PIO.

IPI

Intelligent Peripheral Interface

A hard drive interface used with the larger 8" and 14" mainframe and minicomputers.

L

LANDING ZONE

This is the section of the disk that is designed as the safe zone for head parking

See head parking.

LATENCY (ROTATIONAL)

See average latency.

LBA

Logical Block Addressing

LBA is an alternative disk-accessing method consisting of a logical address number, rather than CHS information. LBA requires a BIOS and drive that support this access method. The BIOS translates CHS parameters from the drive during initialization. All communication between the operating system and drive from that point is accomplished with LBA.

LSB
Least Significant Bit

The bit with the lowest value (1) in the sequence.

LOW-LEVEL FORMAT

The first step in preparing a drive to store information after physical installation is complete. The process sets up the "handshake" between the drive and the controller.

Most newer hard drives are low-level formatted at the factory with special equipment.

LUN
Logical Unit Number

Also called the SCSI ID number. The units device number on a Daisy Chain. Each device on the chain must have its own unique LUN.

Also see daisy chain, SCSI.

M

MEGABYTE

A unit of storage equal to exactly 1,048,576 bytes (sometimes 1 million bytes).

Also see gigabyte.

MFM
Modified Frequency Modulation

A type of encoding scheme that converts the digital bits from the computer into a pattern of magnetic changes or "flux reversals" that are then stored on the hard drive. MFM uses a fixed length encoding scheme that obviates the need for the space-consuming timing signals used in FM. Flux reversals on the disk always will be evenly spaced in time so that the beginning of one bit can be separated from another. This type of scheme allows even single bit errors to be detected easily and corrected by the controller electronics. MFM has since been superseded by RLL recording technology in hard drives, although it is still used in floppy drives.

Also see encoding, FM, MFM, RLL.

MCA
Micro Channel Architecture

The type of BUS used in the IBM PS/2 line of computers. Each MCA hard disk controller board can support two hard disks. If two hard disk boards are installed in a PS/2 system, only one drive may be attached to each controller (you can never have more then a maximum of two hard drives in a PS/2 system, no matter how many controller cards you have). If you have one ESDI and one ST506/412 drive, the MCA architecture always selects the ESDI drive as drive C:.

MSB
Most Significant Bit

The bit with the highest value in the sequence.

MTBF
Mean Time Between Failures

This figure is supposed to indicate how long a drive is expected to last between needing repairs. The figure is normally rounded to the nearest thousand or sometimes even five thousand. To arrive at these figures, the manufacturers perform a battery of stress tests that are analyzed and worked into real-time working-condition hours. MTBF values are measured in power-on hours (conditions with the drive on).

MTTR
Mean Time To Repair

The average time to repair a failed drive. Being that replacement is usually recommended for most failed IDE drives, most manufacturers will list this spec as 30 minutes or less, which is actually *Mean Time To Replace*.

MEDIA

The magnetic layers of a disk or tape.

MEDIA DEFECT

A media defect can cause a considerable reduction of the read signal (missing pulse or Drop-Out) or create an extra pulse (Drop-In). The factories that manufacture the hard drives have equipment that can detect media defects which the standard controller might not. These areas will potentially give the user problems. Even if your own extensive diagnostics find less defects than the list supplied with the drive, enter in all defects when low level formatting to ensure error-free operation.

Also see drop-in/drop-out.

MR
Magneto-Resistive

MR describes a type of material that changes its electrical resistance when exposed to a magnetic field. MR material is used in new read heads designed to be used with extremely high areal density recording media.

Also see heads, inductive.

N

NRZ
Non-Return To Zero

A method of magnetic recording of digital data in which a flux reversal denotes a one bit and no flux reversal, a zero bit. NRZ recording requires an accompanying synchronization clock to define each cell time (unlike MFM or RLL recording). ESDI drives usually use this type of encoding.

O

OEM
Original Equipment Manufacturer

A manufacturer of equipment that is installed in the machine by the factory/vendor.

P

PARITY

A computer data-checking method using an extra bit in which the total number of binary 1's (or 0's) in a byte is always odd or always even; thus, in a parity scheme, every byte has eight bits of data and one parity bit. If using odd parity and the number of 1 bits comprising the byte of data is not odd, the 9th or parity bit is set to 1 to create the odd parity. In this way, a byte of data can be checked for accurate transmission by simply counting the bits for an odd parity indication. If the count is ever even, an error is indicated.

PARTITION

Partitioning divides a physical hard drive into logical volumes. Partitioning was originally intended as a way to divide storage space among the different operating systems that a computer had to use. Partitioning a hard drive is a mandatory operation, even if only one large partition is created. There are different partitioning limitations for each DOS version.

PCMCIA
Personal Computer Memory Card International Association

An interface used to attach small form-factor storage devices and other peripherals to portable computers. PCMCIA (also called PC-Card) also features Plug and Play installation and the ability to "hot swap" some devices.

PIO
Processor (or Programmed) Input/Output

A means of data transfer that requires the use of the host processor, or CPU. PIO is very limited in data transfer rates because the CPU does not communicate with the peripheral (hard drive), meaning the peripheral can only send a minimum amount of data through the CPU during a cycle in order to guarantee transfer. The potential transfer capacity is wasted because the peripheral does not know how much of the CPU's resources are free for data transfer.

Programmed PIO, sometimes called Throttled PIO or Flow Control, is an improved data transfer method that allows the CPU to control data flow.

Also see DMA, IOCHRDY.

PLATED THIN FILM DISKS

Magnetic disk memory media having its surface plated with a thin coating of a metallic alloy instead of being coated with oxide. Plated disks hold far more data than coated media. Also see Platter and Coated media.

PLATTER

The rigid disk, usually made of metal, where the data is physically located. They are usually either coated with an oxide substance (like a floppy disk) or plated.

PLUG AND PLAY

Often seen contracted to **PnP**. An computer industry marketing term that means that a device requires no special hardware or software setup procedures – it is (ideally) ready to go after a simple installation process.

POST
Power-On Self-Test

A series of system tests and initializations performed by the BIOS on power-up. The POST is stored in the BIOS ROM.

PRML
Partial Response Maximum Likelihood

PRML is a type of analog read circuit that overcomes signal overlap and background noise by sampling the signal at several locations along the wave. The PRML circuit then derives the shape of the wave for comparison with subsequent read operations. Curve peaks that are don't match those of the projected curve are dismissed as noise.

Q

QIC-36 Interface

A 50-pin tape drive interface that has become an industry standard.

QIC-02 Interface

Tape drive software command set that has become an industry standard.

R

RADIAL

A way of connecting multiple drives to one controller. In radial operation, all output signals are active, even if the drive is not selected.

Also see daisy chain.

RECALIBRATE

Return to Track Zero. A common disk drive function in which the heads are returned to track 0 (outermost track) to ensure good positioning by having a stable starting point.

RAID
Redundant Array of Inexpensive (or Independent) Disks

A relatively inexpensive way to increase capacity, throughput and reliability in mass storage. Basically consists of several standard hard drives combined to make a large logical unit. In addition to multiplying the storage capacity of drive units, one of the most important features is the ability to guard data against media failure by simultaneously duplicating all information.

Also see SCA, striping.

RWC
Reduced Write Current

A signal input (to some older drives) that decreases the amplitude of the write current at the actual drive head. Normally this signal is specified to be used during inner track write operations to lessen the effect of adjacent bit "crowding." When installing a drive in a system, the number requested is the first track number to begin the area of reduced write current. That track and all subsequent tracks will be written with reduced write current.

RLL
Run Length Limited

A type of encoding scheme that reduces the amount of data-checking information that is stored, and requires less flux reversals (changes in the media) for a given amount of data (see MFM). The logic used is much more complicated than MFM, but allows more data to be placed on the disk. In RLL 2,7 the "run length" of zeros is limited to 7. The codes are chosen so that sequences of zeros in the codes always range from 2 to 7. This allows for a fifty percent increase in disk space over MFM encoding. RLL 3,9 is also available which further increases disk space (up to 100% from MFM).

Also see encoding, FM, MFM.

ROTATIONAL SPEED

The speed at which the media spins. On a 5-1/4 or 3-1/2" Winchester drive it is usually 3,600 RPM.

ROOT DIRECTORY

The root directory is the master directory of the drive from which all the sub-directories will branch out. It contains the FAT and operating system boot files.

S

SA-400 Interface

Shugart Associates designed the SA-400 floppy disk drive in 1978, it was the first floppy drive to gain wide acceptance. This drive utilized a 34-pin cable that is still used in floppy drives today. The interface was later modified for hard drives and this modified version became the ST-506 interface. The SA-400 pinouts have been slightly modified over the years, but the industry standard floppy interface is still referred to as the SA-400.

SCA
Single Connector Attachment

The method of attachment used in SCSI RAID storage systems to connect drive modules to the cabinet.

Also see RAID, SCSI.

SCSI
Small Computer Systems Interface

The SCSI interface is a type of bus that attaches a number of intelligent peripherals, including hard drives, tape drives, CD-ROM drives, scanners, and printers. Each device must have its own Logical Unit Number (LUN) so that the interface can identify it. The number of LUNs a bus is capable of depends on the SCSI revision it supports (SCSI 1-3).

Also see ESDI, IDE, ST-506/412.

SCSI ID

See LUN.

SECTOR

A section of one track is called a sector. Each sector is defined with magnetic markings and an identification number from 0 to 65,535 (this identification number is contained in the sector header). All versions of DOS contain 512 bytes of data per sector (in the data section). All tracks have the same amount of sectors, even though the tracks are much larger near the outside of the platter than the inside. This is only done by DOS to avoid extra complications and as a result, gives up much valuable disk space. More advanced recording methods have been introduced such as ZBR (Zone Bit Recording) in which tracks on the outside cylinders have more sectors per track than the inside cylinders, but each sector still contains 512 bytes of data.

See ID field.

SECTOR HEADER

The address portion of a sector. The sector header (ID field) is written during the format operation. It includes the cylinder, head, and sector number of the current sector. This address information is compared by the disk controller with the desired head, cylinder, and sector number before a read or write operation is allowed.

SECTOR SPARING

This reduces the number of sectors on each track by one and places defect information on it. The application will see less defects, as only the drive is aware of the spare sectors. This reduces the total capacity of your drive, but is useful if the drive has a large amount of defects and your application requires a defect free drive.

SEEK

The radial movement of the heads to a specified track address.

SEEK TIME

Seek time usually refers to the average time it takes the heads to move between one track to another, on average. This is the seek time referred to in the hard drive listings in this book. There is also the track-to-track seek time which reflects how long it takes the heads to move between adjacent tracks.

SERVO

A feedback positioning system. In hard drives, servo information is embedded in the platters. The heads compare position themselves by comparing their position to the location of the servos.

Also see actuator, embedded servo, servo track, voice-coil actuator.

SERVO TRACK

A pre-recorded reference track on the dedicated servo surface of certain disk drives. All data positions are compared to their corresponding servo track to determine "off-track/on-track" position, and correct cylinder positioning.

See actuator, embedded servo, servo, voice-coil actuator.

SKEWING

Skewing is the repositioning of the first logical sector on each track to mask the time required to switch heads or cylinders (tracks). A skew factor is added, when formatting a disk, to improve performance by reducing wasted disk revolutions.

Head skew reflects the time it takes for a drive to switch between head groups. It will be set to 0 if the drive does not support head skewing, and most don't.

SMD

Storage Modular Device

A hard drive interface used in mainframe and minicomputer environments.

SPINDLE

The rotating hub structure to which the disks are attached.

SPINDLE MOTOR

This is the motor that spins the platters. These motors are direct-drive – they never use belts or gears.

SPINDLE MOTOR GROUND STRAP

Most older hard drives had this strap attached to the circuit board pressing against the spindle motor. This dissipated the static generated by operation and grounds the spindle motor casing. This strap sometimes caused high pitched or scraping noises. Placing a drop of oil between it and the spindle or adjusting slightly would usually stop the noise.

ST-506/412 INTERFACE

Sometimes called MFM drives. A very popular format in the 1980s, this interface was developed by Seagate Technologies (originally Shugart) in 1980, solely for use with their ST-506 hard drive (a 5 megabyte formatted drive). ST-506/412 drives are the direct ancestors to modern SCSI and IDE drives.

Also see ESDI, IDE, SCSI.

STEP

An increment or decrement of the head positioning arm to move the heads in or out respectively, one track from their current position. In buffered mode, the head motion is postponed until the last of a string of step pulses has been received.

See buffered seek.

STEPPER MOTOR ACTUATOR

The head actuator is responsible for moving the heads back and forth over the platters. A stepper motor actuator uses a motor that moves the heads by rotating the motor a "step" at a time. By rotating the motor a precise number of steps and then converting these steps into linear motion, the heads are moved. Alignment is assured by a metal band that can cause the drive to be put out of alignment if overheated or worn. Most hard drives, especially inexpensive ones, use this kind of actuator. Floppy drives also use this kind of actuator. Also see Actuator, Voice-coil Actuator.

STEP PULSE

The pulse sent from the controller to the stepper motor on the step interface signal line to initiate a step operation.

STRIPING

The process of interleaving data among drives in an array.

Also see RAID.

SYNCHRONOUS DATA

Data sent, usually in serial mode, with a clock pulse defining the intervals between bits.

T

THIN FILM HEADS

A read/write head whose read/write element is deposited using integrated circuit techniques rather than being manually fabricated by grinding ferrite and hand winding coils. Also see Head.

TERMINATING RESISTORS

Hard drives are always shipped with the terminating resistor in place. This is a small resistor pack usually located near the bottom or near the drive select jumpers. They are usually yellow, and sometimes black or blue. They provide electrical signal termination so that the control signals do not echo along the drive cables. They also provide the proper electrical load for the controller and not using them properly could damage the controller. See the section on hard drive installation for the proper use of these resistors.

TPI

Tracks Per Inch

A measurement of track density, measured along a radius of a platter.

Also see areal density, bit density, track density.

TRACK

The concentric circles that hold data on a disk platter. A track is composed of a circle of magnetic flux changes. Each track is divided into sectors, which are normally 512 bytes in length.

TRACK DENSITY

Track density (or Tracks Per Inch) defines how many tracks can be written onto a disk surface. Track density is radially measured.

Also see areal density, bit density, TPI.

V

VIRTUAL MEMORY

Virtual memory is a scheme used by multi-tasking operating systems, such as Windows, to supplement system RAM with hard drive space. This is accomplished with "swap files," which active applications write-to and read-from instead of system RAM.

VIRTUAL SPLIT

A virtual split is a logical division of the disk drive. Some controller cards support this option when low level formatting to make one physical drive appear as two drives to the operating system. This helps to overcome the partitioning limitations of MS/PC-DOS.

VOICE-COIL ACTUATOR

Voice-coil actuators use a solenoid (a magnet that pulls on a metal rod) to pull the heads toward the center of the platter. The heads are placed on a hinge mechanism with a spring that pulls in the other direction. When the solenoid is released, the heads are pulled back to the outer edge of the platters. The term "voice-coil" is used because this technology is also used in the push-pull action of speaker cones.

Voice-coil technology is vastly superior to stepper-motor technology because it is lighter, faster, and allows very fast and accurate head positioning through the use of servos.

See actuator, stepper-motor actuator, servo.

W

WEDGE SERVO SYSTEM

See embedded servo system

WINCHESTER DRIVE

A term that originated from the old IBM drives in the 1960s that had 30 megabytes of removable media and 30 megabytes of fixed media. Thus the name 30-30, which is the caliber of the rifles made by the Winchester gun factory. The name now refers to non-removable media hard drives found in almost all PCs.

WRITE CURRENT

See Reduced Write Current.

WORM DRIVE
Write Once Read Many

WORM drives contain removable cartridges that can be written to once and read from an indefinite number of times, similar to a phonograph record.

WPC
Write Precompensation

WP is the variance of the timing of the head current, from the outer tracks to the inner tracks of a disk, to compensate for the bit-shifting that occurs on the inner cylinders, which pack more data into a smaller area. Sometimes this number must be entered at the time of low-level formatting, and is only required on some oxide media drives.

X

XT INTERFACE

See IDE, ATA.

Z

ZBR
Zone Bit Recording

Trademark of Seagate Technology. A media optimization technique where the number of sectors per track is dependent upon the cylinder circumference; e.g., tracks on the outside cylinders have more sectors per track than the inside cylinders. The ZBR format is only done at the factory.

Index of Terms and Topics

Notes

Notes

THE HARD DISK

TECHNICAL GUIDE

BONUS CD-ROM

EZ-Drive™

EZ-Drive is a one-step, 60 second IDE hard drive installation and upgrade utility. EZ-Drive makes hard drive installations hassle-free for novices and professionals alike by automatically identifying, partitioning, and formatting any IDE hard drive, making it data-ready in only one minute. It is recommended that you format a floppy disk with the /S switch (FORMAT A:/S) and copy the contents of the /EZDRIVE directory to the floppy. Use this disk, not the CD-ROM, for drive installations. For detailed features and usage information, see Appendix D.

EZ-SMART™

EZ-SMART is a new hard drive tool designed to keep you one step ahead of a disastrous drive failure. When installed on systems with SMART (**S**elf **M**onitoring **A**nalysis **R**eporting **T**echnology) capable drives, EZ-SMART can help warn you of drive performance problems that could eventually threaten your valuable data. While not a guarantee of drive health, SMART technology represents a huge step forward in the evolution of the modern hard drive. Safeguard your data to the fullest with EZ-SMART.

The Micro House® Utilities

To access the Micro House Utilities, make the CD-ROM drive the active drive, then change the directory to "UTILS". For detailed features and usage information, see Appendix E.

Micro House® All Product Demonstration

See why Micro House is the leader in multi-vendor hardware solutions by checking out demos for products like The Micro House Technical Library, an information packed CD-ROM containing technical data, jumper settings, diagrams, memory configurations, and other vital hardware information. A demo for Support on Site™ for Hardware, our flagship information product containing all of the content from the Micro House Technical Library in addition to tens of thousands of pages of real-world problem fixes licensed from the manufacturers themselves, is also included. Finally, take a moment to review the demonstration version of DrivePro™, Micro House's premier hard drive setup and diagnostic utility for all popular drive interface types (MFM, ESDI, SCSI, IDE). Making your multi-vendor computer hardware work together seamlessly has never been easier!

**To place an order for the Micro House® Technical Library,
Support On Site™ for Hardware, or DrivePro™ call 1-800-926-8299.**

Micro House World Wide Web Home Page: http://www.microhouse.com